The Management of People in Hotels, Restaurants, and Clubs

The Management of People in Hotels, Restaurants, and Clubs FOURTH EDITION

Donald E. Lundberg
California State Polytechnic University-Pomona

James P. Armatas
James P. Armatas and Associates, Inc.
Shawnee Mission, Kansas

wcb

Wm. C. Brown Company Publishers
Dubuque, Iowa

wcb

Wm. C. Brown, Chairman of the Board
Larry W. Brown, President, WCB Group

Book Team
Bill Cox, Editor
Patricia L.A. Hendricks, Production Editor
Don Hedeman, Designer
Mary Heller, Visual Research Manager

Wm. C. Brown Company Publishers, College Division
Lawrence E. Cremer, President
Raymond C. Deveaux, Vice President/Product Development
David Wm. Smith, Assistant Vice President/National Sales Manager
Matt Coghlan, National Marketing Manager
David A. Corona, Director of Production Development and Design
William A. Moss, Production Editorial Manager
Marilyn A. Phelps, Manager of Design

Cover Photo:

With the gracious permission
of Lex Hotels, Inc., staff members
of The Whitehall Hotel and Club,
Chicago, were photographed in
the Whitehall Club private dining
room. Photo by John Reilly.

Contents

Preface

Traditionally, management in business has been said to deal with people and the four m's—materials, money, machines, and methods. By all odds the most important and most complicated of these are the people—thinking beings, whose needs proliferate, whose desires change, whose mental and emotional conditions fluctuate, whose feelings influence all behavior. The motivation of people has occupied the best minds since the human race emerged from the lower animal state. All leaders of people are concerned with setting goals and motivating individuals to strive towards those goals. Hotel and restaurant managers are no exception. This book, then, is concerned with people management.

Why not title the book *Personnel Management?* Simply because the subject of personnel management has developed into a discipline aimed largely at persons who intend to work as personnel managers—relatively few of whom are found in the hotel and restaurant business. This book is for every manager and for every supervisor. Theory is illustrated with practice, and practice is drawn from the hotel and restaurant field.

Necessarily the book is based upon an attitude towards the individual and human nature.

Healthy human beings want to work. They need management to help them arrive at goals and encouragement to learn techniques by which those goals can be reached. People are not lazy by nature but may get lazy if they find it more pleasant to avoid certain tasks than to perform them. Hence, the need for the goals—and for achieving them.

Much of the work in the hotel and restaurant field is intrinsically satisfying because it brings employees into contact with other people, mostly in pleasant surroundings, and rewards for performing work for these people—the customers or guests—are forthcoming.

It is difficult to be lonely as a hotel or restaurant employee, assuming the staff is relatively harmonious in and of itself and is free of actual dislike for the management.

Management requires capabilities far beyond those demanded by line jobs in a hotel or restaurant. Not only does management bear more responsibilities than do non-management employees, but the managerial staff performs work which may be just as unpleasant as much of that done by the line employees, and may have to strive harder physically than they do. As a result management should be and is rewarded in keeping with this extra ability and effort.

The goals of hotel or restaurant management are of necessity not the same as those of their staff. It is management's job to try to bring management's and staff's goals into close harmony—as close as will permit maximum productivity and earnings for the hotel or restaurant. To do this requires constant sensitivity to the *human problems,* the definition and redefinition of goals, the constant reaffirmation of the value of the product, and the communication of enthusiasm for the goals of the hotel or restaurant.

Much of management knowledge is intuitive, having grown out of the learning experiences of the individuals as they mature. Though experience in management is essential to the development of a first-class manager, much of management can also be acquired at the same time from books such as this.

Greedy management or ownership can result or has resulted in fortunes. Greed, associated primarily with short-term gains, is incompatible with effective management in the long run. Workers today are selective about where, how, and for whom they work. Management should expect to share the rewards of an enterprise with the staff.

The management of people in any enterprise is perhaps the most complex and demanding aspect of that enterprise. In the hotel and restaurant business the challenge is even greater than in other businesses. People management in hotels, restaurants, and clubs is more complex simply because more cultures are involved.

The sheer size of the industry makes it important. The food-service field itself is the third largest United States industry with approximately 4.1 million full-time employees in both the commercial and noncommercial sectors. The food and lodging industry is the largest employer in the retail trades, followed closely by general merchandise stores and food stores. It employs over 5 percent of all wage and salary workers. Total sales, both commercial and noncommercial, are over $100 billion (estimated for 1978). And it's estimated that 1980 sales will be $122 billion. There are almost 600,000 food-service units, both commercial and noncommercial. The National Restaurant Association estimates that some 25,000 new food-service managers are needed each year.

By 1980 there were about 100,000 hotels and motels in the world, about 45,000 of them were in the United States. These hotels and motels had a total of 2.75 million rooms. There were approximately 7,300 hotels, with a total of 709,100 rooms. Lodging establishments numbered 53,300 with 3,469,100 rooms. Of these totals, it's estimated that there are approximately 37,000 properties with payrolls (i.e., with paid employees) representing about 2 million rooms. The gross annual sales of the lodging industry exceeded $16 billion in 1977. Most hotels and motels are small businesses, but in the United States some 3,000 hotels and motels have 200 or more rooms.

The club industry, while considerably smaller than food service and lodging, nevertheless represents a reasonable share of our country's gross national product.

To thousands of people, the industry offers occupations that are more rewarding than jobs found elsewhere. The industry is made up largely of relatively small establishments, which give the individual ample opportunities for personal recognition. Most establishments offer steady, year-round employment plus the benefits of at least one meal while on the job, uniforms, and other "fringes" not often found in other industries. The opportunity to work directly with people is, in itself, rewarding for the thousands of service employees in the industry.

While management in the hotel, restaurant, and club industry calls for a person with greater-than-average energy, the desire to mix with people, and a willingness to tackle people problems on almost an hourly basis, the financial rewards are probably as great or greater than the same amount of ability would bring in other fields, and there is always the opportunity to go into business for oneself.

The information, techniques, and philosophies expressed in this book are those that can be utilized by a person with a managerial title, by a personnel manager specifically, and also by any person (title or no) who is managing people.

Special thanks to Dr. William P. Fisher and the In-Sink-Erator Division of Emerson Electric Co. for selected excerpts from *Hospitality and You, A Guide to Customer Service;* Chain Store Publishing Corporation for sections of *Today's Waitress;* the Club Managers Association of America; the American Hotel Motel Association; the California Restaurant Association; and the several hotel and restaurant organizations that have supplied ideas and charts for this book.

Appreciation is also due to Professors John Steffaneli and Mel Sandler who made numerous valuable suggestions for changes and additions for this new edition.

The Management Process

1

The accomplishment of objectives requires management and the mobilization of people, money, and things. Management helps to set priorities and goals, determines directions, and promotes incentives and the determination to reach goals.

The manager supervises a number of things, but most importantly, the manager deals with people. To place this book in proper context with the broader subject of management, people management is seen as one of several types of management:

Personal Management
People Management
Time Management
Money Management
Water Management
Energy Management
Product Quality Management
Service Management

In this book we are concentrating on People Management, the subject that in the hospitality business is dominant to the extent that much of the product being sold is service by people to people.

To be a manager of people, one must first manage oneself—personal management. Personal management precedes personnel management. The manager oversees time, money, and an array of functions in a hotel or restaurant, such as menu planning, purchasing, receiving, storing, food preparation, food service, front desk operations, laundry operation, reservations, and sales. Management is the key word—managing self, others, and the delivery of goods and services. In this text, we are concerned with Personnel and Personal Management in the continuing effort to provide food, beverage, and rooms to the public in a hospitable manner and at a profit.

The management of people is a process that goes on day after day, with the manager or supervisor relating to the staff in a number of ways. Basic to management is planning and anticipating the future—both the immediate

Figure 1.1   Management Wheel

and the more distant future. Planning can be formal or informal. Plans can be written down or borne in mind. Planning precedes (or should precede) almost all business action.

In management, communication and decision making come after planning. These three processes are involved in almost every aspect of management.

In the management wheel illustrated (fig. 1.1), planning, communicating, and decision making are placed in the center of the wheel because they are central to and part of the other functions. Around the outside of the wheel we see that management is engaged in recruiting personnel, selecting, training, and appraising them. Management is also involved in setting standards and goals, in delegating responsibility, authority, and accountability, and in motivating people to accomplish the goals and standards that have been set. Finally, management controls people in one or several ways and systematizes actions for efficiency and ease of operation.

MANAGEMENT AND COACHING

In many ways the manager of a hotel, restaurant, or club is like a football coach. Basically both have the same problems: recruitment, training, appraising, delegating, goals, standard setting, motivating, controlling, scheduling, and systematizing. The football coach epitomizes the management process: all of the processes are speeded up and must be performed in the course of one year (much like a seasonal resort hotel). During the off-season he is recruiting and selecting. Preseason practice is given over to training and appraising. At this point the coach selects the quarterback to whom is delegated the responsibility for running the team during the games. The coach and coaching assistants are constantly striving for new standards in blocking, passing, and tackling.

The goal is to win. The coach is constantly motivating, triggering the will to win. Perhaps the feature that distinguishes the superior from the mediocre coach is that individual's ability to motivate the team. This is done by every means the coach can think of, appealing to pride and self-image. Fear and pain are used as instruments. Above all the coach tries to develop the desire in each player to be one of the team, and encourages team spirit.

The coach constantly controls the team, more so than would be possible in most businesses, even to the extent of calling the plays from the sidelines, besides scheduling practices, meals, trips, and games—even off-hours. All of this is tied together with system—training regimens, training tables, systems of play (every play is a system). The hotel or restaurant manager is in effect a coach, playing to win profits and satisfaction for clientele and employees.

Each coach has developed a management style, intentionally or otherwise. Some coaches are autocratic; others democratic; others in between. Vince Lombardi, past coach of the Green Bay Packers and the Washington Redskins, was noted for his dictatorial management style and he was a winner. Other coaches have been notably democratic in style; they also have produced winning teams. In this book we will be talking about management style, the way the manager relates to others in the organization. All winning coaches have one thing in common: they coach. In other words, they show the players how to win, how to block or tackle, or how to set a table.

We'll be talking about motivation, recruitment, selection, and training. Controlling, scheduling, and systematizing will be given less emphasis because other books are available that cover these aspects of management adequately. Neither will this book deal much with marketing, money, materials, or equipment. The emphasis is on *people management*.

DECISION MAKING

In looking at the chart (fig 1.1) listing the various functions in the process of management we see that decision making interlaces with every other function. Decisions must be made about recruiting, selecting, training, and so on. The best decisions bring forth the best results. Decision making runs through our lives. We make a decision to get up in the morning, another to brush our teeth, and still another to dress. Most decisions are buried in habits. We scarcely think about them. Other decisions such as instituting a payroll cost control system, employing a new manager, or selecting a spouse, are major decisions which should be given considerable thought and analysis.

As Freud pointed out, many of the determinants of our decisions are hidden from us but nevertheless influence judgment and action. Our own biology, the way we feel at the moment, our glandular makeup, and the instincts we have as animals color decisions. It might be said that to a large extent we must overcome animal and emotional determinants to arrive at rational decisions. One value of education, supposedly, is to program a person so that when faced with a problem that individual comes equipped with a decision process which in turn makes the person more analytical and gives more options. Presumably the decisions then made are therefore more effective. Some of the techniques for making decisions can be learned from reading and discussion; others apparently must be burned in by experience.

The wise manager recognizes that there is no one best solution for many problems, especially people problems. Too often a manager reviews decisions with the assumption that *the* correct ones were not picked. Life is too complicated—there are too many variables playing in most situations—to be able to pick a perfect solution. Inevitably, there are multiple factors bearing on a problem situation, and these are changing so that what might be a good solution at a given moment may no longer be a good one at a later time.

In making decisions recognize that—

1. in people decisions there is a high risk of failure;
2. the best decision will some day become obsolete;
3. important decisions are generic or strategic in nature;
4. every important decision is chosen from alternatives;
5. major decisions effecting change are seldom welcomed and take courage to implement;
6. organized disagreement usually results in more alternatives and better understanding.

The manager who seeks certainty where there is no certainty cannot help but be disappointed with human affairs, and become discouraged. Rather there are probabilities and the players in the drama of life try to pick the best odds in their favor. To do otherwise creates anxiety, remorse, and dissatisfaction with the self.

TEMPERAMENT AND INSTINCT IN DECISION MAKING

It is apparent to every intelligent person that decision making is heavily colored by feeling and unconscious forces. Sigmund Freud shook the intellectual world with his exposé of the subconscious and its influence on decision making and life in general. William MacDougall, a social psychologist, placed great emphasis on instinct as influencing perception, judgment, and decision making. But his theories were discounted by other psychologists. More recently the *new biology*, which relies heavily on animal studies, has forced a renewed interest in instinct as a determinant of behavior not only in the lower animals but in humans as well. Theorists believe that much of human behavior can be explained by the survival techniques learned in the 15 to 20 million years spent by humankind in evolving from the lower animals. Deep-seated needs to have one's own territory, to belong to a relatively small work group, to fight outside groups, to place one's self in a status hierarchy, and to look to an individual for leadership are forms of instinctive behavior which were developed as man formed hunting packs and defended his territory from other packs and lower animals.

Much of the seemingly irrational behavior that goes on in business can be explained, at least partially, by reference to such notions. More obvious is irrational behavior such as the mass hysteria witnessed at sporting events, rock festivals, and political rallies. Antony Jay postulates that such behavior is an instinctual reaction to the need to depopulate, similar to the instinct that sends the lemmings, when they are overcrowded, marching off to the sea to their death.[1] A similar instinct may be at play when younger members of an organization feel the need to break off into new groups or go to war.

Instinctual needs must certainly play a large part in decision making. The obvious sexual drives and competitiveness help make the world go around and influence decisions at all levels. Who can say that some of the most important decisions, such as those relative to selecting a mate or home, are done on a rational basis? Many management decisions are influenced by the need to achieve power and prestige. The *irrational* is ever present in decision making.

Glandular makeup of the individual affects the decision making. Sanguine persons make decisions in terms of the optimistic future seen by each. The dyspeptic's future is influenced by digestion. The bouyant salesperson needs glandular support to believe in and sell a product. An expanding organization needs the optimist in a key decision-making spot. A more conservative decision maker may be needed at other times.

EMOTION AND DECISION MAKING

Decisions are based on past experience and judgment, and are affected by the amount of steam generated in the emotional system. When a manager works long hours or is under undue stress, that individual's judgment is likely to be less sharp, less focused, and decisions less effective.

The economics of marginal utility relate to the use of one's own energy. Fatigue lowers stress tolerance, resulting in decision making becoming an effort.

Temper is more easily frayed, things are said that often can never be undone, and less appropriate decisions are made which, when added up, have a cumulative deleterious effect.

The manager who takes secret pride in a display of temper over a period of time usually finds that losing one's temper is habit forming; that one day temper will be lost with the wrong people. One becomes less discriminating as to the time and place of daring to display temper, and an explosive level is reached more quickly.

Some executives with low boiling points have learned to recognize the symptoms that precede temper flare-ups. Escoffier, the famous chef, simply walked off the scene, took a turn around the block, got a new perspective, and returned better able to cope with the problem or person at hand. Not a bad technique for anyone with a short fuse!

Managers who cannot control themselves have difficulty controlling others. The famous leaders know when to show anger and often do so for dramatic effect. In other words, a display of anger can be effective at the right moment, more so if the individual concerned has not really "lost" control, but has it well in hand, directing it for a purpose.

Righteous indignation, a reaction to injustice, is a perfectly normal and appropriate response and without it life would undoubtedly be full of more injustice than it is now. The trick is to avoid the smoke point when all of the information about a problem is not in or to know the real intent of a person's remarks which may be taken as offensive. If a manager continually reacts with anger the people around that individual adjust to it, and any possible

---

1. Antony Jay, *The Corporation Man* (New York: Random House, 1970).

desirable effects of stimulating others to greater effort or changing a behavior are soon lost. The manager who cries wolf too often is soon accepted as being overwrought rather than righteously indignant. If one continually spoils for a fight, the strong people in the organization will leave. This results in a weak organization full of yes-people, chameleons who are quite ready to do as they are told, up to a point, but who have no real vitality in their personalities or strength of character to force through necessary changes.

Real anger clouds judgment to the point where precise thinking is impossible, overriding past experience, never allowing good judgment to form. The *big* manager apologizes for actions taken in anger, but a steady diet of eating crow does not build confidence in the person either.

Anger does not permit balanced perspective, nor the consideration of alternatives that may be important. The angry person is not likely to come up with new ideas or new possibilities.

REVENGE IS SWEET AND SELF-DESTROYING

The manager of a resort hotel suddenly found herself with a revolution on her hands, with the entire dining room staff ready to walk out in the middle of a full dining room. Her reaction was to identify the ringleader and fire him on the spot. In this case, ownership did not back the manager and she soon found herself on the way home. While the owners probably should have backed the manager and the manager probably felt "good inside" while doing the firing, this was not the best immediate solution. A desire for revenge on the manager's part often unites the staff, but unites them against the management. "Teaching an employee a lesson" seldom affects only one employee. Every other employee focuses on the action and each weighs the significance of the action in personal welfare terms. The manager has a larger class than she bargained for and may be teaching more about herself than about the subject she thinks she is putting across. While she is involved in such a lesson her attention is monopolized and she is likely to neglect other decision-making areas.

A continuing desire for revenge festers in the emotional system, coloring a person's attitudes toward life in general, and hamstrings one's power to function. A grudge eats away like acid in the person holding it, who, even though "settling the score," really loses in the end.

Often when something is done in anger or in revenge, guilt feelings well up and the person hastens to make amends in one form or another, frequently to the detriment of the hotel or restaurant. A manager may say yes when he should say no, compromising his responsibility.

He may even go so far as to promote a person he has offended even though such a promotion is unjustified. He may hesitate to exercise critical judgment and pays penance for his personal acts.

ANXIETY LOWERS THE SMOKE POINT

The condition illustrated by the military expression "pushing the panic button" can be brought on by extended anxiety or by the buildup of tension as a result of not being able to structure a situation or to formulate a plan of attack on problems. Acute fright paralyzes mental and physical activity and can precipitate action that is unreasonable and completely inappropriate. Taking on too much responsibility triggers anxiety, because the person becomes anxious about jobs that have not been done. The lack of time to complete everything to which one is committed gnaws not only at one's conscience but at one's stomach. The hard-driving manager is likely to take on too much, which is fair neither to the manager nor the hotel or restaurant. That manager has not learned to delegate or feels that asking for an assistant is an admission of inability to take the job in stride. In many instances backing off, absolutely refusing to take on further commitments, or insisting upon having additional assistance, may be the wisest procedure. The competitive desire to take on more than one can handle must be restrained. Hard work may be satisfying, but unfinished work is seldom so.

THE NEED FOR CONSISTENCY IN DECISION MAKING

Human beings want a predictable environment, and the manager of the hotel or restaurant is in a critical position to develop or fail to develop consistency in the environment. Experiments with animals show that they can become conditioned to withstand considerable pain and inconvenience and will accept it; as long as it is predictable. The animal becomes neurotic when it does not know what to expect, even though the inconvenience or pain in itself is not severe. Human beings are much the same, and the capricious manager—the individual who cannot be predicted—keeps everyone in a state of alarm—simply because of that unpredictability. If a manager makes decisions according to the time of the day, level of fatigue, or buoyancy at the moment, employees are hard pressed to figure out the timing and the conditions for approaching that manager. If a person gets a reprimand one day for doing something, a grin the next day for doing the same thing, confusion results. A reprimand would be preferable, if it is predictable. The old saying, "it is not the severity of the punishment, but the certainty of it that is impor-

Table 1.1 Examples of Three Kinds of Decisions

First-Level (broad decisions)	Second-Level (operating decisions)	Third-Level (performance decisions)
Location	Kind of detergent to buy	When to remove a hamburger from the griddle
Sanitation standards	Applicant's qualifications	How to make a soft-serve cone with a twist at the top
Menu	Inspecting deliveries	
Personnel policy	Checking ad results	How to slice an onion
Food quality standards	Whether to fill in for absent employee	How to mop a floor
Advertising and promotion policy		When to mop a floor
Manager's role	Number of portions to produce	When to call a purveyor
Rate structure		

tant," has relevance to all of supervision. The fact that "you can count on old George," even though you can count on him to do the wrong thing, is somehow more satisfying to that person's associates than "you don't know what George will do next."

LEVELS OF DECISIONS

It is useful, when thinking about decision making, to differentiate between decisions according to their importance to the hotel or restaurant, and the magnitude of their effect. By dividing such decisions into three levels, management sometimes can save time by restricting itself to first- and second-level decisions.

First-level decisions can be thought of as those that are most critical for the success of the enterprise. Decisions concerning location, menu, broad personnel policy, and standards fall into this group. Second-level decisions might be thought of as operating decisions, while third-level decisions are routine decisions made by staff members engaged in performing work of a routine nature. Table 1.1 lists some typical decisions that fall into the three classifications. In a chain operation, top management ordinarily deals with the first-level decisions, while store managers or individual hotel managers are concerned with the second level.

UNCONSCIOUS FACTORS AFFECTING DECISIONS

In thinking about decision making it is also helpful to recognize the influence of factors at the level of the unconscious. All of us make important decisions without being completely aware of the influences that directed them.

Figure 1.2 illustrates in chart form how the unconscious mind interacts with the conscious mind in making a decision.

STEPS IN SOLVING THE PROBLEM

Identify the Problem

The first step in the solution of any problem is to identify it and then to try to state it clearly, at least mentally. The next step is to collect information that bears on the problem, and then to frame several solutions. Most businesses are continually making decisions, changing and modifying goals, and are well advised to have not only one plan ready to accomplish a goal, but to have others that can be used in case the first plan fails.

Identify the Assumption

Decision making can be improved by identification of the assumptions being acted upon. For example, the manager who feels that people are generally lazy, indifferent, and ungrateful will come to different conclusions about the development and training of personnel than the manager who feels that people are generally appreciative, ambitious, and willing to work if given the proper leadership. The first manager will probably want to fire the employee who does not produce, feeling that there is no hope for that employee anyway, while the second manager will be more apt to think of ways to motivate the employee and to find out what the trouble is.

Generally speaking, a decision is no better than the information upon which it is based. It should be recog-

Figure 1.2 Example of the Decision-making Process

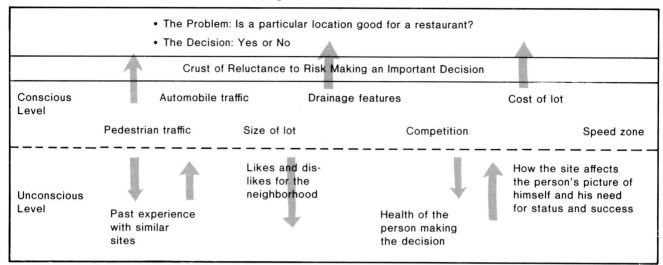

nized, however, that seldom does anyone have all the information that applies to the solution of a particular problem. The executive continually acts in the absence of complete information, using past experience and judgment in arriving at a predictably successful or adequate decision. Then too there is the matter of luck. Once the decision has been reached and has gotten as much approval and cooperation as is feasible at the moment from those who will carry out the decision, the executive goes ahead and acts. Should the decision prove to be the wrong one, little time is spent in reviewing what went wrong or in self-castigation. An executive recognizes that everyone makes wrong decisions, even the most successful of people. One might do well to remember Mark Twain's comment on decision making to the effect that he felt himself lucky if he were right 51 percent of the time.

Of course, the competent manager is not a fatalist and believes that one will profit or suffer from the results of one's decision and actions, and furthermore that one can influence destiny and the direction of the enterprise one manages. This belief in positive action and the power to change the tide of affairs sets off the American businessperson from those of several other cultures, and partially accounts for the difference of industrial growth between the United States and much of the rest of the world.

Analyze into Parts

Problem solvers have long recognized that the important problems today have no clear-cut answers. More often there are pros and cons, or a multifactor problem with several options. The more imaginative the problem solver, the more options that person comes up with. Benjamin Franklin is credited with suggesting a technique for ana-

lyzing problems into parts, dividing the parts into pros and cons as in the example below:

Should I marry the person?

Pros	Con
rich	has a nasty temper
beautiful, handsome	loves others as well
loves me	has bad breath
well educated	hates my parents
has status	could become an alcoholic

Franklin suggested that a problem solver try to cancel out items of about the same weight, and reduce the problem to the point where one side outweighs the other. The technique does not obviate value judgments, but it does break the overall problem down into more manageable parts.

When Is a Decision Effective?

Several techniques for solving problems have been developed using mathematics and logic. When there are complicated problems of scheduling, the technique known as PERT (Progress Evaluation Review Technique) may be applicable. It is a technique that is helpful in solving complicated flow problems. Use of a so-called *decision tree* is another means of anticipating possible options and consequences. Any decision-making technique is after all only a technique, and the decision that is made is in abstract form. Implementing the decision is another matter. Dr. Norman Meier of the University of Michigan proposes that the effectiveness of the decision is in large part measured by its acceptance. His formula is $E = Q \times A$.

In the formula the effectiveness *(E)* of a decision is equal to the quality *(Q)* of the decision times its acceptance *(A).* Implications of the formula are immediately apparent. To gain acceptance of a decision often requires input from the persons who will be involved in carrying it out. *Participative management* is the management style advocated by Meier and others to raise the effectiveness level of decision making in industry.

The effective manager usually is skilled in drawing forth the ideas of associates, and of incorporating them into major policy; however, this is not always the case. There are many examples of highly successful business-persons who were autocrats of the first order, who consulted very few people in making their decisions, and couldn't have cared less if their associates agreed with those decisions. A decision resulting from group thinking may not be as good as one formed in a superior mind. Since most of us don't have superior minds and can have more effective organizations if the people concerned have a voice in the decisions, we do well to learn techniques for getting interest and cooperation.

One way to get other people's viewpoints is to be willing to listen to them, and to listen respectfully. This often takes more time than it is worth, especially when dealing with people who have meager imaginations and little real impact on the effective decision once it is implemented.

Most managers can get more effective results by holding regular meeting of department heads. Often the manager unwisely dominates the group and presents a monologue. After a time such meetings lose their effectiveness except to offer a podium from which the manager gives orders. Department heads may be reluctant to stand up and be counted on any issue, and when asked their opinion of a given subject make a ritualized reply that means practically nothing and commits them to nothing. To avoid such nonproductive experiences, the climate of the meetings must be such that the people with ideas will express them and will learn that they will be rewarded for their ideas.

It may not be effective to go around a conference table and ask for each person's opinion, but it is worthwhile to try to identify those who would express themselves if encouraged. An idea, as presented, may not be valuable, but with slight modification might be of use, and the manager, or whoever is leading the discussion, often can turn the idea presented in such a way that the person presenting it is boosted. This encourages others to step forward and be counted.

There are always some people in a group who speak compulsively, and for them the meeting is a form of group therapy, but their ideas often serve only to confuse the issue at hand.

In some organizations the executive lives on a diet of compromise, since leadership often rests on an amalgamation of opinion and a fusion of standards. Compromise is often the only way to secure group action, and may be much more effective than a more logical idea espoused by one or a few people.

WHAT IS EFFECTIVE DECISION MAKING?

Democratic decision making is difficult to accomplish, but it pays the greatest dividends. From social psychology we are able to examine the interrelated steps that are involved in the decision-making process of a group of individuals.

1. Analysis of background factors. Before we make decisions we must know something about our organization and its people, how they feel about issues, how they are likely to respond to change.

2. Defining factors affecting the problem. This involves not only analytical elements, but the *feelings* of the individuals involved that are likely to affect the decision. Can we identify the sources of resistance we are likely to encounter?

3. The analytical process. Satisfactory problem analysis involves *(a)* problem recognition, *(b)* separating elements of the problem, *(c)* estimating the probability of achieving success, *(d)* listing alternative courses of action, *(e)* trying out and testing possibilities, *(f)* deciding on the most appropriate course of action, and *(g)* relating the action decision to the total organization.

4. Action and reaction. Equally as important as the decision itself, is the actual *implementation.* Whether the decision is actually effective is determined by its result. It is one thing to issue a memorandum that all customers will be served water. Whether the memorandum becomes policy depends upon whether the waitress follows through with the decision. Managers must often spend as much time in follow-up as they do in decision making. The more people involved in the original decision making and the more people who have the responsibility for implementing it, the greater the likelihood that the decision will be followed-up.

A RIGHT TIME AND A WRONG TIME FOR DECISION MAKING

How many decisions have been made in the heat of anger, under the stress of fatigue, or under the necessity for reaching a compromise? There is a right time and a wrong time for decision making. The wrong time is when the individuals concerned are tired, frustrated, and emotionally upset. How much more marital harmony there would be if a decision was reached to never discuss major problems, personal or otherwise, except when both parties are fresh and optimistic. How many bad personnel decisions have been made at the end of a day, when much better ones could have been produced the following morning after a night's rest and reflection?

Departmental meetings wherein important decisions are to be made are better scheduled in the morning when people have the energy to mobilize for problem solving. (Many meetings are held not for the making of decisions but for passing along viewpoints, and these can be scheduled more freely.)

Decisions about personnel matters are almost inevitably better made if some time is allowed to pass between the surfacing of the personnel problem and the making of the decision. Many personnel problems "go away by themselves," if time is allowed. Most personnel problems involve not only a superior and a subordinate, but also the feelings of a group. Some discussion with the group may be needed. Quick personnel decisions have the odds stacked against them.

More on decision making in chapter 8, Management Development.

THE DELEGATION PROBLEM: HOW MUCH AND TO WHOM?

A difficulty experienced by many managers, especially new ones, is the reaching of a decision as to what should be delegated and what should not. The old military manner of delegating was for the superior to parcel out all responsibilities to subordinates, then ride herd on them until the work was completed. The superior decided on what was to be done; the subordinate carried it out. It became the trademark of the military, the subject of jokes, ridicule, and resentment. Such a system assumes that the subordinate has less intelligence and know-how than the superior. This is often a false assumption. False or not, the subordinate resents the implication unless he has been programmed to accept it and takes a certain pride in doing whatever he is told. Such a system fails in that it does not properly use the knowledge, creative capacity, or enthusiasm of the subordinate.

The management training programs of such companies as Marriott, ARA, Gino's, Saga, and Servomation place great emphasis on participative management, involving the worker in the decision and the delegative processes. Participative management assumes that the worker also has valuable input for decisions and for the delegation processes.

The manager is continually faced with the problem of which responsibilities to delegate and which to reserve for

Table 1.2   Assigning Responsibility
Reserved for the Boss
Free to act and decide only with permission
Act and decide only after consulting boss
Acts and decides but keeps the boss informed
Complete responsibility—free to act and decide en toto

management. Some decisions cannot be delegated, and final responsibility for the performance of the unit always rests with the supervisor or manager of that unit. The old military game was to "pass the buck down" so that senior officers avoided responsibilities for failures. It was always someone down the line who had failed, not the colonel, not the general. One reason the colonels and the generals hold their rank is that they probably have an aptitude for looking good in the eyes of their superiors. In a hotel or restaurant the bottom line figure, the profit, makes the shifting of responsibility more difficult. The restaurant either makes money or it doesn't. The hotel either maintains a good occupancy or it doesn't. In the country or city club, profit is not the consideration and the manager bends all efforts to please the members, particularly those in power positions, but the manager is also concerned with meeting budget goals.

In delegating responsibility the manager examines the talents and potentials of the crew and tries to assign responsibilities to those who can best carry them out, though bearing in mind also that people grow by taking on responsibilities they have not had previously. In the learning process, mistakes will be made that must be accepted as part of the manager's responsibility for developing people.

The delegation process can be as simple as "Jack, will you clean out the refrigerator," or as complicated as "Let's all get together the morning of the ninth to discuss the budget." Management styles differ in emphasizing *what* should be delegated and *how* it should be delegated. In some organizations the manager is merely a coordinator. Every responsibility is shared. Other managers delegate a little and make the most important decisions themselves. The trend in recent years is to move toward participative management by which decisions, goals, and the delegation process itself involve the members of the group.

Whatever the management style, the group—be it dishroom crew, kitchen staff, or front office department—should be aware of the delegation process and who is responsible for what. Dr. Gerald Lattin proposes the diagram, table 1.2, as a way of illustrating degrees of delegation. In the diagram, it is seen that some responsibilities are reserved for the boss alone. At another level the person who has a particular responsibility can carry it out as he sees fit but only with definite permission from the boss. At the next level down the person with the responsibility must consult with the boss as he acts and decides in carrying out responsibilities.

Other responsibilities can be assigned subject only to the proviso that the boss be kept informed as things progress. Finally, responsibility can be assigned to an individual for the accomplishment of an objective with no strings attached. The individual having the responsibility acts and decides as best possible, rising or falling on the results.

Common sense says that the assignment of responsibility is an empty process without commensurate assignment of authority and budget. Too often responsibilities are ladled out without giving the wherewithal for the accomplishment of the objective set forth to the person involved. The manager who insists on top-notch housekeeping must also provide vacuum cleaners and detergents. At a higher level the convention sales manager of a hotel must have an adequate travel and entertainment budget for carrying out the responsibility of getting group business. One way to make a subordinate frustrated is to give responsibilities, then to hold back on the resources needed to carry them out. The personnel director cannot be effective without secretarial help. The executive chef cannot keep the kitchen clean if lacking in utility people. The dining room manager cannot give fast service if not permitted to hire enough waitresses or bus personnel.

Delegate Certain Kinds of Authority and Responsibility to the Lowest Level Possible

Certain kinds of authority must be delegated if an organization is to be efficient. The manager of a hotel or restaurant is correct in demanding a voice in all policy decisions and in long-range planning, but all too frequently the otherwise capable executive fails to delegate authority, thereby becoming not only self-hindering, but hamstringing subordinates as well. Valuable time is wasted because all decisions must be cleared through that one person who is taking on work that could be done better by others. Initiative in subordinates is destroyed by the failure to set up the conditions for decision making by subordinates. The restaurant manager who must make out the menu entirely unassisted is doing the chef or the food production manager and himself or herself an injustice. The manager of the hotel who insists on doing all of the employing is knocking the supports out from under the department heads. The chef who insists upon doing the steward's job as well as being chef is destroying the

Table 1.3 To Delegate Effectively
Know what results are expected
Know when they are expected
Know by whom
Follow through and hold people accountable
Delegate in accordance with the person's ability but give him the opportunity to fail, to do things other than routine.

efficiency of at least two people. Delegating authority is one of management's most difficult jobs. It entails accepting responsibility for another's work. It means acknowledging that perhaps there are others who can also make decisions and perform efficiently besides one's self. Only the real executive is big enough to do it well.

Delegated Responsibility vs. Final Responsibility

In delegating authority and responsibility the executive recognizes the distinction between *delegated* responsibility and authority and *final* responsibility for the actions of subordinates. Even though a hotel manager must rely heavily upon the chef to operate the food service of the hotel, the manager must accept *final* responsibility for the food operation as well as for the other departments in the organization.

The delegation process means assigning or jointly deciding what objectives are to be delegated. The power and means of achieving the objective are also assigned. To complete the delegation process one factor is added—accountability. Delegates must come up with results—must be held accountable. Too often goals are set, budgets produced and then the whole process slips away. Definite dates should be set for reporting back.

As in Jesus' parable of the talent, the person given responsibility is held accountable for its exercise. Delegation is a two-way street. The person accepting the responsibility must be aware of the obligation to use it for the benefit of the organization. Delegation is a tool for growth, a way of developing real security in the person. A manager can delegate any function except obligations to people and to the final success of the enterprise.

The delegation process is intertwined with participative management, especially as experienced in *Management by Objective.* In participative management the manager in effect delegates part of the responsibility and authority for setting goals and standards to a subordinate.

MANAGEMENT TRENDS

In modern America, the management of people has been influenced by the Scientific Management Trend and the Human Relations Trend.

The Scientific Management Trend

This movement began almost a century ago and has had a tremendous influence on management practices. The scientific management era has been credited largely to F. W. Taylor and Frank Gilbreth, both of whom were interested in improving the efficiency and technology of industry. Gilbreth, for example, made numerous experiments designed to reduce human exertion in the construction industry. Taylor was for many years involved in the steel industry. Following these two pioneers, the scientific management movement has contributed greatly to the systematization and efficiency of American industry.

Among the improvements resulting from the scientific management movement were the following:

1. Elimination of waste: functionalization, work simplification, motion study, analysis of work flow, standardization, and other systematic procedures.
2. Reduction in the amount of learning required by workers in order to do their jobs.
3. Establishment of clear-cut goals of management.
4. Creation of well-defined channels for communication, decision making, and control.

Serious problems also have been associated with the gains.

1. Pressure has been exerted on workers to produce more; workers have reacted to and resisted this movement.
2. Workers and supervisors have resented someone showing them how "stupid" they had been.
3. People have resented the attitude that their only role was to work, and not that of contributing anything original to their jobs or to their work.

The Human Relations Trend

The second trend developed at the end of World War I as a small attempt to combat some of the problems inherent in the scientific management approach. The most dramatic study giving impetus to the human relations trend was the famous study of the Hawthorne plant of the Western Electric Company, where it was shown that morale and motivation determined how workers reacted to such concrete variables as illumination, ventilation, and fatigue factors. The Hawthorne study and studies subsequent to it showed that workers responded to scientific management principles simply by restricting production to levels that the workers felt were appropriate. They also demonstrated that feelings affect job performance more than was formerly realized.

Human relations is an approach that places a premium on the *needs* of workers. It is easy to be glib in talking about human relations, but humanistic, democratic philosophies of management are difficult to implement. Whether management admits it or not, there are three strong forces in organizations that work against the total success of human relations approaches.

1. Just as employees have their needs, one of the needs of managers is to maintain their power.
2. Companies are geared strongly toward uniformity and conformity; it is an unusual company that can break completely from such chains.
3. All companies have bureaucratic traditions that are extremely difficult to break. Some of these traditions are valuable in maintaining the organization.

Within the bounds of practicality then, *pure* human relations concepts probably never can be implemented in many organizations. Human relations principles, however, are principles toward which all organizations can strive. As such, effective human relations are not seen as ends in themselves but as an approach.

The functions of effective human relations may be conceived of as follows:

1. To promote maximum use of employee abilities. Workers are most effective and most satisfied when they can utilize the maximum of their abilities. Specifically, this means that *assembly line* operations are not conducive to the best human efforts because human beings have the ability "to use their brains" and to become involved with diverse types of activities. From a practical point of view, of course, it is not always possible to broaden responsibilities. As much as possible, management needs to be concerned with providing employees with greater responsibilities within the scope of their interests and abilities, greater involvement in the overall process of the organization, and a voice in decisions relative to their welfare. The rise of automation—contrary to earlier belief—enables management to free employees from activities that formerly required specific and undivided attention.

2. To have concern for the welfare of employees. It is true, of course, that to some extent management has been forced toward human relations by strong labor unions, government regulations, and labor shortages, but in fact most enlightened executives are sincere in accepting their responsibilities for promoting human development and satisfaction.

The human relations trend in American industry is inevitable—a sign of the times. Americans in all walks of life are being allowed greater freedom and responsibility. Few youngsters experience situations in schools or homes where orders are given without some accompanying explanation. The younger generation expects to be involved in the decision-making process. People are motivated to work for many reasons other than the dollar.

3. To promote the maximum of job satisfaction. If one enjoys the work one is doing, if *intrinsic* satisfaction is gained from it, that person is likely to be a successful employee due to being provided a built-in stream of motivation. The problem worker is the one who is interested only in a pay check so that he can hurry out to enjoy himself off the job. He gets *extrinsic* satisfactions from his job. A major responsibility of management is to provide its employees with work they enjoy and find intrinsically satisfying. If the work is not satisfying, management has the responsibility of finding ways of making it more satisfying. This implies that management must *know* its employees and its jobs. It implies that management must recognize that people are different and that they have different interests, needs, and aspirations.

4. To select workers effectively. If it is management's responsibility to make jobs more interesting and satisfying, it is also management's responsibility to select people for the jobs in the organization who are most likely to be satisfied by those particular jobs. The implication of the foregoing statement focuses a major responsibility on management to develop a keen understanding of the problems of recruitment, selection, interviewing, and testing.

The hotel-restaurant-club industry lives with selection and training problems, problems associated with low wages, difficult working conditions, and the fact that many workers in hotels and restaurants are there by default—they could find no other jobs. Hotel-restaurant managers must be practical and realistic in picking the specific person for a specific job.

5. To train and develop.

To be a good supervisor requires sensitivity, ability, ambition, and training. A major role of management is to provide training and development experiences for supervisors and managers within the organization.

6. To provide realistic staff participation. It is unrealistic to assume that the workers at the lower levels of the organization will ever exert much influence in the actual establishment of the overall goals of the organization. On the other hand, it is a basic need of workers to have *participation* in the organization. Those workers who feel they are a part of the organization are more effective and responsible workers.

7. To foster good mental health. It may seem strange to talk about mental health for a hotel or restaurant setting. After all, the person who *breaks down* on the job is a rarity. On the other hand, in an industry that depends on action and speed as much as the food service industry, frayed nerves, frustrations, and anxieties are the rule rather than the exception.

SCIENTIFIC MANAGEMENT vs. HUMAN RELATIONS

Both scientific management and human relations concepts and practices are interwoven into the management practices of successful hotels, restaurants, and clubs. Generally, concepts and techniques related to systematization, work flow, engineering, procedures, and methods represent contributions from the scientific management era. Those philosophies and techniques related to the motivations and needs of individuals generally reflect human relations notions.

MANAGEMENT STYLE AND THE MANAGEMENT PROCESS

Management style reflects attitudes of management and influences the management process. Since about 1960 much attention has been given to *management style,* the characteristic approach taken by a manager in relating to the people who report to him or her. It has been said that throughout history the characteristic management style has been the whip and the carrot (reward and punishment), the kind of management usually associated with training animals. It is based on fear or avoidance of pain and the expectation of reward, psychological or real. Where there has been an oversupply of labor this management style gets results, since the laborer has no other choice. In colonial America and throughout much of America's development the laborer had other choices. One

Figure 1.3 Relations of Manager, Management Style, Management Functions, Clientele

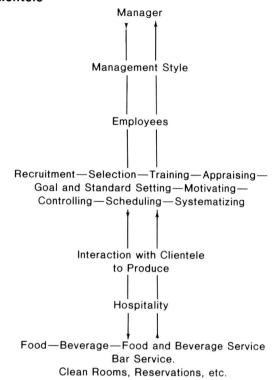

Manager

Management Style

Employees

Recruitment—Selection—Training—Appraising—
Goal and Standard Setting—Motivating—
Controlling—Scheduling—Systematizing

Interaction with Clientele
to Produce

Hospitality

Food—Beverage—Food and Beverage Service
Bar Service.
Clean Rooms, Reservations, etc.

could go West or take up farming. The growth of unions has also acted to prevent some of the worst abuses of people experienced elsewhere in the world.

Scientific management, as a subject, is not ordinarily thought of as a management style, but it tended to look upon people as replaceable commodities. Work done by Kurt Lewin opened up the question as to what type of management or leadership was most effective—autocratic, laissez faire, or democratic. The democratic style of management has been broadened to become *participative management*.

Another style of supportive management has been proposed. It is the kind that looks upon itself as coordinating and supporting rather than directing.

Figure 1.3 is intended to depict the interactions between management style and its impact throughout an organization, affecting people and product, in our case, hospitality, food, and room service.

SUMMARY

Management is a process of planning, communicating, and decision making that takes place in the context of an individual or organizational management style.

Decision making, which interlocks with every other management function, is a complex function that brings into play science, art, logic, and emotion. Many management decisions are group decisions that must be made collectively and that have an impact on several groups of people. Such decisions follow certain interrelated steps: *(a)* analysis of background factors, including knowledge of the people involved and their feelings; *(b)* definition of both analytical and emotional factors bearing on the problem; *(c)* the analytical process involving problem recognition, separating elements of problems, estimating probability of success, testing alternative courses, deciding on the most appropriate course of action, and relating the decision to the total organization; and *(d)* action and reaction involving the implementation and determination of effectiveness.

An ideal organization does not consist of decision makers and implementors. All members of the organization, even those drawing the lowest pay, may have a significant impact on the organization. Since the customer actually dictates the shape of the organization, those working closely with the customer may be the greatest experts on the direction the organization needs to take.

Progressive organizations try to find ways to increase the problem-solving involvement of more individuals. To delegate effectively, a manager needs to know what results are expected, when they are expected, and by whom. The manager needs to follow through and hold others accountable. There is a need to delegate in accordance with the person's ability, but the manager should also give people the opportunity to fail. The delegation process is intertwined with participative management, in which the manager in effect delegates part of the responsibility and authority associated with the position to the subordinate for setting goals and standards.

The management of people has been influenced by the scientific management trend that contributed greatly to the systematization and efficiency of American industry and by the human relations trend which demonstrated that feelings affect job performance much more than formerly realized. Generally, management concepts and techniques related to systematization, work flow, engineering, procedures, and methods represent contributions from the scientific management era. Those philosophies and techniques related to the motivations and needs of individuals most generally reflect human relations notions.

In recent years much attention has been given to management style, the characteristic approach taken by a manager, in relating to the people who report to management. The democratic style has been broadened to become known as participative management, a highly popular management style of the 1970s to be discussed in chapter eight.

Motivation and Management

2

In human affairs there are always leaders, people who set goals and get other people—followers—to accept them and work towards them, or force other people to do their wishes. Even among lower forms of animal life—wherever there is a group of animals—some emerge as leaders and others as followers. Chickens, that have only a glimmer of what might be called intelligence, develop a pecking order among themselves. Moving up the intelligence scale, primates such as baboons organize themselves into social groups with individuals assuming well-defined roles, some leaders, others followers. (The wolfpack always has a leader.) A kind of social organization evolves with a dominant individual at the helm.

Millions of people do the bidding of others, not because they particularly want to, but because they are forced to. People, like the lower animals, are motivated by the offer of reward or by the threat of punishment in one form or another. More important, however, the human being wants self-respect, and goes to great lengths to achieve it—marching into the face of sure death, giving up oneself as a martyr, even committing hari-kari to assure that self-respect will be maintained. "For in each of us," Sigmund Freud said, "there is a desire to be great." Or as John Dewey, the famous educator, once stated, "We are all motivated by the desire to be important, a desire which is almost as potent in the affairs of men as is a need to survive."

People want challenge, want recognition, want to be a part of an organization that has the approval of the community and of society. Most people want to interact with other people and learn to depend upon others for many of the deepest needs.

Using these strong self-realization needs and playing on fears and hostilities, political leaders have motivated masses of people to do incredible things. Men like Julius Caesar, Napoleon, and Garibaldi have inspired common people to uncommon effort. The desire to be somebody, for self-enhancement, lies buried in everyone's mind, no matter how deeply. Toussaint L'Ouverture, once a slave himself, motivated thousands of ex-slaves, arousing them to fever pitch in driving the French out of Haiti. Slaves, brutalized by years of monotonous and heavy labor while forced to exist on a poor diet, rose up against their masters, indicating the divine spark of discontent innate in mankind.

MANAGEMENT AND MOTIVATION

Management assumes motivation. Running through the hundreds of books on the subject of management is the hard core of motivation theory, expressed or implied. To manage people the manager must understand what it takes to arouse them, to turn them on—what kind of environment releases the energies of a person and directs them to a particular goal. Great leaders are necessarily concerned with motivation, and each has developed at least a working hypothesis on motivation. Based on a theory of how some people are motivated and some are not, the manager formulates what has come to be known as a *management style*. The style grows out of a notion about motivation.

At a less sophisticated level the manager merely puts together a number of guidelines and practices, having found that asking may be better than telling; that asking people to participate in decisions which may affect them may be a good thing. Finding oneself to be a model for some kinds of behavior—whose actions are observed and copied by others, and whose attitudes are reflected by employees—is typical of one who holds a manager's job. The manager plays this role without realizing that the role is based on a theory of motivation.

Over the years much of the world's work has been exacted by an elementary theory of motivation based on reward and punishment. Reward people for doing the things you want done. Punish people for doing the things you don't want done. This management style has been called "the stick and the carrot."

Actually there is much to be said for the reward and punish notion of motivation. It works well in animal training and has reappeared in the guise of "behavior modification theory." The punishment aspect can be played down or removed if possible. The behavior modification theory urges immediate, if only token, reward for whatever behavior is desired. The trained seal gets a fish when it jumps through a hoop; the person who is trying to break a chain-smoking habit is self-rewarded whenever the urge to smoke is resisted. The theory is presented in much more sophisticated form in chapter 10.

Scientific management, which grew up around the turn of the century, was an attempt to structure the work situation to the point where motivation by the supervisor was minimized. Frederick Winslow Taylor, the father of scientific management, and his disciples developed the techniques of work analysis, time study, and scheduling for the alleviation of work problems. If, according to them, tasks could be analyzed and broken down, a best way of performing them could be developed and employees could be required to perform in that manner. An assembly line for making automobiles, or a "deassembly line" in a packing plant, where a carcass comes in at one end and disappears at the other, is an institution requiring little supervision. It requires men to perform certain skills over and over again. The big thinking is done by staff and management; employees are interchangeable work units.

Later, in the thirties, various studies by social scientists stressed the importance of feelings of pride, of creativity, and of relations between people, among workers at all levels. Out of this grew the emphasis on human relations. Theories of motivation began to be formulated and management as a discipline was established.

In the discussion that follows, we will look at some of the theories of motivation and how they relate to management style, particularly as the style is seen to be useful in the hotel, restaurant, and club business. It is important to recognize that there is no one theory of motivation, and that all theories have some inherent weaknesses. Nevertheless, the systematic use of a motivational theory can pay dividends to a modern manager.

WHAT IS LEARNED?
WHAT IS INSTINCTUAL?

Fear Is Still with Us

Modern motivation theories tend to play down the role of fear as motivation, preferring to stress positive incentives, such as the need for social intercourse, recognition, approbation, and the excitement that comes from achieving goals. Fear, however, is forever with most of us. Not necessarily in the form of fear of hunger or the other basic needs of mankind, but fear of failure, fear of losing the approval of one's spouse, children, parents, fellow workers, superiors, even one's merit rating. The entrepreneur fears loss of peer approval—the regard of one's fellow club members, one's secretary.

Most of us are trying to live up to an image that was drummed into us somewhere along the line in growing up, drummed in by school teachers, Sunday school teachers, good 'ole Mom, and good 'ole Dad. We all want to measure up to some kind of a standard that has been incorporated into our psyches.

The high achiever fears not winning. The millionaire wants two million. The four-minute miler wants to run the mile in 3.8 minutes. The professor is afraid of failure to get tenure. The unskilled worker is afraid of going on welfare or having to appeal to a relative.

There is something good and wholesome about fear that to some extent offsets its destructive aspects.

A major question in the study of motivation is the one concerned with determining which motives or needs are basic and instinctual, and which ones are learned. What motivations are inculcated by virtue of being a member of a particular cultural group, such as a family, ethnic group, or national group? With what are we born; what do we learn in school or elsewhere?

It was popular at one time to list an array of instinct propensities and proclivities, drives or needs instinctual to humans. More recently the emphasis has been on motivating factors that are learned. Undoubtedly much of the individual's motivation is derived from instincts, universal to all people. The way in which these are expressed, and what comes to be valued, is culturally determined. From a practical viewpoint the manager wants to know what the employee values; what incentives will appeal to the individual.

All theories of motivation face the problem of explaining the causes of behavior and eventually the question "What is learned; what is passed on by heredity?" Two scientists observing the same human behavior may give different interpretations to the motivation for it. On a reflex action level explanation is easier. Many reflex actions are instinctive. On meeting a friend, one smiles and abruptly arches the eyebrows. This is said by one anthropologist to be innate response universally present in humans unless repressed. Human parents apparently have an innate urge to teach their offspring and the offspring to imitate. When a person is surprised there is a reflex intake of breath and the hand starts to the mouth. Opening the mouth is said to be a universal sign of curiosity.

The basic movements of flirting are innate in the human, according to Hans Hass in his book *The Human Animal*.[1] The flirting behavior, he reports, consists of a smile of provocation, an invitation, followed by a "bashful lowering of the eyes, turning away, withdrawal, and apparent tendency toward flight. Visual contact is then resumed and the ambivalent motor sequence may be repeated." Smiling is a reflex action that is accentuated and controlled in the Chinese culture, repressed in others.

According to Hass, curiosity is instinctually motivated in all higher animals, including man. Curiosity might explain inventiveness, the urge to conduct research, even the search for God.

When we try to explain more complicated behavior, the problem of identifying causes grows complex. Obviously we all love, hate, fear, and are anxious. These are the motives that spin the world. Otherwise, how can we explain that greatest of all scourges—war.

Is there an innate urge to be competitive? Competition fuels much of the engine of commerce, sports, educational effort, and much of social life. Whether competitiveness is inborn or acquired really does not matter. It is present. It counts. It is a prime mover of people. Restaurant owners compete with others. Hotel chain executives compete with other chain managers. Within hotels, restaurants, and clubs, department heads compete. Department employees compete within departments.

Competitiveness may be linked to the innate drive to survive, the drive nurtured through thousands of years of struggle on this planet. Aggressiveness is probably an aspect of the will to live, cope, and overcome obstacles and other people. Civilization is a veneer as witnessed by the infighting that characterizes daily life, from the simplest form of working in groups to the board room.

No group of people is immune to the competitive struggle. It exists in the church and the mafia, in the day school and the university. The management problem is not to suppress such motives but to channel them to beneficial ends.

In the search for universal incentives, it is easy to overlook the fact that culture and expectation determines motivation to a large extent. What will motivate a middle-class, white American who has graduated from a school of business will not necessarily motivate the middle-aged member of a less advantaged group. Obviously cultures affect personality and motivation. Studies of national groups and their attitudes toward what is possible within a political system reveal these attitudes to vary widely. A study of five cultures (British, U.S., German, Mexican and Italian) produced these results.[2]

The greater the educational level the more the individual expects responsiveness on the part of elected officials and police; the less education the more the person felt that he could not control the government or the police in any

way, nor could he expect justice. Mexicans and Italians thought they had the least power to control the government. British and American individuals, especially those of higher education, expected the government to respond to them and they expected to join with other people to form groups to make the government respond.

These attitudes towards authority help to explain why individuals raised in certain cultures lack the drive generally associated with the striving middle-class in the U.S. When one feels that he has no control over those in power and cannot expect equal treatment in the eyes of the law or from the establishment, that person is likely to be unresponsive to incentives in terms of advancement and added responsibility.

To repeat, fear as an incentive (or negative incentive) is always with us or at least plays a prominent factor in the behavior of most people. Fear takes many forms: fear of hunger; fear of disease, fear of death. Fear is also present in the form of fear of not winning, fear of losing status, fear of losing esteem of friends, parents, spouses, and children. The over-achiever fears not receiving an "A" in all studies, not making a million dollars this year, not being able to attract beautiful women or handsome men, doing less well than was expected by parents.

It is said that in Japanese society the greatest motivator of all is the fear of failing to accomplish what was expected by the mother, the long-suffering mother who gave everything for the welfare of the child. The Masai warrior is afraid of being afraid, and must prove his courage by killing a lion with a spear. The hotel executive may be afraid of having to tell friends that the job pays less than $30,000; the college professor, afraid because of having been unable to publish during the year; the chambermaid, afraid that she will be unable to pay the rent. Fear is with us all, but in different guises.

Envy too can be a motivator. A large number of German respondents in the study referred to above said that people envy each other in their society and said they tried to live above their stations. Someone always has better clothes, better cars, better homes, more travel experiences, better health, better skills than we do. In a stratified class structure those on the bottom may admire only those with more, whatever the society has in terms of more. In our mobile society the middle-class at least is urged to emulate those with more. "More" is always relative: a person without a car wants one; the untenured teacher wants tenure; the owner of one restaurant wants to own another.

Motivation theorists have tended to downplay the role of money in motivation. One theory calls it a hygienic factor, suggesting that it is not a basic motivator. In our

1. Hans Hass, *The Human Animal* (New York: G. P. Putnam's Sons, 1970).
2. *The Civic Culture,* Almond and Verba (Princeton, N.J.: Princeton University Press, 1963).

society at least, money is a major motivator because it represents so many things—status, winning, approval, new life-style options. Why does any executive require a $500,000 salary rather than a $200,000 salary? Certainly not because of need. The bigger salary is the accolade of success, the symbol of winning, of accomplishment, of recognition by the company.

The question is, will they work harder above a certain salary; will they be more creative for additional money? Are they better leaders with more money? A teenager at a first job in a fast-food operation working for a minimum wage would probably not work any harder if the wage were raised. The teenager, however, might well go across the street to another fast-food enterprise if it offered a higher wage. A restaurant manager takes a much more personal interest in the establishment if a share in the profit is a part of the payment received, especially if those profits are tied to personal effort on the manager's part. That individual may put forth even more effort with pride of ownership.

Expectation and Accomplishment

It is apparent that people tend to try to live up to the expectations of those close to them, as the child to its parents' expectations. If parents expect their offspring to go to college they usually do. A U.S. Marine Corps member tends to act like a U.S. Marine. Ivy League graduates usually expect higher salaries and greater accomplishments from themselves than do state college graduates. They have been conditioned to expect more of themselves and from their society. Conversely persons growing up in less advantaged homes are generally conditioned to expect less for themselves from society. If one never expects to be a manager or particularly affluent, one usually isn't. People seldom exceed their dreams or expectations. This helps to account for the "lack of ambition" (from the middle-class viewpoint) of the less advantaged, the chambermaid, utility worker, the food server, who seem content with their roles.

Only the Incentive "Possible to Achieve" Is An Incentive

Only those things seen as possible can serve as incentives. In the past the British working class seldom attended a university, became officers, or were patented in the peerage. They were conditioned to accept their role in life and looked upon the "upper class" as their betters. The system worked well until recently. There was little envy or antagonism toward the upper classes. The working person took

pride in the job and did not aspire to moving up the class ladder. The corporal may envy the master sergeant, but seldom envies the captain. The captain envies the major because that higher rank is achievable for that individual.[3]

To motivate hotel and restaurant employees the possibility of more money and greater security can be offered to most of them. Promotion to supervisor or manager may have almost no appeal to the majority of these staff members. The risks may be too great for them and their expectations may have never included promotion. For many the tension that goes with supervision and management may be decidedly unpleasant—something to be avoided.

Management must identify those incentives that appeal to the individual. Is it money, security, status, or added responsibility and challenge? Is the individual a risk taker?

Competition can be against a standard, against a level of courtesy, a new record in covers served. Like a football coach the manager arranges the conditions of the game, sets the social climate, trains the players, and calls the signals.

Closely related to competitiveness is the achievement drive, the drive to improve. Competitiveness may be concerned with the battle now—achievement with planning and accomplishment tomorrow or next year.

Research done by McClelland and others at Harvard University has shown that some people have the drive in large amounts; others have very little. Those who have it focus on problem solving and the future; those who lack it are concerned with today and the past. It shows up best in dreams and in projective tests. Some societies have it more than others. Those that have it produce more and rise economically. Those who lack it are relatively stagnant.[4]

Can Achievement Be Taught?

Are humans born to compete, to strive, to achieve? Or do they learn such behavior in a particular society? The answers are not complete, but it is apparent that a desire or need for achievement can be inculcated. Societies differ regarding the need for achievement. Some societies, such as the Hopi Southwest Indian culture, suppress competition in the individual. Other societies, such as the German, Japanese, and American, encourage it. Within any society there is a wide range of achievement drive. The Puritan ethic urges hard work, competition, and conservation of wealth. The person who is completely pro-

3. Hans Hass, *The Human Animal*.
4. D. C. McClelland and D. G. Winter, *Motivating Economic Achievement* (New York: The Free Press, 1969), pp. 14–15, 47, 61.

grammed by the Puritan ethic will be an achiever all his life. Subcultures within the United States encourage less achievement drive.[5]

Within the hotel and restaurant field large numbers of people have little interest in taking on the challenges and problems of management. It is said that not more than one in ten persons has a strong drive for achievement and this in our society which fosters accomplishment.

Most training courses have two components: to develop skills and knowledge and to increase motivation. While many students of human behavior feel that basic human drives cannot be altered greatly in adulthood, others are confident that motivation can be learned and increased. If, argue the latter, it is found that high achievers are concerned with the future and plan for it, then teach the low achiever to do likewise. If it is found that the high achiever has learned to postpone immediate rewards in favor of larger future rewards, teach the low achiever to do likewise.

The importance of the achievement drive cannot be underestimated. Some commentators feel that much of the spectacular economic development of the United States can be directly traced to that drive. With only about 7 percent of the world's population and 7 percent of its land, the United States has accumulated in a relatively short period of time some 40 percent of the world's wealth. It is true that the United States has a wonderful supply of natural resources, but so do other countries. In fact some of the nations rich in oil have a greater financial resource base per capita than does the United States, yet they have done miserably in economic progress.

Part of the achievement drive as expressed in the United States is tied up with the Puritan ethic, which makes hard work a virtue—riotous living a sin. The old sayings put together by Benjamin Franklin, such as "early to bed and early to rise" and "a penny saved is a penny earned" express the essence of this Puritan ethic. Coupling the relatively fluid class structure in this country with the rewards for the able, the shrewd, and the aggressive, the achievement drive has flourished. Some say it has flourished excessively and acquired an unjustifiable mystique.

The Puritan ethic places the emphasis on individual performance. It teaches that individual effort is noble and equates effort and innovation with godliness. It gives short shrift to any belief that man is a pawn of forces beyond his control. Determinism is out, positivism in.

When the ancient Greeks consulted the oracle as to the propitiousness of their next move, they recognized preternatural agencies or forces. The American businessperson will have none of it. It is true that Conrad Hilton offered up prayers following a particularly favorable coup in acquiring another hotel. It is doubtful if he counted much

on divine interference or lessened his efforts before the contracts were signed.

According to the Puritan ethic, it is not considered good form to waste one's substance in expensive living. A died-in-the-wool entrepreneur reinvests. At any given moment such an individual might be worth millions but be hard-pressed to produce cash in any quantity—the person keeps the money working, leveraging it if possible. Ernest Henderson, who was a very wealthy man, set a goal for himself of making at least $10,000 a day for the Sheraton Corporation. He probably felt guilty when the goal was not achieved.

The American ethic includes a belief that almost anything can be done given enough capital, enough know-how, and enough organization. How else would the walk on the moon have been possible? Some 30 billion dollars were mobilized along with thousands of engineers and technicians to make the moon shot possible. Any red-blooded president of a hotel and motel chain believes that the chain can and will grow year after year as the result of the efforts of the people in the organization.

A hallmark of the achiever is the achievement drive. First comes the drive, then the achievement. Few persons rise further than their dreams. Yet achievers hold their dreams within the realm of reality. Not gamblers; they do not rely on luck, but count on their individual efforts for success.

Freudians and behavioral psychologists have recognized the importance of this kind of motivation, but McClelland was the first to attempt to show that the achievement drive can be developed within a short span of time, and by concentrating on training the individual rather than on changing the individual's environment.[6]

Harvard's Department of Social Relations first gave a course on the achievement drive to sixteen managers in a United States company. After two years it was found that these managers had been promoted faster than their matched controls, who had taken the company management course that stressed a "don't rock the boat" policy.

A similar program was tried in India. During a ten-day residential course at the SIET Institute in Hyderabad, American instructors asked small businessmen and middle-level managers from the town of Kakinada to think, talk, act, and perceive like high achievers. They asked these businessmen to write out their plans and goals for the next two years, and they discussed aspects of problem

---

5. The Japanese are addicted to a work ethic, but its origin is different from that of the Puritan ethic. A Japanese must work hard, yet never lose face, for to do so would reflect on the individual's mother, who sacrifices everything on behalf of the child.

6. David C. McClelland (Professor of Psychology and Chairman of the Department of Social Relations at Harvard University), "Achievement Motivation Can Be Developed," *Harvard Business Review,* November-December 1965.

solving: searching for alternatives, overcoming obstacles, getting expert help, planning for possible disasters, minimizing risk, and maximizing profit (minimax). Ten months after their return to their homes, two-thirds of the indoctrination group—double the usual rate—were enterprising and active in achieving.

This is perhaps a more conclusive indication that the achievement drive can be implanted, since the typical Indian businessman doesn't have the high achievement drive found in America. If he has financial status, he doesn't need to work to keep it, due to the loan system; and he is often constrained by the religious and the family system in India. The success of these courses in Hyderabad and later in Bombay suggested exciting possibilities for the development of the individual, especially in poorer countries and in the poverty pockets of America.

Since the Indian studies, McClelland and his associates conducted achievement training courses in Mexico, Poland, India, and Africa. There exist wide differences in motivation drive between the average person in each of these cultures. It was possible to raise the achievement urge among individuals in all of the cultures by using special training methods.

High achievers according to these studies display four characteristic ways of acting:

1. They tend to set moderate goals for themselves and to work harder when the chances of succeeding are only moderately great.

2. They prefer to work at jobs in which they can take personal responsibility for the performance necessary to achieve a goal. They typically avoid gambling situations in which they have no control over the outcome.

3. They like to get immediate feedback as to their performance. They tend to think of money as a symbol of success rather than as a prime motivator.

4. They are constantly on the lookout for opportunities and exert themselves to find opportunity.

Much of the work on raising the achievement motive adheres to common sense. It stands to reason that supervisors and managers at all levels must be concerned with tomorrow. Managers are planners. Planners must think ahead, anticipate the future, and have strategies developed for handling the future. The *foresight syndrome* is a part of every manager's armamentarium. Without it the manager is defenseless and without direction in the face of tomorrow.

Undoubtedly much of "tomorrowness" is a product of the family. If father and mother are oriented to the future, the children are likely to follow suit. If on the other hand the parents feel themselves to be victims of circumstances beyond their control, they may become fatalists, believing that whatever they do has little effect on future events, which are beyond their control. The attitude is easily transmitted to the children.

If indeed the individual is in a restrictive culture, one in which there are few opportunities, it is easy to understand why fatalism flourishes. In a caste society opportunities are blocked off for the lower castes. Fatalism is a natural and perhaps necessary consequence. Indeed it may be a necessary compromise of the psyche with the environment. In some cultures the person actually has very little control over environment. To accept that fact is a rational way to adjust.

Time Perspective

Time perspective obviously influences lifestyle. Clock orientation is a characteristic of our society. Some call it a symptom. The manager, especially the manager in the hotel and restaurant business, is geared to the clock. The meal must be produced in time for the serving period. Deadline follows deadline. The supervisor may be more concerned with two hours from now, the manager with tomorrow, the president with next year. Each has a different temporal outlook. The time perspective for the supervisor who may be concerned principally with today may interfere with the thought for tomorrow.

Need for Affiliation

Another innate drive, according to some psychologists, is the need for affiliation. This can be expressed as the desire to be part of an approving group, the need for friendship, reinforcement of one's ego by group participation. Nearly everyone has such a need. It may be an inborn trait. It is rationally supported in a world of unknowns and uncertainties.

The need for affiliation can be inimical to achievement. Persons overly concerned with seeking and retaining friendship are not of the managerial stamp. Their decisions are cast in terms of their effects, whether people will like or dislike them, and in turn, like or dislike the decision maker. It is possible to operate a hotel or restaurant with happy employees and yet have red ink on the balance sheet!

Effective managers realize that employees welcome challenge and effort if it is presented to them in the right way. True, a "country club" atmosphere may be enjoyed by employees, but they also enjoy pride of accomplishment.

Fortunately, the hotel or restaurant has the ingredients (groups of people serving people) for satisfying the affiliation need. Tie this need to the need for achievement and the organization becomes a team. Team effort can be fun and psychologically rewarding.

Need for Security

Most rational persons have a need for putting something aside for tomorrow and for securing their position among other people. This may extend to securing a favorable position for the family and heirs. Putting something together for tomorrow may mean a million dollars or twenty dollars, depending on the individual. The fatalistic person feels there is no point in concern for tomorrow because fate controls all. One of the problems the Canadian government has had with Eskimos living in the Canadian north is that the Eskimo cannot conceive of concern for the tomorrow. An evidence of this was when the government gave the Eskimos herds of caribou with the expectation that the herds would be built up. What did the Eskimos do but slaughter them for a grand feast.

The manager in a restaurant often is completely puzzled by the behavior of many of the employees who spend every dime they make. Apparently they have learned that there is little purpose in concern for tomorrow, since tomorrow never held much of a prospect anyway. When an individual is raised in a family where there is no piggy bank, no permanent home, no Puritan ethic to bind the person to the future, it is no wonder that the person arrives at adulthood with a concern only for life today. Studies of achievement training have shown that the achiever is different from the nonachiever in that the achiever is concerned with the future, sometimes more than with the present. As Freud put it "he postpones gratification." In the postponement, the person may never get around to enjoy today and tomorrow.

Security is a state of mind that in some individuals is an overriding drive. In others, it scarcely exists. Businesses cannot be built with a complete lack of the security drive and many failures of small businesses can be attributed to a lack of concern for tomorrow. In a hotel or restaurant it is safe to say that at least half of the employees are not security minded in the same way as the supervisory and management personnel. This may account for part of the large number of absentees following payday, a phenomenon which to the middle-class manager is hard to understand. Neither does the person lacking security motivation get upset when late for work. Again middle-class managers have trouble in explaining such behavior unless they move from their own motivational system to that of the employee.

Managers must take into consideration the culture patterns of the group with which they work. In the Spanish tradition, for example, the *macho* is the person who dares, who will fight odds to maintain his dignity or to demonstrate his manliness. Often, at the expense of security or common sense, the macho individual performs in a manly way that may be contrary to what the manager, who could be from a different background, expects.

The security drive that may or may not be instinctual buffers the achievement drive in some cases. Rather than take a chance, one holds on to what one has. To seek a certain amount of security is reasonable and logical in an uncertain world. The person who grows up in an insecure environment may grow fatalistic or the need for security may annoy him. If the parents are insecure the sense of insecurity may be passed on. Or a reaction formation takes place in which the person "cares not a flip" for security. Persons from disadvantaged groups may go either route. The person who is deeply convinced that "it is not worth trying," may live for the moment; tomorrow may never come. Many are the middle-class managers who are genuinely puzzled by employees that fail to save a certain percentage of their income or are not concerned with the future.

The achievement-oriented person may or may not be strongly influenced by the need for security. If one is totally absorbed in achievement, then achievement becomes an end in itself. Money is only a symbol of success and means little except in relation to what competitors are making. No one really needs 10 million dollars or a $500,000 salary. One *needs* such a salary only as a symbol of achievement. What may infuriate the achiever-manager is the fact that the chef is making as much as the manager, though both may be overpaid. In some hotels the sales manager or the chef may receive as much or more than the manager, depending upon the owner's sense of comparative job importance.

The engine behind the drive for achievement is probably the same instinctual force that animals have, a need for survival. In civilized people this animal drive could well take the form of achievement motivation or, more basically, the competitive drive.

Competition against self and others seems to be present in everyone. Family and society encourage or suppress competition. Much of entrepreneurial satisfaction is tied up with the thrill of competing against the person down the street or that other chain. Self-esteem rises and falls in comparing performance.

As compared with the achievement-oriented person, a security-motivated person is patient, uncomplaining, and good humored, having developed such a personality because it was found that this kind of behavior was well received by some bosses and associates. Making no waves makes for security, which is all important for that type of individual. The stereotyped smiling, friendly servant may be security motivated, having learned to accept the status quo philosophically. For this person, such behavior is adaptive and reasonable: helpful, threatening no one, and trying hard to please.

Security is necessarily relative: "Uneasy lies the head of the ruler." The gamesperson playing at or near the top of an organization is continually concerned about retaining that position and therefore may view most of the actions of associates as either threatening or supportive. One of the most powerful persons in history, Stalin was paranoid about his security and ordered the deaths of millions because of his fears. The hotel or restaurant manager can become obsessed with security, may be afraid to try anything new, or be hesitant to take on more responsibility. It can happen to anyone at any level and shows up as free-floating anxiety, the object of anxiety without definite form.

Need for security and its attendant fears and anxieties are not necessarily bad. It is probable that much of the world's work has been generated by just such denigrated motives. In battle, basic motivations become evident. Soldiers seek the ultimate in approval, glory. They also act out of fear, fear of being seen as a coward, or losing face, status, or the friendship of those that they are supposed to support, their comrades. It takes no detailed courses in psychology to recognize the basic security needs and to be able to relate motivation to these needs. Too much security, as in tenured positions and civil service, can be a negative influence on performance. Why work when you don't have to?

Need for Power

Another drive, closely related to competitiveness and the achievement drive, as seen by some psychologists, is the drive for power. Inherent in humans are the needs to be both dominant and submissive. The general aggressiveness developed in the fight for survival as humans emerged from lower forms of life is undoubtedly still with us and helps to explain competitive sports and war. Business rivalries take on the characteristics of war and share the same basic drives. The need for power varies among individuals. It differs from the achievement drive in that power is equated with control, direction, or domination of people. The achievement drive may concentrate on betterment and improvement. Power may be an end unto itself. The person who exercises it may lose sight of the goal. One may relish or love power for itself.

All managers probably have some need for power. Otherwise they would be uncomfortable in giving orders and directing others. It is nothing to be ashamed of; it may be a necessary ingredient of supervision. Only when it is

uncontrolled and dominates the person who has the power can it become dangerous and destructive.

The word *power* has acquired a bad reputation by such aphorisms as "power corrupts; complete power corrupts completely." One might say that without a desire for power little, if anything, is accomplished. Power does not have to be power over people, it can be over things and over one's self. Power is distinctly tied up with pride and ego. To wound one's pride wounds the sense of being able to or interested in controlling the sense of power. Ascribed power, that given by an organization and backed by sanctions, is necessary, except in a few situations, in the hotel and restaurant business. Ideally power should be equated with leadership that is developed by appeals to others' self-interest, ideals, and sense of power. Power of managers in the hotel and restaurant comes from their force of personality, their desire to accomplish, and their urge to carry the employees along with them towards institutional goals.

Power is reinforced by role. Managers play a role that is expected of them as managers. The employee's role is to respond to the manager and most people in our society do so, more or less. The manager wears different clothes, which in part symbolize status and power. Symbols are important in role-playing for manager and employee alike. The male supervisor may wear a tie and a female supervisor, jewelry; the employee, a uniform. The president may insist on wearing a more formal attire and symbols begin at the president's office door: an English secretary, a mahogany panelled office, and an expense account. These symbols may change. This makes no difference as long as the players know their significance.

Can the boss be a friend and still be boss? According to studies of the achievement drive the need for affiliation, friendship, and support from other people varies from culture to culture. It is lower in the United States, higher in such societies as Mexico, Italy, Turkey, or Poland.[7]

In other words the American manager seems to have less need for seeking and holding friends than managers in the other societies studied. Perhaps this is because of the relative independence of the usual American from the extended family, community, and other groups. In less developed countries the individual has fewer opportunities and necessarily relies on friendships and the extended family for security and help, and is expected to reciprocate. More pressures are brought to bear on the Chicano manager or supervisor to hire friends or friends of the family. It would seem reasonable that with such affiliations, standards are more difficult to maintain. In a sense, the manager is fighting the culture.

7. David McClelland, *The Achieving Society* (Princeton: D. Van Nostrand Company, 1961), p. 294.

Need for Prestige

Another motive that probably plays a large part in achievement is the urge for prestige, which by its nature can be endless. Prestige is probably inextricably involved with the achievement drive, at least that part of it dependent upon the feelings of one's peers. If the drive is deepseated and compensatory, it can be a driving force throughout life. Biographical studies show that many prestige-motivated people tend to level off at about middle age in their need for prestige. This may come from a lack of animal vitality or an objective look at oneself and the possibilities. The person has run out of steam, has accepted a certain station in life or quite reasonably says, "this is about it."[8]

WHO MAKES THE BEST EXECUTIVE?

Many management writers have attempted to analyze the managerial personality, to compare the organization person with the entrepreneur, "the autocratic manager" with the "democratic manager." A psychoanalytically oriented study of corporate leaders, using the Rorschach (ink blot) test and intensive interviewing, classified managers into four groups:

1. The Craftsperson—the quiet, sincere, modest, practical type who respects the work ethic and is concerned mainly with building; self-contained; and a perfectionist, unequipped to lead a complex and changing organization.

2. The Jungle Fighter, whose goal is power. Life and work are seen as a jungle, where it is "eat or be eaten." Winner take all. Jungle fighters see their peers in terms of accomplices or enemies—the Machiavellian of today. There are two types: the lions who want to build an empire and the foxes who make their nests in the corporate hierarchy and move ahead by wealth and politicking.

3. The Company Person—is concerned with the human side of the company and with the interactions of people. The company is an ego extension; one shares in its progress and well-being.

4. The Gamesperson—the achievement-oriented individual who likes risks. Life and work is a game. The challenge stimulates and energizes. Like the jungle fighter the gamesman wants to win, but as a team player. Like the company person, what is good for the company is good for the gamesman. People are seen as useful or not useful for the organization, and the gamesman is continually striving and gaining

strength from exercising self-control. The gamesman's enthusiasm imbues others with excitement and ideas.

The successful company needs the Craftsperson and the Company Person, but it also needs the Gamesperson.[9]

President Kennedy was exemplified as a gamesman, the flexible competitive player, a glory seeker. Presidents Johnson and Nixon were likened to jungle fighters. The authors admire the "gamesperson" and feel that person will do well for the organization and for his or her self too. The person is a realist, uses the people in the organization to make the organization win. Business is like a game. There are winners and losers. The gamesperson wants to win and have fun doing so.

MASLOW'S THEORY OF MOTIVATION

The most widely quoted theory of motivation is that presented by A. H. Maslow in his book *Motivation and Personality*.[10] Maslow, like others before him, tried to derive a system of motivation that he believed to be present in every human being. He posited a hierarchy of needs as being the determinants of behavior. Most basic and overriding are those physiological needs necessary for any living being: air, food, and water.

Next in the order of potency in their effect on human behavior are the needs for security and safety. These needs are met by such things as tenure in employment, home ownership, saving accounts, or insurance.

In the following, human needs are ranked according to Maslow, physiological and security needs being most basic.

Self-realization	Work as creative achievement, as fun, as development of the person
Self-esteem	Not satisfied with scientific management
Social	Work in a social setting
Security	Work for survival
Physiological needs	Satisfied with scientific management

From the above it is seen that work may be merely a means of survival and a way of developing security against hunger and the satisfaction of creature comforts. The person who operates a dish machine in an isolated setting

8. Saul W. Gellerman, *Motivation and Productivity* (New York: American Management Association, 1963), p. 154.

9. Michael Maccoby, *The Gamesman, the New Corporate Leaders* (New York: Simon and Schuster, 1976).

10. A. H. Maslow, *Motivation of Personality* (New York: Harper, 1954). For those who are interested in a review of the subject: Motivation, see N. C. Cofer and M. H. Appley, *Motivation: Theory and Research* (New York: John Wiley & Sons, 1967).

may be doing so only because there is no other choice. If other employees are added to the dishroom or the operator interacts with other members of the kitchen, the job takes on social-contact rewards.

For a job to satisfy the higher humanistic needs, the person must be ego-involved, see the job as a challenge, and have the opportunity for creative input. So much depends upon the attitude of the person toward the job. The same job can be exciting and challenging to one and a complete bore to another. It is up to management, at least in part, to *arrange* a job and its *climate,* to allow for individual differences and optimal challenge levels.

So-called scientific management, introduced about the turn of the twentieth century, tended to look upon workers as economic units. Managers and staff were asked to find the most efficient way of performing a job. The employee was expected to perform in the prescribed efficient manner. If the person did not want to conform, there was another who would take that place. The job satisfied the two basic levels of needs but did little to develop the person, challenge him, or ego-involve him to a great extent. Democratic management and the subsequent management by objective is thought to better provide for the higher human needs. The employee takes part in the establishment of goals and is consulted in day-to-day operations, thereby feeling less like a cog in the machine and more like a vital part of a goal-striving group.

MOTIVATORS VS. SATISFIERS

A contribution to motivation theory has been made by Frederick Herzberg and his associates, who point out that many of the factors ordinarily associated with motivation are not really motivators at all. To distinguish between factors which if not met will interfere with work production and those factors that call forth energy and enthusiasm, Herzberg labels the one group *satisfiers,* the other *motivators.* Among those factors that are important for ensuring that work will proceed have to do with physical conditions, a sense of security, wages and salaries, and the social relationships between employees and with their supervisors. Factors that are true motivators, according to Herzberg, are feelings of personal accomplishment, recognition from people who are held in high esteem, participation in making decisions, responsibility, and the opportunity and feeling of growth.[11] The satisfiers or maintenance factors, as seen by Herzberg, are as follows:

Physical conditions	Lighting, temperature, pleasant surroundings, cafeteria food, beauty or lack of it in the work setting.
Security	Sense of enjoyment or contentment within the environment, lack of apprehension over the future.
Economic factor	Wages, salaries and fringe benefits.
Social factor	Relationships with fellow workers and supervisors.

According to Herzberg maintenance factors are not as important for productivity as are the motivators. Maintenance factors, if not met, are cause for complaint. If not acceptable, they interfere with productivity, and they fail to provide interest or enthusiasm for the job.

It can be argued that the economic factor is far more than a maintenance factor, especially for those who view wages or salaries as merit badges or proof of accomplishment. The salary a person gets as compared with the salary received by peers and associates is always important. It matters little that the person may be overpaid as long as a next-door neighbor is receiving more. It may be comforting to owners and managers to assume that the economic factor is only a maintenance factor. Some studies would support such a notion; other studies would not. If wages and salaries are not motivators, how is it possible to get people to sign up for work in Saudi Arabia or at a lonely outpost in the Arctic? At double the salary, there are usually plenty of applicants.

It can also be argued that social conditions of work are more than maintenance factors. Where team effort is called for, it can be a motivator. Studies of soldiers show that feeling for the unit may be the overriding motivator. Many people will work hard to attain security and if this is so, security is a motivator.

It would seem that Herzberg's differentiation between the motivating factors and maintenance factors is useful in thinking about what it takes to stimulate people. In the past overemphasis may have been given to so-called human relations on the job. The manager who is carried away with the belief that human relations will solve everything could end up with a happy but unproductive hotel or restaurant crew. The authors are acquainted with a hotel whose employees receive wages well in excess of the prevailing wage, relatively fine working conditions, an easy relationship between management and employees, yet the establishment is losing money.

The human condition may call for a certain degree of strife, tension, and challenge. Government bureaucracies typically pay as well as or better than industry for work produced at nonmanagerial levels. The maintenance factors are good. Some of the motivative factors may be present but often the achievement and growth factors are not. Consequently, productivity is minimal.

---

11. For a more complete discussion of the *two factor* theory see Frederick Herzberg, *The Motivation to Work* (New York: John Wiley & Sons, 1959), and Frederick Herzberg, *Work and the Nature of Man* (Cleveland: World Publishing Company, 1966).

Table 2.1 Opposing Theories of Motivation	
Machiavellian	**Idealistic**
Humans are selfish, treacherous, greedy, ungrateful, work only for self	Humans are selfless, honest, appreciative, work for the group
Manipulate others	Provide goals for others
Emphasize hate, fear, revenge, punishment, and domination	Emphasize love, sympathy, affection, kindness, rewards
Trust no one	Trust others until proven false

WHAT IS THE BASIC NATURE OF HUMAN BEINGS?

Implicit in any theory of motivation is a view of humankind's basic nature. Is the human being kind or cruel? Self-serving or selfless? Willing to work for the good of others or only for self?

Whatever the basic animal nature of humans, it is instructive to examine history for evidences of what makes human beings go. No doubt human nature does change but written history shows that the calamities of this world have been human-made, brought on by greed, aggression, fear, pride, and ambition. So far the Bible has been right in saying "there shall be wars and rumors of wars." Whatever is in the nature of humankind that brings on war has not changed much since recorded history.

What do the great leaders of history have to tell us about motivation and the management of humans? Consider the motivational theory of one of the greatest religious leaders, Jesus. Compare his thoughts with those of a cynical but highly astute political observer of the sixteenth century, Niccolo Machiavelli, and put the thoughts of both men beside the leadership of Napoleon. Jesus teaches us that human beings are intrinsically good, kind, noble, a part of God. Machiavelli, a jobless Florentine, of the middle-class bureaucracy, wrote a series of guidelines for administrators called *Il Principe*. He advocated manipulation, duplicity, and bad faith. Some of his strategies are highly effective and widely used in management today.

The two notions of humankind's basic nature are seen in table 2.1. The Machiavellian theory is described in the left-hand column as compared with an idealistic viewpoint of mankind as preached by Jesus. Each presents a view of human nature and advice on how to motivate.

Machiavellian is a term of contempt used to describe the sneaky, devious manager who never reveals his true motivation, who seeks to persuade others to his viewpoint by the use of deception and guile. Machiavellian principles may reflect an honest viewpoint of human nature. Some of the so-called positive thinking of today and the earlier Dale Carnegie approach have been analyzed as true

Machiavellian. They attempt to persuade or win people over for one's own ends. They disguise reality in a manner that would be highly approved by Machiavelli. The precept running through the Dale Carnegie approach, "make them think it's their idea," is a Machiavellian characteristic. So too is the precept "make them like you so that they feel obligated to you." If at first you don't win someone over, use any method you can think of and try, try again. Use flattery, gifts, guile. Influence a bit at a time until finally you wear down the person to the point of beginning to feel that your regard is actually genuine. Flatter, ingratiate yourself, extend yourself. When necessary, exert pressures through others with whom the person associates. When you no longer need the individual drop the individual like a hot potato.

Machiavelli saw motivation as manipulation. As such, manipulators never expose their true motivations. Instead they are intent upon influencing another person to do what they want done. To this end the manipulator uses any technique so long as the end is achieved. Carnegie recommends *selling* oneself to his public but the idea has applications in management. A basic tenet in this style of management is appeal to self-interest. Find out what the person really wants—ego enhancement, pride in accomplishment, security—and tie the sales pitch to these wants. Is the person fiercely independent—appeal to one's pride as an individual. If the person's outward appearance is paramount—appeal to self-vanity.

Using this style a manager might adjust the approach for different employees:

"Jack, since you're the strongest guy we've got, would you rearrange the storeroom?"

"Miss Smith, we want someone really efficient at the front desk. Would you be interested in filling in while the others are on break?"

"Mary, you're about the only one around here who understands inventory control. Would you take on the job of making the weekly inventory?"

Machiavelli would favor several of Carnegie's techniques, but he emphasized the value of fear as a motivator.

Machiavelli's dictum was "caress or annihilate." The really good individual in Machiavelli's eyes would be at a serious disadvantage in the world of politics or in the jungle of the corporation executive office.

As seen by Machiavelli, people seldom achieve great wealth or power without duplicity. Cunning, force, and fraud are necessary tools to motivate people. "It seldom happens that men rise from low conditions to high rank without employing force of fraud . . . especially cunning." History is replete with examples. Even though devious, according to Machiavelli, the manager must appear to be trusting, forgiving, and bursting with integrity. The manager must be ever on guard "One must be the fox to recognize traps and a lion to frighten wolves." The really good person is at a disadvantage, according to Machiavelli, therefore "must necessarily come to grief among so many who are not good."

So, according to Machiavelli, the manager should never show irresoluteness. As manager, paraphrasing Machiavelli, you would follow certain guidelines:

1. Do not trust your subordinates. Rely only on cost accounting, original documents, results rather than status symbols or honors—promotions should always be available, even to top brass. (Machiavelli believed in granting rewards a little at a time so that there would always be some left.)

2. Recognize that your top courtiers (your staff and followers) depend upon you for all good things—and expect a sophisticated servility matched only by the limits of imagination.

3. Build your organization around people who are 100 percent loyal to you. If disloyalty in anyone is suspected, eradicate that person.

4. Distrust everybody and be careful of gratitude displayed. Think of people as pawns to be used in your own best interest on your struggle up the social and monetary reward ladder.

Some of Machiavelli's methods are indeed effective. He warned that the real motivations of people change very little with time. "To foresee the future, consult the past . . . for men are always animated by the same passions that produce similar results."

Machiavelli stressed that the manager must always have some rewards available when expecting to have a following. The rewards may be in the form of money or status. Rather than granting large increases even though warranted, Machiavelli would feed them out a little at a time to extend their incentive value.

Professor Richard H. Buskirk has written a most lively book relating Machiavellian principles to modern management.[12] Among the principles upon which he comments are the following:

When it is necessary to punish someone, by discharging the person for example, try to make sure that individual has something to lose by retaliating vengefully. That something can be an unfavorable recommendation or the power you might have in deprecating the person to other people in power.

Be ultra-cautious about putting anything in writing, especially if it is derogatory about another person. Those forthright souls who write letters of recommendation in which they point out the candidates' weaknesses often find that the letter finds its way into the hands of the candidate, who is unlikely to ever forget what was said, and may well seek revenge.

Administrators are wise never to make promises in writing that one may wish to forget later on.

Those people who are most to be feared are those close to the source of power, for they are the ones who can most safely undertake conspiracies against the man in power. Trusted friends, people who have for years buttered up the administrator, loudly extolling that individual's virtues, may be just the ones to act treacherously. Conspiracies can be expected. Some are good, especially conspiracies against rules, regulations, and systems that are nonsensical or repressive, or that interfere with the effectiveness of people. Everyone conspires to some degree—it is a universal human trait. Conspiring may be a valid tactic under certain circumstances.

Always get rid of anybody whom you have injured seriously. Such people carry scars that are not likely to be forgotten. Sometimes a person has no reasonable alternative but to accept whatever benefits can be gotten, and take the accompanying injuries to others in stride. But he warned that, in such cases, the other party will probably seek revenge if given the opportunity.

A correlate to this rule: when taking over a company get rid of all the people you plan to at once. Don't drag out the process.

It may be far wiser to fire workers than to discipline them severely. A person disciplined may wait for an opportunity to get revenge, an opportunity that usually occurs sooner or later.

Don't allow people who have been in power to stay around with reduced power, as is often done when one company takes over another. The person who has had his ego injured will be nothing but a negative on the new team. The principle has particular application in university administration—demoted deans and department chairmen have often mustered dissension that has pulled

12. Richard H. Buskirk, *Modern Management and Machiavelli* (Boston: Cahners Books, 1975).

down administrations. The same principle applies to industry situations generally.

Machiavelli says that at times it is smart to feign folly, merely to please "The Prince," i.e., the administrator. "Yes-People" abound in most organizations. Some of them may not be nearly as foolish as they appear; they are biding their time—merely waiting for the day when they can take over power.

Administrators should make themselves feared in such a way as to avoid hatred, even though gaining no love. It is quite possible for people to respect and fear a boss without hatred toward that individual.

Better a manager be known as miserly than as overly liberal with the organization's money. Too many people are quite ready to give away or use company money whereas they would never think of spending a dime of their own, under similar circumstances, for the good of the organization. "Liberal leaders seldom realize that their generosity to one person robs someone else."

In taking over another company or organization, the manager has the choice of either cleaning house and starting over again, or preserving that organization. If the management style was permissive and democratic it would be unwise to change that style. If the style were to be changed it would be necessary to build a new organization.

"Prudent" men seek no avoidable risks; rather, prudent men trod proven paths: "A prudent man should always tread in the path taken by great men and imitate those who are most excellent, so that if he does not attain to their greatness, at any rate he will get some tinge of it."

It must be recognized that there is nothing more difficult to carry out, nor more doubtful of success, nor more dangerous to handle, than the initiation of a new order of things.

Make sure you have the guns before you go to war; in other words, don't take on a challenge unless you are pretty sure of winning.

If you have been raised by someone in power to a high position, you are at that person's mercy: "Such as these depend absolutely on the good will and fortune of those who have raised them, both of which are extremely inconsistent and unstable."[13]

Don't put your boss in the position of having to choose between you and a number of other people (unless you have another job lined up in advance).

Protect the people who work for you—"woe to the manager who fails to support, fight for the group when the need arises."

If you are in a fight with the management don't expect help from your fellow workers or colleagues. It is everyone for oneself.

Don't ever let the organization feel that they can do without you. They probably will.

The president of a corporation should spend considerable time in "the care and feeding of stockholders," convincing them that the firm has a glowing future. "A pound of future seems to be worth about 3 pounds of present."

"When Princes think more of luxury than of arms they lose their state." If you want to be successful, concentrate on doing so; forget the parties and the pleasure.

You cannot reasonably expect to be obeyed unless you have the power to enforce your own orders. Power comes in many forms such as awards, salary increases, status, a new desk, a committee appointment, fringe benefits, and the like.

A man who wishes to make a profession of goodness in everything must necessarily come to grief among so many who are not good. "A good man may have to do some bad things to save his enterprise. Good must follow a narrow path with few options open to it. While Evil is left free to do whatever it takes to win the day."[14]

Such a view of man and his motives is sacrilegious to the true Christian, yet Machiavellian behavior has paid off rather handsomely for some individuals in business, schools, and churches. Some cultures promote the Machiavellian method as an ideal. A person who can outwit the other person is the clever one to be applauded. In such societies the trusting person is at a severe disadvantage. If the entire society is Machiavellian, the results can be nothing but disastrous. Character and real assassination would be the order of the day. Business would come to a standstill for lack of trust if dictatorship was not on hand to enforce "honesty" by force.

Some businesses may be operated on a Machiavellian philosophy and do well provided the inner circle of courtiers are rewarded with power, prestige, and money. Members of the inner circle must trust one another, at least to a certain extent, for the organization to continue.

It becomes quickly apparent that both theories apply in varying degrees and under special circumstances to most people. There are exceptions. Persons trained in an environment that stresses the Machiavellian approach are likely to look upon it as appropriate for most occasions. Other people have been programmed or conditioned to respond along idealistic lines.

Observations of people in prison camps seem to show that when one is placed under great stress and fears for survival itself, that individual tends to become Machiavellian even though more idealistically inclined under normal conditions of life.

On the other hand most people often want to do things for others. The Christian religion and most other wide-

13. *Ibid.*
14. Niccolo Macchiavelli, *The Prince* (New York: DaCapo Press, reprint 1968).

spread religions are founded partly on this belief. The cynic may retort, "yes, that's the way they get their kicks." Why shouldn't an idealist receive pleasure from such behavior? Perhaps it is instinctual, predicated on the need to band together, to help each other, and to respond sympathetically to others' stress or problems. This is a very necessary instinct for survival as a species.

NAPOLEON'S LEADERSHIP AND MOTIVATION

Napoleon, one of the great leaders of all time, probably had no well-defined theory of motivation, but he knew and understood the kinds of rewards, both psychic and real, that made peasants into brave soldiers. Some of his practices and ideas have relevance for hotel and restaurant management.

1. "A brave regiment cannot exist without a brave colonel." In other words the person at the top of an organization largely determines the spirit and morale of the group. Have you ever seen a really good restaurant or hotel without a top-notch manager?

2. "An army travels on its stomach." The effective leader understands that the basic physical needs must be met if morale is to be high. In today's hotel or restaurant this may mean a reasonably cool or air-conditioned kitchen. It means well-prepared employee meals served in pleasant surroundings, the reduction of unnecessary noise, and well-lighted work areas.

3. "The most effective rewards are those that are given immediately." Napoleon knew that performance and reward must be closely linked. When a man showed particular bravery or skill on the battlefield he was given a battlefield commission on the spot. Most of Napoleon's marshalls were men who had come up through the ranks.

To develop morale in a hotel or restaurant promote from within and promote or give raises for outstanding performance. Do it soon after the performance. Let it be known that anyone in the organization can rise to the top. Too often hotels and restaurants represent caste systems. Unless a staff member has completed college, or even a particular college, that person may be excluded from the upper caste of management.

Provide psychic as well as tangible rewards. Napoleon was quick to give a particularly brave soldier a chased silver musket for all to see. Rather cynically, he carried a bag of medals and ribbons that would be publicly awarded soon after a battle. Most people crave public recognition. The good manager sees to it that it is forthcoming when appropriate.

Create a mystique about the value of the organization. Napoleon was the exemplar of mystical creation. Napoleon fired a nation to the tune of "La Gloire," for the glory of France. The mystique was so powerful that its reverberations are felt in France today.

Effective managers believe, or at least make their organizations believe, that the restaurant or hotel they serve is or soon will be the best of its kind. A sense of mission and purpose is transmitted to the organization. Much of this is done in face-to-face relationships with staff during employee meetings, and in relationships with the public.

Napoleon was able to infuse his elite troops with a burning fervor so that at one ceremony when Napoleon took leave of his troops and burned their standards, some of the men ate the ashes. Some hotels have been able to develop excellent morale displaying a spirit, quickly sensed by the guests, that is a reflection of the fact that a large percentage of the employees have been with their hotels for twenty years or more.

Napoleon knew how to appeal to one's pride and ambition. He also knew that quick tangible rewards induce people to great effort. Titles and wealth were given in abundance to his lieutenants. Rewards went to the brave, the energetic, and the loyal. In 1807 he created eighteen dukes, many of whom had come from the lower classes.

The owner or president of a hotel or restaurant company does well to make sizeable tangible rewards available in the form of stock or stock options to key people. Conrad Hilton has made several people independently wealthy. The Marriott company has a profit-sharing plan that makes it possible for everyone in the organization to benefit handsomely as the stock of the company and its earnings increase. Psychic rewards should be embedded in a solid foundation of money rewards.

THE MANAGER AS A DIRECTOR OF ENERGY

Historically, much of the world's work—and all of its wars—have been motivated by the basic animal emotions: fear, hate, and vengeance. Greed, too, has played a disproportionate role in the affairs of humans. Management today attempts to shift the emphasis from hate, greed, and anxiety to the positive emotions of love, affection, cooperation, and accomplishment. To be realistic, however, much of management will still concern itself with the drives of fear, envy, and greed.

Motivation is defined in a number of ways. Not even the experts agree on a particular definition. One way to

Figure 2.1

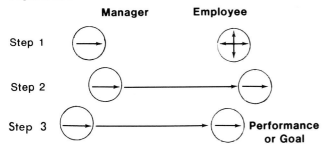

view it is to see the individual with a number of basic needs and drives which are an integral part of that person's animal heritage. The motivator, leader, or manager is seen as reinforcing, suppressing, or channeling these drives to particular performance.

In figure 2.1, we see two individuals, manager and employee. Both have forces within them that will determine their performance. Some are instinctual, some learned. In step 1, the manager has resolved these forces to focus on getting the employee to perform something. The employee is unresolved energy-wise.

With the manager's help, the vectors or forces within the employee are now focused in a particular direction, on a particular goal.

Why belabor this point? To show that managers do not necessarily create forces within the employee and to show that managers help employees to focus toward a desired performance.

Leaders or managers who stimulate or create desires, actually increase the energies of people. Inspiration raises the level of motivation within the person. Great leaders touch off divine sparks and shape and direct the world's work. Some highly effective leaders—Hitler, for example—fuel the baser instincts of hate and greed.

There is nothing magical about leadership, nothing abstruse, nothing beyond the comprehension of the usual manager. The leader triggers or reinforces behavior patterns within the follower. The football coach so conditions his team that when a certain number is called all eleven men simultaneously perform that play. In the restaurant the manager's "team" is trained to prepare and serve a certain menu. The "starting signal" that initiates the food service is the appearance of a patron.

It could be said that the manager programs the operation *and* the employees. Certain signals then call forth programmed responses. The manager might be thought of as a coach or a programmer. Being a programmer implies a kind of step-by-step conditioning; being a coach carries overtones of competition, inspiration, excitement. Perhaps elements of both approaches are needed.

RESTAURANT MANAGEMENT "BY THE NUMBER"

One of the original thinkers in the restaurant field, Harry H. Pope, of Pope Cafeterias, St. Louis, believes that he has condensed management theory for practical restaurant operation into a series of twenty "Guidelines for Food Service Management."

The guidelines, according to Pope, can be used to create "Management by the Number." Similar guidelines have been produced from time to time but none carry the weight of Pope (besides being a management innovator, Pope is an athletic 230-pounder). Operating some thirty cafeterias at maximum efficiency, Pope achieves something most unusual in cafeteria operation—a 28 percent food cost.

The application of "Guidelines" (distillation of Pope's management experience over a lifetime of restaurant operation) in Pope Cafeterias, is simplicity itself. For example: suppose a manager complains that an employee does not know how to work at the food-service counter. Pope calls out, Guideline 5, "Permit no employee to perform any work or task for which the employee has not been trained."

A supervisor reports that volume of sales in a cafeteria exceeded last month's volume but that profit is down. Pope responds with Guideline 20, "We are not trying to see how many customers we can serve. We are trying to see how many customers we can serve without compromising our standards."

To a manager who is constantly smiling and eager to please employees, and who is complaining of impoliteness from an employee, Pope responds, Guideline 18, "All customers and employees have the right to be treated with respect until the right is forfeited through unreasonable attitude or improper actions." In other words, the manager can be too nice and not evidence concern in the form of being displeased, thus standards of courtesy are not being met.

A manager explains that a foul-up that happened the night before occurred after the manager had gone home. Pope calls the manager's attention to Guideline 1, which states clearly "The manager is responsible for the operation of the unit *at all times* whether present or not."

On inspection of a cafeteria, garbage cans are found to be smelly. Pope calls attention to Guideline 2, "At all times someone must be accountable for each item or task in the unit."

A manager explains that an error in the weekly report was a mistake caused by the bookkeeper, to which Pope responds, "Guideline 4 and Guideline 5, Delegation is not abdication," and "Permit no employee to perform any obligation or task for which the employee has not been trained."

The twenty guidelines are as seen below:

Guidelines for Food Service Management*
by H.H. Pope

1. The manager is responsible for the operation of the unit *at all times,* whether present or not.
2. At all times, someone must be accountable for each item or task in the unit.
3. There should be a policy covering everything which happens in a unit. Recipes, schedules, rules, and other policies must be *in writing, communicated,* and *enforced.*
4. Delegation is not abdication.
5. Permit no employee to perform any job or task for which the employee has not been trained.
6. No job or task is so important that we cannot take the time to do it safely.
7. The main responsibility of a manager or assistant manager is to maintain standards *constantly* and *consistently,* by training, developing and controlling the staff.
8. At regular intervals a manager should look at the unit from the guest's viewpoint.
9. During the busy service periods managers and staff should concentrate on service.
10. The secret of productivity is utilization. Available time can always be used for advance production, cleaning, or cross training.
11. The secret of food cost control is utilization. As much as possible, *all* food which is purchased should be sold to the customers.
12. Production should be controlled through advance scheduling, increased production before the rush, and reduced production before the rush is over.
13. There should be a daily review of all portions, involving servers and checkers.
14. The dining room tables must be cleared promptly. Service and production should be geared to the ability to maintain a clean dining room. The staff must be *balanced* at all times.
15. The manager must check production and cleaning with each department head before the department head is scheduled to leave for the day.
16. There should be an objective of reaching a state of perfection. It is easier to maintain perfection than to reach the objective of perfection.
17. The reputation of no individual is as important as the reputation of the company.
18. All customers and employees have the right to be treated with respect, until the right is forfeited through unreasonable attitude or improper actions.
19. The most important obligation in the profession of food service is to protect the health of the customers, by providing good nutrition in conditions of absolute sanitation.
20. We are not trying to see how many customers we can serve. We are trying to see how many customers we can serve without compromising our standards.

HOW TO MANAGE A FOOD SERVICE OPERATION—
Always keep one question in mind: "AM I PROUD OF IT?"
If the answer to this question is "NO," then ask these questions:
1. WHO IS RESPONSIBLE? (See Guideline 2)
2. WHAT'S OUR POLICY? (See Guideline 3)

AGE AND MOTIVATION

Everyone recognizes that age brings declines in energy and reaction time. It also brings declines in sensory acuity. The individual reaches a peak in sensual acuity sometime between twenty and thirty years of age. Top performance in such sports as skiing, tennis, and volleyball is usually reached when the person is also in his twenties. After that, decline in the various senses causes performance to taper off. For example, it is quite normal to require eyeglasses in one's forties.

According to one set of research results, a 50% drop-off is experienced after a number of years in each of the sensory modalities as shown below.

Modality	Years after Top Acuity
Sight	13 years
Sound	15 years
Smell	22 years
Taste	29 years
Touch	60 years

On a more positive note, some of these declines are relatively unimportant. Reaction time to a visual signal is quickest at about age twenty-five when it is about an eighteenth of a second. A seventy-five-year-old person will have a quarter of a second reaction time, which happens to be the same reaction time as that of an eleven-year-old.[15] Vocabulary, general information, similarities, and judgment rise but seldom fall before age sixty. Older persons do better than younger on tests requiring preplanning and decisions as to what is not worth doing.

Ideational, expressional, associative, word fluency, and spontaneous flexibility are generally considered as having to do with creative types of activities. These do not necessarily decline from ages twenty to sixty; sometimes they increase. Most older people are more capable in these respects than they were at twenty years of age.[16] Short-term memory declines with age but such declines are small before age sixty. Tasks requiring speed decline with age

---

*Courtesy of H. H. Pope, Pope cafeterias, St. Louis.
15. *Industrial Gerontology,* no. 12 (Winter 1972): 32.
16. *Ibid,* p. 36.

Figure 2.2 Production curve of kitchen worker working at a normal rate with two ten-minute coffee breaks during a shift.[17]

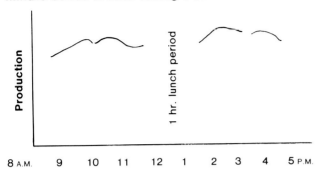

Figure 2.3 Production curve of a bored worker. Note how when worker sees end of shift approaching work production increases.[18]

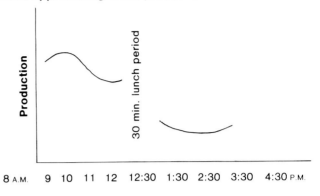

unless they are well practiced. General intelligence declines but for some not until age seventy or eighty.

Motivation must be keyed to ability. The key, then, is to recognize those functions required by a particular job, then to match the faculties that exist within a person with the functions of that job.

Recognizing the normal decline in sensory acuity in the various modalities makes the manager more realistic in recognizing what to expect as to the capabilities of a particular employee. Fast-food operations have found that people over thirty cannot perform well at the speeds required during rush periods. Notice if you will that most of the hamburger restaurants are staffed by teenagers or people in their twenties. In some places, teenagers are more likely to take jobs paying only the minimum wage, which is most often paid by fast-food restaurants.

MOTIVATION AND PHYSIOLOGY

Motivation implies the use of energy and effort. The degree of motivation is obviously related to the state of the organism. In humans the energy level rises and falls daily and waxes and wanes in cycles. Women pass through a twenty-eight day menstrual cycle that affects their motivation. Men, too, are said to undergo periodicity. Spring fever may be the reaction of the body to increased temperatures and longer daylight hours. High temperatures and high humidity depress activity while brisk climates stimulate it.

Individuals differ as to the rise and fall of their energy level throughout the day but enough research has been done to state general principles. Figure 2.2 illustrates a production curve of a kitchen employee working at a normal rate with two ten-minute coffee breaks, one in the morning and one in the afternoon. The employee also has a one-hour lunch period.

Figure 2.2 shows the employee starting work at 8 A.M. and working until 5 P.M. The employee starts at a low level of productivity. The level rises until just before the coffee break at 10 A.M. Following the coffee break the curve rises to its maximum and tapers off just prior to lunch. After lunch there is a warm-up period until 2 P.M. After that, productivity begins to fall off and continues to decrease, except for a brief rise following the afternoon coffee break.

A manager, knowing the typical work curve, would not expect an employee to produce as much in late afternoon as in the morning or at the beginning of the afternoon. The manager would also expect brief work spurts after coffee breaks. Coffee releases stored glycogen, a form of sugar, from the liver and makes more energy available. The break itself is a psychological lift, and the employee returns to work with fresh enthusiasm.

A different work curve can be expected if the work is boring to the employee. In figure 2.3 we see that the curve is almost continuously downward from the time it reaches a peak at 9 A.M. Work spurts, which occur at the end of the morning and afternoon shifts, can be explained by the fact that the worker puts a little more effort into the boring job as he sees the end of the shift approaching.

TENSION LEVEL AND MOTIVATION

The amount of tension or excitement in an individual varies from person to person and also within a person from time to time. The hockey player who must be under high tension for proper body reaction to the demands of the game, therefore needs relatively large amounts of adrenaline and blood sugar. The person crocheting needs relatively little. Too much would interfere with the hand work.

17. Lendal H. Kotschevar, *Work Simplification in Food Service,* (Chicago: Institutions Magazine), p. 21.

18. *Ibid.*

Figure 2.4   How Much Tension?

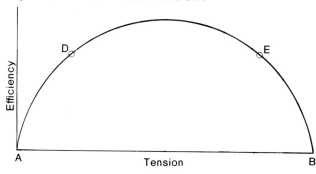

Each job calls for a particular tension level that also varies from time to time.

How Much Tension Is Right?

Every job calls for a certain level of tension if the job is to be done well. The speaker getting up to address an after-dinner meeting cannot do a top job unless keyed up. Opera singers cannot perform well unless their adrenaline is flowing freely and they are more excited than would be appropriate for ordinary living. The soccer player needs to be charged up to run at maximum level and confront the opposition without fear. On the other hand, a person sewing with the same amount of tension would soon be sewing fingers instead of material.

The dining room at the rush period is an exciting place and must be exciting to the waitress if she is to give fast, efficient service. The accountant needs much less excitement. One of the skills needed in a supervisor or manager is the ability to key the excitement level to the demands of the job. In some instances it is the manager's continuing responsibility to dampen excitement. A high-pressure kitchen, for example, needs no shouted orders, no over-wrought chef, no profanity. Auguste Escoffier well understood this and ruled out loud voices and swearing. He also forbade the use of alcohol in a kitchen, substituting instead a barley water that kitchen employees were encouraged to drink.

In the hotel and restaurant business there seems to be more than enough causes for excitement. The manager often is called upon to reduce tension. The deadlines of registration and meal periods are more than enough to create necessary tension levels.

Figure 2.4 is one way of looking at the relationship between efficiency and tension.

As seen in the graph, efficiency is at its peak when tension is somewhere between D and E. When we get up in the morning our tension level is low and we do not really hit our stride until tension builds up to about the point of D. If, however, tension should increase beyond

the point of E our efficiency begins to drop off and hyper-tension results in panic and absolute inefficiency, as seen at point B. We might think of ourselves as walking on a path through a swamp. If we get off the path with either too little or too much tension, we are in deep water and in trouble as regards efficiency and mental well-being. Sometimes under stress we may feel as if we are walking a log over a stream; we have to be particularly careful not to swerve off the log into the water. Psychiatrists have likened the problem of mental health to an escalator. Some people are going up and some people are going down all the time.

Tension Is Communicable

The manager is a focal point of tension. The manager's attitudes, behavior, ways of doing things are copied by other workers. On a less conscious level, stress exhibited in a leader of any kind is picked up by the group. If the leader is anxious the group becomes restive and anxious as well. A calm leader tends to calm the group. A confident leader lends confidence to others.

Some of the symptoms of stress are obvious. Others less so. Stress strains the vocal chords and raises the pitch of the voice. The hunched back, the clenched fist, the stiff posture are signs to others that they pick up subliminally. The tense person tends to overreact, to respond to questions too quickly, to talk fast. This response to tension is innate. If a mother who is afraid of lightning holds her baby during a lightning storm, the mother's tension is communicated to the baby through the tightness of the mother's musculature. When an infant in a group cries the other infants may also cry for no reason except that they have sensed distress.

Sympathetic response probably runs deeper in the human species than is usually recognized. For that reason, a manager who is uneasy or lacking in self-assurance should probably withdraw until composure is regained. Auguste Escoffier understood this well. Whenever he was under stress he did a simple thing. He left the scene of the tension provoking stimuli and took a walk around the block. Not a bad technique.

The environment itself creates tension. Noise is a tension producer. Younger people want more of it than older people. It has been found that noise increases metabolism and the flow of adrenaline. People who live in a city become accustomed to a certain tension level and miss it when not present. While a high level of noise will eventually destroy the cochlea within the ear, it is associated with excitement. Restaurants that cater to the young crowd should see to it that the noise level is fairly high. As the clientele increases with age the noise level should be reduced. The discotheque is wildly exciting to some; to others it can be distressful.

Coping with Tension

A manager knows when to intensify personal tensions and those of others around and when to reduce it. Techniques and skills are used for controlling tension levels.

Each task calls for a certain level of tension. When a manager makes up a work schedule or a budget, stimuli that interfere and excite need to be shut off. There are times when the manager should remain at home or otherwise stay away from the job so that planning and analysis can receive full concentration. Some executives lock themselves into their office and refuse to take calls. Others take a long weekend, sometimes away from home, to do their "big thinking."

In some planning a gestation period is needed. The manager begins to think about a problem, then lets the subconscious work it over. After a day or two attention turns back to the problem, usually with a better perspective and focus. This is not the same as procrastination (refusing to examine the problem until the last moment). Last-minute solutions are usually not as effective and raise the tension level unnecessarily.

The tension level needed for planning and analysis is quite different from that needed for active management during a rush meal period or banquet. Hopefully most of what takes place during such *highs* has been patterned and habituated. The manager and employees are merely carrying out a series of habit patterns that have been developed through practice or training. Physical tension needed to move, to respond to guests' requests, to react to the unexpected is necessarily high. It also burns up physical energy and can be pleasantly exciting in the same way that play is pleasantly exciting. If, on the other hand, the manager or employees have a low blood sugar level, a hangover, or a health problem, the same excitement level is seen as exhausting and frustrating.

ONE PERSON'S STRESS IS ANOTHER PERSON'S FUN

Depending upon one's physical health and glandular condition, the same situation can be seen as distressful or thrilling. This may explain why some people love the food business and become addicted to it in the way that others become addicted to drugs. Of the food business it is often said, "it gets into your blood."

People who really love the kind of excitement found in a hotel, restaurant, or the travel business are those who enjoy a high level of tension over a period of time.

Of course, some bodies are not built to live with a high tension level over a long period of time. The manager who

is that type of person, must then find ways of turning on and off as the occasion demands. Individual differences aside, long periods of stress inevitably produce physical symptoms that vary from person to person. The cold hands, the sweaty feet, the palpitation of the heart, the constriction of the throat, the pain in the neck, and the stomach cramps may be preludes to high blood pressure and a heart condition. Ulcers are almost inevitably connected with anxiety and tension. Long periods of stress will leave the individual wobbly and drained. In effect, the person must pay for high excitement. It creates a debt to be paid back in rest and recuperation.

The well-balanced individual schedules tension level as that individual schedules time. Coffee, alcohol, or cigarettes may create the illusion of debt avoidance, but it is only an illusion.

In planning the day and week, the manager schedules events so as not to experience excessive emotional strain. This is done by balancing out those things that are stressful against those experiences that are recuperative. What is recuperative varies from person to person. For some it may be playing cards; for others, watching TV or drinking a martini. It may be talking with someone well liked and avoiding those people who are not.

A fifteen-minute conference may be highly stressful to one person, exhilarating to another. Committee meetings can be frustrating or pleasurable. Reprimanding an employee may be enjoyable or painful, depending on the makeup of the manager. Sports are a great relaxer for many. Walking, riding a bicycle, playing tennis, or any other sport may be pleasantly exciting and at the same time therapeutic. Paradoxically, perhaps, a high level of physical activity may be tension-reducing in that it wipes the mind free of anxieties and conflicts.

Control the Tension Producer

The manager must be able to identify those persons who enjoy stirring up the emotional pot. The frustrated waitress may get her kicks from creating antagonisms among the group. There are definitely some people who revel in keeping a group on edge. Techniques for doing so may be invidious, sinister, or straightforward.

Have you ever noticed how some individuals excite a group by their mere presence? The sound and pitch of the voice can be an exciter. Speak of sex and the human animal becomes alive. Add an individual to a group and the emotional pot may begin to brew.

Since we live in a competitive society and the individual is trained to be competitive, tension levels can be expected to be above what would be good for normal health in most any successful hotel or restaurant. Add to this the fact that there are so many variables that cannot be controlled completely in the usual hospitality situation that problems are almost certain to arise. Add the dimension of alcohol to the dining room or bar and the measure of unpredictability is again raised and along with it the tension level. Add a hostess or a waiter who is divorced and unhappy, and the tension level again rises.

Symptoms of Tension

Tension symptoms take a variety of forms, some of the more common of which are indigestion, constipation, diarrhea, frequent headaches, difficulty in sleeping, irritability, and a stiff neck or back. Not that every such symptom is caused by tension, but tension could be the cause or contribute to the problem. The person who must have a drink is probably suffering from some psychological problem that produces tension. The person reaches for alcohol as a depressant. Sipping coffee throughout the day is probably adapting poorly to tension or boredom. The chain smoker is obviously seeking reduction of tension.

Chronic restlessness and the inability to concentrate may be part of the syndrome. Physiologically, tension is a means of getting the body ready to protect itself or to strike, a carry-over from our more animalistic days. If the person is able to vent the energy in constructive work, in walking or running, bicycling, or some other form of physical exercise the tension level is likely to be reduced. This does not, of course, get at the root of the tension, which may be excessive ambition, a job that has demands beyond the person's capabilities, hate for one's superior or spouse, and so on.

Ways to Reduce Tension

What happens before an activity and the way it is perceived helps to determine whether an activity is tension-reducing. Ernest Henderson, who built the largest hotel chain of his time, was a great hobbyist. Frequently, he spent a half an hour or so in the morning conversing with friends on a ham-radio hookup before leaving home for his office. Among the ham-radio buffs he was "WIUDY, Ernie in Boston." He found that playing with his radio in the morning relaxed him. Another hobby of his was photography. He liked to take pictures of celebrities for his personal album. He also wrote songs and got a particular thrill when one of them was played by an orchestra in one of his hotels. Collecting antiques and coins were other ways for him to reduce tension.

Managers use various techniques to raise and lower tension in the people with whom they work. Some man-

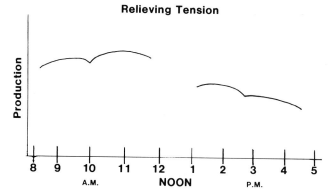

Figure 2.5 Coffee or other breaks make Jack a bright boy.

agers purposely create incidents, drop remarks, or confuse a situation so that people are stirred up. The rationale for such a behavior is that subordinates will try harder. (Withholding information is also a means of insuring one's own power.) Other managers work at reducing stress in their employees by carefully listening to every complaint, sympathizing with employee problems, and discussing decisions in some detail with people who will be affected by them. Of course, this can be overdone.

Some executives believe in keeping their offices minimal and bare. Others purposely introduce conversation pieces such as abstract paintings, aquariums with colorful fish, a vase of fresh flowers, a mounted fish or other trophy, and the like. Comments on such items constitute ice breakers.

A coffee break is a useful device for leveling off tension and for breaking up the work period. As seen in figure 2.5, tension builds up at the start of the work period until about 10 A.M., at which point there is a coffee break. Tension then drops and the cycle repeats itself until the lunch period. The same process occurs again in the afternoon, with the coffee break serving as a goal gradient—something to be looked forward to by the employee, an interruption in the monotony of doing something over and over again—an advantage in making work more pleasant, especially on monotonous jobs.

Work With, not Against, Biorhythms

All of us have daily and long-term biorhythms, ups and downs in the glandular system that vary throughout every 24-hour period and over a few days' cycle, and perhaps a several-month cycle. The jet lag experienced in changing time zones is testament to the way in which the bio-clock we all carry turns us off and on.

If we are used to waking up at about 6 A.M., and find ourselves in a different time zone where it is 3 A.M., the body clock still turns on the adrenalin system, and other glands begin to activate, making it almost impossible to sleep. Similarly, when the body clock tells us it is time to sleep and turns down the glandular system, we are drowsy and can hardly stay awake even though the real clock time is afternoon.

Some of us are night people, some are morning people, and some of us barely get wound up, ever. The morning people are the most alert in the mornings; the night people can only get cracking in the late evening. Whatever the biorhythm peculiar to the individual—work with it rather than against it. Do your heavy thinking when most alert; postpone major decisions during low periods.

WORK ADDICTION

The hotel, restaurant, and travel business is perfect for the work addict. There is never enough time to do everything that could be done. This type of person is admired for endurance and sometimes for productivity. When working for a chain, the goals are set even higher so that the work addict may never experience that final goal. Work addiction is usually self-defeating, if not to the company, certainly to the individual addicted.

Examples of what work addiction can do are plentiful in this business. A young entrepreneur was determined to build a chain of hotels before the age of thirty. He drove himself to the point where his associates had at times to slap him in order to awaken him to sign documents. True, he was successful in that he developed a hotel chain by the time he was twenty-nine years of age. He was totally unsuccessful as a person. He exhausted himself to the point that while eating steak one evening, the steak lodged in his throat and he strangled to death.

One of the most successful chains known in this world was put together by a very talented young man who at the age of thirty-nine died on the tennis courts. (It should also be noted that he was much overweight.)

Ralph Hitz, who was probably the best known hotel man of the 1930s, also died at a relatively early age from driving himself too hard and neglecting his health. Continual demand on the nervous system eventually bankrupts the reserve supply and one or more of the vital organs becomes damaged or inoperative. The Greek truism, "moderation in all things," holds true today. It is all too easy to "burn out" in the hotel and restaurant business.

Again, what is fatiguing for one may be exhilarating for another. A business luncheon may give the appearance of being a productive session and may be so for certain people. For others it is a disaster, the alcohol depresses the mental activities and arouses anxieties and hostilities.

HATE MANAGEMENT

A psychologist is likely to speak a great deal about affection, sympathy, empathy, security, frustration, and anxiety. A psychiatrist is more apt to cut into the emotions more deeply and speak of love, hate, and greed. Civilized human beings are supposed to keep their deeper emotions under control, but this is not always done as manifested in mankind's greatest burden, war. Humankind's natural competitiveness, developed instinctually for survival in the course of hundreds of thousands of years, is still very much with us. *Homo sapiens* is still very much the animal, and as such bands together in cliques and in groups ready to fight other groups. One observer believes such behavior is instinctual dating back to the time when humans banded together in hunting packs.[19]

Any newcomer to an office or a work group is likely to be observed as an outsider, perhaps an enemy, by the group. That is why it is so important to arrange for introductions of new employees to each member of the working group. It is a way of saying "this person is one of your group to be accepted as part of the team" (instead of making life miserable for the newcomer as is often done).

In spite of every effort to think of the hotel, restaurant, or clubs as "family" groups, departments quite naturally unite to form "our group" against "them." Up to a point, such behavior, providing the individual with a supporting emotional base, is desirable. Team effort by setting one department against another, one hotel against others in a chain, is useful to a degree. Carried to an extreme the in-group fights all other groups. Fighting can take the form of sabotage or any of a number of devious ways of making other departments look bad. A typical bureaucracy measures its success by the size of its budget, the number and size of gratuities, and the number of people it has in the department regardless of whether they are needed.

Within a department cliques form, older members may band together against younger ones, ethnic groups pit themselves against other groups, low-status employees may band together against those with higher status. On a managerial level hate runs as deeply, perhaps more deeply, than at other levels. Ambitious people are proud people. Once egos have been bruised their behavior can take on the form of a vendetta.

Part of survival in any corporation is being on the side of the winner. As a company is taken over by another or as a new faction moves into power those on the losing side can expect retribution. Undeclared wars on the corporate level can be as vicious as the real thing. Memos and words substitute for bullets and bombs. Top executives must

19. Anthony Jay, *The Corporation Man* (New York: Random House, 1971).

have the nature of Solomon to bring together warring factions or at least to ameliorate hostilities. In some cases there is no alternative but to dismiss the people most responsible.

During the sixties a large number of hotels and restaurants were taken over by conglomerates. In nearly every case top management was wooed and won with bonuses, stock options, and promises of a variety of perquisites. Very often salaries were increased markedly for key executives as part of the takeover deal. Once a takeover was accomplished many of the management people found they were no longer needed. Often they were given a period of grace as "consultants." More brutally, in a few cases, the employee discovered that the key to the office or storeroom no longer fit. The new management were quick to introduce their own key people and policies. Old allegiances and loyalties were broken up and new ones formed.

Typically, in any organization people at the top are jockeying for power, and enmities among the contenders is high. Once a power shift takes place there is a reshuffling of "corporate friends" and the power structure is realigned. The organization may then go through a period of relative calm and it can be assumed that the power struggle will reappear as ambitious people jab and thrust their way up the corporate ladder. While some observers deplore this kind of behavior others liken it to the survival of the fittest, opining that when the best person wins the organization flourishes. The fallacy in this belief is that the person who wins may be the best at infighting but not necessarily an expert at leadership or high in wisdom.

Some individuals take a pathological delight in stirring up trouble within an organization. They may feel a sense of power or they may just enjoy fighting. In bureaucratic organizations such people are often difficult to drop. Civil service requirements may make it virtually impossible to get rid of such a person. The time and effort required to discharge someone often causes the supervisor or manager to throw up his hands and "bear his cross."

If the supervisor lacks the support of his superior, the troublemaking employee may both bypass and undercut the supervisor. Many executives and administrators secretly enjoy having employees come to them personally with their problems. The so-called open-door policy is dangerous in that it can be a way of undermining the position of the supervisor. The employee soon learns that it is not necessary to work to please the boss if instead one pleases the boss's boss. The supervisor then is left out on a limb. Two choices are open—leaving the firm, or perhaps also playing the same game. The supervisor can go over the head of the person above to gain support.[20]

WAYS TO AVOID OVERFATIGUE

The obvious way to avoid fatigue is to have a healthy mind in a healthy body. This is easier said than done. Each person needs a different number of hours of sleep for normality. The cumulative value of sleep is a great blessing. Sleep solves emotional problems as well as physical. Much research in sleep shows that during sleep everyone dreams unless disturbed. An indicator of dreaming is a rapid-eye movement. When the dreamer is awakened and the dream interrupted, irritability sets in and the dreamer loses the psychic reward of dreaming. Of course, some dreams are frightening and should be interrupted, but most dreaming apparently has the purpose of allowing us to enjoy experiences that we have missed in our waking hours.

A big drain on emotional energy can be caused by resentment, anger, and jealousy. In some cultures great value is placed on revenge and individuals consume a great deal of energy and thought in contriving the means of gaining it. Rage and fear also send adrenaline to the blood, increase breathing, and speed up the heart. Following this excitement the person is left exhausted. Artificial means of stimulating energy such as drinking coffee, smoking, and taking pep pills only create a debt that eventually must be paid off.

One physician says this about coffee drinking, "the coffee drinker is the most tired person around." Coffee releases glycogen, a form of sugar, from the liver and in that sense does provide energy. Eating sugar in any form has similar results. But this, too, builds up an energy debt that must be repaid.

Alcohol masks the feeling of fatigue and in small quantities releases tension for a short time and stops fatigue. The danger in drinking alcohol is that it reduces reaction time and the ability to concentrate. Heavy drinkers are likely to become tired because they substitute the calories contained in alcohol for those in foods that contain proteins, minerals, and vitamins. Alcohol contains about seven calories per gram as compared with carbohydrates, which contain about four calories per gram. It is easy to overstock the "empty" calories contained in alcohol.

Physicians usually agree that exercise is a valuable antidote for fatigue. Walking home from work or engaging in some sport, at least for awhile after work, is stimulating rather than fatiguing, and it sets the body up for a night of good rest.

The time to avoid work is when you are tired. Extra effort is required to do the same amount of work ordinarily done. Coming in early on the job may be a way of getting

---

20. For further reading about tensions and ways of reducing them see Theodore Irwin, ed., *What the Executive Should Know About Tension* (Larchmont, N.Y.: American Research Council, 1966).

ahead of the game. Your desk and ideas are sorted out before the confusion of the workaday world arrives.

The busy executive very often will travel at night in order to save time. This is not recommended, since the body needs regular nighttime sleep.

UTILIZE TENSION TO GET A JOB DONE

To make this discussion of tension and efficiency more meaningful, think how it could be applied to the problem of putting on a banquet, one of a kind which has not been done before. The procedure can be thought of as following four steps.

1. Think the problems through and bring in those who can help. You need help in the form of ideas, information, and hands, plus the imagination of others. Talk it over immediately with the supervisors or other key personnel who will be involved. Remember that you are responsible for forging the final plan, shaping it into a workable form. A strong maitre d' or an exceptional chef may carry the ball and should be in on the meeting. Outline the banquet proposal, ask for suggestions, let the plan set and jell. Come back to it tomorrow after people have had time to mull it over.

Ask questions, modify, change. Let experience, judgment, native intelligence, and energy call the tune.

The menu has been planned, the decor theme developed. Hopefully, everyone is involved (at times this is too much to ask), knows about the plan, and all understand where they're going.

2. Set the emotional stage. A new and different experience calls for a fairly high level of emotional tension in all who participate. Getting the staff keyed up to a football-playing pitch, however, is overdoing a good thing. Too much tension is as bad as too little. People wear themselves out running in place.

To avoid hypertension, stage a trial run. Try out the menu items at home or in smaller quantities. Some changes will always be necessary, and a trial run builds confidence.

Comes "show time," the cast is assembled and pitched to the performance. Expect something to go wrong because something probably will. But, anticipation prevents panic.

3. Lead. Every group effort requires a leader, whether it be taking an enemy pillbox, initiating the *mis en place,* or setting up a cafeteria line. Someone leads,

the rest follow. Most of us are followers and avoid leading, especially when some new behavior is called for.

It is quite natural to fall in behind a leader. For example, the platoon leader gets the best response from the group by saying, "Follow me." Or, a cafeteria manager can exert leadership by stepping up to a salad counter and starting to arrange the salad display. A real supervisor, will ask for the salad server's help; then the supervisor withdraws, letting the server finish the job. Inertia is overcome; action is started.

At the banquet, whoever is in charge calls the starting signals. "Place the juice, lay the service plates."

Suddenly, everyone knows that someone is in charge. Leadership is there. The group relates to the supervisor. Psychologically speaking, the situation has become patterned, there is direction and the individuals form into a group, moving toward a goal.

Once the wheels are set in motion, the supervisor turns attention to other problems—perhaps wishing to be around to identify the unforeseens. A well-planned banquet is like a battle. Once it has started there is little the chief can do to change the course of events. Prearranged plans and procedures take over the role of command.

In the case of a banquet, however, someone must have the "super" vision to spot difficulties and make changes if necessary.

4. Correct and reward. Following any performance on stage, battlefield, or banquet the actors want evaluation. Immediately following the event, what they want most of all is reassurance and praise for things well done. As the manager, following a banquet, circulate around, noticing all the good things: food service, and otherwise. Hold the criticism until the next morning.

People who are tired are hypersensitive to criticism; the ego is not firm enough to take it. The next morning, the postmortem can be held and discrepancies discussed objectively.

Questions are more effective than accusations. "Chef, what did you think of the lemon pie?" Let the chef be the first to point out that the crust was too tough or the lemon flavor too strong. Let the head waiter come up with suggestions for improving the performance. Raise the question as to whether the plates were hot enough, the salads crisp enough, the room at the right temperature.

In the morning, people are fresh and better prepared to self-evaluate. Sometime during the day take the time, as manager, to reassure everyone of your personal interest.

Stop around for a few minutes of small talk, a question about the family. Be sure to chat with those who might have guilty feelings about poor performance or those who have been criticized in the morning meeting. The manager thinks it through, sets the emotional stage, leads off, then rewards and corrects.

CONTROLLED STRESS IS GOOD FOR YOU

Controlled stress provides energy and is a spur for creativity and productivity. Taken in proper doses it may be better than *Geritol*. Some physicians believe that the inevitable physical decline that comes with age can be postponed by activity and moderate amounts of excitement. As the hotel, restaurant, or travel-oriented careerist moves up the management ladder, that individual is likely to become more and more locked into a sedentary role. To combat this, regular physical exercise must be scheduled, exercise not only on weekends but workdays as well. Perhaps it is only walking to work or walking between offices or around the hotel, restaurant, or club. If at all possible some exercise that is fun and has a social component should be scheduled. Tennis, squash, and badminton are excellent. Bicycling and jogging are good.

Importantly, the exercise should be continued right on through life, scaled to the capacity of the body as it ages.

Tension is preparedness for doing something. If something is not done or there is no means of venting the energy created by the tension, the tension will increase. The pole-vaulter must concentrate completely on clearing the bar. One needs all of the concentrated attention one can accumulate for that effort. Concern is part of the thinking of every manager or executive. Excessive concern produces stress. Stress produces tension. We return to the ancient Greek admonition: moderation in all things. What is moderate is the key and will vary with the individual.

Ambitious persons continually urge themselves on. Inevitably there are challenges that cannot be met, which leads to frustration. The psychiatrist tells us to recognize our own personal danger signals: loss of concentration, excessive daydreaming, loss of energy, inability to sleep, and so on. Whatever the symptoms, treat them as cues that must be responded to in a way that will minimize the tension or the anxiety which produces the tension.

In the business world the manager is often called upon to overwork. One of the managers of one of the largest hotels has said that he remains within the hotel for as long as two weeks at a stretch without leaving it. Is this desirable for him or the organization? One person can take on too much responsibility, or another, too little. Excessive striving can result in "burn out."

Whatever the drives which are most important for the individual, it is well if that individual recognizes what it is that keeps him running. Is it the search for power, security, position? Is it the need for challenge, love, acceptance, or is it just escape from boredom?

SUMMARY

Scientific management attempted to minimize the importance of worker motivation by reducing work into small, interchangeable work units. Later research has taught us that people cannot be compared with machines. As a consequence, a major area of study and research related to motivations of workers has developed. By understanding theories of motivation and their relationships to management style, managers can bring some system and consistency into their supervisory efforts.

Some of the most popular theories of motivation concern instinctive-cultural drives or needs of people. Of particular interest is the well-researched need for achievement that D. C. McClelland has shown to be culturally acquired and which also can be altered through intensive training or conditioning. Other needs important for the manager to understand are those for affiliation, security, power, and prestige.

One of the most widely quoted theorists, A. H. Maslow posits a five-level hierarchy of needs. Physiological needs are most basic. In ascending order the higher level needs are for security, social relationships, self-esteem, and self-realization. Once needs at lower levels are satisfied then the individual seeks out higher level satisfactions.

Frederick Herzberg has adapted Maslow's system into a management frame of reference. Herzberg differentiates the *true* motivators of work (Maslow's needs for self-realization and self-esteem) from job satisfiers (Maslow's physiological, security, and social needs). If a person has adequate wages, security, working conditions, and social conditions, this person will probably not be dissatisfied with the job. For one to find one's greatest motivation, one will need a job that provides recognition, participation in decision making, and feelings of accomplishment and growth. Though widely quoted and adopted, the Herzberg model like all theories has its limits. The psychology of individual differences and preferences is not well handled by such a general theory.

Implicit to theories of behavior are notions of man's basic nature. Which philosophy is valid? Is man basically greedy as Machiavelli pictured him, and best managed by manipulation, or does the humanistic philosophy prevail that man seeks positive growth and is best handled with trust, confidence in his abilities, and the provision of opportunities for his self-realization? Managers have gained successful results using both strategies, but the

Figure 2.6 Maslow's Theory of Motivation

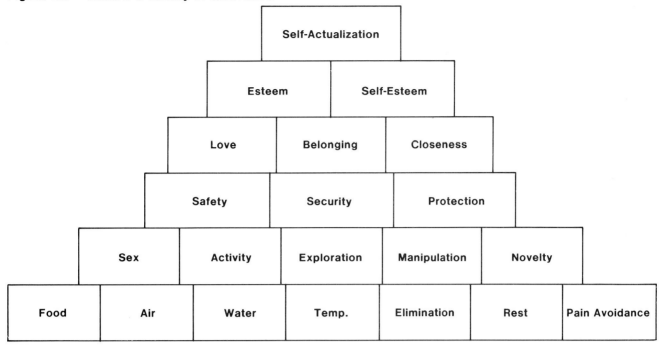

humanistic approach is consistent with most prevailing management theories. In our present society, in which people generally do not feel seriously threatened over loss of physiological and security needs, the Machiavellian approach is dated. Even the worst of despots give lip service to humanistic principles today.

It is not enough for a successful manager to follow blindly certain humanistic principles. One must be sensitive to the needs of subordinates—whatever those needs—and innovative in providing for those needs. An understanding of human physiology is needed, as are lev-

els of tension in individuals, and astuteness in knowing how to create a climate in which the individual can function to maximum capacity.

Tension is pervasive in the hotel-restaurant industry. There is perhaps no industry that demands greater concern with speed, timing, schedules, and detail. Those individuals who do not like tension are probably not cut out for this industry. On the other hand, everyone needs outlets for tension. The manager, particularly if schooled in humanistic principles of management, can be very effective in helping others identify and deal with their frustrations using the skills of listening, understanding, counseling, and handling group discussions.

Organizing People Relations

3

To be effective an enterprise must be organized. People must know the objectives of the enterprise, the lines of communication and authority, and the manner in which their jobs are related to other jobs. Each member should have an understanding of his duties, authority, responsibility, and accountability.

What is organization? It is a structure of relationships that controls a group of persons for the accomplishment of specified ends. The ends for which hotel and restaurant enterprises strive are service at a profit and maximum satisfaction for clientele and employees. Organization is necessary to coordinate the efforts of all the personnel towards these goals. Organization, then, is a means to more effective concerted effort.

Organization proceeds through people. A purpose of organization is to get effective results *with* people. Organization aids and encourages personnel within the organization to utilize their capacities. It also partially sets the conditions for giving people maximum satisfaction in their work and, concomitantly, in life.

Through organization every activity that contributes to an enterprise is brought under centralized direction. This avoids cross-purposes and encourages decisions made from an advantageous point of view for the entire enterprise. Decisions that may appear advisable for certain units may be inadvisable when viewed as a part of the enterprise overall. A separate personnel policy for the person who operates the cigar and candy counter may increase that individual's morale and sales. It may, however, cause enough dissatisfaction among other employees to more than offset the advantages to the *whole* enterprise.

Organization establishes a communication system by which a two-way flow of ideas, suggestions, and information is made possible. It serves as a channel for complaints and grievances.

LINE AND STAFF FUNCTIONS

The functions of line and staff are distinctly different. Line operates; staff supports. The function of the line is to get things done. It carries the responsibility for action. In a military organization the line assumes responsibility for fighting, furnishing ships, or moving supplies, when those are the actions decided upon. In a restaurant, line personnel prepare and serve the food; personnel, purchasing, and marketing support the line.

Staff functions are essentially advisory and supportive. The staff is removed from the line in order to counsel, advise, and assist the line. It carries on research, appraises, and audits the line to see how well the objectives are being carried out and to help determine other appropriate courses of action. In a hotel, the comptroller, personnel director, and sales department are staff, supporting the line.

In the food service industry, line and staff functions are often carried on by the same individuals. Sometimes personnel heads, believing themselves to be strictly in a staff function, find themselves pressed into line actions and perform as line officers.

FORMAL VS. INFORMAL ORGANIZATION

Informal organization is thought of as lacking formal designations of relationships, responsibilities, and authority. There is usually an absence of titles and no clear organizational structure. Formal organization provides a formal designation of individual officers and departments, clear organizational lines of responsibility and authority, and specific delegation and assignment of duties.

Between these two extremes any number of possibilities exist. A family restaurant might operate successfully in an informal manner. Chain operations are usually formalized.

The kitchen operation usually requires some formal organization with an acknowledged leader, the chef. A hotel needs a fairly rigid organization, from general manager to pot and pan washer, but with provisions for easy up and down communication.

FORMAL AND INFORMAL CHANNELS

An organization is not an organizational chart. It is easy to assume that once lines of authority are drawn, the organization will flow smoothly, with the power from the top directing the powerless below. It is surprising and sometimes frightening for managers when they realize how little power they have and how much power is exercised from below. Labor flexes its muscles through slowdowns and strikes to remind management where the real balance of power lies. Individuals steal, "goof off," and do slipshod work to show that they *will not* be pushed around.

The task of management is to find cooperative ways of achieving the goals of the organization. There is no universal set of guidelines. Every major organization in the world has a formal chart of organization, but also important are the informal channels of power and persuasion. Who really makes the decisions? Who do you go to if you want to get something done? Who do you avoid if you don't want an idea stifled? The most effective organizations are those that do not take their structure so seriously that they cannot reexamine it and adapt goals and procedures.

An alert leader comes to understand that the administrative process is not mechanical and that no amount of technique or organization can make one an effective manager. One will also recognize that (a) although major similarities exist in organizations, each differs from another in terms of the methods by which things are accomplished; (b) the only way a manager can understand the organization is by careful observation and analysis; (c) the organizational chart is only a piece of paper that can often mislead a manager if interpreted too rigidly; (d) power and authority reside throughout the organization, not just with management, and all individuals can have an effect on the organization; (e) the *combined powers* of others in the organization is greater than the *individual power* of the manager; (f) power can be neither stamped out nor dispersed—management must learn to utilize power to its maximum; and (g) the manager provides *group leader-*

ship, a more involved task than merely structuring and directing people.

ORGANIZATIONAL PRINCIPLES

Organize Around Functions

Organization must be functional. The functions of purchase and procurement, accounting and auditing, engineering and maintenance, food production, and public relations are separate functions set up according to the purpose of the organization.

Keep organization simple. Do not set up unnecessary levels. Keep the distance between the manager and employees on the lowest rung of the ladder as small as possible so that communication among all levels is kept open, and efficiency is not lost by the inclusion of unnecessary relay stations.

To effect simplicity, promote efficiency, and eliminate unneeded levels of organization, district managers in several fast food chains supervise five to eight stores and also act as relief unit managers. In Hyatt Hotels and some other hotel chains, regional vice presidents oversee several hotels and at the same time are a general manager of a hotel.

Define Every Position

Job analyses have shown that often jobs are not clearly understood. Supervisors do not know the limits of exactly what they are to do and for what they are accountable. What are the porter's duties? Does the job overlap with that of the yardworker? Is the assistant steward aware of having a responsibility for the cleanliness of the dishwashing machine and for the employment of dishwashers, or is this the steward's job? Has the addition of a new wing made the job of wall washing too much for the present crew?

Follow the principle: one person, one boss. Try to avoid having anyone report to more than one supervisor. Every employee from the transient dishwasher to the manager should know whom to report to, and requirements of the job.

A corollary to the dictum "Define everyone's authority" is the equally important precept: "Grant authority commensurate with responsibility." A supervisor without authority is as useful as the extinct dodo bird. An assistant manager who must refer all matters to the manager for decision is nothing but a clearing station or a clerk.

Clarify and Maintain the Organizational Pattern

The nature of a hotel or restaurant business demands flexibility to meet constantly changing conditions. Since organizational structure is functional and depends upon the personalities and goals of the enterprise, it too should be flexible, and easily modified. Hand in hand with flexibility, however, is the danger of misunderstanding the organizational structure.

One of the best ways to define the organizational pattern is to follow it in all personnel practices. A manager should not originate orders except through channels set up by the line organization. Orders from the manager should proceed through the assistant managers, department heads, and supervisors. Supervisors are not representatives of management unless they are given a part in the management process. Bypassing a supervisor destroys the purpose of the organization by creating confusion and undermining the status of the supervisor.

How Many Employees per Supervisor?

A British general Sir Ian Hamilton expressed the idea that the "average human brain finds its effective scope in handling from three to six other brains." He went on to say that there is a rule "whereby from three to six hands are shepherded by one head, each head in turn being a member of a superior group of from three to six. . . ." In other words, there seems to be a fairly well established limit on how many persons should report to one superior. The concept of the number of persons who can be supervised by one person is known as "the span of control."

Instinctively, says another observer, people band together to form working groups of about ten members, or the size of the hunting pack. The human being, evolving over some 20 million years, is still much an animal and feels more comfortable when in a "hunt pack" of ten. The ancient Roman military organization, he asserts, had good evolutionary reasoning behind its organization of tens and hundreds. The basic unit was 10; the centurian commanded 100. The cohort was about 500, or the number that one man could know and they in turn respond to him.[1] The military has experimented with various sizes of squads and platoons.

Perhaps the answer lies more in the complexity of the task at hand and the personalities of the people involved. Some groups, for example, a team of scientists, may be too large at ten. A principal factor in determining optimal size of an organizational unit is how much skilled and technical work is done by the boss. A working chef may be able to supervise only a few cooks and helpers. An executive chef who does no work at the range can supervise a greater number.

It is likely that most management personnel spend more time than they should on nonmanagerial work—skill level and technical. If a president, for example, just loves selling and spends half the time in sales, there is a distraction from the primary job, management. The executive chef who must taste each dish before service sidesteps the management function and can effectively manage fewer people.

It is obvious that in some organizations there are too many supervisors; in others, too few. Where there are sharp lines of authority drawn, such as in the military, the officers and petty officers may be too numerous, leaving the real work to be done by the privates. In bureaucratic organizations there may be excessive paper work for the supervisor or too many supervisors. One of the secrets of the success of several of the fast-food restaurant chains is that there are no executives, only working managers. Managers, at the unit level, step in to operate the cash register, receive food supplies, or work the counter as needed. Employees who feel that they are only thinkers are not wanted.

A common weakness in the hotel, restaurant, and club business organization is the placing of too many subordinates under each department head or supervisor. In a cafeteria, for example, at a given time there is only one manager on duty—supervising perhaps as many as twenty-five employees. It would be far better to establish more supervisors, with someone in charge of the kitchen, someone in charge of the cafeteria line, and perhaps someone in charge of the dish machine room.

In the larger chain organizations it is quite possible for as many as ten or fifteen store managers to report directly to one area supervisor provided that it is not necessary for the store managers to interact to any degree. In fact, most chain-restaurant operations are set up according to a highly standardized plan, which is effected by means of systems and routines that minimize the necessity for consultation in management.

In the late 1960s, the computer revolution reached the hotel and restaurant field, and the routines of accounting and reporting began to be automated to a degree that would have seemed fantastic a few years ago. For example, the Marriott Company has computerized the ordering of food from its warehouse and central commissary and processes payroll and sales statistics as well as inventory control for nearly 150 locations from Dallas to New York City. Oven production schedules are controlled according to a program that is carried out by a computer. All sales of food are entered into the system at the point

---

1. Anthony Jay, *The Corporation Man,* (New York: Random House, 1971).

of sale and transmitted by phone directly to the computer center.

Such a program removes the necessity of the store manager's making dozens of routine decisions each day and permits that manager to concentrate on the other functions of people management.

The amount of supervision needed in a job depends upon the amount and kind of planning, communications, and decisions required to perform the job. Managing a large luxury restaurant is quite a different job from that of managing a McDonald's restaurant. A McDonald's manager has little or no responsibility for purchasing food, planning the menu, making financial decisions, decor decisions, or even decisions about methods of preparation—and little interaction with other McDonald's managers. The span of control of a regional supervisor in the McDonald's system can be much larger than in that of a company like Restaurant Associates, the restaurants which are mostly high styled and individualized.

Similarly, a floor steward in charge of the dish machine crew could conceivably supervise as many as twenty employees without too much difficulty, whereas the executive chef might be overburdened with control over more than five or six section cooks.

The trend in the management of larger restaurants (those doing $1 million plus in sales) is to have a general manager assisted by two and sometimes three other persons with the title "manager." McDonald's employs several "managers" for each store. All but the top manager usually receive hourly wages but enjoy the title of manager and function as shift managers.

Decentralization or Centralization

A problem similar to that contained in the question as to the proper size of the span of control has reference to whether or not a multi-unit operation should centralize or decentralize management. The answer hinges around the definition of management and the type of and character of operations involved. Delegation of authority, responsibility, and accountability should be determined by the reliability and effectiveness of available controls. In other words, decentralization or delegation of responsibility goes hand in hand with the institution of proper controls and, of course, with the availability of managers who have the character, judgment, and skills necessary to carry out the responsibility. Company-operated Holiday Inns, with standardized advertising, menu, and operational procedures relieve the innkeeper of a wide area of responsibility and the necessity for much decision making. Centralized accounting sets up the necessary controls so that the several hundred Holiday Inns can operate effectively as a group. Responsibility, in effect, has been de-

centralized, but accountability has been centralized. This is the key to delegation in multi-unit organizations.

The Hilton Hotels and the Hyatt Hotels comprise many operations each with a separate character. Hotel managers are called upon to accept a wide range of responsibility for maintaining the character and attractiveness of the property they manage. Again, however, accounting controls are centralized and other means of holding the manager accountable are in effect so that decentralization is possible.

Decentralization may work in one company and not in another, depending upon the management style employed at the top management level, the philosophy at top management, and the experience and abilities of the individual hotel managers. In the early 1960s it was decided by Ernest Henderson, then president of Sheraton Hotels, to decentralize. Individual hotel managers were given more latitude and fewer controls. Profits of the company dropped sharply, and it was not too long before more regional supervision and control was instituted.

The Howard Johnson organization, known since its inception for being highly centralized in its management control and in control of operation generally, found it advantageous to decentralize some functions. Advertising, which has been done on a national basis by one advertising agency, is now being supplemented locally, with local agencies called in to produce the advertising material. Managers who had been trained to operate by the book participated in regional seminars held at universities around the country. The seminars allowed the managers to step back and away from their operations and enabled them to "see the forest from the trees." By being physically removed from their restaurants, the managers got a new outlook and a new surge of enthusiasm for the job, according to Howard Johnson top management.

In the case of the Howard Johnson company, the corporation was initiated and got its form under the driving force of the personality of Howard Johnson, Sr. Under the presidency of his son the company took on a more liberal management tone, perhaps one which is more appropriate for a company that has reached a certain stage of maturity, when the decentralization of some functions can be done more gracefully.

EVOLVING THE ORGANIZATIONAL CHART

The organizational chart is devised to reflect power and communication lines. Who is responsible for what? Who reports to whom? Who are the people that are supposed to turn out the organization's principal product—the line

Figure 3.1 Number of Employees Required For 100- and 150-Room Downtowner Motor Inn

Organization Chart for a 100- and 150-Room Motor Inn
Without Food and Beverage Service

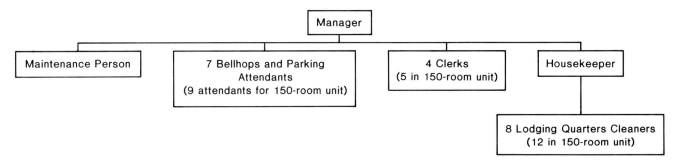

Manager

Maintenance Person

7 Bellhops and Parking Attendants
(9 attendants for 150-room unit)

4 Clerks
(5 in 150-room unit)

Housekeeper

8 Lodging Quarters Cleaners
(12 in 150-room unit)

organization? Who make up the staff personnel, the support group that supplies information and services to the line organization? The military, having had the most experience with organizational problems over the centuries, separate line from staff. Line officers and men are those who actually engage in combat. Staff personnel such as medical, supply, communications, and transport, have one purpose: to support and make more effective the line organization. In hotels and restaurants staff people are represented by accounting, sales, financial, and personnel. In chain organizations staff personnel tend to be concentrated at corporate headquarters; staff personnel are relatively few at the operating unit level. The management of the Stouffer restaurants has no staff personnel assisting in the operation with the exception perhaps of a secretary. The personnel, financial, accounting, control, and other staff functions are centered in the Cleveland home office.

The abstraction known as the organizational chart is an attempt to rationalize the people relationships existing within an organization or those relationships hoped for by whoever devised the chart. Usually a chairperson of the board, board of directors, or president, is at the top of the chart. (Actually the clientele are the ultimate boss.) Boxes are inserted below for vice-presidents, divisional directors, and managers. Solid lines between positions indicate a superior-subordinate relationship, dotted lines indicate a coordinating, staff, or technical relationship. Careful attention must be given to drawing up organizational charts for a number of reasons, the major one being that the status-hierarchy is set down in the chart representing relationships that are loaded with feelings.

"Since when do I report to the comptroller?" "Who gave Julie Brown the title of assistant to the president?" "The chart shows me reporting to Mr. Big's secretary. How silly can you get?"

Some organization theorists place emphasis on the linking relationship between each level in an organization, the so-called *linking pin* concept. Proposed by Rensis Likert, a psychologist, each position in the hierarchy ties together divisions both above it and below it. The person holding the position is the linking pin between the levels, the channel through which communications, authority, and purpose flow. The incumbent is seen as much more than a supervisor or representative of the management above; seen, rather, as the link, the conduit, the person who represents both those above and below. The concept magnifies the importance of middle management in bringing together those at the working level and those in higher management.

Organizational charts institutionalize relationships at a point in time. Because of this, many managements shy away from making such charts. Often lines of authority are not well defined and management would just as soon keep it that way. Job titles at the managerial levels may purposely be left vague. Some organizations change so rapidly that the organizational chart is out of date soon after it is drawn. A number of organizational charts are presented in this chapter. No two are alike, nor should they be. Each chart supposedly represents a blueprint of existing relationships. The chart is a reflection of reality, and hopefully clarifies the ways in which the parts relate to each other.

TYPES OF ORGANIZATION

Simple Organization—A Motor Inn

The organization of a motor inn without a restaurant is one of the simpler types of organization. In figure 3.1, one can see the number of personnel needed for a 100- and a 150-room motor inn.

The figure suggests that there is an optimal size of motel from the efficiency point of view. The cost of labor for operating 50 additional rooms in a 100-room motel is less than directly proportional to the added numbers of

Figure 3.2   Organization of a Large Kitchen in a First-Class Hotel

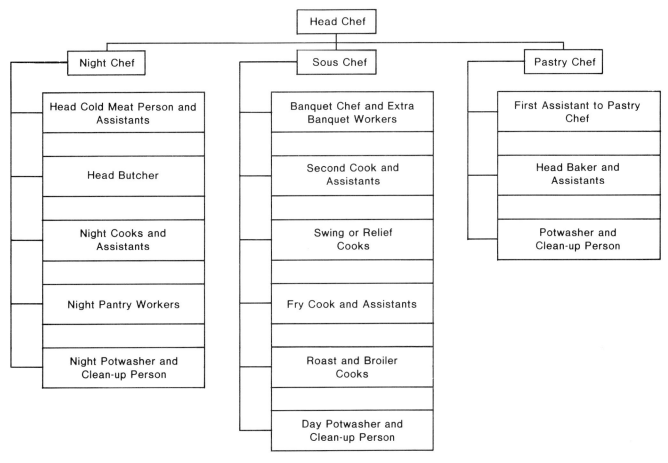

rooms. The extra personnel needed are only two bellmen, one clerk, and four maids. In other words, adding 50 rooms to a 100-room motor inn increases basic payroll costs by a relatively small amount.

No one has determined, by formal study, what the *optimal size* motel, restaurant, or hotel is, but it is fairly apparent that there are several optimal sizes depending upon the market and character of the operation. The 225-room hotel is popular. Often the addition of seats to a restaurant destroys its character or interferes with efficiency, so that the owner would be better advised not to add them even though sales volume would suggest that the addition should be made. On the other hand, many motels that have 100 rooms and are doing capacity occupancies might very well add up to 50 additional rooms if market surveys indicate that they would be filled. The additional rooms would show a higher percentage of profit on the gross income than the other rooms.

Motor Hotel and Hotel Organization

Moving from a motel without a restaurant to a typical motor hotel means the addition of staff personnel and a food and beverage department. Food and beverage service in a hotel may comprise 50 percent or more of total revenue. Under the food and beverage manager comes a section head for general catering.

Depending on the degree of luxury service, employees may number as many as two to a room. The typical full-service hotel employs about .8 to .9 employees per room. In a few luxury hotels the room-employee ratio may reach as high as three. Resort hotels typically have a higher employee-guest ratio than commercial hotels.

Organization of a Large Kitchen in a First-Class Hotel

In a large, first-class hotel kitchen, the personnel become highly specialized. The organizational chart of such a kitchen is shown as figure 3.2.

If the kitchen were staffed predominantly by French and other European-trained personnel, these titles might be changed as follows:

Head Chef—*Chef de Cuisine*
Head Cold Meat Person—*Garde Manger*
Swing Cook—*Tournant*
Second Cook—*Saucier* (sauce cook)

Other titles may also be used, but the job titles seen in the organizational chart are common in the United States kitchens today.

Organization of the Large Hotel

As a hotel increases in size and complexity, so too does the organization. Duties normally performed by one department head in a small hotel are split off and formed into separate departments. The general manager is assisted by a resident manager and an executive assistant manager. Advertising, public relations, and sales are split off and formed into separate sections. Under a director of sales is a group of salespeople and specialized personnel to service conventions. The banquet department is split off from the food and beverage department, having its own manager and staff. The controller is in charge of all accounting and control procedures with specialized personnel in credit, accounting, night auditing, and persons controlling the various cashiers around the hotel.

The dotted line relationship appears on such charts, meaning that the offices connected by the dotted line relate to each other directly in a staff relationship. For example the food and beverage manager relates to the food and beverage controller without having direct supervision or control over the latter. That person reports in a line relationship (supervisory relationship) to the controller.

The director of sales does not supervise the people in public relations, even though working closely with them, as evidenced by the dotted line relationship.

The Sheraton-Boston hotel, 1,400 rooms in size, is part of the Prudential Center Complex in downtown Boston and has experienced one of the highest occupancy rates of any large hotel in the world. Its organizational chart (fig. 3.3) shows it to be part of the ITT-Sheraton chain. It is interesting to note that the controller reports directly both to ITT-Sheraton headquarters, and to the general manager (who also reports directly to ITT-Sheraton headquarters). Where money matters are concerned, the chains usually want a direct line relationship between controller and home office.

It can be seen that in a large hotel such as the Sheraton-Boston, there are a number of specialty restaurants and bars.

Corporate Hotel Organization

Organization at the corporate level of a large hotel chain becomes fairly complicated. Some of the corporate officers have line responsibility, others do not. An executive having line responsibility has direct responsibility for operating results of those divisions and people who report directly to that individual. Staff departments have no such responsibility but often assume it. Staff departments are supposed to support and give technical assistance to operating divisions. It is understandable that when a staff officer sits next door to the president, an individual down the line is likely to act as though the staff person is a line executive and respond to suggestions as though they were orders. The distinction between line and staff becomes very thin and can be a source of confusion and resentment.

Hotel Engineering Organization

The chart identified as figure 3.5 is the maintenance and hotel engineering organization for hotels ranging in size from 200 to 600 rooms (also called Property, Operating, Maintenance, and Engineering [POMEC]). These hotels are part of the InterContinental Hotels Corporation, (a subsidiary of Pan-American World Airways), which had sales of approximately 450 million dollars in 1978. The maintenance and engineering department in IHC Hotels has two functions—the operation of the equipment (energy costs) and the maintenance of the facility (property operation, and maintenance). The department is headed by a chief engineer who is assisted by three to four supervisors.

Hotels, of course, operate twenty-four hours a day, and the department must be organized accordingly. All of the heating, lighting, and air conditioning equipment must be inspected, maintained, repaired, and overhauled. To relieve the chief engineer of routine bookkeeping and administrative chores, a separate division in the department has been established that is responsible for record keeping, filing and work orders, schedules, utility consumption records, equipment records, inventory, and accounting.

Both management and technical assistance come from regional chief engineers and from the staff vice-president, hotel engineering, located in the Pan-American Building in New York City.

Restaurant Organization

The vast majority of restaurants are small and do not bother to draw up organizational charts. Even some of the larger restaurants, those doing over a million dollars a year in sales, lack formal organizational charts. Figure

3.6 might be considered typical of a first-class, high-volume restaurant in the United States. The restaurant is divided into three departments—bar tending, dining room, and food preparation. The manager is assisted by an assistant manager, head bartender, dining room supervisor, and chef. The responsibility is divided between food preparation and food service: everything within the kitchen door comes under the supervision of the chef; everything in the dining room is managed by the dining room supervisor.

Notice the absence of French titles except for the maitre d'. In a French restaurant the maitre d' would be in charge of the dining room. Under the American system the maitre d' may come under the dining room supervisor and acts as a host on the floor and supervisor of service. Employee scheduling in the dining room is the responsibility of the dining room supervisor.

In some restaurants, the hostess is also dining room supervisor, scheduling and supervising service personnel. In other restaurants, the hostess is a minimum-wage employee, acting as greeter and seater, reservations clerk, and ornament.

Organization and Function

Organization and function go hand and hand. Any particular function within an organization can be given organizational structure depending upon the importance of the function. In the Hilton Hotels, the Division of Hilton Hotels Employee Relations and Development is given definite structure, with the Senior Vice President, Employee Relations and Development reporting directly to the President of the Hilton Hotels Division. Four section heads—Benefits and Compensation Planning, Human Resources Development, Industrial Relations, and Affirmative Action—report to the Senior Vice President, Hotel. Personnel managers report to or coordinate with regional directors who in turn report to the Senior Vice President as seen below:

As organizations change—expand, merge, serve different markets—the formal organization structure is usually changed to reflect the changes. The example charts seen here will probably be out of date now, but can serve as examples of organization.

Special Circumstances and Organization

Special circumstances in an organization call for restructuring the organization to fit the situation. Hilton Hotels, for example, have an unusual situation with the two Las Vegas properties, the Las Vegas Hilton and the Flamingo Hilton. In some years these two hotels have generated more than 40 percent of the company profit. The casino operations in the hotels account for the high profits. Casino management and Las Vegas hotel operation call for specialized expertise. These factors are partly responsible for the establishment by the Hilton company of a separate Hilton Nevada Division seen in figure 3.7.

Restaurant Chain Organization

In a large restaurant chain there are necessarily a number of corporate officers who operate in and out of corporate headquarters. Figure 3.8 is the chart for Morrison's, a Mobile, Alabama-based cafeteria, motel, and food-service company which in 1978 had sales of about 217 million dollars. Administration is divided according to function, with line executives in charge of cafeterias, motels, and contract food-service operations. In the home office or in divisional offices, are senior vice presidents for each of these divisions. Under them are sixteen cafeteria regional vice-presidents and three food-service vice-presidents responsible for their own divisions. It is seen that the controller, the vice president of human resources, the vice president of corporate communications, and the secretary-treasurer all report directly to the president.

Small chains of restaurants are often being acquired by large ones and by conglomerates. These changes necessitate structural changes in the organizations. By 1979, W.R. Grace, a conglomerate, had bought five restaurant chains and was seeking more. Since restaurants were but one of some 160 companies owned by W.R. Grace, a separate division within Grace was established headed by a Restaurant-Group executive vice president. More such acquisitions can be expected in the future.

Stouffer Restaurants and Inns was started in 1924 as a $12,000 lunch counter in Cleveland. Mother Stouffer baked the pies that were sold. Dad and the two sons helped run the restaurant. In the late 1960s, as was true of so many companies, the Stouffers chain was *merged* (bought) with a conglomerate—in this case by Litton, later by Nestle, a Swiss-based corporation.

Stouffer Restaurants and Inns in 1979 had organized its Restaurant Division under a "Group Vice President." At the next level down were five vice presidents (industrial relations, purchasing, controller, real estate, and operations), a director of marketing, and a director of corporate facilities design. At the operational level, restaurants were grouped into traditional restaurants, tops (of buildings), and speciality restaurants. This organization is shown in figure 3.10.

Figure 3.3 Organization Chart for Sheraton-Boston Hotel

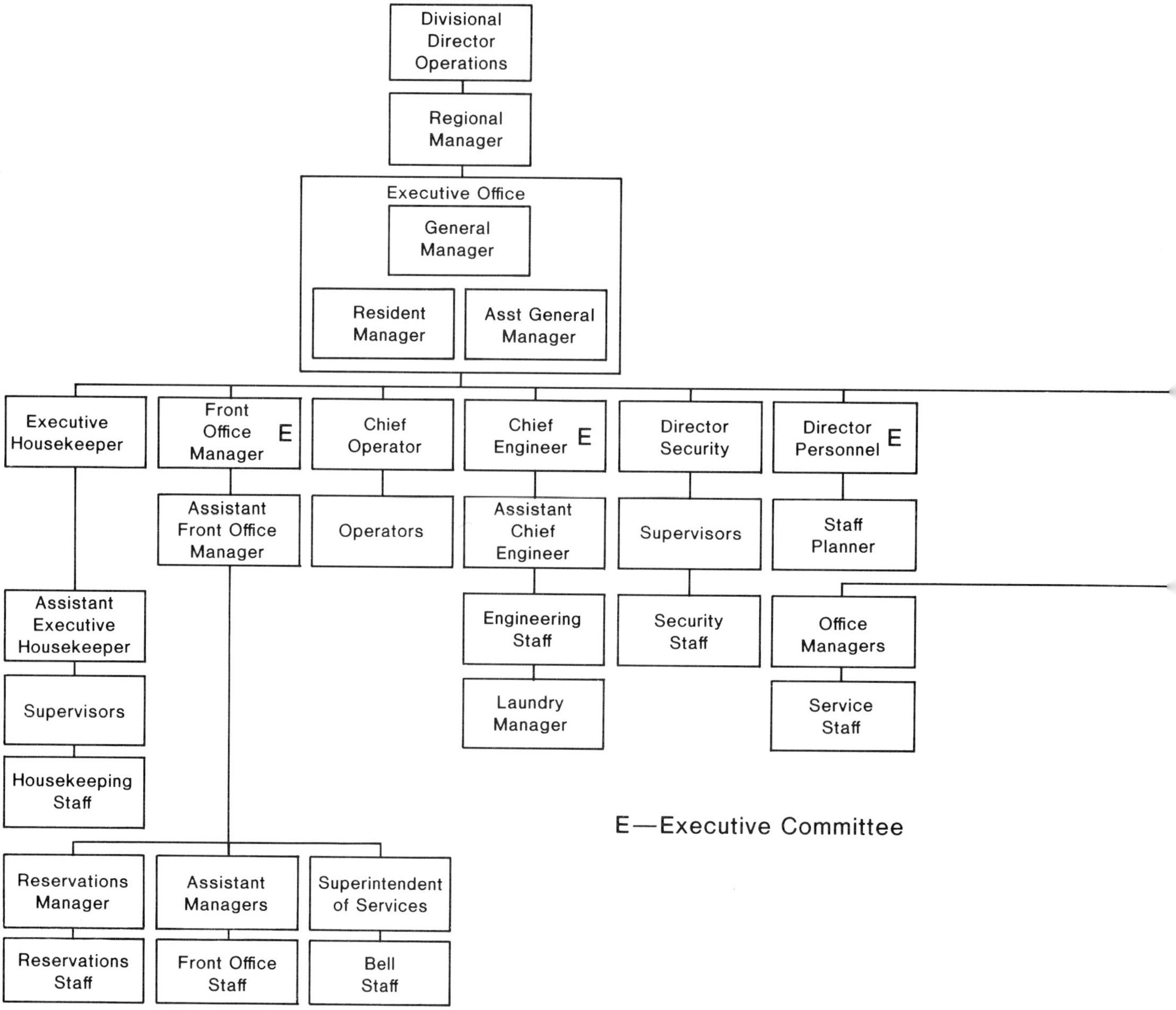

E—Executive Committee

HOSPITAL FOOD-SERVICE ORGANIZATION

A 200-bed hospital dietary department is often headed by a chief dietitian or an individual with the title of *food service director;* a registered dietician (RD) is required by law. Where the hospital has a food-teaching program for nurses or for intern dieticians, a separate division of teaching dietitians may be added. A typical organizational chart for the dietary department of a fairly large hospital is shown in figure 3.11.

Club Organization

For the size of the staff, club organizations can be quite complicated because of the relation between various house committees and operating departments. Clubs are operated for the benefit of their membership, and often the members want a direct hand in the supervision of the various departments. The chairperson of the tennis com-

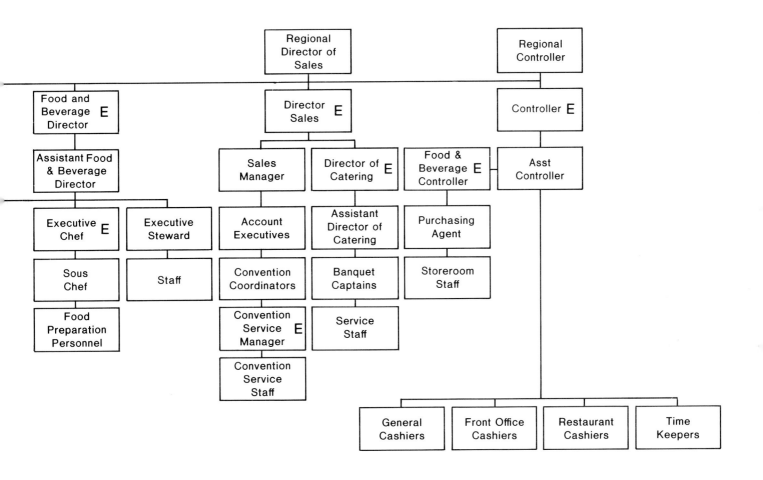

mittee may work directly with the tennis pro, the swim committee works with the pool director, the golf committee with the golf pro, the house committee directly with the office manager. Because of the dilution of responsibility in some clubs the manager's job becomes one highly dependent upon tact, expertise, and personal presence. Many a time a department head can buck the manager, if the occasion arises, by going around that individual to a committee member or to a powerful friend in the membership.

The organizational chart of the Northmoor Country Club (fig. 3.13) illustrates this dual management relationship that exists between department heads and committee chairpersons. It is seen that both the manager and the various house committees have a management relationship with the office manager, the tennis pro, the golf pro, golf course staff, and the pro director. Little wonder that the average country club manager changes jobs about every three years.

Figure 3.4 Organization Chart Hilton Hotels Corporation

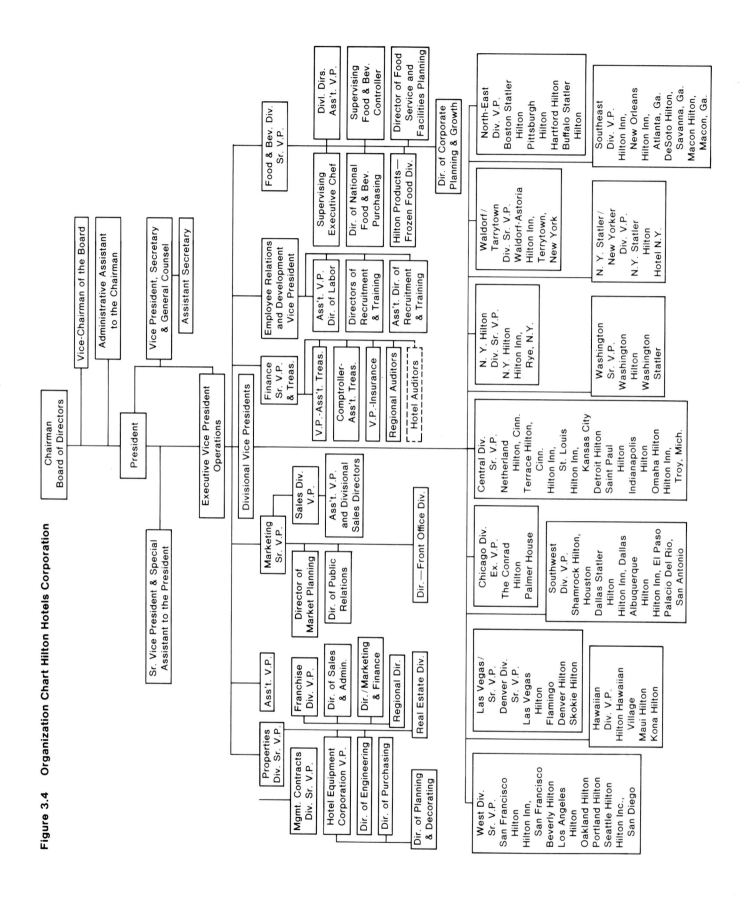

Figure 3.5 Hotel Engineering Organization 200–600 Rooms

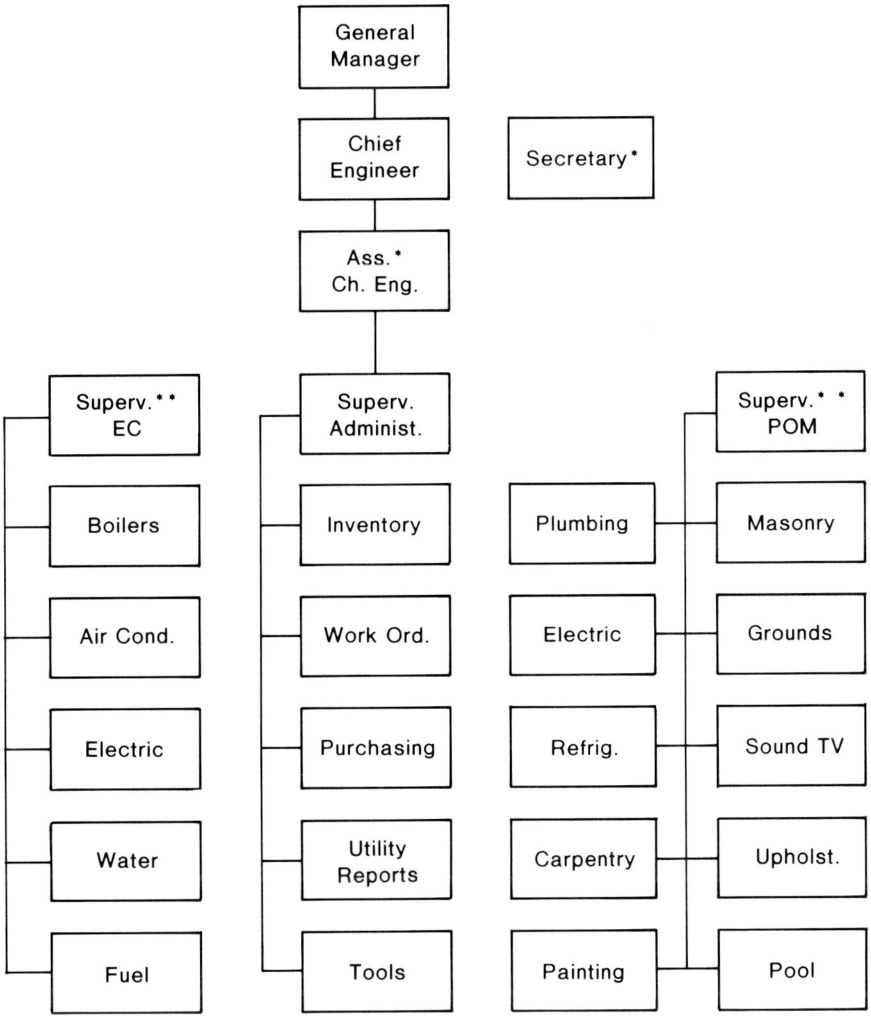

*May not be necessary in 50–150 room hotel
**Possibly additional supervision required in larger properties.

Manning Tables

Staffing or manning tables are often made to accompany organization charts. They list the number of persons on each job and the total number of personnel in each department. The staffing table for a 225-room hotel is shown as table 3.1. Notice that several of the jobs use one-half, one-third, or two-thirds of an employee's time. It is only with such close scheduling of employees that labor cost can be held down and a profit made for the business. Staffing range tables that give the number of personnel needed for various levels of occupancy, food, and beverage sales are more meaningful for purposes of labor cost control. Details of the Harris, Kerr, and Forster labor cost-control system are seen in the appendix.

SUMMARY

Organization is necessary for coordinating the efforts of all personnel toward the goals of the enterprise. Through organization all activities are brought under a centralized direction and a two-way communication system is possible.

Line and staff functions can be differentiated. Line functions have to do with operations. Staff functions are essentially advisory and supportive. Most large companies adhere to formal systems of organization, often reflected in a chart, with clear designation of offices and departments, lines of responsibility, authority, and assignment of duties.

Figure 3.6 Employee Relations and Development

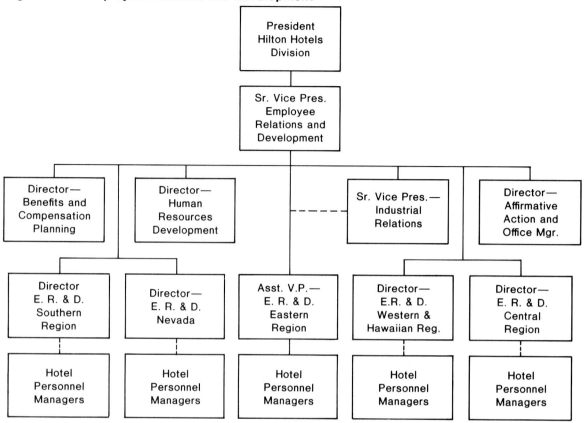

It is important to recognize that an organization is not an organizational chart. People make an organization function. Power resides throughout the organization, not just with the management. The manager's task is to provide group leadership—which is much more involved than merely structuring and directing people.

In order to carry out the principles of organization, certain logical procedures can be followed: (a) similar functions should be organized together; (b) responsibility, authority, and accountability of every position in the organization should be defined; (c) the organizational pattern should be understood functionally, clarified and updated as needed; (d) guidelines should be established concerning the effective span of control of each supervisory position; and (e) decisions should be made concerning the advisability of maintaining centralized or decentralized controls.

An organizational chart is an abstraction of desired relationships within an organization. By necessity the organizational chart must be dynamic in order to reflect the specific interplay of functions within the enterprise. Standard charts of organization cannot reflect the unique characteristics found in various companies and industries. General guidelines are available, however, concerning the organizational structure of some of the most successful large or small restaurants and hotels in America.

Figure 3.7   Hilton Nevada Division

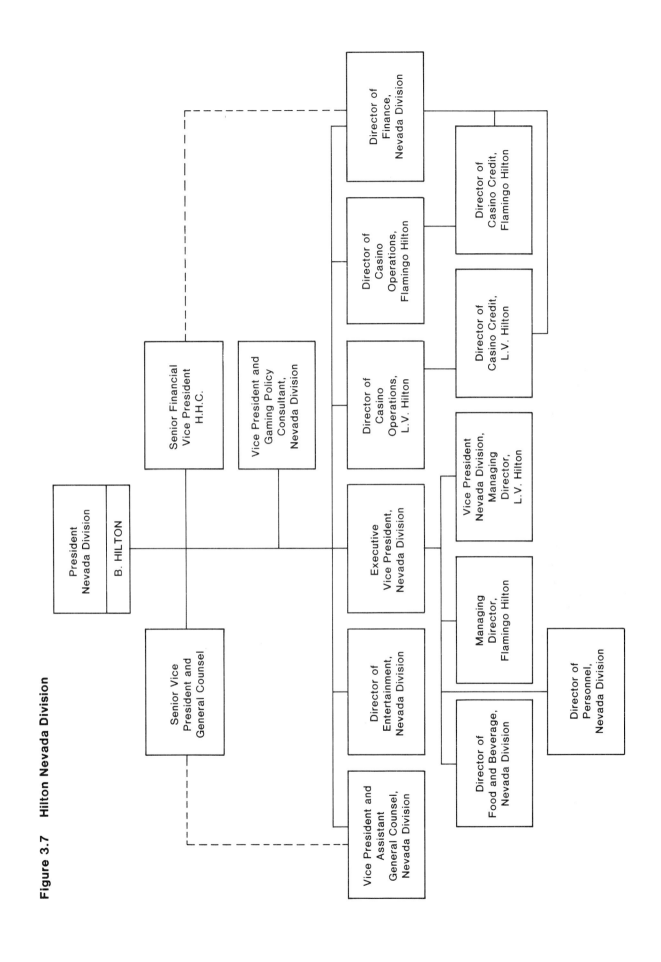

Figure 3.8   Morrison, Inc. Organizational Chart

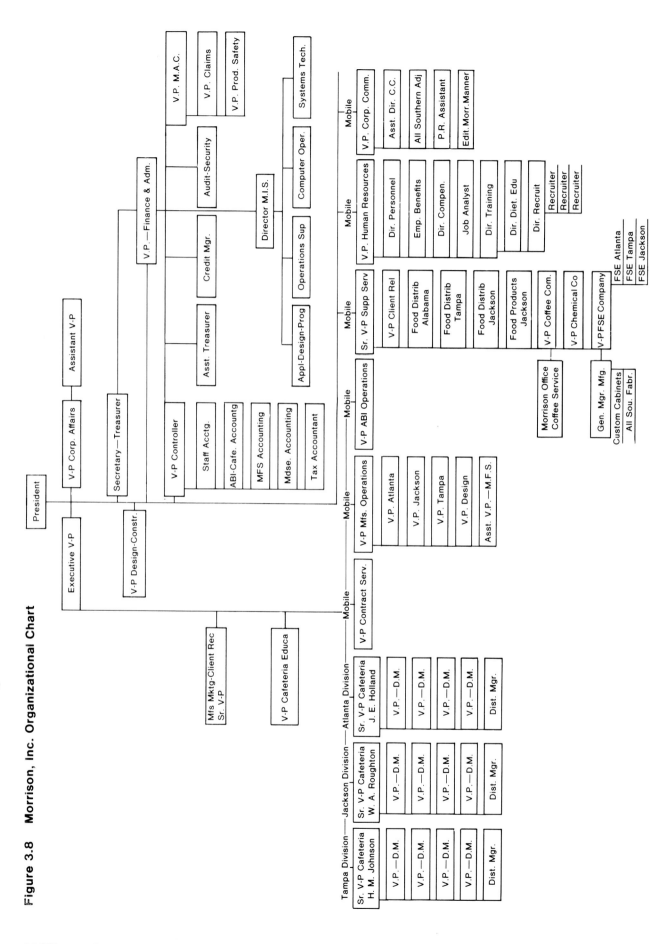

Figure 3.9 Stouffer's Restaurant and Inn Corporation

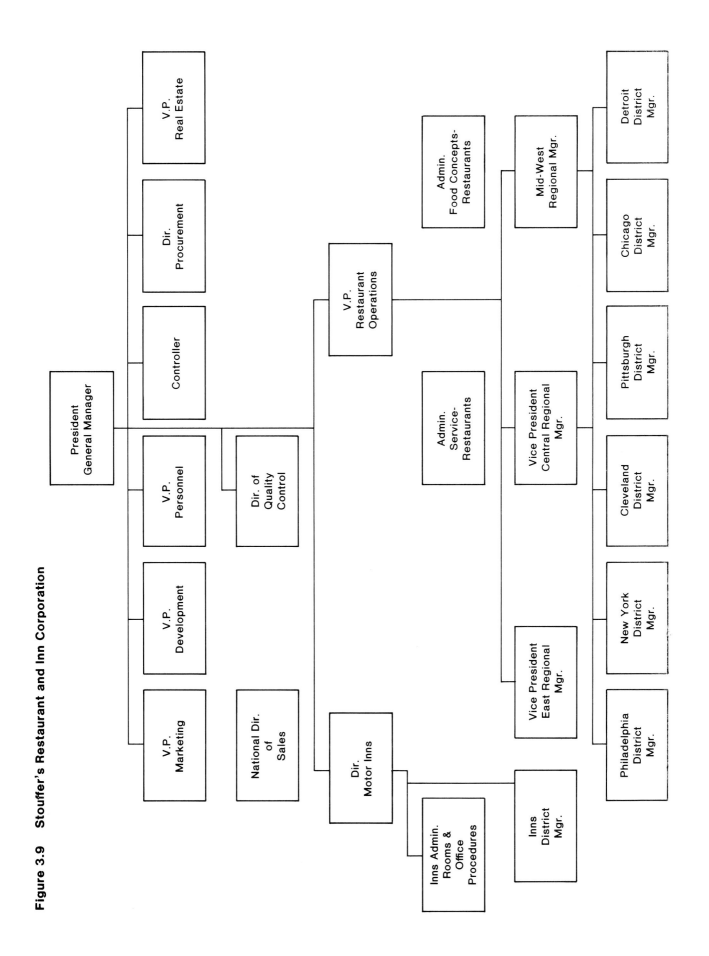

Figure 3.10   Stouffer Restaurant Division

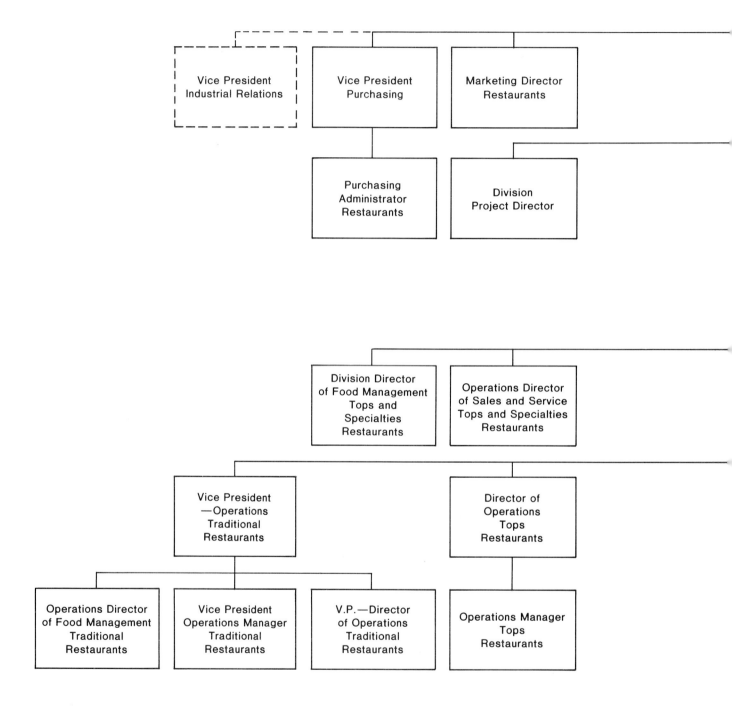

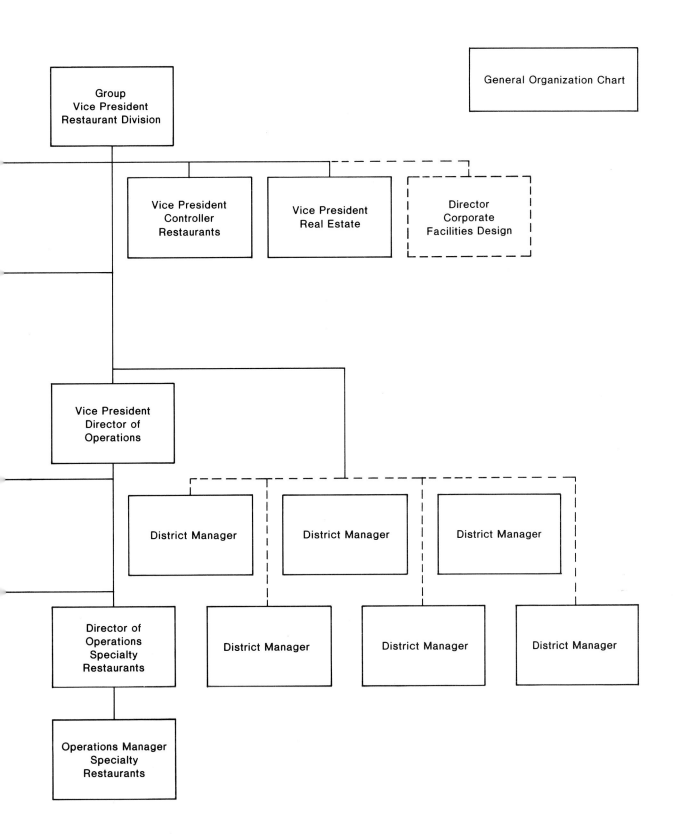

General Organization Chart

Group
Vice President
Restaurant Division

Vice President
Controller
Restaurants

Vice President
Real Estate

Director
Corporate
Facilities Design

Vice President
Director of
Operations

District Manager

District Manager

District Manager

Director of
Operations
Specialty
Restaurants

District Manager

District Manager

District Manager

Operations Manager
Specialty
Restaurants

Figure 3.11   Dietary Department of a 200-Bed Hospital

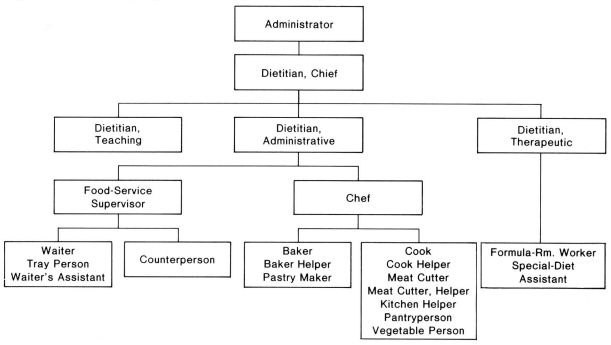

Figure 3.12   Organizational Structure of Northmoor Country Club

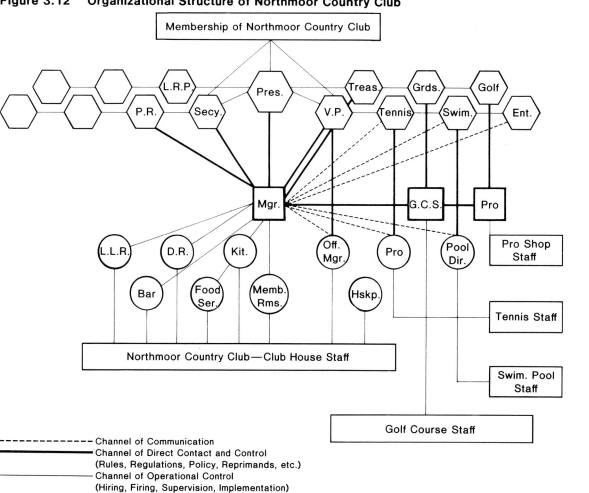

Table 3.1 Manning Table—225-Room Hotel

	Executive Office		Housekeeping
1	General Manager	1	Housekeeper
1	Resident Manager	1	Assistant Housekeeper
2	Secretaries	1	Inspector
4		1	Linen Room Attendant
		1	Linen Person
	Front Office	1	Parlor Person
1	Asst. Mgr.-Room Clerk	1	Night Houseperson
1	Room Clerk	2⅓	Room Houseperson
1	Mail-Room Clerk	1	Parlor Lodging Cleaner
1	Night Auditor	1	Night Lodging Cleaner
2½	Cashiers	3	Relief Lodging Cleaners
5	Telephone Operators	1	Head Night Cleaner
		2	Night Cleaners
	Lounge	17⅓	
1	Manager-Bartender		
2	Bartenders		**Beverage**
½	Bar Porter	1	Beverage Controller
3½		2⅓	News-Pkg. Store Cashiers
		½	Storeroom Porter
	Uniformed Service	3⅚	
1	Superintendent of Service		
3	Bellhop Captains		**Coffee Shop**
15	Bellhop-Porters	1	Manager-Host
2	Doorkeeper	1	Host
9	Elevator Operators	2⅔	Cashiers
30		13	Waitresses
		4	Waiters' Assistant
	Auditing	21⅔	
1	Auditor		
1	Asst. Auditor		**Banquet & Room Service**
1	Food Controller	1	Banquet Hostess
3		8	Waiters
		9	
	Personnel		
1	Manager		**Kitchen**
2½	Timekeeper-Security Guard	1	Chef
2	Night Officer	1	Night Chef
5½		1	Second Cook
		1	Breakfast Cook
	Engineering	1	General Cook
1	Chief Engineer	1	Relief Cook
4	Engineers (Engine Room)	1	Head Pantry Person
2	Engineers (Maintenance)	3	Pantry People
1	Fireman	1	Head Dish Machine Operator
1	Carpenter	2	Banquet Dish Machine Operators
1	Painter	3	Dish Machine Operators
1	Painter's Helper	2	Potwashers
1	Porter	2⅓	Food Checkers
12		1	Night Porter
		1	Store Room Clerk
	Laundry	1	Butcher
1	Manager	1	Baker
1	Asst. Manager-(Washman)	1	Baker Helper
1	Washman's Helper	1	Cook Trainee
2½	Pressers	26⅓	
1	Finisher-Marker		
1	Pants Presser		**Miscellaneous**
1½	Checker	1	Printer
6	Flatwork Ironers		
1	Sewer		
16			

Total Number of Employees: 164 ⅔

Job and Employee Analysis

4

Basic to selection and training procedures is job analysis. Before determining the qualifications or training needed for employees, we must know exactly what work is to be done. Each job is examined and the tasks to be performed listed in an organized form. Each job is inventoried and the job content set down in orderly form called a job description. By using standard terminology and procedure, job analysis is done systematically and efficiently.

Knowing the tasks to be done, the next step is to determine the job skills and personality traits needed to perform the jobs. Job analysis permits the development of job specifications—the kinds of persons and skills needed to perform the work called for in the job description.

After the jobs of an organization have been broken down and written in the form of a job description, an abbreviated form of the job description is made. The abbreviated form is known as a job definition.

Job specifications spell out the personal and skill requirements of the job of lodging quarters cleaner, counter person, roast cook, sous chef, and the other more than ninety jobs to be found in the hotel and restaurant business. The requirements of the job are usually classified under such headings as mental requirements, educational requirements, physical requirements, and personality requirements. A glance at the job specification shows the employer the main requirements of the job. The manager then proceeds to determine if the applicant fits those requirements.

Since particular jobs vary from establishment to establishment, each establishment must often develop its own job descriptions.

Job analysis provides supervisors and other trainers with basic information as to what is entailed in performing a job. Job analysis enables the trainer to prepare job breakdowns, which are step-by-step guides to instructing. The chapter on training shows this relationship between job analysis and training more clearly.

Job analysis defines jobs and lessens confusion and conflict among employees and supervisors. People need to know what is expected of them and where their responsibility begins and where it ends.

Job analysis makes it possible to draw up organization charts showing lines of authority, promotion, communication, and limits of responsibility. Such charts enable the employee to see how he fits into the total picture of hotel or restaurant activity.

Other Uses of Job Analysis

Job analysis is seen as providing backbone information for the personnel- or industrial-relations function. This information can be applied to several functions, as, for example:

1. The work force can be organized on the basis of job duties and responsibilities disclosed by job analysis.

2. More equitable wage and salary administration is possible in which jobs are compensated on the basis of skill required, complexity of duties, responsibilities, and other related job characteristics.

3. Transfers and promotions can be made using job-analysis information as a reference.

4. Grievances can be avoided through careful assignment of responsibilities, definition of tasks and duties, and comparisons of the equity of job with pay rates.

5. Job analysis efforts that disclose unnecessarily hazardous, unpleasant, or unhealthy working conditions can lead to programs of improvement. This aspect of job analysis has become more important with the passage of the Occupational Safety and Health Act of

1970 and with the passage of several state health and safety acts.

6. Production standards can be set through time and motion study based on job analysis.

7. Improved efficiency can result by way of work simplification and methods of improvement based on job study.

8. Collective bargaining is facilitated by having detailed definitions of jobs and the use of accepted standard job titles.

9. Job parameters are established so that the employee knows what is expected. The "eager beaver" employee may do more than what is called for in the job; the "laggard" may do as little as possible. Neither can be faulted if guidelines do not exist.

10. Work performance can be more easily judged when specific tasks are laid out in the form of a job description.

11. Supervisors are virtually forced to better lay out the sequence of work performance and assign tasks in a more logical order. The houseperson's job, for example, can be seen as a sequence of tasks originating on one floor and moving up through others, eliminating unnecessary backtracking.

TERMINOLOGY USED IN JOB ANALYSIS

Some misunderstanding as regards terminology used in job analysis is common. Following are the three principal terms and their definitions.

1. **Job analysis**—a term that applies to the actual procedure of observing the job, interviewing the worker, and recording the results. Job analysis is a procedure designed to discover the facts about jobs, including each job's requirements in terms of the personal qualities of a satisfactory job holder.

2. **Job description**—the organized written form of the results of the analysis, usually done away from the job from notes taken at the job. It describes the work performed, the responsibilities involved, the skill or training required, the conditions under which the job is done, and the type of personnel required for the job.

3. **Job specification**—more properly called a *person specification*, in that it lists the skills and personality traits needed to perform a job. The term has been popularized by the United States Employment Service and further assists in the selection process by outlining the particular working conditions that will be encountered on the job.

The three terms are considered to be parts of the total job-analysis procedure. In terms of the sequence of performance: job analysis (limited sense) is performed; the job description is written from the results of the job analysis; and the job specification is drawn up, describing the kind of person needed to perform the job.

A still briefer form of write-up is the job definition. It is the most concise description of a job possible. Listed following are several job definitions of some lesser-known hotel and restaurant jobs taken from the *Dictionary of Occupational Titles* published by United States Employment Service. The *DOT* contains job definitions of some 20,000 occupations.[1]

GARDE MANAGER *(hotel & rest.)* **cold-meat chef; cook, cold meat.**

Prepares such dishes as meat loaves and salads, utilizing leftover meats, seafoods, and poultry: Consults with supervisory staff to determine dishes that will use greatest amount of leftovers. Prepares appetizers, relishes, and hors d'oeuvres. Chops, dices, and grinds meats and vegetables. Slices cold meats and cheese. Arranges and garnishes cold meat dishes. Prepares cold meat sandwiches. Mixes and prepares cold sauces, meat glazes, jellies, salad dressings, and stuffings. May supervise pantry workers. May follow recipes to prepare foods.

SOUS CHEF *(hotel & rest.)* **chef assistant; chef, under; executive-chef assistant; supervising-chef assistant.**

Supervises and coordinates activities of COOKS (hotel & rest.) and other workers engaged in preparing and cooking foodstuffs: Observes workers engaged in preparing, portioning, and garnishing foods to insure that methods of cooking and garnishing and sizes of portions are as prescribed. Gives instructions to cooking personnel in fine points of cooking. Cooks and carves meats, and prepares dishes, such as sauces, during rush periods and for banquets and other social functions. Assumes responsibility for kitchen in absence of EXECUTIVE CHEF (hotel & rest.). In establishments not employing an EXECUTIVE CHEF (hotel & rest.), may be designated SUPERVISING CHEF (hotel & rest.).

CHEF DE FROID *(hotel & rest.)*

Designs and prepares decorated foods and artistic food arrangements for buffets in formal restaurants: Confers with EXECUTIVE CHEF (hotel & rest.) and SOUS CHEF (hotel & rest.) and reviews advance menus to determine amount and type of food to be served and decor to be carried out. Prepares foods, such as hors d'oeuvres, cold whole salmon, roast suckling pig, casseroles, and fancy aspics, according to recipe and decorates them following customer's specifications, designated color scheme, or theme, using colorful fruit, vegetables, and relishes.

---

1. *Dictionary of Occupational Titles, Part 1, Definitions of Titles,* (Washington, D.C.: United States Employment Service, 1977).

STEWARD/STEWARDESS *(hotel & rest.)* **chief steward/stewardess; executive steward/stewardess; house steward/stewardess.**

Supervises and coordinates activities of pantry, storeroom, and noncooking kitchen workers, and purchases or requisitions foodstuffs, kitchen supplies, and equipment: Inspects kitchens and storerooms to insure that premises and equipment are clean and in order, and that sufficient foodstuffs and supplies are on hand to insure efficient service. Examines incoming purchases for quality and to insure that purchases are as specified in order. Approves invoices or bills for payment. Coordinates work of noncooking kitchen and storeroom workers engaged in activities, such as dishwashing, silver cleaning, and storage and distribution of foodstuffs and supplies. Establishes controls to guard against theft and wastage. Confers with EXECUTIVE CHEF (hotel & rest.), or MANAGER, CATERING (hotel & rest.), concerning banquet arrangements for food service, equipment, and extra employees. May plan and price menus, keep cost records, and establish budget controls to insure profitable food service operation. May perform duties for recreational or business clubs. This job occurs in hotels, as opposed to KITCHEN SUPERVISOR (hotel & rest.), which occurs in restaurants and cafeterias.

STEWARD/STEWARDESS BANQUET *(hotel & rest.)*

Supervises and coordinates activities of kitchen and dining-room workers during banquets to insure that food is served promptly: Consults with MANAGER, CATERING (hotel & rest.) or EXECUTIVE CHEF (hotel & rest.) on such items as serving arrangements and additional employees and equipment needed. Hires and supervises temporary banquet employees. Requisitions table linen, china, glassware, and silverware. Orders preparation of salads and coffee. Observes food being served to insure that food is correctly garnished and arranged on plates.

MANAGER, FRONT OFFICE *(hotel & rest.)*

Coordinates front-office activities of hotel or motel and resolves problems arising from guests' complaints, reservation and room assignment activities, and unusual requests and inquiries: Assigns duties and shifts to workers and observes performances to insure adherence to hotel policies and established operating procedures. Confers and cooperates with other department heads to insure coordination of hotel activities. Answers inquiries pertaining to hotel policies and services. Greets important guests. Arranges for private telephone line and other special services. May patrol public rooms, investigate disturbances, and warn troublemakers. May interview and hire applicants.

MANAGER, GOLF CLUB *(amuse. & rec.)*

Manages golf club to provide entertainment for patrons: Directs activities of dining room and kitchen workers and crews that maintain club buildings, equipment, and golf course in good condition. Hires and discharges workers. Estimates quantities and costs of foodstuffs, beverages, and groundskeeping equipment to prepare operating budget. Explains necessity of items on budget to board of directors and requests approval. Inspects club buildings, equipment, and golf course. Requisitions materials, such as foodstuffs, beverages, seeds, fertilizers, and groundskeeping equipment. Keeps accounts of receipts and expenditures. May assist in planning tournaments.

HOTEL CLERK *(hotel & rest.)* **motel clerk; motor-lodge clerk.**

Performs any combination of following duties for guests of hotel, motel, motor lodge, or condominium-hotel: Registers and assigns rooms to guests. Issues room key and escort instructions to BELLHOP (hotel & rest.). Date-stamps, sorts, and racks incoming mail and messages. Transmits and receives messages, using equipment, such as telegraph, telephone, Teletype, and switchboard. Answers inquiries pertaining to hotel services; registration of guests; and shopping, dining, entertainment, and travel directions. Keeps records of room availability and guests' accounts. Computes bill, collects payment, and makes change for guests [CASHIER (clerical) I]. Makes and confirms reservations. May sell tobacco, candy, and newspapers. May post charges, such as room, food, liquor, or telephone, to cashbooks, by hand [BOOKKEEPER (clerical) II] or by machine [BOOKKEEPING-MACHINE OPERATOR (clerical) II]. May make restaurant, transportation, or entertainment reservations, and arrange for tours. May deposit guest's valuables in hotel safe or safe-deposit box. May order complimentary flowers or champagne for honeymoon couples or special guests. May rent dock space at marina-hotel. May work on one floor and be designated FLOOR CLERK (hotel & rest.). May be known according to specific task performed as KEY CLERK (hotel & rest.); RESERVATION CLERK (hotel & rest.); ROOM CLERK (hotel & rest.) or area worked as DESK CLERK (per. ser.); FRONT CLERK *(hotel & rest.)*.

LINEN-ROOM ATTENDANT *(hotel & rest.; medical ser.)* **linen checker; linen clerk; linen-exchange attendant; uniform attendant.**

Stores, issues, and inventories bed and table linen and uniforms to maintain supply in establishments, such as hotels, hospitals, and clinics: Segregates, counts, and records number of items of soiled linen and uniforms, and places items in containers for transmittal to laundry. Examines laundered items to insure cleanliness and serviceability. Stamps items with identifying marks. Stores laundered items on shelves, after verifying numbers and types of items. Counts and records amounts of linens and uniforms to fill requisition, placing orders on carts for delivery. Conducts monthly and yearly inventories to identify items for replacement. May mend torn articles with needle and thread or sewing machine or send articles to SEWER, LINEN ROOM *(hotel & rest.)*.

MANAGER, HOTEL OR MOTEL *(hotel & rest.)* **manager, general; manager, motor hotel; manager, motor inn; manager, resident.**

Manages hotel or motel to insure efficient and profitable operation: Establishes standards for personnel administration and performance, service to patrons, room rates, advertising, publicity, credit, food selection and service, and type of patronage to be solicited. Plans dining room, bar, and banquet operations. Allocates funds, authorizes expenditures, and assists in planning budgets for departments. Hires personnel. Delegates authority and assigns responsibilities to department heads. In small motels or hotels, processes reservations and adjusts guests' complaints.

EXECUTIVE HOUSEKEEPER *(hotel & rest.; medical ser.)* **housekeeper, administrative; housekeeper, head.**

Directs institutional housekeeping program to insure clean, orderly, and attractive conditions of establishment: Establishes standards and procedures for work of housekeeping staff, and plans work schedules to insure adequate service.

Inspects and evaluates physical condition of establishment, and submits to management recommendations for painting, repairs, furnishings, relocation of equipment, and reallocation of space. Periodically inventories supplies and equipment, and investigates new and improved cleaning instruments. Organizes and directs departmental training programs, resolves personnel problems, and hires new employees. Writes activity and personnel reports for review by management. Coordinates activities with those of other departments. May select and purchase new furnishings. May evaluate records to forecast department personnel requirements, and to prepare budget.

SALES REPRESENTATIVE, HOTEL SERVICES (hotel & rest.)

Contacts representatives of government, business, and social groups to solicit business for hotel, motel, or resort: Selects prospective customers by reviewing information concerning functions, such as sales meetings, conventions, training classes, and routine travel by organization members. Calls on prospects, analyzes requirements of occasion, outlines types of service offered, and quotes prices. Verifies reservations by letter or draws up contract and obtains signatures. Confers with customer and hotel department heads to plan function details, such as space requirements, publicity, time schedule, food service, and decorations. May serve as convention advisor or hotel agent during function to minimize confusion and resolve problems, such as space adjustment and need for additional equipment. May select and release hotel's publicity.

PLANNING A JOB-ANALYSIS PROGRAM

Who should do the job analysis? It is not necessary, as some personnel people believe, that the analyst be an engineer, or have a great deal of training in the techniques of job analysis. The conduct of job analysis does require an above-average, general mental ability plus the ability to observe well and to express what one sees in clear, concise writing. Patience, curiosity, and social skills are needed for questioning workers about their jobs.

Fortunately, in planning job analysis, aid can often be secured from state employment services. Several state employment services have specially trained job analysts whose services can be obtained free of charge. Analysts provided by the state usually act only as consultants or as trainers of persons designated by the hotel or restaurant operator to perform the actual analysis. Individual training is given the prospective analyst thereby enabling the person to conduct the analyses alone and without assistance.

In initiating job analysis it is a good idea to start with only one small department. In this way errors of inexperience can be ironed out before continuing. In an establishment that is just instituting a personnel department, it is good practice to have the personnel director conduct the analysis in person. In this way first-hand knowledge of the jobs and of the organization is gained.

Another consideration in conducting a job-analysis program is its proper introduction to the workers. Any-

thing that hints of an efficiency expert may cause unrest and resentment. The fact that management is studying the worker's job may be taken as implied criticism of the way the job is being done. It may mean an attempt to speed things up. In any event, the fact that the general purpose of job analysis is not known—is sufficient cause for resentment towards management. Where unions are present, job analysis may indicate an attempt to steal some of the union's influence. Union representatives should be informed of the proposed job analysis before the analysis is initiated. The union can be an aid in developing the proper attitude toward the analysis. Union or no union, the workers themselves should be informed of the purpose of analysis and how it is to be performed, with opportunity to ask questions of responsible persons. The proper introduction of job-analysis programs may be just as important as the operation itself.

CONDUCTING JOB ANALYSIS

There are several ways of conducting a job analysis.* One method is to develop a suitable questionnaire form and have the workers fill it out as it pertains to their specific jobs. The job analyst then assembles and compares the forms, selects representative items from the various replies of persons working at the same job and makes a job description. Proponents of this method argue that in the end the worker himself has to tell most of the tasks and responsibilities of his job.

Another method of performing job analysis is to have each department head so trained as to perform the analyses within the department. This method is advantageous in that department heads will necessarily take an active interest in the project and will be more willing to make any changes that they themselves recommend as a result of the findings. Where department heads are already overloaded with work, of course, this method is inadvisable.

A method which has proved workable for the hotel and restaurant is one that is a combination of those already mentioned. One person is responsible for the program, but delegates as much responsibility as possible. All workers and supervisory personnel fill out an itemized analysis questionnaire.

After the analyst has had the questionnaires returned and has made the physical demands appraisal, a preliminary description of each job can be prepared. It is important that this description be considered merely as a rough draft, because the personnel doing the jobs must be consulted and questioned carefully to learn of possible omis-

*See "Hospitality Industry Guide for Writing and Using Task-Unit Job Descriptions," Tourism Education Corp., 200 Park Ave., New York, 10017.

sions. Many tasks within the scope of a job are performed only occasionally. The analyst will probably not observe them. Only through questioning the employee can one learn about these tasks and what they consist of. If the worker regularly performs the tasks, even though it be but once a week, it is a part of the job and should be included in the job description. For example, a dishwasher may be required to empty a garbage can once or twice a day. It is then a part of the job of dishwashing. Perhaps some other employee should rightfully empty that garbage container. Consultation with the supervisor would subtract this task from the job description.

In analyzing a job it is well to itemize every task performed on the job, no matter how inconsequential it may seem at the moment. Once the tasks have been cataloged and are arrayed in front of the analyst, they can be put together into related groups. From these a more general job description can be compiled.

Another reason for listing every task is to avoid omitting from the job description some of the work done. Since every establishment (unless it is a part of a uniform chain) is likely to have jobs that differ from those of other establishments, listing every task will point up the individuality of the job.

As an illustration of the details involved, the tasks that are part of accounting and bookkeeping are given below.[2]

DUTIES OF ACCOUNTANT

1. Accounting

A. *Analysis*
1. Analyzing operating data
2. Analyzing financial data to discover deficiencies
3. Analyzing financial data to discover inefficiency
4. Analyzing financial data to discover fraud
5. Analyzing financial data to discover lack of compliance with policy
6. Auditing all bills
7. Auditing all cash in the cash system
8. Comparing current and previously reported cost data
9. Comparing current and previously reported cost data by functional area
10. Comparing current previously reported cost data by unit
11. Compiling financial reports
12. Compiling financial collection reports
13. Compiling disbursement reports
14. Compiling reconciliation reports
15. Compiling statistical reports
16. Consolidating cost data by functional area
17. Consolidating cost data by account series
18. Consolidating cost data by account sub-series
19. Consolidating cost data by units
20. Determining costs of operation
21. Examining accounting and control procedures to determine compliance with regulations
22. Examining accounting records as to legal compliance

23. Examining accounting records as to reporting policies
24. Analyzing accounting records for useful information
25. Issuing justifications for actual figures being over or under budget
26. Studying problems and recommending action

B. *Bookkeeping*
1. Adjusting control totals
2. Adjusting ledger totals
3. Ascertaining accounts affected by transaction
4. Assess laundry charges
5. Balancing control accounts
6. Balancing disbursements
7. Balancing ledger accounts
8. Balancing receipts
9. Correcting errors in accounts
10. Correcting customer errors
11. Correcting vendor errors
12. Correcting errors, make adjustments (accounting)
13. Handling advance deposits
14. Maintain in-house guest accounts
15. Posting due
16. Posting paid
17. Posting changes to records
18. Posting data to accounts
19. Posting data to customers
20. Posting supply data
21. Posting details of financial transactions
22. Posting expense vouchers
23. Posting expenses
24. Posting payroll deductions
25. Posting payroll to pay records
26. Posting revenues
27. Posting rooms occupied on room occupancy report
28. Posting room rates on revenue reports
29. Pricing inventories
30. Processing bills
31. Recording financial transactions
32. Recording monetary transactions
33. Verifying and balancing entries and records of financial transactions reported and recorded by various depts.
34. Verifying daily balances against predetermined figures
35. Verifying journal entries

C. *Computation*
1. Aging accounts receivable
2. Calculating Travel Agents' commission
3. Computing bills
4. Computing figures for financial reports
5. Computing financial ratios
6. Computing interest changes
7. Computing losses
8. Computing refunds
9. Computing rental changes
10. Computing subtotal averages
11. Computing subtotal costs
12. Computing subtotal percentages

---

2. Compiled by the Job Description Committee of the Council on Hotel, Restaurant and Institutional Education.

THE JOB DESCRIPTION

The written results of the job analysis are put into several forms, the most prominent being the job description, an organized statement of what the job is all about. The form in which it is presented should be one that is most useful for the hotel, restaurant, or club. Descriptions of managerial positions necessarily reflect policy. It is usually found that in the course of job analysis questions are raised that have not been thought out. Sometimes new policies are needed or old ones reworked.

Hotels or restaurants that have been directed by their owners over a period of time often operate "by the seat of the owner's pants." It may be difficult to get an owner to sit down and spell out responsibilities of jobs other than those performed by that very individual. The job-analysis process often results in reassigning of responsibilities and authority. The process can be quite unsettling to an executive who has in the past operated completely on the basis of self-discretion. In one case the chief executive called off the job analysis upon discovering that such an analysis could circumscribe his own role and force the delegation of responsibility he had previously self-arrogated.

Some Guidelines for Writing a Job Description:

A. Describe the job, not the person in the job.

B. Avoid value judgments; for example, in thinking about a room clerk: "Requires advanced education in math and a high degree of accuracy," is not as accurate as: "Must know how to make change; add, subtract, and divide."

C. No attempt should be made to describe the job in fine detail such as might be found in a time and motion study.

D. Sentences should be short, simple, and to the point. Only words and phrases that really contribute to the description should be used.

E. If technical jargon is used, it should be explained.

F. Although job descriptions vary in length, they should be limited to not more than about three double-spaced, typewritten pages.

Information from which job descriptions and specifications can be derived can be systematically collected following a form. The Small Business Administration recommends the forms seen below as guides for pulling together a composite picture of what a particular job entails.* Such information can then be used for constructing a profile of the kind of person who can do the job.

---

*Copies of this Aid are available free from field offices and Washington headquarters of the Small Business Administration. Aids may be condensed or reproduced. They may not be altered to imply approval by SBA of any private organization, product, or service. If material is reused, credit to SBA will be appreciated. Use of funds for printing this publication approved by the Office of Management and Budget, March 20, 1975.

Form 1   **IDENTIFICATION FACTS**

Job Title _____ Location _____

Other titles used _____ Number employed: M _____ F _____

Brief summary of nature or function of job* _____

_____

Code number** _____

Salary range: Minimum _____ Maximum _____
   Average bonus or incentive payment _____
Working hours: Shift: _____ From _____ To _____
   Overtime: ____ never ____ seldom ____ frequent; average hours per week: ____
Misc. _____

*A 1-sentence description, to give a general idea of job.
**Job definition (from the *Dictionary of Occupational Titles*; your local State Employment Service Office can be helpful).

SKILL REQUIREMENTS

Educational Requirements: (general education—grade or years)
    Grammar   High   Business
    School _____   School _____   School _____   College _____
    Specific education for job _____

Job Experience:
    Previous experience required: None _____
        Acceptable type and length _____
    Average length of time with organization _____
    Previous jobs normally held _____
    Next job in line of promotion _____

Relation to Other Jobs: Contacts regularly as part of job:
    Within the Company _____   Outside the Company _____

    _____   _____

Exercises Supervision Over:
    Position of individual: _____
    Subject of supervision: _____

Is Supervised by: *Position of individual*   *Subject of supervision*
    Immediate supervisor _____   _____
    Others _____   _____

Job Duties:
    Regular:
        Before open for business _____
        During business hours _____
        After business hours _____
    Periodic (weekly or monthly):
        Performed on regular time _____
        Performed after hours _____
    Occasional: Performed on regular time _____
        Performed after hours _____

Job Knowledge: *Policies and Regulations*
    General   *Special and Departmental*

    _____   _____

    _____   *Procedures and Methods*
                                               _____

    Technical Information   *Related Information*

    _____   _____

Use of equipment: Types of equipment: _____
    Special operations _____

What previous experience and educational level is required for the job of cook? Does the person exercise supervision over others? Numerous cooks have had little or no education and do well on the job, and provided systematic training is available, a person can be inexperienced and still learn following standard recipes. Since the job of cook varies widely from place to place, each establishment would have to determine the skill requirement needed for that particular establishment. The skill requirements form seen below provides information useful for pulling together a job specification, but it is more useful for the overall job description.

Form 3   **RESPONSIBILITIES**

Direction & Group Leadership:
None _____   Occasional __✓__   Frequent _____   Continual _____

Nature of responsibility _____

Business Operation:
None __✓__   Occasional _____   Frequent _____   Continual _____
Nature of responsibility _____

Care of Equipment:
None _____   Occasional _____   Frequent __✓__   Continual _____
Nature of responsibility _____

Safety and Health of Others:
None _____   Occasional _____   Frequent __✓__   Continual _____
Nature of responsibility _____

Contact with Public: None _____   Occasional __✓__   Frequent _____   Continual _____

Form 4   **EFFORT DEMAND**

Physical Activities

✓ Standing	✓ Turning	✓ Reaching	✓ Pushing	✓ Smelling
✓ Walking	___ Running	___ Throwing	✓ Pulling	___ Testing
✓ Balancing	✓ Stooping	✓ Lifting	✓ Fingering	✓ Hearing
___ Climbing	✓ Sitting	✓ Carrying	✓ Feeling	✓ Seeing

Worker Characteristics

___ Planning   ___ Talking   ___ Making decisions
___ Directing others   ___ Showing initiative   ✓ Working rapidly
___ Writing   ✓ Getting along with people
___ Showing enthusiasm   ___ Working at various tempos
✓ Being well groomed   ✓ Concentrating amid distractions
✓ Controlling emotions   ___ Remembering names and faces
___ Using arithmetic   ___ Remembering details
✓ Working accurately   ✓ Examining and observing details
✓ Discriminating colors   ✓ Attending to many items

Form 5   **WORKING CONDITIONS**

✓ Inside   ✓ Hot   ✓ Dirty   ___ Inadequate light
___ Outside   ___ Cold   ___ Dusty   ___ Inadequate ventilation
✓ Humid   ___ Dry   ✓ Odors   ✓ Working with others
✓ Hazards   ✓ Wet   ✓ Noisy   ✓ Working around others
___ High places   ___ Working alone
✓ Change of temperature   ✓ Working under pressure
Details of Working Conditions (summary based on working conditions) _____
Details of Hazards *Slipping on floors, cutting fingers, back injuries, etc.* _____
Permissible Handicaps: Limb _____   Hearing __✓__   Sight _____

What kind of physical activities are involved?

The job of cook, for example, requires all of the physical activities checked above, an array of physical activities that may be surprising. Certainly a cook must be able to smell, see, taste, finger, and feel. Ordinarily a cook would not need to climb, run, or throw.

What about the working conditions for the cook's job?

It is seen that although the work is inside, it can be humid and present a number of hazards—it can be noisy, dirty. Also, the job of cook requires working closely with others, often under pressure. It is possible that a cook would not have to have normal hearing, communication could be conducted by signing or by writing.

Just what responsibilities go with the job of cook?

To be realistic, a cook need not do much planning if under the direction of an executive chef or food and beverage director. The cook need not write, need not show a great deal of enthusiasm, and may not need arithmetic skills. A cook need not be good at names or faces or necessarily even details if following recipes. Decisions that are made are low order, involving a low level of abstraction. Very important though is that the person be able to work rapidly when the occasion demands speed.

A cook should be able to discriminate colors, show a certain amount of initiative, get along with other people, and be able to change work pace.

In drawing up job descriptions, be careful to emphasize what the job is really about. For example, a busperson can be thought of as a cleanup person. A better emphasis: a person who expedites seat turnover. In the description for a waiter's assistant the purpose of the job might be spelled out: general objective of a waiter's assistant is to speed seat turnover by setting up and clearing tables as rapidly and as efficiently as possible so that seats can be turned over as rapidly as possible without interfering with the comfort of the patrons. By speeding seat turnover, volume of sales and tips are increased.

The club manager's job is beset by conflicting demands and is usually more fluid than in a profit-making operation. All the more reason for developing a clear-cut job description, in this instance, much longer than the previously recommended three-page length. The description immediately following is a good illustration of a detailed job description that can make life easier for the incumbent by listing responsibilities, duties, and various relations. The description is divided into five parts: (*a*) basic functions, (*b*) reporting relationships, (*c*) responsibilities and authorities, (*d*) relationships, and (*e*) planning and establishing standards.

The description is unusual in that it includes the standards of performance by which the manager will be judged.[3] It is also unusually comprehensive, and only parts are reproduced here.

Job Description: General Manager

I. Basic Function

As chief operational officer, he is responsible for the proper management of all aspects of The Club's activities and relationships including, but not limited to, those of members, guests, employees, the general community, taxing authorities, governmental officials, educators, and other members of the industry.

II. Reporting Relationship

Reports to the Board of Directors; fully informs all Committees; cooperates with Club Accountant; hires, supervises and may terminate the services of the:

A. *House Manager*
B. *Night Manager*
C. *Foods Manager*
D. *Dining Rooms Managers*
E. *Beverage Manager*
F. *Membership Secretary*
G. *Reservations Secretary*
H. *Activities Director*
I. *Any other employee designated over which given authority by the Board*

who operate The Club with the aid and cooperation of the department heads, supervisors and employees of The Club.

III. Responsibilities and Authorities

A. As assigned by the Bylaws: these normally specify that the Board shall employ a General Manager, and assign to this person specific authorities and duties. These include such matters as authority to direct and supervise The Club's operations, employ and discharge all club employees except the Club Accountant, to expend monies and make financial commitments in behalf of The Club within budgeted limitations; and to furnish an indemnity bond, at The Club's expense, for performance by self.

B. As assigned by House Rules: these would routinely require the General Manager to enforce the rules of The Club and report member infractions or violations, and to receive and investigate incidences of employee misconduct or inattention to duty reported by members.

---

3. Taken from Henry Ogden Barbour, *Private Club Administration* (Washington, D.C.: Managers' Association of America, 1968) and used by permission with minimal changes.

C. As chief operational employee, properly manages all aspects of The Club's activities so as to insure, over the long term of operations, maximum membership satisfaction; the realization of maximum surplus compatible with the best interests of members, their guests, club employees, and future members; the maintenance and improvement of the quality of products and services; and the security and protection of the invested capital.

D. As chief financial employee, develops, recommends and directs the operation of policies, procedures, plans and programs governing all financial matters of The Club, specifically but not limited to: the receipt, custody, control and disbursement of funds and securities; the choice and use of depositories; the extension of credit; the collection of accounts; assists in the forecasting of cash receipts and disbursements and the maintenance of adequate funds to meet current and future obligations; assists in the selection of sources and negotiation of loans; secures regular analyses of current financial position and recommends appropriate corrective action where necessary; aids in maintaining a proper and adequate insurance program; recommends signature authority; and recommends policies and procedures relative to employee loans, association memberships, travel, entertainment at Club expense, educational programs and attendance thereat; etc.

E. Authorizes expenditures in keeping with the capital and the operating budget after prior approval by Department Head and/or Manager responsible and in cooperation with appropriate Committee Chairperson; observes and corrects cash flow; approves all vouchers before payment; authorizes all salary rate changes of employees receiving less than $500 a month subject to prior budget approval [and along the lines of a stated percentage of employees in the department (perhaps 35%), within a stated percentage of total payroll (perhaps 1½ to 3%), with a minimum amount of increase over base rate (perhaps 5%), and not for any employee who has received an increase within a stated period (perhaps 8 to 16 months); co-signs checks with other selected management personnel of The Club up to a limit of $2,500 per check. . . .

I. Attends all Committee and Board meetings and prepares agendas under supervision of Chairman or the President. Takes minutes of deliberations, may transmit Committee plans and proposals for consideration, with recommendations to the Board of Directors. Keeps Committee Chairman and President informed of progress, coordinates inter- and intra-Committee activities, supplies Committeemen with facts based on Club operations, statistics from other clubs,

membership comments, personal observations and opinions on subjects under discussion. Reports effects of Committee policy or departure from Bylaws, House Rules or Board decisions to the appropriate Committee or the Board of Directors. Coordinates Committee activities. Secures figures and ideas for Capital Budget. Implements decisions and policies established by Board approval.

J. Of assistance in such specific Committee assignments as:
   1. Activities committee
      Coordinates planning and execution of promotional material, entertainers, decorations, special costumes for staff, etc., and may report thereon to the Board of Directors.
   2. Building committee
      Leases suites, rooms and offices; prepares lease forms; prepares proposed work for submission to Committee and Board; works with architects and decorators on planning, improvements and revitalization; takes bids; approves individual expenditures for Capital Improvements; checks job progress and reports to Committee.
   3. Christmas cheer sub-committee
      Has list prepared of employees with position, length of service and amount of bonuses; suggests distribution based on income; coordinates plans for Christmas-Get-Together and executes desires of Committee; supervises mailing preparation and dispatch, and follow-up on member attendance; addresses members and employees at Get-Together on behalf of 'the Management Team.'
   4. House committee
      Discusses services of various departments; secures their aid and advice in selection of brands, types of services, etc. Reports violations of Bylaws or House Rules. Secures ideas of projects for Capital Budget. Suggests possible changes in House Rules; reports and answers complaints and criticisms, conveys suggestions of members and guests. Posts new House Rules when approval is secured. . . .

K. Develops, maintains and disseminates throughout The Club a basic management philosophy expanding upon the Creed and designed to serve as a basic guide to Club operations and to insure on the part of the executives and employees alike:
   The maximum degree of personal satisfaction in the performance of their tasks; the highest level of executive and employee morale; the highest of reputations for The Club among its members, employees, and the general public; proper

and fair courses of employees' and public relations are followed at all times; and that action is taken to correct any unsatisfactory conditions as they arise in any phase of the operations.

L. In cooperation with The Club Accountant, reports the financial progress of The Club and its components to The Board of Directors, including Club performance against budget objectives for sales, costs, net income, investment and growth. Responsible for the planning and approval of all long- and short-term programs of all activities in every sphere of The Club's operational management. Participates in the preparation of plans and programs for the attainment of approved objectives, working closely with Accountant in the development of the Operation and the Capital Budgets including proposed expansion into new fields of activity; severance of unprofitable operations; and planned courses of action for times of economic trial. Recommends such plans and programs as they are developed to the Board of Directors.

M. Acquires, develops, maintains and utilizes to the maximum degree a balanced, efficient and adequate organization with respect to both its proper, sound structure and its personnel. Responsible for the training and guidance of the members of the organization and for the coordination of their activities. Plans for changes in organization required to balance future trends of Club operations. When major re-alignments are contemplated, secures approval of the Board of Directors. Delegates to immediate subordinates the authority for performance of each's assigned functions. Conducts a continuing program of appraisal of management effectiveness.

N. Responsible for the selection, training, upgrading, and development of management, membership relations, activities and entertainment personnel. Supervises all immediate associates in their performance of assigned functions so that the manner of their striving for individual objectives and program achievement is in keeping with the Creed and 'tone' of The Club. Renders advice, assistance and guidance to associates. . . .

T. Responsible for inter-firm relations on all proper matters within the hospitality industry and the community.

U. Presides at Operations Committee (composed of The Managers and The Accountant), Quality Control (Composed of Managers, Department Heads and their Assistants) and Employee Council (one employee elected from each Department) meetings; attends at least one regular meeting of each department at least once a year as well as the weekly combined Dining Room and Food Department Heads' meeting.

V. Handles emergency situations, such as fires, accidents involving personal injury, breaches of security or of House Rules, promptly and in person, but, of course, makes every effort to prevent such situations through training, inspection, and preventive enforcement. . . .

IV. Relationships

A. *The Members*
As Chief Host of The Club greets members and guests by name whenever possible, knows and directs the execution of as many of their preferences as possible; supervises the staff in the execution of the members' desires completely and promptly; observes all Club policies in dealing with the member and sees that all House Rules and Bylaws are respected and complied with; approves the cashing of checks for more than $100.00, and the sending of Club employees on errands away from The Club quarters; approves temporary deviations from House Rules regarding guests, etc., in certain 'one-occurrence' situations; is discreet in conversation with or concerning members or guests; establishes and maintains such relationships with the members of The Club as the Board of Directors may direct for the purposes of maintaining or further developing rapport, understanding, and communication between the staff and the members of The Club.

B. *The Board of Directors*
Having been selected by the Board of Directors, the General Manager is responsible to them through the President for the operation of The Club and for proper interpretation and fulfillment of their policies and of the functions, responsibilities, authorities and relationships of the General Manager's office, (or between meetings of the Board, is responsible to the Executive Committee).

C. *The President (or the Vice-President)*
Reviews major activities and plans with the President to insure that having the benefit of the latter's thinking and is acting in conformity with the Board's views on Club policy. Coordinates efforts with those of these two executives toward the goals of The Club; stands ready at all times to render advice and assistance as deemed necessary.

D. *The Secretary*
Has prepared for the Secretary all correspondence, minutes and all reports of a routine nature; has the Board and Committees informed of all meetings; safeguards all records necessary for the proper maintenance of corporate existence; acts as liaison with The Club legal counsel; directs the maintenance of basic membership records covering receipt, issuance and cancellation of memberships; keeps safely the corporate seal, charter, Bylaws, minutes, property records, powers of attorney, basic contracts and agreements of all kinds.

E. *The Committees*
Acts as secretary to all Committees except the Finance and Entertainment Committee. May submit Committee plans and proposals for consideration and recommendation to the Board of Directors. Secures facts as suggested by Agenda or at request of Committee. Implements the decisions and policies established following Board approval. Schedules meetings and makes Agendas in coordination with the Chairmen. Keeps the Chairmen informed of progress and coordinates Committee activities. . . .

G. *The Accountant and Managers*
The General Manager assists each Manager in the development of a sound and effective organization that:
  1. Achieves the department or division product, service and net income objectives.
  2. Fulfills anticipated growth.
  3. Assures division management of adequate time to accomplish long-range planning.
  4. Develops management personnel in depth and furthers supervisory development.
  5. Develops and constantly carries forward a progressive training program in which the General Manager may participate.
  6. Can afford and does pay adequate compensation.
  7. Handles selections and transfers effectively.
  8. Develops progressive employee and industrial relations.
  9. Utilizes the services of the staff organizations to the fullest practical extent by both the divisions and departments—recognizing, however, that responsibility and authority for operating decisions do not rest with the staff organizations; may underline and reinforce staff suggestions to departments and divisions. . . .

H. *Membership Secretary, Reservations Secretary, and the Activities Director*
  1. Counsels with each to develop a sound and effective organization that will:
    a. Facilitate achievement of service to members' goals within cost objectives.
    b. Disseminate full, prompt, comprehensive, useful information to members, guests and employees.
    c. Maintain records of past events to facilitate the planning or handling of future events.
    d. Insure adequate time for long- and short-range planning, purchasing, implementation and execution.
    e. Continually raise the level of membership facilities, services, decorations, decor and entertainment. . . .

I. *Limitations*
May delegate to management or supervisory personnel appropriate portions of authority but may not delegate overall responsibility for interim or final results or any portion of accountability.

J. *Department Heads*
Counsels with each upon occasion, usually in presence of appropriate manager, encouraging each to work with a view to technical advancement, promotion, better salary and realization of self; makes available both educational and tryout opportunities; conducts sessions in management techniques; helps to coordinate their efforts under the direction of the appropriate manager.

K. *Employees*
Approves all transfers, service awards, and social and recreational activities sponsored by The Club. Sees that all managers, department heads and employees are kept currently informed of Club personnel policy. Stays up-to-date on salary and fringe benefit trends in the hospitality industry; encourages and aids outstanding employees to gain technical advancement, promotion, better salary, realization of self, and perhaps additional education. Acts to insure fair and courteous treatment of employees in safe and pleasant working conditions; counsels in personal problems; acts as a 'court of last resort' on grievance matters.

L. *Professional Assistance—Auditors, Legal Counsel, Protection*
Shares experiences fully with them and aids their search for facts. Listens with an open mind to their findings and suggestions; truly attempts to apply or adapt their suggestions to the operation.

M. *Vendors*
Refers them to the appropriate manager; attempts to insure that none are shown favoritism except that which is earned by maximum quality and prompt service at the minimum final cost consistent with the goals of The Club. Works with Accountant to insure that all accounts are paid on time, with preference if any to those offering discounts.

N. *Professional and Management Associations*
Participates and contributes time to organizations and associations toward maximum professional benefit to self, to the enhancement and progress of The Club, and to their respective memberships. Is active in national, state and local affairs of The Club Managers Association of America.

O. *Civic and Cultural Groups*
Participates in and contributes to the following organizations who enhance the city by their efforts; The United Fund, The Chamber of Commerce, The County Fair or Live Stock Show, the Museum of Fine Arts or Civic Opera Association, and local alumni group of college attended.

P. *Officers and Managers of Other Clubs*
Freely and fully exchanges operational information with them realizing that in the long run it will be The Club that will benefit from such an exchange of operational, promotional, and personnel information.

Q. *The Public*
Behaves in a manner to reflect credit upon The Club and the position held within the organization. May intercede with individuals, upon the request of employees, in the interest of solving employees' personal problems of a business or legal nature.

V. Other Duties

Conducts such other relationships as the Board of Directors may specify.

VI. Planning
In essence, the job is mainly planning—in and for all phases of The Club's life and operation. There is no part of the whole that should not be subject to, and benefit from, the General Manager's thinking, planning, and forecasting.

VII. Establishing Standards
A. Participates with the Committees and Board of Directors in the development and setting of standards of financial or otherwise quantitatively measured achievement.

B. Cooperates with Accountant and Managers in setting standards of financial or otherwise quantitatively measured accomplishments in each division and department.

C. Cooperates with Managers in setting standards of merchandise and supplies purchased.

D. Cooperates with Managers in setting standards for hospitality, surroundings, product (food, beverages, etc.) quality, service, sanitation, environment, etc.

E. Cooperates with Managers in setting standards for recruitment, training, service, appearance and deportment of employees.

VIII. Measures of Performance

A. Membership satisfaction, which may be measured in part by:
   1. Maintenance of membership numbers.
   2. Comparison of Club sales with trends of local sales.
   3. Dollar usage per member.
   4. Visits per member.
   5. Dollar usage per member visit.
   6. Compliments.
   7. Complaints.
   8. New members gained.
   9. Members lost by resignation.
   10. etc.

B. Achievement of Operating Budget Goals.

C. Achievement of Capital Budget.

D. Operating percentages compared to past years and to national and regional figures.

E. The development of personnel from within the organization; low absenteeism and turnover experience figures.

F. Trends of premium rates on Workmen's Compensation and Unemployment Insurance.

G. Promptness, quality of information, forecasts and creative consultative services to The Club and its officers, to the Board of Directors and the Committees.

H. Club's general standing in community.

Other Examples of Job Description

The job of club manager covers a wide range of responsibilities, as do other managerial and supervisory jobs. On a skilled-worker level, the description can and should be much briefer, using just enough words to cover what needs to be covered.

Brevity and conciseness are the hallmarks of a well-written job description. Verbs substitute for phrases. Selection of the best words to describe an operation can delineate the job.

All of the writing should be in reply to the four key questions of analysis. What does the worker do? Why is it done? How is it done? What skills are involved in the doing?

Here, for example, is an illustration of the what, why, how, and skill-involved questions as applied to the job of oysterman or shucker.
Work performed: Shucks oysters and clams (what) to the order of cooks or waiters (why); forces oyster knife between halves of shell, and twists knife, forcing the shell open (how and skill involved); forces knife blade between oyster and bottom half of shell to sever oyster from shell (how and skill involved); the knife may be grasped in the worker's hand, or may be affixed to the workbench (how).

Following is the description for *garde manger* or in American usage, the cold meat and sandwich man.[4]

---

4. Taken from the *Guide to Job Descriptions in the Indiana Restaurant Industry,* Indiana Employment Security Division, Indianapolis, 1957.

Employer Job Title: Garde Manger
Alternate Titles: Cold Meat Chef or Cold Meat Man

I. Work Performed

A. Prepares and garnishes cold food dishes.
   1. Plans future meals. Notes foods left over from previous meals; confers with *chef*, suggests dishes that will utilize as many left-overs as possible; requisitions additional foodstuffs, if necessary, from storeroom.
   2. Carves cold meats. Slices cold roast beef, tongue, canned beef, ham, chicken or other meats, using carving knife or electric meat slicer, places slices of food neatly on plate, decorates dish with lettuce, pickles, relishes or other garnishings; places dish in refrigerator, or on serving table for *waiter/waitress.*
   3. Prepares various dishes. Secures left-over foods from refrigerator or cold storage vault; places food on work table; prepares meat loaves, salads, croquettes, and other dishes that will utilize left-over foods; chops up, grinds, shreds, or dices foods, using knife or electric meat grinder. Chops up onions, celery, potatoes, lettuce or other vegetables; mixes food ingredients. Applies mayonnaise or other dressing or seasoning, molds or fashions mixture in patties or portions of desired size; places food in pan; gives food to *cook* for cooking.
   4. Prepares sandwiches. Obtains prepared ingredients from refrigerator; selects bread; places meat or filling, dressing and seasoning between slices of bread; trims edges of sandwich; slices it diagonally, using knife; lays sandwich on plate and places it on serving table for *waiter/waitress.*
   5. Performs related duties. Prepares salad dressing, such as mayonnaise; mixes ingredients according to recipe and seasons it to taste; prepares appetizers such as canapes, relishes; prepares cold sauces. Keeps work station clean and orderly.

II. Skills, Knowledge, and Abilities

A. Must possess a knowledge of the various cuts of meat, the ability to improvise new dishes utilizing left-over foods, the ability to decorate and garnish dishes artistically and to prepare salads, sandwiches and appetizers; must develop a keen sense of taste to determine when dishes are properly seasoned; must know how to prepare salads for various priced complete meals; must be mentally alert to prepare and adequately season foods; must use considerable independent judgment in the utilization of leftover foods.

III. Details of Physical Activities

A. Stands and walks short distances throughout working day. Constantly handles food and cooking equipment.

IV. Relation to Other Jobs

A. In large establishments there is a *head garde manger* who supervises one or more *garde mangers* and *kitchen helpers* and who is in turn supervised by the *chef*; may be promoted to *second cook.*

V. Job Combinations

A. The duties of this job may be performed by any one of the various cooks in the establishment. In a small establishment a cook may do all types of cooking.

Sometimes other job-related information is included in either the job description or the job specification. Wages paid, training given, hours worked, vacations, and various other details about the job which would be useful to an employment interviewer may be included as indicated below and in figure 4.1.

VI. Job of Houseperson

1. *Training*—first week on the job—one day watching and listening, one day doing and telling why, one day under close supervision, three days working alone with checkup at unexpected intervals.
2. *Possibility of advancement*—to head houseperson.
3. *Schedule of duties*—at 8:00 A.M. report to the Linen Room in uniform for special orders and equipment stored there the night before for repair. Get clean dust cloths. Leave guest room door open (except in stormy weather). Do high dusting first; ceiling lights, draperies, cornices, Venetian blinds (if any), and window screens. Move furniture away from walls. Dust backs of each piece, also wall molding, mopboard and carpet before replacing exactly as before. Start at point farthest from the door and work with vacuum toward door; clean closet light, high rods and shelves, both lights, ventilator and high tile. Dust both sides of door and transom. Make sure the latter works easily. Report damage to furniture or fixtures at once.
4. *Equipment*—for central system. Vacuum hose and attachments, radiator brush, long-handled duster, dust cloth, and stepladder.
5. *Hazards*—only those caused by carelessness.
6. *Duties*—vacuum 117 rooms on three floors in twelve days. This averages nine rooms a day with one corridor. This also includes washing the terrazzo, seeing that adjoining corridors are neat before leaving at 4:00 P.M. This allows for nine check-outs that require special cleaning or other extras during the twelve days. The person working Sunday picks up any rooms omitted or left in bad condition by guests, and also does Linen Room errands.
   To prevent accidents to employees or guests, the striped black and white vacuum hose is placed in the center of the corridors with warning sign in a conspicuous spot.
7. *Special work*—before the beds have been made, vacuum mattress, spring and frame of beds in two rooms each day and help turn the mattresses in two other rooms.

Job of Unit General Manager of Motor Inn Chain

Basic Functions

Plan, organize, staff, direct, and control the operations of the hotel to achieve maximum sales and profits, while keeping guests' needs and objectives in mind.

Specific Duties and Responsibilities:

1. Provide the best of care and services in accordance with modern and scientific innkeeping techniques to assure positive guest satisfaction relationships.
2. Administer and direct the activities of the various hotel departments with the goal of maximizing profits and assuring that guest needs are met.
3. Work closely with the Sales Department to develop, coordinate, and service group movements, conventions, and local sales activities.
4. Determine and recommend sound pricing policy for both the Room and the Food and Beverage Departments, as well as for other income-producing departments.
5. Direct each function of the hotel in an effort to establish just, efficient, and economical operation of each department. Analyze daily, weekly, and monthly reports of each operating unit, and implement policy and procedure to maximize profit results.
6. Recommend, plan, direct, and control the repair and maintenance programs required. Plan and oversee renovation and/or refurbishing activities periodically.
7. Assure a constant source of capable and trained personnel to fill vacancies in supervisory positions, by recruiting, selecting, and training on a continuous basis.
8. Recommend and develop policies to strengthen the operating and financial position of the hotel.
9. Other duties and responsibilities as may be required.

Relationships:

1. Report to: Regional Manager
2. Supervise: Assistant Manager, Maintenance, Catering Manager, Chef, Housekeeper, Sales Manager, Coffee Shop Manager, Night Assistant Manager, Bar Manager, and other executives in the hotel.
3. Other: Work in conjunction with all departments and officials of the Company.

Job of Sales Manager of Motor Inn Chain

Specific Duties and Responsibilities:

1. Develop and keep current a sales filing system of regular and prospective guests.
2. Assist the General Manager in obtaining the maximum sales efforts and services from all employees through proper training and orientation.
3. See that contact is made with clubs and similar kinds of organized groups, travel agents, trade, financial, and professional associations, commercial companies, and airport vendors for the development of future business.
4. Keep files of competitors' activities and prices.
5. Attend the weekly Department Heads meeting and report on sales activity of the past and upcoming weeks.
6. See that all hotels that send along business are kept supplied with current printed promotional materials.
7. Conduct a weekly sales meeting as directed by the General Manager.
8. Prepare a written sales call report on all outside sales calls made each week, and furnish copies to the General Manager, Regional Manager, and Director of Sales.
9. Prepare an outline of all tentative or definite business booked during each week, and furnish copies to the General Manager, Regional Manager, and Director of Sales. Also list all cancelled business, giving reason for cancellation.
10. At the end of each month, prepare a Group and Convention listing of all business booked on either a definite or tentative basis.
11. Prepare a weekly expense report of all expenses involving sales efforts. Submit to the General Manager for approval and reimbursement.

12. Solicit hotel sales by telephone, letter, and personal contact.

   Recommended number of letters per week:

   _____

   Recommended number of telephone solicitations per week: _____
   Recommended number of personal calls per week: _____

13. Coordinate all banquet and catering functions with the Catering Manager or his secretary.

14. Follow up all banquet functions completed and solicit for future business.

15. Assist Catering Department and Front Office in maintaining accurate and complete files on all business.

16. Prepare "confirmation of bookings" letters, and solicitation letters.

17. Receive and answer all inquiries relative to sales.

18. Perform any other duties and responsibilities as may be required:

19. _____
   _____
   _____
   _____

20. _____
   _____
   _____
   _____

Relationships:

1. Report to: General Manager
2. Supervise: Sales Representatives, Sales Secretary
3. Others: Works closely with Front Office personnel, Catering Secretary, and Coffee Shop Manager.

Job of Catering Manager of Motor Inn Chain

Basic Functions

Supervise the banquet service of the Inn, including booking and servicing of banquets, meetings, receptions, etc., whether these functions take place in meeting rooms, suites, or on the grounds of the property (i.e., around the swimming pool or outside the hotel).

Specific Duties and Responsibilities:

1. Hire, train, and direct banquet service people— waiters, bus help, set-up persons.

2. Keep the function book in correct order, seeing to it that all bookings by the Sales Department, and other departments, are properly entered and times for functions are specified.

3. Have up-to-date inventory of all equipment available for meeting and banquet service.

4. After consultation with General Manager, Sales Manager, and Chef, keep banquet menus current insofar as selections and prices are concerned.

5. Keep available for hotel employees and potential guests information on meeting room and banquet room capacities for various kinds of set-ups, including carefully prepared and professionally printed sketches of facilities showing ceiling heights, electrical outlets, complete room dimensions, various seating possibilities, etc.

6. Meeting rooms must be kept clean and set up for viewing by prospective clients at all times. Before staff leaves, after functions held in rooms, the rooms must be cleaned and put in order for the next day's business.

7. Establish files for each function as it is booked. File must include:
   a. Function sheet completed as thoroughly as possible. Information should include name of group, name of contact, telephone number and address of contact, approximate number of guests to attend, exact date and time of function, menu choices (or date when menu mailed), head table or other special needs, copy of confirmation letter, etc.
   b. At conclusion of meeting, details left in file should include actual number who showed up for function, price charged (copy of banquet check very useful), unusual occurrences, and copy of "thank you" letter (which should also include an invitation to rebook the event.)

8. Each Friday prepare and distribute a Weekly Function Schedule, and attach individual Work Sheets of all completed arrangements.

9. Menus for groups must be in the hands of the Chef a week prior to the event to allow time for the purchasing of unusual items not held in inventory.

10. Get guarantees for all food and beverage functions at least 24 hours in advance of the event (48 hours if possible, preferred).

11. Prepare and present checks for all functions at the conclusion of the event. (This is also a good time to solicit comments on service, food, etc., and to rebook the group for its next meeting.)

12. See that all equipment and furnishings used in meeting/banquet service is kept in good repair.

13. Keep at hand list of banquet service people with their telephone numbers and addresses.

14. Explain thoroughly to all waiters and bus help exactly how serving is to be done. (A short meeting prior to table set-up is usually in order.)

15. Assign service personnel according to Food and Beverage and General Manager's direction. (Ratio might be one server to each 25 guests, etc.)

16. Make sure OSHA Regulations are observed. For direction in this important field, talk with the General Manager.

17. Practice energy conservation. Lights and air conditioning should be off when rooms are not in use. The General Manager will give suggestions and guidance in this area.

18. Any other duties as specified by your Supervisor.

Job of Room Clerk of Motor Chain Inn

The Job

Room clerks are usually the first of a hotel's front office staff to greet and welcome the arriving guest. They register guests, and assign rooms considering the expressed preferences of the guests. They also must take into consideration the hotel's best interests both in pleasing guests and in obtaining maximum hotel revenues when making room assignments. They answer questions about room rates and hotel services, issue keys, arrange room transfers, and inform the manager when important guests arrive. Large hotels usually employ several front office clerks who may specialize as key, reservation, or information clerks.

The tasks of room clerks vary with the size of hotels. In small establishments they may process mail, collect payments, record accounts, handle reservations, operate the telephone switchboard, and do simple bookkeeping.

Working Conditions

Most hotels are clean, comfortable, well-lighted, and ventilated. Room clerks work at an enclosed counter located in the lobby. While the work is not physically strenuous, most of the duties require standing. Some reaching and bending may also be required.

Room clerks work under the supervision of a designated head clerk, assistant manager or hotel manager. Teamwork is essential for quality front office work. Clerks must work cooperatively with other hotel personnel to serve guests properly. During peak registration and checkout periods, room clerks work under pressure in order to satisfy the different needs of the clientele.

Establishments which require their front office staff to wear uniforms usually provide them free of charge with cleaning costs included. In some areas of the State, room clerks are highly unionized. The Hotel and Restaurant Employees and Bartenders International is the major union in the hotel industry.

Entrance Requirements and Training

Most employers hire high school graduates who have clerical aptitude and training, particularly in typing, bookkeeping, and office machines.

Neatness, patience, poise, and a friendly and courteous manner in dealing with the public are important personal traits for front office personnel.

There are two methods of entering the occupation. Some hotels follow a policy of promoting employees from within. Bellhops or elevator operators may be promoted to front office positions, depending on their experience, ability, and work performance. However, most hotels hire individuals from the outside, providing on-the-job training for these new employees. In some establishments, trainees start as switchboard operators and key, information, or mail clerks.

Advancement

Advancement often depends on the employee's personal characteristics, experience, training, work performance, and education. A room clerk may advance to chief room clerk, assistant front office manager, front office manager, sales and promotion manager or hotel manager. Top managerial posts usually require many years of experience. Employers are giving increasing attention to personnel with college background for management training positions. Hotel clerks may improve opportunities for advancement by taking college courses in general business or home study courses, such as those offered by the Educational Institute of the American Hotel and Motel Association. In California, two-year courses in hotel operation are offered at Monterey Peninsula College, City College of San Francisco, Orange Coast College, Mesa College, and Los Angeles Valley College.

Source: State of California Employment Development Dept., 1977

Job of Night Auditor of Motor Inn Chain

Specific Duties and Responsibilities:

1. Receive and record guest payments.

2. Prepare for management a daily listing of guest accounts amounting to $100.00 or more.

3. Assign rooms in a courteous and efficient manner to all incoming guests, in accordance with Hotel policy and procedure.

4. Maintain the daily walk-in reservation count sheet.

5. Assume the basic responsibility of seeing that each day's reports and papers are filed. The filing must be kept current at all times.

6. Prepare and have ready by 7 A.M. each day the Housekeeper's Report listing the status of the occupied, vacant, and out-of-order rooms for the night just ended.

7. Maintain a neat and tidy front office.

8. Pay special attention to the phone and follow the basic rules of courtesy.

9. Provide information to any and all guests in a courteous and informative manner.

10. Notify the General Manager of any unusual incident as instructed or otherwise deemed necessary regarding operation, and/or safety and security of Hotel and guests.

11. Complete the night audit by change of shift at 7:00 A.M. Give information to other department heads, especially any information relating to the morning's breakfast business and meeting set-ups.

12. See that all reports and vouchers required are on the General Manager's desk for review and approval.

13. Prepare aging report in triplicate (of city ledger and guest ledger) on the fifteenth and final days of each month.

14. Take room reservations as requested by telephone by completing the standard reservation form or Transaction Form.

15. Instruct and assist the night PBX operator (if there is one) in auditing the monthly telephone bill. If there is no PBX operator this task must be accomplished by the Night Auditor.

16. Handle all internal control procedures as dictated by Hotel policies.

17. Assist the General Manager in the training of management-level trainees, making sure they understand the principles of the night audit and are capable of performing the audit.

18. Discuss what to do in emergency situations with Supervisor. Ask what policies to follow.

19. Perform any other duties and responsibilities as may be requested.

Relationships:

1. Report to: Assistant Manager—Hotel or General Manager.

2. Supervise: Night PBX Operator, Night Security and Bellman.

3. Others: Work closely with all departments to insure overall smoothness of operations.

Job of Floor Housekeepers (Lodging Quarters Cleaners)

Specific Duties and Responsibilities:

1. Clean daily a par of 15 rooms in accordance with the "Daily Schedule of Room Cleaning" list.

2. Take care of all uniforms, equipment, and supplies issued by the Housekeeper.

3. Communicate with the Housekeeping Department while cleaning rooms and call in immediately to the Housekeeper all rooms that have been cleaned.

4. Report immediately all damage found in a room.

5. Report all items missing from your rooms.

6. Load the maid cart twice daily with one-half day's supplies and equipment as issued by the linen room attendant.

7. Make up and notify the linen room attendant of all roll-a-ways and cribs found in checkout rooms, so that they can be picked up and properly stored.

8. Be responsible for a pass key received daily from the Housekeeper. Make sure that it is secured at all times and turned in to the Housekeeper at the end of each day.

9. Turn in immediately, to the Housekeeper, all "lost & found" items, marking down the area or room number where found.

10. Clean thoroughly one room per day as assigned by the Housekeeper.

11. Clean and dry the maid cart at the end of each shift and turn all leftover supplies in to the linen room attendant.

12. Report immediately to the Housekeeper the following;
    (a) No luggage
    (b) No service
    (c) Sleep outs
    (d) Unusual happenings
    (e) Extra guests
13. Use only those cleaning agents issued by the Housekeeper.
14. Perform any other duties and responsibilities as may be required.

Relationship:

1. Report to: Housekeeper or Assistant Housekeeper
2. Supervise: None
3. Other: Work closely with the Assistant Housekeeper.

Hotel and Motel Managers and Assistants

The Job

Hotel and motel managers direct and coordinate activities in the day-to-day operation of their business establishments. This includes the activities of the front office, kitchen, and dining rooms as well as the various departments such as housekeeping, accounting, purchasing and the like. In chain-operated hotels—and the majority of large facilities fall in this category today—policy decisions are made at the corporate level. Of the three types: commercial, residential, and resort, the majority of hotels and motels are commercial, catering chiefly to business and pleasure travelers. Not all hotels and motels require the services of a general manager. Many smaller establishments are owner-operated. Medium-size facilities (50 to 150 rooms) may have an administrative staff of two, a resident manager and an assistant. In large hotels, general managers may supervise several department heads; food preparation may have a special food and beverage manager. There may also be a sales manager to promote maximum use of hotel facilities.

Size and type of hotel determine the scope of the manager's job. In a large hotel the job is primarily administrative. Here, the manager coordinates the activities of the various departments and, for conventions and other special events, delegates responsibilities to the appropriate managers. Usually, the executive assistant or resident manager is the number two person, who assumes control in the general manager's absence. Managers of small or medium size hotels, meanwhile, have more of a direct supervisory role over all functions. When necessary, they may also perform relief work in various activities such as inspecting rooms, setting up tables, and otherwise filling in wherever needed. Managers' duties may also include spending time with business and social groups and participating in community affairs.

Working Conditions

The tempo of work varies. Residential hotels in outlying districts operate at a slower pace than the large commercial hotels. In the latter, the job of hotel manager is both physically and mentally demanding. Problems arise constantly and managers must maintain smooth operation of the establishment while satisfying all of the clientele. Because of these demands and the amount of standing and walking required, normal good health and a high energy level are essential.

Entrance Requirements

In filling a managerial position or selecting a management trainee, employers look for candidates who are familiar with hotel operations—including back-of-the-house departments and front office. These positions are often filled with graduates of specialized programs in hotel administration. The level and specific nature of the beginning job depend on the work experience acquired during or before professional training. Many graduates start in the front office or accounting departments or as assistant to a department manager.

Personal characteristics important to the successful manager include alertness, neat appearance, and the ability to get along well with people.

Promotion

There are no rigid rules regarding the pattern of promotion to the job of hotel manager. A manager or executive assistant is frequently selected from a front office or department head position. Although managers are not always appointed from the ranks in a given hotel, the executive assistant or resident manager is usually promoted from within. Willingness to move is essential for advancement in a chain-operated hotel.

Training Requirements

A college education is highly recommended. Courses in hotel administration and accounting are especially useful. Also helpful are courses in business administration, law, labor relations, economics, and industrial psychology. Many managers stress, however, that college training should not make the beginner scorn the menial entry-level hotel jobs.

Source: State of California Employment Development Dept., 1976

The Job

All-around cooks are skilled in all phases of the culinary arts and can prepare any item on the menu of a full-service restaurant. This type of restaurant offers complete meals and wide variety, including dishes which require lengthy or elaborate preparation. All activities and all personnel in the restaurant kitchen are under the direction of a *CHEF,* or *head cook.* It is the chef's responsibility to see that distinctive, high quality food is produced, consistently, efficiently, and economically.

Job Duties

Job duties vary from one restaurant to another, with size an important factor. In smaller establishments, a *working chef* presides over the kitchen as both supervisor and head cook. Duties include planning menus, ordering supplies, hiring cooks and other kitchen staff and supervising their work. The chef also performs complex cooking tasks, prepares the specialties of the house, and may develop unique or original recipes. In large hotels and clubs, an *executive chef* oversees the purchasing and preparation of food for all food services operated on the premises. Typically this includes one or more restaurants, a coffee shop, and a banquet or catering department. Usually there are several kitchens. Within each kitchen one chef, called a *sous chef,* acts as supervisor, while cooking is primarily handled by a skilled *second cook.*

Most full-service restaurants that serve lunch and dinner, or dinner only, have a day and an evening shift. The working chef, second cook, and/or several other all-around cooks come in early in the day to start the sauces, soups, casseroles, roasts, and other slow-cooking items needed for the dinner menu. They may also prepare or supervise the preparation of lunch, cut and portion meat, or bake bread. On the dinner shift, one or more *dinner cooks* and/or the *night chef* make final preparations and then do all the broiling, sauteing, and other to-order cooking required during the evening meal service.

In very small restaurants, there may be only one all-around cook handling all cooking duties on each shift. In larger establishments where there are several cooks, each may be assigned to a separate "station" where a specific cooking operation, such as broiling, is performed. All-around cooks must be capable of rotating to any of the stations. However, in very large first-class establishments, station cooks tend to be specialists. They do not normally rotate from one station to another and therefore, while they must be highly skilled, they are not necessarily all-around cooks.

Cooks are on their feet and in motion throughout their shift, and during mealtimes must work under pressure. They are exposed to such hazards as cuts, burns, and scalds and to the stress of extreme temperature change when moving from a hot stove to a walk-in refrigerator.

Entrance Requirements, Training, and Advancement

Cooks need an excellent sense of taste and smell. They must be healthy, agile, alert, and dependable, and work well with others. In addition to being expert and creative all-around cooks, chefs need a sound business sense, organizational ability, and supervisory skill.

All-around cooks have traditionally learned their craft by means of informal on-the-job training. Starting as *cook's helpers,* they observe and assist at various stations and advance as their skills develop. It may take years of informal training and many job changes to accumulate the well-rounded experience needed to qualify as an all-around cook. More concentrated training is provided by a formal apprenticeship program, specifically designed to prepare all-around cooks for first-class hotels, restaurants, and clubs. Three years of carefully supervised on-the-job training are supplemented by formal instruction in all phases of cooking and kitchen operation. Apprenticeship openings are limited and competition for admission to the program is keen. However, additional opportunities are expected during the next few years, due to special federal funding for this purpose.

Community colleges offer Certificate and Associate Degree Programs in either food preparation or hotel and restaurant management. Some qualified graduates get beginning jobs as cooks; others enter the apprenticeship program, or a four-year restaurant management school. A variety of high school and adult education food preparation courses are also available. While differing in detail, all emphasize basic kitchen and communication skills. These courses prepare students for entry-level kitchen jobs, apprenticeships, or college-level training.

Advancement for the all-around cook may take the form of a higher, more responsible position within the same establishment, or a similar position in a larger or better restaurant. Experienced all-around cooks with demonstrated supervisory ability may eventually become chefs.

Source: State of California Employment Development Dept., 1977

The Job

Short order cooks prepare, cook, and assemble individual orders of fast-cooked and precooked food. They work in coffee shops, fast-food restaurants, and similar establishments, which feature simple food, informal style, and moderate price.

Job Duties

The work performed and the skills required depend on the restaurant's menu. In establishments where the menu is varied, the cook's activities tend to be diverse and complex, requiring considerable expertise. By contrast, in fast-food operations with limited menus, the work is more routine, requiring a lesser degree of skill.

Varied-menu establishments range from small coffee shops to large ''family-style'' restaurants. Typically they serve breakfast, along with other meals and snacks, throughout the day. Although certain types of orders predominate on each shift, cooks may be asked to poach, fry, or boil eggs; cook hot cakes, potatoes, meat or seafood in a skillet, on a grill or in deep fat; broil steaks, chops, hamburgers; and prepare hot or cold sandwiches, beverages, and desserts. They season the food as it cooks, and must take care to cook it exactly as ordered. They must know which side dishes to prepare along with each main dish, and schedule their work so that all items are done at the same time. Cooks also arrange and garnish the completed order on the plate.

During slack periods, cooks perform additional tasks. For example, they may slice and preportion food, bread, meat or fish, mix waffle and pancake batter, or restock and clean their work station. Cooks working behind the counter in a small coffee shop may wait on customers directly, compute their checks, and receive payment.

In specialty restaurants, where food is prepared to the customer's order, cooks need more skill than is required in take-out establishments, where food is ordinarily cooked according to company specifications. Busy take-out operations increasingly use assembly line production methods and push-button equipment. Employees in take-out operations are typically classified as ''food service technicians'' or ''crewpersons'' rather than as cooks. They may take orders, perform busing services, or handle deliveries, storage, and stock in addition to preparing food.

Working Conditions

Cooks are on their feet and in motion throughout their shift. They are exposed to extremes of heat and cold and such hazards as cuts, burns, and scalds. Some restaurant employers have agreements with locals of the Hotel and Restaurant Employees and Bartenders Union (AFL-CIO). Employers provide uniforms and free or reduced-price meals.

In fast-food operations, most jobs are part time. Full-time cooks work eight hours a day, five days a week, generally including weekends. In 24-hour establishments, cooks may work on any of three shifts; beginners generally start on the night shift.

Entrance Requirements, Training, and Promotion

All cooks must be healthy, agile, alert, dependable, and work well with others. Short order cooks need above average coordination, a good sense of timing, and the ability to work under pressure.

Employers hiring cooks look for previous experience in establishments with a similar menu and pace. Thus, fast-food, dinner house, or institutional experience alone would generally not be considered fully qualifying for a busy 24-hour coffee shop.

Many employers prefer not to hire from outside, but to train and promote employees. Beginners usually start as dishwashers, observe and assist the experienced cooks, and advance as their skills develop. Persons with some related experience may start as cook trainees. For example, fast-food workers who have mastered the techniques of hamburger grilling are frequently trained as grill or broiler cooks in fast-service limited-menu steak houses.

Fast-food take-out establishments ordinarily hire inexperienced young people and teach them all aspects of their job. Many fast-food and family restaurant chains have formal comprehensive training programs.

Promotional opportunities for short order cooks include transfer to a better paying establishment or to a position as dinner house or hotel fry cook. Employees of chain operations who demonstrate supervisory ability may be trained to manage one of the units.

Source: State of California Employment Development Dept., 1978

Job Description Manual

Once job descriptions have been made, they can be assembled in mimeograph form into a three-ring notebook, a notebook that permits easy removal of pages and replacements as changes are made. Each employee should receive a copy of his own job description when hired, and all department heads should have at least the master file for the jobs over which each one has supervision. The manual then serves as a basic list of tasks to be performed, a reference for the worker, the supervisor, personnel persons, and managers.

The Job Specification

Closely related to the job description and sometimes combined with it is the job specification or person specification. Once the tasks performed in a job are described, a separate form can be developed, *the job specification*. The tendency is to "over-specify," to blow up the job skills and the kind of person needed to perform those skills. Many jobs do not require a knowledge of reading and writing, and it should so be noted. The kitchens of numerous restaurants in the Southwest are staffed by Mexican-Americans who, though they speak no English, do their jobs effectively.

Remember, no job requires *all* the faculties of the individual, which means that many jobs can be performed by people lacking in several abilities, or handicapped so that they cannot perform certain tasks. Many jobs can be done by mentally or emotionally handicapped.

Figure 4.1 represents an example of a job specification.

Figure 4.1   Job Specification Sheet

Job Title: Vacuum operator.

Employed Number: Six.

Hours: Eight hours daily; 8:00 A.M. to 4:00 P.M. 40 hours, weekly.

Day Off: Sunday, except once in six weeks—Monday.

Vacations: One week after one year, two weeks after five years; three weeks after ten years.

Nationality: Citizen or working toward citizenship.

Mental Qualifications: Average intelligence or slightly below, ability to follow directions.

Personality Requirements: Good disposition, dependable, careful and cooperative, even-tempered.

Contacts: Other workers, guests, management.

Type of Labor: Unskilled.

Supervisor: Inspector.

Salary: $30 per day, paid weekly.

Maintenance: Uniforms furnished and laundered; lunch the only meal.

Experience: None required.

Education: Preferably grammar school. Will hire the disadvantaged. Some mechanical ability.

Physical Qualifications: Ability to operate a vacuum cleaner and ability to see well enough to clean carpets.

Responsibility: Own work, equipment, furnishings, guest's belongings.

Working Conditions: Pleasant.

CAREER OPPORTUNITY LADDERS

From job analysis to job descriptions and job specifications it is a logical step to develop career ladders, showing normal progression from one job to another. "Career ladders" are useful in showing the relationships between jobs. More importantly, they show employees the avenue to higher skills and greater responsibility. The examples below, developed by the California Employment Development Department, show the usual steps up a career ladder for the jobs of cook apprentice to executive chef, waitress to atmosphere restaurant manager, bus boy to maitre d', hotel and kitchen helper to head broilerman.

To show multiple routes of progress from job, to job up and sideways, within a large food-service establishment the U.S. Department of Labor funded research which resulted in the "progression chart" seen below. The chart breaks down a large food-service organization into four function areas: support, food production, control, and service. Dotted lines show the routes up and the lateral routes that can be followed by a worker either at the entry level or at a higher level. For example, a dishwasher could move up within the support area to become a utility assistant, an assistant steward, to kitchen steward. Or the person could move sideways into one of the other three areas.

The chart points out that a waitress, for example, could move out of service into food checking or storeroom keeping. A pot washer has the possibility of moving laterally into food preparation, control, or service. Such charts can illuminate possibilities for someone who formerly felt limited in job potential.*

*See "Career Ladders in the Food Service Industry," National Restaurant Association, Washington, D.C.

Broiling

This area of work involves the cooking of meats and seafoods on a broiler and is usually found in dinner houses and specialty restaurants.

CAREER LADDER OPPORTUNITIES

HEAD BROILER MAN

BROILER COOK

KITCHEN HELPER

Besides Kitchen Helper, this career ladder could also be applicable to other entry occupations such as Bus Boy, Dishwasher, or Cook Helper. Kitchen Helpers perform a number of tasks including washing work areas, walls, equipment, utensils, cookware, and mopping and sweeping floors. They also assist Cooks, when required, by washing, cutting, and portioning food items. After a period of satisfactory job performance, a worker could be promoted to Broiler Cook.

Broiler Cooks start the broiler and regulate the temperature. They clean and portion the foods, and make batters, sauces, and gravies. They place meat and seafood on the broiler and determine degree of doneness by touching it with a cooking utensil or by examining it visually. Several years of experience would qualify a worker for promotion to the job of Head Broiler Man, when an opening exists.

Head Broiler Men have the final responsibility for the quality of the food and the profitable operation of the kitchen. They perform the same duties as the Broiler Cooks as well as supervising and coordinating the activities of the employees that work in the kitchen.

KITCHEN HELPER TRAINING
5 to 6 hours of on-the-job training.

HIRING REQUIREMENTS
1. Able to stand for long periods of time.

2. Able to tolerate heat and humidity of kitchen.
3. Temperament to perform efficiently during rush periods.
4. Able to lift and carry 50 to 80 pounds.

Restaurant Service

This area of work is involved with the serving of food to patrons in restaurants that have formal dining rooms.

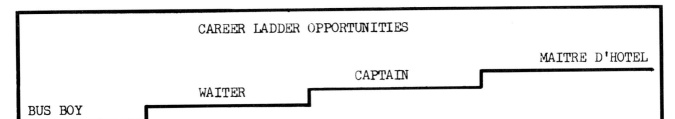

CAREER LADDER OPPORTUNITIES

MAITRE D'HOTEL

CAPTAIN

WAITER

BUS BOY

Bus Boys perform a variety of tasks such as removing used dishes from tables, wiping off tables, and replacing linens. They reset tables with clean dishes and fill water glasses. After a period of satisfactory job performance, plus an indication that the worker has a personality that is suitable for the occupation of Waiter, a worker could be eligible for promotion.

Waiters take the patrons' dinner orders, unless this is done by a Captain, and serve the prepared food. They give work directions to Bus Boys to insure that the tables are set and cleared according to established practice. They also confer with the kitchen personnel to verify that the food is prepared according to the wishes of the customers. After several years of experience, plus an aptitude for supervision, a worker could be promoted to Captain.

Captains supervise the activities of the Waiters and Bus Boys in an assigned area. They escort customers to their tables and may take the customers' cocktail or food orders, recommending dishes and wines. In some restaurants the Captain, or Waiter, also carves meats and prepares flaming dishes at the patrons' tables. Many years of experience plus an indication of managerial potential could qualify a Captain for promotion to Maitre D'Hotel, who is responsible for the over-all operation of the dining area and is in charge of assigning tables, accepting reservations, and coordinating the activities of the dining room with those of the kitchen.

BUS BOY TRAINING
4 to 5 hours of on-the-job training.

HIRING REQUIREMENTS
1. Able to stand for long periods of time
2. Grooming and disposition suitable for public contact work.
3. Temperament to perform efficiently during rush periods.
4. Able to lift and carry 50 to 80 pounds.

Bus Boy placing dish of butter on table.

Management — General Atmosphere Restaurant

This area of work is involved with the management of a general atmosphere restaurant for a large chain organization. This career ladder is generally not applicable to independent restaurants, because most of the managerial functions are performed by the owners.

CAREER LADDER OPPORTUNITIES

```
                                                                    MANAGER
                                      ASSISTANT MANAGER
                    HOSTESS
WAITRESS
```

Waitresses take orders and serve meals to the customers. They insure that all of the tables have the proper settings and condiments. They prepare some food items such as toast, fountain drinks, or desserts. They total the customer's bill and bring change. After a period of satisfactory job performance, plus a demonstrated talent for dealing tactfully with people, a worker could be promoted to Hostess.

Hostesses escort the customers to their tables and take their cocktail orders in establishments where drinks are served. They coordinate the activities of Waitresses and Bus Boys and ring up sales on a cash register. Workers with a couple of years experience as a Hostess, who have acquired a background in business management could be promoted to Assistant Manager.

Assistant Managers perform the duties of Manager when the Manager is not present. They also assist the manager in preparing and submitting regular reports to the chain headquarters concerning such topics as costs, profits, personnel, and special problems. After several years as an Assistant Manager, a worker could be promoted to Manager who is responsible for the hiring and overall supervision of all employees of the establishment. The Manager also coordinates the operation of the kitchen with that of the dining area to insure that the restaurant functions efficiently and profitably.

WAITRESS TRAINING
2 to 3 days of on-the-job training.

HIRING REQUIREMENTS
1. Able to stand for long periods of time
2. Grooming and disposition suitable for public contact work.
3. Able to work efficiently during rush periods.
4. Able to perform simple arithmetic and make change.

Waitress taking customers' orders.

Gourmet Cooking

This area of work involves the preparation of classic dishes and luxury type foods that are found in gourmet restaurants and hotels.

CAREER LADDER OPPORTUNITIES

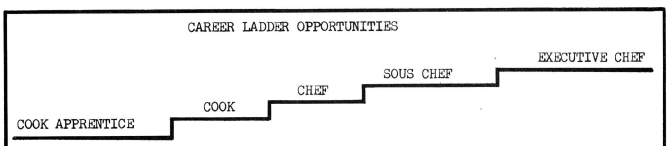

EXECUTIVE CHEF

SOUS CHEF

CHEF

COOK

COOK APPRENTICE

Cook Apprentices receive on-the-job training and instructions in different aspects of food preparation such as broiling, roasting, meat cutting, salad making, fry cooking, and soup and sauce making. After an apprenticeship of about three years, a worker is considered a journeyman cook. A number of years of additional experience, plus demonstration of the ability to prepare gourmet foods and sauces, could qualify a Cook for promotion to the position of Chef, who is expected to be capable of preparing all the items on the menu.

Several years of successful job performance as a Chef, plus an indication of supervisory potential, would enable a worker to be promoted to Sous Chef, who supervises and coordinates the activities of Chefs and all other employees who work in the kitchen. Many years of experience, a display of managerial ability, plus the successful completion of courses in restaurant management would enable a worker to be promoted to Executive Chef.

An Executive Chef supervises and coordinates the activities of the Sous Chef and has the ultimate responsibility for the operation of the kitchen. They plan and organize such things as menus, recipes, and manner of food preparation. They must also be aware of costs, because the Executive Chefs are responsible for the profitable operation of the kitchen.

COOK APPRENTICE TRAINING
Applicants receive on-the-job training throughout the course of their apprenticeship.

HIRING REQUIREMENTS
1. Applicants must be at least 17 years of age.
2. Able to lift and carry 50 to 80 pounds
3. Able to stand for long periods of time.
4. Able to tolerate heat and humidity of kitchen
5. Temperament to perform efficiently during rush periods.

Cook Apprentice portioning food.

JOB ANALYSIS AND WORK SIMPLIFICATION

The primary purpose of job analysis is to secure accurate descriptions of the jobs in the establishment being analyzed. In performing job analysis, however, the analyst recognizes many situations in which operations are being performed inefficiently. Poor work scheduling and inefficient work methods often come to the attention of the analyst during the course of the analysis. By pointing out these discrepancies and seeking better methods, the analyst becomes in effect a work-simplification person as well as a job analyst.

Job analyses performed in hotels and restaurants usually result in work simplification brought about by eliminating unnecessary motions and tasks and by suggestions for better organization of workers and work that has been acted upon. The consequent savings in wages and increased production usually more than pay the cost of the job-analysis program.

This means, however, that unless care is taken some employees will be abruptly thrown out of a job. It will pay the hotel or restaurant to make every effort to transfer, upgrade, or otherwise find employment for employees who have been displaced as a result of job analysis or work simplification. It is only by following such a policy that the cooperation of the employees can be obtained in a continuing method-improvement program.

How Job Analysis Resulted in Work Simplification

An illustration of how work simplification results from job analysis was strikingly shown in a job-analysis program conducted at the Hotel Radisson in Minneapolis a number of years ago.

One of the questions asked in the course of the job analysis was, "What time do you come to work and why?" No one, it seemed, knew the answer. Further analysis revealed that while in the preceding ten years offices and department stores had adjusted their opening hours from 8 to 9 or 9:30 A.M., the hotel continued to require their employees to report to work at the same time they had been reporting for the previous twenty-five years. A large majority of employees were required to be on the job at 5, 6, or 7 A.M. Since the stores and offices of the city were not open, the patrons of the hotel were not up and requiring services. The hotel employees did practically nothing productive their first two hours on duty.

The service elevator operator, when asked, "Why do you come to work at 6 A.M.?" replied that he had been so instructed fifteen years ago when hired. When asked what he did the first thirty minutes between 6 and 6:30, he replied, "Nothing." Further questioning disclosed that between 6:30 and 7 he took a few employees to the locker room, a half flight up.

An outstanding case of inefficiency appeared in the job of steam fitter. The hotel had absolutely no need for a steam fitter. One Sunday's, "work" by the steam fitter consisted of repacking two faucets, for which the individual was paid $23. Needless to say, the job of steam fitter no longer appears in the hotel's organizational chart. Other examples of poor scheduling of hours were found. Job analysis enabled the management to rearrange hours and require the presence of employees only when needed. By this method the equivalent of forty-six persons were eliminated from the payroll.

Job analysis showed that security officers and lodging quarters cleaners were duplicating each other's work in reporting occupancy of rooms. The cleaners spent about thirty to forty-five minutes each morning checking their sections for occupancy. Security officers made the same report every hour. Prior to the job analysis the security officer's reports were filed away in the assistant manager's desk and forgotten. Under the new procedure this report reached the room clerk four hours earlier and the forty cleaners were each saved at least 30 minutes per day. They now spend their first half hour doing hall cleaning, thereby eliminating the need for hall persons and some housepersons.

The same analysis pointed out that although the wages of bellpersons had been raised substantially, yet they no longer supervised the cleaning of the lobby and were "too busy" to relieve the elevator operators during their rest periods, most of their time was spent in delivering hotel property to customers for a gratuity. Two night housepersons spent six of their eight hours performing extra services for guests and two hours working for the hotel. By actual count the two night housepersons delivered fourteen extra easy chairs, five floor lamps, six extension cords, three bridge tables and chairs, and two card tables with chairs. One guest alone asked for and received twelve extra chairs. The house received no revenue for this service and lost the time spent by the employee. Moreover, the equipment had to be removed the next day by employees who were not working for tips.

SUMMARY

Basic to several personnel procedures is job analysis, a process that takes inventory of the work done to accomplish the objective of the enterprise. The process of job analysis has three related parts: (1) *job analysis*—a term that applies to the actual procedure of observing the job,

Figure 4.2 Functionally Integrated Career Progression Model for a Food-Service Facility

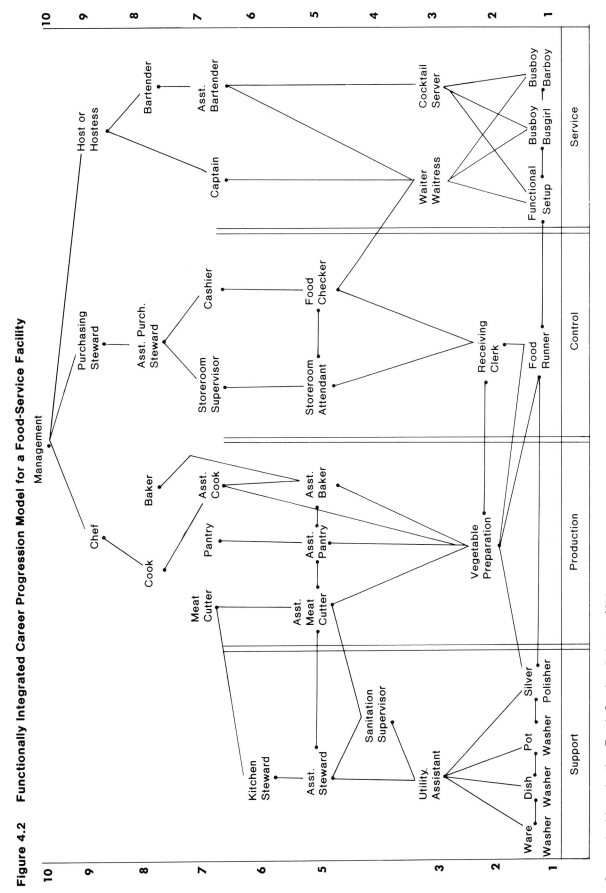

Career Ladders in the Food Service Industry (Chicago: National Restaurant Association, January 1971).

interviewing the worker, and recording the results; (2) *job description*—the organized, written form of the results of the analysis that describes the work performed, the responsibilities involved, the skill or training required, the conditions under which the job is done, and the type of personnel required for the job; (3) *job specification*—the person specifications that list the skills and personality traits needed to perform a job and outline particular working conditions that will be encountered on the job.

With the basic information obtained from a job analysis, a variety of functions concerning personnel and industrial relations can be performed, including the drawing up of organizational charts; listing the organization of the work force; making wages and salaries, transfers, and promotions more equitable; handling grievances in an objective manner; uncovering hazardous or unpleasant working conditions; establishing production standards; setting up work simplification improvements; and facilitating collective bargaining by standardizing job titles.

Planning for job-analysis can be carried out by existing personnel in any organization without specialized skills. State employment agencies may provide valuable assistance. The analysis should start experimentally in one department and then spread as the analysts gain greater experience and a better system. Clear communication of the purpose of the analysis within the organization is essential in order to enlist cooperation and to avoid resistance.

A number of different forms and procedures are available to serve as guidelines in the undertaking of the job analysis. Forms and examples of actual job analyses are found in this chapter to provide assistance to the prospective job analyst.

The Selection Process

5

From a letter written in 1917 by Ellsworth Statler, premier hotelman of his day, to all the managers of his hotels, we read:

> "From this day you are instructed to employ only good-natured people, cheerful and pleasant, who smile easily and often. This ought to go for every job in the house, but at present I will insist on it only for people who come in contact with guests.
>
> It does go, from this day, for all department heads, front office people, cashiers, captains, elevator men, porters, telephone operators, and other employees who have to deal directly with patrons.
>
> If it is necessary to clean house, do it. Don't protest, get rid of the grouches, and the people who can't keep their tempers, and the people who act as if they are always under a burden of trouble and feeling sorry for themselves. You can't make that kind of person over; you can't do anything with him profitably, but get rid of him. Let the other fellow have him, and you hire a man who can be taught."

Every organization must be staffed initially, and new persons brought in continually to replace those who leave and to fill newly created jobs. In staffing a new hotel or restaurant hundreds of applicants are screened, sometimes thousands. For the opening of a new hotel in Mexico City 50,000 people made application for employment. Summer resorts typically screen hundreds of applicants each spring, and in new properties it can be expected that at least half of the employees will be gone at the end of six months or a year. In well-established hotels and restaurants it is not unusual to have a turnover of 50 to 100 percent within a year. Despite an unemployment rate of more than 7 percent in the U. S., it is not unusual to find as many as thirty or forty positions vacant on any given day in a large city hotel. Most of this turnover, it should be pointed out, takes place in the entry or semiskilled jobs. Even in the best-operated clubs, hotels, and restaurants, the turnover could be a minimum of 5 percent a year to take the place of those who are ill, pregnant, or those who retire. The selection process is therefore continuous and involves recruitment, interviewing, testing, and placing employees on the job.

Like the football coach, the hotel or restaurant manager is constantly searching for good potential "players," people with the attitudes and energies to produce a good team effort. The selection process brings the potential players in so that the manager and department heads can train and inspire them to produce hospitality and the other goods and services offered in hotels, restaurants, and clubs.

RECRUITING

Attracting personnel and placing them in the jobs most appropriate to their skills and personalities is a function so important that often the success of the enterprise hinges upon it. No enterprise can long survive in a competitive economic system, no matter how favored, if poor personnel selection and poor placement are in effect for any length of time. If not convinced of this, examine the costs of labor turnover, the cost of dissatisfaction arising out of placing a person in a job for which that individual has no interest, or the losses resulting from inefficiency because of the absence of requisite abilities.

Resistance to trial-and-error methods of employment is increasing in hotels and restaurants, which are striving towards stability of employment. A mistaken placement may have years of bad effects. Organized labor is demanding more security in tenure of employment. Unions negotiate clauses that make it difficult for an employer to discharge a worker. Competitors, using expert methods of choosing employees, force the hotel or restaurant manager who has not adopted similar methods either to adopt them or be satisfied with employees found unsatisfactory by others.

There are, of course, many employers who pirate trained employees from neighboring hotels and restaurants. This can prove satisfactory provided the pirates pay a higher wage or if tips are higher.

One well-known restaurant and hotel firm sends its executives out to meals at competitors' establishments where the more desirable waiters and waitresses are told, "If you think about moving, come and see us." The executive leaves a business card. Not wholly ethical, but effective!

Recruiting can be a complex task. To take applicants as they come off the street may be disastrous because inefficient workers may result from those hired hastily. On the other hand, a similarly disastrous result may occur if "good" people are recruited without prior consideration being given as to how such people are to be used.

Farsighted recruiting requires (a) consideration of people power needs; (b) knowledge of the promotional ladder within an organization; (c) a prediction of future turnover rates on the basis of past experience and future growth expectations; and (d) understanding of the type of person who seems to be best suited for specific positions in the organization.

Recruitment problems differ among various hotels and restaurants. Each organization, on the basis of its experience, must come up with certain philosophies, standards, and policies relative to its recruitment program. In standardizing policies, it is recognized that some degree of inflexibility ensues, but too much flexibility removes the value of system. The following standards, or policies need to be established in developing a recruitment program.

1. What are the minimum skills and requirements of each job? These are normally in the form of job specifications. It is a needless waste of time, money, and energy to recruit individuals who will not be hired ultimately.

2. Is promotion to be from within or from outside? An organization that develops its supervision from within exclusively may be crippling itself in the long run if it recruits individuals who do not have long-range potential, even though these individuals may have excellent qualifications for the available position. On the other hand, where potential for growth and advancement are limited, a recruiting program that focuses on individuals with proven records of growth-seeking, such as college students or those who leave jobs for better positions, is unrealistic and leads to labor dissatisfaction and turnover.

   Many hotels seek a balance whereby both systems are used. This avoids moving unqualified people up purely because of labor shortage and at the same time avoiding the lethargy that develops in organizations where people lack advancement possibilities. In chains of hotels or restaurants some positions call for skills and experience that are not developed within the chain. Therefore some recruitment for higher-level jobs from the outside is necessary.

3. Prior to recruitment, everyone in the hotel or restaurant who will be affected should be informed of the jobs to which new employees will probably be assigned. This helps keep the organization stable in the eyes of present employees and prepares them for the changes to come.

SOURCES OF EMPLOYEES

The first step in the employment procedure is to secure a supply of desirable recruits. Part-time employees are usually needed for banquets, conventions, and other heavy-volume periods.

As a matter of practicality hotels, restaurants, and clubs often draw most recruits from among friends and acquaintances of present employees, which can be both an advantage and a disadvantage. A position opens and quite naturally other persons on the job are among the first to know about it. If present employees like the establishment, they are likely to tell relatives, friends, and acquaintances about the opening. The new employee is more readily accepted into the work group and feels more welcome if acquainted with someone already employed. The friend is more likely to help the newcomer adjust to the work situation and may act as informal tutor. Such practice tends to perpetuate the kind of employee presently on the job. It may encourage the employment of members of the same family or an extended family who are self-protective. It can perpetuate work attitudes and habits, which may be unfavorable since a friend or relative quickly picks up the attitudes of the sponsoring individual. On the other hand, the "good" or "model" employee is likely to want to add persons of similar motivation and abilities to the organization. "Friends of friends" often prove to be excellent recruits.

Recruitment from within avoids several of the usual costs of recruitment. And too, where there is good morale, present employees can act as a continuous recruitment cadre, relieving management of much of the problem of recruitment.

Promotion from Within

Recruiting is always easier when the organization needing people has a reputation for fairness and opportunities for advancement. Career ladders chart specific promotion

Figure 5.1   Career Training and Progression in a Model Organization

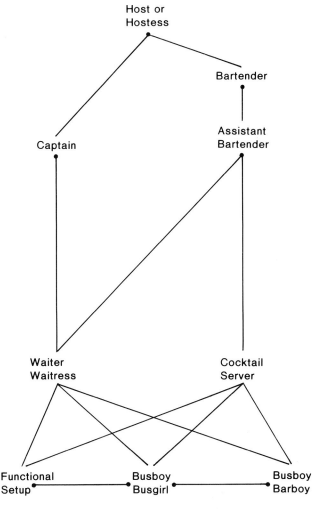

opportunities to help insure that a steady supply of desirable employees apply.

Career ladders specifically designed for an organization show the employee the opportunities and benefits that can be accrued from a commitment to a career that is headed "up" the ladder.

Figure 5.1 is a chart showing the various possibilities for career training and progression in a model organization. Note that training opportunities can be made available for the various steps up the ladder.

Recruitment through Newspapers

Hotels and restaurants often depend upon newspaper advertisements for attracting new employees. For some jobs, newspapers are satisfactory. They are particularly useful in attracting the unskilled and young people whose knowledge of employment opportunities is meager. In some places, newspapers are a relatively poor tool for securing supervisory personnel or highly skilled workers. In other places, the newspaper is highly effective. They should be used with caution in times of business recession, for they are likely to attract many unqualified workers who if refused employment will resent the refusal. Moreover, time taken to screen the qualified from the unqualified is costly.

A different type of personnel is attracted by the various newspapers in the same labor area. One type of worker reads the sensational tabloids, another reads the conservative newspapers. The choice of the newspaper as an advertising medium should depend upon the type of job to be filled.

"Inexperience is an asset!" says the waiter ad for one restaurant chain. Other ads ask questions such as, "Do you want to make money?" and "Do you like to meet people?" "Compare your salary for waiting on tables with that of the secretary next door—you're almost sure to come out the capitalist of the pair." Ads seeking part-time waiters might start with, "Do you want well-paying, part-time work?"

Placing a classified ad as close as possible to the beginning of the ad section has the advantage of immediately catching the eye of people who are scanning the classified ads. An ad for a meat cook could appear in the list as "Cook, Meat." Combination ads such as "Porters and Waiters" do not pull as well as when the heading lists only one job, "Porters" or "Waiters."

A tight labor market may call for a larger ad. Display ads, large ads with white space, have been effective for some hotels and restaurants; for others, the effect has been no greater than with the classified ad. Running an ad continuously is thought by some to give the implication that all is not well with the personnel policy of the company. One study, however, showed that when an ad was discontinued for a few days the number of applicants did not increase after the ad again appeared.

Older people are attracted by words such as "steady" or "permanent." A hospital dietary department might use a caption, "Do you want to be a friend of the sick?" This would attract a different type of person than the usual "Kitchen Help Wanted" ad caption.

Since many hotels and restaurants prefer to train their waiters, the lack of experience as a waiter is no serious liability. An ad that stresses the need for good health, a pleasant appearance and speaking voice and points out that experience is not required attracts a better person than is likely to otherwise apply.

A run-of-the-mill advertisement usually attracts a run-of-the-mill worker. If the hotel or restaurant wants a high type of employee and has something tangible to offer, such as unusual working conditions, high pay, or benefit plan, these advantages can be listed in the advertisement. Listing advantages builds public relations in general.

Wording the Employment Ad

The employment ad may provide the only information about the restaurant available to the potential employee. Like a television commercial, the employment ad is brief and attention-getting. To attract, it appeals to the reader's self-interest and perhaps self-pride. What kind of ad appeals are effective?

Remuneration—
    top wages
    top dollars $$$
    excellent pay
    pay while training
    profit sharing
Benefits—
    paid holidays
    paid vacation
    free health insurance
    free dental insurance
    free meals on the job
    discount on all meals
    prestige restaurant
    free uniforms
    choice of hours or days
Work Environment—
    excellent supervision
    friendly co-workers
    newest equipment
    homey kitchen
    air conditioned kitchen
    variety of duties
    cheerful decor
Opportunity—
    for a food-service cashier
    for advancement
    for added responsibility
    to make friends
    to develop new skills
    to add to your family income
    to use your free time
    to work without previous experience (we train)

Examples of "No No" Ads

The ads below were once considered well done and perfectly acceptable to U.S. government regulatory agencies. What is it that makes them unacceptable today?

Waitresses
18–25

If you are a high school graduate, like people and are interested in a position offering steady work, the best of working conditions, meals and uniforms, apply for Stouffer Girl work. Experience not necessary. Salary while training. Openings for both full-time and part-time work. High paying positions plus meals and uniforms. No Sunday or holiday work.

High School Graduates
18–25
What do you want in your job?
High Wages
Security
Congenial Surroundings
Chance for Advancement
Opportunity to Meet the Public
Meals Furnished
Inquire About
Stouffer Girl Work

In light of the Equal Employment Opportunity and Age Discrimination laws, the ads discriminate with regard to age, sex, and the educational background required. The ads also discriminate against men, against age groups other than the 18–25 age bracket, and against persons without high school diplomas.

In composing help-wanted newspaper ads, avoid including anything that conflicts with the laws, such as listing requirements as "young," "men only," or "recent graduate." Include the statement "An Equal Opportunity Employer" at the bottom of the ad.

An Acceptable Ad

The ad below is acceptable and effective.

Waiters/Waitresses

We are looking for attractive, peppy, versatile servers to join our opening team. You must have an outgoing, friendly, vivacious personality. Dependability is a must. We start training January 8th.

You will be paid while learning our system. Enjoy good earnings, all new facilities, helpful, friendly management. Hours are varied, and flexibility is important. We will be closed Sunday.

An Equal Opportunity Employer

List Qualifications Needed

It is only fair to the reader that ads specify the kinds of skills and personal qualities needed to perform the job. These could include:

Alertness
Attractiveness
Over 18 or 21 for liquor service, depending upon
    state law

Must like working with the public
Certain work experience needed
Pleasant personality
Must have own transportation
Must have completed certain culinary training

The "Right" Job Titles

According to the personnel staff of Stouffers, each city is different in the way people respond to job titles. Experiment with job titles, they say, to find out which titles used in the employment ad will attract the most applicants. Their list of most-used titles and possible alternatives follows.

Titles Often Used:	Alternatives:
Cook	Food Preparer, Kitchen Helper, Dietitian's Helper, Food Handler, Food Trainee
Waiter/Waitress	Stouffer server
Pantry	Food-Service Bar, Service Bar, Pantry Server, Steamtable, Salad Maker
Host/Hostess	Receptionist, Greeter, Dining Room Supervisor
Bus	Bus Person, Dining Room Bus, Utility Helper
Dishwasher	Dish Machine Operator, Kitchen Helper
Office Clerk	Bookkeeper, Typist, Figure Clerk
Janitorial	Cleaner, Handy-helper

Recruitment through Radio Advertising

Radio advertising has been found to be effective in recruiting extra and part-time employees, especially chambermaids. The radio reaches listeners not actively seeking employment and who would not usually read a newspaper Help Wanted column. By radio they can be reminded they already have skills such as cooking and housekeeping which can be exchanged for extra money and still have time to keep up their own homes.

Employment Agencies

Public employment agencies are little used by hotel and restaurant employers except in particular localities. Often the employer finds that referrals from public agencies have not been screened, perhaps because the agency is more concerned with placing the applicant in a job than with ascertaining the individual's job qualifications. Charitable employment agencies sometimes operate in a similar fashion, giving little thought to the needs of the employer. In some cities, however, the public employment services are highly satisfactory.

The state employment services are public employment agencies that have the tools to do a first-class referral job. The states must meet certain standards and cooperate with the federal government to be eligible to receive federal funds. The United States Employment Service acts as a clearing house of employment information, conducts research, develops employment tools, and is a nonfee referral agency for workers.

The USES also has developed aptitude tests for various blue-collar and white-collar jobs. (These tests are based on the tests developed for the U.S. armed services during World War II.)

The major testing procedure usually involves administering the General Aptitude Test Battery to prospective job candidates. There are twelve parts to this test, including such things as verbal tests, spatial perception tests, manual and finger dexterity tests, and the like.

The battery usually is used in guidance and counseling (e.g., a high school counselor might administer the whole battery to a soon-to-be-graduate to uncover potentially beneficial areas of employment aptitude).

A job candidate who is interested in hospitality employment typically takes a Specific Aptitude Test Battery, which is nothing more than one or more parts of the General Aptitude Test Battery. Norms have been established for most hourly and a few professional jobs in the hospitality industry. The job candidate's score is compared to the norm established for the hospitality job under consideration. A favorable comparison is indicative of an aptitude for that job.

These norms have been revalidated (some are still under the process of revalidation) to remove cultural biases and other prejudices.

Private employment agencies sometimes provide a valuable source of recruits. Again, research will show the merit of each employment agency. In the past some unscrupulous employers entered into fee-splitting agreements and other nefarious arrangements with unethical employment agencies.

Schools and Colleges as Employee Sources

Schools and colleges are sources of recruits for jobs demanding special skills and/or supervisory talents. Hotel and restaurant chains employ recruiters to appraise and employ graduates of hotel and restaurant courses. A few months before each graduation period the recruiters personally interview prospective graduates. This proves valuable to both the prospective graduate and the business sending the recruiter. Students are informed of the available jobs, and employers have the opportunity to find those qualified to fit their particular needs.

Recruiting college students for summer jobs has also proved advantageous to the employer and to the student. From the employer's point of view, a high type of employee is had at a relatively low wage. Students majoring in hotel and restaurant administration bring fresh ideas and in many cases are more proficient than the regular employees, especially in auditing and other front-office jobs. Because students want a variety of work experience, they can be used to replace regular employees on vacation and they can be rotated in several jobs. Some students who have had several summers of experience have successfully managed resort operations and summer clubs during their senior year. Most resort operators find students proficient in waiting on tables. Hospitals have found students effective in the kitchen and business office.

Usually a recruiting program for summer employment is instituted by which contacts are maintained with several schools. Fraternities and sororities can provide a constant supply of recruits. Where conditions of employment and pay are desirable, college students return year after year until their college work is completed. Many later become patrons. Guest comments, such as "the most attractive people at this resort are the help," attest to the success of the idea of using students as summer employees.

Other Sources of Recruits

Numerous other sources of recruits are often overlooked. For a particular hotel or restaurant one or more of such sources may prove excellent. Some of these are foreign language newspapers, state boards of vocational education, veterans' organizations, YMCAs, YWCAs, Catholic and other denominational organizations. Some restaurants have found the best recruits in the suburbs of cities and in small, country towns.

HIRING THE HANDICAPPED

Since it is true that almost all jobs require only certain faculties and skills, it is a sound personnel policy to employ physically handicapped persons for certain jobs. For example, it has been found that a hearing impairment does not affect performance on such jobs as houseperson or wall washer. Handicapped employees are usually more dependable and have better absenteeism and tardiness records than nonimpaired employees. A dish room crew of deaf and dumb is regularly employed by a summer hotel, with excellent results.

To show the number and variety of jobs that have been satisfactorily filled by impaired personnel, the following list shows the results of successful placements of handicapped persons in the Statler Hotel Company, now part of the Hilton corporation.

Food and Beverage Departments

Assistant Steward—Right leg stiff—must be dragged.
Night Kitchen Runner—One eye.
Cook—One eye.
Yardworker—One hand paralyzed.
Glass Washer—Deaf mute.
Dish Washer—Fingers missing, deaf mute, crippled back, one short leg.
Pastry Cook
Vegetable Person
Coffee Person } Defective hearing.
Salad Person
Bar Porter
Silver Cleaner } Deaf.
Food Runner
Silver Drier—Infantile paralysis (uses crutches).
Cashier, Cafeteria—Arthritis, deformed joints.
Hostess, Cafe Rouge—Artificial leg.
Head Room Service Waiter—Artificial leg.
Waiter, Terrace Room—Wired shin bone.
Night Restaurant Auditor—Arm off at elbow and artificial leg.
Waiter—One finger missing.

Service Department

Elevator Operator (passenger)—Artificial leg, one arm, short leg.
Elevator Operator (freight)—Short left leg, one arm.
Doorman—Four fingers off left hand.
Lobby porter—Paralytic leg.

Housekeeping Department

Wall Washer—Deaf mute, short arm, one arm.
Houseperson—Spinal disorder (hunchback), palsy.
Vacuum Person—Twisted leg.
Night Cleaner—Both feet partly amputated.
Floor Housekeeper—Defective hearing, paralyzed arm.
Lodging Quarters Cleaner—Hunchback.

Laundry Department

Sewer—Deaf and dumb.
Worker—Defective hearing.

Engineering Department

Plumber—Short leg.
Electrician—Short leg.
Painter—Defective hearing.

Clerical Workers

Night Auditor—Artificial leg.
Mail and Information Clerk—Deformed arm.
Operator, Telephone—Deformed arm.
Clerk, Valet—One arm.

Totally blind persons have been highly proficient dishwashers.

Several other jobs in the hotel, restaurant, and club business can be successfully performed by the visually handicapped. The switchboard operator of a private club, totally blind, has become a beloved member of the staff over a period of years. Members have gotten to know this individual, who recognizes each member by voice, thereby personalizing the operation. In the laundry the person who folds towels and washcloths could be totally blind. The flatwork ironer or feeder needs only enough vision to detect holes, tears, and stains in materials. The person who tends the machine that automatically folds shirts could also be totally blind. In the kitchen, in addition to some of the crew on the dish machine who may be blind, a blind person may fill the job of pot washer, especially if not required to collect pots and pans from various parts of the kitchen.

A number of other jobs in the hotel, restaurant, or club require only travel vision, enough sight to move about and generally see what is going on. Among these jobs are waiter's assistant, kitchen helper, banquet houseperson, pantryperson, porter for room service, houseperson, bellperson, and several of the jobs in the laundry that do not require inspection of the cleaned linen.[1]

It should be pointed out that though many jobs can be filled by handicapped persons, such persons must have the personal attributes and abilities to do the work. Blind persons should accept themselves as persons with visual limitations and be able to handle personal and social relations without undue embarrassment or stress. Probably needing help from co-workers, they should be able to request such help and to work as a team member. The individual's mental ability must be high enough to handle the work assigned, coupled with mobility such as to be able to get to and from the place of work (perhaps with help from rehabilitation personnel).

The employment of the mentally handicapped in the hotel restaurant and club business has probably been in effect ever since such businesses began. Several jobs in the business require perseverance, energy, and the ability to work in unpleasant conditions but only a relatively small amount of general intelligence. A pot and pan washer can be illiterate or slow thinking as long as the person is willing to take directions and withstand the heat, humidity, and restricted working area. Socially, this individual is at the very bottom of the ladder, with wages that are among the lowest. Anyone with options ordinarily does not stay on the job. Similarly the job of dish machine operator is hot, noisy, demanding, and low paying. A retarded person who has few choices may be a much better employee than an unimpaired one. The mentally handicapped if given the opportunity of being a contributing member of a work group may be delighted with the work, receiving wages and more self-respect than if unemployed or in an institution.

Very often the problem faced by impaired persons is not on the job but off the job. Life in a city can be frustrating for a normal person; for an impaired person, it may be impossible. With the help of special agencies the impaired can be given support outside of work and helped to get to and from work. The work itself may be one of the most satisfying experiences that such people encounter.

The Role for Marginal and Deprived Workers

American culture tends to view health as an ideal but normal state. Illness is something to be endured without complaining. There is even the vague feeling that illness is the fault of the victim. An ill or disabled person is expected to exert every opportunity toward achieving a complete recovery. Disabled individuals by definition are culturally suspect, but they can gain some acceptability if they can *prove* to others that they are striving for normality by showing motivation and independence in their efforts. Disabled individuals who are dependent, unsure of themselves, bitter, or too focused on their disabilities are quite likely to be rejected as poor employment risks.

How accurate are these biases? What can be done with disabled or marginal people who "won't help themselves?"

One of the authors was involved in a major research project that attempted to rehabilitate permanently institutionalized individuals into roles in which they could work and function independently outside of an institution. All of the candidates in the program had lengthy histories of social maladjustment and all had been institutionalized

1. See American Foundation, "The Visually Handicapped Worker in Service Occupations in the Food Service and Lodging Industries," American Hotel and Motel Association, Hilton Hotels Corporation, Rehabilitation Corporation, 1968.

in Veterans Administration hospitals and domiciliaries for lengthy periods. The program required each candidate to be involved in an intensive one-year program that provided vocational training, human-relations laboratory training experiences, independent self-government living experiences, individual counseling and psychotherapy, group therapy, and community-placement services.

An important methodological aspect of the research was the fact that no interested candidates were eliminated. Everyone who wanted to try the program was given an opportunity. A large number of individuals who expressed pessimism about their chances were encouraged and coaxed into participating. Unlike most employment selection situations, it was possible at the end of the program to determine whether the individuals who were picked as poor prospects or who labeled themselves as poor prospects had actually failed. Also, it was possible to check the accuracy of the professional staff in predicting success for those candidates who initially looked *good*.

The results of the study were quite interesting and dramatic. It was demonstrated that permanently institutionalized and chronically disabled individuals can be productive workers when they have been through a rehabilitation-oriented training program. Secondly and surprisingly, the candidates who generally were considered as the best prospects initially turned out to be the dropouts. The candidates who generally were considered to be the worst prospects turned out to be the most stable and productive. In analyzing this surprising result, it was discovered that the assessors—all professional psychologists or personnel administrators—were biased by the candidates' assessment of themselves. Most of the eventual dropouts presented themselves in a highly optimistic manner, denying the existence of problems or potential problems. In short, they actually *distorted reality* in that by the very nature of their predicament their situation was difficult and problems should have been expected. Men who actually did complete tended to be pessimistic and negative about their condition and about possibilities for success, but at least they were in touch with the *reality* of their situation.

An important lesson can be learned by personnel administrators from this study. One should not be unduly critical nor skeptical about marginal or minority employees because of anticipated adjustment problems or conflicts. The very fact that one recognizes one's dilemma and realizes the likelihood of having the problems is already a positive sign that the person will be amenable to adapting to or coping with problems as they arise. One must be much more suspicious of the person with obvious potential problems who chooses to deny or distort them. Many prospective marginal employees who are being screened as too dependent, too bitter, and too unsure of themselves will prove to be capable employees if given the chance.

Many employers have become disenchanted with "hire the handicapped" or "hire minorities" campaigns simply because they automatically expect individuals from those groups to adapt automatically to the norms and ways of their present employees. Prospective employers must recognize that these individuals have special needs and problems that take time, support, and encouragement to resolve. If the effort is expended by the employer, however, the dividends in having long-term, stable, capable employees will be well worth the effort.

Members of any minority or marginal group, be it racial or disability, experience problems of isolation and of "not belonging." Those individuals comprising the majority feel support from their culture, which enables them to endure stress. They do not experience identity problems because their own identity is firmly grounded in the fact that they are *not* marginal. The individual who is in some manner a member of two cultures that are often in conflict is usually exposed to a relatively high risk of some sort of psychological adjustment problems. It is often the rule rather than the exception that a new job experience poses a number of job-related personal and physical problems for a dual-culture member. It is important for employers to recognize that the experience of problems is not an abnormal situation but, rather, is expected behavior. At such times employers need to be particularly supportive and reassuring in helping the individual to overcome isolation and to feel a belonging with that individual's new group.

Hiring the Handicapped

A summary of points to consider in hiring the handicapped is seen below:

1. Hire for the faculties that are needed on a job. Forget those faculties that are not needed. For example, if sight is not needed for the job, good vision is not a consideration. Perhaps only one arm or one leg is needed to perform a particular job. The job specification will spell out those faculties that are needed. Match job specifications and applicant.

   Most jobs in a hotel or restaurant do require reasonably good health. In a kitchen, obesity, back trouble, or foot trouble are definite handicaps. The ability to resist high temperatures and humidity may be important.

2. Check all references by phone. Ask for the applicant's strength and weaknesses, also about honesty.

3. Avoid the "job hopper," who will probably hop right on through your place as well.

4. Check transportation. How is the person going to get to and from work? Any considerable commuting distance constitutes a liability.

Figure 5.2   Two Examples Showing Averages and Proportions

Example 1

Average Number of Customers Served by Waiters Recruited from Three Different Sources

Source 1		Source 2		Source 3	
Waiter	Customers Served	Waiter	Customers Served	Waiter	Customers Served
A	490	K	316	R	531
B	263	L	385	S	290
C	654	M	473	T	386
D	732	N	911	U	940
E	556	O	522	V	622
F	755	P	460	W	341
G	692	Q	623	X	333
H	784			Y	418
I	760				
Total	5,687		3,690		3,861
Average	631.88		527.14		482.63

Example 2

The Difference Between Proportions of Serving Personnel Recruited from Different Sources Who Were Promoted During the First Year

	Source 1	Source 2
Total Number of Employees from Each Source	30	36
Employees Promoted During First Year of Service	24	27
Proportion Promoted	0.80	0.75

5. Are children cared for? Children are a blessing, but also a liability, especially for a person who has several and only limited energy.

6. Be honest about the job: night shifts, house rules, no smoking rules, weekends and holidays.

7. Explain the wages fully: days off, union costs, and benefits.

EVALUATION OF THE RECRUITMENT PROGRAM

The most important contribution of a personnel worker is not the discovery of employee resources but rather the evaluation of these resources. Some determination must be made as to where the most satisfactory employees for each position are obtained.

To do such evaluation, a criterion of satisfactory performance must be obtained in terms of the quantity of work performed and in quality of work performed.

In evaluating sources of recruitment, it is only human nature to remember the good employee who came from one source or to remember the poor employee from another source and then to generalize by a stereotyping of these two sources, each of which in reality may be no better or worse than the other. To discover if one source is really better than another, all of the people from each source must be evaluated. Because of the effects of stereotyping, it is always best to learn the *significance of a difference* between sources. These differences are expressed by comparing the *average* performance of workers from different sources or in terms of the *proportion* of differences in the performance of workers from different sources. Figure 5.2, example 1 shows how averages can be used, and example 2 shows how proportions can be used.

In example 1, the total number of customers who were waited on by three groups of waiters in their first week of employment were averaged. The groups represent the sources from which the waiters were recruited. It was recognized that it is difficult to evaluate *any one* waiter with any other waiter in terms of the number of customers served, because the number of customers served on the various shifts differs. Groups of waiters can be compared because it can be assumed that the individual differences will be averaged out.

Example 2 was taken from the personnel records of a hospital food-service division in which the criterion—promotion during the first year—was used to differentiate successful from unsuccessful serving-line recruits. Employees from two sources were thus compared in terms of the differences noted in the *proportions* of relatively successful employees obtained from each source.

Statistical significances of the differences can be computed for examples 1 and 2 by the more sophisticated personnel researcher or by those with the time and inclination to dig out the methodology from statistics books. The most statistically unsophisticated, however, can quickly see that in example 1, source 1 is by far the best source of recruits—*even though* the worst worker came from that source, and neither of the two best workers came from that source.

In example 2, it is obvious that there is not much difference between source 1 and source 2 since the difference between proportions of 0.80 and 0.75 is slight. The implication of this finding should caution management against accepting either one of these sources to the exclusion of the other.

Comparisons of averages and proportions are but two evaluation techniques. In terms of establishing recruitment-criterion measures, employees may be classified by such measures as employee turnover, accident rate, ratings of performance, absenteeism, wages earned, test scores, grades made in training courses, and other variables.

THE APPLICATION FORM

A means of securing standard information about applicants is the application form. Although the application form basically is considered a selection tool, it is discussed in this section because it generally accompanies all initial contacts with potential employees. It can be used as a permanent personnel record and the information it provides can be used in conducting research. The application form saves the interviewer time and gives the interviewer an idea of the applicant's literacy.

Questions to be included on the application form depend upon the type of work the applicant is seeking. Every item should serve a purpose. No item should be included unless the information it calls for is useful either for research purposes or for determining the applicant's eligibility for the job. Any item that can be shown to discriminate against any individual on account of race, color, religion, sex, or national origin is forbidden under the Civil Rights Act of 1964. The same prohibition is extended to classified advertising. Under this Act photographs may not be required as part of the application. The United States Equal Employment Opportunity Commission (EEOC) has been set up to enforce the Act.

For purposes of filing, one of the first items on the application form should be the type of work desired by the applicant. A number of biographical and statistical items should be included if there is any reason for using such data in keeping the personnel file or in research. Some suggested items:

1. Name, social security number, and date of filing application
2. Address and telephone number
3. Whom to notify in case of emergency
4. Health card, if required
5. Working papers, if a minor
6. Work desired

From these data it is possible to determine something about the type of employee who will be satisfactory in a particular job. For example, in one hotel studied by the writers it was found that lodging quarters cleaners were more likely to be satisfactory and remain on the job if they were between the ages of thirty and fifty-five and had either few or no dependents. In other hotels investigated, these facts were of no value in selecting cleaners.

Another section of the application form can be used to learn something of the applicant's experience and reputation. For many unskilled jobs in the hotel and restaurant, secondary or college education may be undesirable unless the employer believes such candidates may soon be promoted. For supervisory and sales positions, the educational section questions should inquire as to the specific courses taken in schooling, the place of schooling, and the grades received. Previous work experience information is also valuable. Questions concerning place of previous employment, type of work performed, wages or salary, and reason for leaving can be of use if properly followed up. The use of references will be discussed later.

A sample application form, developed by the Educational Department of the National Restaurant Association, is shown as figure 5.3.

Figure 5.3   Application Form

NOTE: This Application Form outline for nonsupervisory employees was developed by the Educational Department of the National Restaurant Association after a survey of similar forms revealed that all of them requested the basic information called for below. It is *not* suggested that this outline be used "as is." In practically all cases it will be advisable to include some of the additional questions that are printed on the back of the form, together with any special questions that can help determine whether the applicant qualifies for your type of operation.

Position Desired _____   Date _____

Name _____   Social Security No. _____
      Last   First   Initial

Address _____   Phone No. _____

Height _____   Weight _____   No. of Dependents _____

☐ Single ☐ Married ☐ Divorced ☐ Widow ☐ Separated

Circle Highest Grade Attended in School = 1 2 3 4 5 6 7 8 9 10 11 12 College 1 2 3 4

Person to Notify in Case of Accident _____

Address _____   Phone No. _____

Experience

(List Last Employment First)	Dates	Type of Job	Reason for Leaving
Firm _____	**From**		
Address _____			
_____	**To**		
Salary _____			
Supervisor _____			
Firm _____	**From**		
Address _____			
_____	**To**		
Salary _____			
Supervisor _____			

Comments of Interviewer: _____

Family
List ages of dependents and relationship to you: _____
Are you related to any employee of this company? _____ Who? _____

Living Conditions
How long have you lived at present address? _____ In this community? _____
How would you come to work? _____ How long does it take? _____

Interests
What are your hobbies? _____

Other
Are you employed now? _____ By whom? _____
What led you to apply for work here? _____
Have you been employed here before? _____ Position: _____
Are you willing to work nights? _____ Salary desired? _____
Size uniform? _____ Right or left handed? _____ Can you type? _____
Are you a U.S. citizen? _____
Have you served in U.S. armed forces? _____ Rank? _____
Are you interested in company's group insurance plan? _____
I certify that the above facts are true to be best of my knowledge and understand that misrepresentations are sufficient cause for dismissal.
Signed: _____

Revision of Application Forms

Because of increased emphasis by state and federal government on the necessity for avoiding discrimination in employment, application forms must be carefully worded so as to avoid requesting information that could lead to discrimination. The question "Date of birth" is revised to read "Are you at least 18 but less than 66 years of age?" It is illegal to discriminate because of age, and persons 40 to 65 years of age are specifically protected by law. Any preemployment question that tends to elicit an applicant's age is prohibited by the Age Discrimination Act.

Questions concerning citizenship are also changed from "U. S. Citizen?" to "Do you have the legal right to work in the U. S.?" In California, for example, it is not necessary to be a U. S. citizen to qualify for state employment and it is illegal to require a noncitizen to produce an Alien Registration Card prior to hiring.

The question that appeared in many application forms in the past, "Physical Limitations?" is changed to "Do you have any physical condition that may limit your ability to perform the type of work you are seeking and which should be considered for purposes of proper job placement?" Employers are required by law to provide reasonable accommodation to the physically handicapped, including, in some cases, special toilet facilities. Drug addicts and alcoholics are considered handicapped, and it may not be easy to deny employment on these grounds alone.

Whereas in the past receipt of compensation for a job-related injury might have a bearing on employment, it no longer can be so considered. Consequently, the question "Have you ever received Workmen's Compensation?" has been removed.

Police records are also subject to careful handling. It is legal to ask, "Have you ever been convicted of a felony crime?" but a conviction does not automatically disqualify an applicant from receiving consideration. The law in California prohibits asking if an individual has ever been arrested. "Conviction," if used as an employment factor, must be related to a job requirement. For example, a bank embezzling charge would be job-related to performing as a cashier.

THE EMPLOYMENT INTERVIEW

The Role of the Interview

Aids such as the application blank, tests, and references are used in selecting employees, but no one device is more important or more widely used than the personal interview.

The interview allows two human beings to meet face to face in order to explore possibilities for employment.

No other technique offers the flexibility and the depth of the interview. Unfortunately, the interview is also one of the most complex and difficult techniques to master. There is no mechanical way to interview. Interviewing requires intense concentration, perceptiveness, time, sensitivity, and training. There is no short cut to good interviewing, but once a person develops interviewing skills, that individual's value to an organization is considerable.

A common mistake made by the interviewer is to proceed blindly without recognizing the barriers that exist between interviewer and candidate. Aside from the complex differences in personality, there are two main barriers: (1) the professional problems of the interviewer and (2) the psychological constants found in the interview exchange.

In the professional role of an interviewer, whether recognized or not, every practitioner experiences some degree of conflict concerning one's competence. In truth, no one can be completely correct in one's personnel judgments. This conflict may be manifested in a tendency to be overly self-conscious or to overevaluate one's skill—either of which interferes with good interviewing. In addition, all interviewers have built-in expectations of candidates: The interviewer expects the candidate to talk, to be truthful, and to provide information that is relevant. It is an established fact that when interviewers are thrown off guard by candidates who do not conform to these expectations, the interviewer unconsciously tends to react negatively toward the candidate basically *because the interviewer feels uncomfortable.*

Relative to the psychological constants in the interview, candidates for jobs are at a decided disadvantage. They find themselves *giving* and *revealing* but the interviewer is not required to give anything.

Candidates ascribe to interviewers these characteristics. (a) Interviewers are seen as being *voyeuristic;* they are psychological "peeping Toms." (b) Interviewers are *autocratic* individuals who tend to dominate and to control situations. (c) Interviewers are *oracular;* they give the impression of being omniscient and all-knowing. (d) Interviewers are *saintly* individuals who are helpful, but always in a detached "holier than thou" manner. It is easy for the interviewer to assume any or all of these roles. Such roles are traps; the degree to which an interviewer falls into the trap is the degree to which that individual will be a poor interviewer.

The employment interview gives the interviewer an opportunity to evaluate the applicant's appearance and manner, something of the person's general temperament, and the first impression the applicant will create in meeting customers and fellow workers. The work record gives a prognosis for future performance.

On the other hand, the interview has weaknesses and may mislead the interviewer. At best, the interview can give the interviewer only a superficial insight into the total personality of the applicant. It has little value for determining such traits as honesty, reliability, perseverance, mechanical skill, and mental ability. As a means of gaining a rough appraisal of the applicant's first impression, conversation facility, physical appearance, and skill in social participation, it surpasses any other convenient means of appraisal. It has distinct advantages and serious limitations.

The employment interview is an occasion when not only the employer but also the applicant consider each other's mutual problems and interests. The employer is not granting a privilege, nor is the applicant asking a favor. Each has something to offer—the employer, the job, and the applicant, services.

The interview is a two-way communication device, the interviewer stating the nature of the vacancy, the applicant, qualifications. In order to enable the applicant to make an intelligent decision as to whether the job is acceptable, the interviewer must detail the hours of work, the physical exertion and mental effort required, and the general benefits and disadvantages accruing from work with the company.

If the applicant appears to meet the qualifications of the job being sought, the other details of interest should be given. Days off, information on paydays, when and where to report for work, and the special advantages the enterprise offers to employees—all are points of information. To avoid overlooking certain items, a checklist form is useful. Too often the interview is a quiz session during which information passes but one way—from applicant to interviewer. At this point, the interviewer may turn salesperson and try to insure that the applicant takes the job.

When communication is one-way, the interview also fails on two other points: the establishment of rapport and the promotion of goodwill towards the enterprise. The interview can be a means of establishing a cordial understanding between the applicant and the management. The conduct of the interview can assure the prospective employee of the good intentions of management; later, if the applicant is found qualified and is employed, relations between this person and management will have gotten off to a good start. The employment interviewer is a representative of management; the interviewer's manner and behavior reflect management's attitudes to the applicant.

The other point at which the interview can fail, if the two-way communication is not maintained, is in its public relations aspects. Some of the best public relations people a hotel or restaurant has are its own employees. The employment interview is the first step toward making future employees want to advertise the enterprise.

Regardless of whether the interview culminates in employment, the attitude with which the applicant leaves the employment office will sooner or later be reflected in the general reputation of the hotel or restaurant. By accepting the applicant as a conversational equal, avoiding cross-examination methods, and generally encouraging two-way communication, the interview is an effective means of promoting public relations.

Points to Consider in Employment Interviewing

Before the Interview

1. Determine the goal of the interview: evaluation, information, selection.
2. Prepare an outline to guide you during the interview.
3. Schedule the interview at a time that is convenient for both you and the interviewee.
4. Inform the interviewee of the purpose and kind of interview, and the papers and all other pertinent information that may be needed.
5. Study all pertinent information about the person you are interviewing; take notes so that you do not forget your data.
6. Provide plenty of time for the individual.
7. Provide conditions of privacy for the interview.

During the Interview

1. Be yourself.
2. Let the interviewee settle down before beginning.
3. Be direct in your questions when possible.
4. Make your questions open-ended—do not be content with simple "yes" or "no," answers, but ask questions that require explanations and descriptions.
5. Try to get pertinent and accurate answers to the questions you ask.
6. Give the interviewee enough time to think about a question before giving you an answer.
7. Be a good listener, not a talker.
8. Do not interrupt the interviewee. Always let the person finish what was started if possible.
9. Make frequent use of "why?" and "how?"
10. Let the interviewee finish answering one question before you ask another.
11. Use simple language.

12. Do not let the person know your sentiments. You want to find out about the interviewee, not how well that individual can discover your own biases.

13. When in doubt about what the interviewee is saying, summarize the statements made by the person. Be careful to give what you feel has been said, without putting words in the person's mouth.

14. Avoid taking sides on issues. Don't badger or harangue.

15. Do not hesitate to probe.

16. Be in control of an interview. You are there for a purpose. Both your time and the interviewee's time are valuable.

17. At the end of the interview, give the interviewee an opportunity to ask questions.

18. Keep alert before and after the formal part of the interview. All aspects of your contact should be "evaluative" in nature.

Questions to Avoid

As is the case with the application form, certain questions may not be asked in the interview because they may provide information that would lead the interviewer to discriminate against the applicant on the basis of race, color, religion, sex, national origin, age, physical or a mental handicap—unrelated to performance on the job.

The interviewer may ask about military experience or training, but not about the applicant's "general" military service. Nor may the interviewer ask about the type of military discharge unless it has a valid relationship to the particular job. Applicants may not be asked if they have ever been arrested. They may be asked about conviction for serious crimes and the when, where, and disposition of such offenses if the job in question involves responsibility for money or security.

After the Interview

1. Review and organize your notes immediately.
2. Try to answer questions you have raised to yourself about the interviewee.
3. Try to see a pattern to your analysis; try to develop an integrated picture.
4. Check on references.
5. Having summarized and evaluated your facts and attitudes, arrive at a decision.
6. Advise the interviewee of your decision.

Training of Interviewers

Some significant research findings have emerged in terms of what seems to be the best way to train interviewers and counselors.

1. The techniques of interviewing are not as important as attitudes. The interviewers' basic attitudes must be *genuine*.

2. The interviewer clarifies personal attitudes toward himself, towards others, and towards the work. Sound techniques are thus developed.

3. The interviewer needs the self-experience of knowing what it is like to be interviewed by someone who has an understanding of that interviewer as a person. It is valuable for interviewers to seek constructive evaluations of their skills from others, to do role-playing with others, and to maintain a learner's approach to their work.

Characteristics of Good Interviewers

The criteria for deciding who makes a good interviewer or counselor are vague. At the present stage of our knowledge, the criteria adopted by the American Psychological Association seem most applicable:

1. Superior intellectual ability and judgment.
2. Originality, resourcefulness, and versatility.
3. Fresh and insatiable curiosity; self-learner.
4. Interest in persons as individuals rather than as material for manipulation; a regard for the integrity of other persons.
5. Insight into one's own personality characteristics and a sense of humor.
6. Sensitivity to the complexities of motivation.
7. Tolerance; "unarrogance."
8. Ability to adopt constructive attitudes; ability to establish warm and effective relationships with others.
9. Industry; methodical work habits; ability to tolerate pressure.
10. Acceptance of responsibility.
11. Tact and cooperativeness.
12. Integrity, self-control, and stability.
13. Discriminating sense of ethical values.
14. Breadth of cultural background; an educated person.
15. An interest in psychology and understanding people.

Quickie Interviews

Managers of restaurants and department heads who have interviewed over a period of time often shake down their interviewing system to a few key questions and observations. When hiring counter persons for a fast-food operation, it takes no great philosophical pondering for the employer to recognize that they are looking for personable, presentable, prepossessing persons, people who come across to the general public as bright, shiny, healthy, and outgoing. The interviewer can usually identify such persons quickly. No previous work experience may be required, so if a person seems eager to work and looks the part, the person is usually hired.

No matter that the person may stay only a few weeks, there is a well-defined training program to develop new employees and applicants waiting in line.

Conducting the Employment Interview

If the interview is to be successful, there are several preliminary steps to be taken. One of these is to provide pleasant physical surroundings for the interview. Well-furnished, adequately lighted waiting rooms, a supply of popular magazines, ashtrays, washrooms, and toilet facilities will tend to reduce any anxiety the applicant may have and create a favorable and lasting impression. In the applicant's mind the confusion, noise, and cramped quarters of many hotel and restaurant employment offices are a reflection of the enterprise in general. The interview itself should be conducted in privacy or semiprivacy, in a room that is quiet.

The interviewer plans the interview and attempts to make provision for increasing the objectivity of the observations. One tries to recognize prejudices and discount them in one's observation.

The interviewer knows what jobs are vacant and the job specifications. The type of questions are planned so as to set limits on the interview and secure only pertinent facts. Depending upon the number of applicants waiting and other duties, the interviewer schedules time so that applicants are kept waiting no longer than necessary.

In opening the interview it is usually well to begin casually with a friendly greeting such as, "Good morning, Miss Wells. Please make yourself comfortable." Opening questions should be nonthreatening and perhaps non-job related, but should avoid generality. A request such as "Tell me about yourself" might be answered by an intelligent applicant by "What part? Do you have a few weeks? Where shall I begin?" A better opener would be to ask something concerning the type of work the applicant is seeking. Questions requiring a "yes" or "no"

answer should be avoided. Give applicants a chance to express themselves on a topic they know, so they can gain confidence in themselves, which will be reflected in the interview.

Other ways of building the applicant's confidence are to give the appearance of being unhurried, to avoid asking leading questions, and to not overtalk the applicant. By using simple words the interviewer can avoid embarrassing the less educated. Some don'ts for the interviewer include the dictum, "never talk down to an applicant or moralize." Avoid giving personal advice and never criticize the applicant. Do not display authority, and never argue.

Selling the Company?

Should interviewers think of themselves as being ambassadors of goodwill for the company or should they consider themselves merely as screens for sorting out the wheat from the chaff? Professional recruiters who visit various college campuses leave widely different impressions upon the students. Some are so enthusiastic about their companies that nearly everyone who is interviewed wants to go with the company. Other interviewers turn off the students so that even though the company has a good reputation the students lose interest. Some interviewers play God and expect a certain kind of dress and behavior. If the applicant shows up in jeans and/or without a resumé in hand, the interviewer refuses to consider the person seriously. One such recruiter feels that it is the recruiter's responsibility to educate all student applicants in resumé writing, dress, and decorum. Though that recruiter may have been right about such standards she should not have been surprised when student interest in her company dropped sharply.

Reference Guidelines

If a personnel person is conducting an interview and does not have information available covering key factors important to the selection for a particular job, it is wise to talk briefly with the department head who will be making the final decision as to what kind of person is needed. The department head, too, may draw up a list of key factors for personal reference that can be used during an interview. Such reference lists may seem superfluous, but it is easy to get sidetracked during an interview and to overlook the obvious—for example, that anyone with back trouble probably cannot perform as a room clerk since that job calls for long hours standing on one's feet in a relatively small space. On the other hand, it is easy to "overhire" and insist upon qualifications not needed in the performance of a particular job. A purchasing agent does not need two arms; a cashier can operate from a wheelchair; a lodging quarters cleaner, the dish crew, or the entire kitchen crew need not write or speak English as has been demonstrated manyfold in the restaurants and hotels of southern California and the Southwest. Neither do they need good hearing. Deaf mutes can operate a dishroom.

A sample of the kind of checklist that might apply in the selection of candidates for room clerk follows.

Factors in the Selection of Candidates for Room Clerk

Education: High school assumed, two years of college preferred, simple math skills necessary.

Experience: Desirable but not mandatory.

Initiative: Some initiative desirable. Person should be able to work without direct supervision, make routine decisions on basis of house policy. "Sell up" when appropriate.

Mental Fatigue: Stress may be extreme at times. Candidate should be even-tempered, have strong ego, an interest in pleasing people, have high frustration tolerance.

Physical Demands: Standing and walking during most of shift. Stamina essential.

Responsibility for Work Flow: Candidate must be able to communicate quickly and effectively with bell captains, reservations workers, and with housekeeping department.

Guest Relations: Human-relations skills all-important. Candidate's personality all-important. Must be able to sell, coax, persuade, and accept criticism in contacts with guests.

Physical Appearance: Well-groomed individuals are most desirable for this type of work. Good taste in language, manners, and dress required.

Interviewing is partially an art and as such hinges on subleties of facial expression, bodily postures, gestures, and inflections. The interviewer must play a role, the role of the interviewer, and must act the part. Of course playing a role does not preclude honesty and sincerity, but the interviewer must remember that one's very manner is an integral part of interviewing. The interviewer's mood can easily reflect itself unfavorably by tone of voice. The question "Are you unemployed now?" may sound sarcastic, accusing, or friendly, depending on how it is expressed. Similarly, overcordiality may imply to the applicant that employment is a "sure thing," when actually the qualifications may be unsuitable.

Interviewing requires the ability to observe carefully without the observation's being unfavorably apparent. The capable interviewer soon learns that what the applicant does not say may be more important than what is said. A short answer to the question, "How did you like your previous employer?" may to the alert interviewer imply a positive and deep-seated dislike for the previous employer, although not so expressed in words. The good interviewer also makes mental notes of gaps left in the applicant's account of work experience and notes conflicting or incongruous statements. The interviewer does not mention such lapses.

Small bits of behavior sometimes are clues to the applicant's personality. They should be carefully verified before reaching conclusions. Obvious characteristics may exclude the applicant from certain jobs. Nervousness on the part of the applicant that might be embarrassing socially would probably be sufficient reason to exclude the applicant from positions demanding a smooth sales manner. The same behavior has little or no significance for certain skilled jobs in the house. Again, the applicant's chronological job record is probably the best information base.

The Patterned Interview

The underlying premise of the patterned interview is the following. The best basis for judging what a person will do in the *future* is to know what that individual has done in the *past*.

In conducting a patterned interview, the information the interviewer seeks to discover is seldom brought to light by asking the applicant a direct question. For example, it is not advantageous to ask an applicant, are you honest? are you intelligent? can you organize? and so on. Rather, this information is found through a discussion of job history, educational background, family relationships, and feelings on other issues.

In a patterned interview, interviewers must recognize that sound conclusions cannot be drawn from the answer to any one question. The questions that are asked should be thought of as straws in the wind. A straw is tossed into the wind and drifts to the east; several other straws are tossed and the majority of them also drift toward the east. It is then possible to make a fair assumption that the wind is blowing from the west. The same analogy can be used in interviewing. If several questions are asked and the applicant's answers all seem to be pointing in the same general direction, then it is assumed that a pattern of behavior has been developed and that a prediction based upon it stands a good chance of being correct.

Figure 5.4 is an example of a patterned interview. In this instance, an interview for the job waiter/waitress,

Figure 5.4 Interview Pattern for a Waitress

The following interview pattern if followed carefully, will give you many valuable clues to the applicant's personality traits and attitudes which will affect her performance.

Question:	Purpose: Weigh her answers to determine:
1. How did you happen to apply here?	How does she feel about working here?
2. What do you consider to be the most important responsibilities of a waitress?	What are her attitudes toward the job?
3. Who has the greater responsibility, a waitress or a cook? Why?	Does she have the proper appreciation for cooks?
4. What do you consider to be the greatest causes of failure among waitresses?	Does she recognize the pitfalls of the work?
5. What do you consider to be the most important qualification of a good waitress? Why?	Does she understand the full responsibility of the job?
6. How does your husband feel about your working as a waitress?	Will there be domestic difficulties?
7. Do you feel waitresses are usually fair to each other?	What is her attitude toward other waitresses; will she get along with the others?
8. Why do so many waitresses look down upon their jobs?	Will she look down on her job?
9. Suppose a male guest makes insulting remarks to you. What would you do?	How would you handle difficult situations? Is she easily upset?
10. Suppose the hostess insisted you do a certain thing in a certain way, when you know definitely there is a better way? What would you do?	What is her attitude toward supervisors and authority? Would she be stubborn?
11. What do you think about waitresses who change jobs often?	Is she a "job-hopper?"
12. Please pardon this personal question, but why did you decide to get a job and work?	What motivates her? Will she be with you a long time?
13. Why do waitresses so often have crying spells?	Is she emotionally stable?
14. Which do you consider more important, courteous service or prompt service?	What is her attitude toward both factors?
15. Suppose you were asked to spend 2 days in the kitchen watching food prepared: What would you think?	Would she try to know the product she sells?
16. Suppose you have a regular guest who always complains about something? How would you deal with him?	Would she resent complaints? How would she handle them?
17. How would you handle the guest who never tips?	Would she be loyal to your restaurant?

Figure 5.4—*Continued*

18. What would you do if you suspected the hostess of playing favorites in assigning stations and seating guests?	Is she suspicious and picayunish? Is she negative—"imposed upon?" Or does she emanate good will?
19. What would you do if your tips were falling off?	Is she willing to admit her mistakes?
20. Suppose the hostess "bawled you out" in the presence of your guests. What would you do and say?	Is she easily upset, or would she be calm in difficult situations?

Suggestions

1. After each question, use such follow up questions as:
   "Why do you think so?"
   "With what purpose in mind?"
   "What other things might you do?"
   "Why do you feel that way?"

2. The answers within themselves are not important. You are interested only in the personality traits and attitudes they bring out.

3. Neither agree nor disagree with the answer. Merely ask questions. Be polite and courteous, but keep a straight face.

4. Interview privately.

5. This interview requires only twenty minutes, but can point to potential problem areas the employee will encounter in getting started on the job.

twenty questions are asked the applicant. The interviewer is reminded to interpret the answers to each question. For example, the first question "How did you happen to apply here?" is an attempt to arrive at the candidate's feeling about the particular hotel or restaurant. Does the person view the hotel as prestigious, as a place that has a good reputation for clientele and for employees; is the person favorably disposed towards the establishment?

As each question is asked by the interviewer and answered by the applicant the interviewer jots down impressions of the response. A code could be developed to speed up the interviewer's response. The interviewer could assign three pluses (+) as the maximum favorable response, three negatives (−) as the maximum negative response.

The pattern interview includes factors ordinarily overlooked in the usual interview. It also presents the opportunity for correcting misconceptions about the establishment and creating a more favorable attitude.

Every restaurant operator with a service dining room has ideas, some more valid than others, about how to select waitresses. Height, weight, hair color, number of dependents, age, and other factors are considered.

Certainly waiters should be selected to fit a certain clientele. Carhops catering to family groups can be older and more mature than in fastfood establishments. A resort hotel that has guests over fifty has mature persons of forty and up waiting on tables, but brightens up the dining room by hiring teenagers for passing rolls and relishes.

Eugene Laitala has done research on biographic information as related to success of waitresses. In examining the record of 2,000 waitresses who were college students and worked in summer hotels, he found significant correlation between age and size of community from which the women came rather than between those who were college students and those who were noncollege students.

1. Young women under eighteen were not successful at waiting on tables in one-third of the cases.

2. Women who came from cities over 100,000 population did not work out in forty percent of the cases.

3. Women over twenty-two, those who had finished college and were looking at the waitress position as a "last fling," were problems in one-third of the cases.

4. Women away from home for the first time were a greater problem than those who had lived on the campus.

He reasoned that girls from larger cities were not as likely to conform as those from smaller towns where social mores and customs were more stable than in the cities.

In another study of waitresses in resort hotels the following items were of significance.

1. **What was the previous work experience?**
   All persons who had no previous work experience of any kind proved unsatisfactory as waitresses. Sixty-nine percent of those rated as outstanding by their supervisors had previous work experience which pertained to the serving of food.

2. **What objections do you have to working broken hours—no objections, minor objections, strong objections?**
   None of the outstanding workers objected to broken work hours, but 29 percent of the unsatisfactory had strong objections.

3. **Are there many kinds of work you would not do because they are not good enough for you?**
   Forty-three percent of the unsatisfactory waitresses answered yes to this question as compared to 6 percent of the outstanding.

4. **Is she shy, bold, or at ease?**
   Being at ease proved to be indicative of job success. A few shy persons were found in each rating group, but only the unsatisfactory group encompassed persons described as *bold*.

The Multiple Interview

To increase the validity of the interview, two or three interview sessions are often scheduled. The multiple interview gives both the interviewer and the applicant time to think over the proposition. Nervousness, untruthfulness, and other weaknesses that go undetected in the single interview often show up. Sometimes the veneer of the "personality individual" wears thin and the real person is revealed in the second or third interview.

Sky Chefs, Inc., a nation-wide chain catering to airline passengers, tried several variations in the interview for selecting employees over the country. In Denver, a most intensive program was set up to select the 120 best qualified food-service employees. "Display ads" one column by six inches were run in the classified section of the newspaper for a period of three months. Each warned that the applicant must have a pleasing appearance and personality and a willingness to undergo a thorough screening program. Four thousand applications were received. Each applicant completed an application form of over 225 questions.

Most prospects were given three interviews. During the first interview the personnel director explained the Sky Chefs' programs, history, and methods and asked a series of questions. If deemed satisfactory, the applicant was requested to return anywhere from one day to a week later for a second interview. The interim period was in itself a selection device, since those not really interested in working for the company failed to return for the second interview. In the second interview, the questioning was even more intensive. A third interview provided the opportunity for a final decision.

Testing the Interviewer

One way to develop skill in interviewing is to test the skill of the interviewer by evaluating results.

A common statistical test determines how successful the interviewer is in discriminating between desirable and undesirable applicants. The process requires the analysis of numerous cases; a few individual cases cannot provide sufficient information.

Nancy Brown, interviewer for the XYZ Restaurant-Cafeteria Chain, decided to determine her effectiveness in selecting cashiers and checkers for a two-year period. Each of the cashiers interviewed prior to employment was systematically rated on a five-point scale: (1) Acceptable—excellent; (2) Acceptable—good; (3) Acceptable—average; (4) Acceptable—borderline; and (5) Nonacceptable. Since the nonacceptable candidates were not hired, her skill in predicting failure was not determined.

If Ms. Brown were a good interviewer, then theoretically the best employees should perform best on the job and the worst employees should perform least effectively on the job. In order to establish a criterion of performance, she asked the managers of three operations in the XYZ chain to rate all the cashiers and checkers hired during the two-year period who had worked six months or longer. Ms. Brown presented the following instructions to each manager:

> For this study please consider as one group all of the cashiers hired by the XYZ Chain during the past two years who have worked at least six months and who are working now or did work under your direct supervision. From this group, rate the employees in terms of whether you consider them to be among the top, the upper-middle, the lower-middle, or the lower 25 percent of the total group of cashiers and checkers under your supervision.
>
> In other words, if ten new employees who met the description worked directly under you, then you would necessarily have to assign at least two of these employees to each of the four categories. The extra two employees obviously would have to be assigned to whatever category seems appropriate; *however,* in the case of having two extra employees to assign, *always* assign one candidate to one of the two categories representing the highest rated two groups and assign the other candidate to one of the categories representing the lowest rated two groups. No category should ever contain more than *one* employee more than is contained in any other category. Use the following rating system to assign employees to categories:
>
> A—top 25 percent; B—upper-middle 25 percent; C—lower-middle 25 percent; D—lower 25 percent.

Table 5.1	A Comparison of the Interviewers' Evaluation and the Ratings of the Managers				
Restaurant Groups	Interviewer's Category	Number of Candidates	Manager's Rating	
			High	Low
Rest. A	1. Excellent or Good	12	42%*	58%
	2. Average or Borderline	15	53%	47%
Rest. B	1. Excellent or Good	18	72%	18%
	2. Average or Borderline	16	37%	63%
Rest. C	1. Excellent or Good	17	41%	59%
	2. Average or Borderline	22	46%	54%

*This number indicates the *percentage* of the cases in this category who were rated high by their supervisors.

When Ms. Brown received the ratings from the supervisors, she made the analysis seen in table 5.1 using her evaluation ratings prior to hiring and the ratings made by the managers at least six months after the candidate was hired. For purposes of comparison, Ms. Brown combined the workers she had evaluated as number one and two and called them the best employees, and she combined the workers in categories three and four and called them the worst employees. She also combined the ratings made by supervisors into high and low ratings, including together all of those workers rated in the highest and upper-middle 25 percent as high-rated workers. All of those rated lower-middle and lowest 25 percent were grouped as the low workers.[2]

From table 5.1 it can be seen that Ms. Brown was partly successful and partly unsuccessful in predicting the future success of interviewers. Her predictions for Restaurant A and C do not appear to be any better than chance. In Restaurant B, however, her predictions appear to be quite significant. Seventy-two percent of those she rated as having the highest potential actually turned out to be the highest performing employees, and 63 percent of the employees rated as having the lowest potential turned out to be the lowest performing employees.

It is obvious, from the table, that Ms. Brown is an interviewer with a problem. Should she forget about her interviewing altogether? should she interview only for Restaurant B? or what?

Ms. Brown sought to discover *why* her evaluations seemed inconsistent. To do this, she went to the managers doing the performance ratings to discover the characteristics managers were looking at when they evaluated their employees.

To Ms. Brown's enlightenment, she discovered that true to her own job specifications, the manager in Restaurant B rated employees in terms of their technical competence, their ability to perform their work without making mistakes, and their efficiency as workers. It did not surprise her that she and the manager of Restaurant B were in agreement, because those were the areas in which Ms. Brown also placed primary emphasis in her evaluation interview.

In Restaurant's A and C, Ms. Brown found that *personal* factors, such as ability to get along with customers, friendliness, attractiveness, and youthfulness were the factors that those managers were considering in their ratings. Technical competence did not seem to be accorded much emphasis.

Because Ms. Brown was a good personnel interviewer who *evaluated* her skill and who tried to *improve* her function, she was in a position to solve a severe selection problem. Assuming no basic shifts occurred in the managers' attitudes Ms. Brown would know that she should use different criteria in assessing cashiers and checkers for locations A and C than she does for location B.

---

2. It should be noted that the scaling and rating categories discussed in this problem are arbitrary and could just as easily be modified in a number of other ways.

Figure 5.5   A Temperament Profile

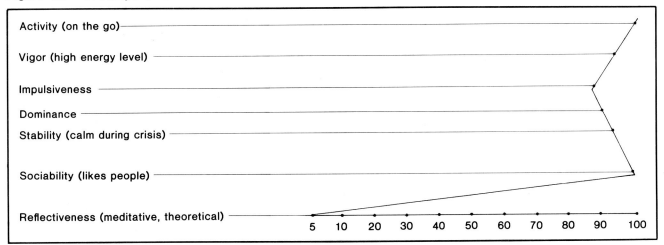

SELECTING DECISION MAKERS

Many people feel that they could make excellent hotel, restaurant, or club managers, as witnessed by the kinds of criticism freely given by the public and by club members. Relatively few of them could effectively manage. In several ways an effective manager is an exceptional person. The physical demands of the job are high, requiring stamina and a high level of energy. The manager must have strong resistance to frustration and be able to brush off criticisms and problems that would injure a tender ego or a thin skin. A person must be able to maintain a pleasant manner and appearance, retaining poise under trying conditions.

A person need not be intellectual; in fact the intellectual is not likely to make a good manager. Figure 5.5 is a temperament profile based on tests of dozens of managerial personnel in a large hotel and restaurant company. It shows the manager as being highly active, vigorous, and rather happy-go-lucky, though quite willing to dominate a situation. This individual has the glandular makeup and personality to remain calm under stress and is, of course, highly sociable. Such a manager is not reflective, meditative, or inclined to the theoretical.

In selecting anyone for a position that calls for considerable responsibility in terms of making decisions and working with other people, the interviewer must make assessment in terms of three factors: one's abilities, what does one want in life, and how does one go about getting what one wants. Abilities for jobs in the hotel, restaurant, and club business hinge around IQ (intelligence quotient), SQ (social quotient), and energy level. Ability to get along with and work through other people may take precedence over IQ, although certain minimum IQ is needed for each job. The Army found a long time ago that to be a successful officer required an IQ of somewhere around 110, meaning that the person should have above average ability for problem solving and adaptability. Successful managers usually have above average energy and are able to focus it on a range of problems over a period of time.

What a person wants in life is often a secret, even to the individual. Perhaps it is a drive for prestige or power. Maybe the security need is all-important. In others it may be the need for affiliation with and approval from certain people. Some individuals spend a great deal of time and effort proving their masculinity or femininity. Knowing what a person really wants goes a long way toward predicting how that individual will direct efforts and make decisions.

Knowing a person's abilities and wants, we can then examine the characteristic ways in which the person goes about getting these wants. Has a person gotten ahead by being a sycophant, ingratiating oneself with those in power? Is the person a bulldozer, driving through to the very end, regardless of the consequences? Or is the person a manipulator? What do such people do when they fail? Some people work even harder, others collapse. Is the person imaginative in seeking to overcome people or other kinds of problems? Is the person typically a compromiser? This may be called for in some jobs; it may be disastrous in others. How shrewd or astute is the person? Does one see through the motivations of others or is one taken in by a manipulator? The way a person behaved in the past is the best key to the way that person will behave in the future.

How can the kind of information suggested above be obtained for making an assessment? Much of it never will be found because our society trains us to hide our true motivations. Some of the information can be derived from previous employers and associates. Use the telephone for getting such information, since few people will commit that kind of comment to writing. In telephone contacts, phrase questions in terms of strength and weaknesses of candidates. Otherwise previous employers are likely to generalize and avoid comments on any shortcomings the candidate may have.

Don't expect a doer to be loved and respected by previous employers or employees who worked with that person.

Assessing People

1. Abilities
   - IQ
   - SQ
   - Energy level

2. What does the person want?
   - Proof of masculinity/ femininity
   - Identity
   - Recognition
   - Approval
   - Power
   - Independence

3. How does the person gain a desired end?
   - Ingratiating oneself
   - Bulldozing
   - Manipulation
   - Leading
   - Playing the long shots
   - Hard work

Look at the record of accomplishment if seeking performance. Some clubs and other operations are not really seeking a performer but rather a caretaker, a coordinator, a supporter, or a nice person. If that is what is needed, then look for that type of individual. Some operations have arrived at a state of maturity wherein little change is needed or desired. Placing an achiever as director of such an organization is misplacing talent. Similarly, placing the "country club type" in a hard-driving, profit-oriented hotel or restaurant chain is a mistake for all parties concerned.

Oddly enough a few managers can do well in a large organization as head of the organization and fail miserably in a smaller organization. The general manager of a 1,000-room hotel who relies heavily on experienced, capable department heads may fail in a 100-room house

where the manager is called upon to have much of the expertise of daily operations. In a large operation the general manager may be more of a coordinator and public relations figure. In the smaller operation, the manager must take a hand in menu planning, promotion, and daily personnel affairs at all levels.

Renewed Emphasis on Honesty and Integrity

Some hotel and restaurant companies are again emphasizing the view that the hospitality business is a service industry, an industry that requires managers and employees to do things for and to please people who are away from home. Therefore, management and employees should have a basic dedication to the principle of service to others.

While much is made of the need for innovation and the need to include the maverick on the team, many companies seek a relatively conforming person, one who is quite ready for and comfortable with playing a prescribed role. That person, they believe, is essentially moral and committed to the middle-class, American value system. Such a person is felt to be more predictable, better integrated as a personality, and better able to produce the kind of effort needed for service to the public.

TESTING

A personnel manager, learning that one of the company's best workers had scored very low on a test that eventually would be used in selecting future employees, nearly discharged the worker. ". . . the tests really opened our eyes about her. Why, she's worked here for several years, does good work, gets along well with the others. That test shows how she had us fooled!"[3]

The foregoing anecdote may sound facetious, but it is not fictitious. It is but one example of how people in responsible positions grossly misunderstood and misuse tests. Tests can be valuable tools of selection, but unless understood and used properly, are dangerous and misleading.

---

3. H. B. Lyman, *Test Scores and What They Mean* (Englewood Cliffs, N.J.: Prentice-Hall, Inc., 1963).

What Is a Test?

Testing is an *indirect* method of measurement that by definition cannot be as valid as a direct measurement. Knowing the limitations of a test, it can be seen how illogical the personnel manager's reasoning was in the anecdote related. Tests properly used in industry are a step in the selection and placement program, but they can only supplement selection and placement of people.

One way to hire good workers is to hire everyone who applies and observe them as they perform on the job. In time, certain people emerge as the good workers. Of course, an oversupply of poor workers would be carried to the detriment of the organization. Obviously, profit-making enterprises and those interested in efficiency cannot afford such a luxury and look for methods to avoid hiring the ineffective. One such method makes use of psychological testing.

Historical Development of Tests

The use of psychological tests dates back to pre-World War I times with the concept of the IQ test developed by Alfred Binet, a French psychologist. For the first time it was possible to rank individuals on a scale, high to low, on a measure called *general intelligence*. Following Binet, Louis Thurstone, an American psychologist, and an English psychologist Charles Spearman, discovered that it was possible to measure individuals not only in terms of general ability but also in terms of several specific abilities such as manual dexterity, perceptual ability, and verbal ability.

It was assumed by some that tests were the answer to all of the problems in industry. They thought that tests, by providing measures of the factors discovered in job analysis, were considered essential for success. Unfortunately, it was discovered that tests could not measure such intangible but essential variables as motivation and personality. Some individuals, for example, score well on tests, but do not have the desire to work; others score poorly on tests, but compensate for their possible lack of skill by their desire.

Up to the present, industry has not been successful in utilizing tests to measure personality variables except under specific research conditions. Such variables are usually investigated through an interview or through clinical tests that are interpreted by a professional psychologist who is intimately familiar with the job-analysis criteria.

The tests to which industry has addressed itself successfully are paper-and-pencil tests measuring *maximum performance*.

Maximum-Performance Tests

A maximum-performance test is one in which each item has a correct answer and in which the person tested is required to do as well as can be done by that person. An intelligence test is a maximum-performance test in the sense that each item has one correct response and any other response is scored as being incorrect. If two people are taking an intelligence test and one person gets more answers right than the other person, we can say that the person with the most answers correct is the more intelligent.

Contrast such a maximum-performance test with a "typical performance" test, such as a personality test. A typical personality test item may be the following: *Do you like grouchy people?* Yes or no. The "correct" answer to such a question is very speculative. Also, a testee may fool himself or lie. On an intelligence test, there is no way to lie—the person either knows the answer or does not know it.

Because tests such as personality tests are consciously or unconsciously distorted by test takers and because the variables measured are so vague, personality tests are all but useless in employment situations except under specific research conditions.

The various types of maximum-performance tests used in industry are the following:

1. **Intelligence Tests**
   These indicate the level of problem-solving ability a person may possess. They indicate how quickly the individual should be expected to catch on to the intricacies of a job. They will not reveal *how* a person will use his intelligence in terms of judgment, creativity, and orderly thinking.

2. **Aptitude Tests**
   These are designed to measure the probable rapidity and success an individual will attain in a specific activity, assuming constant motivation and other factors. The tests are available in a number of areas, such as mechanical, physical science, engineering, medical, etc. The most widely used general aptitude tests (i.e., measuring more than one aptitude) are the Differential Aptitude Test published by the Psychological Corporation and the General Aptitude Test Battery used by the United States Employment Service.

3. **Achievement Tests**
   These are available to measure the degree of skill achieved in specified areas such as typing, shorthand, welding, spelling, comptometer operation, etc.

Basic Attributes of Tests

All tests have three attributes that need to be considered: validity, reliability, and usability.

Tests must also be used in relation to developed "norms."

Validity

This is the most important consideration in any test; i.e., whether the test is really measuring what it purports to measure. There are no set rules for deciding what is "good" validity; such decisions take time and experience. There are many guidelines, and test users need to know the different ways to consider test validity.

1. **Face Validity**

   This means simply that the test *appears* on inspection to make sense and to be valid.

2. **Content Validity**

   In such validity, a check is made to see if the content of the items covers the points that seem to be essential for success on the job.

3. **Empirical Validity**

   This tells how closely the test relates to some criterion (i.e., to some standard of performance, such as supervisor's ratings or production standards). It is the most important kind of validity since it sets a rigidly objective requirement on the test. As a general rule, anyone using tests in an employment situation should insist that the tests bought be subjected to empirical validation by the publisher.

4. **Construct Validity**

   This form of validity also requires correlation between test scores and another variable, which usually is a complex psychological variable. This type of validity is not typically found in employment tests.

5. Test Validity must be done in accordance with standards set by the Equal Employment Opportunity Commission if they are to be used in industry. Validation must be in terms of the actual work performed on the job, and "cultural bias" in test items must be avoided.

Reliability

Reliability refers to the consistency of measurement. A test cannot be valid unless it measures something consistently; however, a test can be reliable without measuring the characteristics it purports to measure.

Reliability may be evaluated statistically in either an absolute or a relative sense. For assessing absolute reliability, a measure called the *standard error of measurement* is used. Relative consistency provides an index of overall dependability of scores in the form of a correlation coefficient. The main considerations to remember about reliability are:

1. Tests are not reliable if they are not taken under *standardized* conditions. They must be administered to all testees under the same conditions.

2. Tests are not reliable if they are not scored properly and consistently.

3. Tests usually are not reliable if: the test is not administered according to the author's instructions; testees have prior information about the test or coaching; unfavorable physical conditions exist (e.g., poor lighting or ventilation); testees experience personal illness.

4. In general, the longer a test is the more reliable it will be.

5. The more random, diverse, and heterogeneous the subjects making up a test group, the more reliable will be the correlation between the scores made by the group and a criterion measure.

Usability

This means that there are many practical considerations in testing. Because of time problems, costs, or other factors, it may be necessary to sacrifice some desirable features. It is important for test users to understand the relative merits of the tests they employ.

Norms

Norms frequently are forgotten or overlooked in discussing tests, but the fact remains that such terms as reliability, validity, and test scores are always *relative* to those ratings made by a group of individuals to whom the test was administered previously. No test score makes sense unless the norm group relative to that score is known. For example, Joe may score at the ninetieth percentile on an intelligence test. The first reaction might be, "Not bad—that's higher than 9 out of ten." A more important reaction would be, "ninetieth percentile of what?" For example, to score higher than 90 percent of the applicants for a pot and pan washing job may not be very good if Joe is being considered for a supervisors' job. To score higher than 90 percent of all high school graduates, on the other hand, may be very good.

As a general rule, the most relevant norms are those that come closest to representing the person with whom we are concerned. For example, if we want to know what a good score is for Joe, we should try to compare him with persons who are his own age and who have his social and educational background. All organizations need to develop "local" norms for every test used. Local norms are ones collected about present employees. No norms will be more relevant for selection purposes than the norms of present employees.

Possible Tests for Use with Hotel and Restaurant Workers

In this section a number of the tests that lend themselves for use with hotel and restaurant workers are reviewed.

Intelligence Tests

Conservatively speaking, there are over one hundred paper-and-pencil group tests of intelligence on the market. Generally there is considerable similarity and overlap in these tests in the sense that: (a) most of them are weighted heavily with items measuring vocabulary and arithmetic skills and (b) most of them depend for their validation on a correlation with older, more basic intelligence tests such as the Army Alpha or the Stanford Binet.[4]

One of the most important considerations in an intelligence test is applicability. Some tests are too verbal and too difficult for people who apply for lower-level jobs; other tests are too easy for college-level people and for those applying for management-type positions. It also should be remembered that although intelligence is one factor for success on many jobs, it is not the only factor. The most commonly used intelligence tests in industry are the following:

1. **The Otis Self-Administering Test of Mental Ability** (World Book Co.)
   This test (several forms) contains seventy-five mixed items arranged in order of difficulty (arithmetic, spatial, vocabulary, sentence meaning, analogies, etc.). It may be administered as a twenty-minute or thirty-minute timed test. The test has good reliability and is appropriate for use with high school students and adults. Although its validity leaves something to be desired, as is the case with all paper-and-pencil intelligence tests, the validation of the Otis by virtue of its longtime use is relatively good.

2. **The Wonderlic Personnel Test**
   There are several forms of the Wonderlic, each containing fifty items. Because of the ease with which it can be applied and administered, the Wonderlic, a twelve-minute revision of the Otis, is probably the most widely used test in industry. It is used by one well-known hotel school as an aid in selecting students for admission. Unfortunately, it is frequently misused also. It is slightly more difficult than the Otis and is best suited to adults with at least a high school background since it is highly weighted with verbal concepts. It is not at all suited to the rank and file food-service applicant. The validation on the Wonderlic is surprisingly skimpy considering its general usage.

3. **The Army General Classification Test** (Science Research Associates)
   This is a civilian edition of the popular test routinely used for Selective Service during World War II. It is a forty-minute timed test consisting of three parts: vocabulary, arithmetic, and a task requiring the viewing of objects spatially. A considerable amount of research has been done with the AGCT. It is best suited to noncollege groups, since it rates slightly lower in difficulty than does the Otis. The AGCT is slightly more usable with food and hotel workers than the Otis.

4. **The Personnel Tests for Industry** (The Psychological Corporation)
   The PTI consists of a series of three measures, all scored and used separately, which are designed for workers at an entry level. Good initial research and norms have been established for these tests. They include a verbal test (five minutes), an arithmetic test (fifteen minutes), and the following oral directions test (fifteen minutes).

---

4. Ibid. It is interesting to note that the concept of "intelligence" is very difficult to define; most test constructors do not try to define it, but rather arrive at their test validation indirectly by correlating the scores subjects make on their tests with the scores made on earlier intelligence tests even though the earlier test constructors themselves had the same problem of not being able to define intelligence.

Aptitude Tests

1. **The Differential Aptitude Test Battery** (The Psychological Corporation)

   The DAT comprises eight separate tests designed to measure eight separate abilities or aptitudes: verbal reasoning, numerical ability, abstract reasoning, space relations, mechanical reasoning, clerical speed and accuracy, and language usage (two parts: spelling and sentences). The time limits set vary from six minutes to thirty-five minutes for each of the subtests. The total testing time is three hours and six minutes. The DAT is a well-constructed battery and the research that has gone into it thus far has been systematic and good. It has two major limitations for use in industry: (a) its length and (b) the adult norms are not adequate since it was developed for high school use. The industrial users of the DAT should take a research approach, i.e., find out which subtests seem applicable and collect normative data.

2. **Purdue Pegboard** (Science Research Associates)

   The Purdue Pegboard is a test of arm and hand dexterity and finger dexterity. It consists of a pegboard with pins and washers. The total test administration takes less than ten minutes. The Pegboard is a widely used test. The validity on any pegboard task varies quite considerably, depending on the groups tested and the criterion measure. A few studies are reported covering food service or hotel workers.

3. **Minnesota Rate of Manipulation Test** (Educational Testing Bureau)

   This is another form of board test, which consists of either placing or turning disks into holes. The test takes less than five minutes. It is considered a test of manual dexterity. It has been validated on such occupational groups as butter wrappers, food packers, bank tellers, typists, and garage mechanics. Cafeteria management in a large department store is enthusiastic about the test. It is reported that persons scoring in the upper 20 percent of all those who take the test and who have at least dull normal intelligence make the most satisfactory dishwashers. On the other hand, persons with low dexterity as measured by the test plus very low intelligence are definitely poor employment risks.

4. **The Minnesota Clerical Test** (Psychological Corporation)

   This is an adult test to measure clerical aptitude. It has face validity for use in selecting bookkeepers, secretaries, cashiers, and clerks. It is a fifteen-minute timed test that consists of two parts, the numbers test and the names test. The numbers test offers two sets of numbers such as the following: 8749–8794, 4892–4892. The examinee must decide which pairs are identical. The names test offers two names; A. G. Smith—A. C. Smith. The examinee must decide if the names are the same. This test has been widely researched and seems to have good validity for routine clerical jobs requiring speed and accuracy.

5. **Other Clerical Tests**

   The Psychological Corporation publishes the *General Clerical Test* and the *O'Rourke Clerical Test,* both of which are similar to the Minnesota Clerical Test. Both offer more complex reasoning items than does the Minnesota test, but neither has had widespread use, study, or validation. The O'Rourke test has been used with reported success by a large Boston hotel. A validation research was conducted that showed test results to correlate highly with job performance of clerical workers.

Achievement Tests

There are no specific achievement tests applicable to the hotel-restaurant-club industry, although the following tests have application in specific contexts: The Blackstone Typewriting Test, The Blackstone Stenography Test, The Seashore-Bennett Stenographic Proficiency Tests, The Elwell-Fowlkes Bookkeeping Test, and Interview Aids and Trade Questions.

Achievement tests can be developed by an organization to determine its own needs. The school lunch rooms of Chicago developed and used such a test for selecting cooks in 1950. Each applicant was required to prepare dough for a two-crust pie and to mix and serve a beef stew. Unseasoned peas, carrots, and other ingredients had been cooked early in the morning by the regular school lunch employees. The applicants were given ten minutes to mix the stew, season it, and dish it up. The stew was then graded by a committee using these criteria.

1. Are the ingredients mixed in proper proportions?
2. How is the working technique?
3. Is the stew served attractively on the plate?
4. Did the candidate finish in the allotted time?
5. How does the stew taste?

The final judgment was in terms of "good," "passing," or "fair." The written examination was a trade test including questions on cookery, cooking equipment, personnel and human relations. The examination time to test the 200 applicants was seven hours. Those who were waiting to take the exam were shown movies on nutrition, food buying, and food preparation.

Written examinations used previously had proved unsatisfactory. Of the persons who had passed the old written exam, only one had proved satisfactory during the six-month probationary period. On the other hand, competent cooks who had worked for years were unable to pass the written exams.

Interest Tests

Although not typically considered good selection tests because of their vulnerability to manipulation by the examinee, interest tests provide some measure of a person's relative interest for certain fields of endeavor. Interest tests are perhaps best used in an intuitive sense as a gross screening measure. For example, if a waitress does not show an interest in people, the personnel worker may want to place special emphasis in his interview on deciding whether or not the applicant would have difficulty working with people.

There are three main interest tests on the market. All are untimed and take from one-half hour to one hour to administer.

1. **The Strong Vocational Interest Blank** (Stanford University Press)
   This is one of the finest tests on the market in terms of its validation and research; unfortunately, it has limited use in most industrial situations except under skilled interpretation. It was developed primarily to compare the individual interests of college students with the interests of people successful in professional fields. It is applicable only to higher level, management applicants. A skilled clinical interviewer can make good use of the Strong in combination with the data acquired in the interview.

2. **The Kuder Preference Record** (Science Research Associates)
   This is the most widely used test in industry, primarily because of the ease with which it can be scored and interpreted. The test requires approximately forty-five minutes to administer. Scores are obtained indicating a person's relative interests compared with a norm group in ten broad areas of activity: outdoor, mechanical, scientific, computational, persuasive, artistic, literary, musical, social service, and clerical. It is applicable to nonprofessional groups.
   Some research with the Kuder in defining the successful student majoring in hotel administration has been done by Dr. Gerald W. Lattin.[5] Working with hotel students at Cornell he found that the

successful students tended to place high values on power, control of others, society life, and personal recognition. Unsuccessful students tended to value comfort and the intellectual life. Successful students scored higher than average in computational and persuasive interests. They scored lower than average in scientific, mechanical, and social service interests and about average in musical, clerical, artistic and literary interests.

Statler Hotels (now part of Hilton Hotels) did research in the selection of room clerks. These psychological tests were used: the Kuder Preference Record; the Wonderlic Personnel Test; and the O'Rourke Clerical Test. They found that their best room clerks scored high in computational, persuasive, social service, and clerical interests. In the Wonderlic Personnel Test a cutting score of twenty-five was used, i.e., one was employed if one scores less than twenty-five on the test.

Consideration was given to the applicant's work experience and to his educational background. The most successful room clerks had about two years of college and have taken mostly liberal arts subjects.

3. **The Lee-Thorpe Occupational Interest Inventory** (California Test Bureau)
   The advantage of this test lies in its length (requires approximately thirty minutes to administer) and in the ease with which it can be taken (understandable by junior high school students). It measures six broad fields of interest. The Lee-Thorpe lacks the general acceptance and research data of the Strong and Kuder tests.

"Honesty Tests"

Lie detector tests have not found wide application in the hotel and restaurant field. Studies of the results of introducing honesty tests for use with bank and department store employees show a general tendency of employees towards petty pilfering and a marked reduction in stealing after taking the honesty tests. It has been found that persons making complete confessions usually prove better risks than do unexamined and untried persons. Hotels and restaurants with inordinate linen, food, or silver losses might well try an honesty test. TGI Fridays, a chain of high-volume restaurants, ask all employees to take a lie detector test.

---

5. Gerald W. Lattin, "Factors Associated with Success in Hotel Administration," Doctoral Dissertation, Cornell University, 1949.

The honesty test is usually a combination of several physiological measures—blood pressure, pulse rate, breathing, and the resistance of the skin (due to presence or absence of perspiration) to electric current. If handled by a well-trained person, the honesty test (or lie detector test) can indicate within a margin of error whether or not the subject taking the test is responding honestly to the questions.

The administration of honesty tests should be made only with the consent of the majority of employees. If employees feel they are not trusted by management, this feeling may be more costly than the costs of pilfering. If the personnel see that management is asking their cooperation to detect certain individuals who are harming the reputation of all employees, the detector test should accomplish its purpose.

Measures of Job Performance

Test validation is not possible unless a measure of performance is available. Job-performance measures are difficult to attain, but they can be extremely useful, particularly if research and experience demonstrate behavioral or test score differences between individuals who fall into different performance categories, such as high-rated or low-rated, promoted or not promoted, long-term employee or short-term employee.

The following variables can be used as possible measures of job performance in trying to come up with test criteria or other criteria to use in evaluation of prospective candidates.

1. *Dismissals and releases.* In test validation, there should be a difference in test scores of those fired compared with those maintaining their jobs.

2. *Transfer and relocation.* Can differences be detected between those employees who will accept or not accept transfer? What type of employee seeks out a transfer?

3. *Wage and salary increases.* Theoretically there should be measurable differences between employees who have had their salaries raised versus those who do not receive raises.

4. *Promotions.* This is potentially a very good criterion in which comparisons are made between those promoted and those not promoted.

5. *Production.* These are hard to obtain in the hotel and restaurant fields because of the diversity of requirements in each position. Anything that can be measured directly, however, is a potentially valuable criterion measure; for example, number of

pies baked per hour, customers served, trays washed, telephone calls handled.

6. *Turnover or tenure.* What are the characteristics that differentiate long-term from short-term employees?

7. *Ratings and performance evaluation.* How do supervisors rate employees? Care must be taken to eliminate any bias in ratings and to get supervisors to give accurate ratings of their feelings.

8. *Job knowledge.* Many predictive tests are based on the premise that those potentially successful in a given field should have a better understanding and knowledge of that field than people not involved in that field.

9. *Waste.* Some individuals can cost a company much money because of their sloppy or wasteful habits. Can systematic relationships be found between certain factors and the amount of waste?

How to Evaluate the Usefulness of a Test

Theory

1. A test never gives you concrete information but only probability; i.e., chances are two to one, three to two, three to one, etc., that a person will turn out as the test predicts.

2. To be of use, all that can be required of a test is that it increases one's ability to predict outcome over that of using chance alone. (If a test allows us to state that a worker has a two to one chance of being successful, this is a great improvement over just taking a fifty-fifty chance on that person.)

Technique

There are certain required steps and conditions that must be met in evaluating a test.

1. A group on which to try out the test—this should contain at least twenty people and the people should function on comparable jobs (treat management and worker groups separately).

2. Test scores—record all of the scores.

3. Ratings—have the supervisor who knows the workers best rate all of them in terms of their overall work performance, e.g., good, fair, poor (it is best to have the same person rate all workers; in addition, if several raters are in agreement as to the rating of each worker, the validity of the rating is increased).

4. Table or chart results—make a table to determine whether the test correlates with the ratings of supervisors. If it does, then you have a useful test.

5. Once you have established the test as useful and you know what kind of scores to expect, you are ready to use the test on new applicants.

6. Plan to reevaluate the test as soon as you have hired enough new applicants who have worked long enough to be rated (usually about a year).

Examples of How to Chart Results

1. In Restaurant X it was discovered that one of the most important abilities for success as a kitchen helper and server was the ability to follow oral instructions. Each of the people currently employed was administered a test measuring this ability and sixty-four scores were accumulated, one for each worker. The tester ranked the scores from highest to lowest and divided the workers into three groups: those who scored in the highest one-third, those who scored in the lowest one-third, and those who scored in the middle one-third. Three raters working independently put each of the workers into one of three categories of performance: low, average, or high. Once ratings were made, the raters got together and resolved their points of departure so that they were able to come up with an agreed-upon rating for each worker. The results were charted as follows:

| Test Score Results | Proficiency Rating | | |
	Low	Average	High
Upper ⅓	18%	33%	50%
Middle ⅓	29%	36%	28%
Lowest ⅓	53%	33%	22%
Number of Workers	17	39	18

In the chart it can be seen that 50 percent of the workers who scored high on the test were rated as the highest employees, but that only 18 percent of the workers who scored high were rated as poor employees. On the other hand, 53 percent of the workers who scored low were rated low, and only 22 percent were rated high. On the basis of the results shown by the chart, this test would be very useful in the selection of food-service workers. If all future applicants were required to score higher than the lowest one-third of workers on the test, then over 50 percent of the worst employees would be eliminated with very little loss of good employees.

2. All 191 workers below a management level in an organization were given a test of numerical reasoning and were rated as to whether they were acceptable or nonacceptable employees. On the basis of their test scores, they were assigned to one of four groups. The results are charted below.

Test Score Results	Number of Workers	Percent Rated Nonacceptable
26-up	19	6
18-25	49	14
10-17	60	36
2- 9	63	73

On the basis of the numerical reasoning test, it can be seen that if all prospective applicants were required to have a score of ten or higher, over half of the unsuitable candidates would be eliminated.

3. In the *mean difference method,* the test scores of workers are recorded in one of two groups. Group A consists of those workers performing at a level considered below the midpoint when compared with other workers. Group B consists of those workers rated above the midpoint. The test is a measure that is administered at the time of hiring. Analysis consists of recording separate group test scores and calculating means (arithmetic averages).

Group A: those below average in job performance
Group B: those above average in job performance

Group A		Group B	
Person	*Test Score*	*Person*	*Test Score*
A6	5	A7	9
B7	6	A5	7
A3	5	B2	8
A2	4	A1	9
B1	5	B5	6
B6	3	B3	11
B4	3	A4	8

$$\Sigma X = 31 \qquad\qquad \Sigma X = 58$$

$$\text{Mean}_L = \frac{\Sigma X}{N} = 4.43 \qquad \text{Mean}_H = \frac{\Sigma X}{N} = 8.29$$

Group B has the highest mean score on the test; therefore, high test scores tend to be associated with high performance ratings.

The examples given are but three of the ways that tests can be evaluated against ratings. Until you do such evaluations, however, you never really know how good the tests you use are. Many times after you have done an evaluation you will find that the test is even a poorer predictor than just chance alone! Once you are willing to spend time and energy evaluating tests, you will find that they are a worthwhile aid to selection.

The more research-oriented readers will be concerned with conducting more statistically refined validation studies in which validity coefficients will be computed between test scores and a criterion of performance. A question frequently asked is, "How high should a validity coefficient be in order to be acceptable?" The answer to this question is variable. Tests with relatively low validity coefficients may be useful. As a general rule of thumb, it is important to do both validation studies as well as the less formal expectancy table research described in the foregoing examples. Only then is it possible for the researcher to make a relative judgment concerning the usefulness of the test.

For those interested in the statistical tools needed in working psychological tests, see the Appendix in this book.

TESTING AND FAIR EMPLOYMENT PRACTICES

In recent years selection testing has come under much scrutiny and some attack from the government—minority groups, and unions claiming discrimination in testing. The discrimination is alleged to be of two kinds. One source is from the user who sets unrealistic standards or who uses tests not relevant to the job. The other source is in the tests themselves. It is argued that tests are inherently discriminatory to anyone who has not had the full advantage of a free exposure to American culture. In a landmark case against the Motorola Corporation, it was determined that the intellectual measures used in hiring were inherently discriminatory.

The Equal Employment Opportunity Commission (EEOC) and the Office of Federal Contract Compliance (OFCC) have issued rulings on employee testing and other selection procedures. The regulations are designed "to insure that examining, testing, and other employment practices are not affected by discrimination on the basis of race, color, religion, sex, national origin, partisan political affiliation, or other nonmerit factors."[6]

Because some discrimination in tests can be found does not mean that tests should be abolished. In fact, soundly constructed and well-validated tests are likely to be our best assurance *against* discrimination in hiring. Employers have always and will continue to use some form of selection process, sometimes no more than a first impression feeling during an initial interview. Valid selection tests reduce the number of errors made in selection due to ineffective testing or interview procedures. The company is saved time and expense, the unfit worker is spared the turmoil of trying to fit a job beyond his capabilities, and the qualified worker is not unfairly displaced.

The key to nondiscriminatory testing lies in (1) selecting tests that are known to be well constructed and valid and (2) conducting validation studies. Tests from established publishers, such as those listed in this chapter, generally meet the criterion of being well-constructed, researched, valid, and reliable. It is important to recognize, however, that no matter how valid a test may be in one situation, it may or may not be valid in another situation. Test users *must always* determine how useful the test is in their own particular situation. Those test users who develop local norms on their employees and who validate the usefulness of their tests are not likely to engage in nor to be guilty of discriminatory practices.

In order to validate the use of a test, a person does not need to be a trained statistician or personnel specialist. The section of this chapter, "How to Evaluate the Usefulness of a Test," is designed to show simple, effective, step-by-step methods of validating a test.

When large groups of candidates are tested, the scores of minority or deprived groups may be lower than the scores of other groups. When this occurs, it does not mean that one group is inferior to the other, only that the test is more difficult for one group. The recommended procedure is to collect *different* norms for each group. A minority group member is not compared with people in general but only with other minority group members. The same procedures for validation described above are still required.

Actually, the concerns raised about testing by various groups are basically good in the sense that companies are being forced to proceed with validation procedures—something that is essential regardless of circumstance.

---

6. Department of Labor, Title 41, Public Contracts and Property Management, Part 60–3. "Employee Testing and Other Selection Procedures," Code of Federal Regulations (36 FR 7532).

Guidelines to Use in Minimizing Possibility of Bias in Testing

1. Maintain detailed job descriptions on each job for which testing is used.

2. Allow for retesting when requested by the applicant. It is a good idea to select tests with alternate forms.

3. Assure objectivity in the administration and scoring of tests.

4. Establish local validation and norms for every test used. This is an essential procedure that will more than pay for itself in eliminating potentially ineffective workers.

5. Establish separate norms for minority groups by sex. Once norms have been established, they can always be combined at a later time.

6. Whenever possible, have tests or programs developed by professional consultants.

7. Be able to show that intentional discrimination has not existed by keeping all data on individuals who applied and were hired.

The Induction Process

The induction process can be considered a part of the selection process. If the hotel, restaurant, or club is large enough to support a personnel department, the personnel manager or interviewer can be assigned the formal responsibility for inducting the new employee. The purpose of a formal induction is to relieve anxieties, answer questions, and make the newcomer feel welcome. Any new employee from dishwasher to manager needs some reassurance in the first days on the job. Details about hours of work, benefits, and the nature of the job may have been covered in a general way during the employment interview. Once hired, the person needs to know a number of details about the hotel or restaurant, details that may be overlooked: where is the lavatory, where is the employees' cafeteria, what should be done in case of illness, how are the time cards handled?

To insure that some part of the induction process is not overlooked, some companies draw up a brief checklist as a guide for the personnel department. Such a checklist follows.

Induction Checklist

1. Explain the philosophy of the company.

2. Explain the pay rate and various deductions. Use a dummy paycheck that includes the deductions.

3. Explain hours of work and the necessity for calling in as soon as possible in case of illness or emergencies.

4. Explain the various benefits: health insurance, life insurance, hospitalization plan, dental plan.

5. Describe rest and lunch periods and how meals are paid or accounted for.

6. Explain the importance of checking in and out and penalties for falsification of work time.

7. Explain the use of uniforms, towels, and other working gear, and the importance of conserving their use.

8. Explain the policy of eating on the job.

9. Introduce the new employee to the supervisor and see to it that the supervisor introduces the employee to other workers. Make it very clear who is the boss.

10. Discuss transportation possibilities to and from work; help with car pool if necessary.

11. Ask if employee has any questions.

12. Invite the employee to come back to the personnel office the next day for a few minutes if there are any questions.

13. Visit the employee on the job sometime during the first day.

14. Visit the employee on the job sometime the next week.

As stated elsewhere, the first few days on the job are critical. In the hotel and restaurant business it has been found that if the employee stays through the first week the odds of the individual's remaining go up markedly. If the employee remains as long as three months the odds of the person's becoming a valued and permanent employee rise again. By spending time on induction and follow-up on the employee's progress, much turnover can be avoided and morale increased.

Checklist for Employees

Using a different approach, another way to help insure that the new employee has gotten the information needed for the job is to provide a checklist of information important to every new employee. At the end of the first week of employment an interview is scheduled with the new employee. The interviewer can be the supervisor, someone from the personnel office, or some other designated person who goes over the checklist to see that the new employee has the information needed to feel a part of the organization and to be able to do the job effectively. The checklist, of course, does not take the place of on-the-job or other types of training.

Checklist for First Week Interview

For your guidance, please check the items on which you would like more information when we talk about you and your job.

Signed _____

My Job

_____ Schedule of Hours—Lunch and Rest Periods
_____ Work Assignment
_____ Supervisor
_____ Departmental Organization
_____ Wages
_____ Automatic Increases
_____ Pay Day
_____ Deductions (Paycheck)
_____ Time Card
_____ Overtime
_____ Union Membership
_____ Transfers
_____ Probationary Period
_____ Other: _____
_____

Company Benefits

_____ Vacation Policy
_____ Sick Leave Policy
_____ Leaves of Absence
_____ Holidays
_____ Insurance Plan
_____ Effective Date
_____ Insurance Office Location
_____ Retirement Plan
_____ Where Meals Are Taken
_____ Publications
_____ Other: _____
_____
_____
_____

Company Programs

_____ Safety
_____ Department Committeeman
_____ Educational Refund Plan
_____ Eligibility
_____ Training Department Location
_____ Suggestion System
_____ Location of Suggestion Form Boxes
_____ Performance Review
_____ Purpose
_____ My Participation
_____ Scholarship Program
_____ Other: _____
_____

Company Rules and Regulations

_____ Smoking
_____ What Areas
_____ Identification Cards and Badges
_____ Reporting Absence
_____ Whom to Call
_____ Use of Telephones
_____ Change of Address
_____ Whom to Notify
_____ Security Regulations
_____ Parking
_____ Other: _____
_____
_____

General House Policies

Some managers are reluctant to tell employees what they can and cannot do, believing that doing so smacks of authoritarianism. By doing so, however, many problems can be averted. A short handout sheet, mimeographed or printed, can be drawn up in the form of "general house policies."

Such policies should include a statement covering the dressing and grooming standards expected. Some restaurants even describe the way an employee should dress going to and coming from the restaurant or hotel.

SUMMARY

Selection is an ongoing process generally consisting of recruiting, interviewing, testing, and induction. Guidelines are presented for each step in the selection process, but the most effective manager evaluates and compares the various techniques and tools available. In addition to describing various selection procedures, the chapter provides research techniques for evaluating a recruitment program, the effectiveness of different interviewers, and the usefulness of tests.

An important source of selection information is the application form. In addition to being a time saver, it can be used as a permanent personnel record and its information used in conducting research. Sample application forms are included.

Interviewing is a highly important and specialized skill that should not be taken lightly. Good interviewers can be trained. More important than the techniques used, attitudes must be *genuine*. Before one gets to be a good interviewer one needs to clarify personal attitudes toward self, others, and the work itself. Interviewers must allow their techniques to be evaluated by others and constantly try to improve personal skills through such divisions as role playing. Once a person has skill and experience, different techniques of interviewing can be mastered.

A highly effective technique of interviewing is the patterned interview, in which the interviewer systematically seeks out information concerning the candidate's work, education, health, family, and social adjustment. A multiple interview technique has been successful in some organizations in which the candidate is brought back for several interviews.

Interviewers cannot operate in the dark. The more information they glean from job-analysis studies and from research on the effectiveness of various workers, the more effective they will be in their efforts. In assessing for management positions, an interviewer needs to systematically seek answers to the questions: (1) What abilities does the candidate possess? (2) What are the candidate's wants, needs, and goals? (3) How are the person's wants achieved?

Intelligence tests, aptitude tests, and achievement tests (i.e., maximum-performance tests) have been used successfully in industry for over fifty years. Subjective tests, such as those measuring personality and attitudes, are too vague and too subjective to be effective except under research conditions.

A number of useful, well-researched tests may be ordered from test publishers. No test should ever be used indiscriminately. Test users must understand the conditions under which a test is practical, the need for tests to be administered and scored under standard conditions, and that the norms used must be relevant to the individuals being considered. Once a test is selected for use, it must be validated for the new population group on which it is being used. A simple validation procedure is offered.

In recent years employment testing has come under scrutiny from the government. Minority groups and unions claim discrimination in testing. Although discrimination is possible, the fact remains that soundly constructed and well-validated tests are likely to be our best assurance *against* discrimination in hiring. The key to nondiscriminatory testing for an employer lies in (a) selecting tests that are well-constructed and valid and (b) conducting validation studies.

Once a person is hired the formal induction process helps to relieve anxieties, answer questions, and make the newcomer feel welcome. Checklists of items worthy of discussion and clarification are included.

References

Buros, O. K. *Mental Measurements Yearbook.* 7th ed. Highland Park, N. J.: Gryphon Press, 1972.

Cronbach, L. J. *Essentials of Psychological Testing.* 3d ed. New York: Harper and Row, 1970.

Kirkpatrick, J.; Ewen, R.; Barrett, R.; and Katzell, R. *Testing and Fair Employment.* New York: New York University Press, 1968.

Training

In the early development of the hotel and restaurant business in this country there was little need of formal techniques for training employees. The early American tavern was usually operated by the owner assisted by family and perhaps a few servants or apprentices. The proprietor learned innkeeping from his father or through a long period of informal apprenticeship. The host's wife cooked, the children and an occasional servant or apprentice were instructed by the host and his wife in housekeeping, food preparation, and service.

The late nineteenth century brought many changes. The introduction of new equipment, machinery, and an interest in scientific nutrition and sanitation made formal training a necessity. Large units employing tens and, in a few cases, hundreds of employees created many problems, among them the need for job training. Tavern keeping changed to hotel and restaurant operations.

Until the restriction of immigration from Europe went into effect in the 1920s, the training problem was not severe. Europeans trained in the trade since childhood were eager to come to America and take jobs as chambermaids and kitchen employees. Many skilled artisans, chefs, and journeymen sought jobs in America. Immigration laws, however, practically cut off this source of supply and left hotel and restaurant operators little choice but to train new employees.

The full effect of the immigration restriction was not immediately felt. During the thirties skilled and intelligent workers from other trades were forced by the depression to seek work in hotels and restaurants. With World War II, however, the training problem became acute. The biggest boom the hotel and restaurant business had ever experienced found it faced with a need to expand while losing experienced personnel to the armed services or to high paying war jobs. The need for employees was tremendous. Almost anyone was hired, as the saying went, "who was warm and had a pulse." Needless to say, inefficiency was great. Some of the larger hotels had to employ

as many as a third more employees than previously to do the same amount of work. The hotel and restaurant business became training conscious.

The situation, of course, was not unique to the hotel and restaurant business. The federal government appropriated $100 million to expand and speed up training in industry generally. A training-within-industry service was established to set up and administer a vast job-training program. It did a remarkable service. Out of the experiences of this program have developed valuable training techniques described in this chapter.

Particularly in the sixties, the larger companies such as Marriott, ARA, Inter-Continental Hotels Corporation, and the hundreds of public sector food-service operations employed training specialists and in some cases established training departments. A few state restaurant associations arranged for waitress training and food sanitation training, and government health departments, city and county, have in some places offered food sanitation (food handling) courses since the 1930s. Much of the effort of the larger companies went into management development, readying personnel for supervisory and management positions. In the United Kingdom industrial training boards were established, funded by taxing all hotel and catering establishments. Those establishments that did not take advantage of the training simply subsidized training for their competitors.

In the United States much of the federal government's efforts in training have been to subsidize training of disadvantaged persons by contracting with hotels and restaurants. In effect, the federal government has encouraged the employment of unskilled persons and has subsidized their living expenses while learning and at the same time paid employers for their training efforts.

Training has become such an important part of chain operations that numerous training departments have been established and "Council of Hotel and Restaurant Trainers," CHART, was formed in 1971. By 1977 it had seventy-five members. The organization is intended to provide a forum for the exchange of ideas and for the professional advancement of its members.

CHARACTERISTICS OF HOTELS AND RESTAURANTS THAT INCREASE IMPORTANCE OF TRAINING

A large majority of jobs in hotels, restaurants, and hospitals deal directly or indirectly with the public. A flaw in a piece of machinery or poor workmanship in a pair of shoes is not nearly so noticeable to the consumer as a piece of hair in the guest's soup or a dirty sheet on his bed. The hotel and restaurant business hinges on a face-to-face relationship with patrons. A mistake, or inefficiency of one employee, may lose a customer forever.

Waiters, hosts, room clerks, and telephone operators deal directly with the public. Their work is under the constant scrutiny of the guests. They are inspected not by one supervisor, but by all of the public they serve. It is imperative that they know precisely what to do and how to do it. A hotel cannot afford to have an untrained telephone operator or room clerk. A club cannot afford to have a disinterested receptionist.

Characteristic of a large number of hotel and restaurant employees, especially in recent years, is their tendency to float from one job to another, to have a relatively meager educational background, and to be somewhat emotionally unstable. This is not true of employees in many well-run establishments where careful selection and management prevail, but generally among hotel and restaurant employees there is a high turnover caused in part by those characteristics. This is especially true of unskilled jobs such as dish machine operator, pot and pan worker, kitchen helpers, and cooks. The jobs of waiters and waiter's helpers have a high turnover. A large percentage of wait personnel consider the job pass-through an interesting, fun job for a few months or a few years. In the approximately five thousand resort hotels in this country only a fraction of the employees can be expected to return after a year. These facts indicate strongly that a great deal of training is necessary to produce the desired level of job performance.

Many hotel and restaurant employees lack any real motivation for their work other than economic necessity. About 48 percent of the 1.6 million employees in the lodging industry are women. About 48 percent of the 3.4 million employees in restaurants are women. About 30 percent of restaurant employees are teenagers. Only a small percentage look forward to making hotel or restaurant work a career.

Detailed instruction is necessary. A Florida State sanitarian tells this incident, which illustrates the point. A manager of a well-run restaurant was showing the state sanitary inspector and the county sanitarian his new and expensive dishwashing equipment. The equipment fairly gleamed; the water temperature of the rinse was the approved 170° to 180° and the demonstration was a success—except for one thing. The machine operator, caught in the rush period, was stacking cups in the dish racks three deep. The bottom spray of the dish machine washed the insides of the bottom layer of cups, and the top spray washed the outside of the top layer of cups. The insides of the top two layers of cups, of course, were left uncleaned. The operator solved this by toweling the sugar out of these cups by hand.

Another and similar incident serves to show why it cannot be taken for granted that the employee knows even the basic elements of a job. A fine restaurant with all new equipment was inspected by a government sanitarian. Despite two booster heaters that raised the dishwashing water to 190° at the hot water storage tank, the temperature at the dish machine was 153°, seventeen degrees less than the approved 170° to 180°. Dishwashing with 153° water had been going on for several months, with apparent satisfaction on the part of the management and the dish machine operators. No one, it seemed, had even noticed the temperature gauge on the machine, even though the 170° mark was signaled with a red arrow. The reason for the low temperature was a 250-foot run of uninsulated piping between the hot water storage tank and the dish machine.

The average semiskilled hotel or restaurant employee is not eager for any instruction resembling the usual classroom situation. The usual employee is interested only in training that has a real, immediate objective. Theory and abstraction have little place in employee training. It is almost impossible to create interest without an immediate objective. The employee must be continually reminded of how the training will solve problems, increase security, make the individual a more valuable employee.

Most useful hotel and restaurant training will involve teaching new skills that are immediately applicable. For supervisors, the skills may be how to give orders, how to reprimand, how to put over a new idea. For employees, the skill may be that of cutting steaks, making a bed, operating a PBX, or preparing a crêpe Suzette.

Table 6.1	Departmental Pattern for a Full-Service Hotel Including Representative Jobs	
Department		**Percent of Work Force**
1. Administration— Management and Control Hotel Manager Controller Front Office Manager Director of Sales Bookkeeping—Machine— Operator		3.7
2. Front Office—Desk and Telephone Front Office Cashier Room Clerk Telephone Operator		10.3
3. Service—Porter, Bellperson, Room Service Bellperson Doorperson Head Porter House Officer		19.3
4. Housekeeping Lodging Quarters Cleaner / Section Housekeeper Housekeeper Houseperson Linen-Room Person		26.8
5. Restaurant Dining Room—17.4% Waiter's Assistant Host Waiter Kitchen—16.7% Cook Dishwasher Kitchen Helper		34.1
6. Maintenance and Equipment Operation, Including Heating Equipment Carpenter Electrician Fireman Painter Plumber		5.8

MOST HOTEL AND RESTAURANT JOBS REQUIRE ON-THE-JOB TRAINING

A Department of Labor study showed that nearly all women in hotel occupations were thirty-five years of age or older. Almost half of the women were forty-five or over.

Men also were a somewhat older group, considerably more than half being thirty-five years or older. Workers who enter an occupation at an older age usually are less motivated in learning the job than those who have selected a trade while young. More training is needed for the older group.

According to the late Fred Eckert, hotel consultant, 62 percent of the total payroll of a hotel is unskilled manual labor and semiskilled service labor, who must be trained in the hotel and instructed on the job. Of this percentage, two-thirds are unskilled workers: lodging quarters cleaners, waiters, waiter's assistants, dishwashers, housepersons, porters, cleaners, yardpersons, firefighters. The other third are the front office clerks, cashiers, bellpersons, elevator operators, telephone operators, food and bar checkers, storekeepers, security persons, and junior supervisory department heads.

Table 6.1 provides a typical departmental breakdown taken from a United States Employment Service report. The chart shows clearly that, except for a small percentage of administrative and maintenance jobs, the bulk of hotel jobs are of a service or semiskilled nature for which there is little training available outside the hotel.

Classroom instruction is rare except in a few companies that have systematic training programs for management trainees.

Realistically, final responsibility must rest with the supervisor, not with a traveling trainer or someone from the personnel department. It is the supervisor who rewards and punishes the employee, who benefits or is handicapped by training, or the lack of it. Since most hotel and restaurant jobs are of a semiskilled nature, they can and should be learned on the job. Management training and training for chefs and bakers is something else again, requiring several months even when presented systematically.

Advantages of Training to the Enterprise

A few of the gains that accrue as a result of training employees are:

Increased Learning Rate

The learner does not have to proceed by trial and error. One's rate of learning increases under instruction and one is brought to efficient performance sooner. Through an effective training program the new employee becomes adapted to the work situation faster. Emotional tensions are reduced by helping the learner to avoid mistakes.

Interest shown by the instructor acts as a stimulus to learning. The learner reaches full production more quickly.

Increased Quality of Performance

Because of being taught the correct way to do a job the learner avoids learning incorrect ways. Teaching implies imparting the best methods found through the experience of a number of persons. Only the best ways are taught.

Decreased Breakage and Spoilage

Most jobs involve some breakage or spoilage, be it the job of cleaner, dishwasher, or fish butcher. An untrained and inexperienced worker can cost the operation much money. A study of New York State industries showed that training reduced spoilage by 73 percent. Training can be insurance against breakage and spoilage. Wise management pays for insurance.

Reduced Number of Accidents

In some studies in industry it has been found that accidents among untrained persons are almost three times those among trained persons. This is true particularly among employees working around dangerous machinery. In addition to the fact that untrained employees do not know how to manipulate the equipment, the nervous strain brought on by not knowing is an important cause of accidents. It would be folly to put an inexperienced worker in charge of air conditioning maintenance or to hand over the job of oysterperson to an untrained worker. Hazards in a hotel and restaurant are of a different type than those in a general factory. Every job in a hotel or restaurant has hazards of some kind.

Reduced Labor Turnover

Studies in industry have sometimes shown labor turnover among trained employees to be one-half as great as that among untrained employees. Some of the reasons for making the employee more stable will be discussed later.

Reduced Absenteeism

A survey conducted during World War II among sixty-three New York State plants showed a 38 percent reduction in absenteeism among pretrained workers. An employee who does not know what is supposed to be done is more apt to find a reason to stay at home rather than appear for work.

Increased Production

The most obvious reason for training is increased production. The trained waiter can handle several more tables than the untrained one. The trained cleaner can do fifteen rooms instead of ten. The skilled painter can paint twice as many rooms as the unskilled one. Much training cannot be measured directly but is reflected in guest satisfaction. Training given the bellperson is not measurable in increased production but its effects are readily discernible in the tone of the house. Similarly, it is virtually impossible to credit the presence of a gracious host as the reason for a certain number of regular patrons, but the person's importance to the business is obvious.

The productivity of any organization depends on teamwork, morale, management direction, capitalization, equipment, and some other factors. Boiled down into a simplified formula, productivity equals competence times motivation: $P = CM$. P can stand for performance, proficiency, productivity, knowledge, and profit. Competence implies knowledge, education, and particularly training.

Advantages of Training to the Employee

Trained employees are not only more valuable to the enterprise, but are worth more to themselves. What are some incentives that can be used to motivate the trainee to learn?

Increased Earning Power

The new employee may be trained to produce efficiently sooner. The old employee may learn more effective ways of doing his work. Increased earnings should result in both cases.

Prepares for Advancement

Training enables employees to learn their own jobs well and begin to learn the next job above. If employees have the ability, training can prepare them for supervisory positions.

Enhances Self-respect, Increases Feeling of Security and Economic Independence

Trained workers meet one of the ideals of our American culture. Relatively free to make their own decisions, they can feel pride in their work, and have a relative sense of security. Each one is a freer individual. The electrician has a trade that may be contributed to the success of a business. A skilled cook is the backbone of a good restaurant. Training makes workers self-respecting, self-reliant, participating employees.

The Triad of Training

Training can be thought of as dealing with three levels of change in the human organism: conceptual, human relations, and technical skills. Conceptual skills are those dealing with ideas and concepts, the kind ordinarily thought of as being taught in colleges and universities. All concepts are abstractions. Some, such as mathematical symbols, seem more distantly related to human behavior than others such as ideas of justice, peace, and harmony. The human relations skills—being able to control and influence feelings (ours and others)—have always been important to the guest-employee relationship and in the tension-ridden atmosphere of a busy hotel or restaurant. Technical skills are those having to do with the performance of the repetitive aspects of a job: typing, accounting, and making reservations are examples.

As a person moves from being a worker to a supervisor the human skills assume more and more importance. In management the conceptual skills of planning, decision making, and other forms of abstract reasoning assume greater importance.

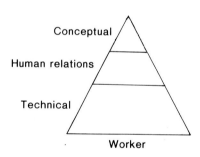

Conceptual
Human relations
Technical

Worker

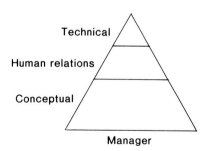

Technical
Human relations
Conceptual

Manager

SOME LEARNING PRINCIPLES

Learning usually involves perception, thinking, and motivation. The instructor is concerned with all three. Some of the basic principles of learning are presented as an introduction to the training process.

Individual Differences in Learning Ability

Obviously some persons learn a great deal faster and retain what they learn longer than others. Even in college classes where one would suppose that students are fairly well matched regarding learning ability, large individual differences are found. It is not unusual for some students to learn twice as quickly as others. Since this is true in the college population, the great differences that show up in the general population can be surmised.

Psychologists have found that fast and slow learning ability, and all degrees in between, are distributed among people according to pattern. This pattern, when plotted in the form of a curve, is known as the *normal distribution curve*. If we could measure by a standard intelligence test the learning ability of 1,000 persons who represent a sampling of the general population, we would find that they could be plotted on the normal distribution curve. About 500 would have average learning ability, about 150 would be above average, and another 100 would learn much more rapidly and could solve much more difficult problems than the average person. Similarly we would find about 150 who were slower than average in learning and could not solve as difficult problems. Another 100 could be classified as feeble-minded and some of these would be found to be institutionalized. The curve would look similar to the one in figure 6.1.

Aptitude for Skill

Likewise, results of tests of finger dexterity, personality characteristics, and mechanical aptitudes would show wide individual differences. Some learners are endowed with aptitudes and capacities for learning certain skills and types of knowledge quickly. Others have less aptitude and a few can never be taught.

The Prospective Learner Must Have Incentives for Learning

Unless trainees are shown how training will be of benefit to them, they are likely to have little interest in learning. Creating interest is the mark of a good teacher. Some spend one-half of the total teaching time in arousing interest, the other half in giving the subject matter. The desire to learn is brought about by a number of motivating factors: the learner's entire past experience, the way the learner looks at life, values and personal adjustment, general health. These factors determine the meaning the learning situation has for the trainee. The trainee by virtue

Figure 6.1   Learning Ability

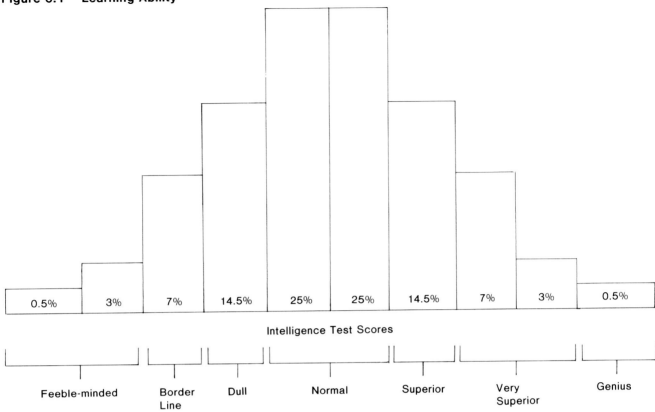

Intelligence Test Scores

| 0.5% | 3% | 7% | 14.5% | 25% | 25% | 14.5% | 7% | 3% | 0.5% |

Feeble-minded   Border   Dull   Normal   Superior   Very   Genius
                     Line   Superior

of being alive has a desire to act. How one will act toward the learning situation will depend partly on whether the instructor can make the trainee receptive to learning and create a desire to learn.

To make a person work cheerfully and effectively one must connect with these internal directive powers. This means that the teacher, supervisor, or personnel director must be familiar with the energizing drives or forces that cause people to do the things they do. People tend to repeat and learn those things that are accompanied by a satisfying state of affairs and tend not to repeat or learn those activities that are accompanied by an annoying situation.

The social motives consist of the urge to secure those things that might build up one's ego or self-respect, such as winning in competition, receiving praise, the feeling of accomplishment, avoiding censure, obtaining security, or being respected and understood by the teacher. Learning involves the whole person, one's need for social participation and social approval. Take account of the person as well as the material or skill to be taught. In our society the physiological needs such as the urge for food, sleep, shelter, etc., are taken care of as a matter of course when jobs are available.

Thought should be given to incentives that arouse these energizing influences. Money awards appeal to most people but have their limitations and are not always available. Security, at times a powerful incentive, is relatively less important in our present setup. The improvement of status, however, when judiciously employed by a respected supervisor, or the opportunity for advancement on the basis of merit, or even personal recognition, are incentives that pay big dividends not only in learning situations but in all human relations.

Should the Rate of Learning Be Uniform?

Having a good approximation of the trainee's general intelligence or special aptitudes needed for the learning task aids the instructor in predicting the learning time that will be required. A general knowledge of how learning takes place also aids in predicting learning time. Learning motor skills such as those involved in dishwashing, salad making, or pastry cooking usually follows a general pattern regardless of the particular trainee. Knowing this pattern will help the instructor to anticipate learning rate

Figure 6.2   Learning Time

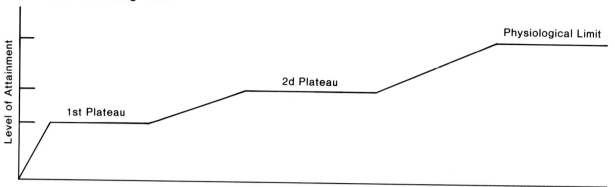

and keep both the instructor and the trainee from becoming discouraged at certain times.

In the first stages of practice of a motor skill, learning proceeds rather rapidly, followed by slower learning in the later steps. The fast learning is due to the acquisition of a few simple patterns, many of which are similar to or the same as patterns learned previously. Also there is a minimum of the boredom and fatigue that often characterize later stages.

In many jobs learning will show no increase for periods of time. The learner will have reached a "plateau," and neither the instructor nor the trainee should be unduly concerned. Some plateaus serve to integrate earlier acquisitions. Others may be due to lapses of attention, fatigue, waning effects of incentives, and contentment with the present level of attainment.

Figure 6.2 is a hypothetical learning curve of learning a new motor skill.

In this case the learner experiences two plateaus during which time the person is unable to perform better. Finally the learner reaches the point at which higher attainment cannot be reached—the physiological limit.

Other types of learning, such as changing attitudes, memorizing, and organizing abstract materials, also proceed by patterns. The instructor will not find uniform learning ability among individuals or a uniform rate of learning within an individual, nor should either be expected.

Distributed Practice Is More Efficient than Continuous Practice

In teaching a new skill, the subject matter of sanitation, or almost any type of material, the employee will learn more efficiently if the instruction is spaced through several periods rather than presented all at once. In teaching sanitation, for example, the employee learns faster per given length of time and remembers the material better if the lectures are spread out so as to be given in several periods of less than an hour each. An entire afternoon or morning in a training session is usually inefficient. It is characteristic of most learning situations that interest is difficult to sustain for any length of time. In some types of training, such as that of teaching an employee to operate a machine, it is sometimes most efficient to space the training in periods as short as ten or fifteen minutes, once per day. Whether this should be done depends upon the learner's motivation and past experience with the skill to be learned, or with similar skills, and upon the complexity of the skill to be learned.

Evaluating the Employee's Progress Aids Learning

Learning proceeds more quickly when the employee is provided with a standard for indicating specifically what progress is being made. In teaching by the lecture method, periodic examinations are valuable in pointing out the learner's mistakes and in stimulating interest. In teaching motor skills, approval should be given whenever any part of the skill has been mastered and the learner should be again shown just how to continue so as to master the other parts. When the trainee is given a precise achievement goal toward which to work, learning is facilitated.

Step Up the Goal Gradually

Set up goals that the learner can reach quickly. In training a salad maker, for example, set the number of salads for the first day within the grasp of the new employee. Implying that Mary the new salad person should be as expert as Tom the old employee only discourages Mary. As the new employee learns, step up the goal gradually until standard production is reached. A new cleaner may do well to clean ten rooms a day the first week on the job. The next week the new person might be encouraged to do twelve a day and by the third week the standard of sixteen a day. Setting the goals too high means that the goal is no longer a goal for the employee. A goal is a goal only as long as the employee thinks it is.

Absolute Standards

Heavy industry, when beset by slipshod work practices and faulty inspection practices, began to emphasize the necessity of setting absolute standards sometimes called *no fault* or *no error standards.* This concept can be easily applied to the hotel and restaurant business, especially insofar as sanitation practices are concerned. In other words the learner is told from the outset that there are certain absolute standards that cannot be abrogated or changed in any way. If "absolute standards" are introduced immediately and driven home with repetition and encouragement, the employee is more likely to believe and act as if there are no lesser standards. Such standards do not mean that a learner cannot show a gradual increase in the number of units produced. Insisting that there is an absolute standard of so many covers to be produced, so many salads, or so many breakfast rolls would be a mistake. On the other hand, insisting that not one fly, not one cockroach, not any kind of litter on the floor will be tolerated, is a standard that can be established immediately—a first and easy step towards higher goals.

Every fine kitchen supervisor insists that each plate that leaves the kitchen looks perfect; the rim of the plate is wiped completely clean, asparagus placed in the right spot, potatoes placed attractively, the sauce barely masking the meat, and so on. Set the standard early and adhere to it. Allow no deviations; and everyone concerned becomes programmed to believe there is no other standard. The waiter is not permitted on the floor if his shirt is not absolutely clean and pressed, his hair trimmed to the standard desired by the restaurant, shoes shined, and body deodorant used. The waitress is never permitted a run in the stocking, long fingernails, rundown heels, or unkempt hair.

The desk clerk is never allowed to lean on the desk; never, never, never.

The reservationist must always say "good morning," or whatever is appropriate for the time of the day; always, always, always.

No one allows the phone to ring more than two times if one is anywhere within the vicinity of the phone.

The garbage pail is always washed after use.

The floor of refrigeration spaces are always clean.

Use of Cues in Training

The Industrial Training Board for the Hotel and Catering Industry of the United Kingdom has sponsored considerable research into training and the development of various training materials. One result of this research has been to identify visual and other cues that act as stimuli to a worker to initiate or otherwise change behavior while performing a task. Cues enter the nervous system via any of the sensory modalities—touch, hearing, kinesthesis, sight, sound, pressure, and others. The skilled individual has undertaken to mold self-behavior into precisely patterned forms that give the person extraordinary control over a limited set of conditions—the task at hand. The cook learns "how it feels" to beat an egg effectively, recognize when peas are done by pressing one of them, knows that steak has reached a certain stage of doneness by pressing it with a fork.

The skilled individual has learned to react to various cues which, when the learning has proceeded to the level of a true skill, recedes into unawareness. The skilled person performs a program, a series of connected responses each triggered by a cue or a previous response. An individual may not be aware of the cues to which he/she is reacting. To speed training a trainer should be well aware of those cues that are important in performing a skill and point them out to the learner. For example, in beating an omelet the kinesthetic cue is the "feel" of the mixture as it is getting thicker reflected by the amount of pressure exerted by the muscles to maintain beating. Visual cues are the bubbles that break to the surface and the manner in which the mixture drips from a whip.

Related tasks are strung together to form a job. Cleaning a room is a series of tasks, such as replacing a pillow case, spreading sheets, mitering sheet corners, washing the toilet, vacuuming the floor, and so on. The job can be thought of as a repertoire of subskills. The subskills are linked together into larger and larger units of behavior. Eventually a complete hierarchical plan for the performance of a job is developed. Studies show that under stressful conditions the complete skill breaks down in a way opposite to the way in which it was built up. The control over the larger units of behavior disintegrate and the performer concentrates on carrying out the suboperations, which normally he/she would not think about.[1]

To illustrate the cue concept, look at the task breakdown for cooking fresh peas as seen in figure 6.3. Under the column "Cues to Support Decision Making," it is seen that visual cues are the color of the peas and the presence of any insects.

---

1. *Research into Training for Skills in the Hotel and Catering Industry,* 2d Progress Report (London: Ealing Technical College, April 1968).

Figure 6.3

Operations	Decisions	Cues To Support Decision Making	Cooking Time	Standard
1. Shell peas	Quantity	Check production requirements		Bright green in colour and nicely seasoned, the cooked peas should be crisp to the bite. The addition of butter, the ratio of salt and sugar used is at the discretion of employer.
2. Inspect	Reject substandard	Black/discolored or peas with (weevils) or grub holes; powdering can often be seen		
3. Wash	How	Running water in colander		
4. Prepare pan, season water		Water must be boiling		
5. Cook peas	Method	Add peas to pan, bring back to boil quickly. Control temperature till boiling steadily. Lid off pan. Water must cover peas.	15–20 mins.	
6. Remove when cooked	When	Test sample for taste and "bite."		
7. Drain using colander	How long	No water present.		
8. Finish and serve	According to requirements			

Courtesy of the Industrial Training Board for Hotel and Catering Industry, United Kingdom.

Another visual cue is seen when the water reaches the boiling state, at which point the peas are added to the water.

Another cue is the depth of the water in the pan. The final test for doneness is the "bite" test: the cook bites into a pea for taste and to measure the resistance of the pea to the pressure exerted by his teeth on the pea.

Identification of Sensory Cues

One way to recognize the importance of cue identification in the training process is to analyze a simple skill and pinpoint the operational cues important for carrying out the skill. The chart in figure 6.4 is set up to identify cues in the five sensory modalities—smell, vision, kinesthetic, touch, and taste. Time also could be a cue. For example, in griddling a hamburger the cook has a pretty good idea how long a half-inch hamburger takes to cook. Other cues would involve the juices turning brown, the meat itself turning from red to brown, the discontinuance of the flow of juices from the interior of the meat, and the resistance of the meat to the pressure of the spatula.

Front-office skills would include learning to respond to verbal cues such as: "Do you have a room for the evening?" "What is the room rate?" "Will you take a personal check?"

A good room clerk also reacts to a number of less obvious cues, such as tone of voice and posture of the registering guest.

The waiter must learn to react to almost imperceptible cue behavior on the part of the patron. After studying a menu, a guest may lay it down on the table indicating a readiness for ordering. Raised eyebrows may indicate a desire to communicate verbally. A frown while eating an entree may suggest that something is wrong with the food, at least in the patron's mind.

It is suggested that the reader perform cue analysis by charting the performance of a simple skill such as frying eggs, making a white sauce, or deep frying potatoes.

Training against a Standard

Some skills are judged against a running performance standard, others against an end result. Handling an irate guest is a running performance against a standard of mollifying, satisfying, or pleasing the guest. Production of a cake is against a standard of cake that has a certain height, crumb, appearance, and taste. Grilling a hamburger involves time and the reaction to various cues—temperature, color, and resistance to pressure. The following diagram illustrates the process:

Grill Hamburger
Standard Product

Cue (Griddle Temperature)	**Cue** (Color of Meat)	**Cue** (Resistance to Pressure)
	Time	

Figure 6.4   Chart for Recording Sensory Cues Associated with Operations

Symbol	Mode	Task

Symbol	Mode		
△	—Smell		Subject
⬡	—Vision		
△	—Touch	Observer	
▢	—Kinesthetic		
D	—Taste		Date

Level	Mode	Nature of the Cue.	Notes
Operation			
1.			
2.			
3.			
4.			
5.			
6.			
7.			
8.			

Courtesy of the Industrial Training Board for Hotel and Catering Industry, United Kingdom.

Figure 6.5   Fruit Salad Making

Operation	Steps	Key Points

1. Preparing the lettuce.	1. Make lettuce cups of head lettuce.
	  a. Make single cups out of large curly leaves.
	  b. Make single cups out of small curly leaves combined together.
	  c. Lay aside outer flat leaves for shredding.
		Be sure head lettuce is clean, crisp, and not deteriorated. Be sure to shake off excess water.
		Cups should curl up around fruit and not lie too flat on plate.

2. Arranging fruit in lettuce cup.	1. Place heavy, firm fruit in lettuce cup to make the foundation. 2. Place less firm and smaller fruits on top of heavy fruits. 3. Place more colorful and decorative fruits on top of salad.	Keep a light touch and an artistic sense. Decide where fruit goes and put it there. Make every motion count. Remember, the basic appeal of the salad is freshness, crispness, good flavor, and beauty of arrangement. Finished salad weights: Plate _____ Salad order _____ . Half (or junior) order _____ .
3. Marinating the salad.	1. Stir French dressing thoroughly each time you serve from it. 2. Dip out dressing and drip it over the fruit.	Use short, quick motions to blend completely the oil and seasonings. Do this only after the salad is ordered, because on standing, dressing wilts the lettuce and draws juice out of fruits. Use enough dressing to season each piece of fruit but not so much that it will run off onto lettuce cup or plate.
4. Serving Salad.	1. Serve at once to the customer or put it in the refrigerator.	Seconds in a hot kitchen affect the crispness and freshness.

Standards must be determined but this can be a participative decision involving employees and in one way or another the consumer. Chili made in Texas may call for a large amount of chili pepper, less if served in New England. Steak broiled in Texas usually calls for the well-done stage; in New York City, many customers want a rare steak. Some companies now include a color photograph of the end product as part of the recipe card. The photo provides cues at least as regards arrangement and color.

Standards of cleanliness vary. Nothing is clean to the point of sterility. How often should blankets be washed? How often should bedspreads be changed or dry cleaned? How often should mattresses be turned? Unless these standards are incorporated into the training program, they are likely to be overlooked.

PREPARATION FOR INSTRUCTION

Preparation for instructing takes a much longer time than the actual instruction. For a particular job each step must be laid out in sequence. A sample job breakdown, taken from a government publication, *Establishing and Operating a Restaurant,* is shown (fig. 6.5) for the task of Fruit Salad Making.

In preparing job breakdowns, department heads should be asked to participate. The results should be kept in loose-leaf form and be thought of as subject to change or modification. By placing emphasis on the desirability of preparing careful job breakdowns, emphasis is at the same time placed on training and training techniques.

A guide for preparing the job breakdowns appears in *A Manual for Training Hospital Employees* drawn up by the Cleveland Hospital Council. Sections covering housekeeping, laundry, and dietary are applicable to hotels and restaurants. Figure 6.6 is a sample job breakdown taken from the manual.

Figure 6.6   Wet Mopping Floors

Equipment:
2 Pails
2 Wringers
2 Mops
1 Hair push brush or
1 Dust Mop
Dust cloth
Supplies

Important Steps	Key Points
Assemble equipment.	_____ Listed above.
Sweep floor with hair brush or dust mop.	_____ To remove surface soil.
Prepare cleaning solution and rinse water.	_____ According to type of floor.
Dip mop into cleaning solution.	
Operate mop over convenient area of floor.	_____ Around floor adjoining wall—into corners first.
	Use continuous overlapping figure eight movement.
	Avoid splashing baseboard and furniture.
Return mop to cleaning solution.	
Wring mop dry—return to floor.	_____ To pick up excess moisture.
Rinse dry.	_____ Use clean mop partially wrung from clean water.
Return mop to rinse water.	
Wring mop dry—return to floor.	_____ Absorb all moisture.
Repeat mopping and rinsing of areas adjoining.	_____ Overlap areas until entire surface is cleaned.
	Do not touch walls.
	Mop toward door.
Use damp cloth, wipe baseboards, and pick up surplus moisture left in corners by mop.	
Clean and replace equipment.	

JOB INSTRUCTIONS

Job instructions are detailed lists of duties to be performed and a description of how they are to be performed. At best they are dull and dry and when turned over to an employee for his own study are not too effective as training materials. As with so many training aids, the manner of use is as important as, or more important than, the material itself.

Pope's Cafeterias, headquartered in St. Louis, have broken down all of the jobs found in their establishment and have made detailed job instructions that are handed to the new employee and for which the employee signs. Tests are given to the employee a few days later covering the information on the job instruction folders.

A valuable aspect of job instruction is that it is the result of someone in management being forced to sit down and list everything to be done on a job. Even though the new employee may not learn much by reading the instructions, the sheet is valuable in that it can be a reference for the supervisor as a list of points to cover in training.

Many visual aid materials are available at reasonable prices. Job instruction sheets constitute a minimal effort in formalizing and systematizing training. If mimeographing the sheet is too much of an effort, type a few copies and cover them in plastic, to be used whenever a new employee is hired.

Included as a part of job instructions can be such information as standard portion sizes to be used. The information following was developed by the management of a roadside restaurant to be handed to new fry cooks as a part of job instructions.

Portion Sizes as Part of Job Instructions

Portions

1. Cooked French Fries
   a. Sandwiches   2 oz.
   b. Dinners   3 oz.
   c. Side orders   5 oz.

2. Cooked Hash Browns
   a. Dinners   4 oz.
   b. Sides   4 oz.
   c. Breakfasts   2 oz.

3. Chef's Salad
   a. Line 8″ bowl with leaf lettuce, fill bowl with chopped salad; cut 1 slice of cold ham in strips and 1 slice of cheese, wedge ½ tomato and one tomato and one boiled egg

4. Stuffed Tomato Salad
   a. Line plate with leaf lettuce
   b. Shredded lettuce
   c. One tomato cut as prescribed
   d. Fill tomato with 4 oz. tuna salad
   e. One lemon wedge
   f. Top with mayonnaise and cherry
   g. Pickle

5. Cottage Cheese and Peach Salad
   a. Line plate with leaf lettuce
   b. Shredded lettuce
   c. Three #20 scoops cottage cheese
   d. Two peach halves—cut each in three wedges
   e. Arrange in cottage cheese in prescribed manner
   f. Top with mayonnaise and cherry

6. Cottage Cheese and Pineapple Salad
   a. Same as Cottage Cheese and Peach Salad
   b. Use two pineapple rings

The El Torito chain, part of the W.R. Grace Company, has developed detailed job instructions, one of which is seen below. It is an excellent example of how job instructions can provide the framework for job knowledge.

Procedure for Cocktail Waitress*

. . . The one area that sets us apart from any other restaurant is our cocktail lounge. Our major competitors, even the more expensive steak and prime rib restaurants, do not even pour as fine a quality house liquor as we do. We pour a double shot of Chivas Regal, Jack Daniels, Beefeater, and Smirnoff brands. Thousands of dollars could be saved by just changing the brand to one slightly cheaper, but this has never been tried. Unfortunately since our restaurant chain has become so large, most of our customers are not familiar with our reputation and do not know the scotch they are drinking is Chivas Regal.

It is the responsibility of the cocktail waitress to inform our customers. She can do so by saying when a man orders a scotch, "We pour Chivas, will that be all right?" When she is placing several drinks on the table, she may recite them back saying, "Beefeater martini, Smirnoff Screwdriver and a Daniels on the rocks." Psychologically the drinks will taste better, the customer will feel he is getting a bargain and he will be more likely to do the rest of his evening's drinking with us instead of moving to the next bar. Our bar business depends on service and a quality drink, not on entertainment and dancing.

Cocktail waitresses carry a lot of responsibility:

1. When taking a drink order, your friendly attitude is very important. Always remember to smile and greet the customer before asking them if you may bring them a cocktail.

2. Know exactly what the customer wants, i.e., if a man wants a martini, find out if he wants vodka or gin, up or on the rocks, with an olive or a twist. If a customer orders a Margarita, sell him a large one.

3. Know the brands of the liquor in our bar. Don't waste the customer's time checking with the bartender. (This includes wines).

4. Make the mention of our bar brands an unbreakable habit.

5. Place the cocktail napkins on the table with the logo facing the customer. Napkins should be changed freely; whenever they are soiled, and always when a new drink is served.

6. Be completely prepared before you approach the bar to give your order. Don't spend a bartender's time unnecessarily. If the red line system is used, there will be no conversation at the bar at all.

7. Watch the bartender as he pours so you will not have to ask him what each drink is.

8. Check your drinks for proper garnishes (they are an essential part of the recipe), straws, and stir sticks.

9. No drink may leave the bar without a ring on a bar check. Wait for it to be rung and take it with you.

10. When serving your drinks, know where each drink belongs. You should never have to ask.

11. Common decency and the health laws forbid you to touch the rim of the glass. This includes empty ones.

12. *You must show the bar check to the customer when you are stating the amount of the tab.*
    a. If the guest is paying with cash, verbally recite the amount of tender, i.e., "out of ten dollars."
    b. If a guest is paying with a credit card (we accept Visa, American Express, and Master Charge) ask if they would like to run a tab or close out the account immediately.

---

*Quoted from an instruction sheet for cocktail waitresses. Courtesy of a highly successful restaurant chain.

When handling credit cards you must remember certain things:

1) Make sure the card is in the machine when running off the draft. Also, don't forget to remove the card.

2) Print card on back of bar ticket.

3) Check expiration date, circle, and initial.

4) Check to make sure the number is not in the cancellation bulletin.

5) If the amount is $50.00 or over, take it to the manager. He will call the credit card company for a guarantee number.

6) When charge voucher is presented to customer, present bar ticket also.

7) Make sure the customer signs the voucher and totals it. If he has not totalled it, you must put the total in before handing him his copy. The signature must match the signature on the card. Wives may not use husband's card unless their signature appears on the card. If a guest insists upon transferring a tab to his dinner check, you may say that you prefer to clear the tab in the cocktail lounge. If he persists you must immediately comply by taking his tab to the dining room.

13. When all your tables have been serviced, stay in your station, not at the bar.

14. The time to check back is when the first customer's glass is getting low. Don't embarrass the fast drinker by making him call you. Be available at all times without actually intruding.

15. Never allow dirty ashtrays to remain on the table. Change them by capping them with a clean ashtray, remove from table, and put the clean ashtray back down. This prevents drinks from being ruined by flying ashes.

16. When guests are having several rounds make a point to remember their order. You will be intruding if you have to ask repeatedly.

17. During cocktail hour and after serving hors d'oeuvres, clean away empty plates and dirty napkins immediately.

18. Know what food items can be served in the bar area and recommend them to your customers. When serving these items don't forget napkins and utensils.

19. It is against the law to serve or allow alcoholic beverages to be consumed by a minor. Failure to comply with this law may result in the restaurant losing its liquor license and the waitress and/or bartender being arrested or fined.

The Company Policy on checking ID's is as follows:

a. The person must be checked if appearing to be 25 years old or under, regardless of how offended parents or other older adults become.

b. Never serve a drink to a person that is not present at the table.

c. Valid ID consists of:

1) A current valid driver's license.

2) A state-issued current nondriver's identification card.

3) Valid passport.

4) A current military I.D., birth certificates, temporary drivers license, college cards, and work I.D. cards are not acceptable. Out of State drivers licenses that have no photographs should be referred to the Manager.

d. When in doubt about the identification, check with the Manager.

e. Don't allow a minor to drink from someone else's glass.

f. You are responsible for the drinks at your table even if they were purchased from another cocktail waitress or from the bar.

g. Never worry about offending a person by asking for their ID. Generally speaking, a person is only offended if they don't have proper ID.

20. When removing a glass from the table, ask the customer "May I take this drink?" "Are you finished with this drink?" The customer may feel that his drink is still good when it may appear to be only ice.

21. When clearing a table after customers leave, notice whether the chairs and sofas should be brushed off.

22. Anytime you're busy and cannot wait on a table, acknowledge the customers with "I'll be right with you."

23. Use a tray whenever delivering or picking up empty glasses.

24. When not busy, keep an eye on the appearance of the lounge. Fluff pillows, put matches out, straighten bar stools.

25. Have all house promotions okayed by Manager.

Opening Procedure

1. Wipe down tables and check chairs for crumbs. Dust other furniture.

2. Light candles and supply ashtrays and matches.

3. Supply back-up cabinet with cocktail napkins, straws, stir sticks, matches, and extra candle refills.

4. Check lighting and listen for music.

5. Sign out for bar and bar food checks.

6. Have bank ready to go with the proper amount of change.

7. Make sure the side station is stocked with chips, salsa, bowls, saucers, baskets, napkins, and forks.

8. Change date in the charge machine and fill supply of vouchers.

9. Make sure your cocktail and tip trays are clean.

Closing Procedure

1. Wipe down each table thoroughly.

2. Take ashtrays to the dishroom.

3. Blow out all candles and turn off fireplaces.

4. Help bartender with glass drying if necessary.

5. Run a tape on your checks. You must have 2 identical tapes. Pay the bartender the total and put checks in numerical order. Sign checks in and check off the used checks on the security guest check sheet.

6. Punch out and give time card to the manager before changing to go home.

Training is made much more effective if done systematically, by the numbers if you will—programmed, planned, systematized, step step step. It may appear "Mickey Mouse" to list everything that has to be learned on a job but some details are likely to be overlooked if such lists are not developed and kept updated. Illustrative of the detail encompassed in a management-training program is the list (fig. 6.7) developed by the management of the Grinder Restaurants, a coffee shop chain in Southern California. Item after item is listed, but more than that—the trainer must check off each bit of learning as it is accomplished by a trainee. The list is an indication

Figure 6.7

Name: _____

Mgmt. Training			
	Your Initial	Authorized by	Date
II. Misc. Mgmt. Preparation Locations of breakers, on-off-how, roof vaps, motors, pumps, filters, etc.			
Store security measures, emergency and home phone numbers			
How to count readings and prepare $100.00 drawer			
How to count safe and when, etc.			
Cash short and over-steps to take, forms to fill out, etc.			
When to count drawers, each reading, etc.			
Accepting checks, cashing checks, safe loans, etc.			
Store keys authorized for emp. to use or keep			
Employee phone #'s and availabilities			
Store diary—purpose, use of, etc.			
Guest checks—daily control, distribution, procedures, etc.			
Accidents—procedures, where to send injured, etc.			
In case of a hold-up			
In case of fire (hood and portable ext., etc.) automatic gas shut-off			
Thermostat settings, vents open, balance of air			
Sidework manual—how to assign, check, use, etc.			
Thawing procedures—amt's, when, who, etc.			
Back-up list—when, who, etc.			
Meat, pork, produce, poultry—weights, quality, yield, etc.			
Deliveries—how to accept, what to check, etc.			
Equipment breakdown—steps to take			
Manager's hourly routine—purpose, explained, etc.			

Figure 6.7—*Continued*

	Your Initial	Authorized by	Date
File cabinet—explanation of files, filing procedures, etc.			
Problem employees—handling, steps toward correcting			
Mgmt. and store evaluations			
Mgmt.—proper dress			
Wait. stations—how to make out, change, why, etc.			
All posted bulletins—purpose, explained, etc.			
Times necessary for a mgr. to be on floor			
Guest complaints—how to handle, etc.			
Hostess and mgr.—who seats, who takes cash, why?			
Salesmen, charities—what to do, why, etc.			
Cig. machine refunds, how, etc.			
86 ing items—authorized items, why, to prevent, etc.			
Water softener, water heater—where, etc.			
Cash register—date, year, numbering, hand crank, tape, etc.			
Loitering of employees, how to handle			

Mail this form to main office after obtaining authorized signature below

Supervisor: _____ Date: _____

Figure 6.8 Cooks Training Program

Name: _____

Cooking Equipment and Related Facilities Properly Cleaned.

	Authorized By	Date
1. Microwave	_____	_____
2. Cutting boards	_____	_____
3. Toaster	_____	_____
4. Hot drawer	_____	_____
5. Reach-ins	_____	_____
6. Bread shelves	_____	_____
7. Back-up area	_____	_____
8. Steam table	_____	_____
9. Broaster	_____	_____
10. Heat lamp and inserts under	_____	_____
11. Deep fryers	_____	_____
12. S.S. trash and grease cans	_____	_____
13. Grills and gutters	_____	_____
14. Refrigerated drawers	_____	_____
15. Cold table	_____	_____
16. Broiler	_____	_____
17. Salamander	_____	_____
18. Oven	_____	_____
19. Open burner	_____	_____
20. Hood, s.s. wall	_____	_____
21. Slicer	_____	_____
22. Sm. freezers	_____	_____

of the detail involved in management training for a relatively simple restaurant operation, a coffee shop. Nothing is left to chance. The trainee must be shown where the breaker switches are and go over the rooftop evaporators for the compressors, locate the motors, the pumps, and the filters.

After every task or learning segment has been completed, the trainer lists those areas in which the trainee is weak and the steps that should be repeated. Store unit managers are selected as trainers for their ability and interest in training.

The list of items shown in figure 6.7 are only about one-third of the total with which the trainee must become familiar in the Grinder Restaurants.

The cook's training program has a similar set of details to be learned, one part of which is to become familiar with the twenty-two pieces of equipment as in figure 6.8.

Nothing is left to chance. Employees are rated after each performance. The host and hostess report, for example, lists these factors as being important for the work habits:

—Station cleanliness during shift
—Shift-ending condition
—Proper greeting
—Proper seating
—Rotation of seating
—Properly takes cash
—Properly takes care of "to go" items
—Smiling, courteous, polite
—Teamwork—manager and waitpersons
—Organization during shift
—Strengths and weaknesses

INSTRUCTING THE EMPLOYEES ON THE JOB

Who Instructs?

There have been many discussions as to who should train employees. Should it be the manager or an assistant? Should it be the department heads or a special training officer? Should the training be given by one of the highly skilled employees already on a particular job, and, if so, should that individual receive extra compensation for teaching?

Like it or not, the supervisor—the person who is in day-to-day contact with the employee—must take the major responsibility for training, whether it be formal or informal. Characteristically, in hotels and restaurants, training is informal, haphazard, and unsystematic. Charitably, it could be called coaching, with the employee thrown into the job, under fire almost from the moment hired. The supervisor then gives pointers, corrects, and demands, until the employee performs to the supervisor's standards.

Chain organizations usually have traveling chefs, salad makers, bakers, and dining room hosts and hostesses who move from unit to unit, acting as trainers. They are most often used in opening a new restaurant or hotel, frequently acting as line supervisors until the new operation has shaken down.

Figure 6.9

Job Instruction

When to Instruct

New crews needed
A new employee
Corrective measures
Upgrading

Prepare to Instruct

1. Know the job yourself—quality, quantity, and method.
2. Break down the job—steps in order, key points; safety factors (how and why?).
3. Set a schedule—(accuracy and speed), date or hour to be ready.
4. Arrange work station—tools, equipment, materials, and supplies.
5. Get everything ready—as the worker is expected to keep it.
6. Approach to the learner—friendly, helpful, patient attitude. The learner wants to learn.

How to Instruct

1. Prepare the learner—Put the person at ease (Break the ice). State the job and find out what the individual knows about it. Explain purpose and importance of job to get the person's interest. Place in proper position.
2. Demonstrate the operation—Show, tell, illustrate each move. One step at a time. Stress key points, safety factors. Slowly and patiently. No more than the person can get at one time. Repeat the demonstration.
3. Application or try out—Have the person do the job. Watch for and correct errors. Compliment and encourage. Have the person repeat operations, explaining steps and key points. Question person during procedure. Repeat job until both you and the person are sure.
4. Follow-up (supervise)—Put person on self-help regimen, but advise where help can be gotten. Check frequently, encourage person, invite questions. Taper off coaching as individual progresses.

The learner can perform if the instructor has taught.

Who Actually Does the Training?

Few restaurants or hotels have specialized trainers. Rather, experienced employees or supervisors who enjoy and are good at training are invited to perform that function as a part of on-the-job training. Waiters or waitresses who are effective trainers may be paid up to fifty dollars a week extra for training a new person, and also receive all the tips generated by the trainee during that training period. In other establishments, lead employees act as trainers without additional compensation.

Conditions for Effective Training

1. The trainees must want to change. They must feel a need for training. If this need is not there, the problem is to discover why it is not there and how it might be put there.
2. The program must be geared to the needs and problems of the trainee.
3. The trainees must seek out the answers and conclusions. People learn by *experience* and *involvement.*
4. Human relations training is more effective if conducted in groups. Research shows that group decisions are more effective in modifying behavior than are individual approaches.
5. A training program can provide trainees with opportunities to let off steam. Human relations involves feelings and emotions. Typically, behavior changes only after an emotional experience in which a person may feel quite angry or frustrated, or quite fearful, in the process.
6. It is important not to strip trainees of their old modes of operation and defense. Let the training add to but not take away from. As trainees feel more comfortable with new roles, they can be expected to change their old patterns more permanently.
7. Training should lead to *usable* skills; platitudes about loyalty, incisiveness, and so on are less meaningful.

The Four-step Job Instruction Method

The Training Within Industry program of World War II developed an abbreviated formula (fig. 6.9) for instructing. It has been adapted for training in hotels and restaurants.

Other Methods of Training

Orientation Lectures and Tours

In larger organizations, such as Disney World, a systematic orientation program is instituted of which lectures, movies, and tours are a part. Some hotel and restaurant chains have orientation films that show the new employee the scope of the organization, its varied activities, and something of the part the employee will play in the organization. Such films, when done well, are an excellent means of getting the employee off to a good start. A few hotels and restaurants have set up a lecture and tour program. Building tours can be conducted, and something of the architecture of the building and a simple description of department organization can be mentioned. After the tour there was an opportunity for discussion and comments. A smaller organization could combine similar orientation procedures with periodic employee meetings.

Sponsor Training

The new employee is usually confused and ill at ease. An effective way to make that individual feel a part of the organization is to provide a period of orientation during which personal support is given the new person in making adjustment to the enterprise. This is successfully accomplished by providing a sponsor. The sponsor shows the new person where the rest rooms, eating places, lounges, and locker rooms are located. The sponsor also introduces the new person to associates, thereby serving as an entree to the *esprit de corps* of the organization. Persons especially suited for serving as sponsors may be so designated and given a small merit increase in wages. Sponsors may also be able to act as instructors.

The Stouffer Company makes good use of sponsor training by asking an experienced waitress/waiter to help the new one along. After preliminary training in table setup, the new waiter/waitress is given a few tables to handle. The new person gains confidence in the job by assurance from the neighbor-sponsor waiter/waitress. Induction is gradual and more satisfying.

Role-playing and Skits

A teaching method that combines fun with learning is dramatization. Three or four waiters/waitresses may put on a skit showing their way of serving a guest. The others may criticize. Sometimes the wrong way and the right way can be dramatized. An instructing chef can show how not to cut a roast, followed by the right way. The housekeeper can demonstrate the wrong way and the right way to change a bed. Humor can be used and is an effective means of driving home a point.

Dramatizing is also a good means of changing undesirable attitudes. Having various employees play the roles of others can often give them insight into their own and others' problems. Having waiters/waitresses play customers or dishwashers, and vice versa, will often strengthen cooperation and clear up hidden feelings of resentment.

Problem Situation Training

Another training technique is to provide problem situations, either at formal training session meetings or in the form of booklets for personnel. The National Restaurant Association has produced a number of training aids. One of these, produced by In-Sink-Erator in cooperation with the NRA, poses problem situations and asks the employee to make a judgment about the appropriate way to handle each problem.[2]

As an illustration of this kind of training, four problem situations are taken from the NRA booklet:

1. It's dinner hour. The lights are dimmed for candlelight dining. Unnoticed by the other waitresses or his parents, a child at a table adjoining your station spills ice cream on the highly polished center aisle.

   You:
   A. Quickly place a chair or other obstacle over the food to prevent someone from slipping on it.

   B. Return to the kitchen immediately and have the proper busperson handle it.

   C. It isn't your station, but when you have the opportunity, call to the waitress or busperson responsible and say there's been an accident.

   D. Stand guard by the spillage to caution customers and co-workers, while you send word of the accident to the kitchen or nearest busperson, and someone comes to properly clean the aisle.

   Answer to Situation 1:
   Safety and sanitation are the two foremost considerations of all food service establishments, and in this instance the safety of customers and co-workers is threatened. Thus, immediate attention is required. You cannot wait until you return to the kitchen or ignore the spilled ice cream. On the other hand, it would be inconsiderate to the parents for you to call the attention of everyone in hearing distance to the fact that the child has spilled food. Placing a chair or other obstacle over the slippery area may not be the most desirable action, as the chair might be moved or someone could stumble against it. However, since this may be the only logical course open due to press of duties, give yourself 10 points for either (A) or (D).

   Did you choose the right answer?

---

2. *Hospitality and you . . . A Guide to Customer Service,* In-Sink-Erator in cooperation with National Restaurant Association, Chicago, Ill., 1971.

Chef/Instructor Walter Schreyer instructs a student in the art of cocoa painting, while another student puts the finishing touches on a wedding cake.

Chef/Instructor Bruno Ellmer supervises the platting of a variety of Middle-Eastern delicacies that the students in the International Kitchen have prepared.

A chef/instructor conducts a class in one of the demonstration kitchens at the Culinary Institute where students can observe a full menu being prepared.

Demonstrating blending techniques in sauce making, a Health Care Division food service director instructs his cooks.

A chef demonstrates garnishes in the Buffet Catering kitchens of the Culinary Institute.

New franchise holders attend classes at "Hamburger University" to learn the daily details of operating a **McDonald's restaurant**.

Alumni Hall, formerly a Jesuit chapel, is the site of many gala events at The Culinary Institute of America. The flags represent the major wine producing countries of the world.

2. One of your regular customers has ordered the "Bigger Burger" without looking at the menu, as he knows what he wants. However, when you present the check, he says, "I believe you've overcharged me 10 cents." The price has only recently been raised, and you point out the new one on the menu. By this time he is embarrassed and slightly angry.

You say:

A. "I'm terribly sorry, sir, I only work here. Our manager sets all the prices."

B. "I'm sorry that you didn't know about our price change. It's really my fault for not calling it to your attention."

C. "I'm very sorry you weren't told about the price change. But we will let you have it at the old price this time as a special favor."

D. "Let me call the manager. Perhaps the manager will give it to you at the old price since you've been a fine customer of ours."

Answer to Situation 2:

Menu price increases can present difficulties, particularly with regular customers. And there is little really you can do to prevent a situation such as this, because to mention the increase when a person is ordering may bring an "I can afford it" retort. You must then answer the customer in a manner that will neither antagonize nor place the person in an awkward position. You cannot alter the check, as pricing is a function of management only; neither can you ask the manager to give this customer a special price, as this would embarrass both the customer and manager. We feel that the best solution is to place the blame on yourself (B) for not calling the new price to the customer's attention. By shouldering this burden, you will probably win the admiration of the customer.

Did you choose the right answer?

3. Mrs. Rose is a daily customer at your restaurant, and is usually served by Mary, a long-time employee who handles the station nearest you. When you take her order, she requests an extra roll and pat of butter with her luncheon special. Then she is furious when you add it to

her check as a separate charge. She says she has never before been charged for this by Mary, yet you know that restaurant policy calls for an additional charge.

You say:

A. "I'm sorry, but Mary is wrong if she doesn't charge you. She knows it's called for on the menu."

B. "I didn't realize that this was Mary's policy with you, and I'll certainly take it off the check."

C. "The manager insists upon this additional charge; it's out of my hands."

D. "Perhaps Mary is acting on instructions from the management that I don't know about. I'll check with the management immediately to make sure."

Answer to Situation 3:

Here you are faced with an unpleasant situation because a fellow worker has either been making a serious error, or has seen fit to alter management policy to suit her personal desires. The problem is really twofold; how to impress upon the customer that she cannot be given preferential treatment, but doing so in a manner that will discredit Mary only as a last resort. You certainly should not follow Mary's lead, as this breaks a management policy that involves honesty. Yet there's no need to be flippant, and say the manager told you to. The best solution is (D) to offer to check with the manager on approved special arrangements. Chances are the customer knows Mary is wrong and won't want to incriminate her. Whether this is the case or if the customer is bluffing, she won't want this done, and will, hopefully, stop expecting special prices.

Did you choose the right answer?

4. This fellow's name should have been Sidney Skinflint. He comes to your restaurant for dinner at least once a week and never leaves more than a 5 percent tip. Everyone tries to avoid him, but he usually ends up sitting at your station.

You:

A. After he has finished his meal, pick up the 20¢ and stare at it long and hard right in front of Sidney.

B. During the meal, be somewhat reserved, and perhaps slightly inefficient, hoping he'll get the point.

C. Give him the same kind of service you give anyone else.

D. Just come out and tell Sidney that if you had to make a living off his miserable 20¢, you would have to apply for relief.

Answer to Situation 4:

It has been said that each of us has a cross to bear. You might have more than one, but you do have Sidney, and you must bear him. So you must treat him as you would anyone else. Answer (C) is correct.

Did you choose the right answer?

Dialogue Training

Another form of training closely related to the problem-situation technique is that called *dialogue training* as explained by Joseph W. Thompson. Verbatim transcriptions of conversations that have taken place on the job between guest and employee are used. If a conversation indicates a recurring problem of lack of knowledge or poor attitude on the part of the employee it is selected for discussion.[3]

Situations that illustrate lack of courtesy, or poor attitude or sales approach are selected. Others, illustrating lack of knowledge, should also be selected. Those selected are then placed on slides and used as springboards for discussion at employee-training meetings. The fact that problem situations presented are taken from real life add interest.

The trainer presents the situation and asks what was right, what was wrong, was the guest satisfied, what could have been done to increase sales, what should the employee have said. Dr. Thompson reports that the use of such dialogues as problem situations is effective in changing behavior to the extent that the employee comes up with the "right" answer for improving service to the guest. Samples of dialogue collected by Dr. Thompson are seen below.[4]

Training Procedure

Here is the suggested procedure for the complete training:

1. Trainer presents a brief explanation of the dialogue situation prior to presenting the dialogue and explains the viewer's role.

2. Dialogue presented on screen. Dittoed copies handed out.

3. Silent period during which trainees study the screen and their copies of the dialogue. They think about what was wrong and what should be improved—the proper way to have conducted the dialogue.

4. Trainer now proceeds to ask questions of the group such as "What was wrong?" "Do you think the employee said the correct thing?" "Was the guest satisfied?" "Could an additional sale have been made?" "Could the conversation be improved?" "How?"

5. Group members give their ideas as to how the dialogue should have been conducted. Trainer should try to involve *every* person in the discussion. If some don't speak up, the trainer should call on them and ask for their opinions.

---

3. *Recruiting and Training Employees in the Service Industries,* Extension Bulletin 44 (Michigan State University: Coop. Extension Service, July 1966).
4. *Ibid.,* pp. 9–10.

6. The trainer then presents a brief review of the dialogue and summarizes the consensus of the group as to what the best way would have been for handling the particular situation presented in the initial dialogue.

7. The above steps are repeated for each dialogue projected on the screen.

Some Results

The objective of dialogue training is to teach employees to think about typical situations they encounter on the job and about the best possible dialogue to use in each particular situation. Actually, it is the fact that dialogue training is based upon real-life customer/employee and supervisor/employee situations that makes it so interesting and enjoyable. No unrealistic material dulls the learner's interest. The employee enters into the training experience enthusiastically, sensing that the material presented is exactly what really happens. The learner's interpretation of what would have been said and done makes a lasting impression. This type of thinking strongly motivates the person to try to handle the situation correctly at the first opportunity that presents itself. Thus, dialogue training helps the person to understand a situation thoroughly, making for greater self-confidence, assurance, and capability.

Remember, though, that the immediate purpose of dialogue training is to give the guest and customer *better service*. Better and more satisfying service results in greater sales and profits.

Sample Dialogues

In order to furnish guidelines toward organizing a training program, nine sample dialogues are given. Dialogues 1 through 4 involve waitress and guest; dialogues 5 through 9 relate to reservations or room service.

1. **Knowledge of the menu.**
   Waitress: May I take your order now?
   Guest: I see you have lasagna on the menu. What is this dish anyway?
   Waitress: Well . . . ah . . . now I don't really know just what that is. . . . Let me go and ask the chef.
   Guest: Never mind, I'll take a cheeseburger and a cup of coffee.

2. **Making suggestions.**
   Guest: What do you have special out there tonight?
   Waitress: We have all kinds of good stuff.
   Guest: I notice you have chicken cacciatore on the menu. Is it good? How does it look?
   Waitress: Everything is good.
   Guest: Bring me some of that chicken cacciatore.
   Waitress: (No reply, writes notation on check and leaves table.)

3. **Increasing sales through suggestions.**
   (Guest escorts his best girl into fine restaurant for dinner. There is an attractive display of wines near their table.)
   Waitress: Are you ready to order now?
   Guest: Yes, we would like that sirloin dinner for two, medium, with the chef's salad, lima beans, and coffee.
   Waitress: Thank you. It will take a few minutes to prepare your steaks.
   Guest (to girl friend after waitress leaves): I would have ordered wine, but she didn't ask me if we wanted any and I'll be darned if I'm going to beg her to sell us a bottle.

4. **Responding to suggestions from supervisor.**
   Hostess: Mary, Mr. Hanson (the manager) would like to increase the sales of soup, and we are stressing this for the next two months. When you are taking orders, why don't you suggest a delicious cup or bowl of soup?
   Mary: That's fine. Are we going to have a special card on the menu about the soup?
   Hostess: Yes, there will be a different soup each day.
   Mary (to the first guest the following day): We're featuring garbanzo soup today, have you tried it? It's delicious.
   Guest: Never heard of it; what's it like?
   Mary: It's a Spanish soup. It has beans in meat broth and flavored with chorizo sausage.
   Guest: I'll take a chance; bring me some.

5. **Being polite, use of words (front desk).**
   Prospective guest: I'd like to register for a room.
   Desk clerk: Do you have a reservation?
   Prospective guest: No.
   Desk clerk: Then you will have to step over to the reservation desk.

6. **Being helpful and polite (front desk).**
   Prospective guest: Do you have a room?
   Desk clerk: I'm sorry but we are all booked up for today.
   Prospective guest: Well, where could I find a room?
   Desk clerk: As far as I know, every place in town is filled.

7. **Room sales technique (front desk).**
   Prospective guest: What are your rates for rooms?
   Desk clerk: Well, sir, how many are in your party?
   Prospective guest: Just the wife and myself.
   Desk clerk: That will be $25.

8. **Guest's complaint.**
   Guest (to desk clerk): That shower head in my room just doesn't work correctly.
   Desk clerk: Oh my! Did you get *that* room? I'll put it down again and see if we can't get it fixed this time.

9. **Guest courtesy.**
   (Bellman near front desk, greeting guest with considerable luggage)
   Bellman: Good afternoon, sir, may I help you with your luggage?
   Guest: Yes, that will be fine.
   Bellman: You are in 631. You take the passenger elevator to the sixth floor. I'll take the freight elevator and you meet me on the sixth floor.

Figure 6.10   Examples of Comment Cards

the MCL real cafeterias
- the Sherman
  sherman drive & 38th
- the Ripple
  2121 east 62nd st.
- the Arlington
  arlington & 10th

Do we meet your high standards and respected requirements?

Your suggestions are appreciated. Do you have any ideas to help prevent our human errors and omissions?

Please indicate with check (✓) marks and drop in suggestion box near the door.

Service	Food
☐ Excellent	☐ Excellent
☐ Good	☐ Good
☐ Fair	☐ Fair
☐ Poor	☐ Poor

_____ Time of day _____ Date

Remarks and Suggestions: _____

_____

_____

Signature and Address: (Optional)

_____

_____

Thanks and please come in again, soon!

the MCL real cafeterias

Room _____

Because . . . we want to be perfect in your eyes, please tell us how we rate with you.

	Excellent	Average	Not satisfactory— comment
Rooms			
Room Clerk			
Garage			
Doorperson			
Concierge			
Bellperson			
Room Service			
Phone Service			
Valet—Laundry Service			
Lodging Cleaner Service			
Gourmet Room			
Pink Kitchen			
Cloakroom			
Swimming Pool			

Comment Cards

Perhaps the simplest yet one of the most effective devices for gaining the continuous training interest of employees in the effect they make on customers is the comment card (see fig. 6.10). The cards are placed on each table and in each guest room in the hope the guest reacts to the service by completing the card.

In the case of a restaurant the completed card is handed to the manager, cashier, or dropped into a box located near the exit. The hotel guest leaves the completed form on the desk where it was found, at the front desk, or returns it by postage-paid mail.

Guest comments are read at employee meetings. Employees receiving favorable comments are praised publicly; those receiving adverse comments talked to privately.

The owner of a Miami chain of table service restaurants believes the comment cards to be the most effective personnel control device. He states that he can keep his finger on the pulse of management in each restaurant merely by reading the cards. He keeps the key to the card collection boxes and collects the cards weekly.

In a business where it is difficult to keep employees continuously concerned with service, the comment cards act as a device to exert pressure for service awareness.

Programmed Instruction

Programmed instruction is a technique of presenting material to be learned in a manner which if well done increases the amount learned and its retention. In the early 1960s the cooking process was analyzed and presented in programmed form. Since then a number of programmed training materials have appeared.[5]

Programmed instruction is designed to break complex ideas into smaller parts and take the learner through the reasoning process to develop the entire concept. It is also a way of reinforcing learning by insisting that the learner react to each piece of information as it is presented. Programmed instruction can be highly effective; it can also be very boring.

Rather than try to explain the technique, two samples of programmed instruction material are presented here.

Meat Cookery

"We can make a cook, but a roast cook must be born."

A few years ago meat cooking was indeed artistry. Thermometers were seldom used, and cooking information based on research was scarce. Although we still need much more information, we are today cooking meats more precisely and according to research-based knowledge than in the past.

1. To understand how to achieve maximum acceptability and yield in meat, we must know something about its composition and structure and what happens in the cooking process.

Muscle is composed of about 60–70% moisture by weight, the amount varies inversely with the amount of fat present. One of the problems in meat cookery is to achieve at least 140°F internal temperature in meat, an attractive brown surface, high palatability, low shrinkage, and to retain as many nutrients as possible. Some loss of moisture is inevitable through *shrinkage* caused by evaporation and denaturation. Because of denaturation, meat will shrink even though cooked completely immersed in liquid. A freeze-dried or dehydrated meat will absorb some moisture in cooking. The term for loss of weight experienced in cooking is *shrinkage*.

In cooking all but dehydrated and freeze-dried meat, some .... is inevitable. (shrinkage)

2. Meat begins to cook at about 140°F, a process in which the flavor of the meat changes. Meat proteins coagulate at from 165° to 175°F, denaturation occurring before this. Normally, then, we would think that meat cookery begins at .... °F and ends at .... °F. (140°F, 175°F)

3. In the cooking process, the protein fibers pull away from the bones and shrink when heat strikes them. Moisture is forced out, denaturation occurs, and the juices flow from the meat as meat drippings. Therefore, if meat is to be cooked, some .... (technical term) is to be expected. (shrinkage)

4. Of the solids in meat, about 80% are protein and 20% fat, although pork may have a slightly higher fat ratio to proteins. It would be expected as a part of shrinkage that in cooking some of the .... would be melted and lost from the meat. (fat)

5. Evaporation takes place when meat is browned; the color pigment, mostly myoglobin, changes to brown and the small amount of sugars present are caramelized. As the juices come to the surface, they too are evaporated. Some .... of weight by evaporation occurs in browning.[6] (loss, shrinkage)

The second example is taken from *Today's Waitress, A Self-instructional Training Program.*

Children can be a problem. They can, for example, order dishes their parents don't want them to have. A wise waitress, therefore, tactfully consults the mother when she takes a child's order.

If a child orders filet mignon the waitress should:
A. Take the order immediately.
B. Look to the mother for approval.
C. Tell the child the dish is too expensive for him.

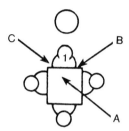

Correct answer: B. Look to the mother for approval.

Once the orders are taken and are prepared by the kitchen staff, begin serving.

Where it is convenient, serve all food from the guest's left and work clockwise. Choose the arrow indicating the side from which you would serve guest 1 the appetizer.

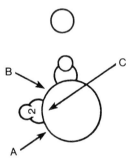

Correct answer B.

Beverages, however, are served from the guest's right. Choose the arrow indicating the side from which you would serve guest 2 a glass of milk.

5. Some of the programmed materials are Amendola and Lundberg, *Understanding Baking* (Boston: CBI Publishing, 1971).
6. *Understanding Cooking*, rev. ed. (Holyoke, Mass.: Marcus Printing Company, 1976).

Correct answer A.

Remember food is served from the _____ and beverages from the _____ .
Correct answers: Left, right.

Liquor Liability Training

Restaurant and bar operators have suddenly become much more aware of the responsibility they are charged with: refusal of service to persons who appear to be verging on drunkenness. In a few cases bars and restaurants have been sued after a customer has left the premises and become involved in an auto accident, so-called third-party liability. Restaurant operators serving alcoholic beverages are urged to institute affirmative, ongoing educational programs for training employees to be more alert as to when and how liquor service should be refused. It is the licensee's (operator's) responsibility not to sell alcoholic beverages to obviously intoxicated persons or to allow employees to encourage overconsumption. The bartender treads a fine line between good hosting and censoring, between salesperson encouraging drinking, and responsible citizen working for the public well-being. (In 1978 the California legislature relieved the situation in that state somewhat by passing a law removing the right to sue the "third party," for example, a tavern operator for liability who had served a person who later became involved in an accident.)

Courtesy Training Programs

Courtesy training is a continuous effort in the hospitality business. Some of it is done formally, but most of it informally. Hilton Hotels Corporation spends hundreds of thousands of dollars annually to stress the asset value of its staff, a staff that management says is not only courteous—but caring too. Their advertising program theme: You Make the Difference. Externally—for advertising directed towards the public—the theme is: "For Every Three Guests There Are Two Hiltons," meaning two Hilton employees for every three guests. Attitudes, according to the program, are responsible for 93 percent of innkeeping success, compared to 7 percent for knowledge and skills.

General Managers are urged to visit every department each day and to "show interest in staff members and what they are doing. Your actions will create a reaction called inspiration. . . ." Managers, the program contends, cannot demand courtesy; they must live it. In other words, the General Manager is the model of courtesy for others to follow.

A courtesy committee is suggested for each hotel, comprising the General Manager, the resident and/or Executive Assistant Manager, and the Personnel Director. Departmental meetings are held by department heads and films are shown. The program includes a question-and-answer session, role playing, and demonstrations of problem solving pertaining to guest relations. Employee participants are shown how to identify and handle guest problems; how to use a telephone effectively; how to project a Company image by exemplary personal conduct; and how effective teamwork can be achieved within each department, and among departments. Employees are sensitized to an awareness of when to initiate and when to follow to achieve maximum guest satisfaction.

Photographic messages on motivation are supplied each Hilton Hotel from headquarters, and awards are given to the Courtesy Employee of the Month at each hotel. Winners (selected by employee ballot) for each month are invited to an Awards Luncheon hosted by the General Manager. Each winner receives a special badge; a letter of appreciation is sent to the winner's home; a memento is given to the winner's spouse; and a savings bond is awarded. Each of the twelve winners is eligible for the hotel's Employee of the Year Award, the winner of which receives Hilton stock and personal letters from the President and Divisional Vice-President, plus a personal plaque. The Employee of the Year for the entire corporation gets a trip plus generous cash allowances.[7]

Transactional Analysis Training (TA)

A number of leading hotel and restaurant firms have introduced transactional analysis training on a company-wide basis. TA, as it is called, is first presented to management, then carried on to the employee level via one-, two-, and three-day sessions. Such companies as Howard Johnson's, Holiday Inns, and the Little America chain have developed films and complete TA training programs for both management and employees. The book *Front Office Human Relations* contains a detailed description of TA concepts especially applied to the front desk.[8]

7. *Lodging,* American Hotel & Motel Association, September 1977.
8. Donald E. Lundberg, *Front Office Human Relations* (San Marcos, Ca.: Nu Pak, 1979).

Security Training

Fully aware of the constant increase in robbery, thievery and other hazards to guests, hotel management is putting progressively greater emphasis on security training for personnel. Western International Hotels, for example, defines security as "the safety of our guests and their possessions, and the safety of our employees and their possessions."[9] Security is seen as the responsibility of all employees, and of guests as well. In the 1970s, security was seen as challenging Energy for the title of Number One Concern of the lodging industry. Corporate-level committees have been established to coordinate security and safety programs, as well as to make provision for a number of physical safeguards, such as double locks, night chains, and observation ports for each guest-room door. Security training is being combined with safety training—administered as a single program.

Front staff are trained to issue guest keys only upon verification by name and room number. Keys left in guest rooms and those left on the front desk are retrieved quickly to avoid their being picked up by dishonest persons.

Written procedures are provided for turning in found articles to a specific person. Anything found is tagged and logged with a description of the article, where it was found, when, and the name of the finder.

Security personnel have regular procedures for checking guest rooms to see that they are secure. Western International Hotels requires that security persons, when on regular patrol, test each door with the palm of a hand. If the door is found ajar, the personnel person goes to the house phone and calls the guest room. If there is no answer, the security person inspects the room to insure its security and records that activity in a Daily Activity Report.

Special procedures are followed by lodging quarters cleaners during the routine room-cleaning process:

If a room is occupied but the guest is out, the door is closed and a notification card placed on the knob on the corridor side of the door.

If the room is occupied with the guest in the room, the door is left open.

If the room is vacant, the door is left open while cleaning goes on.

In no case does the cleaning person use the radio or television in the room.

Policies are established to protect employees from obnoxious guests. The Western International Hotel policy is designed to avoid any kind of physical altercation between employee and guest. If the staff are threatened in any way, they are instructed to:

Refrain from being heroes.
Retreat as necessary.
Defend themselves only as a last resort.

In other areas of the hotel, threatened employees are told to:

Retreat and call security.
Avoid development of a situation.
Protect themselves only as a last resort.

FOOD SANITATION TRAINING

The United States Public Health Service (PHS) believes that about one million cases of food poisoning occur in this country annually, 30 to 40 percent of them occurring in food-service establishments, largely the result of food mishandling. The case reported below is not typical, but points up the danger:

"In 1975, 343 passengers and 1 crew member aboard a chartered commercial aircraft were served a snack of ham and omelets. Shortly before the plane landed, the crew member and 196 of the passengers were afflicted with a gastrointestinal illness characterized by diarrhea, vomiting, abdominal cramps, and nausea. Most of these persons required hospitalization. One death was later reported: that of the manager of the catering firm responsible for the food's preparation. He had committed suicide."[10]

As new information is made available about food protection, ordinances relating to food handling change. Some of the recent changes:

Frozen foods should be stored at 0°F or below.

Essentially hazardous foods requiring cooking shall be cooked to heat all parts of the food to a temperature of at least 140°F, which means that if the rule were strictly applied roasts would not be taken out of the oven when the center is less than 140°F.

Dry milk and egg products, if reconstituted, should be heated to 140°F before being served.

Poultry, poultry stuffings, and stuffed meats must be cooked to heat all parts of the food to at least 165°F, with no interruption of the cooking process.

Pork and pork products should be cooked to heat all parts of the food to at least 150°F.

Two bacteria are responsible for more than 75 percent of the reported and confirmed cases of food-related diseases: staphylococcus for approximately 55 percent and salmonella for about 21 percent. Both germs are passed along by unsanitary conditions and by food handlers who have not taken proper precautions to keep their hands clean and out of food materials.

---

9. "Security Is Everybody's Job," *Lodging*, September 1977.
10. Quoted in Clinton L. Rappole, "Sanitation in the Food Service Operation: The Implications of the Proposed Sanitation Ordinance," *Cornell Quarterly*, August 1977.

Technically, the Federal Drug Administration has the responsibility for inspecting all food-service establishments; in practice the primary responsibility for regulation of the industry remains at the local level. The National Institute for the Food Service Industry has produced an excellent training course for food-service establishments and a number of local governments have similar courses.

Enforcement of the regulations has been tightened. For example, the Public Health people will not permit tables to be set prior to serving a meal with glasses, cups, knives, forks, and spoons unless the glasses and cups were inverted, and the knives, forks, and spoons wrapped or otherwise covered. Nor may any bread or rolls that are left over from being served in a basket at a table be served or used again in any way. Leftover butter chips may not be used. In the past, these were fairly common practices.

In a study in New York City, fifty-eight cases of illness were traced to one cook who had prepared a certain dressing. The staphylococci of the dressing that had caused the illness was found in the mucous membrane of his nose. Needless to say, that restaurant lost considerable business. In another case, twelve people in the state of Washington were taken violently ill with gastroenteritis. The cause of the illness was traced to a particular restaurant kitchen. General sanitation was fair. There was no noticeable filth. The chef merely had a cut finger from which staphylococci flowed to poison the twelve guests of the restaurant. This is an illustration of personnel not knowing proper sanitation precautions.

Lack of sanitation control results in legal claims. One restaurant chain, which served over 5 million meals in one year, had these claims brought against the company.

Bone in seafood cocktail	3
Piece of metal in food	1
Piece of casserole dish found in food	1
Chicken bone cut roof of mouth	1
Allergic to seafood cocktail	1
Piece of glass in grapefruit	1
Glass in fruit cocktail	1
Tooth broken on chicken	1
Alleges food poisoning account of fish served	1
Lost filling while eating candy cane	1

Because of the importance sanitary food handling has for the health of the general public, the United States Public Health Service has developed a Food-Sanitation Training Course that is being used by the restaurant industry. The course is divided into seven lessons, presented in three lecture periods, as follows:

1. **Bacteriology.**
   History, nature, growth, reproduction, shapes, and habits.

Communicable diseases.
Relation of bacteria to disease; method of disease transmittal; causes of decay and fermentation.
Insect and rodent control.
Spread of disease by insects and animals; life cycle, habits of insects and animals; contamination and destruction of food.

2. **Sanitization of eating utensils.**
   Effects of various agents on bacteria; proper disinfection of utensils and equipment.
   Food handling and public health.
   Food spoilage, refrigeration and preservation; relations of animal life and bacteria to food poisonings and infections.
   Personal hygiene.
   Hand washing, rest room sanitation, uniforms, personal appearance, use of side towel.

3. **Detergents and methods of sterilization.**
   Proper use of detergents; application of steam, chlorine, etc. Lecture and demonstrations designed for those actually employed in this important phase of operation.

Another food-sanitation course is available from the National Institute for the Foodservice Industry (NIFI).[11] Government approved, this course is widely used. The Educational Institute of the American Hotel and Motel Association, East Lansing, Michigan, also offers a food-service sanitation course based on the NIFI course.

Food sanitation and general cleanliness are vital to restaurant success in this country. The major food-service chains such as Howard Johnson's, Denny's, Sambos, and Big Boy are all well aware of sanitation—and the image of cleanliness—as major appeals to the dining-out public. As the American public grows more sanitation-minded, the restaurant operators have no alternative but to reflect this sanitation consciousness.

Sanitation practices and attitudes are the result of what has been learned in the home and school. In restaurants the manager is the key person. What the manager does or does not do is reflected by the employee.

The Subconscious Overview

The experienced manager is constantly alert for sanitation errors and reacts automatically to cues that say something is wrong:

Soiled uniforms?
Any body odors?
Dirty hands or fingernails?

---

11. NIFI.

Hairnets or other hair restraints being worn as required?

Is someone fingering a pimple or scratching one's head or face?

Smoking in the dining room or kitchen?

Is anyone sneezing in their hands?

Who is wearing an ornate ring or a dangling bracelet, which could get into the food, or be a hazard around moving equipment?

Does someone have a bad cold and need to be sent home immediately?

To emphasize the importance of cleanliness, Howard Johnson, founder of the chain, would appear unannounced at a parking lot or in a restaurant and pick up loose paper or cigarette butts, a practice certain to be instructive to the manager. Sanitation starts with the manager, who is the model for others to follow or, better yet, emulate.

In some locations, food-service establishments will necessarily have to supply showers and clean uniforms, for the simple reason that employees may not have bathing facilities in their homes. This is especially true in developing countries. (In some countries the managers find it necessary to provide vitamin pills to employees with their meals to keep the employees healthy on the job.)

Learner-Controlled Teaching Material

Since most hotels, restaurants, and clubs employ relatively few people it is seldom feasible to employ a full-time trainer at a particular property. To insure uniformity of training and educational materials, and as rapid progress as possible, many of the materials have been individualized and put into a form that permits the trainee to proceed at the individual's own learning rate, and on a self-learning basis. Learner-controlled materials have been produced by several chains and by outside companies. The materials are presented in the form of programmed instruction, video cassettes, microfiche, cassettes that can be played on tape recorders, sixteen mm films, slide film packages, and others. The learning materials often come packaged as modules, some ingeneously devised. Their novelty value alone creates interest for a time at least.

Learner-controlled instruction, however, lacks the kind of motivation possible in a face-to-face, teacher-to-student relationship. The old saying, "the best teaching arrangement is Mark Hopkins on one end of the log and the student on the other" is probably still valid—one teacher, one student. The teacher in a classroom with several students is next best for maintaining motivation and interplay between instructor and trainee. Such arrangements are not always practical.

Cassette Training Materials

Holiday Inn owners in the United States and Canada are required to buy a training program on tapes, Vid Net, covering such areas as General Training (train the trainer, first aid, safety); Housekeeping (cleaning, supplies, storage); Front Office (operations, checkout procedures, machines); Food and Beverage (table service, lounge service, food preparation, suggestive selling); and Empathy (human relations skill training).

The human relations segment presents a series of well-acted situations in which employees are confronted with typical problem guests—"Mr. D. Manding," Mrs. Delight (wants continuous attention and approval), The Drunk. Other situations are dramatized to show how to improve interdepartmental communication, self-control, and handling of group business.

Two-day programs covering the application of transactional analysis to motor hotel operation are made available on a per-person basis to Holiday Inn management personnel.

Each Holiday Inn pays $1,000.00 for the tapes and $850.00 for a video player—a small investment according to the Director of Education Program Production when put into proper perspective; that the system will better train employees to run a two-million-dollar (or more) operation.

The Best Western Professional Development Program is assembled in a series of film strips—small, self-contained cartridges, each with a program of about ten minutes. The projector resembles a small television set, weighs only fifteen pounds, and can be easily moved from one location to another. The programs available in 1977 dealt with the training of cleaners and front desk personnel and the handling of reservations.

Training Schedules

To press for the accomplishment of training, some organizations regularly ask supervisors to assess their employee in terms of skills, and to check off those skills that need development. Sheraton Hotels, for example, sets up a training schedule that lists employees and indicates the skills of each that need sharpening. One of their training schedule forms is shown as table 6.2. Notice that the skills in need of polishing are indicated by having the supervisor name the date the training for each will be completed.

Table 6.2   Training Schedule

Department   Town Room   Date 4/16/78

Jobs Performed	1 Rule, Regulations	2 Town Room Uniform	3 Floor Plans	4 Table Setup	5 Menu Reading	6 Taking Orders	7 Writing Checks	8 Ordering Food	9 Pick Up	10 Serving Guests	11 Side Work	12	Remarks
Average Training Time Hours	2	½	1	4	4	2	2	2	2	4	1		
1. Mary Jones	X	X	X	X	X	X	X	X	X	X	X		
2. Pat Hendricks	6/18	X	X	X	X	6/19	X	X	X	6/24	X		
3. Julie Kennedy	X	X	X	X	X	X	X	6/23	X	X	X		
4. Joyce Smith	6/18	X	X	6/18	X	6/19	X	7/1	X	7/1			
5. Robert Gregg	X	X	X	6/18	—	—	—	—	—	7/1	6/25		
6. David Corona	6/18	6/18	6/18	6/18	6/19	6/19	6/20	6/23	6/23	6/24	6/25		
7.													
8.													
9.													

Code: X Can do the job satisfactorily.
      — Doesn't need to do the job.
      Insert the date training will be completed.

_____
Supervisor

Test Yourself—Are You a Good Trainer?

1. Do you consider preparation to be the first step in instructing an employee? Do you spend as much or more time in preparation—getting things ready—than you do in actual instruction?

2. Do you prepare job breakdowns for what you are going to teach? Have you listed the key points around which you will build the instruction?

3. Do you devote any time to explaining to employees how they will profit from learning what you have to teach?

4. Do you determine what the employee already knows about the job before you start training?

5. Do you set up a timetable showing the time you plan to use in job instruction day by day, and when you expect the training to be completed?

6. Do you expect that there will be periods in the course of the training during which no observable progress will be made?

7. Do you expect that some employees will learn two or three times as fast as others?

8. Do you both tell and show the employee how to do the skill involved?

9. When the employee performs incorrectly, do you say, "No, not that way!"

10. Do you give instructions so clearly that no one can misunderstand what is intended?

11. Do you ask the employee to try out the skill and to tell you how to do it?

12. Do you use praise frequently?
(All of the questions should be answered yes except number nine.)

THE NATIONAL APPRENTICESHIP TRAINING PROGRAM

The National Apprenticeship Training Program offered by the Educational Institute of the American Culinary Federation is a three-year, or 6,000-hour, on-the-job-training program. The initial 500 hours constitute a probationary period. Apprentices must be sixteen years of age or older and have completed high school or its equivalent. The program is set up to be worked in conjunction with a post-secondary educational institution. The standards of accomplishment to be attained by the apprentice have been developed in cooperation with Bureau of Apprenticeship and Training of the U.S. Department of Labor, and much of the funding comes from that Department.

On-the-job training has been carefully described in terms of basic competencies expected as a result of the training. As an illustration of the competencies required of the learner, the sections on stocks and soups, sauce cookery, and garde-manger section are as follows:[12]

Stocks and Soups 6% or 360 hours	1. Complete knowledge and experience in the preparation and use of the stockpot.
	2. To gain vast experience in the preparation of various soups that will include the following: cream soups and veloutes, strained and pureed soups, various vegetable soups, cheese soups, and national and specialty soups.
	3. Experience in consommé preparation.
	4. Experience in various clarifying processes for stocks and soups.
	5. A complete working knowledge and understanding of proper soup garnishing.
Sauce Cookery 10% or 600 hours	1. To gain a substantial mastery of the major classifications and uses of sauces.
	2. Experience in the preparation of all the basic sauces that will include the following: brown sauce, the white sauces, tomato sauce, butter sauces, compound butters, specialty sauces, and cold sauces.
	3. Knowledge of the uses of bases and flavorings for the preparation of various sauces and gravies.
	4. Gain experience in the preparation of gravies and glazes.
	5. Be able to record a substantial amount of experience in all preparations of soups, stocks, and sauces.
The Garde-Manger Section 8% or 480 hours	1. Gain a summary knowledge in order to be able to supervise and direct the preparation of vegetables and fruits, breakfast setup and production, sandwich and salad station setup and production, operation of the entire pantry section, and the preparation and display of cold canapes and hors d'oeuvres.
	2. To understand and experience the art of buffet presentation and basic uses and preparations of various decorations.
	3. To work with and appreciate the combinations, various shapes, sizes, and colors of the items used on the buffet table.
	4. Preparation and use of the Chaufroid and Aspic pieces.
	5. Preparation of simple model pieces and various gallantines used for buffet display.
	6. To gain experience in the use and preparation of all popular appetizer selections and the preparation of all condiment items necessary for production of a la carte appetizers.
	7. Experience in the preparation and production of various non-baked hot and cold desserts.
	8. To develop competent skills in the handling of related tools and in the artistic preparation and presentation of all food items used in this section.

How to Use Visual Aids

Too often the showing of a movie or filmstrip finds part of the audience asleep when the lights go on. To be effective, visual aids must be a part of a carefully planned program. Learning is not a passive affair. The instructor should get the audience to participate by pointing out things to look for in the films and by asking questions concerning key points in the film. Often a film may be most useful as a kickoff to a discussion. It is always good teaching to summarize a film after its showing and to show how it is related to problems at hand.

For teaching a particular operation the filmstrip or slide presentation is effective. One frame is shown at a time and the commentator has as much time as is needed to drive the point home. Movies can be excellent devices for showing large-scale operations or for morale purposes.

---

12. From: National Apprenticeship and Training Standards for Cooks, The American Culinary Federation, East Lansing, Mich., 1977.

Orientation films that give the new employee an overall picture of an enterprise can be effective.

Summarizing techniques of presenting instructional films, we can itemize the following steps:

1. Stimulate a readiness to learn. Pose searching questions on the film that the employee should keep in mind while viewing it. Relate the film to the past experience of the employee. Point out the advantages the film can offer. Give a verbal synopsis of the film and, if possible, a written synopsis.

2. Show the film.

3. Immediately start a discussion about the film. Ask for criticisms of techniques presented. "Are there better techniques?" Ask for comments as to the usefulness of the practices presented to the present situation. Ask the employees to paraphrase the important points presented. Summarize the discussion, emphasizing key points.

4. If necessary repeat the procedure at a later date.

ANNOTATED LIST OF FILM STRIPS AND FILMS

Film strips and films, when relevant, add to any training program, but are not usually substituted for discussion and lecture. Using "loop" film strips and films makes for easier instruction of one or a small number of employees at a time. The loops, which usually come in cartridges, can be plugged in to a projector, after which they run automatically. One of the advantages of the loop is that the film can be repeated as many times as required by the learner. Another advantage is that the machine can be controlled by the learner who can repeat the film without the embarrassment of having to admit to not getting what was needed from the film the first time it was shown.

Films and film strips for the hotel and restaurant business have been usually produced by companies wanting to sell a product. Some are excellent. Numerous films and film strips are now available that contain no such bias.

Recommended film strips and films annotated below are those distributed by the National Restaurant Association, One IBM Plaza, Suite 2600, Chicago 60611.

CASSETTE TRAINING PROGRAMS

FC 02—*The Angry Flame*: Preventing fires in food-service establishments requires advance planning. Train employees "what to do" in an emergency fire situation (10 minutes).

FC 03—*Behind the Line*: Training for cafeteria service personnel . . . Greeting customers, suggestion selling, the importance of appearance, attitude, and actions. Special emphasis on career opportunities (13 minutes).

FC 04—*The Server Assistant*: Emphasizes attractive appearance through personal hygiene and grooming . . . courtesy . . . attitude toward work, customers, fellow workers. Details duties . . . table setting, assisting waiters/waitresses, table cleanup (12 minutes).

FC 12—*The Freeloaders*: Emphasizes the factors that cause pests to enter, stay, and multiply in the establishment. Film stresses the good practices that must be observed in order to deny them attractions (10 minutes).

FC 17—*Protecting the Public, Part 1—Personal Side*: Stresses personal hygiene all personnel should follow before coming to work and during work (10 minutes).

FC 18—*Protecting the Public, Part 2—Food Protection*: Rules for sanitary cooking, reheating, serving, and storing are illustrated. The way in which time and temperature affect germ growth is explained simply but thoroughly (10 minutes).

FC 19—*Protecting the Public, Part 3—Establishment and Equipment Sanitation*: The proper cleaning and sanitizing of equipment and reasons why sanitizing is a serious business are brought home forcefully to viewer (10 minutes).

FC 20—*Smart Waitress, Part 1—Personal Presentation*: A reminder that personal appearance starts with the daily tub-bath or shower; that deodorant advertisements aren't all exaggerated (10 minutes).

FC 21—*Smart Waitress, Part 2—Attitude*: Film emphasizes that their "attitude" is essential— shows how it affects them and the customer (10 minutes).

FC 23—*Smart Waitress, Part 4—Teamwork*: This film shows how important *teamwork* is to the smooth operation of a restaurant. Nonteam waitresses and unpleasant undercurrents disturb staff (10 minutes).

FC 27—*Work Smart—Stay Safe*: Training program packed with information on how to prevent accidents caused by unsafe work habits (10 minutes).

S 803—*Waste Prevention*: Cleverly dramatizes methods used to avoid wasteful practices. The Waster is shown discarding perfectly good food, ignoring portion control, and being careless and wasteful while handling and storing food, dishware, utensils, etc. (10 minutes).

S 808—*Storage and Receiving Procedures*: Covers the basic principles of receiving and storing foods. Shows the importance of using proper procedures when checking the quality and quantity of goods received. Includes a detailed explanation of both dry and refrigerator storage to prevent contamination, waste, and pilferage (10 minutes).

S 812—*Food Presentation*: Professional waiters and waitresses are shown serving a wide variety of menu items. Stresses imaginative employment of color using garnishments, condiments, and accompaniments (7 minutes).

16MM, VIDEOCASSETTE, OR 8MM CARTRIDGES

B 402—*Handling Complaints*: An ideal film for all personnel who must deal with customer complaints. Through a series of dramatic vignettes this film illustrates a basic principle involved in handling a complaint.

B 403—*Handling Money*: Creates real-life situations involving cashiers and clerks. Presents in detail proper methods of counting money, making change, and avoiding errors commonly caused by interruptions. Shows how to spot marked, altered, or counterfeit money and illustrates the artifices of the short-change artist.

B 404—*Handling Checks*: Teaches basic procedures for handling checks, with emphasis on customer courtesy. Short, incisive episodes bring essential steps of inspecting checks and validating signatures into sharp focus. Helps establish standards and procedures of check handling to save money by reducing losses.

B 405—*Handling Credit Cards*: A must for all organizations accepting credit cards. Shows all steps in a credit card transaction. Each step is illustrated by a dramatic episode with special precautions highlighted. Provides an effective, routine procedure for reducing risks of handling credit cards.

M 301—*Eye of the Supervisor*: Equips supervisory personnel to review and evaluate employee performance. Emphasis is placed upon collecting all information before reaching a conclusion. Tips on self-evaluation, self-improvement as well.

M 303—*Preventing Employee Theft*: Basic principles of theft prevention are dramatically illustrated: reducing temptation, limiting opportunity, establishing controls and communication. Surveillance devices.

M 304—*Discipline—A Matter of Judgment*: Emphasizes paramount need for objectivity and impartial judgment when issuing a reprimand or terminating an employee.

M 305—*The Training Memorandum*: Dramatization takes a supervisor who is skeptical of training through a series of experiences, outlining the many benefits to himself, his workers, and his company.

M 306—*Increasing Productivity*: Directed at opening the minds of viewers to increase productivity through motivation, systems analysis, job planning and organization, and the creation of an enriched and nourishing work environment.

M 307—*Flight Plan*: Dramatically introduces the manager to the purposes of planning, what it accomplishes, and essential elements of a good plan. Through a series of flight sequences a successful manager illustrates elements involved in the planning process.

M 308—*Delegate—Don't Abdicate*: Illustrates that successful delegation is something managers must plan and work for in order to make the best use of their time, build teamwork, and produce results.

M 309—*Successful Persuasion*: A new approach to salesmanship. The buy-sell relationship for sales personnel, managers at all levels, and others. The dynamics of the "persuasion transaction" to convince people of the value of ideas, products, services.

M 310—*The Time Game*: Teaches time management by taking its audience through a card game in which the stakes are managerial success and the chips are segments of time. Stresses keeping a personal time log, controlling crises, establishing priorities.

M 312—*The Peter Hill Puzzle*: An open-ended, engrossing drama about the impact serious cost management and accountability problems can have on the lives of every person in an organization. An important tool for organizational development in such areas as problem solving, leadership, decision making, and cost management.

SUMMARY

Many hotel and restaurant jobs involve unskilled manual labor or semiskilled service labor in which little training is available outside of the place of employment. Realistically most training must rest with the supervisor.

Definite advantages accrue for an organization from a training program in the form of increased employee learning rates, increased quality of performance, decreased breakage and spoilage, reduced number of accidents, reduced turnover, reduced absenteeism, and increased production. Most importantly, the hotel guest and restaurant patron receive a better product with more hospitable service.

For the employee, training offers the advantage of increased earning power, preparation for advancement, enhanced self-respect, and increased feelings of security and economic independence.

From research and experience in the training area, certain principles and findings can be generalized: (*a*) As persons move from being workers to supervisors, they need fewer technical skills and more conceptual and human relations skills; (*b*) realistically all people are not endowed with the same potentials for learning; (*c*) much of effective teaching lies in creating incentive and interest for the trainee; (*d*) norms can be established by which to gauge the progress of individuals in mastering certain skills; (*e*) distributed practice is more efficient than continuous practice; (*f*) learning proceeds more quickly when the employee is provided with a standard for indicating progress; (*g*) goals should be stepped up gradually; (*h*) skilled individuals learn to make maximal use of sensory cues in understanding the task at hand. Effective training orients the trainee to the use of such cues.

Certain conditions must exist for meaningful training to take place: Trainees must feel a need for training, and the program must be geared to the needs and problems of trainees. The training should lead to usable skills. A human relations model is desirable in which trainees seek out answers and conclusions on their own through involvement with the tasks and their own experience; group learning processes are utilized; and opportunities are provided for the expression of feelings and emotions.

A well-established plan of training is the four-step, job-instruction method involving preparing the learner, demonstrating the operation, having the learner try out the procedure, and following up to determine and enhance progress. Other methods found in hotels and restaurants include lectures and tours, sponsor training, role playing and skits, problem-situation training, dialogue training, and programmed instruction.

Training obviously depends on the trainer's skill and motivation. Attention needs to be given to help trainers develop confidence, skill, and consistency in following through on schedules. A diverse supply of audiovisual aids—all readily available—can be a valuable source of support to the trainer while at the same time providing interest for the trainee.

References

Martin M. Broadwell. *The Supervisor and On-the-Job Training.* 2d ed. (Reading, Mass.: Addison-Wesley Publishing Company, 1975)

————. *The Supervisor as an Instructor.* 3d ed. (Reading, Mass.: Addison-Wesley Publishing Company, 1978)

On-the-Job Training: A Practical Guide for Food Service Supervisors. (Chicago: Hospital Research and Educational Trust, 1975)

Training and Continuing Education. (Chicago: Hospital Research and Educational Trust, 1970)

Training Food Service Personnel for the Hospitality Industry. United States Department of Health, Education and Welfare, O E–82018, Washington, D.C.: United States Government Printing Office, 1969.

Employee Appraisal

7

Management, alert to the growing demands for more effective personnel programs, has in some cases turned to merit rating as a method for insuring that promotions in classification and pay be placed on as fair a basis as possible.

Proponents of formalized rating systems—variously called merit rating, performance review, personnel rating, and service rating—proclaim many advantages. They argue that by using scientific ratings, management benefits by insuring a better selection of supervisors. Workers are better satisfied when they feel that their opportunities for advancement depend on an unbiased appraisal of their abilities. Employees, it is pointed out, are stimulated to higher standards when they know that they are subject to periodic rating. It is further believed that merit rating reduces grievances by promoting communication, especially when ratings are discussed between rater and ratee.

Employee rating is not without opponents. Some of the opponents have as evidence a history of unsatisfactory attempts to use personnel ratings. Some have found that merit rating has been a source of labor unrest and has increased grievances rather than diminished them. Several large industrial plants have tried and discarded well-known plans. Appraisal systems can take an inordinate amount of time to administer, especially in a bureaucracy that feeds upon red tape. Political considerations often override merit.

The fact of the matter is that everyone who manages personnel uses a system of rating. Every military system and every business that has supervisors and workers uses ratings to determine wage payments and promotions. Two primary differences stand out in the various forms of rating: one, the degree of complexity of the rating device, and two, the degree of subjectivity on the part of the rater. The unanalyzed ratings made by the old-time boss is a rating to be sure, but is likely to be biased. An effective rating system can aid in making the judgment less biased and more reliable. Since we must appraise people, a method by which more objectivity is attained should be welcomed—provided it is not too complicated or time-consuming. To be efficient the method must be accepted by those being evaluated.

INHERENT WEAKNESS IN ALL RATING SYSTEMS

Any system by which a superior rates a subordinate is likely to cause resentment in the person being rated or anxiety in the rater. As has been said many times, few people like to play God and sit in judgment on others. Every rating system contains this element, even though it is not visibly apparent. The rater may become anxious because the person being rated will expect a performance rating higher than justified. Who can be completely objective about oneself?

To overcome some of this hostility and anxiety, various plans have been proposed by which the person being rated participates in setting up the criteria of performance and in effect rates himself/herself against the criteria. In such cases the supervisor is supposed to be more counselor than judge. This seems to be stretching the point too far. Individuals will probably never have goals completely common with those of the firm. They have their own private dreams of themselves, their role in the company, and in the eyes of their friends and family. To permit every individual in a firm to set goals or criteria by which one is judged is unrealistic. Hotels and restaurants in this country are established for the most part to make a profit, and it is difficult to see many individuals, especially the person at the bottom, subordinating personal goals completely to a profit objective. In a club where profits are not a goal, management and employees cannot be expected to willingly subordinate their own satisfactions to those of the club membership.

This does not mean that persons being rated should not have a voice in establishing objectives and criteria and that there should not be discussion of the rating. Participative management (as discussed elsewhere in this book) moves in that direction. Management by objective is an attempt to give the person being rated a voice in establishing the evaluation criteria. Management by objective has a rating scheme built into the system; the subordinate makes progress, reaches or exceeds the objective that has been jointly established by the supervisor and the subordinate. It has the great merit of avoiding the necessity for a formal, ritualistic rating system by which one person judges another. It emphasizes performance rather than traits. It does not point out a person's weaknesses but gives the person more latitude in identifying personal weaknesses and doing whatever is necessary to reach an objective. In this sense it has a great psychological advantage over traditional systems by muting hostilities and anxieties arising from person-to-person rating. Another tremendous advantage is the fact that the subordinate is invited to help set objectives that then become one's own rather than something imposed from above. A discussion of management by objective is seen in chapter 8, "Management Development."

THE FUNDAMENTALS OF A GOOD RATING DEVICE

Basically, all formal rating systems are alike. They provide a means of comparing one employee with another or a group of others doing a similar job. If the method aids the person doing the appraisal by making that individual more critical, thus better able to give judgments that are more consistent and accurate, it is a good system. It should be simple enough to be explainable to the employee—and should not require an inordinate amount of time. Again, the device is only effective if it is accepted by the person being evaluated.

Since all rating devices are attempts to compare employees reliably, the manner in which they vary is in the way in which the employees are compared, the factors or criteria being compared, and the acceptance of the employees being compared.

Absolute Rating Scales

In absolute rating scales the judge assigns an arbitrary value to the trait being rated. One judgment is made for each case involved. This may take the form of assigning a certain numerical score to a person for each trait rated. For example, if it is decided to assign a perfect score on

neatness a weight of ten, the rater may judge a particular ratee as being worth a score of only seven. This type of device may be varied by placing the absolute judgment on a linear scale.

1	2	3	4	5	6	7	8	9	10
Unkempt				**Neatness**					Very Neat

A problem with absolute rating scales of any type is that of defining the factors used. What is initiative? What is adaptability? Does a particular job call for much initiative or none at all? How adaptable should a person be to fill particular jobs? Does a pot and pan worker need adaptability or is that a liability? The performance-appraisal form, table 7.1, is intended to be facetious. It points out how an employee rating system can become ridiculous.

A serious example of the absolute rating scale is seen as table 7.2. A critic of absolute rating can immediately spot difficulties with such a form. Each of the factors deals with an abstraction that undoubtedly means something different to each rater. "Kitchen expertise," dealing with the actual skill of food preparation, is a broad subject in itself. A person can be skilled at cutting onions and lack skill in rolling out pie dough. Different raters may disagree as to the importance of various manual skills.

The construction of the rating form in itself weighs some factors more important than others. If, for example, more items are included in the category *knowledge,* that factor is more important.

In using an absolute rating scale it is important for the users to recognize that the scale itself determines how various factors are weighed. Raters can agree among themselves that the knowledge factor may be given a weight of 60 percent, other factors 40 percent. They may agree on any other relative weights. Obviously different operations would call for different weights of the various factors. A chef in a posh restaurant might be expected to run the whole kitchen, in which case knowledge assumes major importance. In another food-service operation the chef may actually be a working chef, cook, or a lead cook in which case knowledge covering nutrition, pricing, and cost control would be relatively unimportant.

The rating form can be changed to emphasize factors that are increasing in importance to an operation. Suppose an operation has taken on more catering, in which buffet presentation is important; the factor *presentation* could be given more weight in the rating process. If the price of food increases, more emphasis may be placed on the chef's knowledge of cost control and pricing.

Table 7.1   Guide to Employee Performance Appraisal

Degree of Performance
Please Check Appropriate Box

	Far Exceeds Job Requirements	Exceeds Job Requirements	Meets Job Requirements	Needs Improvement	Does Not Meet Minimum Requirements
Quality of Work	Leaps tall buildings with a single bound	Leaps tall buildings with a running start	Can leap short buildings if prodded	Bumps into buildings	Cannot recognize buildings
Promptness	Is faster than a speeding bullet	Is as fast as a speeding bullet	Would you believe a slow bullet?	Misfires frequently	Wounds self handling a gun
Initiative	Is stronger than a locomotive	Is as strong as a bull elephant	Almost as strong as a bull	Shoots the bull	Smells like a bull
Adaptability	Walks on water	Keeps head above water under stress	Washes with water	Drinks water	Passes water in an emergency
Communication	Talks with God	Talks with angels	Talks to himself	Argues with himself	Loses arguments with self

Will be revised only if necessary

A. D. 1974

Signature of Employee _____
Signature of Supervisor _____
Witness _____

Table 7.2   Rating Form (Chef)

Factor	Rating				
	1	2	3	4	5
Kitchen Expertise (Knife skills, hand-eye coordination, motion economy)					
Creative Imagination Shown (Originality in recipe, decoration)					
Presentation and Appearance of Food (Color, shape, interest)					
Organoleptic Quality of Food (Flavor, compatibility of flavors, texture, etc.)					
Knowledge					
Forecasting					
Menu construction and planning					
Nutrition					
Pricing					
Cost control					
Employee scheduling					
Cooking process (heat transfer, practical food chemistry)					
Use of leftovers					
Clientele relations					
Company policy					
Weighted Overall Rating					

Checklist Method

By the checklist method the rater is given a list of traits and is asked to check those that apply to a particular employee. The checklist might contain such descriptions as *always on time, treats the customers courteously, does not cooperate with other employees, uses intoxicants on the job.* This method has the advantage of pointing out one's weak and strong points to the employee. It has the disadvantage, however, of having to be translated into another system so that comparisons between employees can be made.

The checklist rating device is also a simple and easily understood device. Figure 7.1 shows a checklist rating device designed for use with kitchen personnel.

Different departments will require different qualities in their personnel. Checklists can be made to fit the needs of any department. This should be done by consultation with the departmental supervisors concerned.

The items included in the checklist rating scale can be weighted so that certain items are given emphasized consideration. However, it is simpler to add additional items of a similar type if the rater wishes to weight certain qualities. By giving one point for each item, the rating is simply the total of the items checked. By making the items statements of desirable behavior, the rater is given an opportunity to check as many as are believed appropriate rather than being required to subscribe to statements that are derogatory or unfavorable to the employees being rated.

Critical Incident Method

Where performance is difficult to quantify the supervisor is sometimes asked to note examples of good or bad performance during a specific period. This method is really a sampling technique and is no more reliable than overall judgment, except that the supervisor is required to actually record observations made from time to time that can be referred to at the time of the rating. The biased supervisor can easily show a biased record by selecting those incidents that favor the bias.

Work Sample and Measure of Productivity Methods

Closely related to the *critical incident method* is that of the *work sample method* whereby the rater makes a brief formal examination of the workers' ability to perform a set of prescribed tasks.

Figure 7.1 Personnel Rating

Department ___Kitchen___   Date _____

Employee _____

1. Reports for work on time.
2. Begins work promptly.
3. Turns out the required amount of work.
4. Turns out more than the required amount of work.
5. Does neat work.
6. Organizes work well.
7. Calm and steady during rush periods.
8. Works well on own responsibility.
9. Shows good judgment in routine application of kitchen rules.
10. Capable of assuming higher responsibilities.
11. Accepts responsibility for own errors made.
12. On lookout for shortcuts and ways of bettering job.
13. Keeps self personally neat and clean.
14. Maintains cleanliness in work.
15. Courteous.
16. Self-reliant.
17. Use of intoxicants does not affect work.
18. Does not waste materials.
19. Does not waste food.
20. Follows instructions carefully and accurately.
21. Does not allow emotions to interfere with work.
22. Cooperates effectively with others.
23. Keeps equipment in good working condition.
24. Capable of assuming higher responsibility during absence of superior.
25. Gives other employees recognition for good work.
26. Shows a great deal of patience.
27. Has a pleasing, friendly manner.
28. Learns new tasks quickly.
29. Takes the initiative in getting work done.
30. Is entirely honest.

Signed _____

In the *measure of productivity method,* a rater examines performance that can be measured quantitatively: how many covers were washed in an eight-hour period, how many glasses washed? how many pies produced? how many reservations handled?

Order of Merit Method

This method consists of ranking the members of a group from high to low. Members are assigned positions such as first, second, third, fourth, etc., according to the judgment of the rater. The objection to this is the difficulty of considering the whole group at once and yet keeping the individual in mind in a position relative to the others. It is fairly easy in a group of sixteen to pick the top two or three and the lowest two or three. Ranking the others accurately is virtually impossible.

In hotel or restaurant operations wherein the supervisors are loathe to do "paper work" ratings of employees, it might be well to employ a simple *forced distribution* type of rating. The supervisor is asked to place each employee in the highest 10 percent, the middle 65 percent, or the lower 25 percent. The form that might be used is shown as figure 7.2.

Method of Paired Comparison

By this technique each individual in a group is compared with every other individual. May is compared with Jan, with John, and with Sally. The rater asks "Which of these persons is best performing the job?" Because there has been no easy way of combining the results of these comparisons, the method has the disadvantage of being cumbersome and time-consuming. It has value in that raters are not required to keep all of the ratees in mind at once. Each ratee is compared separately with every other ratee.

An example of *paired comparison* might look like this:

Task: Place the initials of the best supervisor in a pair at the intersection of comparison with every individual.

	JJ	PP	RR	SS	33	Score	Rank
JJ	—	JJ	JJ	SS	JJ	3	2
PP		—	RR	SS	WW	0	5
RR			—	SS	RR	2	3
SS				—	SS	4	1
WW					—	1	4

The *paired comparison method* is an excellent technique but it gets highly involved if many people must be rated. To make ratings when many people are involved, the formula $\dfrac{N(N-1)}{2}$ must be used to discern how many comparisons need to be made. For example, if eight people were being compared, twenty-eight different comparisons would be needed.

RECENT STATISTICAL DEVELOPMENTS

Recent investigations of rating scales that include a number of factors in the rating suggest that actually raters consider only two or three basic factors. For example, in

Figure 7.2   Personnel Rating

Personnel Rating

Department _____ Date _____

Group 1
(Highest 10 Percent)

List in this group the outstanding employees under your supervision, those who are best suited for promotion, most loyal and dependable, and those who contribute most to the efficiency of your department.

Name	Position

Group II
(Middle 65 Percent)

List in this group the average efficient employees under your supervision, the ones who are not outstanding but can be relied upon to do their work well.

Name	Position

Group III
(Lower 25 Percent)

List in this group the lower 25 percent of your employees, the ones whom you feel could probably be replaced by others more efficient and responsible.

Name	Position

one study it was learned that although the raters were asked to rate on twelve different factors, they were actually rating only two basic ones. In this study the two underlying factors that were common to all of the twelve were "the ability to do the present job" and "likelihood of being promoted."

APPRAISAL AS A MEANS OF IMPROVING PERFORMANCE

When appraisal is thought of as merely a process by which a superior judges or measures the performance of a subordinate, the results may be only frustration and tension. The superior may feel guilty. The subordinate may resent the implication of imposed inferiority and also of being judged by a superior. The rating process, as it is in the military and various bureaucracies, including universities, can degenerate into a game in which subordinate is pitted against superior. Instead, the purpose of ranking the individuals regarding performance should be a way of identifying areas in which further training is needed. Therefore, much of the sting of the rating is removed, and the person being rated may come to see it as a means of self-improvement. This can be more easily done in dealing with professional and managerial personnel.

To turn the appraisal process from rating to self-improvement the complete philosophy of appraisal is changed. No one is looking down and judging someone on a lower level. Rather, there is a mutual discussion between superior and subordinate with regard to what conditions must be altered to change or upgrade performance. Both parties may find that each has had a different performance standard in mind—perhaps both have been wrong. In many cases it is the rater, not the ratee, who must change.

In the waitress evaluation chart (table 7.3), the form has been changed. The device is not seen as a way of assigning a performance score or of making comparisons between one person and the group. The focus is to identify those spheres of behavior that should be changed in light of certain standards of courtesy, cleanliness, attitude, and technical skill.

Ideally the evaluation would result in setting down various objectives such as attending a charm school, seeing a doctor, introduction of a weekly meeting to improve technical waitress skills and knowledge. In this sense the evaluation can take on aspects of management by objective.

INSTALLING A MERIT RATING SYSTEM

As with any new personnel program a merit rating system should be introduced only with the cooperation of those who will participate. In setting up such a plan, a "less busy" time of year should be picked and the department heads and other supervisors invited to sit in on the discussion as to what form of rating device is most suitable for the business. When the various devices have been debated and a device agreed upon, mimeographed copies of the form can be made and distributed for use.

The rating form used should be thought of as tentative, subject to change if experience with it indicates a need for corrections. Meetings with supervisors should be held so that agreements can be reached concerning the terminology employed. It will be found that the term *good employee* has many different meanings, depending upon who is using it, and how it is being used. Questions as to how excellent is *excellent* and what constitutes *leadership* may arise should these terms be used in a rating form.

Employee meetings are also desirable if the rating is to accomplish the purpose of pointing out to employees areas in which they may need improving. Supervisors must understand the rating device.

How Often to Rate?

To be effective, and yet to avoid their being done mechanically, ratings probably should be made every six months. If there is too much of a time gap between ratings, there is a danger that the rater may forget some incidents or may emphasize recent incidents too much. If appraisal is seen as a means of self-improvement, new employees should be reviewed after two or three weeks.

Because of the time it takes to rate employees, some hotels have found it advisable to include only certain job classifications in their merit rating practice. One chain excludes all service jobs in which gratuities figure as a part of the wage and all semi-skilled positions such as the job of lodging quarters cleaner. According to the general manager of the chain, persons holding jobs, payment for which depends in part upon gratuities, in effect rate themselves by the size of their tip income.

This is no doubt partially true, but it should be pointed out that there are instances where tip employees receive large tips at the expense of the hotel in terms of guest attitude and the overall good of the enterprise. Such cases, of course, can be identified and usually corrected by proper supervision.

In jobs such as cleaner, several chains have instituted what amounts to an automatic merit increase based solely on experience on the job. All receive a merit increase after forty-eight full working days on the job. Such a system serves as an incentive to stay on the job, but it does not reward the expert or the energetic.

Since merit rating is often linked with wage payments in that merit increases are given for more efficient performance, a method for payroll control is needed. This has been accomplished simply and effectively by setting a ceiling for each grade of merit rating. In some departments it may be advisable to permit 90 percent of the department to receive the highest pay for their classification; in others, 80 percent. If a department head exceeds the determined limit, the excess is readily noted.

Who Shall Do the Rating?

In determining who should do the rating of a particular employee, it can be agreed that the employee's immediate supervisor should be one of those involved. Usually the supervisor and two or three other management representatives comprise a wage or merit rating committee. Some industrial organizations have found it advantageous to include a union representative or some other employee representative. The wage committee as set up in one hotel

Table 7.3   Waitress Evaluation Chart

Date _____

Name of Waitress _____

Name of Supervisor _____

To the Supervisor: Before asking the waitress what she can do to improve, ask yourself what you can do to help her improve.

Suggestions: Use this chart as a guide for a friendly discussion between you and your waitress. Your purpose is to set an atmosphere in which mutual problems can be approached and to change attitudes and behavior. Get the waitress to suggest changes. Let her do most of the talking.

	Needs Much Improvement	Needs Little Improvement	Excellent
Health and Appearance Is she pleasant looking: Nails, skin, teeth, clothes, posture? Would an improved diet help? Would more regularity in sleeping and other personal habits help? Is different makeup or clothes indicated? Are her vision and hearing adequate? Is there a possible need for glasses or a hearing aid?			
Job Attitudes Could she improve manner toward guests? (a) Does she make guests feel important in a graceful manner? (Improve how?) (b) Does she seem to enjoy serving people? (Why or why not?) Could she improve her relations with her associates and superiors? (How?) (a) Does she feel she is "better" than many of her associates or her supervisors? (Why?)			
Job Skills Does her diction or speaking voice need improvement? Could she improve her day-to-day knowledge of the menu? Does she know the most efficient ways of doing her work? (Which skills need improvement?) Does she know how to approach guests so that they feel they are in competent hands?			
Personal Adjustment Is she able to withstand the psychological pressures of the job? What personal problems stand in her way? (What can be done about them?) Is she fairly self-confident and self-sufficient? (What needs to be done to improve her confidence?)			

Plans for improvement as decided together with person being rated:

1. _____

2. _____

3. _____

organization is composed of the department head, the hotel manager, the comptroller, and the personnel manager. All merit rated positions that have not reached the maximum are reviewed at least twice a year. Ten days before the meeting of the wage committee, the department heads make recommendations. Within that ten-day period the personnel manager prepares a report on the employee from the standpoint of punctuality, conduct, etc. On daily inspections of the hotel the manager makes it a point to observe the working of the employee, and the comptroller observes the level of the payroll and whether or not the department head has a tendency to be too generous or not generous enough. The employee does not know the meeting is going to take place and is unaware of being under observation. On the day of the meeting the department head tells the story; there is a general discussion; the department head refrains from voting; and the three other members of the committee determine whether there shall be an increase, and if so, how much.

Training Raters

An appraisal system is no better than the appraisers. To make a rating program effective, supervisors must be convinced of the worth of the program and understand its purposes and mechanics.

The best way to promote supervisor understanding of the present rating system is to allow supervisors to help devise the system and to change it as necessary. Frequent conferences will be necessary to keep the supervisors' support of the program. Discussion of the possible errors of rating is a painless way of instructing the supervisors in good rating procedure.

Three errors are common:

1. **The halo effect**

   Many of us have a tendency to judge other people by their most noticeable characteristics. A chef with a pleasing personality is more likely to be judged a competent cook than one who is obnoxious in social relations. If one of our pet peeves is tardiness, an employee who is late is likely to be judged by us as having something less than true ability. The noticeable trait colors and biases the entire judgment. We are all prone to label a person good or bad, failing to differentiate among many traits and evaluating them separately. The halo effect is a weakness most of us have in judging a person on the basis of one or two traits. It is as though the one or two traits were a halo obscuring one's critical ability. The halo may be either favorable or unfavorable. A way to avoid the halo effect is to consider each trait separately. Go through the list, rate every person on one trait, then go through the list again, marking each on the next trait, and so on.

2. **The leniency error**

   Another common tendency is to want to be a good fellow and rate everyone higher than the person deserves. This practice is especially prevalent in rating supervisors and department heads. Of course, this does an injustice to the superior person. By placing the mediocre in the same category as the best, the superior person is not given sufficient recognition.

3. **The error of central tendency**

   Another failure in rating appears where the rater tends to think of everyone as being average and rates each one as such. Everyone on the list of persons is checked as average or close to it. This may be a defense on the part of the rater who fails to admit that there are people in the division who are superior, or for that matter, who are inferior. In discussing rating it can be pointed out that in any group there usually are individuals who are the poorest in the group in several traits by a ratio of two to one or more.

A way to reduce these errors is to analyze the ratings made by each rater. Omitting names of the rater involved, all raters can be asked to discuss the ratings made. Criticisms made by the group are likely to be accepted and to be more effective than those made by top management.

ATTEMPTS TO MAKE RATINGS MORE RELIABLE

Several methods have been used in attempting to make ratings more precise. One method has been to rate the individual on a number of factors rather than on one overall impression. Following this logic the number of factors that went into the rating was increased. Whereas formerly an employee may have been rated on efficiency, he may now be rated on knowledge of the job, accuracy, initiative, leadership, and personality. Some lists include as many as twenty-eight factors.

Elaborate statistical techniques have been applied to ratings, but the application of these techniques does not improve the validity of the device. Certain factors have been given double the weight of others. Numbers have been assigned and summed to give a supposedly accurate total appraisal. Depending on the job the ratee may be given 20 points for courtesy on the job, 20 points for neatness, 50 points for initiative, 50 for quality of work performed, and so on into any number of possible arrangements. Unfortunately, these attempts have not proved too fruitful.

Table 7.4 Total and Systematic Errors of Three Raters

Example 1

Data: Ratings (assumed for illustration) accorded ten ratees on a single trait by three raters.

	Ratings					Errors		
	Rater A	Rater B	Rater C	Total	Mean M_r	Rater A	Rater B	Rater C
A	7	7	4	18	6	1	1	−2
B	6	5	7	18	6	0	−1	1
C	8	7	6	21	7	1	0	−1
D	8	8	5	21	7	1	1	−2
E	9	8	10	27	9	0	−1	1
F	4	5	3	12	4	0	1	−1
G	6	6	3	15	5	1	1	−2
H	3	4	2	9	3	0	1	−1
I	9	9	6	24	8	1	1	−2
J	5	4	3	12	4	1	0	−1

Total Errors: $T E = \dfrac{\Sigma[R - M_r]}{N}$

Rater A: T E = 6/10 = 0.60
Rater B: T E = 8/10 = 0.80
Rater C: T E = 14/10 = 1.40

Systematic Errors: $S E = \dfrac{\Sigma(R - M_r)}{N}$

Rater A: S E = 6/10 = .60
Rater B: S E = 4/10 = .40
Rater C: S E = −10/10 = −1.00

Taken from D. Yoder, *Personnel Management and Industrial Relations,* (New York: Prentice-Hall, 1968).

Evaluating the Accuracy Ratings

Often raters agree as to the general pattern of the ratings they assign a specific ratee, but one rater may be consistently higher or lower than the other rater. This is what is known as a *systematic error* of the rater. By measuring the systematic error, it is possible (*a*) to adjust the rating of a discrepant rater to coincide with other raters or (*b*) to make a rater aware of being out of step with other raters. Another way of showing raters their deficiencies is to calculate their *total errors*. This technique shows how close an individual rater comes to the average.

The techniques described are not complicated, but they must be applied to an individual trait rather than to a total rating. The following steps are necessary to implement the technique of calculating total errors and measuring systematic errors:

1. Discover the mean, or average, rating on that characteristic for all of the raters (designated as M).

2. Note the individual rater's ratings on the trait (designated as R).

3. The total for each rater on the trait is the following:

$$T E = \frac{\text{Sum } [R - M]}{N}$$

where differences (R − M) are added without sign and N is the number of persons rated.

4. To find the systematic error on each trait:

$$S E = \frac{\text{Sum } [R - M]}{N}$$

where the differences are added algebraically and N is again the number of persons rated.

Example 1 (table 7.4) illustrates the method of measuring total and systematic errors of ratings. The total error is most suited for determining the most dependable rater.

In Example 1 it can be seen that rater C is the least dependable rater—consistently rating higher than raters A and B. Two approaches can be used to rectify the situation: (*a*) all of C's ratings can be lowered one scale score (as shown by C's systematic error), or (*b*) C could be trained to correct the existing rater bias in future ratings.

RECORD KEEPING

Employee record keeping has always been part of the responsibilities of the management. In fact, such federal statutes as the Walsh-Lee Public Contracts Act, the Fair Labor Standards Act, and the Civil Rights Act of 1964 require the reporting of information to the personnel service.

The computer has rapidly developed into one of the most valuable tools available to the supervisor. Not only does the computer reduce the onerous task of storing and retrieving records, it is also a powerful offensive tool in helping managers to understand and cope with a wide variety of problems related to unit levels of employees' turnover rates, employee attitudes, absenteeism rates, and personal characteristics of employees.

What information is valuable to managers in trying to understand their personnel? The answer to this, of course, will vary with each company and its needs. Listed below are a series of possibilities that might apply to company situations.

1. Personnel data from the application blank.

2. Recruiting and hiring data—including source of recruitment, dates of interview and hire, reason for selection or rejection, test scores and interview rating, and number of other applicants for the same position.

3. Work, education, and related experience—including not only schools attended, military experience, and previous employers, but also specialized skills and hobbies.

4. Compensation/work assignment data—including wage classification, salary rate, date and amount of next salary increase, all previous increases, title, ID number, record of hours worked, seniority date.

5. Evaluative/promotable data—including work preferences, goals, rank in current work group, date of last appraisal, appraisal results, growth potential rating, special awards and recognition, promotions or demotions, test scores, evaluative interview ratings.

6. Data relative to employee attitude or morale potential—including measures of productivity or quality of performance, absenteeism, tardiness, suggestion plan activity, grievance activity, attitudes toward supervisory practices, understanding of management philosophy, attitudes toward job.

7. Safety or accident data—including a record of the injury classification, physical limit, and any workmen's compensation claims.

8. Benefits data—including medical and life insurance plan, participation, retirement, savings plan, reasons for time not worked, suggestion plan activity, unemployment compensation claims data, other benefits.

9. Turnover data—including reasons for leaving, forwarding address, possible pay increase on the new job and its amount, confirmation of pay with new employer if possible, and statement concerning eligibility for rehire.

10. Characteristics of the employment environment—including average educational level of coworkers, turnover rates, accident frequency, personal characteristics of the supervisor, frequency of disciplinary actions, amount of overtime usually worked, and amount of employee dissatisfaction with working conditions.

11. Position or job history—data can be accumulated concerning the date the position was established, the identity of past incumbents, the types of changes involved for each person leaving (quit, lateral transfer, promotion, or other), source of each new incumbent (such as newly hired, lateral transfer, or promotion).

12. Labor market data—including a description of the personnel pool in the area in which new employees are drawn. Unemployment levels can be broken down by skill, age, and sex.

SUMMARY

Rating systems though necessary are not without critics. By definition a rating forces one person to sit in judgment of another, a system that often creates anxiety or resentment in the participants. Participative management concepts minimize some of the sting of the rating process by giving the person being rated a voice in establishing the evaluation criteria.

Various rating possibilities exist. Absolute rating scales assign arbitrary value to traits being rated, but such scales are not meaningful unless the trait can actually be measured absolutely. Most traits cannot be so measured. The very selection of traits to be rated also brings a bias into the rating. A checklist rating method points out in behavioral terms areas where an employee is strong or weak. Its disadvantage lies in the difficulty of making comparisons between individuals. Other techniques include the *critical incident method* consisting of a series of examples or critical incidents concerning an employee which the supervisor accumulates in order to evaluate performance; the *work sample method* involving a brief formal examination of the workers' ability to perform a set of prescribed tasks; the *measure of productivity method* examining performances that can be measured quantitatively; the *order of merit and forced distribution methods* ranking members of a group from high to low; the *method of paired comparisons* requiring each individual in a group to be compared with every other individual.

In order to reduce the frustrations, tensions, and hard feelings often created by appraisals, there is much merit in using the process merely to search for areas wherein further training is necessary. The stage can be set for mutual discussions between superior and subordinate in which both parties may find that each has had a different performance standard in mind.

Employee record keeping has always been part of the management responsibility. The computer has greatly facilitated the procedures and possibilities of record keeping. Records are a burden that must be borne with, but they are a valuable offensive tool for the manager in making plans in areas related to personnel—recruiting and hiring, acquiring descriptive information, compensation, evaluation and promotion, attitudes, safety, benefits, turnover, environment description, job history, and labor markets.

Suggested Readings

Bellak, Alvin O. "Performance for Hourly Employees." *Personnel Journal,* June 1971.

Management Development

8

Management development—preparation of hourly-wage employees for increased responsibilities—has been given considerable emphasis since 1965 by such companies as Saga Food Administration, the Marriott Corporation, Gino's, and ARA. In some cases budgets amounting to several hundred thousands of dollars have been established so that staffs of management development specialists could conduct management-development courses around the country. Courses come under various labels: training, management-development, organization development, career progression, and so on. The purpose is to improve management performance, and to identify potential management personnel, and provide them with management skills and motivation for management. A few companies have sent their management personnel to sensitivity training sessions, the so-called *T groups*, the purpose of which is to free people for easier and more honest people-to-people communication.

Participative management has been stressed in most management-development courses. Emphasis has been placed on how to gain acceptance of ideas, on decision making, and on the usual management skills of selecting, training, organizing, delegating, systematizing, and so on. Management development has been a necessity for those rapidly expanding companies that can expand only as rapidly as management personnel are available for expansion.

Management-development courses differ from the usual classroom course in that considerable emphasis is placed on changing attitudes, building confidence, and imparting a management style. Discussion and debate are a large part of these courses, with the trainer avoiding the lecture method to a large extent.

An Educational Division manager discusses employment opportunities in Saga Food Service with student employees at a Saga-served campus, thus helping personnel managers with their recruitment efforts. The Division serves more than 400 schools across the nation.

HUMAN RESOURCE ACCOUNTING

Human resource accounting attempts to place a dollar value on the people in an organization. The attempt often reveals new perspectives of the organization. Putting dollar signs on people emphasizes the importance of training and management development. The waiter who with training can produce $200 in sales in a shift and the assistant manager who can run a 30 percent food cost and a 20 percent labor cost are obviously worth more than less productive people.

Human resource accounting may lead to planning for replacement of key personnel by promotion from within: "Manager X is being groomed to be a district supervisor. Assistant manager Y is being readied for a move to manager. Supervisor Z is learning the responsibilities of the assistant manager.

167

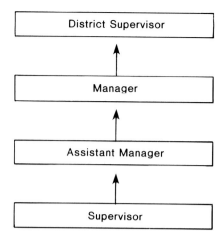

District Supervisor
↑
Manager
↑
Assistant Manager
↑
Supervisor

A hotel or restaurant is comprised of two principal resources—facilities and people. The facility—the hotel, the motel, restaurant, or club building—has value within itself, but can be made functional only through the use of management and employees, the people. It is quite possible to have lovely facilities—a beautiful hotel, restaurant, or club—which quickly becomes a liability if the human resources are deficient. Most of the larger hotel chains and many restaurant organizations do not want to own the facilities—rather they are offering their human resources and their systems of operation to the owner or lending agent for a hotel, restaurant, or club. In these instances, the human resource factor is paramount.

Human resource accounting is a relatively new technique for keeping an inventory and placing a value on the human resources of the organization. The value of human resources in a hotel or restaurant can be expressed in several ways: the total cost of developing the present organization; the cost of replacing the present people; the discounted cash flow value of what the people will be worth to the organization in years to come.[1]

When European chefs hired on with a complete brigade to operate a kitchen, the value of that brigade was obvious, especially if it decided to leave en masse without notice. Resort hotels often employed a chef who brought along a brigade or at least key employees. The kitchen crew considered itself a unit whose allegiance was to the chef. Where the chef went they went. The management company resembles the kitchen brigade in the sense that it provides a ready-made package of people and systems. One of the more important systems delivered by the management firm is likely to be the marketing and promotional system, often part of a national or international marketing/referral organization.

In some operations the human resource team is much more important than the systems or the facility. In others, human resources are of less importance. The fast-food hamburger restaurant may need only one or two knowledgeable management people plus an attractive facility, an advertising program, and a good location to be successful. Most of the employees are teenagers, who are quickly trained and easily replaced. A large, first-class hotel relies much more heavily on the human resources, the key people, the desk, housekeeping, engineering, sales, and food-service personnel.

In other words, human resources can be examined in the same way that physical resources are checked. The value of people in the organization can be accounted for in somewhat the same manner as buildings, beds, butter and eggs.

CHARACTER OF THE DEPARTMENT HEAD

The department head in the hotel and restaurant is in many ways a key to the success or failure of the business. No matter how sound the management's plans and policies, they cannot be effective except as instrumented by the department head. A chef unskilled in human relations can destroy a food business. An inept night manager of a hotel can disrupt morale and lose many guests for the hotel.

In the eyes of the employee the supervisor is management. The face-to-face relations between first-line supervision and the employees are the only realistic gauge the employees have of management. First-line supervision is the bedrock of morale.

In the hotel and restaurant field the supervisor has a bigger job than in most other businesses. The job has not been functionalized as it has been in the steel industry, where the crew supervisor has a few specific tasks to perform and is aided by time study persons, control personnel, and planning and engineering departments. In the hotel and restaurant field the supervisor holds a multiplicity of jobs. The executive chef of a medium-sized restaurant, for example, is responsible for the operation of the kitchen, and in addition, often does personnel work: hires, promotes, demotes, fires employees; arranges for vacations, rest periods, and lunch periods. As a department head much time is spent in conference with other junior executives and with the manager. Too, the executive chef is an engineering officer: if the dishwashing machine breaks down this same individual is supposed to know something about fixing it, and if there is any work simplification done, the chef directs it. The executive's chef's list of duties may ever be extended.

The housekeeper of a large hotel is another example, being responsible for accounting and purchasing of sup-

1. Savich and Ehrenreich, "Costs/Benefit Analysis of Human Resource Accounting Alternatives," *Human Resource Management*, Spring 1976.

(Above) A remote control computer terminal, located in Saga's Personnel Department, works in conjunction with the main computer. Up-to-the-minute personnel data can be transmitted into the files or extracted instantaneously through this unit. (Right) Programmers update Saga Administrative Corporation's computerized personnel records system located at the corporation's national headquarters in Menlo Park, California. The computer memory bank maintains data on more than 1,100 Saga food service managers located throughout the country.

plies, of decoration in rooms, and of upkeep and maintenance of equipment. These last duties are in addition to training new cleaners, scheduling their work, and making daily reports.

A Person in the Middle

The supervisor is in many ways a person caught in the middle. While representing management, this individual also represents the employees. When top management neglects to inform a supervisor of plans and policies and fails to support the person in relations with employees, that supervisor is indeed caught in the middle. To increase confusion the supervisor in the hotel or restaurant has a third party to please—the guest.

The supervisor is expected to be not only a leader but a follower. While planning and coordinating activities, the supervisor looks to management to determine policies and originate orders. In addition, in relations with other supervisors this individual is expected to act as if on the same level of authority and responsibility as they are. The supervisor plays a variety of roles, but the position is not always clear-cut. The supervisor is in a hazardous position from a personal stability point of view.

A Dealer in Human Relations

An important aspect of the job is human relations. The supervisor must be friendly and still maintain discipline—must understand the individual and yet treat that individual as a member of a group. It is necessary to be able to praise people without flattery. Orders must be clear and forceful yet must avoid the implication of command. While being a leader the supervisor must consider the wishes and suggestions of the employees by appealing to ambition but avoiding promises, the carrying out of which may be uncertain. Competition is encouraged but so also is team spirit. The supervisor is expected to be firm and consistent, yet flexible; is supposed to be interested in detail, yet full of enthusiasm and ready to think in broad terms. The supervisor, in other words, is expected to be one step lower than the angels.

Desirable Traits

What are some of the traits the supervisor should have or can learn in order to be successful? It must be admitted that some of these traits are largely the result of personality development over the course of years, but most of them can be developed, at least to a degree.

Ability and Attitude to Plan

Planning is the thinking that precedes the actual performance of work. It facilitates the avoidance of mistakes in practice by running over them in thought. It establishes goals towards which efforts can be directed.

Planning ability is not the same as intelligence. A genius according to the results of an intelligence test may be a poor planner. Planning is partially an attitude that can be acquired. It is a habit that can be encouraged in anyone.

Sound supervisory planning proceeds by definite steps. It requires the consultation and suggestions of everyone who will be affected by the plan. Sound planning welcomes modification.

An office manager sees the necessity for revising working hours. The manager discusses this necessity with the office employees, and also with top management, then reports back to the employees; a decision is thus reached that is acceptable to everyone, or at least much more acceptable than if the decision were entirely arbitrary.

Decisions that effect a major change should always be based on planning consultation. On the other hand, day-to-day decisions that implement plans already agreed upon are properly the supervisor's. To consult in such cases may be a waste of time, destroying the supervisor's rule as leader.

Ability to Set an Atmosphere of Approval

An atmosphere of approval is a social climate in which there is a minimum of resentment and insecurity and a maximum of personal satisfaction. The supervisor has so arranged the human relations that each employee feels that, despite one's mistakes and weaknesses, the supervisor believes in the individual, and the individual's value to the enterprise. A housekeeper makes the cleaners regard themselves as friends, and all consider the housekeeper as always being behind them. The host gets across the idea of siding with the waiters. The service superintendent has so acted that the service clerks believe they are respected and appreciated.

This means that the supervisor is friendly, but not familiar. It means that the supervisor goes out of the way to do favors for the employee, but does not make a practice of drinking beer or becoming intimate with employees.

It means that the supervisor calls the employee by name frequently, but may not approve of the employee's getting on a first-name basis. The supervisor visits the sick employees; is interested in vacation experience; is interested in the new car.

Some of the acts and attitudes that make for an atmosphere of approval are:

1. Recognition of each employee as an individual. Respect for the person's opinion. Recognition of each employee's contribution, and frequent expression of that appreciation. This does not mean unwarranted flattery. It does mean an attitude of looking for and speaking about acts or traits that warrant praise.

2. Consistent, predictable behavior on the supervisor's part. The supervisor works at maintaining a stable manner of acting in supervisory relations. Employees know what to expect. They feel secure in their relationship with the supervisor.

3. Maintenance of a stable, well-defined work environment. All changes of any importance are introduced gradually and with the approval, or at least acceptance, of the employees. Wages and promotion are clearly defined. Each employee knows what must be done to win a wage increase or a promotion. Orders are planned. They are stated in a definite form. The person receiving the order is given the reason for it. The person receiving the order is encouraged. The order is followed up. Similarly, other relations are planned and introduced with a minimum of confusion and anxiety.

The Desire and Ability for Leadership

In our culture it is tantamount to being un-American to deny a desire for leadership. Yet a minority of people have any real desire to take on responsibility, to plan, to take the blame for others' failures, to assume the guilt feelings that result from discharging or reprimanding an employee. Many other persons who have the desire for leadership do not have the ability, and no amount of education or training will equip them for leadership.

The requirements of leadership vary with different jobs. A chef need not have the same kind of leadership as that demanded of the hotel manager. The host requires a different kind of leadership ability than the sales manager. Some leadership jobs emphasize planning ability; others, face-to-face relations with people. The job of host requires the ability to work under social pressures; in the job of sales manager this factor is not as crucial as imagination and perhaps congeniality and enthusiasm.

Assuming the supervisor has the desire and native capacity for leadership, what traits and skills should be developed to enhance that leadership?

We have been discussing planning ability and the factor of setting an atmosphere of approval. These are requisites of leadership but are considered separately because of their individual importance. Later chapters will discuss means of creating personal satisfaction and attaining cooperation—also factors in leadership.

1. **Initiative and ideas.** Leaders are distinguished by their self-starting, their desire to get things done, their willingness to take on responsibility. They have ideas that, though often mistaken, stimulate others to thinking. Leaders develop initiative in others by delegating responsibility. They encourage others to take on responsibility. They have enthusiasm.

2. **Decisiveness and firmness.** Once a program of action has been decided upon by the group, the leader is decisive and firm in carrying it out. This applies to work standards and discipline in general. Personnel do not want lax discipline. They admire and follow decisiveness and firmness.

3. **The problem-solving attitude.** The leader sees employees and events as problems to be solved. An employee who is recurrently late is a problem to be solved, not an object of scorn or of retribution. A broken-down refrigerator is something to be fixed and to be prevented from breaking down in the future. The leader does not cry over spilt milk, being oriented to the future.

4. **The multiple-track mind.** The supervisor to some extent and the executive in a large degree each need to develop a multiple-track mind. Any job of importance requires that several projects be developed simultaneously. The executive must be able to switch from one thought and one project to another, painlessly and efficiently, keeping all in their proper perspective.

MANAGEMENT AND COMPROMISE

Good management does not necessarily mean that the manager has the ideas, then sells them to the staff, lock, stock, and barrel. Compromise and modification usually are needed. Often the best results are obtained when the manager's idea is amended in the light of the employee's reactions to it. The Hollywood version of the executive spending nights dreaming up wonderful new sales and production plans, putting them into effect the next day sometimes happens when the executive is brilliant and forceful, but this is atypical. The introduction of new ideas must always include prior consideration to existing habits and beliefs and so building on them.

Aside from encountering the usual resistance to all major changes in behavior, new ideas and behavior must also be fitted into what is already established. The manager's idea of where the new electric range should be placed will be only as good as the chef's acceptance of the idea. Probably the best location will be a joint decision growing out of consultation with the chef by the manager.

A good manager knows when to compromise and recognizes the optimum degree of compromise. Take as a case in point an occurrence in a British hotel where both the housekeeper and the hostess were unusually competent persons. As is often the case, in similar circumstances, some professional jealousy existed. The housekeeper, an old employee, resented the recognition of any newcomer in the organization, and, as was inevitable, an incident resulted.

The housekeeper's daily duties included placing flowers in the lobby. Her aptitude for flower arranging consisted of stacking them pell-mell in the receptacle, nothing more. The hostess, it happened, was an artist with flowers, and on seeing the disarranged flowers in the lobby, arranged them into a delightful floral ensemble, then left. Soon the housekeeper returned, and being only human, restacked the flowers as before. Later, the hostess returned, became perturbed, and trouble brewed.

The manager decided that one of the dissidents would have to go; however, both were competent, valuable employees. The manager talked the problem over with an assistant and received the suggestion that the two employees should be called in and counseled to see if they could not be brought into friendship.

The next day the assistant housekeeper was taken ill and could not report for work. The manager approached the hostess asking if she would be willing to help the housekeeper out of a jam. He spoke to the housekeeper intimating that the hostess desired to learn something about housekeeping. Could the housekeeper help? Indeed she could. The manager modified the original decision. The women became good friends and the organization was strengthened.

RELEASING HUMAN ENERGIES

Human beings have within themselves wellsprings of energy which, if tapped and directed, will accomplish individual growth and the satisfaction of human needs. If misdirected the energies destroy not only the persons involved but seriously interfere with the growth of people around them.

Improving the person means releasing energies, developing enthusiasms, directing these energies to useful purposes. In other words to improve the person we increase efficiency, we promote desirable goals, and we stimulate enthusiasm. How?

First by recognizing that to increase personal efficiency and build enthusiasm we appeal to the person.

And what is the person? A bundle of energies, guided by instinct and learned social needs. Each person is somewhat different, but enough like others of a similar background to be fairly predictable. To reach the person we must have some idea as to what makes one tick; what one wants today, tomorrow, and next year.

These things we know about all people, whether they be Eskimos or south Floridians; everyone needs some tension, some relaxation, some frustration of a kind that is challenging but not disorganizing, in order to give and get love and affection, and to experience the creature comforts and satisfy the other creature urges at least in part.

Everyone, be he president of General Motors or an Iowa farmer, needs a fairly predictable environment. Everyone needs relative security, the sense that one's major needs will be satisfied.

In this country most of us have come to place high value on these ten goals—each person ranking them according to one's own experience and physical makeup:

1. Economic security consistent with the level of anxiety over prestige, status, and protection from want (related to class position in the culture, deprivations experienced, resistance to frustrations, level of aspiration).

2. To know what is expected from one's superior; to be able to predict within reasonable limits the behavior of the superior.

3. Rewards: to know what will be forthcoming in the form of salary increases, promotions, commendations, etc., provided we exert our best efforts. To know that punishments in all forms (loss of prestige, loss of approval, etc.) will be forthcoming if we fail.

4. To know that one's associates are predictable.

5. A personal philosophy compatible with the social environment.

6. To "belong" and be accepted in one's social group.
   a) Participate in decision making and in the growth of organization.

7. To belong to a family (for some this may have more liabilities than assets insofar as stability is concerned).

8. To be successful in the eyes of those who count—superiors, one's neighbors, one's associates, the community—to achieve in one's own eyes.

9. To carry a favorable picture of one's self (self-esteem, self-respect).
   a) Maintain personal integrity, individuality, value as a person.
   b) To maintain consistent personal integrity in one's attitudes, beliefs, values.
   c) To at least "feel" that we are partially independent agents, that we have some share in making decisions that affect our own welfare.
   d) To experience the feeling of accomplishment.

10. To be able to express consciously our loves and hates (aggressions). To make a "reasonable" adjustment to the reality of one's culture.

To improve a person, capitalize on that person's constructive energies. Tie in the goals of the program with personal needs. Work can be seen as drudgery or as highly exhilarating activity. The way one sees one's work will determine that individual's performance to a large degree. When a program is seen as a means of achieving the following seven goals, the wellsprings of creative energy will be released.

1. Creating economic security
2. Gaining prestige and admiration
3. Gaining and giving love and affection
4. Performing work that is esteemed
5. Participating in sports and recreation
6. Acquiring knowledge
7. Aesthetic and spiritual development

All well and good. But how about specific do's and don'ts? Here are a few.

1. Define goals as a group. When a new kitchen range is needed get everyone in the kitchen in on the problem—even though you already know the best buy.

If there's a bottleneck on the serving counter—pose it as a group problem at your next meeting. We must feel close to our work team. We need to feel as though our thoughts on a common problem are important.

When there's a special dinner to be served—ask all of the personnel involved to decide who should work, how much each can do. Almost invariably goals set by the group are higher than those set by the supervisors. Group standards usually carry a lot more weight than supervisor standards.

Share decision making with your immediate subordinates. Encourage them to do likewise with their subordinates.

2. Hold out the carrot, but be frank about wages. Let employees arrive at the idea that their work is to a large degree like that of a minister or a nurse—their job affects the physical development and well-being of the community.

3. Give every person a "responsible part." Delegate responsibility even if it's only responsibility for measuring and controlling the temperature in the rinse compartment of the dish machine.

To develop responsibility, delegate. Expect mistakes at first. Ask people to do things. Praise results in public, discuss discrepancies in private.

4. You can help create a stable working environment by expecting crises. In the food business, crises are a part of the job. Expect them, anticipate them, and your adrenal glands will not be overworked.

5. Talk progress. Point out progress. Goals that have been reached do not motivate people. It is progress toward a goal that sparks an operation.

6. Keep the goals within the range of achievement. Impossible or long-range goals don't have much pulling power for most of us. To talk of what we should aim for next year has much less potency than to talk about what we're going to do tomorrow.

7. As a group, set up definite goals for each week; to lower this week's food cost, to paint the kitchen walls, to overhaul the ice machine, the target for next week is. . . .

8. Propagate the idea that this operation is going to be the best in the state, a good program with good people in it.

9. But don't be disappointed when everything is not the best. Perfectionism has no place in most supervision. Getting everything exactly right may be exactly wrong.

10. Improving the person improves the program. The best way to improve the person is to improve the program.

MANAGEMENT STYLE

As mentioned previously, the manner in which a manager manages can be termed *management style*. Style of management evolves from the manager's own philosophy and how that individual sees human nature. Style can also be taught, and most management development courses in the hotel and restaurant business today are featuring participative management as having a number of advantages over traditional styles. The authors take the viewpoint that management style should be related to the individual and group concerned, that one style of management may be effective with an individual who has a certain level of sophistication, another style more effective with a less sophisticated individual. The same individual may prefer one style of management one time; another, at another time. Much of what is said about management styles is based upon speculation. This matter of style will be reviewed within the chapter.

Management practices until fairly recently tended to emphasize the boss or owner as doing all of the planning and decision making. Employees were there to carry out the plans and wishes of the employer. The good employee was the obedient worker.

During the industrial revolution, there were more people seeking employment than there were jobs, especially in Britain. The worker knuckled under, or else. Labor unions were nonexistent. The individual did as told, or was replaced. In this country plentiful land and relative labor scarcity gave the employee more options. If unhappy with a boss, a person could change jobs, perhaps go West and take up farming.

Extreme labor scarcity during World War I and the growth of labor unions were instrumental in the giving of more thought about means of gaining maximum productivity from employees. Scientific management and the conveyor belt had dramatically increased productivity per person-hours but had tended to overlook the workers' feelings and needs for creativity and participation. It was time for the social scientists, fledglings though they were, to begin serious study of the human as related to work.

In the late 1930s a German psychologist, Kurt Levin, and a number of his students working at the University of Iowa and elsewhere conducted studies with children and teenagers to learn what type of leadership was best for a particular purpose. Groups of boys were given three styles of leaderships: laissez faire, autocratic, and democratic. The studies seemed to show that autocratic leadership would produce a high output but did not develop the capabilities or decision-making skills of the participants. Laissez faire leadership led to almost no production and the breakdown of the groups. Democratic leadership seemed to be most effective for personal development and, over a period of time, for productivity. Other psychologists studied leadership under various grants and came to shift the emphasis from considering the individual as having certain traits that were desirable for leadership to emphasizing skills that could be developed for setting a climate of leadership or management.

Implicit in the new thinking about management was the idea that the greater the participation in decisions by whomever is to carry them out, the better. An attempt was made to move from the old-style boss who gives orders to a new style facilitator who arranges for the best talents of the people in the group to be developed and expressed.

Contrasting Styles of Management

It is popular to contrast authoritarian and democratic styles of management, the assumption being that managers tend to fall into one or the other. Such contrasts are provocative even though they may be misleading. The authoritarian style has come to be known as *Theory X* as

proposed by Douglas McGregor in his classic book, *The Human Side of Enterprise.*[2] The democratic style of management is labeled as *Theory Y*.

As a means of sharpening the distinctions between the authoritarian (Theory *X*) and the democratic manager (Theory *Y*) the paradigm is shown as follows.

In describing management's task under Theory *X*, McGregor listed certain inherent propositions:

1. Management is responsible for organizing the elements of productive enterprise—money, materials, equipment, people—in the interests of economic ends.

2. With respect to people, this is a process of directing their efforts, motivating them, controlling their actions, modifying their behavior to fit the needs of the organization.

3. Without this active intervention by management, people would be passive, even resistant, to organizational needs. They must therefore be persuaded, rewarded, punished, controlled; their activities must be directed. This is management's task—managing subordinate managers or workers. It is often summed up by saying that management consists of getting things done through other people.

Behind this conventional theory there are several additional beliefs, less explicit, but widespread:

4. The average human being is by nature indolent, working as little as possible.

5. The average person lacks ambition, dislikes responsibility, prefers to be led.

6. The average individual is inherently self-centered, indifferent to organizational needs.

7. The average person is by nature resistant to change.

8. The average person is gullible, not very bright, the ready dupe of the charlatan and the demagogue.

Authoritarian	Democratic
People want to have situations well defined and to carry out orders.	People have creative capacity and want to use it.
Some people are strong, wise, aggressive, and creative.	Most people can be developed to be strong, wise, and aggressive.
A manager gives orders, does not explain.	A manager encourages participation in all decisions and at all levels.
People want to be controlled and directed.	People want to make their own decisions and resent coercion.
People are happy when under tight and wise control.	People are happiest when given wide responsibilities and will rise to the occasion with experience.

2. D. M. McGregor, *The Human Side of Enterprise*, proceedings of the 5th Anniversary Convocation of the School of Industrial Management (Cambridge: Massachusetts Institute of Technology, 1957).

According to McGregor, much of the conventional practice in management is fashioned from Theory *X* propositions and beliefs. By implication, then, the only decisions one need make as a manager relate to whether one should be *hard* or *soft* in one's approach, or perhaps as to whether one should take a middle position by being firm but fair.

By contrast with the Theory *X* approach, the Theory *Y* or human relations approach has come to question the basic tenets underlying Theory *X*. Do people really need to be directed? Do we get more productivity from people by treating them as tools or are there more effective ways of motivating people? What in fact *does* motivate people?

McGregor feels that humans strive to satisfy their basic needs. He utilizes the famous need hierarchy of the late Abraham Maslow to explain a person's needs (discussed in chapter 2, on motivation). There are five levels of needs. Once the needs at one level are satisfied, man seeks satisfaction at a higher level. These levels are as follows:

1. **Physiological and safety needs**
   The needs for protection against danger, threat, deprivation.

2. **Social needs**
   For belonging, for association, for acceptance by one's fellows, for giving and receiving friendship and love.

3. **Ego needs**
   Those needs related to one's self-esteem—needs for self-confidence, for independence, for achievement, for competence, for knowledge; and those needs related to one's reputation—needs for status, for recognition, for the respect of one's fellows.

Unlike the lower needs, these are rarely satisfied, but they do not appear until the lower needs are satisfied. Organizations offer few opportunities at worker levels for their workers to satisfy ego needs.

4. **Self-fulfillment needs**
   The needs for realizing one's own potentialities, for continued self-development, for being creative in the broadest sense of the term.

In a tight labor market, management might motivate workers by threatening their physiological and safety needs. When jobs are relatively abundant—as they generally have been since the start of World War II—workers are not likely to be satisfied nor motivated simply because their wages are adequate and their working conditions good, unless they also can receive some satisfaction of their higher level needs.

According to McGregor, the times of Theory *X* management have run their course. Modern managers need to become acquainted with the concepts of Theory *Y,* which operates on the following assumptions:

1. Management is responsible for organizing the elements of productive enterprise—money, materials, equipment, people—in the interests of economic ends.

2. People are *not* by nature passive or resistant to organizational needs. They have become so as a result of experience in organizations.

3. The motivation, the potential for development, the capacity for assuming responsibility, the readiness to direct behavior toward organizational goals—all are present in people. Management does not put them there. It is a responsibility of management to make it possible for people to recognize and develop these human characteristics for themselves.

4. The essential task of management is to arrange organizational conditions and methods of operation so that people can achieve their own goals *best* by directing *their own* efforts toward organizational objectives.

Theory *Y* then represents what has been called *management by objectives* in contrast to *management by control.* It focuses on the creativity of management to provide opportunities for employees to receive ego satisfactions. It charges management with the task of learning to decentralize jobs so that greater numbers have responsibility for decision making, to enlarge the responsibilities and decision-making possibilities within jobs, and to bring employees into the process of setting goals and of planning ways to implement those goals.

According to researchers who study management style, authoritarians, if died-in-the-wool autocrats, tends to shut themselves off in later life from new ideas and to resent anything that might be construed as criticism. If one owns the operation and can establish the rules and has most of the power, that individual's orders are simple, open, and direct. The employees know where they stand and may enjoy the kind of well-structured relationships engendered by the autocrat. Persons who have been dealing with craft and subtlety in management relations may welcome an autocratic climate.

The true autocrat makes the rules, obeys them, and expects everybody else to do so, while taking the responsibility for change and for failure. This individual may sincerely believe that employees, without one's paternal guidance, would be lazy (perhaps they are).

Under autocratic management employees more or less expect the boss to see to it that they are busy. When the boss is not around they may feel quite justified in relaxing or doing nothing.

The authoritarian manager may run an efficient operation; morale may be high; the customers may be highly pleased. Theorists declare that under the autocrat, employees do not "grow." It can be said with assurance that autocratic managers may be depriving themselves of ideas and enthusiasms from employees who have both to offer. This may be the case. It should be pointed out, however, that people can learn management skills and develop themselves under a variety of management styles.

Autocrats are likely to surround themselves with employees who respond to the autocratic style of management. An employee raised in an autocratic atmosphere may be conditioned to feel at home in such an atmosphere. This person feels less than comfortable if placed in a democratic climate. Employees who resent authority will leave, given other employment options. If employment opportunities are limited, such employees are likely to swallow their resentment and remain on the job. Knuckling under produces frustrations for such employees, but routine jobs may not interfere with their actual production to any great extent. They do it or else. Those who feel "right" under an autocrat may model themselves after the boss and, when promoted, step right into the boss role, giving orders, demanding loyalty and obedience.

Good autocrats feel that they know best. They may take parental pride in their operations and their employees. "Papa or Mama knows best." Some such autocrats take a deep personal interest in their employees and are more generous than managers who subscribe to other forms of management styles. The autocrat may develop a notion that the establishment is a "big happy family"; the manager is the parent.

The authoritarian style of management has advantages. Many successful hotels and restaurants around the world are run by autocrats. If the autocrat is well-trained, has imagination, is energetic, and knows the business, the hotel or restaurant may be extremely efficient. It may even be most satisfying to the guest or patron.

In the tradition of rugged individualism entrepreneurs dream their dreams, plan their strategy, and shape their individual organizations to the entrepreneur's will, producing a better product at lower cost and forcing competitors to the wall. That is the tradition of John D. Rockefeller and Henry Ford. In the hotel business competitors were not necessarily forced to the wall, but men like Caesar Ritz, Ellsworth Statler, and Conrad Hilton dominated their empires. In the restaurant business, Howard Johnson and J. Willard Marriott were in the same tradition. The antithesis of the corporation person, such persons rely little on committee or staff recommendations preferring to trust their own intuition and judgment. From the employees' viewpoint, from potwasher to vice-president, it's "what the big boss wants."

The X-run hotel or restaurant is the reflection of one man's imagination, drive, and dedication. In Valle's Steak Houses, for example, Mr. Valle often decided the price of the stuffed peppers, on the spot. His image and force of character was seen in almost every detail of operation even though the enterprise might include thousands of employees. Major decisions (and many small ones) are usually made by the central personality.

The same approach exists to some degree in the company founded by Howard D. Johnson. The rapid expansion caused much of the operation to become systematized. Purchasing, advertising, menu-planning, and much of the food preparation is done on a nationwide scale to insure consistently top quality. Operations at the unit are simplified and standardized.

The individual manager is given food and labor cost control targets that are tied to a bonus plan. A unit manager's primary function is to act as people manager by hiring, training, scheduling, and motivating. At this unit level, the nature of the management style is a direct reflection of the individual operating within a proven system.

Perhaps both X and Y theories are right. Inherently a person is curious and to a certain extent inventive. Cultures vary in terms of favoring one theory over the other. Parental influence is also a factor. When individuals mature and work in a certain type of environment they may be conditioned to move toward either X or Y. Being part of a conveyor belt system necessarily suppresses Y. Any time a person is substituted for a machine or forced to do completely routine tasks, it is psychologically important for the person to adapt to that environment. So much of work is a deadly routine.

Fortunately, in the hotel and restaurant business there is a minimum of routine, especially in guest contact relations, where every contact calls for adaptability on the part of the employee. Guest relations presents a constant challenge; it takes wit, flexibility, and energy to satisfy a guest.

Personality and Leadership Style

A 1977 study of nineteen hotels and twenty-two restaurants in the New Orleans area used the same conceptual framework, stating that "A highly independent person can be characterized as an individual who attempts to use job-related activities to fulfill higher order needs, such as the egotistic need. A highly dependent person will view a job only as a means of fulfilling lower order needs like food and safety. The individual with a highly independent personality will tend to be an initiator on the job, will want to take command, and will be interested in achieving and progressing. A highly dependent individual on the

Management Style
X/Y Continuum

X ←————————————————————————→ Y

Unilateral decision making

Gives orders

Makes demands

Raises questions

Sets climate for participating
decision making

Shows respect for others' input

Asks for opinions

other hand will tend to view a job only as a means of making money."[3]

According to researchers Nebel and Stearns, a participative-leadership style best suits an independent individual, while an authoritarian leadership style results in conflict. A dependent person welcomes structure and direction from above. Too much freedom or too much responsibility tends to frustrate such an individual. In their study it was found that the less education the employee had the greater the dependence on others, and consequently the need for a directed type of leadership.

The X-Y Continuum

Possibly the best way to look at management leadership behavior in terms of the *X* and *Y* Theory is to think of that behavior as being on a continuum, ranging anywhere from strongly authoritarian to completely democratic. At one end of the continuum would be the pure-*X* type behavior, the manager making the decisions and expressing commands for immediate compliance. At the other end of the continuum would be the manager who consults, asks, develops a group decision, and expects group action as a result.

The same individual could well go back and forth on the continuum, sometimes an autocrat, sometimes in between, sometimes a complete democrat. The situation determines to a large degree the most appropriate leadership style, where on the continuum the manager should fall in terms *X-Y* leadership. In observing managers in action it is seen that effective ones may run the gamut from *X* to *Y*, ordering, cajoling, pleading, asking, or merely presenting problems to be solved. At the *Y* end of the continuum the manager may be seen as a stimulator, a coordinator, a resource person posing questions, making arrangements so that conditions are such that the people who will carry out decisions will also participate in making them.

It is quite possible that in the hotel and restaurant the manager/leader is seldom pure *X* or pure *Y*. A manager can be characterized as more *X* than *Y*, somewhere in between, or more *Y* than *X*. The pure autocrat would probably not do well on the American scene. Neither would the pure *Y* type. The hotel and restaurant business is too much deadline dependent to permit the pure *Y* type of leadership for any period of time. There is also the matter of personnel turnover that requires rather strong direction of new people. Moreover, since a large percentage of hotel and restaurant employees come from less advantaged groups, groups that have been found to be comprised of more dependent types, the *X*-slanted style of management may be more appropriate, at least initially.

Whatever the theory, effective hotel and restaurant management personnel can be observed being primarily *X*-oriented. Salespersons may operate much more effectively under a *Y*-oriented style of management, although not necessarily so. Probably the really effective manager slides across the *X-Y* axis behaving as the situation dictates.

Nebel and Stearns conclude their study of leadership in the hospitality industry by saying that management has a responsibility for choosing a leadership style most appropriate to the circumstances. Three factors, they say, should be considered.

Employee factors, situational factors, and organizational factors.[4]

The employee factors that would favor a participative approach exist when employees have:

—High needs for independence;
—A willingness to assume responsibility for decisions;
—A high tolerance for ambiguity;
—A sincere interest in job problems and their solutions;

---

3. Eddystone C. Nebel III, and G. Kent Stearns, *Employee Characteristics and Personnel Practices in the Hospitality Business,* University of New Orleans, 1977.
4. Eddystone C. Nebel III, and G. Kent Stearns, "Leadership in the Hospitality Industry," *Cornell Quarterly,* November 1977.

—The experience and knowledge necessary to deal with job problems;
—And expectations of sharing in the problem-solving process.

Management-level employees and probably front-desk employees are more likely to fit these factors than are entry-level employees, such as dishmachine operators, lodging room cleaners, waiter's assistants, and cooks. The maintenance job with full responsibility for making up maintenance schedules, spotting mechanical problems, researching purveyors for replacement parts, and the like necessarily calls for a more independent personality. Department heads necessarily are more independent, problem-solving individuals if they are to be effective.

Situational factors that affect managerial style include:

—Work that tends to be unstructured and ambiguous; the nature of the problems faced by the group require the knowledge of the members of the group;
—The group has functioned together effectively for some time and can be expected to communicate and cooperate in a group problem-solving effort;
—The organization has a value system and management philosophy fostering a participative-management style; and
—The pressures of time are not intense, so that subordinates can be allowed to participate in the decision-making process.

The day-to-day operations of a dining room do not lend themselves to the participative style of management; employee meetings, however, present situations in which the participative style can be employed if other factors are appropriate. The housekeeping department of a large hotel employing disadvantaged groups who lack personal confidence and may have problems in coping with life generally, is not a situation conducive to participative management. "Different strokes for different folks." The host who is well educated, aggressive, and socially poised may respond to a participative management style, whereas the trainee-cook, with minimal education, may well expect and welcome a more directive approach.

Management climate of an organization also influences leadership style. Nebel and Stearns suggest participative leadership to the extent that the organization managers:

—Feel strongly that the employees should share in the decision-making process;
—Have a great amount of trust and confidence in their subordinates;
—Feel comfortable allowing subordinates a greater degree of latitude and freedom from supportive decision making; and

—Are able to cope with the increased uncertainty and ambiguity inherent in a participative approach to decision making.

Strong leadership at the top of an organization may have experienced success with a hard-nosed approach to people—do it or else. The president's style spreads up through all the ranks and influences the management style throughout the organization. On the other hand the company whose top officials have been influenced by management courses taught in colleges and universities are likely to favor the more participative style.

Much of the rationale for participative management is based on the rights of individuals to dignity and a voice in their own affairs. It is a movement away from treating the worker as a commodity or a replaceable part of a system. While system technology and scientific management have brought unparalleled prosperity to parts of the world, it has also dehumanized the worker in many instances. The highly paid employee on the Detroit assembly line feels a loss of identity and looks upon work as a necessary evil, a means of getting money. The tyranny of the assembly line is largely absent in the hotel and restaurant business, and for that we can be thankful (the conveyorized dishwashing machine comes close to it), but there are plenty of jobs that are oppressive. Try standing in front of a broiler for eight hours in a kitchen that is not air-conditioned.

Attempts to add interest to work and to give the employee a feeling of craftsmanship and completion is a movement toward humanizing the job. In the Volvo automobile plant in Sweden, for example, workers are put together as teams and assemble a whole car as a team rather than repetitiously adding a carburetor or a piece of upholstery time after time. It is reported that turnover has been reduced from 50 to 25 percent per year. This kind of job enlargement can be done in the hotel and restaurant business by having a dish crew rotate jobs, asking them to set their own standards of cleanliness, and performing their own quality control in terms of seeing to it that the rinse water remains at 180°F temperature. In the housekeeping department, team cleaning has been tried and under some conditions has worked well.

THE MANAGEMENT GRID

A clever device for placing one's self in either the autocratic or democratic camp was developed by Blake and Mouton.[5] They developed a leadership questionnaire that gets at the dimensions of autocracy versus democracy, in their terms *task-oriented or people-oriented*. According

5. R. R. Blake and J. S. Mouton, *The Managerial Grid* (Houston: Self Publishing Co., 1974).

to the way a number of questions are answered the person can place himself on a grid, seen as figure 8.1. The grid allows scoring on two scales, *T* and *P,* standing for task-minded or people-oriented. The highest score possible is nine on each scale. A score of five indicates average concern. According to the authors a nine-nine placement on the grid is ideal. It represents high concern for both people and production. A one-one slot would reflect a laissez-faire state of abandonment. A one-nine scale overbalances in the direction of care and comfort for the employee, while a nine-one location on the grid indicates autocratic management.

Concern for production or task and concern for people are often incompatible. This is one of the reasons why supervision is complex. If we had no production goals and management involved only in keeping people satisfied, our task would be less complex. Likewise, if we operated a completely computerized operation in which we only had to push buttons, our supervisory responsibilities would be relatively easy.

There is no best balance between production and people; the correct balance must be worked out within each organization. As already discussed, certain supervisory styles are more effective than others. Before people can change to new supervisory styles, however, they need to recognize their present supervisory styles. The *T-P Leadership Questionnaire* can be helpful in pinpointing styles.

To test yourself complete the T-P Leadership Questionnaire that follows these scoring instructions:

1. Circle the item numbers for items 1, 4, 7, 13, 16, 17, 18, 19, 20, 23, 29, 30, 31, 34, and 35.

2. Write a 1 in front of the circled items to which you responded S (seldom) or N (never).

3. Write a 1 in front of the items not circled to which you responded A (always) or F (frequently).

4. Circle the *1's* you have written in front of the following items: 3, 5, 8, 11, 12, 15, 17, 19, 22, 24, 26, 28, 30, 32, and 34.

5. Count the circled *1's*. This is your person-orientation (P) score. Record the score in the blank following the letter P at the end of the questionnaire.

6. Count the uncircled *1's*. This is your task-orientation (T) score. Record this number in the blank following the letter T.

Figure 8.1   T-P Leadership Questionnaire

Name _____   Group _____

The following items describe aspects of leadership behavior. Respond to each item according to the way you would be most likely to act if you were the leader of a work group. Circle whether you would be likely to behave in the described way *always* (A), *frequently* (F), *occasionally* (O), *seldom* (S), or *never* (N).

If I were the leader of a work group . . .

A F O S N 1. I would most likely act as the spokesman of the group.

A F O S N 2. I would encourage overtime work.

A F O S N 3. I would allow members complete freedom in their work.

A F O S N 4. I would encourage the use of uniform procedures.

A F O S N 5. I would permit the members to use their own judgment in solving problems.

A F O S N 6. I would stress being ahead of competing groups.

A F O S N 7. I would speak as a representative of the group.

A F O S N 8. I would needle members for greater effort.

A F O S N 9. I would try out my ideas in the group.

A F O S N 10. I would let the members do their work the way they think best.

A F O S N 11. I would be working hard for a promotion.

A F O S N 12. I would be able to tolerate postponement and uncertainty.

A F O S N 13. I would speak for the group when visitors were present.

A F O S N 14. I would keep the work moving at a rapid pace.

A F O S N 15. I would turn the members loose on a job, and let them go to it.

A F O S N 16. I would settle conflicts when they occur in the group.

A F O S N 17. I would get swamped by details.

A F O S N 18. I would represent the group at outside meetings.

A F O S N 19. I would be reluctant to allow the members any freedom of action.

A F O S N 20. I would decide what shall be done and how it shall be done.

A F O S N 21. I would push for increased production.

A F O S N 22. I would let some members have authority that I should keep.

A F O S N 23. Things would usually turn out as I predict.

A F O S N 24. I would allow the group a high degree of initiative.

A F O S N 25. I would assign group members to particular tasks.

A F O S N 26. I would be willing to make changes.

A F O S N 27. I would ask the members to work harder.

Figure 8.1 — *Continued*

A F O S N 28. I would trust the group members to exercise good judgment.

A F O S N 29. I would schedule the work to be done.

A F O S N 30. I would refuse to explain my actions.

A F O S N 31. I would persuade others that my ideas are to their advantage.

A F O S N 32. I would permit the group to set its own pace.

A F O S N 33. I would urge the group to beat its previous record.

A F O S N 34. I would act without consulting the group.

A F O S N 35. I would ask that group members follow standard rules and regulations.

T_____ P_____

_____   _____

Name   Group

Locating Oneself on the Grid:

Directions: In order to locate oneself on the Leadership Grid below find your score on the Person dimension (P) on the horizontal axis of the graph. Next, move up the column corresponding to your P-score to the cell that corresponds to your *Task score* (T). Place an *X* in the cell that represents your two scores. Numbers in parentheses correspond to the major management styles in Blake and Mouton's Managerial Grid.

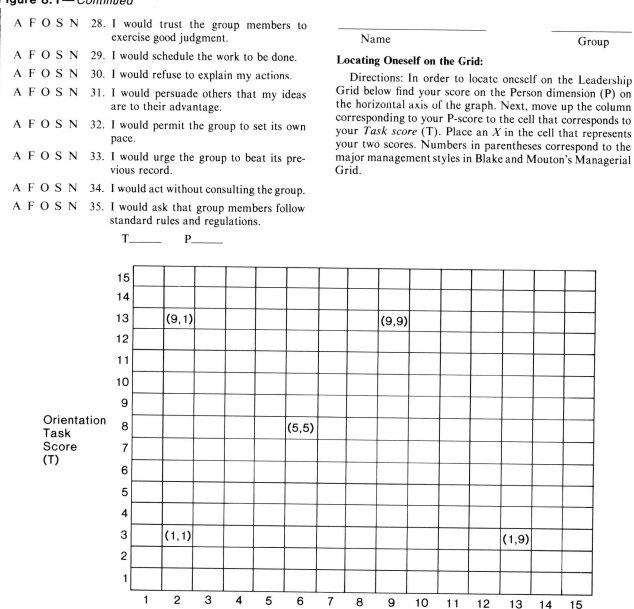

The management grid and its assumptions make for an interesting discussion among supervisory or management people. It can be used as a springboard for teaching management theory and as a training device.

PERSONALIZED MANAGEMENT

So far we have discussed Theory *X* and Theory *Y* and managerial strategies related to these two theories as proposed by Douglas McGregor. Contrasting the Theory *X* individual with the Theory *Y* is an excellent way to dramatize the two ends of the continuum of management style. A further refinement is needed, however, to translate the theory into practice, for the simple reason that very few people, employees or managers, fall directly into either camp. Even Adolf Hitler was not strictly a Theory *X* manager, for he used many of the techniques on his generals that a Theory *Y* manager is supposed to use. Neither does Machiavelli fall under the Theory *X*.

We all know from personal experience that different strategies are needed for different people and for the same person at different times. Personalizing management according to the conditions existing and the personalities involved calls for the greatest of skill, and not a little intuition. This is where management becomes an art rather than a science.

Professor Clare W. Graves proposes that individuals exist on one of several levels of human behavior, depending upon their health, sophistication, and personal adjustment.[6]

Recognizing that classification is always arbitrary, he suggests seven levels of existence, each level calling for its own management style:

1. Autistic behavior (barely alive). At this level the organism is so ill that the person can produce nothing. The only kind of management appropriate would be that of parent caring for an infant. Such people do exist in underdeveloped parts of the world and among people who are seriously ill mentally or physically, or nutritionally weak.

2. Animistic existence (belief in mystic forces). This is the unsophisticated person, hagridden by superstition or taboo, whose concept of time, space, quantity, materiality, and the like exists only vaguely. The manager of this type of person must accommodate to the individual's style of life and understand that the usual incentives do not apply. Force will work as long as it does not conflict with strong religious or other beliefs.

3. Awakening Level (need for structure). At this level a person needs an orderly, predictable, and unchanging world based on a predestined order. Millions of people in India and Africa live in such a world. Management should be tied to rigid rules of what to do and what not to do. Such a person is confused by being asked to participate in management decisions. Theory is inappropriate.

4. Aggression and Power Level. At this level the person believes in being able to control events and other people. Power is important. Management and employees joust for power. Union leaders may be of this type and may see relations between management and employees as a matter of who dominates who. A manager operating in level 4 may do quite well as long as he can manage level 3 people.

5. Social-centered level. At this level the worker has moved beyond level 4 and seeks a congenial atmosphere and a comfortable work place. The person slows down his work and concentrates on satisfying social needs. At this level an employee does not believe it is one's moral duty to do one's best as does the level 3 worker, but will, however, be responsive to group incentives and group decisions.

6. Aggressive individualism. The employee has lost common fears and refuses to be dominated, believing that the goal is important, not how one gets to it. Management is to provide the support and wherewithal to do the job. The goal can be set jointly, but management must not prescribe the way to the goal. This person resents both the social leader and the authoritarian. The level 6 person may both threaten and confuse the conventional manager.

7. Pacifistic individualism. This is the highest level in which the individual is not particularly aggressive or resentful, but insistent on an atmosphere of trust and respect. This person resents domination of any kind. Management must fit the organization to that person—not the other way around. Many professional staff people, for example, are at level 7, and deeply resent autocracy in any form.

Relation to Theory X and Y

In reviewing the seven levels it is seen that neither Theory X or Y would work with level 1, the person who is barely alive.

Theory X would work with levels 2 and 3, and in some cases with level 4 people.

Theory Y would be the most appropriate for level 5, but a new type of management that fits itself to the individual is more appropriate for levels 6 and 7.

At these latter two levels the so-called *supportive management* is most appropriate.

What further complicates management theory is that people move from one level to another, according to their energy level and personal needs at the moment. A person may welcome a highly structured organization when first moving into a hotel or restaurant, but later resent it. The person who has had a bad night may not want to participate the next day. At times nearly everybody needs a parent figure, and would welcome "big daddy" or "big mommy" as a boss. At other times they will quit a job if such a management is even hinted at.

Theory X is based on these assumptions about the universal drive in humans:

1. The average person dislikes and will avoid work.

2. The person therefore has to be forced, controlled, and directed to work.

3. The person prefers to be directed and has little ambition.

4. The person seeks only security.

---

6. Clare W. Graves, "Deterioration of Work Standards," *Harvard Business Review,* Sept.-Oct. 1966.

Theory X would relate well to at least the first three levels of existence. At higher levels it would not be as appropriate.

Theory Y supposes that the expenditure of effort at work is natural:

1. External control and threat are not good means for producing work.
2. People will exercise self-control and self-direction if their ego and actualization needs are met.
3. The average human will seek responsibility under proper conditions.
4. Employees will exercise imagination and ingenuity when managed not by external direction and control but by self-direction and self-control.

Theory Y is not necessarily appropriate for level 5 where the person is mainly concerned with satisfying social needs. Many bureaucratic organizations are happy organizations because they are clubby and socially centered. Little if anything is produced. The employees are busy enjoying each other and satisfying their own personal needs. This may explain in part why it is possible for a takeover company to eliminate millions of dollars in staff salaries and still increase production.

The bureaucratic organization tends to operate at level 5, especially if level 5 people are employed. The good bureaucrat is a level 5 individual. One of the main sources of achievement is to beat the system, extract more vacation days, use up one's sick leave, get a merit increase regardless of merit. Level 5 proliferates administrators who only make work for each other and those who report to them. Budgets increase and departments enlarge so that eventually they are like the crew of a Navy vessel, everyone working for everybody else and very little coming out at the end of the line. People are busy reporting to each other, coordinating, writing memos, building fences, entertaining the right people, pleasing the boss.

All this says is that management calls for a great deal of insight into one's own personality and into the personalities of associates and employees. Management style is an interaction between the manager and those managed. What style is the effective one depends upon the two parties concerned. Asking a person right off the street to respond to participative management is false idealism. Expecting military-type management to work with a highly trained professional may be equally bad, although some professionals may expect and enjoy autocratic management if other conditions are right.

The level 6 and 7 persons are those who are positive, growing, eager for part of the action. They are genuinely uncomfortable when unchallenged. They seek the approval not only of peers but of the boss. These persons do not need close supervision or rigid controls. To be boxed in with bureaucracy is stultifying to them as personalities and as producers. They resent being told minute details of what should be done and what should not be done. The authoritarian is resented. Presumably they will respond positively to a system that helps fulfill their needs for self-respect; since such persons are going to be on the job a good share of their lives they want work that is intrinsically satisfying. Too often in the past work has been seen as a necessary evil, necessary as a means of getting the wherewithal to do the things one wants to do.

The Theory Y person may be framed too idealistically. Certainly much of the work done in hotels and restaurants must be accomplished by system. There is no great demand for innovation, at least on a day-to-day basis, except in the realm of human and guest relations. Even the brain surgeon gets bored.

In many hotel and restaurant work situations boredom is minimized by the fast pace demanded of the situation. The teenager working in a McDonald's restaurant has no time for boredom. In fact, the job is so demanding that few people over thirty can stand the pace.

Whether or not a person is comfortable in a particular management climate depends a good deal on level of energy, imagination, expectations, and the life-style grown up into. Presumably everyone has the God-given force within to grow, to take on challenges, to be competitive, to enjoy activity. Society places constraints on these forces in school and elsewhere. Disadvantaged homes may produce the kind of apathy or fatalism that makes the person something other than a clear-cut exemplar of the kind of person who does well under Theory Y or at levels 6 and 7.

EXECUTIVE COMMITTEE MANAGEMENT

A number of hotels and hotel chains have introduced the idea of Executive Committee management, a plan under which the general manager meets weekly with divisional or major departmental heads for a discussion and possible resolution of hotel problems. In the Hyatt Hotels, for example, the Executive Committee is made up of the divisional managers (Rooms, Food and Beverage, Engineering, Sales, Comptroller, and usually one or two other departmental heads). The group meets every Monday morning to review problems and plan for the future. The Executive Committee arrangement does not relieve the general manager of final responsibility for all decisions, but it does allow for first-hand information about problems to be brought forth at the meeting and it facilitates the resolution of problems.

This arrangement is a form of participative management. When extended down through the departmental heads and into the various departments by other meetings and discussions, it spreads participative management throughout the organization. The management style of the general manager, of course, influences the degree of participation that takes place. If nothing else, the establishment of an Executive Committee arrangement at least sets the stage for a participative management and provides a structure through which participative management is encouraged. The Executive Committee arrangement is not democratic management, a form that would be ineffective in a hotel or restaurant. Meetings are held behind closed doors. Majority opinion does not rule. The general manager is still completely responsible for results, must still stay on top of the operation, and should continue to insist on peak performance.

MANAGER-ON-DUTY PROGRAM

Another related program in the direction of participative management is the "manager-on-duty" scheme used in many Hyatt Hotels. According to a schedule, each departmental head assumes the role of general manager for a weekend. While largely relieving the general manager of weekend responsibility, department heads get top management experience. When scheduled for weekend duty, the departmental head in effect becomes general manager. A manager-on-duty becomes a manager-in-training.

To make the program more attractive to departmental heads, they are invited to move their families into the hotel for the weekend. There, they are treated to the best suite available, all food and beverages, and the use of all hotel services. Mondays, following the weekend duty, are days off for the departmental head.

THE "DIRECT LINE" PROGRAM

Establishing a structure for communication outside of the formal organization is another way of gaining interest and participation. Hyatt Hotels have set up "Direct Line" committees, which are comprised of one appointed employee from each department. Membership is rotated quarterly. Usually the most vocal employees are selected and encouraged to speak out concerning problems and grievances.

MOTIVATION AND BUREAUCRACY

Qualities needed in a bureaucracy may be considerably different from those needed in a vigorous, expanding organization. The bureaucracy may value cooperativeness, the ability to work with others, and skill in pleasing a number of people, but it values especially skill in pleasing the immediate boss. The driving, energetic gamesplayer could feel stifled in an old-line organization with a flat growth. The ambitious restless individual who possesses much self-confidence will probably not remain long in the flat-growth bureaucracy. Bureaucracies attract people with a high need for security, those who are not overly concerned with productivity—their own or others—and those who are patient. In a full-blown bureaucracy the ambitious individual may need to wait for years to make major changes or advance. The military is a good example of this sort of bureaucracy. Small talk at the Pentagon centers around retirement. Not much is said about goals and results. A good bureaucrat knows how to get things done in spite of others. The aggressive person may be used, then discarded.

Conversation with an executive recruiter:

"We are looking for a young person to come into a 100-unit fast-food organization, someone who is aggressive, driving, who can take over the organization within fourteen months. The individual will be in a training position for about a year, at which point the salary will be increased. At the end of fourteen months the increase will be substantial as the person assumes the presidency."

"Are you interested in someone who is aggressive to the point of being abrasive?"

"Yes, indeed, that is the kind of individual we need to get the organization rolling. After it gets going the person can be fired."

The recruiter is saying that the overly aggressive person can be hired for a purpose, then released when the purpose has been served.

MANAGEMENT DEVELOPMENT FOR MINORITY GROUPS

In the 1960s management in the hospitality business began to think seriously of ways to move members of minority groups into management. The countrywide emphasis on civil rights under the leadership of John F. Kennedy and Lyndon B. Johnson gave rise to civil rights legislation and encouraged minority groups to press for greater recognition and the possibility of moving from menial jobs into supervisory positions. The riots in several of our cities were at least partially responsible for the desire on the part of many managements to have at least a few minority members in positions visible to the public, such as in the front desk and in the personnel department. In the early 1960s Jackie Robinson, a former baseball great, was given the title of personnel director of the New York-based fast-food chain Chock-Full-of-Nuts, and several of its units were managed by blacks. By and large, however, relatively few members of minority groups are in management.

Motivating trainees from minority groups for management positions may present special problems of learning. Hispanics may have English language handicaps. Expectations and confidence levels may be low. The achievement may be less than necessary for management, and needs for affiliation and security may override other considerations. To explore the problems of moving members of minority groups into management in the hospitality field, two studies were funded by the Statler Foundation.[7]

What follows is a statement of some of the assumptions made in conducting the studies and some of the conclusions drawn based on the studies.

LEARNING TO PLAY THE ROLE OF A MANAGER

Anyone who moves from worker to management level must learn to play a new role, that of a manager. To be effective the role must be more than concerned with using certain phrases, accents, dress, and manner. Most important for the role of manager is to think like a manager, with a sense of being positive about problem solving and planning, and to have an attitude that makes for pleasure and excitement in achieving. McClelland and his associates at Harvard University have used a projective technique to illuminate the trainees' present motivations and to impel them to think and act like managers. It is an interesting and challenging mode of training.

The particular projective technique used by the McClelland group is a modification of a well-known device, the Thematic Apperception Test. The subject is presented with a series of unstructured pictures and asked to tell a story about what is taking place in the picture. Usually the subject is not aware that in fabricating the story one is telling about oneself—one's own problems and aspirations.[8]

The stories are analyzed in terms of four motivations: achievement, affiliation, power, and security. After a discussion of how the various motivations influence behavior and relate to managerial success the subjects are asked to retake the same test. In the second testing the subjects are requested to respond to the pictures as though they were high achievers. In effect, they are asked to role-play the part of the high achiever. In so doing they change their own perspective and presumably begin to think, talk, and act like achievers.

The purpose is to get the nonachiever to set achievement goals and to search for the means of attaining them. They supposedly pick up the kinds of attitudes necessary to overcome obstacles; they learn habits of getting expert help. Most importantly, perhaps, their time perspective

changes. Instead of living for the now, or in the past, they develop concern for anticipating tomorrow and avoiding disasters in the future. Role playing using the "Exercise of Imagination" (as the modified TAT is called) has been able to effect changes in individuals' achievement drive in various countries where the achievement training seminars have been conducted.

The "Exercise of Imagination" test was used in the second phase of the Statler Advancement Program. It is interesting to note the variation in response among subjects to the same picture. As an illustration: the last picture in the series is that of a man sitting in a relaxed position in an airplane seat. All of the pictures are purposely vague.

1. Subject 1 interprets the picture as: "Mr. Thompson who is on a plane smiles to himself after reading a book concerning the ways in getting the job done and with less cost to the company at the same time."

The interpretation of this response is highly favorable in terms of the achievement drive. It represents the kind of thinking intended by the course. The subject sees and projects a personal need for achieving into the picture and does so in positive concrete terms. "Getting the job done with less cost."

2. Subject 2 has these reactions to the picture: "Not too many people can have this kind of happiness. A man away from home is back in town again. In these days to go from one place to another does not take long because of the giant planes we fly. In two minutes we will be landing at the airport. My wife and my son probably will be there waiting for me. Then I'll be a happy man."

The need projected by subject 2 is primarily concerned with "affiliation" and "security." This one sees the person in the picture as getting satisfaction from having the support of one's family. The subject is probably insecure at the moment from being in a strange environment—the course itself.

3. Subject 3 says: "This is a manager trying to make a success at his new job, but seems to have doubts and lacks confidence and courage to go on."

The subject reflects self-doubts and insecurity, perhaps lack of confidence in the new role being presented in the course.

---

7. The studies were conducted at the University of Massachusetts in 1971, and at Gettysburg College in 1972.
8. The theory behind the use of the test is seen in these books by David McClelland: *Motives and Fantasy and Action* (New York: Van Nostrand Reinhold, 1958); *The Achieving Society* (New York: Van Nostrand Reinhold, 1961), *Motivating Economic Achievement* (New York: Van Nostrand Reinhold, 1969).

4. Subject 4: "This picture is saying that the man has made it in life. This person is thinking about the hard times he has had but is not lying back taking it easy thinking how far he has moved up in life."

The subject here is reflecting on a personal long struggle to achieve and is "backward-oriented," at least in this response.

5. Subject 5: "A hard working and busy manager has completed a very profitable job and is returning home to his wife and family with a feeling of well-being and accomplishment. He is thinking ahead of more goals to start on the next day."

The subject reflects the achiever type of thinking.

6. Subject 6: "I've reached my goal. My family is secure and I'm thinking back about the hardship and suffering I went through to achieve this goal. Now I'm beginning to realize what hard work brings, how do I tell my children in order that they may achieve this goal more easily. My decision will be education, experience, and desire to want to be a part of society."

Running through most of the responses was a great emphasis on security, having arrived, and a need for affiliation. Several apparently felt that leaving the worker role with its union protection for a management position decreased security.

In reviewing the responses there was little evidence of the need for power, although two of the subjects displayed considerable aggressiveness in class as regards a need to exert "leadership" within the group. This was evidenced by their monopolization of the discussion at times, sitting at the head table at the time certificates were awarded, and generally "taking charge."

Another recurrent theme evidenced in the responses was an apprehension over becoming a manager. Most of the subjects felt that they had been tagged for a promotion either to supervisor or a higher rung in the management ladder. This apprehension was again understandable.

It is suggested that the test of imagination has considerable potential value for any course in motivation training. Care should be taken, however, in presenting the test so that it does not threaten the subject.

HOTEL AND RESTAURANT MANAGEMENT RELATED TO OTHER DISCIPLINES

One of the most interdisciplinary of studies, hotel, restaurant, and club management draws on a number of other disciplines. The subject of management itself draws upon the more basic disciplines of psychology and sociology. The hotel, restaurant, or club manager is knowledgeable in food preparation, control systems, design, and tourism. These in turn draw upon more basic disciplines. For example, food preparation is based on food science, nutrition, chemistry, and microbiology. Hotel and restaurant control systems are based on computer technology, finance, mathematics, and accounting. Tourism draws on areas of travel, transportation, history, government, and destination development.

Figure 8.2 represents one attempt to show the relationships between the various disciplines that together comprise hotel, restaurant, and club administration. It is included here merely to show the complexity of the field and the necessity for being versed in a number of areas of study. The chart suggests the challenge of the field.

COLLEGE AND UNIVERSITY EDUCATION

Beginning in 1922 colleges and universities in the United States offered four-year courses in hotel and restaurant majors leading to a bachelor of science or bachelor of arts degree.

Today, some fifty universities offer four-year degree programs in food-service management, hotel management, or both. A few offer a masters degree program. The Council on Hotel, Restaurant, and Institutional Education publishes a directory of these schools. The *Directory of Hotel and Restaurant Schools* can be obtained by writing to the Council on Hotel, Restaurant, and Institutional Education, Henderson Human Development Bldg., Penn State University, University Park, Penn. 16802.

Institutional management, a related field, is offered at about 100 colleges throughout the country. Institution management trains dietitians and food-service managers in hospitals, schools and colleges, hotels, restaurants, in-plant feeding operations, and in research.

It is difficult to know exactly what hotel and restaurant executives would like to see offered in a university curriculum. Some favor sales, others finance, still others food and beverage knowledge. A survey of twenty leading hotel chains in the United States revealed that 89 percent of the respondents felt that a bachelor's degree in hotel administration was valuable; 56 percent favored a master's degree in Business Administration. All placed high value on experience, and most arranged for job rotation, understudy, and on-the-job training experiences for junior management. Table 8.1 shows what the respondents believe to be major skill requirements for future hotel executives.[9] It should be pointed out that at the time of

9. Anton W. Gotsche, "Executive Development in the Hotel-Motel Industry," *The Cornell Hotel & Restaurant Quarterly*, February 1972, p. 77.

Figure 8.2   Relationship of Academic Disciplines to Hotel, Restaurant and Travel Administration

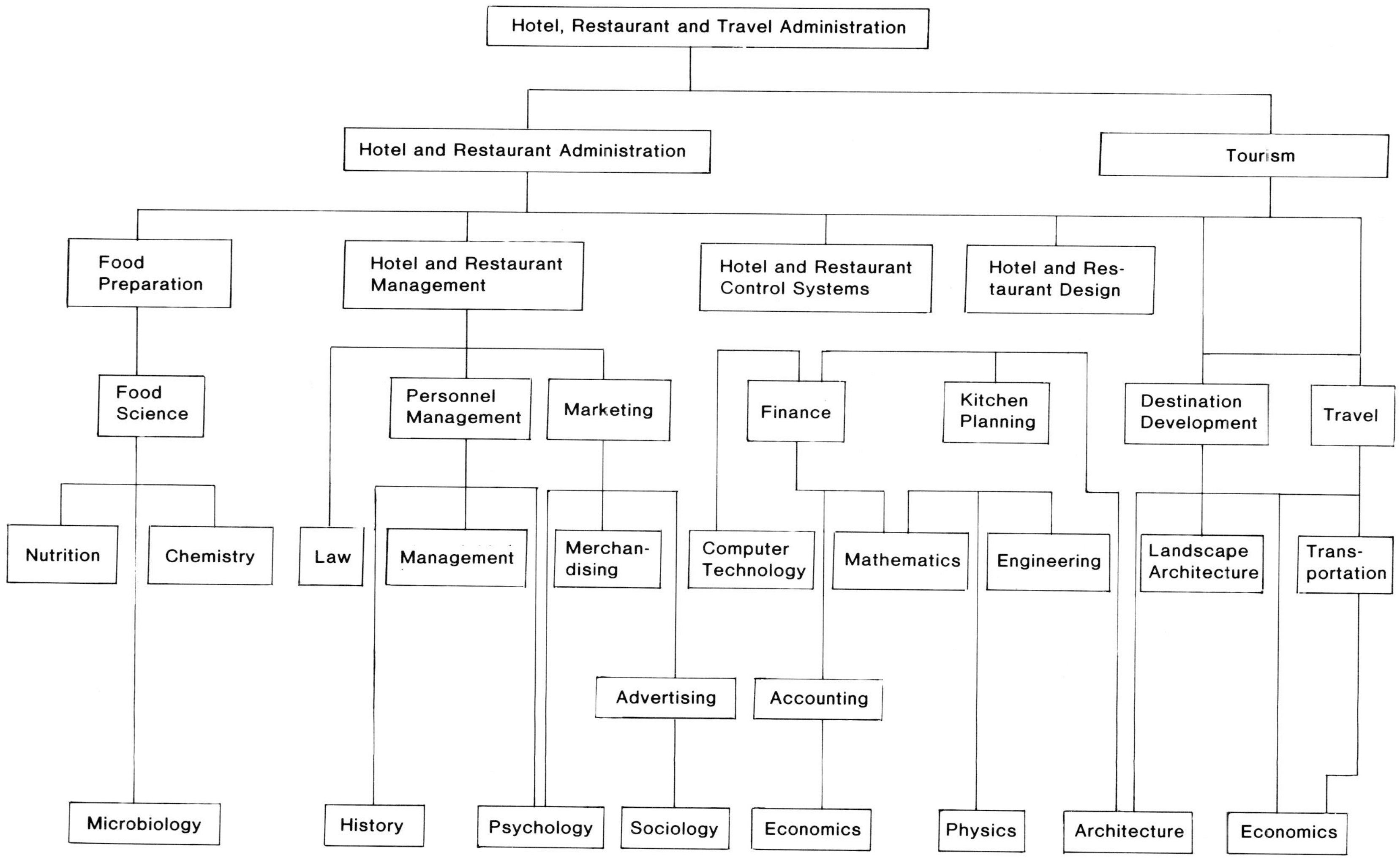

One of about 50 universities offering hotel and/or food-service management courses, California State Polytechnic University, Pomona, headquarters its hotel and restaurant program in Kellog West, a beautiful conference center that provides a "living-learning" center for students.

Table 8.1	Major Skill Requirements of Future Hotel Executives	
Skills Required	Number of Companies	Percentage of Companies
Financial management	17	94.5
Decision making	16	89.0
Human relations	16	89.0
Marketing management	16	89.0
Accounting and controls	14	77.8
Written communications	14	77.8
Public speaking	12	66.7
Food and beverage management	12	66.7
Legal background	10	55.6
Sales management	10	55.6
Quantitative analysis	8	44.5
Computer programming	8	44.5
Systems management	8	44.5
International management	7	38.9
Economics	1	5.6

the survey hotel occupancy was down, which might have affected the ranking of the skills required.

It could be expected that the ranking would be different if done by proprietors of motels and restaurants. Club operations would place much less emphasis on financial management and very little, if any, on marketing management. Food and beverage management would probably be moved up towards the top in importance.

Curricula Offerings

College-level hotel and restaurant courses can be divided into five areas:

1. Management

2. Accounting and control

3. Foods: preparation and service

4. Engineering

5. Travel and tourism

The emphasis on these areas varies with the school. All of the schools insist on practical training along with theory. Summer work is encouraged or required, and work in the kitchens and dining rooms of the colleges is possible for most students desiring it.

University level courses in Hotel, Restaurant, and Travel Administration must be designed to provide both skills and theory. If the course of study is weighted in favor of skills, academicians are likely to fault it for being vocational. If weighted heavily in favor of theory the student and the industry feel that it is impractical. Courses like *Front Office Management, Housekeeping,* and *Cooking* come in for considerable criticism from some students and from educators who favor theory. On the other hand, most students resent having to enroll in courses such as physics, chemistry, and higher mathematics, feeling that courses like these are not relevant to the practice of management. Nearly everyone has a bias in favor of one subject or another. Some favor heavy emphasis on sales, others on computer application, some on accounting and control. Since employers expect graduates to have a certain basic knowledge of pricing, controls, and operations, the hotel and restaurant educator finds it impossible to present a curriculum that is well received by everyone.

For example, in a doctoral dissertation, it was found that while chief executive officers in hotels and restaurants rated social sciences and humanities to be of little or no importance in the curriculum, educators in the field (perhaps because of pressures from their colleagues) were more favorable to the inclusion of such subjects in a hotel and restaurant curriculum.[10] The majority of educators, chief executive officers, and chief personnel officers did not believe instruction in the liberal arts to be important in the development of the potential executive for the hotel and restaurant industry. Chief personnel officers would emphasize human relations skills, while chief executives would stress improvement in communication skills. Chief executives would emphasize development of creative thinking, inspiration, and initiative. The teaching of advanced management techniques was ranked low by educators, personnel officers, and executives.

The statement that follows is a viewpoint as to what Hotel, Restaurant, and Travel Administration education should be on a college campus.

As a field of study, Hotel, Restaurant, and Travel Administration is interdisciplinary. It draws upon economics, psychology, management, food technology, food chemistry, microbiology, physics, engineering, architecture, accounting, marketing, law, and transportation. From these disciplines are formulated approaches, systems, and analytical tools for the purpose of providing satisfying emotional experiences and services for people in the context of lodging and food service away from the home. Figure 8.7 represents an attempt to show how the study of Hotel, Restaurant, and Travel Administration draws on more basic discipline for information and expertise.

Recognizing that the person trained for today is out-of-date tomorrow, the teaching emphasis at the universities is on principles and analytical tools, processes, and systems. These change relatively slowly. While, for example, it is not necessary for the usual hotel and restaurant graduate to be a computer expert, he should know the capabilities, limitations, and (to some extent) about the language of the computer.

It is recognized that at least a minimal exposure to the skills and knowledge that make up the present state of the art is necessary for an understanding of the principles. Skills such as typing, NCR operation, ice carving, bartending, busing, and dishwashing are seldom taught at the university level. But, for example, hygienic principles of food handling are taught, and the student is asked to apply this knowledge in the dishroom and in general sanitation in the food service.

In teaching about food at the university level, there is little interest in teaching cooking skills but much interest in having the student understand the rationale of cooking. Food purchasing, preparation, and service is taught along with the role of food in history and in society as part of a total dining experience.

Accounting principles are included in the curriculum but students are expected to learn front-office procedures on the job. The theory of management is taught knowing that only in the crucible of work as a supervisor can the graduate learn to be a manager. Food chemistry and heat transfer are presented, and the student is expected to round out knowledge of cooking while on the job as it applies to a particular style of operation.

The place of the hotel in society is stressed, rather than a particular building design, although both are important. An understanding of the forces of society that make vacationing possible are as much a part of our field as the pricing of a menu.

It is said that "the past illuminates the present." The development of the hotel and restaurant field, the men and their ideas who have innovated, are considered important for an understanding of the field today and the direction it may take tomorrow. The economics of travel and innkeeping are seen as a reflection of the total economy, interrelated and sharing in the broad forces which form our society.

It is recognized that students are composites of many talents and that in the restaurant, hotel, and travel field

10. Robert Lukowski, "A Comparative Study of Attitudes toward Undergraduate Education for the Hotel and Restaurant Industry" (Ed.D. diss., University of Massachusetts, 1972).

pure academic ability—the ability to learn and handle abstractions—may not be any more important than the ability to withstand stress, to maintain moral stamina, and to be able to force one's way to a hard but necessary decision.

No one personality type is prescribed for success in the field. The accountant in a hotel is likely to be a different personality type than the manager, the sales manager different than the food and beverage director. Special opportunities exist in the expanding area of public food service, in health care, nursing homes, and schools. Travel agencies and airlines offer appealing positions for individuals who take the travel and tourism area of concentration. For the sports-minded, there careers open in ski lodges and stadium food service operations. The outdoor type will probably prefer the resort to the downtown hotel.

Consideration is given to the moral and ethical aspects of management, since every personnel decision has moral overtones.

Research is another function carried on as a means of developing new information and involving students and faculty in the excitement of discovery.

The hotel, restaurant, and travel field is intrinsically exciting. Students who elect the field as a career can participate in this excitement and in so doing transmit some of this excitement and its pleasures to the traveling public.

FROM COLLEGE TO CAREER

The thousands of students enrolled in the two- and four-year Hotel and Restaurant programs around the country are often unprepared for the transition from college to the workaday world. That transition is made easier for the student when the individual's educational program has had close ties with industry and when the student has been required to work in the industry during summer vacations and/or part-time during the college years. A number of the four-year programs require the student to complete 800 to 1,000 hours of work experience to qualify for graduation. Seen by many students as an imposition, the requirement is to the advantage of the student, enabling the person to gain first-hand experience in the field, in a way that is nontraumatic should the student decide that the field is unsuitable. If the person's capacities and interests lie elsewhere, no one is hurt seriously.

The student work experience enables the person to learn the "dog work," the "nuts and bolts," basic skills that the college graduate should have salted away in the nervous system before graduation—busing, waiting, basic cooking, front desk clerking, stewarding, cashiering, hosting—jobs a general manager must know something about.

Students also work as trainees during the summers in hotel sales, as reservation clerks and in a variety of other positions; the greater the variety the more valuable for the student.

Having learned the basic skills in and out of school, the student, once graduation rolls around, is often bewildered by a number of avenues open and uninformed as to the best way to proceed. The new graduate produces his resumé and often mails a number of them broadcast to the headquarters of a variety of hospitality businesses. When only a few reply the applicant becomes discouraged.

The applicant must keep in mind that the hospitality business is to a large extent people-related and that it would be foolish for a personnel director or manager to hire anyone solely on the basis of a resumé. The new graduate should also keep in mind that anyone successful in the hospitality business has to be assertive and aggressive, reflecting these qualities is the manner in which an applicant goes about getting the job. Will the person call, make an appointment, and appear in person on time, well groomed, responsive, eager to please, self-contained, and ready to present oneself in the best possible light? Too often recent graduates have exaggerated notions of their value; at least that is the impression they leave on the interviewer. The applicants should strive to present themselves realistically, with emphasis on their positive qualities. They should be self-possessed, confident, mannerly, and thoughtful towards the other person. A person who is over-aggressive may be just right for the job but turns off the interviewer. Controlled ambition and a readiness to work within the parameters of a particular organization are usually the best tactics for those seeking management positions.

The usual large organization recognizes that new graduates are best placed in training positions for a few months, a time for each party to learn about and test the other. The expectation of the independent enterprise often exceeds what the graduate can accomplish. At times a new graduate is highly elated to be placed in a very responsible position, one which after a few weeks or months overwhelms the person. Too bad. Both parties suffer. The recent graduate has learned but at the expense of some emotional scars. How much better to move up only when ready.

Another traumatic situation can occur when a recent graduate sets up in business before being ready. Not only is the experience traumatic; it can be costly, a cost that could hang like a millstone around the person's neck for years in the future. It has happened many times. The best way to go into business is to first learn a format thoroughly and then copy or adapt it. That way the little things like buying the right product, having a reliable supplier, having the right menu, the right location, etc., have already been learned. Any one of a multitude of factors can become a major problem if something similar has not already been experienced. Better to wait a few years and have more than adequate contingency financing to cover the unforeseens.

THE RIGHT SPOUSE

Hotel and restaurant people are known for their high divorce rate, a fact that is quite understandable in the light of the demands made by the business—constant pressure, odd work hours, long work hours, anxieties, people frustrations, the depression that comes from overwork. Physical attraction is not enough to hold marriages together when hit by the onslaught of the kinds of tensions that can be characteristic of the hospitality business. Common goals, common interests prove the better cement for marriage survival. Many successful motel and restaurant businesses represent the combined efforts and enthusiasms of a couple. In restaurants the wife often does the bookkeeping and handles the personnel while the husband is concerned with the operations. It is not uncommon to find that the wife is the better operator and front person, while the husband takes on a specialty, such as purchasing, bookkeeping, or public relations. Gender does not necessarily determine the best choice of role. The wife may be the leader, the husband the follower; accept it and exploit it. If the wife is the retiring, number-minded person, let her be the bookkeeper; if she "just loves people," maybe she fits as the official host for the whole operation. If he is mechanically minded and just loves yard work, that is where he belongs—in the yard and with the machinery.

THE RESUMÉ

Just prior to graduation the student often sees the outside world as coming up fast, formidable, confusing, challenging. How best to present oneself to the waiting business world? A resumé is in order but how to draw it up. Is it so complicated that one must turn to a resumé specialist? Is a resumé really needed? If the student has been working with a company while in school, the logical move is to go with that company if both parties like each other. Even so it is well to have a resumé on hand that can be updated as necessary.

A resumé is no more than a succinct information sheet of interest to a prospective employer. As such it makes sense that the resumé may require tailoring to the particular job opportunity. In most cases one asks oneself "What does the prospective employer want to know about me?" Resumé formats vary, but can run something like this:

Resumé

Name	Residence	Phone

Personal data: Date of Birth.* If married—name of spouse, and names and ages of children (if any).

Height and Weight; State of Health, Religion.*

(*An employer may not legally ask about such things as religion or age, but it may be wiser to include such information to avoid joining a company that is prejudiced in those areas.)

Academic experience: Year of graduation from high school; name of high school.

Years of graduation and names of higher educational institution(s). Listing of courses completed that seem particularly relative to the job in question.

Grade point averages attained if above average.

Work experience: List all work that has been accomplished and detail relevant responsibilities.

References: List those persons who would be certain to give a favorable reference. Avoid listing anyone whom you might have reason to believe would not give a favorable reference. Include addresses and phone numbers.

(If already employed it is sometimes better to specify "References upon request.")

Honors received: List awards, commendations, offices held, scholarships won, membership in the elite organizations, etc.

If an Eagle Scout list it, if President of a student organization, name it.

Hobbies and sports: List participation in sports, team or otherwise.

Hobbies, such as English History, stamp collecting, racing cars, repairing old automobiles, bicycle touring, etc.

By all means carry a resumé to every interview, and hand the interviewer a copy. Doing so saves time, is businesslike, and creates a favorable impression with the interviewer. Some recruiters for large companies mark down anyone who appears for an interview without a resumé.

THE PROBLEM OF YOUTH

Many recent hotel and restaurant graduates are moved into management positions within a year or so and find themselves supervising people much older than themselves. The younger persons are put on their mettle to behave in a way that avoids the appearance of immaturity or lack of leadership, or ability, and gains the respect and confidence of the older persons. Throughout history, political, military, and business leadership has not necessarily been related to age, although the appearance of dignity and maturity is more important in some situations than others. There have been major generals, self-made millionaires, and city mayors in their 20s. The younger person may need to work at presenting the mature image, but the most important thing is to show determination, enthusiasm, and flexibility. A willingness to ask questions and to show appreciation for advice is helpful. The cocky young graduate with all the answers can be a liability to himself or herself and to the organization. The young manager has to work harder, longer, and with greater purpose than others and be able to communicate to others the desire to achieve. Push without being pushy. Be willing to retreat when necessary, ask questions, respect others, and recognize that the college education provides only a base upon which to build and from which to grow.

Dietetic Internships

The American Dietetic Association (ADA) has an intern plan for training dietitians. A postgraduate program provides the student who has the baccalaureate degree with training in one of three different kinds of internships: hospital, administrative, or food clinic. Most approved courses last one year. Membership in the ADA is highly recommended.

Management Correspondence and Home-Study Courses

Several motel-management correspondence courses were developed in the 1950s and more in the 1960s. Some have depended upon high-pressure salesmanship plus the implied promise of employment following the completion of the course.

The least expensive and most comprehensive correspondence courses for the hotel and restaurant field are available from the Educational Institute of the American Hotel and Motel Association, headquartered at 1407 S. Harris Road in East Lansing, Michigan. Programs of study offered by the Institute include the following:

1. *Management and Administration*
   Introduction to the Hospitality Industry
   Organization and Administration in the Lodging Industry
   Motel-Motor Hotel Management

2. *Professional Development*
   Human Relations: Supervisory Development I
   Communications: Supervisory Development II
   Training in Coaching Techniques: Supervisory Development III

3. *Technical Management*
   Basic Sanitation for Food-Service Employees
   Hotel-Motel Law
   Food and Beverage Management and Service
   Hospitality Industry Accounting I
   Food and Beverage Purchasing
   Food Production Principles
   Front Office Procedure
   Hotel-Motel Sales Promotion
   Supervisory Housekeeping
   Maintenance and Engineering
   Tourism and the Hospitality Industry
   Convention Management and Service

The Institute offers a diploma program under which the enrollee may receive a diploma upon completion of ten of the Institute courses, provided the courses completed were so selected as to represent each of the three major areas of course offerings: Management Administration, Professional Development, and Technical Management.

A recent home-study course has been developed by the National Institute for the Food Service Industry (NIFI). The main thrust of their instruction, though, centers around food-service sanitation. In fact, their course on sanitation is used by many states and municipalities for certifying food-service managers.

SUMMARY

More organizations are providing management-development programs for both salaried and hourly employees.

The importance and complexity of the role of the supervisory personnel or department head is being increasingly acknowledged. The supervisor must be a dealer in human relations with the ability and attitude to plan and to set an atmosphere of approval and the desire for leadership. Good supervisors make judgments, arrive at compromise solutions, anticipate crises, and establish climates in which others can feel secure and effective. They recognize individual differences in employees and are sensitive to special needs of people: the young, elderly, minority, or handicapped workers.

To encourage ambition and growth among employees, the development of career ladders is recommended to provide a route of promotion and movement. Formal programs of training, development, and progression can be established.

Management styles differ. It is important to recognize various prototypical positions of management, such as those popularized by Douglas McGregor as *Theory X* (authoritarian) and *Theory Y* (democratic). Industry today is moving toward Theory Y, toward management by objective rather than management by control. With such movement, management's task is to show creativity in providing opportunities for employees to receive ego satisfactions through such things as decentralizing jobs, enlarging responsibilities and decision-making possibilities within jobs, and bringing employees into the process of setting goals and of planning ways to implement those goals.

Unfortunately, Utopias do not exist in the hotel-restaurant field. An effective manager must be eclectic in adapting different styles to different situations and different people. We need to recognize that Maslow's level of self-realization is a potential, not a fact, in most individuals. Until a person feels comfortable in a structured environment, that individual is not likely to feel comfortable in an unstructured environment. The effective manager must use different styles for people at different levels of development. The more managers understand the different styles, the more likely they are to understand their own individual style. Once one can recognize one's style, then one is in a position to alter, adapt, or develop that style.

Human relations exercises—as discussed and presented later in the book—are designed to help managers understand their styles and to experiment with change. The T-P Questionnaire, to signify *task-* or *people-orientations,* is presented as an exercise to help supervisors understand their management styles in terms of the Management Grid concepts of Blake and Mouton.

The use of Executive Committees in hotel operations is a move in the direction of participative management. The general manager of the hotel enlists the interests and knowledge of key departmental heads but retains final responsibility for all major decisions.

Special emphasis needs to be given to the management development of minority groups. Few members of minority groups are found in management at present. In addition to problems of discrimination, minority group members often are lacking in educational skills, experience, and confidence for handling management positions. Studies demonstrate that groups can change historical and cultural attitudes, such as reflected in low levels of aspiration and needs for achievement, if a supportive environment is provided with the definite purposes in mind

of raising expectations and ways of thinking. With a critical amount of intellectual ability and energy, many persons can be trained to be managers and leaders. What is important is to provide individuals with practice in thinking like managers and wanting to be managers.

The field of education in hotel-restaurant management is expanding broadly. With expansion come inevitable questions concerning curriculum, areas of emphasis, and student selection. One of the major struggles—not unlike that found in all disciplines—involves the balance desired between theory and practice. At present most college-level hotel and restaurant courses can be divided into five areas: management, accounting and control, foods, engineering, travel and tourism. As the field expands more and more opportunities for training exist at all levels.

A HOTEL MANAGEMENT DEVELOPMENT PLAN

A few of the larger hotel chains have developed comprehensive management training programs lasting from a few months to a year, time enough for the trainee to move through the various departments of the hotel and actually work many of the key stations. Hyatt Hotels is typical. The program lasts one year. It takes the trainee through rooms division, the food and beverage division, the sales department, the controller's division, the engineering department, and work with the personnel director and at various kitchen stations. About four months are spent in the rooms division, four months with the food and beverage operations, and two months in the other departments. An additional two months are scheduled in the area in which the trainee wishes to build a career following completion of the program.

Under the Hyatt plan, a trainee may receive a management assignment in the front office, reservation, housekeeping, or guest services. The rooms division includes the jobs and the functions seen in the chart below.

Rooms Executive		POSITIONS HELD
Front Office Manager Housekeeping Manager Hotel Assistant Manager		
PBX Bell Service Concierge	Security Reservations	EXPOSURE
Hotel Law Contracts	Budgeting Forecasting	SPECIAL KNOWLEDGE
Involvement Leadership Ability to Communicate	Empathy Adaptability	PERSONAL QUALITIES

Working with the Food and Beverage Director, the trainee goes through the positions seen in the following chart.

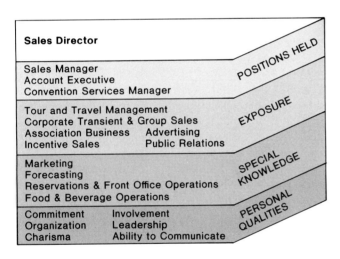

The Sales Department trains the student in market forecasting and provides exposure to work with reservations and front office operations (see the chart).

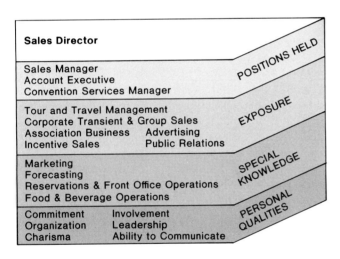

The assignment with the Personnel Director the trainee covers the areas indicated in this chart.

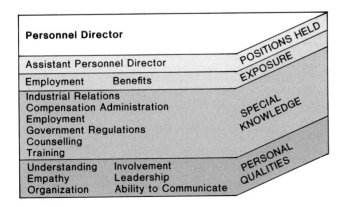

Each Hyatt Hotel has a Controller in charge of accounting and bookkeeping. The trainee covers the functions as seen in this chart.

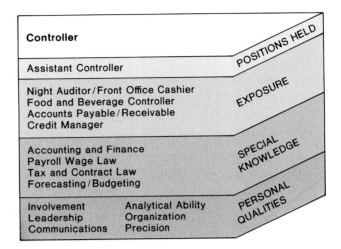

A stint with the Chief Engineer involves the kinds of functions seen here:

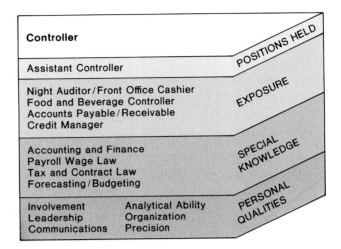

In the kitchen, working under the Executive Chef, the trainee is exposed to the functions seen here:

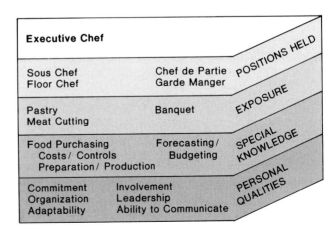

PERSONNEL PROBLEM CASE STUDIES

Two personnel problem situations, representing actual cases are described below. Based on your study, identify and analyze the real problems. Then, think of possible alternative solutions and finally select the solution you believe would be most effective. Be able to produce reasons for your decisions, and describe how you would implement them.

There is rarely a totally correct answer to such situations since each tends to be unique.[11]

The House of the People

Sidney West recently was hired as president of one of the "grand" hotels in the world, located in a major east coast city. His selection was unusual, as West had no previous experience in the hospitality field beyond that of a professional guest. He had been a successful advertising executive.

The hotel, The Court Arms, was a landmark, known for excellent service, tradition, and a certain ambiance. When West became president, employee performance relative to this image was poor, as shown by increasing numbers of guest complaints and a decreasing percentage of return reservations. Guests were becoming used to curt answers, indifference, and a lack of courtesy from the services staff, which included the front desk, waiters, bellmen, door attendants, and cleaners.

His first month was spent walking around the property, investigating complaints, and interviewing as many employees as possible. He found some major problem areas. The employee locker room was in disgraceful condition. There was trash on the floor, no soap or towels in the restroom, toilet seats were missing, and locker doors were broken. Other employee areas were in similar disarray, with paint and plaster peeling from the walls. West visited the employee cafeteria, where he found the food unpalatable and the utensils bent and dirty. The cafeteria was inadequately lighted—dark. In essence, he felt that the employees lived better at home than at The Court Arms. West could well imagine a room service waiter bringing fine food to a suite and then returning to a dungeon where he could not adequately or comfortably wash his hands.

When he questioned the personnel office, which was located at the rear of the hotel in the basement, about the orientation program, he was shocked to find out that the program consisted of signing a W-2 form and immediate assignment. The formal training program featured only on-the-job training for a three-day period and had no performance evaluation, except comments from the immediate supervisor. Moreover, a bulletin board planned for the outside of the personnel office had never been installed, and important employee notices were posted in a haphazard manner.

West soon discovered that a language barrier was partly responsible for poor communication. Five hundred employees out of 1,500 could not read, write, or speak English. Spanish was their primary language. The hotel's house organ was of little use as it was written in English and featured only management receiving awards and industry accolades. All departmental and interdepartmental memos and notices were solely in English. Also, he found that employees in the same department and throughout the hotel knew their fellow members by face, not by proper name.

In his rounds of the front of the house, he noted that the desk clerks and the reservationists had never seen a guest room, much less spent a night as a guest of The Court Arms. How could they effectively show enthusiasm about the rooms and special features to a prospective guest? In a similar vein, the managers of the six restaurants in the hotel ate only at their own restaurants. They neither knew about the merits (or lack of them) of the other five restaurants, nor had they investigated their competition outside the hotel. The hotel department heads also were unfamiliar with the internal workings of the other departments. Poor communication and coordination had led to many disruptions and embarrassments for the departments, and for the guests caught in between.

West had a monumental task in front of him. How could he achieve a smooth-functioning internal hotel team at The Court Arms, where the employees would be proud to work and where the guests would be treated as well as the employees?

Questions for Discussion

1. How should West define priority areas of concern?

2. In each priority area so designated, outline several methods that West could utilize in order to find solutions for these problems.

3. What should an orientation program include?

---

11. Eight additional case studies taken from real-life situations in the hotel and restaurant business are available. These cases focus on personnel problems relating to motivation, responsibility, authority, organization, orientation, recruitment, selection, training, grievance procedures, and company policy. Such case studies can provide insights into decision making in the hospitality business. The cost of the studies is $5.00, and they can be obtained from John R. Hendrie, Personnel Department, The St. Francis Hotel, Union Square, San Francisco, CA 94119.

4. How could West motivate his service staff in order to instill a pride in their performance? Where should he start?

5. What role should the personnel department play in West's reorganization of and reemphasis on the employees?

The Rooms Department

Mr. Harold Kline is the Rooms Manager of the Skycrest Hotel in York, Pennsylvania. He supervises eight employees in his department and knows that different leadership styles and inducements will encourage these subordinates and upgrade their performances. These are the employees:

A. Juan Gomez (21)—Elevator Operator. He has been with the hotel for three years, since arriving from Puerto Rico and has been taking English and math courses by correspondence in hopes of a high school equivalency diploma. Juan will be married in four months.

B. John Sims (35)—Assistant Rooms Manager. John is married with three children, ages 5, 7, and 9. His wife is experiencing a difficult fourth pregnancy. He has worked at Skycrest for seven years, having started as a desk clerk.

C. Millicent Fernis (23)—Secretary. A recent college graduate who just recently joined the staff, Milly is an avowed activist. Noted for her independence, she also has a high absenteeism rate and frequently takes a long lunch hour. Millicent has been accused of creating dissention in the department, but is regarded as a proficient secretary.

D. Harry Cotter (48)—Bell Captain. Harry, a black, has worked for this hotel for 24 years, having started as a bellman. Unmarried, Harry knows "where the action is" for lonely guests. He performs his duty with ease and confidence, spending off hours with his sick mother.

E. James Schmidt (26)—Front Desk Clerk. James, a veteran, is completing college at night. He has worked at Skycrest for the past year. Management feels that he has great potential, as he is punctual, honest, and very thorough. His wife is a secretary in the sales department.

F. Salena Goertz (33)—Cashier. Salena is fairly new with Skycrest, although she had a similar position with another hotel. She is considering marriage to an accountant and leaving to become a housewife. As she is a new employee, Salena has yet to have complete authority or responsibility for her position as cashier. Her dissatisfaction with the training period, considering it to be too lengthy, has been heard by some department members.

G. Sean O'Neill (51)—Doorman. Sean has worked at Skycrest for over 20 years. Lately, management has heard some complaints about his being gruff to guests, and his behavior when not on duty being boisterous. He holds another job as a bouncer for a nightclub.

H. Ted Hart (38)—Front Desk Clerk. Ted is very quiet and goes about his job in a routine manner. He is married and has two children. Management felt that Ted was ready to advance a year ago.

For each employee, choose a style of leadership (paternal, authoritarian, etc.) and at least three incentives from the following list:

Incentives

1. More recognition
2. Major Medical insurance for family members
3. A raise in salary
4. Overtime beyond straight salary
5. A more flexible work schedule
6. More supervision
7. Threat of separation
8. Threat of demotion
9. A title
10. Educational benefits for family
11. Less supervision
12. Greater decision making
13. Job enlargement
14. Job rotation
15. Interdepartmental or inter-hotel transfer
16. Profit sharing
17. A management trainee program
18. Reimbursement for night school courses

Improving Morale

9

MOTIVATION VERSUS HYGIENE

Let's return again to a discussion of the motivational theories of Frederick Herzberg, discussed in chapter two.[1] It was noted that the factors that lead to satisfaction and high motivation in workers are different from the factors that lead to dissatisfaction and low morale. People who are happy with their jobs generally feel they are successful in the performance of their work and that they have the possibility for professional growth. Conversely, those individuals who are unhappy with their jobs—who have low morale—have feelings that are usually associated with the conditions that *surround* the doing of their work. For some reasons they regard their work environment as psychologically unhealthy.

Undesirable work factors may be thought of as *hygiene* factors in the sense that hygiene operates to remove health hazards from the environment. Hygiene is not curative; rather, it is preventive. Factors of hygiene included in work are supervision, interpersonal relations, physical working conditions, salary, company policies and administrative practices, benefits, and job security. When any of the hygiene factors deteriorate to a level unacceptable to a worker, then poor morale and job dissatisfaction are likely to occur. The reverse, however, does not hold true. Just because hygiene can be maintained at an acceptable level does not mean that employees will have positive attitudes toward their jobs. They will have only an absence of low morale and dissatisfaction. Positive satisfactions are related to opportunities within the job itself for self-realization and feelings of personal accomplishment.

Much of this book is aimed at the methods by which management can provide a climate where workers can maximize self-realization possibilities. Concepts related to management by objective, job enlargement, Theory *Y*, democratic and humanistic management are all concerned with the problems and methods of establishing satisfactions for workers.

This chapter, by contrast, deals with hygiene and is concerned with (*a*) recognizing those factors that can contribute to low morale and (*b*) describing programs and techniques that can contribute to increased morale.

Some symptoms of low morale:

1. An unusual number of disciplinary problems and grievances
2. Low output, featherbedding, or slowing down
3. Unusually high absenteeism and tardiness rates
4. Lack of interest and inefficiency
5. High sickness rate
6. Evidences of fatigue without apparent cause
7. High turnover, bickering, and internal fighting.

If communications are effective in an organization, potential morale problems can be identified quickly before they get out of hand. Informal communication meetings will point out such problems, and employees are likely to bring problems into the open at group meetings.

THE LOW TURNOVER FALLACY

Personnel experts have for many years lauded low turnover, holding it up as an ideal and denouncing the hotel and restaurant business as a turnover nightmare. In fact, many jobs are better performed by persons who are "pass-

---

1. Frederick Herzberg, *The Motivation to Work* (New York: John Wiley & Sons, 1959), and Frederick Herzberg, *Work and the Nature of Man* (Cleveland: World Publishing Company, 1966).

ing through." One has only to compare the flight attendant of the 1950s and 1960s with the flight attendant on the preferred routes of today. Before airline unions became so strong, flight attendants could not marry or be of a certain age and meet other stringent qualifications. The younger flight attendant looked upon the job as a fun thing, an opportunity to travel, to meet a prospective spouse, an adventure. After a few years, the adventure part wore thin, the attendant married, had a family, and the job became a big drag. The cute, young individual who said "Coffee, tea, or me" now says "Coffee, coffee, coffee." The eagerness to please is not there. Yes, the new attendant is professional, but impersonal and bored.

Much of the hotel and restaurant business depends upon young people for its high gloss, enthusiasm, and warmth. The front desk clerk who is a careerist can scarcely be expected to be excited and eager after three years of the same thing. Many of the best waiters are young, college women and men who, if they became careerists would be less than good.

Depending upon the job, high turnover or low turnover may be good or bad—bad if it is a reflection of poor management, poor wages, poor working conditions; good if it brings fresh enthusiasms into the business, fresh perspectives, fresh aspirations. The hotel and restaurant business has been uniquely valuable to our society in that it provides entry positions for young people, jobs that introduce them to the work ethic under favorable conditions. The fact that the young people do not envision the job as a career may be a plus factor for the business.

Certainly high turnover among chefs, department heads, and managers is not conducive to efficient operation. A reasonable turnover figure for managers might be 10 percent a year, as compared with 100 percent turnover among teenagers in a fast-food operation. Teenagers who receive the minimum wage, experiencing their first work, may find the experience salutary. The general public gets quick, pleasant service, and food at reasonable prices.

There is much to be said for rotating managers and supervisors from one unit to another. Some hotel chains have an established policy of moving managers every two to three years. Management personnel in expanding chains, especially restaurant chains, move much more frequently. Management personnel may learn from each move. The potential for boredom or complacency is greatly reduced. In a growing restaurant chain, assistant managers may find themselves general managers in new stores within a few months; district managers of five to ten stores within a year or so.

Having said this, we can also say that labor turnover can be a clue to morale.

LABOR TURNOVER—PRO AND CON

As defined by the United States Department of Labor, labor turnover is either the percentage of total employees hired in a month, or the percentage of total employees leaving in a month. Whichever percentage is smaller is the turnover rate, in this case called the *net turnover rate*.

The costs of turnover are sometimes overlooked. Some of the costs are hidden. To itemize a few may emphasize the costs.

1. Recruitment costs—newspaper and other advertising costs.

2. Induction costs—clerical help, interviewer's time, department head's time, stationery, costs of checking references, physical examinations.

3. Training costs—time of trainer, cost of training materials, supervisor's time.

4. Production losses—losses resulting while new employee's learn to perform efficiently. Losses entailed by other employees in having to work with or teach new employees. Loss of patronage because of poor service. Loss of production between decision to quit and actually quitting.

5. Breakage costs—breakage of dishes, breakage of equipment due to lack of skill.

6. Accident costs—higher accident rates of unskilled employees reflected in direct or indirect workmen's compensation insurance cost.

7. Over-all costs—breakdown of social organization that is reflected in overall loss of morale and efficiency.

Total turnover costs run from a minimum of about $50 for a new kitchen helper to several thousands for a top executive.

High turnover rates in themselves do not necessarily mean poor management. First of all rates must be considered relative to the hotel and restaurant business.

Turnover rates must be viewed in the perspective of the locale and of general business and world conditions. Turnover rate is much higher during and following a period of war. One would also expect a higher turnover rate in a metropolitan district than in a smaller city or town. Turnover is high when unemployment is low. Nevertheless, labor turnover can be an index of morale. When there is a spurt in the labor turnover rate of a particular department, it is time for the personnel director to look into the supervision, wage rates, and other conditions of employment in that department. Likewise, when turnover

Table 9.1	Labor Turnover Report		
Department	No. of Employees	No. Hired This Month	Percentage
Coffee Shop	21⅔	14	64.6*
Laundry	18	4	22.2
Personnel	4½	1	22.2
Uniformed Service	31	6	19.3
Kitchen	26⅓	3	11.3
Housekeeping	34⅓	3	8.7
Front Office	12½	1	8.0
Barber Shop	4	0	0
Banquet	9	0	0
Auditing	3	0	0
Indian Room	3½	0	0
Engineering	12	0	0
Executive	4	0	0
Beverage	3⅚	0	0
Printing	1	0	0
Total	189⅔	32	16.8

*14 ÷ 21⅔ = 64.6%

Labor turnover is expensive to the hotel, as new employees are inefficient until they learn to perform their duties. Untrained employees cannot give good service to the guests. We must try to keep our employees.

Courtesy J. B. Temple.

jumps for the entire organization it is time to make an investigation.

A certain amount of turnover is to be expected. Marriage, retirement, employees quitting to continue their education, sickness, or other reasons are a part of the dynamics of a healthy organization. To be meaningful, the rates should be further refined. Unavoidable separations should be listed separately from avoidable separations. Where the business is a rapidly expanding one, it is probably better to keep the separation rates apart from the accession rate.

Turnover of personnel often occurs in only a few jobs, while the majority of jobs remain stable. In a Fort Worth hotel, for example, it was found that 26 percent of the jobs accounted for 90 percent of the turnover. Identifying these jobs and working on them can sharply reduce turnover.

Turnover usually occurs in the first few weeks of employment. One chain found that 75 percent of their turnover took place among employees who had been working in their hotels for less than six months. If the employee could be made productive and satisfied within that period, the likelihood of a good stable employee was greatly increased.

One way of drawing attention to the turnover is to compile a monthly Labor Turnover Report (see table 9.1). This is sent to department heads and serves to point up the problem for both the department head and management.

ABSENTEEISM AS A MEASURE OF MORALE

As is true with labor turnover, a certain amount of absenteeism is to be expected. The common cold probably keeps more persons from work than any other malady. It is just about as common in California as it is in New York. However, in the fast-growing study of psychosomatic medicine, it is being proven that a large proportion of our ills, including the common cold, are psychosomatic. Persons who are tense and fearful are more susceptible to colds and other diseases than are those who are relaxed and well adjusted.

Many cases of absenteeism because of sickness can be traced directly to the morale at the place of work. In other words, sickness can be the result of poor supervision, poor placement, or other work-related reasons.

A room clerk who is annoyed with a supervisor is more likely to find it necessary to stay in bed because of a headache, or to take a driver's test, or to do other important business, than if relations with supervisors are pleasant. Absenteeism can be an index to personnel relations.

The manager or the personnel director can often spot departments that need particular attention by keeping records of absenteeism by departments. For example, in a large metropolitan hotel it was found that whereas the absenteeism rate for all employees averaged but 4 percent per day, the housekeeping department had a consistently high absenteeism rate of about 10 percent.

It will be discovered that even with the best efforts, absenteeism will be regularly higher in some departments than others. By keeping graphs of the number of absentees, a rough base rate can be established. Although it will change with the conditions of the labor market, it can serve as a standard.

Absenteeism rates also may be expected to follow a weekly pattern. Depending upon the weekly work schedule and the day on which payday falls, a characteristic curve of absenteeism throughout the week is established. Other factors such as weather conditions, the effect of convention business, epidemics, and the caliber of supervision will influence the curve without necessarily changing its basic shape.

It is an interesting piece of research for the person responsible for coordinating personnel to keep graphs of absenteeism on which are also recorded weather conditions, conventions, paydays, and local events of unusual character. It can be expected that absenteeism climbs on cloudy or cold days, that it climbs following payday and that following the annual employees' dance a large number of persons can be expected to be sick with "colds." Such records are helpful in formulating a program for reducing absenteeism.

Figure 9.1 is a graph showing the record of absenteeism plotted for the month of March in a large Eastern hotel. The effect of unfavorable weather and the occurrence of paydays on the absenteeism rates are particularly noticeable.

The hotel from which this data was taken was able, by means of a systematic program, to reduce absenteeism from a rate of 6 percent to one of 2 percent in a period of twelve months.

The program and its results are outlined below.

Steps Taken

1. Required submission of daily reports to Personnel Department
2. Departments and/or Personnel Department contacted all absentees
3. Department Heads interviewed all absentees
4. Personnel Department interviewed all chronic absentees and those out for three or more consecutive days
5. Personnel Department revised orientation talks for new employees to place greater emphasis on regular attendance and prompt reporting of illness, etc.

Results

1. Realization of ill effects of absenteeism on their department by department heads

2. Greater interest in regular attendance by employees due to emphasis placed on attendance by department head and/or Personnel Department during personal interview
3. Reduction of absentee rate from 6 percent to 2 percent in twelve-month period
4. Reduction in overtime payment due to absence.

THE EXIT INTERVIEW AS A BAROMETER OF MORALE

In addition to saving many good employees for the organization, the interview conducted at the time an employee is being separated is a way of gauging morale. When leaving the employee usually feels there is nothing to lose so why not tell the company what is wrong with it. Often the individual is under emotional stress and will give information which would not otherwise be given. Much of what is said may be biased, but the skillful interviewer takes this into account. Exit interviews may point to areas that need immediate attention or may point up needs for a long-term reorientation of personnel relations.

The interviewer does not argue with or evaluate the employee's statements, as the employee may resent the slightest suggestion of criticism. The interviewer remains an interested, uncritical listener doing a skilled job, one that requires definite techniques. The interviewer's opinions should be saved for later investigation.

Regardless of whether the employee is right or wrong, whether leaving for reasons that have nothing to do with the hotel or restaurant itself, whether the individual is worth saving to the organization, it is good public relations to show the employee that you are interested in and value the suggestions or criticisms. The exit interview is a *must* in any personnel program.

An exit interview form is shown as figure 9.2.

FACTORS AFFECTING MORALE

Hotel and restaurant work provides many employees with personal satisfactions found in few other industries. The fact that the hotel and restaurant is often a center of community affairs and good fellowship is reflected among employees. The ebb and flow of people, the excitement of meeting and working with new persons, and the absence of routine specialization in most hotel and restaurant jobs can lead to a warmth of living which makes for personal satisfaction and efficiency. Together with its advantages, hotel and restaurant work offers disadvantages, at least some of them peculiar to the industry: long and irregular hours, low pay, unusual demands, and low social status.

Figure 9.1 Graph of Absenteeism

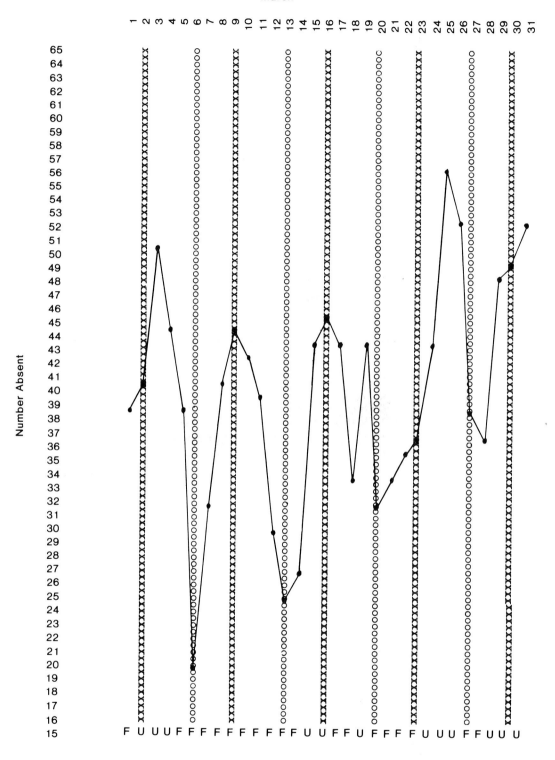

F — Favorable weather
U — Unfavorable weather
x — Sunday
O — Pay day

Figure 9.2   Exit Interview Form

Name _____   Date _____

Address _____   S. S. No. _____

Last Day Worked (or to work) _____   Time Card No. _____

                                          Time Card No. _____

Reason for Separation (check)

Quit
( )   Has another job
( )   Work unsuitable
( )   Family reasons
( )   To return to school
( )   To return to self-employment
( )   Leaving city
( )   To get another job
( )   Unknown
( )   Pay

Laid off
( )   Lack of work, dismissed
( )   Incompetence
( )   Attendance
( )   Intemperance
( )   Discipline
( )   Misconduct
( )   Sick
( )   Continued absence

Statement of Employee

Statement of Superior

Remarks

The hotel and restaurant industry offers a great challenge to the manager with appropriate skills and talent to exploit the positive aspects of the work environment and to compensate for the negative aspects. Possibilities for reducing, neutralizing, or preventing morale problems follow.

Job Titles

The title of the job may in itself be a stimulus of interest. Who would not like to be a vice president? Banks and advertising agencies have dozens of them. One means of identifying people in our culture is by the job they do and by the title of the job. It is only natural that workers tend to identify themselves with their jobs and to feel elevated or depressed by the manner in which the job is regarded by others. Waiters sometimes have feelings of inferiority because they are *servants,* though they may earn more than their patrons. No one wants to be a dishwasher or pot and pan washer. Few individuals, regardless of their status in our society, like to be called maids. *Line person,* or *counter person* is a more preferable term than counter girl. Some hotels title bellmen *service clerks.* Setting up appropriate job titles can have decided advantages.

An illustration of this is an incident that happened in a leading airport restaurant chain. By eliminating all dishwashers the turnover rate among those who washed the dishes fell sharply and there was less trouble in recruitment for the job. The new title, *plane equipment sterilizer,* was just as appropriate as dishwasher and a much, more desirable title. Other restaurants have changed dishwashing to *machine operating,* thus bolstering the ego of those who did the work. Machine operator is actually a better description of the job since machinery has been introduced, than is dishwasher. Machine operator is more democratic, dignified, and descriptive of the work performed.

Persons who work at the less desirable jobs can be classified as floorpersons and utility persons. Counter girls are classified as salespersons. Where manual jobs are not made into semi-skilled or skilled jobs, changing the job title to one with more favorable connotations may not appear entirely ethical. Since a job title change harms no one, the authors see no reason for not making changes that result in making people more satisfied with their jobs. Using euphemisms is an old English custom that reduces tension in a great many areas, including many outside of industry.

Instead of placing the usual small advertisement—chambermaids wanted—in the classified ad section, the management of a Minneapolis hotel showed a picture of a neat, well-dressed woman and asked for floor housekeepers. The hotel had no scarcity of first-rate applicants.

A hotel had difficulty in keeping an employee on the job of garbage burner. The difficulty was quickly eliminated when the garbage burner became an incinerator superintendent.

The Use of Rest Periods and Task Changes

Where work is of a continuous, unchanging kind, rest periods have been shown to increase efficiency, interest, and in most cases, overall production. Moreover, it is argued with some justification that whether or not there is a scheduled rest period, workers will take them anyway. If rest periods are scheduled, the employee is not required to break a written or unwritten rule. Because of the service nature of most hotel restaurant work, the rush and slack periods, and in many places absence of close supervision, rest periods are not necessary for many jobs. Places such as the laundry and the clerical and accounting offices can profit by scheduling rest periods. Rest periods for cleaners are especially desirable. Their job is a lonely one, providing few contacts with patrons and fewer associations with the other employees. Rest periods give a needed pause for conversation and social intercourse. The ten to fifteen minutes lost in the morning at 10:00 and the afternoon at 3:00 is more than compensated for by a reduction of monotony and increased interest in the work.

Where jobs are deadly routine it often helps to arrange for a job change periodically. Sometimes the arrangement is official; sometimes the employees themselves arrange for trading jobs. This tends to break the monotony and to refresh interest.

In laundry jobs it is often possible to shift on jobs every two or three hours. The deadly office job of filing can be lightened by having persons agree to take it on a rotation of two or three days at a time. Many jobs in the kitchen can also be shifted.

In addition to maintaining interest, job shifting creates a reserve of trained personnel who in emergency can take on jobs other than their regularly assigned ones.

Flexitime Versus the Four-Day Week

Flexitime is a concept that, when put into practice, gives employees considerable latitude in selecting the hours they work. Many hotels permit cleaners to leave, once their quota of rooms has been completed—a form of flexitime. Most hotels and restaurants require an employee to appear for duty at a certain hour; for many jobs this is an absolute necessity. Where a certain latitude is possible, as in the housekeeping department, cleaners could be permitted to arrive at work at any time between 7 A.M. and 10 A.M. and remain eight hours, or go home early if their work is done. Hours can be accumulated against more vacation time or days off. Sales offices might operate just as well on flexitime based largely on the discretion of the employees. The manager's secretary and engineering might also be on flexitime.

In part, restaurants operate with flexitime already. In many restaurants waiters are scheduled according to their wishes (within limits).

As compared with the four-day week, flexitime is said to be more productive. For many jobs the ten-hour day proves excessively long. It is quite possible that some jobs should last no more than four to six hours a day, since the demands and energy drain are so intensive. Chains like McDonald's have recognized this and seek to employ most employees on a part-time rather than full-time basis. Four hours on a deep-fry kettle is enough for most anyone. Four or five hours under the high-tension conditions of some fast-food operations exhausts a person, even a teenager. Fast-food operations thrive on young, enthusiastic people who see the work as fun, but who would see it as drudgery if required to work on a full-time basis.

Sound Promotion and Transfer Policies

One of the marks of a growing, progressive operation is an adequate promotion policy. Most ambitious people, particularly younger ones, are more concerned with opportunities for advancement than they are with present wages and conditions of work. The effects of a policy of promotion based upon ability can be seen not only in increased executive ability but as an electrical wave that sparks the entire enterprise.

Often undue weight is placed on seniority and experience. Some old-line managers believe that no one can possibly exercise proper supervisory control without having ten or fifteen years of experience on the job under constant supervision. This is a costly and mistaken idea. Studies have shown that there is such a thing as too much experience. A competent individual who in the job of steward has been at the job for ten years has probably ceased to grow in the last five of those years. The extra five years may serve only to dull that person's ambition and crystallize routine habits of thinking. In many cases too much experience is just as bad for the organization as too little. When a job takes on an entirely routine nature for a person, it stymies flexibility. One of the most progressive

and fastest-growing chain of hotels in the country publicizes the fact that the vast majority of its executives are under the age of forty.

Obviously all employees are not capable of being supervisors and executives. Promotion, however, can still be offered as an incentive, for promotion is whatever the individual receiving it believes it to be. For most employees an increase in wages is a promotion. For others a transfer to a more desirable working environment is a promotion. As discussed previously, changing the title of the job is considered by many to be a promotion. If the change is one desired by the employee, it is a promotion; if not desired, it is a demotion.

The importance of placing the employee in the job for which the person is best suited was brought out in chapter 5 on selection and placement. Even though we use the best selection and placement techniques available, there will be many employees placed in the wrong positions. Techniques of placement are, at best, tools that can facilitate proper placement. Such techniques cannot measure the subtle personality characteristics of the supervisor and the employee that must be taken into account if good job relations are to be obtained.

Unconscious prejudices, quirks of personality, unforeseen emergencies—any of these may seriously upset the equilibrium between supervisor and employee. If the difficulties cannot be remedied by counseling or other means, it may be well to transfer the employee to another department. The stress and excitement that press on the chef, cooks, and other employees of a kitchen may set off an emotional explosion that cannot be explained on rational grounds. Wounded vanity or a thrust at one's ego is often enough to set up a condition better settled by a transfer. To fire the employee is unfair and lowers the sense of security of the remaining employees.

Transfers must be carefully arranged and caution taken that offense to either party be kept at a minimum. Transferring every employee who requests it without careful investigation undermines the supervisor and creates dissension and lack of discipline. When a transfer appears advisable, the supervisor for whom the employee is working should be consulted and, if possible, permission for a transfer obtained from that supervisor. The supervisor of the receiving department must also be consulted. If that supervisor objects, the transfer to that department must be deferred until consent is given, or transfer to a different department considered.

Of course, there are employees who for emotional reasons or lack of ability cannot fit into the hotel or restaurant at any point. Management must be prepared to discharge them.

Incentives for All

Why not incentives for everyone in the restaurant or hotel? Various operators provide financial incentives for everyone in the kitchen:

a. Dishmachine operators receive a few cents per cover served during the course of a shift;

b. Meatcarvers in some of the newer chains receive a few cents per order after a base volume has been passed;

c. Cooks receive a few cents per cover after base is reached. In some restaurants the chef receives 25 cents per cover served.

Most waiters and waiters' assistants are already on a tip incentive basis. Front desk personnel receive bonuses based on percentage points of occupancy above a norm. Lodging quarters cleaners receive 50¢ or more a room, above a norm. Restaurant management often receive bonuses based on the control of food costs, labor costs, and other costs.

Once a week the cleaner with the cleanest room can be paid a bonus. The bonus may be based on the least number of discrepancies found during an inspection. Nonwinning cleaners are shown the inspection sheets listing the discrepancies, a procedure that becomes a method of instruction and a means for setting cleanliness standards.

Salespersons may receive a weekly bonus based on a percentage—say 10 percent—of meeting room rentals generated for that week.

Laundry personnel may receive a bonus at the end of each month if the cost of laundry supplies remain below a fixed figure.

For any incentive plan to succeed, ways to avoid people's "beating the plan" must be considered.

For example, the laundry crew may not use enough detergents to clean the linen; or a chef or manager receiving a bonus based on food cost savings may "save" too much—cutting portions to the base, buying inferior food.

Bonuses based on labor savings can result in short staffing or overworking a crew—low labor cost but poor service and poor morale—while a front desk bonus based on occupancy can mean that low-rate rooms are pushed at the expense of better rooms.

Incentives to Reduce Costs

Incentives to reduce costs not only save money but raise morale. Everyone likes a contest if it is stimulating and fair. Incentives can be set up in the form of competing with past records. The dish pantry is a good place to start. It is at the soiled dish and loading table that 75 percent of the breakage and chipping occurs. Breakage costs average between 0.5 and 1 percent of the gross revenue in most commercial food operations. This may appear small, but where there is a $100,000 monthly volume, the breakage may add up to more than $500 a month!

To reduce breakage costs, consider these ideas:

1. Set up a display of china showing the cost per item. When employees see that some of the plates may cost as much as $3.75 each, they may be more careful.

2. Place one person in charge of the dish pantry. Give this person the feeling of responsibility for reducing breakage costs.

3. Install duckboards on the floor around the dish machine. They will reduce slipping on wet floors.

4. Install a neoprene mat near the loading end of the dish machine. If dishes are dropped, the chance of breakage is reduced.

5. Give special attention to the night operation of the dish pantry. Studies have shown that carelessness during night operation is likely to be greater than during day operation.

6. Have the waiters and waiters' assistants presoak the dishes together. Do not bus glasses and dishes together.

7. Use plastic-coated racks and conveyors to reduce chipping and scratching of the glasses and dishes.

8. Install an overhead rack above the soiled-dish table for cups, glasses, creamers, etc.

9. Around coffee urns where high breakage occurs use lowerators for cup and saucer storage.

Research has shown that dishwashing costs break down into these percentages: labor, 70.0 percent; indirect costs, 11.5 percent; dish breakage and replacement, 11.5 percent; hot water and detergents, 7.0 percent. Any or all of these costs can be reduced through an incentive plan. Here is a plan that was used by a large Midwestern hotel:

The cost of the breakage was computed over a six-month period and found to be about $4,800—approximately $200 per week. Some of the loss was believed to have been caused by a poor physical setup and inadequate supervision and training. Most of it, however, was due to a high turnover of low paid, rather poor caliber personnel.

Corrective measures entailed three changes: (*a*) closer supervision and more thorough job instruction of the dishwashers; (*b*) a planned change in the physical setup; and (*c*) the introduction of an incentive system, whereby dish and glass washers were urged to competitively lower their previous breakage records. As an incentive they were paid a percentage of the savings resulting from the reduction in breakage. In this way both management and employees would share in the increased efficiency.

Additional savings to the hotel were made because the turnover rates were materially reduced. Finally, breakage costs were established at about $90 per week.

Some difficulties were encountered in administering the plan. Dividing the incentive money equally among the employees did not work because some of the employees were far superior to others. Arguments, sometimes violent, were precipitated among the dishwashers over the operation of the plan and the speed of the department was reduced because of the extra caution taken in washing the dishes. Most of the difficulties probably could have been eliminated had a management-employee committee been designated to administer the plan.

Other hotels and restaurants have established similar breakage-reduction plans successfully. One successful plan pays employees 60 percent of the savings occurring. Where management is not prepared to continue the incentive payments and uses the plan just to set up lower breakage figure as a standard, the plans will result only in ill will.

Several restaurants have increased the interest of waiters in their work and improved the quality of work by sponsoring a monthly contest in which prizes are given to those who receive the most compliments on service. The compliments must be made through a host or cashier. Prizes of $50, $25, and $10 are given to the three winners. Incentive plans can be set up in any department. By paying a $10 or $15 bonus to bartenders who surpass their previous gross sales, the sales figures jump markedly. By paying a percentage of the reduction in food costs to kitchen employees, food costs have been cut as much as 15 percent. The contests more than pay for themselves in increased patronage. Waiters formerly disinterested in spots on the silverware and glasses take the dishwasher to task. Salad arrangement and attractiveness of food become incentives.

Incentives for Attendance and Punctuality

Characteristically hotel and restaurant managements have depended upon disciplinary measures to keep attendance at a high level and tardiness at a minimum. Because discipline often has unpredictable and undesirable results, some managements have set up positive incentives for insuring attendance and reducing tardiness.

In jobs with high turnover it usually pays to give a bonus at the end of a month. Figuring the price of turnover as at least fifty dollars, a bonus of a few dollars builds stability at low cost. The amount of the bonus is not as important as the idea. A housekeeper in a Mississippi hotel increased both stability and good workmanship by giving a 10 percent monthly bonus to housepersons and cleaners. A bonus of 10 percent is paid each month that the cleaner or houseperson is never absent or late and when the room-inspection reports show *excellent*.

The Harding Restaurant Company at one time gave employees merit points for continuous service, punctuality, and attendance. The merit points could be exchanged for a wide variety of nationally known products at wholesale prices. Good Time Charlie's Restaurant in Las Vegas gives a one-day incentive bonus if the employee has perfect attendance for three months.

Incentives for Cleaners

A job that many managers stoutly maintain can never be placed on an incentive basis is that of a room cleaner. Some managers report that they have tried incentive plans with cleaners and that the plans have failed. Cleaners, it is averred, can work only under strict supervision; they will work only so fast. This does not appear to be true since the quota of rooms a cleaner is assigned varies in different hotels and in different parts of the country.

A Minneapolis hotel investigation was conducted by announcing on a Sunday that cleaners could leave as soon as their rooms were completed. All of the cleaners were finished and gone by one o'clock. A hotel in Boston had practically no turnover among cleaners. One of the reasons for the low turnover was explained by the fact that they were permitted to "keep their own hours" as long as their work was completed so as to fit the hotel schedule. Some of the cleaners come in at 9:00 and leave at 4:00, others take longer. The arrangement allows for individual differences in initiative and skill and places the responsibility for elapsed time differences on the employee.

Several hotels pay extra for each room done above quota. Some maids regularly do twenty-five rooms a day under such a plan. Many hotels hold contests in which the individual doing the best job of cleaning is given a prize or a paid day off. Such plans undoubtedly stimulate interest and morale when conducted fairly, and the prizes are distributed so that everyone has an opportunity to win once in a while. (Interest soon wanes if the same few people win all of the time.)

Some small motels schedule cleaners to work in teams of two. Beds are made by both cleaners working together, since two working together can make beds faster than can two working singly. After the beds are finished, one does the bathrooms while the other finishes the rooms. The one who gets finished first helps the slow one. Each can be trained to check the other's work.

In other operations a team of two cleaners works together on stripping and making beds. They go from room to room stripping linen—then backtrack and make the beds. Some hotels specialize tasks in room cleaning. Housepersons do the bed stripping and the heavy vacuuming; room attendants follow, completing the room.

It can be argued that two people working together are likely to spend too much time in conversation, to develop animosities, or to overlook parts of their job. It would be worthwhile for a personnel director to try the plan out on one floor only and to record the results. Cleaners requesting the arrangement should be permitted their choice of companions, care taken that two aggressive, persuasive persons not be paired.

Other Incentives

To remove the stigma of the term *waiter* some restaurants call them salespeople and build their service around a sales plan. By guaranteeing salespeople a 10 percent service charge, they have removed the necessity for *gratuities* and all that the term implies. A restaurant manager equipped all dish personnel with instruments for taking bacteria count. The dishwashers then became quasitechnicians and morale went up accordingly. The same manager had an unusual scheme for keeping the kitchen immaculate. A white line three to six inches wide was painted around each piece of kitchen equipment, the idea being to keep the white line spotless. In so doing the rest of the kitchen was kept clean. This manager avers that if one cannot spend two or three days a week golfing or fishing one is "no good as a manager."

A simple and readily understandable incentive plan that equates bonus payments with the room count was used in an Atlantic City hotel. Bonuses were divided into four classifications: A, B, C, and D. The bonus classification that applied was dependent upon the room occupancy above a standard figure. All employees of the hotel were covered by the plan. When the room count went a certain figure above the set standard, all employees received a small bonus payment. The bonus payment increased as more rooms were sold. Employees had ready access to the room-count record.

Since there was a direct connection between room count and wages, there was a great deal of interest in keeping room occupancy high, which was advantageous to all concerned.

Service teams in dining rooms are effective. In a number of restaurants, waiters, and waiters' assistants cart persons work as teams. One assistant works with two waiters, and removes soiled dishes to either of two wheeled carts. The carts, which have removable shelves and hold soiled dishes and silver from forty tables, are moved by two other employees. As each cart is filled, it is rolled to the dish pantry where the full shelves are exchanged for empty ones. Waiters are kept free for taking orders and delivering food. Assistants set up the tables, clear, and wipe them.

A 132-room inn in East Memphis, Tennessee, has established incentive programs for the front desk, housekeeping department, laundry department, and for the sales representative. Every day that the front desk crew rents 129 of the 132 rooms the front desk employees on duty that day receive additional pay. According to the management the clerks work more closely together to reach the bonus figure and tend to pace themselves more carefully. If one clerk makes a mistake on a reservation, a skip occurs; or if a guaranteed reservation is not honored and the guest is "walked," the day's bonus is forfeited. A danger, management says, is that unless checked by a supervisor, the clerks may become unconcerned about the room rate average and sell most the minimum rate rooms first.

The housekeeper and the assistant housekeeper receive weekly bonuses if their cleaners take care of an average of fourteen rooms or more a day for the week. Once a week the cleaner with the cleanest room receives a bonus.

The laundry department bonus is based on the use of laundry chemicals. If the cost is ten cents per room or less, each full-time laundry worker receives a bonus for the month. The hazard involved is that workers may skimp on the chemicals in order to win the bonus and sacrifice cleanliness and fluffiness of the linens.

The sales representative for the hotel receives a weekly bonus of 10 percent of the meeting room rentals generated that week. It is easy to give away meeting rooms and several local organizations were taking advantage of the lenient policy of complimentary meeting rooms. The salesperson is now motivated to sell the meeting rooms, and as a consequence meeting room rentals doubled.

Physical Factors in the Work Area

Walk from the impressive, beautiful lobby of many hotels into the back offices and work areas—from beauty to drabness. Poor working conditions do not lead to first-class service in any business. Badly lighted, poorly ventilated upholstery shops do not turn out quality repairs. Worn-out tools save no one money. Outmoded equipment does not reduce costs. Poor working conditions do not promote loyalty. Layout planning is just as important to the restaurant, the laundry, the kitchen, and the other working spaces as it is to the industrial manufacturing plant. Some kitchens are so poorly planned that the employees expend most of their energy in overcoming the results of the planning, or lack of it. Where waiters must climb stairs between the kitchen and dining room, efficiency naturally decreases.

According to its management, the Shoreham, because of a shortage of men waiters, attempted to hire women, but the women refused to carry the trays weighing twenty to twenty-five pounds up the stairs. An escalator for food handlers saved many man hours per day, resulted in a marked saving in breakage, and became the biggest morale builder in the hotel's history. Installing the escalator also saved much energy and made for more alert employees.

Often simple routing plans save many hours of labor. By having waiters sort their dirty dishes into appropriately arranged racks, trays of dirty dishes do not pile up at the dishwashing counter, nor do the waiters have to stand in line to dispose of their dirty dishes on the counter. The old system of merely heaping trays full of dirty dishes onto the counter and waiting for the dishwashers to sort and remove them leads to congestion and confusion.

New equipment may often change a job from a monotonous, laborious task to one requiring skill and responsibility.

Included in pleasant working conditions are the employees' cafeteria and its management. Just as much attention should be given the employees' restaurant as to the guests' restaurant. It is not necessary that the food be lobster Newburg and steak, but it should be of high quality and sufficient quantity. Its preparation should be under the direction of the chef. Planning the serving of the food is important. At one large hotel, employees were allowed thirty minutes for lunch. A checkup by the personnel manager revealed that many of the employees were standing in line waiting to be served for thirty minutes. By handing employees time checks while in line and picking them up when the employee emerged from the cafeteria it was found that the total time to eat in some cases ran to one hour and a half. The employees were not benefiting from the time lost. They were just as dissatisfied as was management when it learned of the situation.

This situation was not of recent origin. It had been going on for a number of years. After meal hours had been staggered for the various departments, employees were able to eat without wasting time. True, some had to break their habit of eating at twelve and change to eleven, but this was no great problem.

In the investigation of the employees' cafeteria it was also learned that all the cleaners ate lunch at the same time. This left no cleaner on any floor in case one was needed. By planning, it was possible to arrange that there was at least one maid on; the result—a smoother-running organization.

Work Week

In 1850 the average employee worked sixty hours per week. By 1920 this had dropped to fifty, and in 1941, to forty. During World War II, however, some employees in certain key industries worked as many as eighty hours per week. Now the nation's average is back to forty hours or less per week. The hotel and restaurant industry has an average that is considerably higher. Many hotel and restaurant employees regularly work more than fifty hours per week. Do such long working hours make for efficiency?

Extensive studies conducted by the government during World War II revealed some remarkable facts. Where some industries were working seven days per week, a reduction to six days actually increased production. The studies showed that there is no optimal number of hours for all jobs. Depending upon the amount of physical exertion and other factors, the number of hours during which maximum efficiency can be maintained varies from job to job. The optimal number of hours for most jobs varies between forty and fifty. For a few jobs, it drops to thirty and sometimes less. To be sure, overall productivity may be greater for fifty-five hours work than for forty-five, but productivity per hour will be significantly less.

Hours worked beyond high-efficiency levels are usually costly to management. Overtime wages are seldom profitable to an enterprise. The average employee who does not have adequate time from his work for change, rest, recreation, and relaxation does not have high interest in his work.

Sometimes management has superstitions about hours of work, believing that employees must stay on the job regardless of whether the work is complete. Most dishwashing jobs are placed on an eight-hour day basis. Since there are few restaurants that maintain a schedule by which there are always dirty dishes to be washed, there are sometimes long periods when the dishwashers have nothing to do. This is especially true when banquets do not begin until after the time planned. Dishwashers, or more correctly machine operators, may stand around for several hours. This is not conducive to morale. "Old line" management may declare that there is always something to be done. This smacks of the regimented and distasteful "made work" to be found in the armed services. Waiters work split shifts with no ill effects. Why not permit machine operators to leave when their work is completed?

In recent years many notions about the proper number of working hours for hotel and restaurant employees have been changed. The job of bellperson, for example, has traditionally been one of long hours, six days a week. In the Hotel Roosevelt of New York City their hours were reduced to forty per week. Surprisingly enough, the bellpersons who depend almost entirely upon tips for their income made as much in five days as they formerly did in six. They were fresher and could handle more patrons in a given time. Being more alert, they gave better service and received higher tips. A reoriented outlook concerning hours of work and productivity in the hotel and restaurant business is indicated. Union contracts now specify that time-and-a-half be paid after forty hours per week, which is another inducement to keep hours down.

Vacations

Vacations with pay for employees are an investment by management in the health and morale of the individual employee. Vacations can give the employee a new lease on life. Change of scenery, change of interests, travel, rest, and relaxation are no longer considered a gift from a benevolent employer. Vacations with pay are part of our democratic way of life. In cold dollars and cents they are an investment that pays off in production and efficiency.

Typically, employees are granted one week of vacation after one year of service and two weeks of vacation after three years of service. A few managements give three weeks' vacation after ten years of service. The trend is to increase the number of days of vacation.

Some restaurants shut down their complete operation and all employees go on vacation together. Often remodeling or extensive maintenance work may be scheduled during this period. Most hotels and restaurants try to plan their vacation schedule so that vacations are spaced throughout the summer months. Some take on additional summer employees to fill in for regular employees who are vacationing. College students are often used to replace vacationing employees.

By publicizing vacation trips in the house organ, their value to morale is enhanced. Management may aid employees in vacation planning. Some provide summer camps for employees or secure special rates for them at the seashore. Hotel or motel chains can give their vacationing employees reduced rates, especially at resort hotels during the off-season.

Assuring the Employee of Regular Employment

Surprisingly, the hotel and restaurant business which, generally speaking, offers one of the most stable employment records in business, makes little of this fact and fails to use it as an inducement in securing and keeping employees. Most of the larger hotels have an "old timer's club" it is true, but they do not publicize the regularity of employment offered, nor do they give assurance to employees that, provided their services are satisfactory, they are guaranteed employment.

For a person to be an efficient and enthusiastic employee, requires a sense of security. A complete sense of security is probably impossible in our culture and may not be desirable, but there is a minimum sense of security that the hotel and restaurant business can provide by merely publicizing what is already true.

The employee who is insured against the whimsy, personal feelings, and caprice of a department head is a more stable worker. A Los Angeles hotel provides a control that helps insure job security. No employee can be discharged, not even by the president, managing director, or manager of the hotel, if the "special" board of directors disagrees. The board of directors consists of five members elected annually from the working personnel by a general election of employees. Employees who receive notice that their services are no longer required and feel that their dismissal is unjustified may, in each case, present the evidence to the board of directors for their decision. A special meeting of the board is called, and a thorough investigation made for each employee, who may appear before the board, present any evidence considered desirable by that employee, and summon any witness that employee considers advantageous to have for strengthening the case against the department. Likewise the head of the department concerned is requested to appear and present any evidence and witness to justify the action.

Credit Unions

Credit unions can serve as one of the many *security measures* that reflect themselves in higher employee morale and efficiency. More important, credit unions can keep employees out of the hands of loan sharks. By providing a relatively convenient and low-cost type of credit, the credit union removes many expressed or implicit fears from the minds of workers. (Faced with the possibility of an emergency need for money, many employees do not possess the frame of mind needed to maintain wholehearted interest in their work and the self-confidence necessary for many hotel and restaurant jobs.)

True, employees who need money for medical or other emergency bills can turn to the personal loan services; but often an employee who has met these gentlemen will find the acquaintanceship difficult to drop. Loan sharks have been known to keep workers in their debt for years. Credit union interest is never more than 1 percent per month of the unpaid balance, and the unions operate so that they do not infringe upon the individual's self-respect. It is common for a credit union to lend as much as $500.00 on the borrower's signature, and much more with security.

In addition to providing low-cost credit, credit unions foster thrift among the employees participating. Those who invest in the credit union share in the profits of operation. Thrift promotes stability and reduces turnover figures.

From the point of view of the employer, the credit union provides training and experience and a sense of responsibility for the employees who are elected to manage the credit union. The board of directors, the officers, the credit committee, and the educational committee provide management with an opportunity to observe latent potentialities and leadership in employees whose regular work gives them no opportunity to assume responsibility. Officers of credit unions are called upon to preside at meetings and to practice cooperation. They gain experience in decision and policy making; they are made to feel important, which is important to them and to the enterprise.

Antagonism between employers and employees over garnishments of wage can be partially avoided by the establishment of a credit union. Loss of employee working time caused by creditor's telephoning and visiting can be reduced. The ill feeling that results from refusals to repeated requests for advances in wages can be avoided. Unfavorable public relations, the result of employees' failure to meet their obligations, can be eliminated. The employer stands to gain as much as the employee.

Credit unions operate under federal or state laws. Federal credit unions were authorized by the Credit Union Act of 1934. Some hotel and restaurant credit unions operate under the federal law, others under their respective state laws. Credit unions have a remarkable record for repayment of loans: less than one-half of one percent are not repaid.

To encourage credit unions, employers often publicly endorse their organization and provide other aids such as free office space, payroll deductions for payment of loans, and grant some company time in which to perform work in connection with the credit union. The personnel office and the credit union can be mutually helpful.

Since much of the value of the credit union results from the participation and responsibility of employees, organization and management should be left largely in the hands of employees. This, of course, does not mean that an employer who feels there is a need for a credit union cannot actively encourage its organization. Full information as to purposes of a credit union can be had free of charge from the Federal Deposit Insurance Corporation, Washington, D.C.

The Suggestion System

The suggestion system is usually thought of as a method for securing ideas that may prove beneficial to the organization. It can be more than this; it can be a device for securing employee participation and cooperation.

The history of the formal use of a suggestion system in hotels and restaurants is one of excellent results and of dismal failures. Much of the failure of suggestion systems in the hotel and restaurant industry can be traced to the manner and spirit in which they are conducted. If management considers the suggestion system merely as a cheap means of securing ideas for increased efficiency, the plan is likely to fail. If it is looked upon as one way to

secure the worker's interest and participation and a way to share with the employees the rewards of increased efficiency, the suggestion system has a chance to be successful. No suggestion system is any better than the effort put into it by management.

Payments for ideas accepted in hotels and restaurants are made in a lump sum—usually $5 to $15. If you were an employee would you submit a $1,000 idea for a possible reward of $10? Probably not. Successful suggestion systems usually pay a generous proportion of the savings resulting from the suggestion. In industry, the percentage paid is as much as 50 percent of the savings: Many suggestions are paid for even though they may not have an immediate value to the organization. Employees are thus encouraged to do constructive thinking about their jobs and about the company.

All suggestions, accepted or not, should be answered—usually within two weeks. Reasons for their acceptance or rejection should be given in writing or by personal interview. Award winners should receive publicity. Repeat winners can be pictured in the house organ. Acceptable suggestions should be published; personal letters can be written to explain why the others were not satisfactory.

To enhance the feeling of participation, at least one employee who is not a representative of management should sit in on the committee that accepts or rejects suggestions and determines their value to the hotel or restaurant. Employees should be rotated so that participation can be extended. Perhaps the employee is not qualified to judge the value of a suggestion. The presence of that person, however, assures enthusiasm in implementing and carrying out the decisions. People who are encouraged to take on responsibility develop responsibility and learn to understand democratic procedures and to understand the value of group participation.

SUMMARY

Work hygiene is concerned with the environment surrounding work, such as supervision, interpersonal relations, physical working conditions, salary, company policies and administrative practices, benefits, and job security. When any of the hygiene factors deteriorate to a level unacceptable to a worker, then poor morale and job dissatisfaction is likely to occur. However, the reverse does not hold true. Positive satisfactions are related to opportunities within the job itself for self-realization and feelings of personal accomplishment.

Indications that may be symptomatic of low morale are disciplinary problems and grievances, low output, high absenteeism, lack of interest and inefficiency, high sickness rates, fatigue, turnover, and bickering.

Labor turnover statistics can help managers note trends and identify special problem areas. Absenteeism statistics can be compiled as an indicator of morale level. The exit interview can be used as a barometer for identifying problems. In an organization with good communications, morale problems will surface quickly at staff meetings and in informal conferences.

Management can take many positive steps to reduce, neutralize, or prevent morale problems from developing. The following are examples: improve job titles, use rest periods and work changes, establish sound promotion and transfer policies, use incentives, improve physical areas, stabilize the work week, establish vacation policies, assure regular employment, share profits, establish insurance and pension plans, and set up suggestion systems and credit unions.

Behavior Modification Theory
and Techniques of Supervision

10

PRINCIPLES AND TECHNIQUES OF BEHAVIOR MODIFICATION

Very few parents go to school to learn how to raise children. They just do what comes "naturally"—sometimes rewarding, sometimes punishing—in trying to shape the behavior of their children. Of course, sometimes the system of rewards and punishments they use can get out of balance and then parents need to analyze—often with professional help—just what went wrong and what they can do to get back on course. The problems of getting on course are quite often complex. Children are complex. Each has a unique personality and each lives in a complex social environment. With such complexity it is not surprising that so many people have problems in relating to others and in adjusting to various aspects of their lives.

The task of a supervisor is not unlike that of a parent, when trying to shape the behavior of the workers and using a broad system of rewards and punishments ranging from the giving of money and recognition to firing and criticizing. In many ways the supervisor's task is even more difficult. The controls of a parent are lacking and subordinates come to the job with habits and behavior patterns that are firmly established.

Behavior modification is based on a theory developed in animal studies that showed that behavior is modified when a particular act is reinforced; it is gradually extinguished, or fades if the behavior is not rewarded or punished. Punishment is used in the broad sense: anything that is perceived as being unpleasant or nonrewarding. The supervisor saying "Good morning" to an employee is a reward. Saying nothing can be construed as a punishment. The notion is almost too simple, yet it is effective and has proved so in a number of business situations and in treatment of deviates as well as normal people. When a waiter sets up a table quickly, efficiently, and in the right way, the supervisor says "That's good." The "that's good" is reinforcing correct behavior, a form of reward.

When the utility person cleans a floor, the supervisor notes it at once and says something to the effect of "That's very clean." Again a reinforcement. The cleaner makes a bed correctly and does it quickly and efficiently; the supervisor says "What a beautiful bed." The key is to continue reinforcement time and time again until the correct procedure has been implanted in the nervous system and the individual does it automatically. Critics may say that the technique is too obvious—too unsophisticated. Yet it works on all levels.

Nearly everyone wants praise, wants approval—wants it now, not sometime in the future. Praise immediately follows the act, for the "immediacy effect." The same technique is applicable in any similar situation. Develop the wanted behavior, explain it, and reinforce it time after time after time.

In recent years a field of study specifically concerned with behavior modification has shown promise as an aid to parents, supervisors, teachers, and others interested in shaping behavior. This field of study known generally as behavior modification has its roots in experimental psychology. Of particular interest in behavior modification is the development of an understanding of how individuals acquire their various behavioral habits in order to teach the individual how to break old habits or acquire new ones. It is felt that all individuals learn according to basic laws and principles of behavior.

Before we can modify the behavior of others, we must be able to recognize the behavior we wish to change. Therefore, the first steps in behavioral change have to do with careful observation, recording, and providing consequences. This process will be referred to as pinpoint, record, and reward or punish.

Pinpoint

Pinpointing is very simple. It simply involves identifying a completed movement cycle by an individual. We know a cycle has occurred when we can observe the beginning and the end of the cycle. An example of a behavioral cycle is the crying sequence of a child. The total sequence includes the event that precipitated the crying, the actual crying, the termination of crying, and the immediate event that followed the crying. An angry flareup could also be pinpointed in the same manner. One does not have to restrict pinpointing to emotional situations. Any behavioral sequence can be pinpointed, such as sequences of rudeness to a specific customer, slowness or sloppiness in mopping a floor, non-job-related talking, smoking a cigarette, or leaving one's job area.

Record

Once we have pinpointed a behavior our next step is to record it. For example, in a given time period we know that Mary talks to others in situations unrelated to her job. Each time she talks, we have observed one sequence. If we want to alter her behavior, then each time we observe a sequence it is important for us to record the sequence. It is only after we have a total picture of the number of talking sequences that we are able to determine whether or not a problem of behavior exists. In this manner we have tangible data with which to confront Mary. It is also only when we have a record that we and Mary are able to determine whether subsequent improvement has been made. The recording can be done with a counter or with a simple tally sheet.

Only after we have recorded the behavior should we alter it. The ways of altering behavior are many and varied. In the sections to follow we will enumerate them systematically. In most practical situations the best way to alter behavior is to allow the person whose behavior is to be altered to make the decision as to the direction the change should take. If the supervisor has done a good job of pinpointing the behavior and has recorded the observations made, that supervisor has done the job. The subordinate will be the "expert" in determining the mode to use in bringing about changes.

The simple technique of pinpointing, recording, and rewarding is an extremely powerful technique for bringing about specific behavioral change. It is also a highly effective way for a supervisor to evaluate accurately the performance of subordinates. Many times a supervisor will make a generalization that "Mary talks all the time." When the supervisor actually records the number of times that Mary talks, that supervisor may find that one incident has served as the base of perception, and that Mary actually does not talk excessively.

TYPES OF STRENGTHENING BEHAVIOR

To bring about behavior changes we usually operate under certain behavioral laws involving reinforcements (rewards and punishments) and extinctions. If a person shows a behavior that we feel is good and we wish to strengthen this behavior so that it will be continued in the future, then we would provide a positive reward or reinforcement immediately after we observe the good response. In practice, if we wish to strengthen the performance of a person who has mopped a floor and has just done a good job, then immediately after the performance the reward is given (e.g., with a statement of "Good job" or with a monetary reward or an extra amount of "break" time, etc.). If we wish to weaken an inadequate performance and bring about a change, then immediately following a specific behavior sequence we could use a negative reinforcer (i.e., a punishment). For example, if the mopper did a sloppy job, we could "punish" with critical remarks, deprive the mopper of extra pay, require that the task be performed again, etc. If we wish a behavior pattern to "go away," then we extinguish that behavior by simply not responding in any fashion. In time, behavior that is not reinforced will diminish.

The principles of behavior modification are usually not utilized in any systematic way in supervisory practice. In an informal way, however, any time a supervisor has an interaction with a subordinate, a law of behavior is in some way being utilized by that supervisor. Each time praise or criticism is given some mode of behavior is reinforced. Unfortunately, supervisors, by not being systematic in their approach, are often guilty of reinforcing the wrong behaviors. Further along in this chapter a specific program is offered that can teach supervisors specific techniques for relating to their subordinates. The section that follows immediately gives general examples of techniques that can be developed by management for use in training employees more effectively.

Positive Reinforcement Techniques

Increase Social Responsiveness

A number of research studies have demonstrated that it is possible to increase the level and quality of social responsiveness. The effectiveness of a waiter, host, or other worker in direct contact with the public is related strongly to that person's skill in social interactions.

Here is an example of how a supervisor can increase social responsiveness in an employee:

> Harry, the manager, was interested in getting Alice, his night hostess, to be more socially responsive to customers. Alice was very competent and efficient. It was not that she

could not be sociable and friendly, but she was not as consistently outgoing as Harry felt was desirable. Following the lessons of behavior modification, he observed her behavior for several days and pinpointed a number of desirable social behaviors she showed during the period of observation. These behaviors included such things as special concern she showed for a customer's health or welfare; friendly, casual comments about current events or the weather; helpfulness in doing an extra favor for a customer beyond her regular duty; and periodic inquiry concerning the customer's satisfaction with the service.

Once Harry could pinpoint the behavior he felt was desirable, he next recorded over several days the actual number of times Alice showed desirable behavior. This allowed him to establish a *base rate*. Once the baseline was established, Harry discussed the study with Alice. He let her know which behaviors he felt were desirable. As an incentive he told her that he would give her a monetary reward that would be proportional to the amount of improvement she showed in desirable social responsiveness above her base rate.

The preceding example is but one way that social responsiveness can be improved. Once a base rate is known, a variety of rewards could be used to increase social responsiveness, including verbal praise, recognition through winning in competition with one's peers, or special awards. The important thing about getting an employee aware of an ability to show progress in social responsiveness is that the mere attainment of progress becomes a powerful reinforcer for that individual toward the continuation of socially responsive behavior. Everyone has seen an example of a person who blossomed socially simply because of having developed self-confidence in social interactions.

The example given above obviously requires a considerable amount of an observer's time. When an observer is not available to record behavior an effective technique is to have the employee become a self-observer—recording each positive response by using a counter that can easily be kept in a pocket. This technique constantly reminds the employee of the need to maintain the desirable behavior in all interactions with others.

"Token" Economy System of Reward

Recently the *token* system has been utilized with considerable success in motivating workers toward specified desirable behavioral ends. The system requires the immediate rewarding of desirable behavior with a token that later can be exchanged for money or a prize. The tokens can be presented by each person's supervisor whenever the person has performed a desirable function; they can be presented at random times by an unknown judge who poses as a customer and who gives them as a special reward when the employee fulfills a desired performance; or they can be given on the basis of letters of praise from the clientele being served. Several of the airlines have utilized the token system to advantage.

Assertiveness Training

Many employees do poorly in specific jobs because they are fearful of certain features of the job. For example, it is well known that some employees who do extremely well behind the scenes do not do well in "front of the house" situations, or certain employees who work well with people do very poorly when it comes to performing some of the technical functions required in a job. The fact that one has a fear of the tasks that one is poorest at doing usually means that skills will remain undeveloped, and eventually, because of not being well rounded, this person will be bypassed in gaining a promotion; or if given a promotion, that person will be seriously lacking in certain required skills.

Assertiveness training is designed to help one identify one's fears, and then to systematically encourage the person to learn to be more effective in the performance of the feared act. The principle is one of compensation by which one overcomes a weakness by continually practicing the very thing in which one is weakest. If, for example, it is discovered that a person is fearful of getting in front of a group to talk or lecture, then a program is developed to help this individual acquire skills in getting before a group. A series of progressively difficult steps are established and some reward is given each time a step is mastered. The first step in the given example requires the subject to practice alone in front of a mirror, pretending to be talking in front of a group. To help in gaining confidence one is required to learn thoroughly what is to be said. When the first step has been accomplished to satisfaction, a reward is given. The second step involves the same performance in front of one or two people. Eventually, as progress is made, the person will be required to give the same performance before a large group of people and ultimately will be required to speak extemporaneously before a large group.

Negative Reinforcement Techniques

Generally speaking, negative reinforcement is not as desirable as positive reinforcement in modifying behavior. It is, however, an extremely effective technique if not done harshly, and if the punishment is something that the subject understands in advance (thereby coming as no shock or surprise). In the supervisory training sections that follow, negative reinforcement is used as an effective tool by which employees come to understand the meanings of rules. Once a rule is established and the supervisor is consistent in interpreting that rule, then a principle of negative reinforcement is being utilized. In this example, however, it is important to recognize that the punishment is not coming from the supervisor per se, but is coming as an effect of the rule. The supervisor is only an instrument by which the punishment is being administered. In this case, there is nothing personal between the supervisor and the employee; merely an instance of the supervisor "doing a job." A wide variety of punishments can be used effectively. For example, a person can be deprived of a reward such as extra money, time off, praise, or any desirable goal. One can also remove a person from the surrounding in which an undesirable behavior takes place, such as setting apart two employees who are talking or if an employee is smoking in an area in which smoking is not permitted, one can move the employee to a different work area. Another technique of punishment is to make the offending individual aware of the behavior by requiring extra efforts from that person, such as extra work, extra study, a more difficult assignment, etc.

One of the most creative examples of punishment being used to modify behavior is the *double bind*. Very frequently people show undesirable behaviors or habits that they wish to change, but unfortunately they do not have the persistence to change; nor is help immediately available at the time they have shown the undesirable behavior. In such situations the double bind approach is useful. In that approach, the responsibility for providing punishment is left completely up to the individual. It is therefore important that the person show an interest in modifying the behavior in question. In planning the initial strategy, one makes a concerted effort to change one's whole pattern of behavior. If the individual succeeds, then the program is quite successful. The change in behavior is attributed to the threat of punishment, which was sufficient to bring about a new motivation pattern in the person. If one persists in one's old behavior, then that person is subject to "self-punishment." The trick in the double bind approach is to pick a punishment that will be helpful and not harmful to the person. For example, if a person tries to modify a behavior of getting to work late, the punishment might be to spend one hour in the evening reading a book on supervision for each tardiness. In this way, even if one does not change one's pattern of being late, the person at least has acquired some knowledge that ultimately may be helpful to the individual and to the organization.

The double bind approach is an extremely useful and promising technique—double bind because there is no way for the subject to beat the system. No matter which way one goes, one will always help oneself. In practice, dramatic results can be obtained very quickly. Once a person has mastered a specific habit, then other habits can be picked to modify. Of course, the punishments will vary according to the individual need of a particular subject. The punishment that is always picked is one that will be helpful to the individual in reaching one of that

person's specific goals. It should be something that the person wants but usually does not have the time to pursue.

Extinction Techniques

From the study of human behavior we know that much behavior can be modified, not by reward or punishment, but simply by discontinuing the positive reinforcement that is maintaining the behavior. As such, in order to use extinction as a behavioral change technique, the most critical factor involves careful observation and pinpointing in order to be sure that we understand *what* is reinforcing the undesirable behavior. Any parent is readily aware that certain behavior in their children is directly related to the resulting action of the parent. For example, Johnny cries every evening before he goes to bed. Mother sits in his room every night until he goes to sleep. One night Johnny cries and his mother no longer sits in his room. Eventually Johnny goes to sleep. In a few nights Johnny goes to sleep immediately without crying. This is an example of how Mother ended Johnny's crying behavior by simply no longer rewarding Johnny for crying by being present in his room.

In the units to follow on supervisory training a number of examples are given to show how supervisors can alter undesirable behavior in their subordinates. The general law to be learned is that any behavior will be weakened and will likely disappear if it is not recognized. In supervisory practice this means that supervisors must learn to ignore behavior that is irrelevant to the task at hand no matter how disruptive it may seem at the time. For example, if the supervisor expects Mary to sweep the floor and if in the process of sweeping the floor Mary complains and is sarcastic, the supervisor might get into an argument with Mary concerning her attitude. Mary will learn that her complaining behavior will always result in an argument with her supervisor. This, in turn, may teach her how to avoid doing chores such as sweeping the floor. If, instead of arguing with Mary about her attitude, the supervisor will simply ignore her complaints, then the complaints will most likely go away because Mary receives no reward for them. If Mary fails to sweep the floor, however, that is a different problem. The supervisor will need to deal with the relevant issue of Mary failing to comply with a firm requirement.

GUIDE TO SUPERVISORY TRAINING

The remainder of this chapter consists of a practical guide to supervisory training that can provide the reader with information or be used specifically to train prospective supervisors. It is geared primarily to the supervision of the task-oriented worker typically found in the hotel-restaurant field. It is broken down into four sections for ease of presentation.[1]

The guide that follows makes specific use of the behavior modification theory and techniques described in the first section of this chapter. Although all of the practices described below are based on theory, the material is practical and presented in a "how-to-do-it" style.

Consistency in Supervision

A powerful law of behavior states: (*a*) any behavior is strengthened and likely to reappear when we expect some result to happen and it actually does happen; (*b*) any behavior is weakened and likely to disappear when we expect some result to happen and it does not happen.

In supervisory practice one expects one's actions to result in a certain response from one's supervisor. In this manner supervisors can strengthen or weaken certain behavior in their employees by controlling their own response to the behavior. This law of behavior can be seen operating in the behavior of young children or in supervisory-subordinate relationships. If one child teases another child and the teased child becomes upset, it is a fairly sure bet that the child doing the teasing is likely to persist. If the teased child does not react, the behavior of the teaser will cease. In a supervisory situation, if the subordinate comes to the supervisor continually to receive instructions, it is a sure bet that the subordinate will always be dependent. If, upon coming to the supervisor for instruction, the subordinate does not receive the expected, that individual is likely to seek out other means of solving that and other problems.

It is extremely important for supervisors to demonstrate that they are consistent in their behavior. Consistency is the *absolute* predictability of a supervisor's behavior. To the subordinate it means, "every time I fail to report to work on time I am docked" or "every time I get loud I am reminded." To the supervisor it means, "every time two of the subordinates get loud I will remove one of them" or "I will never allow the subordinate to leave without cleaning his area."

Why is it important to be consistent? One of the vital needs of people is the need for safety. It is important for each person to have reassurance of just what can and cannot be done. If one does not have reassurance and must always be on the alert to defend oneself, one's life will be in a constant state of turmoil. By being consistent in their relationships with their subordinates, supervisors provide the opportunities for their subordinates to avoid being defensive in order to grow and develop on their jobs.

Although as adults we like to think of ourselves as independent, one of the reasons we can be independent is the knowledge and confidence we have that we can predict certain aspects of our behavior and the behavior of others. We have this confidence because we have learned to accept certain consistent facts of life. If we know what to expect from our supervisor, we do not have to spend all of our time trying to figure out what the supervisor is going to do next. We are free to explore new aspects of our work and to be more productive employees.

If supervisors are unpredictable, a subordinate feels chronically anxious. If a supervisor states a rule, the subordinate must always test that rule at least once. And every time the supervisor does not enforce the rule, the subordinate is less responsible, and may in time become a master of manipulation. If one learns to manipulate, one has little time or energy to learn more constructive skills.

Of course, by talking about the importance of predictability we do not mean to imply that the world is or should be perfectly predictable. In fact, the world is a highly inconsistent place. Because life is so unpredictable it is important for supervisors to behave consistently even if only in terms of one or two forms of behavior. Then a subordinate can afford to give up many testing behaviors, and so be more effective in actions.

Examples of being consistent on the part of the supervisor are the following:

1. Insisting that the pantry be cleaned every Saturday rather than whenever it becomes intolerably dirty.

2. Providing exactly fifteen minutes for a work break at a prescribed time and not allowing the taking of a break when the work slackens.

3. Setting up for the noon rush exactly at eleven o'clock as opposed to starting when other chores are completed.

Why is consistency so important? To answer the question look at the results of inconsistency. From a wide variety of research in the behavioral sciences, we have come to recognize that much abnormal, psychopathological, and defensive behavior is a result of inconsistency in the child-rearing practice of parents. Even in the most normal of human development, the inconsistencies one experiences in life are related to defensive behavior the individual develops in order to cope with the inconsistencies.

---

1. The material in this section was adapted from J.M. Smith, and D.E.P. Smith, *Child Management: A Program for Parents* (Ann Arbor, Mich.: Ann Arbor Publishers, 1966).

Defensive behavior is used to describe an individual's reaction to unfamiliar and thus unpredictable changes in life. Children often defend themselves with temper tantrums or illness, while adults often show their defensiveness with anger, frustration, fear, illness, or irresponsibility. When some consistency or predictability develops, the defensive behavior usually subsides. By being able to understand defensive behavior and to recognize that defensiveness is inevitable in the face of unexpected changes, it is usually easier for a supervisor to tolerate defensive behavior in a subordinate.

Examples

1. Mary, a supervisory waitress, noted, "Every time I feel bad, the girls under my supervision are at their worst. Sally and Betty argued all morning and Alice didn't get set up on time."

The subordinates are not just "waiting" for Mary to feel bad so they can act up. They are merely reacting to the changes they see in the way Mary looks and acts.

2. Fred received a raise of fifteen dollars but he had figured on twenty. He became quite angry.

His anger does not reflect ungratefulness and selfishness, but is a result of a strong expectancy on his part that was not fulfilled. Such behavior may arouse anger on the part of the supervisor, but Fred's reaction is normal and predictable when one understands his expectancy.

3. One day Al, a bellman, came to Tom, his supervisor, with some suggestions for improving efficiency. Tom became angry.

It was not Tom's fear of Al's taking his job that led to the angry reaction. Tom was preoccupied with another problem and resented the interruption—he was unprepared for dealing with the unexpected.

Most good supervisors intuitively know that the first few days of work for new employees are not a fair test for them, because new employees are likely to be nervous and upset until able to predict how they will relate to the new work situation. Good supervisors also are aware that once employees learn a certain job they are extremely reluctant and defensive in taking on a new assignment. It is not that they are disloyal or stubborn but rather that they are comfortable and relaxed in a situation in which they know what to expect.

We may conclude that it is especially important for supervisors to be consistent whenever changes occur in the work situation that could lead to defensive behavior. Unfortunately, these are the very times when many super-

visors tend also to be inconsistent. They are likely to be too busy to enforce the usual rules, or feel hesitant to be consistent because the employee has so many other demands, or hesitate due to a feeling that the employee may be ill because of the individual's strange actions. The important point for supervisors to remember is not that new situations are undesirable but that change from old to new results in defensive behavior.

Examples

1. The kitchen crew had a substitute supervisor and they were "cutting up." Their behavior resulted not from a dislike of the supervisor but rather from an attempt to discover which rules were still in force.

2. John was dining room manager. When Bill the waiter was late to work one day, John decided not to make an issue of it because he knew Bill was having some domestic problems. Finally after three or four infractions, John confronted him. Bill "blew up" and accused John of picking on him.

Bill's behavior did not represent poor training. He undoubtedly was upset by his domestic problem, but he was further upset by John's inconsistent response to his being late. By being inconsistent, John only further increased Bill's anxiety.

Whenever new situations arise, new rules must also be developed such as: "In the new dining room, no smoking will be allowed." The new rule will be tested several times before it becomes "real." If the supervisor enforces the rule constantly, it no longer will be tested.

The Use of Rules

From the preceding section we know that supervisory consistency is important and that supervisors can become more consistent by establishing a few rules and enforcing them absolutely. Most supervisors have far too many rules, none of which are enforced consistently. Such rules make life more complicated for everyone. This section deals with the kinds of rules that need to be established and describes how they should be enforced.

Most supervisors feel uncomfortable or guilty in the making or enforcing of rules. They are often not aware of the importance of rules. To relieve their guilt some supervisors never tell but ask "would you like to help in the kitchen?" A supervisor needs to be polite, of course, but if the only acceptable answer is yes, then it would be less confusing to say, "John, I want you to help in the kitchen."

Some rules are "long-term" and must be enforced repeatedly. These usually govern the performance of a routine chore.

1. You must clean the storeroom every Saturday.
2. Each employee must be in complete uniform before reporting on the floor.

Short-term rules or *commands* are spontaneous decisions of supervisors made in specific situations. They require consistent enforcement but are difficult if not impossible to enforce because they are not well planned. For example:

1. Clean the storeroom this afternoon.
2. I want you to come in at eight o'clock tomorrow.

What Kind of Rules to Establish

A rule must fulfill three requirements. It must be *definable, reasonable, enforceable.*

Definable

The floor supervisor tells a subordinate, "I'm dissatisfied with your appearance. I expect you to look decent at all times." Only the supervisor knows what "decent" means and this is likely to change from day to day. The subordinate will not be able to predict what it takes to pass inspection. This rule is worse than no rule.

A rule must be well-defined so that a person is instantly aware of the infraction when breaking it. One may argue that the rule is unreasonable, but one cannot argue about whether or not he completed the task. For example:

1. "Fred, before you leave each night you must clean the utility room. I will post this checklist of what must be done."
2. "Mary, Thursday afternoon you are to wash all the tables and chairs with warm, soapy water. Wash the tops, sides, and legs of the tables and wash the chair completely except for the bottoms. After you have washed each table or chair, buff it with a soft rag in order to remove any soap film."

Reasonable

A reasonable rule takes into account (*a*) the *time* the task will take and whether sufficient time is available and (*b*) the capability and skill of the person doing the task. A worker may eventually be able to perform the requirements of a task with much skill, but initially will need explicit instruction.

It is wise to actually watch the person do specific steps initially, but to allow the individual to perform the task without being helped. It is the finished product that is important. If the person has failed to complete the task, he or she can be told simply, "you haven't finished." If the task was not performed skillfully, you can simply

perform the task on the person's behalf so that it can be observed by the individual, who will then be left alone to practice.

Enforceable

A supervisor must anticipate any subordinate breaking a rule; therefore, the supervisor must be certain that the rule can be enforced consistently. If not, then the rule should not be made. The key question to be answered in order to decide whether a rule is enforceable is the following: *Will you know a rule is broken every time without having to depend on other people's testimony?*

Examples of nonenforceable rules are

1. "I don't want you girls to argue anymore."
2. "I want you to really work hard today to prove your ability."

Examples of enforceable rules are

1. "Albert, the trash must be emptied every day by two o'clock."
2. "You are not to wear anything but a white uniform."

Enforcement of Rules

There are three steps to the enforcement of rules: (1) set a time limit; (2) make sure that the task is carried out; and (3) ignore irrelevant behavior.

Set a Time Limit

Yes: "You must clean the table before you eat dinner."
No: "You must clean the table soon."
Yes: "The windows must be washed by noon on Saturday."
No: "The windows must be washed once a week."

Make Sure the Task Is Carried Out

John was told that he must wear a clean white shirt to work each day. He appeared with a blue shirt. The supervisor said, "John, you cannot work today without a white shirt."

John replied that he didn't have a clean one and that they were shorthanded today and he was needed. The supervisor said, "We do need you, but you will not be allowed to work unless you have a clean white shirt." John returned home to get a white shirt. He never attempted to come to work again without being dressed appropriately.

Ignore Irrelevant Behavior

Although it is difficult for most supervisors to accept, the most powerful technique for eliminating many behaviors is simply to ignore them. Whenever a rule is set one can expect considerable fuss, turmoil, excuses, and other signs of defensive behavior. All of these behaviors are normal and expected, but they are irrelevant to the task requested. They should be ignored. Examples of behavior to be ignored:

1. William says, "It doesn't make sense to empty the trash tonight. The baskets are only partially full."

2. Betty hates to put equipment away at the end of the work day because she feels that isn't part of her job. However, the rule states that she is to do it. She does comply with the rule but is vocal in her complaints and works slowly. Her behavior should be ignored so long as she is completing the assigned task.

Ignoring behaviors, of course, is not an easy task, especially for supervisors who feel they should make some response to all actions of their subordinates. It is difficult not to respond to sarcasm, arguments, or pleas—unless one practices. Then it becomes easy. A supervisor must simply act as if the irrelevant behavior was unnoticed. If the behavior is particularly upsetting, the supervisor may want to become busy with some other task or to walk slowly and unconcerned out of the room.

It is important to remember that the anger shown by the irrelevant behavior of people is probably not a personal attack on the supervisor. When the subordinate becomes upset, comforting the individual is likely only to make the matter worse.

Problem Rules

When rules are difficult to enforce with time limits, such as in a situation of a person having a habit of being late or of cursing, it is best to simply tell the person without making a rule. If the behavior persists, then it may be necessary to establish a rule.

As near as possible, such rules also should be definable, reasonable, and enforceable. Of course they will be more difficult to enforce than those with strict time limits. Below are listed steps that can be taken in order to deal with problem rules.

1. Ask for a restatement of the rule. In an unemotional way this simple technique has been found to be more effective and easier to use than any system of punishments and penalties.

2. Ignore irrelevant behavior.

3. Enforce by establishing routines.

Enforcement of Commands

When a supervisor issues a command such as "clean this area" or "don't go out into the dining room" the command must be enforced much as long-term rules. A time limit can be set making sure that the task is carried out, ask for a restatement, and ignore irrelevant behavior.

If commands given on any one day were counted the supervisor would be amazed at the number. Since the carrying out of each command properly requires a considerable amount of the supervisor's time and energy, the secret is simply to give as few commands as possible!

Outcomes of Consistency Training

Initial Expectations

1. **Start with one rule at a time, not many rules.**
   If enforcing rules has been a problem in the past, much energy will be expended in enforcement. The first rule is the one in which you establish your consistency. Remember also that each rule changes the worker's environment. Time is needed by the individual for adjusting to each change. It takes time for people to remember rules. Once the rule is mastered then you go on to other rules.

2. **Expect difficulties initially.**
   When rules are established, there is always a testing of limits and things often get worse before they get better. Sometimes things go well and then all of a sudden the rule is broken in every way imaginable. It is important to simply "have faith" and to be completely consistent in carrying out the rule. The testing behavior will eventually diminish. Many supervisors are guilty of abandoning a rule when it is tested. They fail to realize that testing of a rule is a normal process. If the subordinate shows anger or anxiety over the rule it is not actually a personal response to the supervisor.

3. **The rule setter is likely to change also.**
   It is not uncommon, after the struggle and upset caused by a rule enforcement has passed, that the supervisor recognizes many of the actions taken were not as reasonable as had been previously assumed. Many of the rules of supervisors frequently arise from their own frustrations and inadequacies.

The Supervisor's Role

We have discussed in other sections of this book the notions of *Theory X* and *Theory Y* supervision as espoused by McGregor.[2] Theory X supervision of course is con-

---

2. D. McGregor, *The Human Side of Enterprise* (New York: McGraw-Hill, 1960).

cerned with watching, telling, and directing others. Theory Y supervision is concerned with providing an environment in which one can grow and develop personal satisfaction and responsibility in one's work. The approach to supervision espoused in this text is compatible with Theory Y. Although most supervisors agree with Theory Y, in practice they often act as if their main function was to prevent bad habits in workers and to instill good habits. Most of their time is spent in offering good advice and warnings to prevent any experimentation on the part of the subordinate. The subordinate has little opportunity to discover the consequences of one's actions on one's own. As a consequence, the individual has little confidence in personal judgment. If supervisors spent more time in providing a stable environment free of unnecessary tensions for subordinates, and if they spent less time in giving specific instructions, both supervisors and subordinates would be much more effective.

Examples of how to create a healthy work environment rather than to control specific behavior are

No: The supervisor requires Walt to fill out timecards whenever the supervisor is too tired or busy to do them himself.

Yes: The supervisor requires Walt to fill out timecards every Monday, knowing that Walt needs the consistency provided by the rule.

No: The management holds an employee meeting every week to spell out the rules to employees.

Yes: The management holds an employee meeting every week. Employees are encouraged to question any rules and to air complaints, to seek information, and to offer suggestions that might lead to change. Rules of management are also clarified.

No: The supervisor gives Jane a job and tells her exactly how to do it.

Yes: The supervisor gives Jane a job and tells her the goals expected. The supervisor's job is to minimize the obstacles that Jane is likely to encounter in reaching the goal. If Jane needs specific help, the supervisor provides it.

A Growth-Development Environment

A growth-developing environment contains three essential characteristics.

1. A *model* (i.e., a person after which one can pattern oneself)
2. *Limits* (i.e., rules)
3. *Freedom to discover.*

Thus far we have discussed in detail the aspects of a growth environment that are related to limits or rules.

The characteristics encompassing the needs for a model and the freedom to discover are equally important.

The Supervisor as a Model

When a subordinate has a choice to make in a work situation, that individual is likely to act in a way consistent with the way the *model* would act. This model is most likely to be the way one of the supervisors acted.

A distinction is being made. The subordinate acts the way the supervisor *acts,* not the way the supervisor *tells* how to act.

In a given situation a subordinate may not know what to do, but can usually think of a similar situation concerning the supervisor that will assist in the making of a decision. For example, Lee was given responsibility over a small crew of workers. One of the workers displeased him. When Lee displeases his supervisor the supervisor yells at him. Lee therefore yelled at his subordinate.

Providing Freedom to Discover

Let's follow Mrs. Jones, a food-service supervisor, around. She talks to the dishwasher: "Dont't stack the glasses that way—you'll break them." "Mop up this water on the floor—you'll fall." "Don't stack your dishes that way—they look terrible."

She next goes to the salad girl: "Don't cut like that—you'll cut off your fingers." "Stop talking—you can't do your work."

She moves on into the storeroom. "Hurry or you'll make everyone late." "Look how messy you are. If you don't clean up, no one will like you."

Anyone following Mrs. Jones would notice two things about her behavior in attempting to direct her subordinates. First, she is extremely ineffective. Day after day she says the same thing and day after day her subordinates perform in the same way. Second, much of her advice just is not true. The dishwasher has never fallen down. The salad girl has never cut herself. The storeroom keeper has a large number of friends, regardless of his messiness.

One may ask why the supervisor persists in such frustrating and ineffective behavior. In part, her behavior results from her own feeling of responsibility for her subordinates. She may also feel guilty because she realizes that she has little actual control over her subordinates' behavior. In order to "do her job" she feels compelled to give verbal warnings and advice.

Nagging is poor supervisory practice. It fails to give positive results, but even worse, it has a number of negative effects. No one likes to be nagged. The person who submits to nagging usually feels resentful and often rebels. What can supervisors do other than nag? They usually are not nagging out of spite but rather they have a genuine concern for their subordinates. In fact, most naggers do not want their subordinates to dislike them—they nag so that subordinates will not have to test the rules that are laid down by the naggers themselves.

Supervisors must learn that they are not responsible for everything subordinates do. It must be the subordinates, not the supervisors, who take the responsibility for their own behavior.

Supervisors are responsible for being effective in what they can do. They must be responsible for creating a healthy work environment by enforcing limits consistently, by providing a model for the subordinate to follow, and by allowing subordinates to discover things themselves. Also, they can relieve the subordinates of guilt by not expecting them to follow rules that are impractical or impossible to follow.

Summarized below are some important steps for supervisors to keep in mind.

1. **Subordinates must learn for themselves the consequences of their own actions.**

   Learning for oneself is not only the best way to learn, it is the only way one can learn. A subordinate can never learn the consequences of a rule without having broken the rule.

   Yes: John put off his cleaning until quitting time. He will have to complete it after quitting time.

   No: John's supervisor tells him, "If you don't get started on your cleaning, you won't finish by quitting time."

   Yes: Martha was late for work.

   No: Martha's supervisor warned her repeatedly not to be late for work.

   Yes: Al fell on the wet floor.

   No: Al's supervisor told him, "Keep this area dry. You'll break your neck."

2. **Select rules that can be enforced by natural consequences.**

   A rule of a natural consequence can be enforced even when the supervisor is not present. These are by far the most effective rules to establish.

   Yes: Mop the floor every Saturday morning.

   No: Mop the floor when it needs it.

   Yes: Stay out of all work areas other than your own.

   No: Don't argue with other employees.

3. **Do not set unnecessary and impractical rules.**

   Before rules are set, they should be considered carefully. Can any benefit come of the rule other than *self-discipline*? (Self-discipline can only be imposed by oneself.) If the rule is broken, will the result really be as disastrous as we allege? Is the rule really worth the effort required to enforce it consistently?

SUMMARY

Theories of learning can be applied to supervision. All individuals learn according to basic laws and principles of behavior.

Before we can modify behavior we must be able to recognize the behavior we wish to change. The first steps in behavioral change have to do with careful observations, recording, and providing consequences for change.

Behavior develops under laws involving reinforcements (rewards and punishments) and extinctions. A behavior pattern persists and is strengthened if a positive reward follows the behavior. A behavior pattern weakens and changes if a negative reward follows. A behavior pattern weakens or extinguishes if no reinforcement follows.

Positive reinforcements can be effective in bringing individuals to show increased social responsiveness, to develop desirable work habits, and to show greater assertiveness and less fear. Negative reinforcement is a tool to help employees come to understand the meanings of rules and to help break undesirable habits. Extinction is important in conditioning both supervisors and subordinates to separate relevant work from irrelevant work behavior.

A how-to-do-it guide to supervision is presented utilizing behavior modification principles.

1. Consistency in supervision is achieved if the following law is applied: (*a*) any behavior is strengthened and likely to occur when we expect some result to happen and it actually does happen; (*b*) any behavior is weakened and likely to disappear when we expect some result to happen and it does not happen.

2. A rule must fulfill three requirements. It must be *definable*, *reasonable*, and *enforceable*.

3. There are three steps to the enforcement of rules: (*a*) set a time limit; (*b*) make sure that the task is carried out; (*c*) ignore irrelevant behavior.

4. Initial expectations of consistency training: (*a*) start with one rule at a time, not many rules; (*b*) expect difficulties initially; (*c*) the rule-setter is also likely to change.

5. A growth developing environment contains: (*a*) a model, such as a supervisor, after which one can pattern oneself; (*b*) limits; i.e., rules; (*c*) freedom to discover for oneself one's possibilities.

6. Supervisors need to keep in mind: (*a*) subordinates must learn for themselves the consequences of their own actions; (*b*) select rules that can be enforced by natural consequences; (*c*) do not set unnecessary and impractical rules.

Techniques of Group Leadership
and Decision Making

11

In recent years theories of teaching, counseling, and supervision have undergone dramatic changes as emphasis has been shifted from the teacher, counselor, or supervisor to the group receiving the instruction. Research consistently has demonstrated that group decision-making methods are definitely superior to the lecture procedure in getting groups to make use of information presented to them. Appropriately enough, one of the first studies that demonstrated the superiority of group methods involved the changing of food habits of housewives during World War II.

Since World War II and the rise of the Human Relations movement, the small group has been recognized as a powerful force for human change and development. As individuals we learn and maintain our patterns of behavior by virtue of playing roles in family groups, social groups, work groups, and other significant groups in our lives. Since groups are instrumental in molding our behavior, it is only logical to assume that groups can also be instrumental in bringing about behavioral changes.

A field of study and research devoted to training possibilities within small groups has grown over the past twenty-five years until graduate programs and courses are now offered in most universities. American industry makes extensive use of Human Relations training laboratories and seminars conducted under the auspices of the National Training Laboratories (NTL) and the American Management Association (AMA).

Although supervisors work continuously with small groups and hold many employment meetings, systematic techniques and theories for working with groups have often been overlooked in their training. They simply *play by ear* or model what their previous supervision has taught by example. This chapter presents theory, technique, and exercises designed to increase knowledge and skill in working with groups.

FREEZE . . . UNFREEZE . . . REFREEZE

All groups of people have problems.

These problems can range from minor irritants to very serious dilemmas that potentially can destroy the groups themselves. Some groups are able to solve their problems, no matter how severe. Other groups never seem to resolve their problems. They keep coming up with the same inadequate solutions time after time, or they simply run from the problem by not facing it. One common way of running from a problem is by "giving" it to someone outside the group to solve.

Psychologists have learned a great deal about group problem solving. One concept of behavior that can be useful to any group in solving problems deals with a theory of change, which has three stages, called *freeze—unfreeze—refreeze*.

For example, suppose we have a twenty-five pound piece of ice in a cube and we want to make it round. We must first unfreeze or melt the ice before we can fit it into a new mold. Once we have fitted it in the new mold, we must refreeze it in its new form. Human behavior can be shaped just like ice. When we act habitually in the same manner, making the same assumptions and exhibiting the same old attitudes, we are showing *frozen* behavior. We usually fall back on the same old habitual ways of dealing with problems and dilemmas no matter how ineffectual these ways have been in the past.

Two typical ways of dealing with problems are to force solutions that have never worked in the past and to run from them. Occasionally, we get tired of beating our heads against a wall and we question our old practices and attitudes. At such times we are passing into an *unfrozen* state. Whenever we start discussing problems from new perspectives, we are creating conditions under which we can question old habits, assumptions, and attitudes.

The idea of *invention* is essential to unfreezing. We need to brainstorm—to seek out alternate ways of doing things before deciding what should be done. Although unfreezing is essential, we need to be aware that being in an unfrozen state is highly uncomfortable and that we probably experience more confusion than understanding. Confusion results, along with feelings of discomfort, when we begin to abandon the security of old habits and assumptions. Nevertheless, if we are to change frozen patterns of behavior, we must pass through the stage of unfreezing. We must stay unfrozen until we can invent new ways of responding to replace the old, ineffectual ways.

Feedback from others in the group and from experience in trying out our ideas can be used to tell us if our new methods of behavior are achieving the results we intended. If the feedback indicates that our new behavior is not effective, then we should remain unfrozen and try further experimentation. If the feedback is positive and indicates that we have obtained desired results, then we can profit from our feedback and make appropriate generalizations. We apply our new behavior to actual situations. We then start to *refreeze* our new behavior.

So much for theory. Let's put the theory into practice. Here is a step-by-step program each group can use in solving any problem or dilemma.

1. Identify the problem during a meeting attended by all. Often some of the biggest problems in any group are that the members lack the courage to bring a problem into the open or they lack confidence in other members to deal effectively with the problem.

2. Describe on paper how you have attempted to solve the problem in the past. Why didn't the solution work? Did you avoid or run from the problem?

3. Brainstorm! Invent new solutions to the problem. You should really struggle to come up with at least three sound solutions.

4. Try out the first solution in action so that you can get feedback and see if the solution will work. Don't fall into the trap of saying, "Oh, that will never work," before you try it. If after you have tried the solution and it doesn't work, try the second solution, and so on. If no solution works, go back to the drawing board and brainstorm again.

5. When you find a new solution, profit from it! Pat yourself on the back. Analyze again what you did. Recognize how you overcame your own inertia, by yourselves. Gain confidence that your group can solve any problem. You really can if you will only learn to *unfreeze* and *refreeze*!

The following model illustrates the relationship between freeze-unfreeze-refreeze and dilemma-invention-feedback generalization.

GROUP GOALS AND FUNCTIONS

Any time you are with more than two people you are in a group. Of course, you are aware that not all groups are identical. Some are very formal, others are completely informal, and others are not clearly defined. Generally groups have three kinds of meetings—mechanical, "bull," and organic. A mechanical meeting is well-defined with set procedures established for decision making. A "bull" meeting is very informal and does not lead to decisions. An organic meeting hopes to establish goals and decisions through group consensus. It is a prototype of democratic action. The organic group also serves as a prototype of the group-process human-relations training groups try to achieve.

Mechanical Meetings

1. Group has a goal, often set up in advance of interaction and frequently determined by a chairperson or an executive committee.

2. Decision-making group: decisions made by mechanical means, such as voting.

3. Designated chairperson: role of chairperson filled by one person elected or appointed for meeting.

4. Functions performed by chairperson such as summarizing, testing for feasibility, or calling for a vote.

5. In order to move group towards the goal, the chairperson follows *Robert's Rules of Order* or some other explicit act of rules governing procedure and interaction. Chairperson at a large meeting may be assisted by a parliamentarian or sergeant at arms.

6. Members get permission from chair to speak.

"Bull" Meetings

1. No shared group goal except the desire on the part of individuals to express general interests.

2. Not a decision-making group.

3. No chairperson.

4. Functions, such as summarizing, testing for feasibility, testing for a consensus, or taking a vote, not usually performed.

5. Method of interaction is on an individual "win-own-points" basis. One person wants to talk about a subject, so presents the issue, provokes controversy, and fights to win point.

6. Members speak when they desire.

Figure 11.1 Freeze, Unfreeze, Refreezing Theory

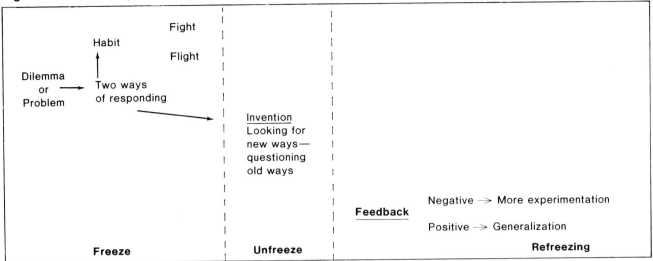

Organic Meetings

1. Group has an emergent goal, determined through interaction of members.

2. Decision-making group: decisions made by consensus.

3. Role of chairperson: filled by different members, depending on the needs of the group.

4. Functions, such as summarizing, testing for feasibility, testing for consensus, etc., are performed by various members depending on the requirements of the situation.

5. Members move toward goal consistent with the needs of the situation rather than under the direction of an elected person.

6. Communication pattern is self-regulating, with each person taking responsibility for coordinating participation.

TASK FUNCTIONS

In order for a group to have direction and movement, certain functions—*task functions*—need to be performed. In a mechanical meeting, task functions are usually performed by the chairperson. In an organic meeting they are performed by the group members. Regardless of who performs them, the following task functions can help a group move toward its goal more effectively.[1]

Stating the Problem

One function is concerned with influencing group action by posing the problem or stating an issue for the group to discuss. In discussion groups, which start without a formally designated or indicated leader, it is necessary for somebody to state an issue or formulate a concern so that the group can move. One member might state an issue. Although not the designated or elected leader, this individual has the skill of stating an issue that will magnetize the group around that point. A group member can test whether the person has been consistently stating issues for the group to discuss or whether that person has been doing so much that others do not have an adequate opportunity to influence the course of group events.

Giving Procedural Suggestions

The next function is concerned with giving suggestions as to how the group should proceed. Groups are confronted continuously with the problem of how to proceed, whether a certain action is suitable, or whether some other procedure would move the group along more effectively.

Asking for Information

Another item sharply distinguishes between a mechanical and an organic meeting. The leader of any group has the privilege of interrogating others. This is an extremely powerful position. The interrogator does not show a hand, but pierces into other people with an arrow. Either they yield and tell the interrogator the answer or they resist and refuse to cooperate. The interrogator is in control of

---

1. The sections titled "Task Functions," "Maintenance Functions," and "Content and Process" are based on the proceedings of Participants' Training Laboratory, Veteran's Administration Hospital, Houston, Texas.

what they do through the interrogation process. Interrogation can be a highly desirable activity in a group because it provokes all kinds of thinking. It is only when all of the interrogation originates from one person, who has other powers in addition, that the group is likely to be maintained in a state of dependency on one person. In addition when the responsibilities for digging and ferreting out new information are lodged in one person, the person's human frailty may result in the critical questions that would really move the group toward effective decisions not being asked.

Summarizing

The role of summarizing can be an extremely powerful group role. A member, after listening and participating normally, finally gives a really good summary that ties the package in a neat knot. This means that the solution is apparent to all. The solution is crystallized; the discussion is over. The other people look to the summarizer because this is the person who really knows what has been happening. More weight is given to the summarizer's participation by the other members. A group member can test whether the summarizer has been listening to group activity, whether a summary would have helped the group find its direction again, and whether a summary was provided when needed.

Testing for Feasibility

The next function is concerned with testing the feasibility. A group might consider discussing some topic that is highly abstract. The individual participants really do not have the intellectual competence to deal with the topic effectively. Therefore, the discussion wanders for lack of feasibility. The group needs someone to say, "We don't have the intellectual skills among us that would permit this to be an effective discussion." This should help the group to get in touch with its major problem of being concrete and realistic with respect to resources available to it.

Testing for Consensus

This function involves taking responsibility for finding out if a group is in agreement by testing for consensus. If *A* is talking and it looks as if there is some emerging agreement, this person may say, "It looks as though we are moving toward an agreement. I wonder if we are in agreement on this point?" What has happened? Now everyone's attention is locked on *A* as the person who saw that

the group was ready to agree and who brought the group together. To test for consensus is a more powerful group function than simply to give an opinion, to answer an interrogation, or to respond when somebody else states an issue. It is a very powerful social role. Invariably, leaders in mechanical meetings feel an obligation to test for agreement. Yet, the person who is formally designated as the leader of the meeting is so involved as to be unable to see an emerging agreement. One or more other members may better test for consensus. This is another group function that can be shared between group members.

Standard Setting

Once a group has made a decision to pursue a topic and come up with an examination of it, the group has made a commitment to which it is obligated unless the group releases itself. The person who keeps the group together in a mechanical meeting is almost always the designated leader, the one who rules remarks as out of order. Standard setting as a means of staying on the topic does not need to be spotted in one person; it can be done by whomever or at whatever time one sees that the group is beginning to stray off the target.

In a mechanical meeting the group functions usually are held by the official person in charge, such as the leader, chairman, or president. By comparison, in an organic meeting such functions are distributed according to the ability and insight of the individual members.

MAINTENANCE FUNCTIONS

Maintenance functions are those actions that are necessary for enabling the group to move along at the highest level of efficiency and learning. These functions are aids that must be provided by members of the group if the group is to work efficiently and if learning is to take place.

Gatekeeping

A simple technique to help make a group more effective has to do with *gatekeeping*. Gatekeeping is based on the notion that the best kind of a group is one in which all members are willing to assume responsibility for the group's actions. An effective leader of a group must realize (and help others to realize) that each member is responsible for making a contribution to creative group thinking, decisions, actions, and feelings. It is important to recognize also that groups must deal not only with topics and items from an agenda, but must deal also with feelings of the members of the group, and be able to recognize barriers stemming from feelings that may interfere with group harmony.

Since total group involvement is critical, the gatekeepers try to keep the channels of communication open. The gatekeeper must be sensitive to the feelings of all group members and usually try to get each member of the group to share personal feelings with other members. A good gatekeeper will "close the gate" on a member who dominates a discussion. For example, the gatekeeper may say, "That's fine John, but let's hear how some of the others feel."

A good gatekeeper will "open the gate" for silent members, perhaps saying, "You have made some good points, John, but we need to have other opinions. Jane, you have been quiet. How do you feel about this issue?"

Whenever in a meeting, each member of the group should try to observe what is happening. A member should take notice when people try to force decisions. One should count the number of times important issues are sidestepped or dropped simply because no one took the initiative to pursue a touchy problem. One should note how many members "me too" what other members contribute but are reluctant to initiate ideas of their own. Each member of a group needs to try to be a gatekeeper. It only takes one perceptive and persistent gatekeeper to bring about some dynamic changes within a group.

One maintenance function is *listening.* Have you ever sat on a bus, or a train, or at a baseball game and tried to talk to the person next to you who just sat there like a "bump on a log?" It is pretty hard to maintain any kind of interacting relationship with a person who will not listen. One method of supporting a person when the person is talking in a group is by listening, particularly when it concerns an idea that the listener is trying to make work. It is important to understand what is being said. If a person keeps "running off," it doesn't really matter whether that person is listened to or not. But if one is really trying to express oneself clearly, then that individual needs someone who will listen. Have you ever found yourself wondering if people in a group are listening to you or not? You try to make sense if you think others are interested and listening.

Another maintenance function is carried out by a person who helps others become less dependent on the leader of the group, the expert. Industrial groups try to extract words of wisdom from the experts. They inquire, "How are we doing?" This is a very legitimate question; they just may be going to the wrong source to find the answer. Maybe the source is in their own group. It is not easy to learn how to use this source. One of the maintenance functions is to devise the kind of support that will replace the disappointment created when expected leaders don't perform as expected. When the people who are expected to act as experts do not act, group members must provide this function in the group. This is an extremely important maintenance function. It is a kind of *replacement* if the expert is not there when needed.

Another maintenance function in the group is *encouragement.* We do not have to agree with a person, but by helping one to say what one thinks might help the group clarify problems. People can say, "Is this what you mean, or do you mean this?" Encouraging other people to bring out their ideas and their feelings is an important maintenance function, but it demands a tremendous amount of insight.

A person needs to be logical and know the facts. This is important. One has to have a more legitimate basis for ideas than what one feels, but we need to understand the feelings as well. Expressing genuine feelings holds a very high value in our background and training. Yet, feelings are what confuse thinking. A human relations group tends to encourage the expression of feelings, to make people judge the appropriateness or genuineness of feelings, and to explore the implications of expressing feelings. The testing of the appropriateness of feelings as related to problems is an extremely important maintenance function. A human relations group gives the chance to explore these implications of feelings, their meaning in terms of problems people are trying to state and how to deal with them. *Legitimizing* feelings is another maintenance function.

A person tries to give an opinion. We may not agree with it, but the person is making this offering to the group. To *validate* one's efforts and *accept* them is another important kind of maintenance function. Often there is a person in a group whose ideas are not going along with those of the group. In such cases it is not up to any one individual to override the person's ideas or invalidate them. It may be that the person's ideas are out of order. If they are, then this is a group problem. It may be, though, that others are also out of order. Maybe several are wrong and by looking at it together, a true picture of what the problem is may develop. The *giving of acceptance,* accepting the person's offering to the group, is another maintenance function.

All of these maintenance functions aid the group in working *as* a group. If they are performed, they help individuals function as real group members. The group, as well as its members, stands to benefit from the effects of well-performed maintenance functions. Once the significance of these functions is understood, and their implementation practiced, the performance of a group is significantly effected.

Following is a brief summary of the various maintenance functions.

Function	Description
1. Gatekeeping	Gatekeeping is a technique of bringing silent members into the group action. "Kathy, we haven't heard anything from you in the last thirty minutes. Do you have anything to say?"
2. Task orientation	This function is one of keeping the group working on the topic or problem.
3. Facilitating understanding	The function here is to help people to communicate more clearly, particularly when people are not understanding each other. "It seems to me that Jack is talking about something different from what Ann is referring to in their argument."
4. Emotional support	The function needed here is to help others to express ideas, plans, and purposes that are often difficult to express because of the person's emotions.
5. Participant-Observer	This function involves not only the individual behaving in the group, but also observing one's own behavior. In this way, learning to observe one's own behavior assists in better understanding oneself.
6. Assisting others to test their private assumptions	Often, people are making decisions on the basis of irrelevant data or false assumptions about what is going on. Assisting others to test their assumptions facilitates group learning and decision making.
7. Giving acceptance	The accepting of other people's opinions skillfully, without rejecting the person, or disagreeing in a manner that causes the person to think about the disagreement and not of being rejected, helps maintain group effectiveness.

CONTENT AND PROCESS

Talk in a group may focus on two types of issues. Discussion may focus on *content* issues or on *process* issues. It is possible to consider both of these simultaneously.

Content is the *what* of the discussion; content is the essence of the discussion. It may concern events, problems, or issues arising out of, or caused by, the group's activity. The content is of a "here and now" group-related nature. On the other hand, content may concern events, problems, or issues that do not arise out of the group's activity. Such outside events that do not depend on the group for their origin and are not related to the group's activity in a causal relationship are considered "then and there" issues.

Process concerns *how* the group is working together. It covers issues of procedure, organization, performance of group functions, relationships between group members, and decision-making procedures. When a group's members discuss *how* they are working together, they are occupied with "here-and-now" issues that arise out of the group's working together.

When a group focuses its talk primarily on the process employed by the group in a meeting, it is moving in the direction of analyzing its process. When certain procedures are identified and discussed, questions regarding the effects of these procedures arise. In identifying and evaluating various procedures and their consequences, a group is making a process analysis.

The question may arise as to why a group should spend its time analyzing its processes. Many groups have worked together efficiently without knowing that process analysis even exists, much less seeing a need to make one. The reason for emphasizing process and its analysis is really a means of quality control. Groups that are not concerned about their process may perform well, but those who put their process in the test tube for observation learn to perform better. When a group begins to evaluate its process systematically, it frequently discovers reasons for its problem as a group—blocks to communication, decision-making procedures—that prevent total support, and individual procedural errors that affect that person's relationship with the group.

In other words, process analysis involves all the procedures that govern the development of a bunch of individuals into a group or a team. It also has an influence on how *well* the group will eventually learn to work together. Process analysis is a tool available to groups for evaluating the procedures they use and their effectiveness. Such an evaluation, if coupled with understanding and incentive, usually leads to an increase in group cohesion, efficiency, satisfaction, and effectiveness.

In summary, discussion in a group is of two major types. Discussion may focus on:

1. **Content**

    Content is what is being discussed. It is what you are talking about. It is the issue under consideration. Content issues can be further broken down according to what point in time they cover. When content issues deal with outside, back-home problems, politics, sports, etc., these represent "then and there" issues; that is, these are issues that arise *outside* the group, and the group's activity did not cause these events in any way. When the content issues deal with problems arising because of the group these are here-and-now issues. These issues concern events caused by the group and directly related to group activity.

2. Process

Process is *how* the discussion is handled. When the effect of a member's behavior on the discussion is considered, when problems between members arising out of discussion are considered, when decision-making procedures are considered, *process* is under consideration. It is by taking a close look at *how* a group works together that the members really develop into an effective group.

Here are some common examples of *content* and *process*. When a group is talking about home problems in connection with past life, situations in the family, on the job, problems like the status of American education, problems of communities, or the effect of religion on behavior, that is not process. Those are *what* topics of discussion, *content* issues.

Such discussions may produce needs for a chairperson, or voting; they may produce feelings of anger, or cause a person to flee, another to *fight*, or another to *invent*. When these are happening in the group and are discussed, these are *how* topics—*process* issues.

When the group stops talking about a content topic to talk about how the members are working together—that is process. When the group stops talking about a content topic and starts talking about how members are feeling towards one another and how these feelings affect the group's activity—that is process. When the group stops talking about a content topic and starts trying to figure out why some members are silent, or others are talking quite a lot, or getting angry at one another, or are bored—that is process. When a group stops talking about a content topic and starts to analyze who is controlling, whether or not to have a chairperson, why people voted rather than decided an issue by getting everyone's agreement—that is process.

Content issues provide a vehicle for group activity. Process determines the direction and speed of the group's development.

The Art of Listening

Effective communication goes both ways. Giving instructions is downward communication. Listening is upward communication. Upward and downward communication go hand in hand and both are more effective if done by the *same* person.

Good listening is an art that, if properly applied, becomes a general attitude. Day in and day out, the supervisor or manager who is willing to listen to the other fellow's point of view and who tries to take it into account before taking action will find the role easier. The problems of making work changes and of handling supervisory problems will not be so traumatic. If, in addition, the supervisor has worked hard to earn the confidence of subordinates by *consistently* showing them that their feelings and ideas are valued, that supervisor's role is more effective. If communications are blocked, situations such as the following can develop:

> The most frequent complaint was that although orders and instructions about work traveled easily enough, it was difficult to take up ordinary feelings, especially if they were critical about the job or about life in the factory. The main stumbling block in getting such feelings resolved was the reticence about communicating them upwards. The reticence was said to be due to the fact that if a person tried to express to his superior his feelings about the job, or about the superior himself, it was all too likely that the superior would argue with him and try to show him that his feelings were unreasonable and that they did not tally with the facts. Having the existence of one's feelings denied in this way only made things worse. The resentment against his superior arose for not understanding the employee and not helping him to get at what was disturbing him.[2]

Supervisors who are well accepted and seen as good counselors must be cautious to avoid getting involved in the personal lives of subordinates. They should restrict themselves to listening; avoid giving advice. Even when the advice is successful, there is a risk of forming a dependency relationship with the subordinate. Above all, a supervisor should never play amateur psychologist with someone with a deep-seated personality problem. Besides taking up too much time, this may prevent the person from getting professional help.

The Teaching of Counseling and Listening

The technique recommended is called *nondirective* because it puts the responsibility on the person who is speaking. It has three functions:

1. It allows the listener to understand what the other person really thinks and feels. It is thus a valuable way of getting *information*.

2. It allows the other person to *release* pent-up feelings.

---

2. Jaques, Elliot, *The Changing Cultures of a Factory* (London: Tavistock Publications, 1951).

3. By expressing oneself and having the listener *reflect back* feelings, one is able to develop greater *insight* into one's own problems.

Stages in a Problem Listening Session

1. The speaker is encouraged to a release of feelings, and the listener encourages their release. The listener *accepts* everything heard regardless of personal reaction; the listener *does not pass judgment* on the speaker and needs to believe, *basically,* that the speaker is capable of solving purely personal problems.[3]

2. *Facts* are collected. Having let off steam, the listener can ask questions to bring out more information. The listener may also give information.

3. *Solutions* are formulated. Once the facts are assembled, the speaker is in a position to weigh the various solutions and to pick one. The listener's role is to make sure the speaker has all the facts.

These are the three main phases of the problem listening session, but of course the phases are not arbitrary; there may be considerable shifting throughout the session.

By following these steps, both the speaker and the listener work at (1) clarifying the feelings so that they color the facts minimally and (2) not jumping to conclusions before all of the facts are accumulated.

Understanding others is a difficult art that can be learned best under practiced supervision. Each individual may have a different style. In general, here are a few summary points to remember.

1. *Encourage the other person to talk.* This means the listener must curb the natural impulse to talk. In addition to listening, the listener must concentrate— must be *interested* in what the other person is saying and try to *understand.*

2. *Reflective summary.* An effective way of encouraging others to talk is by summarizing the person's feelings, disregarding the facts. For example,

   Speaker: "Yes, I'm thinking of quitting. I don't seem to be getting the hang of the job. At least that's what people around here seem to think."

   Listener: "You feel people are sort of down on you?"

A reflective summary serves a number of purposes: (1) it shows the other person that the listener understands and is fair; (2) it allows the other person to restate an attitude if under the impression that the listener did not understand; (3) it highlights what has been said. People often are surprised to learn what feelings were behind their words when their words are reflected back to them.

3. *Probe.* The listener's role is to understand. If one does not, one should feel free to solicit information by asking questions.

4. *Weighing alternatives.* The listener wants to help the other person make a decision, but does not want to make the decision for the person. The other person may even make a very poor decision. The listener does have the responsibility of helping the other person make a good decision by asking questions when the decision is made, such as:

   "What probably would be the effect of that?"
   "Is that the only solution?"
   "How would that help?"

AN EXERCISE FOR INCREASING PROBLEM AWARENESS

Invisible Committees

When one finds oneself in a new human relations group, that person is influenced by numerous sets of forces that have a bearing on the individual's behavior in the group. One brings with one to the group situation:

1. Theories, assumptions, values, beliefs, attitudes about self (self-concept), others, groups, organizations, and cultures. These serve as one's *frames of reference* for one's behavior.

2. Loyalties to other outside reference groups; i.e., one's family, profession, religion, political affiliation.

3. A repertoire of behavior skills that permit or prevent one from doing what one really wants to do (diagnostic skills, listening skills, etc.).

4. More or less realistic expectations, hopes, and anticipations concerning what the group experience will be like.

These forces, in evidence for each person, form one's invisible committees. At the beginning of the life of a group, people know little of each other's invisible committees. The ambiguity of this situation may create feelings of discomfort and confusion.

---

3. This section is based on material from Department of Human Relations, University of Kansas.

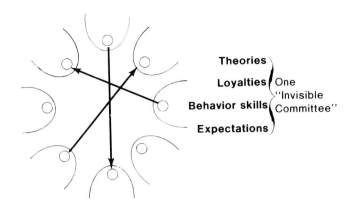

Theories ⎫
Loyalties ⎬ One
Behavior skills ⎬ "Invisible
Expectations ⎭ Committee"

Johari Window

The Johari Window (named after Joe Luft and Harry Ingham) was first used in an information session at the Western Training Laboratory in Group Development in 1955.

Interaction in the Human Relations Group (as well as in other group situations) can be described in terms of a single individual and that person's relationship to others. The four quadrants of the Johari Window represent the whole person in relation to others.

Area 1 is behavior and motivation known to self and known to others. It shows the extent to which two or more persons can give and take, work together, and enjoy experiences together. The larger this area, the greater the individual's contact with the real world, and the more available are the person's abilities and needs to self and others.

		(k) Known to Self	(u) Not Known to Self
(k)	Known to Others	Area of Free Activity 1	Blind Area 3
(u)	Not Known to Others	Hidden or Avoided Area 2	Unknown Area 4

Area 2 is behavior and motivation open to self but kept away from others. In a new group this is a large quadrant because we do not know much about each other. Another illustration is the person who knows well that a particular remark is resented but keeps it inside. This is also the area of the hidden agenda.

Area 3, the blind area, represents behavior and motivation not known to self but apparent to others. The sim-

plest illustration is a mannerism in speech or gesture of which the person is unaware, but is quite obvious to others. Or an individual may have a need to run the whole show and not be as aware of this as others are.

Area 4 is the area of unknown activity wherein behavior and motivation are known neither to ourselves nor to others. We know this area exists because both the individual and the persons associated with discover from time to time new behavior or new motives were there all along. An individual may be surprised and surprise others by taking over the groups' direction, or another person may discover that the individual has great ability in bringing warring factions together. This person was never before seen as a peacemaker either by self or others.

The human-relations group method is designed to encourage freer, more open communications of ideas—meanings as well as feelings. If successful, the Johari Windows of various individuals *vis-a-vis* each other should change through time from Form 1 to Form 2. (See diagrams below.)

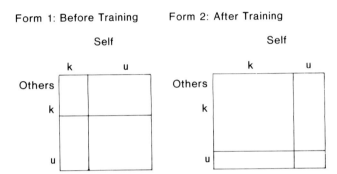

Form 1: Before Training   Form 2: After Training

Self   Self

k   u   k   u

Others   Others

k   k

u   u

Congruence

Congruence (a notion developed by Carl Rogers) is essential before meaningful communications between a person and self or between two or more people is possible. Thus the first quadrant in the Johari Window will be enlarged. Congruence implies that both parties in the communication process permit themselves (*a*) to become aware of what they experience and truly feel and (*b*) become willing to share their awareness in a free and nondefensive manner.

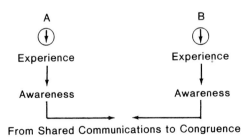

A   B

Experience   Experience

Awareness   Awareness

From Shared Communications to Congruence

Thinking of congruence as having two aspects is helpful. First, it has to do with the agreement between one's self-image and the way one is. By interpersonal experience, particularly as one sees oneself through the eyes of others, the aspect of congruence can be increased. Second, one can think of the amount of congruence between people in their conceptions of some third experience—person, problem, group, idea, etc. Constructive interaction can lead to a reduction in incongruity and to more adequate conceptions.

Exercise

Each person in the class or group is asked to write anonymously on a card something about one or more of the motives and characteristics that the individual consciously tries to hide from others. These cards are collected by the leader who reads them aloud to the group. The large group then breaks into smaller groups to discuss the lecture and the material on the cards.

Alternate Exercise

The Johari Window approach offers an excellent tool to help a group recognize and resolve many of the critical but unspoken problems that are found in organizations. Rather than to write about personal motives and characteristics, each member of the group is instructed to write anonymously on a card something negative (that the person ordinarily would not make public to others) about the organization for which that person works. This exercise is best suited for groups all working in the same organization. The cards are then collected by the leader who reads them aloud to the group. Each statement is then used as a point of general discussion by the total group.

The technique described above has been used extensively by one of the authors with significant success. The statements are usually candid and offer important shortcuts to resolving many of the important problems that arise in organizations. It usually takes many meetings to discuss the statements that are presented; therefore one Johari Window exercise can provide discussion topics for several developmental meetings.

WHAT CAN BE GAINED FROM HOLDING EMPLOYEE MEETINGS?

Depending upon how they are conducted and upon the caliber of the overall employer-employee relations program, employee meetings can have a number of values.

A Means of Putting across Changes

It is one thing to have ideas, another thing to implement them. The manager or the supervisor may be the most intelligent, the most highly educated, and the most experienced person in the organization, yet one whose *good* ideas may fail to achieve what is desired because the ideas are not accepted. One reason for failure is that the ideas are not those of the people expected to carry them out. They are those of the manager/supervisor.

Ask yourself which of these two ideas you would be more likely to accept.

1. "From now on you will turn in a report on every ounce of cooking fat you use!"
2. "We have a problem of keeping track of the cost of cooking fat. Can I get your ideas as to how we can remedy the situation?"

Perhaps some people would prefer the first. Most will go along quicker with the second approach. The superior-inferior relationship is almost always resented. When ideas are presented in the context of such a relationship, enthusiasm for them is almost invariably certain to suffer.

Asking people's opinions is a subtle form of compliment that all enjoy. Dishwashers and assistant managers, janitors, and food supervisors all react alike in this regard.

When ideas are presented in employees' meetings "for your criticism and suggestions," the ideas are likely to be accepted. Many times the manager or supervisor's idea emerged from an employee meeting in practically the same form as it would have been detailed by the manager or supervisor in private. So much the better. The value of the idea is multiplied because now it has employee interest and is well on the way to action.

A Means of Getting the Best from Employees

Every manager or supervisor should realize that one primary function in supervision is to utilize others' abilities and enthusiasm. Managing means working through other people, drawing upon their skills, their experience, and their ideas. The employee meeting can be a device for drawing out and utilizing the talents of many.

The employee meeting led by a competent supervisor can stimulate critical thinking and new ideas. It can enlarge the individual's perspective and aid in recognizing one's job as a part of the department. One is helped to see one's problems as they are related to those of the department and to the total organization. In a hospital, for example, the overall goal of making the patient well is often forgotten by the maintenance person or the vegetable preparer. The porter in a hotel often forgets the main purpose of the hotel—service at a profit and personal enjoyment in the doing. The employee meeting can reorient and restructure the goals for everyone concerned.

Following is an excerpt from an employee meeting held in a midwestern hotel. It illustrates how the employee meeting can enlarge the participant's perspective.

At a regular kitchen meeting a wall washer, whose assignment included the kitchen area, was sitting in on the meeting.

Steward: Now, does anyone have any gripes? . . .
(Pause, followed by some laughter)

Wall washer: Yes, I have one. Why can't the food runners be a little more careful in the way they knock their trucks up against the walls?

Runner, (half in earnest; half kiddingly): If we did that, you wouldn't have anything to do.
(Laughter)

Wall washer: Anything to do—why I can't keep up with the upstairs rooms I've got, let alone keep the kitchen clean.

Runner: Oh, I thought when you left here. . . .

Steward: Yes, Jonesy (the wall washer) does the kitchen and also a lot of rooms upstairs.

Runner: Okay, we'll be more careful with the trucks.
(Other runners nod in agreement)

In a discussion in which many competent people participate, ideas are forged that stand the test of practicality. Every idea that concerns a department as a whole should be subjected to the bombardment and modification of discussion. In addition to gaining acceptance of changes, discussion subtracts unworkable parts and implements the desirable parts.

Following is an illustration of how it pays to use everyone's ideas. The scene took place in a cafeteria's employee meeting.

Supervisor: We've got a bottleneck in getting clean trays. We haven't got room in our present setup for another tray-wiper, and we've got to have the trays dry. They come out of the dishwashing room plenty fast. Has anyone got any ideas? (Long pause) How about you, Mr. Small (the tray-wiper)?*

Mr. Small: I'm going as fast as I can already.
(Another pause)

Mrs. Katsch (a counter person): I worked at the Longbow last year and the person who wiped the trays there has a system of wiping with both hands at once, which was supposed to be a lot faster.

Mr. Small: You can't wipe with both hands. You've got to pick them up and turn them over with one hand.

Mrs. Katsch: Yes, but the wiper there had a sponge in each hand and wiped the top of one in one job and the bottom of another in the other pile at the same time.

Mr. Small: I don't think it will work.

Supervisor: Maybe Mrs. Katsch will demonstrate after our meeting and see what Mr. Small thinks of it. Would you be willing to give it a try, Mr. Small?

Mr. Small: Why yes, we can try it anyway.

Later the new method was installed and increased the number of trays wiped by more than one-third at no increase in energy expenditure.

A Means of Building a Cooperating Work Team

Cooperation comes from the attitude to cooperate and experience in cooperation. The employee meeting can help to build both. The face-to-face relations that result when people sit together in a meeting provide an emotional experience that ties an aggregate of people together into a group of people enjoying the experience of association. Through competent leadership the group takes on common goals and solves common problems. A discussion of proposed kitchen layout with kitchen personnel is not only a means of solving the layout problem but is a means of drawing the group together. A discussion among cleaners concerning the best way to clean a room is not only a training session but also a period of tightening the emotional bonds so necessary for teamwork.

Employee meetings can give experience in how to give and take. Cleaners who work all day alone have little practice in cooperation. The storeroom clerks are practically isolated. While kitchen personnel interact at a high rate, they often do so under stressful conditions that may destroy cooperation. Employee meetings can bring people together in a relaxed, friendly, problem-solving atmosphere. They provide a workshop in which to learn to work together.

---

*Note: Some of the newer and larger dishmachines are equipped to blow-dry trays automatically.

A Means of Releasing Tensions and Resolving Personal Problems

Frustrations are inevitable on any job. The employee meeting provides a means of relieving part of the day-to-day job frustration. Here is an illustration of how it has worked in a waitress meeting.

Hostess: Well, that about winds up the discussion of today's menu. Is there anything further we should talk about?

(Pause)

Waitress: Is there anything we can do about that Beau Brummel who makes a pass at me every day at 12:15?

(Laughter)

Another Waitress: Stop swinging your hips.

(More laughter)

First Waitress: But I don't swing my hips.

Another Waitress: Then you should try.

(More Laughter)

Hostess: What can you do to politely discourage mashers?

Voice: Send them to me!

Hostess: How would it be if I always manage to seat the gentleman, and I know who you mean, at Charlotte's table.

First Waitress: Fine, he really gives me a bad time.

Hostess: We'll try it anyway, and if he bothers anyone else I'll talk with him, and if need be, talk with Carlisle (the manager).

PLANNING EMPLOYEE MEETINGS

There are two schools of thought on planning employee meetings. The first subscribes to a carefully planned meeting. The other subscribes to an informal, *regularly scheduled,* but unstructured meeting. The rationale of the unstructured meeting is that it is more democratic and provides more opportunity for employees to accept responsibility. Of course, an unstructured, unplanned meeting may have slow periods. On the other hand, such periods may be advantageous in that the members of the meeting become embarrassed and uncomfortable—in a sense they are subtly forced to become involved with the meeting. Either the planned or the unplanned meeting can be effective, provided the leadership truly makes it an *employees' meeting* and not an *employer's meeting.*

The advocates of a carefully planned meeting adhere to the following guidelines.

1. Have definitely in mind what you wish to accomplish in the meeting.

2. Prepare an outline or agenda for the meeting.

3. Schedule the meetings at least a day in advance. Arrange for a quiet, well-ventilated room in which to hold the meetings.

4. Schedule the meeting during a lull in working hours. Avoid the first and last hours of the day for holding the meeting.

5. When possible, include employee representatives in the planning of the meeting.

The supervisor can gain employee participation by:

1. Presenting the problem and asking for opinions. The problem may be of any nature that affects the employees and which is within the supervisor's compass of responsibility. It may be merely the introduction of a new cooking range, a proposed change in working hours, the problem of courtesy, the problem of breakage, or of work simplification. When discussion touches upon areas of responsibility that are not within the supervisor's scope, this should be made clear.

2. Refraining from giving answers even though having the answers.

3. Asking pertinent questions and giving illustrations that are related to the discussion.

4. Suggesting alternative solutions to the problem presented, but only if none are forthcoming from the employees.

5. Making certain that no personal embarrassment is caused an individual by:
   a. Making efforts to save face by "covering up" obviously mistaken ideas and rephrasing them in more suitable form.
   b. Avoiding humor that may be at some individual's expense.

6. Allowing every person their say even at the risk of creating uncomfortableness in the group by allowing an unwise or overly emotional person to monopolize time.

7. Making use of the "reversible why." That is when questions are directed to the supervisor, who throws them back to either the questioner or to some other discussant.

8. Assuring the employees that their suggestions will be followed up. When suggestions concern policies that are not the supervisor's responsibility, the supervisor should make it clear just what will be done to bring the ideas to the attention of a superior. No promises should be made as to what reception the superiors will give the suggestions.

9. Keeping the meetings short and to the point. The supervisor should announce at the beginning of the meeting the time the meeting will end, and stick to this decision as closely as possible. An hour is a reasonable time for most meetings.

10. Follow-up. Report back to the employees the progress being made on the ideas growing out of the meetings. Also report on failures to follow through on ideas and give an explanation.

THE CONFRONTATION MEETING

Unrest, breakdowns in communications, or serious problems periodically come to the attention of top management. The usual response will be to take such long-term actions as holding top-management meetings and then lower-management meetings, holding general communication-improvement meetings, or conducting attitude surveys. All of these responses are positive but time consuming.

The Confrontation Meeting[4] is a direct, immediate technique for allowing management to identify problems, establish priorities, increase total management participation, and gain increased involvement in organizational goals.

The Confrontation Meeting is designed to take place in an intensive, one-day meeting in which all managers are called together. In larger organizations this may consist of large groups of 100 or more. Specific phases of activity are covered during the day.

1. **Phase I—Climate setting**
   The top manager sets goals for the meetings, expresses concern for free discussions, and assures everyone that no punishments are in order for open confrontations. (forty-five minutes to one hour)

2. **Phase II—Information collecting**
   The total group is divided into smaller groups of seven to eight people with instructions along these lines. Think of yourself as an individual with needs and goals. Also, think as a person concerned about the total organization. What are the obstacles, "demotivators," poor procedures or policies, unclear goals, or poor attitudes that exist today? What different conditions, if any, would make the organization more effective and make life in the organization better?[5] (one hour)

3. **Phase III—Information sharing**
   Each reporter writes about his group's complete findings on a flowsheet tacked around the room for a general session of all participants. An attempt is made to break the problem into six or seven major categories. (one hour)

4. **Phase IV—Priority setting and group-action planning**
   This after-lunch session includes a brief general meeting and then people are assigned to their natural work units (e.g., accounting, production, customer-sales, etc.). Some units, of course, may be very small while others will be large. The task of each group is to discuss problems in its specific areas, to set priorities, and to decide how to communicate results of the session to their subordinates. (one hour and fifteen minutes)

5. **Phase V—Organization action planning**
   At a general session each group gives its report and sets priorities. The top manager reacts to these reports and makes specific commitments for actions. (one to two hours)

6. **Phase VI—Immediate follow-up by top team**
   After the conference meeting ends, the top-management team meets immediately to plan first follow-up actions to be reported back to the total group within a few days. (one to three hours)

7. **Phase VII—Progress review**
   Follow-up with total management group four to six weeks later. (two hours)

The Confrontation Meeting has been highly effective, but some caution is in order. If the top-management team does not really use the information or facts to follow through, more harm than good will develop. On the other hand, because of the enthusiasm that can be generated at such meetings, care must be taken that unrealistic or impractical goals and commitments are not made.

THE CASE STUDY

The case-study approach popularized at the Harvard Business School presents managers and prospective managers with detailed information of actual concrete cases. From group analysis and the interchange between participants and trainers, considerable practical learning takes

---

4. Richard Beckhard, *Harvard Business Review* 45 (1967): 149–55.
5. *Ibid*, p. 154.

place. Implicit to the case-study approach is the realization that no "best solution" exists.

The cases are usually quite lengthy, running to twenty pages or more. They usually contain a problem a company is experiencing, and the strategies and objectives to be pursued. The case describes in detail the existing organization, operation, and employment practices. Pertinent data relative to financial structure is also included.

Armed with the facts, the trainees then proceed toward a solution. One of the stimulating aspects of the Harvard cases lies in the fact that a solution that actually was worked out in practice is often available so that participants can evaluate some of their own decisions. Cases can be obtained from the Harvard Business School for use in developing training seminars.

Multiple Role Playing

A variation of the case-study method is to write a short case depicting some problem area of management. These can be related to developing leadership, improving sensitivity to the feelings of others, learning ways for dealing with hostile persons, gaining appreciation for decision making, or any number of concrete problem situations that actually exist in the organization.

The technique calls for a case to be presented to a group of supervisors. Five or six roles are described for discussion of the case. The supervisory group is broken down into smaller groups so that each supervisor will have a role to play. The case is conducted for thirty minutes. All supervisors meet again for thirty minutes to one hour to discuss the case, reach consensus, and, if the case relates to an actual problem situation, to make recommendations to management.

Here is an actual exercise, the case of George Arnold.

George is the fifty-three-year-old manager of a coffee house in the XYZ chain of coffee houses. He started working with XYZ as a kitchen helper, right out of high school thirty-five years ago. Over a ten-year period he worked his way up to assistant manager and then twenty years ago was made manager. The old timers in the organization recognize that George's strength always had been his "back," his ability to work hard, his reliability. He never was creative or original; he never showed much ability to anticipate or to plan ahead; he was never too sensitive to the needs of his employees. At age fifty-three, George is still reliable, but his energy seems to have given out. Now he seems only to go through the motions.

For the past year, Bill Baker, the assistant manager, has taken over much of George's responsibility. When difficult problems arise, the employees come to Bill. It is Bill who anticipates the need for supplies and who is concerned with personnel placement and efficiency. He is the person who prevents and resolves crises. It is common knowledge among employees that without Bill the coffee house would be in trouble.

George's name came up at a recent meeting of the top management of XYZ. One idea discussed was that George should be made to accept an early retirement, but it was felt that the financial and psychological loss would be too severe for him. Consideration was given to demoting him, but there really were no jobs available for him. Also, it was felt that such a move would affect the seniority policy of the organization and demoralize other employees. Finally, management decided to leave George in his present position. Bill's problem was discussed, but it was decided to postpone action until he expressed dissatisfaction with his situation.

The management group felt it had solved a surface problem. But did they really? Actually, they brushed over two fundamental problems.

1. How much importance should management place on efficiency as against human satisfaction, and where does one draw the line?

2. Assuming that management can resolve the first problem, what are the best ways of achieving maximum efficiency and maximum human satisfaction?

In Arnold's case a number of problems were not faced. Was the company being fair to itself, to Bill Baker, to the other employees, to its long-range goals? What does a company owe its employees? Are the retirement benefits in line?

It is obvious from the case of George Arnold that simple management problems may be tied in with not so simple problems that relate to promotion policies, fringe benefits, job evaluation, recruitment philosophies, organizational structure, individual needs and motivations, and employee attitudes.

Now that you have read the case concerning George Arnold here are your role-playing instructions.

All roles in this case will be the same. You are a member of the management group. Mr. Carter, the President of XYZ, has decided that the management group needs to reconsider George Arnold's problem within a broader context. A meeting of the management group has been called. Your role is to contribute your ideas to this meeting.

SITUATION TRAINING

A type of training widely used as a part of management development in some of the larger hospitality operations is called situation analysis. The participants are presented with a problem. The participants form broken groups and each group is asked to produce a solution. Situation analysis has several advantages:

1. Participants learn to solve problems as a group. Such experience is good practice in developing participative management skills.

2. It is readily seen that different groups will come up with different solutions to the same problem, which points up the fact that for many problems there is no one "best" solution. The best solution may be that one that has the whole-hearted support from the group that produced the solution.

3. It is readily seen that people problems usually involve moral questions with no easy answers.

4. It can be pointed out by the instructor that group decisions may be far more effective than individual decisions for certain kinds of problems, particularly people problems.

5. It can be pointed out that the situation calls for various types of inputs—expert opinion, facts, and judgment. The group can gain practice in identifying the various types of input. Which is opinion; which is factual; which is judgment.

An Incident for Group Discussion and Decision

The type of problem used in situation-analysis training is described below. The problem calls for moral judgment in a highly dramatic setting. The group is asked to decide whether to take a chance on losing two men in outer space forever as opposed to definitely saving the other four men involved. This kind of incident touches deep-seated human values and calls for decisions not unlike those made by military leaders in time of battle. Participants see that human problems often involve risk and are matters of conscience as well as profits.

The Group

Each of you is a member of NASA. More importantly, you are a member of a group referred to as the "Brain Trust XX"—the decision-making group of NASA for the Apollo XX flight. Your group has been called into an emergency session to make a decision regarding a problem that has arisen during the Apollo XX mission.

The Incident

Four astronauts had spent ten days visually observing the moon from sixty miles away. They had been directed by your group to make the final maneuver to land on the dark side of the moon. Two members of the crew successfully landed on the moon via the Lunar Exploratory Module (LEM). While returning to the mother capsule, the LEM lost power about twenty miles from union and is now unable to reach the mother craft for the flight back to earth. The Apollo craft could make an extraordinarily difficult maneuver to recapture the LEM. However, the chances of recovery, though not hopeless are calculated at only one in six. If an attempt is made at recovering the LEM, and the plan fails, four men and two crafts will fall into non-Earth-directed orbits and be doomed. If no attempt is made at recovery of the LEM, only that craft and two men will be lost; the mother craft will be saved and most of the scientific and financial objectives of this mission will have been achieved. If an attempt at recovery is made and is successful—WOW!

The Problem

Should Apollo XX be directed to recover the LEM? The timing of the orbits requires a decision within thirty-five minutes.

Bringing the situation closer to home can arouse a number of management questions and relate to company policy. An example would be a problem dealing with Charlie, age fifty-five, with four dependent children. Charlie is only 50 percent effective because of failing health. Should he be discharged, pensioned, kicked upstairs?

Closely related to situation-analysis training is what has been called Laboratory Assessment Training. A member of the group is asked to assume the position of an executive who is faced with a number of problems represented by the contents of an overflowing in-basket, and who sits at a desk and examines the mail and memos in that in-basket. The other members of the training group observe how this individual handles the situations as represented by the papers in the in-basket. Are all of the problems examined before any are acted on? Does the person organize those problems according to importance, tackling the important ones first, leaving the lesser important ones until later? Does the person call on experts for assistance? How is delegation handled? The observers note the person's behavior and produce a critique. In the process they themselves are learning.

The Attitude Survey and Group Discussion Meetings

A direct way of setting an agenda for discussion meetings is through an attitude survey. In addition to helping identify situations or problems that need to be discussed, the employees feel that management is interested in them and their opinions about the operation of the hotel or restaurant. The morale survey is probably the most direct method of securing information about morale. If carefully conducted it can be highly valuable. If injudiciously conducted it may not serve its purpose or it may backfire. Interpretation of the survey is just as important as the manner in which it is conducted.

Figure 11.2 How Do You Feel about Your Job?

Following you will find a number of statements which represent opinions frequently expressed by hotel and restaurant employees. You are asked to express agreement or disagreement with each statement of opinion **by circling one of the five numbers which precedes it**. The following key shows the meaning of each number.

    2 **Strong Agreement** with the statement; agreement without reservation.

    1 **Moderate Agreement**

    0 **Undecided**; no definite opinion upon the issue involved.

   −1 **Moderate Disagreement**

   −2 **Strong Disagreement**; complete rejection of the proposition which is stated.

There are no right or wrong answers. This is **not** a test of information, but only an expression of **your** opinion about debatable issues.

    Please do not sign your name. We are not interested in the opinions of specific individuals, but only in those of the group as a whole. You therefore may express yourself frankly and without reservation.

    Read each statement carefully, but do not spend time debating it. **Respond on the basis of your first impression.**

2 1 0 −1 −2 I feel that I really accomplish something in my job.
2 1 0 −1 −2 My associations with other employees are satisfactory.
2 1 0 −1 −2 I am seldom overworked.
2 1 0 −1 −2 There is little monotony connected with my job.
2 1 0 −1 −2 There is little danger of injury in my job.
2 1 0 −1 −2 I receive about as much training on the job as I need.
2 1 0 −1 −2 My job is very monotonous.
2 1 0 −1 −2 My supervisor never bawls me out in front of others.
2 1 0 −1 −2 My supervisors do not try to impress me with their superiority.
2 1 0 −1 −2 I can usually find out how I stand with my supervisors.
2 1 0 −1 −2 The management sincerely wants to know what employees think about the way things are done.
2 1 0 −1 −2 Most supervisors are as courteous as one could wish.
2 1 0 −1 −2 Most supervisors are careful to consider the employee's suggestions.
2 1 0 −1 −2 Supervisors for whom I work usually make the correct decisions.
2 1 0 −1 −2 I feel as though I am really a part of the organization here.
2 1 0 −1 −2 The management appreciates my work.
2 1 0 −1 −2 My supervisors keep their promises to employees.
2 1 0 −1 −2 The management here treats its employees better than do managements in most other hotels and restaurants.
2 1 0 −1 −2 An employee can get ahead if that person tries.
2 1 0 −1 −2 The promotion policy here is fair as it takes experience into account.
2 1 0 −1 −2 Politics play little part in promotions here.
2 1 0 −1 −2 There are enough recreational facilities here for the employees.
2 1 0 −1 −2 Satisfactory eating places for employees are provided.
2 1 0 −1 −2 Suitable places for meeting and relaxing are provided employees.
2 1 0 −1 −2 My living conditions are about as good as can be expected.
2 1 0 −1 −2 The food served employees is below average in quality or preparation.
2 1 0 −1 −2 Comparatively speaking, I am paid about as well as I can expect.
2 1 0 −1 −2 On the whole, the plan for pay increases is fair.
2 1 0 −1 −2 I can feel reasonably sure of holding my job as long as I do good work.
2 1 0 −1 −2 One of man's greatest satisfactions is his work.
2 1 0 −1 −2 If I had it to do over again and were not under economic pressure, I would still work in the hotel and restaurant business.
2 1 0 −1 −2 If I had it to do over again I would still work in this establishment.

Morale surveys do not give anything more than indications of trends. The results therefore should not be interpreted literally or strictly. It may be found that of 500 employees, 30 to 50 are dissatisfied with almost everything the morale schedule mentions. This is no cause for alarm. One anticipates a certain amount of dissidence. Opinion questionnaires, the usual type of schedule used in a morale survey, seek to tap attitudes. Attitudes are based on emotion and consequently rather ill-defined, and they change somewhat from day to day.

This is not a criticism of the attempt to measure attitudes, since emotions, attitudes, and feelings determine the way we all see things. The physical working conditions of a kitchen may be ideal, but to the vegetable preparation person who cannot stand the sight of the vegetable chef, the conditions may be terrible. The morale survey attempts to get at these feelings.

Figure 11.2 is a form that can be used in measuring employee attitudes regarding job satisfaction. As is seen, the schedule deals with overall job satisfaction: satisfaction with training, with supervisors, with employee services, with interest in the job. The schedule can be cut down or supplemented to fit the individual establishment.

In asking employees to fill out such a questionnaire the first time a survey is made, some suspicion on the part of employees may be encountered. It is a good policy to introduce the idea of the survey several days in advance, either personally or via the house organ. Union representatives will usually aid in selling the idea if approached properly. Making it clear that the survey is a group project—that management is interested in knowing employees reactions to their jobs and in assuring anonymity by having no names signed to the schedules—will help assure the success of the project.

If management is confident and entirely aboveboard, it will post the results of the survey or publish them in the house organ. Periodic surveys will keep management informed of marked changes in morale.

If changes are to be made as a result of the survey, management should follow through and also see to it that the changes have been made.

AN EXAMPLE
OF ORGANIZATIONAL CHANGE

Many hotel and restaurant firms are operated "out of the owner's hip pocket." As the organization grows administrative personnel are added and the organization is divided into more units. One of the great problems in building an organization comes in adding intermediate layers of management between the major decision makers and the unit managers. As a company expands and matures, staff personnel are likely to be added and levels of management introduced between the top level and unit manager and the unit. The situation exists until an economic recession takes place or until the company is bought by a larger one. Then suddenly numerous well-paid executives and staff personnel are released; they are no longer needed. In one case headquarters staff, to the tune of 1 million dollars in salaries, were dropped when the hotel chain was bought by another. Problems of organizational contraction can be as wrenching as that of expansion, and much more painful.

Sonesta Hotels is one of the more innovative companies in hotel management organization and style. Mr. A.M. Sonnabend, the founder of the company, purchased his first hotel, the Somerset, in Boston in 1947. "A.M." was a wheeler-dealer, a shrewd businessman, who went where the opportunities were. At one time, he bought a bankrupt company, Childs Restaurants, for the tax loss they "owed." Under him the company expanded rapidly. Following his death in 1964 his three sons took over control of the company.

Roger P. Sonnabend, then president, introduced many of the concepts advocated at the Harvard Graduate School of Business, which he attended. He was particularly impressed with behavioral science and the ideas of Management by Objective and Theory Y discussed in the chapter on motivation.

Sonesta Hotels has undergone several major changes. At one point it expanded rapidly into the motor hotel field. Later it sold most of the motor hotels, redefining its objective as being to operate luxury hotels in major cities. It once operated the Carlton Towers in London and was involved in a hotel in Milan. Its major property was The Plaza Hotel in New York City, which was sold to Western International Hotels for $25 million.

The case that follows was adapted from an article by Richard Beckhart, a consultant who helped in changing the organization and management style of the Sonesta Hotel.[6] The case is presented in this chapter as an example of how some of the techniques and practices of human relations training described in this chapter can be incorporated into major organizational changes consistent with Theory Y, Management by Objective concepts.

In the introduction of change to the Sonesta, steps were taken to define the change problem, to evaluate the existing interpersonal systems in the organization and their readiness for change, and to determine appropriate change objectives. The types of changes designed had to do with (a) *organizational climate* reflecting the organizational practices, communications, and ways of handling conflict, (b) *attitudes* and *values* of people, and (c) *skills* in problem solving and maintaining working relationships.

The first phase of the program involved information collecting, feedback, and action planning. The consultants held interviews with key management staff and with samples of subordinate staff. Material was collected relative to communication lines between the president and his staff, line-staff communications, location of decision making, role clarification or confusion, and communications procedures.

In a three-day meeting with top management the findings were presented and free discussions focusing on both content and process issues (facts and feelings) were held. Content and process are discussed more fully in an earlier part of this chapter. Because of the openness of the communications, and the emergence of concrete plans of action in which all managers were in agreement, these sessions were felt to be highly productive. It was also felt that similar sessions needed to be held with managers at all levels from the lowest manager to the president. These "confrontation" meetings were intended to provide a means by which the total organization could quickly

6. "An Organization Improvement Program in a Decentralized Organization." *The Journal of Applied Behavioral Science* 2, no. 1 (1966).

engage in a process of self-survey and action planning. (A prototype of a confrontation meeting is described earlier in this chapter.)

The outcome of the various feedback and confrontation meetings led to a decentralization of authority within the organization, with greater job enlargement for each subordinate manager. In order to prepare managers for such responsibility, a series of training surveys were developed to acquaint each manager with a Management by Objective, Theory *Y* orientation. In addition to human relations training, technical sessions were held dealing with such areas as food and beverage preparation, budget and controls, audit procedures, and other technical functions. Goal-setting programs were carried out throughout the organization utilizing Management by Objective philosophies. According to the authors, the effectiveness of the program was demonstrated by a dramatic improvement in earnings, lower turnover, and increase in performance effectiveness of most units in terms of costs as related to sales, more efficient staffing, and reduction of costs with no appreciable decrease of service.

Consistent with the theory described earlier in this chapter in the Freeze-Unfreeze-Refreeze model, the Sonesta study reflects a process of change that is basic to an understanding of human relations principles. A group or organization is first confronted with a problem or *dilemma*. Next the group must overcome habitual ways of responding to the dilemma in order to *invent* new approaches. *Feedback* is essential. If the feedback is negative the group or organization must continue to experiment. If the feedback is positive, then the learning that took place can be *generalized* to new experiences and situations with which the group or the organization will have to deal.

SUMMARY

Since World War II the small group has been recognized as a powerful force for human change and development. Today human relations courses and seminars are taught to students, civic leaders, and corporation executives throughout the country.

A number of techniques and exercises teaching group process have been developed. Central to the notion of group decision making is the model Dilemma-Invention-Feedback-Generalization. Group process can be broken down into task and maintenance functions. Task functions are concerned with keeping a group oriented to the task at hand. Maintenance functions are relevant to the group's maintaining a healthy climate and good working relations in order to reach goals. Talk in groups may focus on *content*—what is being discussed—or *process*—how the discussion is handled. Effective listening is a learnable skill that can be a significant aid in helping a person to understand and relate to others.

Exercises can be useful in helping individuals in groups to relate. The Johari Window is a technique for helping people and organizations develop greater understanding of self-disclosure and self-knowledge.

Individuals with group skills can be effective in conducting employee meetings. These meetings can be valuable in bringing about changes, getting the best from employees, building cooperation, and reducing tensions.

A number of special types of meetings are possible. The confrontation meeting is a highly unique method for getting to the heart of complex problems in a direct, immediate way by having an all day, organized session of all managers. Special training meetings involve the case-study approach, multiple role playing, situation-analysis training, and group discussion meetings centered around an attitude survey.

Management by Objectives

12

The books on formalized goal-setting systems are legion in number, but Peter Drucker and Douglas McGregor are generally credited with providing the foundation for management by objectives systems in use today. "Management by Objectives," or MBO, is a management concept that has gained considerable popularity since being introduced by Drucker in his 1954 writings on "Management by Objectives and Self-Control."[1] In 1960, McGregor wrote about two sets of assumptions—Theory X and Theory Y—in *The Human Side of Enterprise.*[2] According to Theory Y,

1. The expenditure of physical and mental effort in work is as natural as play or rest.
2. . . . [individuals] will exercise self-direction and self-control in the service of objectives to which they are committed.
3. Commitment to objectives is a function of the rewards associated with their achievement (esteem and self-actualization, for example).
4. The average human being learns, under proper conditions, not only to accept but to seek responsibility.
5. The capacity to exercise a relatively high degree of imagination, ingenuity, and creativity in the solution of organizational problems is widely, not narrowly distributed in the population.
6. Under the conditions of modern industrial life, the intellectual potentials of the average human being are only partially utilized.

Management by Objectives is a process by which work is organized in terms of achieving specific objectives within set time limits. Most authors agree that in the system of MBO, the superior and subordinate jointly:

1. Specify, in writing, the major functional areas of responsibility for the subordinate, including goals to be accomplished in terms of results, and

2. Determine how and within what time frame the agreed-upon standards should be achieved, so that the superior and the subordinate can periodically evaluate progress.

If the conditions of MBO are satisfied, then the following expectations result logically:

1. The decision-making and control processed within the company should show direct improvement, and
2. Employee satisfaction increases as a by-product.

For a concept as popular as MBO, validation research is somewhat sparse. The research that has been undertaken does demonstrate that the act of setting clear goals on an individual's job, as opposed to only broadly defining that individual's areas of responsibility, generally results in increased performance.[3]

Although many of the practices possible within a participative management frame of reference have been shunned by many managers, particularly in the fast-moving hotel-restaurant field, MBO has enjoyed widespread acceptance.

Unfortunately, many managers erroneously view Theory Y assumptions as being overly permissive. Part of the misunderstanding arises from the difficulty most managers experience in trying to translate management theory into practice. By contrast, Management by Objectives is a common sense, "how-to-do-it" approach to management that can be readily understood, implemented, and evaluated. MBO, in practice, is "hard-nosed" participative

1. Peter F. Drucker, *The Practice of Management* (New York: Harper and Row Publishers, 1954).
2. Douglas McGregor, *The Human Side of Enterprise* (New York: McGraw-Hill, 1960).
3. R.M. Steers, R.M. and L.W. Porter, "The Role of Task-Goal Attributes in Employee Performance," *Psychological Bulletin,* 81 (1974): 434–52.

management in which the manager expects responsible performance, makes sure that feedback is always available, determines that the results of all objectives are evaluated, and shows continuous interest in the growth, development, and full utilization of the people under that manager's direction.

The following section presents a "how-to-do-it" approach to MBO that enables the reader to set up a personal approach to the sequences of MBO, namely Goal Setting, Periodic Review, and Summary Appraisal. The reader should recognize that MBO is not within the special province of any one theorist, but that many systems of MBO exist. The common denominator of all goal-setting systems lies in the assignment of "task goals" to the various members of an organization or department. Task goals may be defined as relatively specific targets or objectives that an employee (or a small group of employees) is responsible for accomplishing within a specified time period. In order to provide meaningful feedback concerning the results achieved through completed task goals, the goals need to be tied in to some form of systematic performance appraisal and review.

Chapter 10 of this book emphasizes that behavior can be controlled when we can experience direct consequences for our actions, in terms of either rewards or punishments. In order to establish a system of behavior control, we must follow relatively straightforward but careful procedures having to do with observing, recording, and providing consequences for behavior. Briefly, we must be able to pinpoint or identify the behavior we wish to control, and we must have a reliable way of measuring the behavior to determine whether the performance is improving, staying the same, or deteriorating. Once we have a measuring instrument, we are in a position to give feedback to others concerning their behavior in the form of a reward or punishment consequence.

Management by Objectives, simply stated, is a form of behavior control in which the subordinate participates with the superior in describing the behavior pattern (or goal) the subordinate wants to achieve. Both the subordinate and the superior agree on the measuring instrument that will be used to determine whether the goals are achieved. Both the subordinate and the superior recognize that the measuring instrument will provide feedback concerning the progress the subordinate achieves. Both are aware in advance of the potential consequences for the subordinate who achieves the predetermined goals, or for that subordinate if failing to achieve those goals.

GUIDE TO MBO

This section consists of a practical approach to Management by Objectives that can provide the reader with information to be used specifically to set up an operational MBO program. The section consists of three parts: Objective Setting, Periodic Review, and Summary Appraisal.

The material that follows makes specific use of MBO theory and techniques described in the first section of this chapter. The material is practical and presented in "how-to-do-it" form.[4] Specifically, three guides are presented to assist the manager in discussing and evaluating employee performance.

Each guide is self-contained, but together the guides represent an overall cycle of activities related to performance, as follows:

1. **Objective Setting.** This involves discussion between the supervisor and subordinate in which specific job accomplishments of the subordinate are determined and a time frame established for their completion.

2. **Periodic Review.** This is a discussion concerning progress made toward the objectives and any adjustments or actions that need to be considered.

3. **Summary Appraisal.** This is a discussion of the overall aspects of performance and the value of the contribution relative to salary action.

The relationships between these three performance discussion approaches are shown on table 12.1.

OBJECTIVE SETTING

Much of management in the hotel-restaurant field involves putting out "fires" and "doing," as opposed to planning and setting goals. Too often managers get into the same day-by-day ruts, and soon the same problems and lack of progress become apparent year after year.

Objective setting, important for both supervisors and subordinates, helps supervisors (a) plan and schedule the departmental workload; (b) budget and allocate resources; (c) measure and reward effective performance. Objective setting helps subordinates (a) plan their own work and time; (b) know the expectations of the jobs; (c) evaluate their own progress and effectiveness.

---

4. The material in this section was adapted in part from the extensive literature on MBO and in part from practices within the General Electric Company presented by Dr. Emanuel Kay.

Table 12.1 Summary of Performance Discussions

	Objective Setting (OS)		Periodic Review Session (PRS)		Summary Appraisal (SA)
Purpose	To determine specific accomplishments for a given time period (up to 12 months)		To review progress		To summarize results
Issues	—Individual goals —Establishment of standards to measure accomplishments —Mutual agreement		—Open exchange of job related information —Validity of objectives can be reevaluated —Determine problem areas and support needs of employee		—Evaluation of performance —More objective basis for salary action —Personal development and promotability
Outcomes	A written agreement enabling you to: —Plan time —Establish priorities —Allocate resources —Relate to organization goals		—Solution of job related problems —Action steps for performance improvement —Support identified needs —Identified causes of performance problems		Written record of: —Performance —Support for recommended salary action —Areas for improvement
Hypothetical Fiscal Year	AUG	NOV	FEB	MAY	AUG
	OS	PRS	PRS	PRS	SA OS

What Is An Objective?

Objectives can vary among such classifications as operational objective, short-term objective, critical objective. All objectives have in common the quality of being a SPECIFIC STATEMENT OF AN EXPECTED OUTCOME.

A "specific statement" should relate to a *single desired result* that also can be *measured* or that has a established standard so we know when the objective is completed successfully.

Here are some examples of "acceptable" or "unacceptable" objectives.

Unacceptable	*Acceptable*
To provide better customer service during the current fiscal year.	To submit progress reports on customer complaints each Monday morning.
To improve the efficiency in the department by making sure employees are satisfied in their jobs.	To reduce employee turnover by the end of the fiscal year, staying within current budget.

The acceptable goals contain *both* a *single desired result* and a *specific standard or measurement*.

Objective Setting from the Supervisor's Perspective

The intent of an objective-setting session is to arrive at a mutual *agreement* on the employee's expected performance and how that performance will be evaluated. The meeting itself should be planned in advance so that the subordinate has time to give consideration to the role, responsibilities, and the objectives considered important by that individual. To have overall guidelines, the employee needs to know the goals of the organization as a whole and those of the department.

During the actual objective-setting session, the supervisor's role is to help the subordinate be specific in the formulation of objectives, to guide the individual in setting objectives that may not have come to mind, to clarify any uncertainties concerning areas of responsibility, and to suggest ways to measure the accomplishment of objectives. Each supervisor must recognize that a certain amount of "negotiation" is involved in discussing targets, priorities, and standards of achievement that will be mutually agreeable to both the supervisor and subordinate.

How to Write Objectives

An objective is a *specific statement of an expected outcome*. It must be written in simple, precise language so that it is easily understandable and leaves no room for misinterpretation.

1. An objective is achieved as the result of some action. Therefore, the first step is to begin with "to" followed by a verb—to achieve/compile/reduce, and the like.

2. The action should relate to a *single desired result* so that everyone knows when the objective is met. "To open a new unit by June 1."

3. The objective should include as many *quantitative* factors as possible, such as sales, costs, time, length.

4. The objective should specify the "what" and "when" rather than the "why" and "how." For example, "To reduce employee turnover by 20 percent by the end of the current fiscal year," rather than "To reduce employee turnover through improving working relations."

5. The objective must be *understandable* to those who will help meet it.

Sample Goals

1. To achieve a 15 percent return on investment within four operating quarters.

2. To complete training program A for all assistant managers by the first of the year.

3. To reduce breakage of dishes in kitchen by 10 percent within one operating quarter.

SETTING STANDARDS

A standard is the gauge of acceptable performance that lets us know when a goal has been accomplished. A standard is established in terms of a desired end result. It provides the supervisor with a precise measure of a subordinate's work, a way of valuing work and a means of relating merit increase to accomplishment. The subordinate knows whether adequate progress toward planned goals is being made and has a means of evaluating and correcting personal performance.

A standard can be stated in terms of volume amounts, units of production, time units, frequency rates, ratios, and percentages. Specifically, here are a number of measurements that could be used to establish standards of performance in the hotel-restaurant field.

1. **Costs and profit**
   —sales volume
   —labor costs
   —customer complaints
   —sales growth rates
   —overhead cost levels
   —net profit as a percentage of sales
   —food costs
   —frequency and size of check
   —percentage of return on investments
   —percentage of share of actual and potential markets
   —cost of employee recruitment
   —customer sales per employee ratios
   —net operating income

2. **Productivity**
   —time required to prepare order
   —time customer waits before being served
   —ratio of experienced help to new hires
   —percentage of sales volume against forecasts
   —output/input correlates between equipment utilization and labor capacity
   —people-hours per order
   —prep time rates

3. **Efficiency**
   —percentage of error in taking and filling orders
   —percentage of waste
   —amount of equipment downtime
   —customer flow through the operation
   —time customer waits before being served
   —time to prepare order
   —percentage of items prepared at standard
   —percentage of returned orders

4. **Manpower Management**
   —labor turnover
   —before and after training scores
   —absenteeism time ratios
   —number of disciplinary cases
   —average tardiness rates
   —grievances
   —suggestions submitted and implemented
   —accident frequency
   —percentage of MBO objectives achieved

Priorities

All objectives do not have the same value and importance. Cost and consequences will vary for *not* accomplishing some objectives. It is important to rank-order objectives and to assign subjective values for each goal.

Objective Setting in a Restaurant Environment

Long-range planning is difficult to achieve in a restaurant environment. Most of the activity requires a rapid response, readiness for action, and flexibility of service. The specific actions of food-service work do not take much time, but volume is usually high and time is at a premium. Whether one is a waiter, cook, dining room host, or unit manager, the press of customer needs keeps everyone on a high pitch of alertness and pressure.

A key use of objective setting in an environment as demanding as a restaurant is to maintain a *balance* between short-term activities and longer-range needs. The restaurant manager can use objective setting in a way that keeps longer-range work from being sacrificed continually in favor of shorter-range work. To maintain such a balance requires considerable effort and discipline from the restaurant manager. Managers must show continued interest and involvement, provide information and data for subordinates, show firmness in their expectation on priority setting, and place strong emphasis on setting objectives for long-range improvements. When individuals are performing high volume, short-term work under pressure, they are unlikely to develop planning perspective and may receive discouraging signals from associates who are pressing for their short-term output.

What Should Be in the Individual Employee's MBO Plan?

1. Start with the day-to-day work that makes up the main part of the job and agree on how and when it will be measured and who will do the work and measuring. Come up with several objectives. (Example: Reduce china and glass breakage by 20 percent by such and such a date as measured by the daily breakage report and the weekly inventory report.) Do not elaborate on the steps for reaching a goal unless a special need for clarification exists.

2. Then pick one work activity that might be improved profitably and set a goal for its *improvement*. (Example: Reduce number of customer complaints in the dining room by 15 percent by such and such a date as measured by the daily complaint tally.) Have the employee write up a brief plan for accomplishing it.

3. As success is gained in improving one objective, add a new objective.

4. As success is gained in improving ongoing activities, set objectives for updating the employee's knowledge and skill in areas related not only to that individual's own direct work efforts but also to other related jobs.

(Example: Waitresses to participate with kitchen personnel in a three-hour per week, x number of week's task force to improve the system of order flow. Objective—reduction in time of 10 percent from time order is received to time order is placed on customer's table as measured by periodic time-study samples. Note that this procedure could easily be incorporated in the chapters of this book on management development or organizational development. Possibilities are created for participative management, job enlargement, creative problem solving, group interaction, improving communications, and the gaining of a better understanding and rapport between two traditional adversaries—servers and kitchen workers.)

5. Finally, the manager should see to it that the objectives accomplished can be part of an effective routine, which then reduces the time required of the employee for that function. In effect, the target is to reduce the time devoted to day-to-day activity so that more time can go into long-term improvement projects. The amount of time left over after the day-to-day work is done determines how many longer-term objectives an employee can carry on at any one time. Usually only one or two objectives are involved. It is better to complete one longer-term goal successfully in a short time than to spread it out more over a longer time period.

Other Considerations

1. Most organizations have a number of valuable measures, standards, and systems. Build on existing plans and systems as often as possible.

2. Do not give up existing practices, but do look for ways to integrate objective setting into ongoing practices.

3. For long-term objectives, set specific times for meetings between supervisor and subordinate (a minimum of three to four times a year).

4. Objective setting is more than having schedules that the superior checks. The aim is for the employees to become involved in planning for results to which they are committed fully. This means the manager must spend considerable time to meet with and help personalize the objectives of each employee.

PERIODIC REVIEW SESSIONS

The Periodic Review Sessions of a manager and an employee provide an opportunity to assess the employee's progress, identify problem areas, find ways for resolving problems, and reassess and reestablish priorities. Managers are concerned with helping their employees progress toward their objectives. Three to four review sessions during the year are suggested as a minimum, though more should be held with newer or marginal employees.

The Helper Role of the Supervisor

There are two main roles required of a supervisor. The role the supervisor plays reflects the way that individual evaluates employee performance.

The first role is a *judicial* one, in which the supervisor is required to evaluate objectively the results achieved versus the objectives established. Did the employee accomplish what was pledged in the contract? In a judicial role, the supervisor is expected to praise or criticize, reward or punish. The judicial role is most prominent during Summary Appraisal Sessions.

The second role is that of a *helper*. The helper role is the dominant one expected during the Periodic Review Session. This role involves supporting decisions and proposals made by the employee, solving job-related problems, and assisting and advising the employee. The helper role may be conceptualized as providing "coaching" and "counseling" to the employee.

Much like a coach, the manager may need to guide employees, give them suggestions, help them plan, or provide resource material to them. In a counseling role, the manager can help employees elaborate on their solutions, draw out their thoughts, ideas, and feelings, and act as sounding board for some of the alternatives with which they may be struggling. The counselor helps individuals arrive at their own conclusions and decisions.

What Is Done in a Periodic Review?

1. The session should be employee-centered. The supervisor plays the role of helper and concentrates on listening from the employee's frame of reference (see chapter 11). The employee needs to "level" with the supervisor. If the employee has problems or if the supervisor is creating road blocks that prevent the employee from reaching objectives, the supervisor must be made aware of the dilemma. Realistically, employees are not likely to "level" unless they are encouraged to do so and know from previous experience that they can trust the supervisor. To bring about employee participation, the supervisor must encourage a full discussion of progress, feelings, and problems. Such involvement obviously requires a mature, confident, and trained supervisor who is well versed in many of the human relations skills referred to in the various chapters of this book.

2. The attitude of supervisors should be *constructive* and *supportive*. The supervisor does not have to admonish the employee. The measuring device provides a fairly direct way of letting employees know whether they are meeting their objectives. If an employee is failing in meeting an objective, the problem will be obvious. The supervisor should be concerned with finding out how to be of help to the employee.

3. In areas in which improvements are needed, the supervisor must focus on the *problem*, not the employee. The supervisor can be helpful both in identifying causes of performance problems and in coming up with possible ideas for resolving dilemmas.

4. The supervisor needs to *maintain objectivity*. The supervisor needs to seek information and to get as many facts as possible, but should be careful not to criticize, accuse, or prejudge.

THE ROLE OF POWER IN THE SUPERVISORY RELATIONSHIP

In the area of human-relations training, considerable observation, experimentation, and research has been directed toward examining the use of power in the relationships between supervisors and subordinates. Much of the research centers on investigating three conditions under which supervisors exert differential power roles with their subordinates:

1. In "Authority-Obedience" situations, in which supervisors assume all of the power;

2. In "Joint-Determination" situations, in which supervisors share their authority equally with their subordinates; and

3. In "Laissez-Faire" situations, in which supervisors abdicate their power, thus forcing their subordinates to assume total departmental authority.

The experimental research generally shows the following results:[5]

1. Laissez-Faire leadership does not lead to effective performance from subordinates.

2. Joint-Determination is consistently most effective. Although the quantity of work performed under the Authority-Obedience condition is highest, work continues only in the presence of the leader. When the

---

5. R. White, and R. Lippitt, "Leader behavior and member reaction in three 'social climates.' " *Group Dynamics Research and Theory*, ed. Cartwright and Zander (New York: Row, Peterson and Co., 1960), Chap. 28, pp. 527–55.

leader has left, the work declines. Work established under Joint-Determination continues at the same rate, even when the leader leaves the room. Originality in problem solving is highest under Joint-Determination.

3. Authority-Obedience conditions create much hostility and aggression, including aggression against scapegoats. It also creates passive submissiveness to authority. Aggression is *thirty times* more frequent in Authority-Obedience than in Joint-Determination situations. The aggression is directed not so much toward the leader but toward other followers or outsiders.

4. Authority-Obedience can create discontent that is not apparent on the surface. For example, high degrees of absenteeism and turnover arise from Authority-Obedience situations. When asked, nineteen of twenty individuals preferred Joint-Determination over Authority-Obedience leaders.

5. More dependence and less individuality exists in Authority-Obedience situations. Conversation is less varied and more confined to the immediate situation. In short, a definite loss of individuality is apparent.

6. More group-mindedness and friendliness is apparent under Joint-Determination conditions. The relationship between supervisor and subordinate is characterized by mutual praise, readiness to share, friendly remarks, and general cooperation.

From the research, it should be obvious that a participative relationship between manager and employee is not only desirable—it is essential. Historically, managers have operated under the false assumptions that they will be tested continuously by employees unless they exercise their authority in a strong fashion. Research refutes this notion. Once managers identify their authority, their subordinates generally respond positively, except to managers who are unusually weak, Laissez-Faire, or inconsistent.

SUMMARY APPRAISAL

From the discussion of the Periodic Review, it was seen that the manager plays the Helper role, in it attempting to coach, counsel, advise, suggest, and generally to function as a resource person to assist the employee in achieving objectives. By contrast, during the Summary Appraisal session, the manager's main focus is to evaluate results and end-product achievements of the subordinate in reaching objectives. On the basis of the Summary Appraisal, the employee receives concrete feedback concerning performance, effectiveness which may or may not be reflected in a salary action.

Using the Periodic Review as a basis for salary review is not without its problems. Research studies generally do not demonstrate that salary reviews based on performance appraisals actually lead to greater productivity; in fact, evidence exists that performance appraisals often affect adversely the manager-employee relationship, particularly in situations in which the employee considers the evaluation to be unfair. Among organizations actually using Summary Appraisal systems, advocates can be found that relate salary review to performance appraisal, while others do not relate salary review to performance appraisal.

In chapter 10 relating the Behavior Modification Theory, it was noted that supervisors must be consistent in their behavior with subordinates. If one's supervisor is unpredictable, one feels chronically anxious. Every time a supervisor fails to enforce a rule or a commitment from a subordinate, that subordinate becomes less responsible, perhaps learning to become a master of manipulation with little time or energy to learn more constructive skills.

The Summary Appraisal provides a systematic tool for reducing much of the unpredictability in the work situation for the employee. The employee knows clearly the level of personal accomplishment and the reward or lack of reward provided, which in turn is likely to reduce the anxiety concerning the management decisions that arise from the performance.

Steps Taken During Summary Appraisal

1. Performance results of the position description items not covered by MBO objectives are discussed. Greatest emphasis is given to those items in which performance was best or poorest.

2. The job description is updated as needed.

3. Performance results of MBO objectives are discussed. Again, emphasis is placed on the extremes of performance, i.e., those objectives in which performance was best and where it was poorest.

4. Identify and discuss personal and situational factors, such as skills, application of effort, resources, and relationships with other departments that may have affected performance.

5. Plan specific actions that will lead to improved performance in the future.

6. Discuss the career interests of the employee and plans for achieving them.

Table 12.2   Putsch's, Incorporated: Management Development Program

Job Description Assistant Manager*	Management Training Program (Classroom)*	Evaluation Procedure**	MBO Expectation**	MBO Evaluation Criteria**
1. Conduct formal and informal group meetings in order to encourage and capitalize on concepts of participative management.	1. Six hours of instruction and participation in group dynamics, group structure and participative management with outside readings.	1a. Written examination. 1b. Observation of the trainee conducting an employee meeting at his work unit.	1a. To conduct weekly communication meetings of 45 minutes duration with subordinates. 1b. To contribute two improvements per month in efficiency or productivity based on ideas from communication meetings.	1. Documentation submitted to the Unit Manager.
2. Enlarge and enrich functions of subordinates in order to maximize productivity and efficiency and to increase satisfaction.	2. Three hours of instruction and participation in job enlargement theory and practice.	2. Observation of trainee utilizing job enlargement practices at his work unit.	2. To enlarge the work scope of two subordinates per month and to demonstrate an increase in efficiency or productivity of 10% for each employee.	2. Documented results submitted to the manager.
3. Enforce rules and employee expectations as established by the manager.	3. Six hours of training in techniques and theory of Behavior Modification in Supervision including lecture, readings, workshop training and practice in the unit.	3a. Written examination. 3b. Assigned project work.	3. Increase the performance of subordinates in areas of importance designated by manager (e.g.) sanitation, tardiness, personal hygiene, friendliness toward customers, etc.	3. Documented results submitted to the manager.
4. Provide effective human relations and counseling support in dealing with employees.	4. Six hours of training and role playing in individual counseling and motivational techniques. Selected readings.	4a. Written examination. 4b. Observation.	4a. Maintain a standard level of employee satisfaction. 4b. Maintain a low level of employee turnover.	4a. Employee attitude survey. 4b. Exit interview.
5. Select competent employees and trainees.	5. Three hours of training and role playing in employment interviewing and selection skills. Selected readings.	5a. Written examination. 5b. Observation.	5. Select individuals at a standard level of efficiency, performance and work stability.	5. Performance and turnover results of employees hired.

*Existing Procedure
**Projected Proposal

Table 12.2—*Continued*

Job Description Assistant Manager*	Management Training Program (Classroom)*	Evaluation Procedure**	MBO Expectation**	MBO Evaluation Criteria**
6. To initiate constructive change and to create an environment conducive to new ideas and improvements of employees.	6. Nine hours of training on participative management tools for bringing about constructive changes within organizations.	6a. Written examination. 6b. Observation.	6. Utilize a group problem solving technique to increase efficiency, production and satisfaction of workers.	6. Documented results collected by the manager.
7. To set and attain constructive personal work goals, to encourage goal setting by employees, and to provide a system of measurement and reward for the attainment of goals.	7. Six hours of training on the setting of objectives, evaluation procedure and the use of MBO.	7. Written MBO exercises.	7. Development of a series of personal work goals and a series of goals for the department and for each employee.	7. Documented measures of attainment for each goal established.

The Written Summary Appraisal

Once the Summary Appraisal is completed, the manager asks the *employee* to write a summary of the appraisal discussion to be completed within two weeks. The summary should cover the following points.

1. Performance results not covered by MBO objectives.
2. An updated position description if necessary.
3. Performance results of MBO objectives.
4. Personal and situational factors that influenced performance.
5. Specific action plans for improving performance.
6. A statement of the employee's career interests and plans for achieving them.

Both the manager and the employee review and sign the summary. The summary can then be made part of the employee's personnel file and reviewed at the next Summary Appraisal session.

Outcomes of Summary Appraisal

For the supervisor, the Summary Appraisal offers a written record of a precise evaluation of employee performance that can relate individual contributions to departmental and organizational objectives. For the subordinate, there is a written performance record and a clearer picture of where that individual stands in the department and the organization. Due to the objectivity of the Summary Appraisal, the employee usually feels satisfied that the appraisal provided a fair measurement of performance.

MBO AS PART OF MANAGEMENT DEVELOPMENT TRAINING

In order to make more relevant both Management Development Training and MBO Training, Putsch's Incorporated, in consultation with one of the authors of this book, developed a unique program. The program seeks to prepare assistant managers for carrying out their human relations responsibilities by spelling out these responsibilities in job descriptions and by providing human relations and MBO experiences that specifically prepare the assistant manager to perform work according to the job description. Table 12.2 outlines the program.

Practical Examples

One way to understand MBO is to learn the mechanics. The three examples are hypothetical: one shows the kinds of goals that might be established by a restaurant manager working with the chef; another shows the kind of goals that might be established by an area vice-president working with a restaurant manager; the last is an illustration of the kind of goals or results that could have been drawn up between an area vice-president of a hotel chain and a unit hotel manager.

Management by Objective (Hotel manager)

Goals	Results
Increase total sales to $2.5 million	Sales are $2.6 million
Increase profit from $50,000 to $60,000	Profit remained at $50,000
Drop 2 menu items that contribute the least profit	Dropped roast beef special on Monday nights but returned it because of so many complaints
Hire female desk clerks	Accomplished
Reduce bar costs from 34% to 30%	Costs reduced to 32% by discharging Joe, but bar sales dropped $5,000
Change 10 guest rooms to sample rooms	5 rooms have been converted
Replace lobby carpet	Still not done

Management by Objective (Chef)

Goals	Results
Reduce utility costs from 5% to 2% of sales	By cutting off burners and range tops when not in use, utilities cut to 3%
Attend 1 course in food preparation	None available
Replace charcoal broiler with gas fired broiler	Done
Reduce the average temperature in kitchen from 90° to 80°	Added large window air conditioner and turned off equipment when not in use, still too hot
Find dishwashers who will stay on the job	Using no one who scores about 8 on Wonderlic test, but must pick up and deliver such people from their homes. Very stable

Introduce 1 new menu item	Tried Veal Scallopini, Broiled Columbia Salmon, and Chicken Cacciatore—Cacciatore has 33% food cost, constitutes 10% of sales

Management by Objective (Restaurant manager)

Goals	Results
Increase sales to $200,000	Sales were $205,000
Hold food costs to 38%	Food costs were 39.5%
Hold training sessions for cooks every Monday morning	Held 18 sessions, then ran out of material
Replace F & B manager	Was unable to find suitable candidate but believe incumbent more motivated
Read 3 new management books	Read 1
Replace conventional ovens with convection oven	2 ovens were replaced
Decorate banquet room	Decoration plan has been drawn up

Like so many techniques, follow-through is an important part of the operation of the technique. Definite review periods are part of the plan. Goals are set, results measured and reviewed. The cycle then begins over again with new goals being established over a definite time period. The review process again takes place, and the cycle repeated.

The "how to" of achieving an objective can also be spelled out as a joint venture between superior and subordinate. Or the "how to" may be developed later. An example of a more detailed plan of action is seen on the following page.[6]

6. From Ackermann and Welch, "Management by Objectives: The Task Unit," *Cornell H & R Administration Quarterly,* May 1973, p. 45.

Problem: Food cost is 2% too high

Owner-Manager	Program: Reduce food cost by 2% before next P & L Statement	**Salad Preparer**	Tasks: 1. Wash lettuce with anti-oxidizing agent 2. Bag produce and refrigerate promptly
Food Production Supervisor	Projects: 1. Tighten portion control 2. Tighten receiving procedures 3. Reduce waste of produce	**Storeroom Porter**	Tasks: 1. Weight in meat 2. Complete receiving report 3. Rotate oil merchandise
Hostess	Projects: 1. Reduce waste of condiments 2. Reduce waste of butter 3. Reduce time between production of order and service of that order	**Waiter 1** **Waiter 2** **Waiter 3** **Waiter 4** **Waiter 5**	Tasks: 1. Return condiments to refrigerator 2. Serve correct amount of butter 3. Serve food promptly
Cook 1 **Cook 2** **Cook 3** **Cook 4**	Tasks: 1. Use scoop to portion mashed potatoes 2. Pre-portion turkey & beef using scale 3. Portion French Fries with scoop	**Waiter's Assistant 1** **Waiter's Assistant 2** **Waiter's Assistant 3**	Tasks: 1. Salvage unopened crackers 2. Assist Waiter in carrying large orders

Performance Planning Cycle

The Management by Objective scheme as employed by Saga Administrative Corporation has built a recurring cycle into the plan. Diagrammatically the Saga Performance Planning Cycle is seen as:

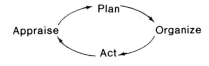

Ideally every employee is asked to sit down with the supervisor and together plan for desired results in a given time span. Each supervisor and employee together identify what is to be accomplished in key result areas. In the case of managerial employees the employee is asked to allocate efforts to three areas: managerial effectiveness, financial, and personal development. A new manager may be asked to attend so many days of management development classes and read a number of textbooks concerned with human relations. If the manager is weak in the financial area, the goal may be to complete a course in accounting and improve skills in budgeting. Each year the amount of effort allocated between the three areas will change:

Key Result Areas	Key Result Areas
Managerial Effectiveness	Managerial Effectiveness
Financial	Financial
Personal Development	Personal Development
Year X	Year X + 1

At the end of the performance cycle the employee reviews performance with the supervisor to see if the objectives which they both have developed have been completed. In some cases the employee may have exceeded the performance plan; in other cases, the target figure may not have been reached. Performance planning supposedly can be done with all levels of employee from pot and pan washer to president. In each case targets are set and commitments made. People are emotionally involved in attaining the objective since they have had a hand in determining it. Performance planning is a way of quantifying performance and of gaining participation in decision making. It is in the stream of participative management, which is a way of gaining employee involvement, interest, cooperation, and ideas.

Criticisms of MBO

Critics of MBO point out that some sophistry is involved in MBO in that supervisor and subordinate recognize that the objectives are not something that the employee, having a completely free hand, would set. And why should one? Anyone working for an organization should be realistic enough to recognize that in committing oneself to the organization for pay, one is giving up some of one's own cherished secret goals in return for the opportunity to be part of an organization and its goals. The goals of an organization, be it hotel, restaurant, or club are not the same as those of the individual. The corporation must be profitable to survive. The club must provide services and satisfaction to its members. The individual may feel that for one to reach complete fulfillment one should work only three hours in the morning and be free to pursue personal interests in the afternoon. One may feel that weekends should be reserved for family. Perhaps some day when the leisure society has arrived this will be possible, but not now. In the meantime the employee, hourly or salaried, makes a contract with the employer to subordinate some personal interests to the purposes of the organization. The fact that an employee is invited to help set objectives as they pertain to the job and is given some latitude as to the manner in which those goals are achieved, is a step forward from the old type of dictatorial management wherein the goals were set by management, and the work done by the employee.

A legitimate question can be raised about the relevancy of MBO to such routine jobs as dishwasher, potwasher, porter, cashier, counter server, fry cook and similar jobs that are repetitive in nature and have little room for innovation or room for any large degree of change. How much participative management can be applied to counter persons in a McDonald's restaurant? The system is well established. The productivity standard is largely set by the number of customers lined up in front of the counter. The employee could be given some responsibility in deciding how clean the establishment should be kept, the kind of behavior that is seen as courteous, or the degree of personal grooming.

MBO Related to Control Systems

Management by Objectives is like older control systems in some ways. It establishes goals, sets a time limit for reaching the goals, and compares performance against targets. Under MBO it is assumed that goals will be changed during each performance cycle. The traditional control system is different on two counts: participation in establishment of the standards is not a central part of the traditional control system.

Performance standards in the traditional control system are relatively fixed.

In a table-service restaurant, dish machine operators can be asked to report on the menu items that show up uneaten on the plates, to keep records of the amount of detergent used, and to help in setting up guides for controlling hot water use.

Using the scientific management approach, standards could be set by operations analysts or industrial engineers. The person who will be working to the standard does not necessarily have a voice in its establishment. MBO requires subordinate participation in goal setting and as such is a management development system. Everyone participating in MBO gets practice in goal setting and decision making.

Cost-control systems of the traditional type have been effective in controlling costs and were a step forward in science of management. In the 1950s the Hilton Hotel Corporation, which has become known for its use of industrialized methods, asked the Harris, Kerr, and Forster Company to produce a labor cost-control system. This system gave the Hilton Hotels Corporation a decided competitive edge. In an industry where sales volume fluctuates sharply from day-to-day, week-to-week, and month-to-month, a system that concentrates on reacting to these variations is valuable. The Harris, Kerr, Forster payroll cost-control system is included in chapter 15 as an illustration of a complicated cost-control system, one that has proved highly useful in the hotel business. By routinizing what could be a cumbersome and time-consuming chore, this cost-control system insures that attention will be given to the effort. Decision making concerning labor cost control is systematized and the responsibility for carrying out the system is placed with the operations analyst and the department head. Top management is freed to do other things.

SUMMARY

Management by Objectives (MBO) is a management concept that has gained considerable popularity. The subordinate participates with the supervisor in establishing specific work goals and in determining how and by what time frame the goals will be achieved.

MBO is seen as a cycle consisting of three parts: Objective Setting, Periodic Review, and Summary Appraisal. Objective Setting is the process by which goals are determined and a plan established. Periodic Review Sessions provide a systematic opportunity to review programs and to take actions for improving performance. The Summary Appraisal provides an evaluation of performance and a written record of performance that can point to future areas for improvement and serve as a basis for recommended salary review.

Specific procedures allow a supervisor to learn how to identify and write objectives and to arrive at clear measures for evaluating performance. During the Periodic Review, the supervisors play helper roles in which they try to focus on problem issues and not on employees. The power of the supervisor must be used constructively and with restraint. The Summary Appraisal provides an avenue for evaluating employee performance and for planning future actions and goals to further the employee's performance and career achievements.

MBO offers a number of practical applications for the hotel and restaurant field. Examples of its use in management development, performance planning, and control systems are discussed.

Organizational Development

13

The management environment of today is dramatically different from that of any time in the past. It has been estimated that more new knowledge in technology has been developed in the past ten years than in all of the previous history of mankind. Ninety-three percent of all scientists who ever lived are alive today. Not only has technology changed; the work force has changed to keep up with technology. Workers today are more knowledgeable, independent, and professionally oriented.

Dramatic changes have also taken place within the hotel and restaurant industry with the advent of fast foods, franchises, gigantic corporations, and the ever-changing and demanding tastes of American consumers. One of the main keys to success in the hotel and restaurant field, as in all American management, has certainly been receptivity to *change*.

For many years, the Human Relations movement was seen as the salvation for enlightening managers on modern concepts of managing their most precious commodity—human resources. Through the National Training Laboratories, the American Management Association and a myriad of programs established in universities around the country, the modern manager has been able to receive sophisticated training based on modern theories of human relations management and on the utilization of experiential and participative techniques of learning. That the experience has been rewarding and invaluable to the participants cannot be denied. The sheer magnitude of the training available attests to its popularity. Its popularity notwithstanding, Human Relations training has not altered significantly the management practices within organizations for two main reasons: (*a*) training per se does not necessarily lead to behavioral change and (*b*) the training of individuals apparently does not directly imply the bringing about of organizational changes.

Growing out of and away from the inadequacies of the human-relations training movement has come the management process known as *Organizational Development,*

or OD, which has evolved over the past ten years. Formally stated, Organizational Development is, first of all, an educational strategy adopted to bring about a *planned organizational change.* The strategies for bringing about such change differ enormously, but OD takes place *within* an organization in a real life setting rather than in an abstract laboratory setting. Secondly, the changes sought for in OD arise directly from the *exigencies* of problems or crises with which the organization is trying to cope. These crises usually revolve around one or several of the following situations:

1. Problems of destiny, i.e., growth, identity, revitalization;

2. Problems of human satisfaction and development; or

3. Problems of organization effectiveness.[1]

This chapter reviews some of the technology and practice of Organizational Development that has application to the hotel and restaurant field. The specific targets for change among OD practitioners fall mainly in the following areas:

1. Bringing about some decentralization of decision making to lower levels within the organization.

2. Bringing in more democratic forms of leadership.

3. Eliminating classes of citizenship.

4. Bringing about an overlapping of organizational families on projects and functions in order to improve communications.

5. Opening systematic avenues for communications.

6. Role enlargement in order to increase the sense of participation by workers.

---

1. H.A. Hornstein et al., *Social Intervention: A Behavioral Science Approach* (New York: The Free Press, 1971).

7. Group responsibility for tasks to insure greater psychological involvement of the individuals.

8. Making more explicit the nature of organizations so that individuals can have flexibility for action rather than feeling rigidly governed.[2]

TECHNIQUES OF CHANGE

Techno-Structural Interventions

All organizations are by nature bureaucratic. In principle, most bureaucracies are open systems offering considerable possibility for change and flexibility. In actual practice, most organizations often become closed and rigid, bound by the very rules and regulations that were developed originally to make the organization run smoothly. In the high labor-turnover hotel and restaurant field, each new employee is often greeted with, "Don't ask me 'why?' That's the way we've always done it."

Techno-structural interventions are directed at reorganizing organizations to make them more flexible, relevant, and effective. Such reorganization can involve changing the organizational structure (such as centralizing or decentralizing managerial decision making) or the physical environment (such as redesigning machines or architecture). These interventions are not attempts to change individual behavior directly, but research evidence shows that individual behavior does change as the structure in organizations requires different behavior of individuals.

An Example of a Decentralized Reorganization

Putsch's is a Kansas City-based organization that operates cafeterias, coffee houses, and specialty restaurants. Prior to 1971, it was privately held. The management structure was highly centralized, with most of the management decisions being made by a few individuals. Most of the units were in close proximity, and general management personnel were able to spend considerable time in the units. Because of the direct involvement of general management with unit operations, the need for formal systems was not critical. In 1971, Putsch's was acquired by Marcor. In the acquisition, the Putsch organization was granted complete autonomy and only one requirement for change was anticipated. As a privately held company, Putsch's was not oriented to increase the number of units significantly. As a publicly held company, rapid expansion was anticipated. An excerpt from a report made to the company regarding status of management development within Putsch's as of 1976 follows.

At the time of its acquisition by Marcor in 1971, the Putsch organization recognized that its centralized organizational structure was not conducive to optimal growth. Although the management structure was not altered at that time, a major decision was made relative to the hiring practices of management trainees and assistant managers: No longer would individuals be hired to fill slots, but each candidate was considered on the basis of his/her potential to become an independently functioning unit manager or higher. New selection criteria were established for those executives doing the final assessments. Management training positions were established to prepare new recruits with a variety of on-the-job training experiences.

By the start of 1975, a major reorganizational decision was made which involved working toward the establishment of a more decentralized organizational structure with the unit manager taking on a greater independent responsibility. In order to accomplish the reorganization in a systematic manner, it was recognized that two preliminary steps were of critical importance: (1) A centralized system of controls needed to be upgraded in areas of finance, quality assurance, and personnel and (2) An essential part of the management development program was to include training in management by objective philosophy and skills in anticipation of MBO being utilized as a company-wide tool of management. It was also recognized that the ultimate success of MBO would depend on the development of meaningful company-wide financial information and controls.

Management development training has included (1) Formal management, supervisory and human relations training; (2) On-the-job training in management, food and technical aspects.

Starting in 1975, weekly 3-hour meetings were established with unit managers and general managers in order to facilitate communication, discussion, decision making and training among managers. In 1976, on alternate weeks, a 10-session, 3-hour per session training program was developed and conducted by a psychological consultant. The format followed a laboratory training model in which training exercises were conducted in a group setting, but in which each participant was expected to utilize in a work setting the techniques and procedures learned in the laboratory. The following areas were covered:

1. Theories and practices of management including humanistic and behavioristic approaches (i.e., Maslow, McGregor, Herzberg, Skinner, Blake and Mouton).

2. Group process and decision making.

3. Organizational development concepts related to job enlargement and job enrichment.

4. Behavior modification principles in supervision and rule setting.

5. Human relations skills and the effective use of power in motivating others.

6. The development of counseling skills for use in supervision.

7. Employment interviewing and selection skills.

---

2. P. Katz and R.L. Kahn, *The Social Psychology of Organizations* (New York: John C. Wiley and Sons, 1966).

8. Theories and techniques for bringing about effective change in organizations.
9. The setting of objectives, evaluation procedures, and the use of MBO.

Once the unit management group completed the management development program, the program was initiated for assistant managers. With assistant managers, an attempt was made not only to present ideas and techniques, but also to tie the training in with job duty requirements, to measure effectiveness of each trainee in learning skills, to measure effectiveness of each trainee in applying skills in his/her work setting and to demonstrate future effectiveness in operating under an MBO framework.

Job Enrichment

Since the early Hawthorne studies on employee production emphasized the importance of human organizational factors,[3] considerable attention has been given to the concept of Job Enrichment. In brief, Job Enrichment involves broadening an individual's work role to provide more opportunities for decision making and greater diversity of action. Logically it follows that Job Enrichment should result in greater satisfaction for the individual employee and greater productivity for both the individual and the company.

A number of major research studies have demonstrated the validity of Job Enrichment concepts. A.K. Rice of the Tavistock Institute has published classic papers on increasing productivity and satisfaction of workers through job redesign in such diverse and complicated organizations as weaving sheds in India and British coal mines.[4] More recently, two Swedish automobile plants, Volvo and Saab-Scandia, have been studied extensively for their pioneering efforts in their industry in creating "job shop" type environments rather than assembly lines, which provide considerable choice and broad involvement to assembly workers.[5]

By now the research evidence is clear. In situations wherein management is *committed* and willing to work toward its success, Job Enrichment can pay significant dividends. The hotel and restaurant industry, with its concern for worker involvement, quality service, and opportunities for employees to move up the vocational ladder, offers an excellent environment for use by management of Job Enrichment approaches.

Job Enrichment does not involve a series of universal steps; rather, it reflects an attitude and a willingness to experiment on the part of management. There follows a series of actual cases that resulted from a seminar on Job Enrichment held with a number of restaurant managers and assistant managers. As part of the seminar, participants were required to inject Job Enrichment ideas into the positions of employees actually reporting to them.

—A pot and pan washer was trained to assume responsibility for the storeroom in addition to pot-and-pan responsibilities. Through better scheduling, the individual was able to handle both functions, thereby receiving more pay, a new title, and an opportunity that helped move that individual into management training. The company converted a mediocre employee into a productive and highly involved employee and reduced labor cost by eliminating a half-time storeroom person.

—A waitress was given additional responsibility to assist as a hostess. She was able to advance more quickly up the career ladder.

—A senior serving line cafeteria worker was given responsibility for "managing" the line. This person was encouraged to make out schedules, have employee meetings, develop a team, work out problems with the kitchen, and generally to become involved in whatever needed to be done in order to make the unit more effective. Morale and efficiency increased significantly on the line.

—The bus help was given the additional responsibility for being "data collectors" for a number of specific studies undertaken to evaluate customer behavior and performance patterns of staff. The bus workers became quite involved in the whole project and developed a number of excellent suggestions for studies. Their contributions were made as additions to their regular duties. They seemed more involved with their work, and "horseplay" decreased considerably as unscheduled free time diminished.

TEAM DEVELOPMENT

Most organizations consist of overlapping teams, sometimes called family groups. These groups may be permanent parts of the organization (e.g., a dining room manager and key subordinates or a cross-departmental team—the general manager, the kitchen manager, and the dining room manager) or they may be *ad hoc* committees, task forces, or project teams.

The team is often the backbone of the organization, and team development is a major focus of organizational development intervention. A popular technique for team building is a two- or three-day off-site meeting of key

3. F.J. Roethlisberger and W.J. Dickson, *Management and the Worker* (Cambridge: Harvard University Press, 1939).
4. A.K. Rice, "Productivity and Social Organization in an Indian Weaving Shed," *Human Relations* (1953).
5. Editor "Job Redesign on the Assembly Line," *Organizational Dynamics* (1973).

personnel to consider a reorganization or to work through problem situations. Skill training is often used to enhance team development in areas related to understanding group process or in establishing greater efficiency in decision making. The section following includes techniques groups or teams can use to enhance their effectiveness.[6]

1. *The Manager's Diagnostic Team Meetings*
   Simply stated, the Diagnostic Team helps the top manager check the health of an organization. The team checks to see if the organization is proceeding toward its goals and entertains possibilities for change. It usually meets once or twice a year for several sessions and allows the manager to get feedback from a collective group of key individuals. Team members usually consist of department heads, staff assistants, outside consultants, and respected members of outside organizations. The team has no executive powers but functions merely to evaluate and advise. Four steps are usually involved in the process of a Diagnostic Team's functioning.
   a. A meeting is held in which information is pooled and general observations shared.
   b. The team picks target areas in which specific information is sought and selects methods for collecting information, e.g., interviews, questionnaires, group discussions.
   c. A period of data collection.
   d. Team meeting to review data, reevaluate goals, and make future recommendations.

2. *The Family Group Diagnostic Meeting*
   This group diagnostic meeting gives the individual manager an opportunity to critique the performance in specific work areas with the people working directly under him. These meetings are held periodically with groups of up to thirty employees for periods of two to four hours. They try to focus on understanding and problem solving rather than on criticizing and defending. They are most effective with some structuring of topics, e.g., planning, future goals, what do we do best, what do we do worst, problem areas. Often data feedback is provided on the basis of studies made prior to the meeting (see the section in this chapter on Data Feedback).
   The Family Group Diagnostic Meeting is a quick way to establish a group rapport, but it is only a beginning. Such a meeting implies that some action will be taken by management, so that a manager must be ready to follow up in providing feedback to the group.

3. *Family Group Team-Building Meeting*
   The team-building process involves a more elaborate sequence of procedures than does the diagnostic meeting. During a period of approximately three days, the team-building groups meet with the expectation of:
   a. capitalizing on group talents in identifying problems and opportunities;
   b. establishing group commitment to change and new actions;
   c. improving working relationships; and
   d. building tight team identifications.
   The procedure for a team-building meeting generally adheres to the following format:

   a. *Setting the Objectives of the Meeting*—Team-building meetings are usually conducted by a third party from outside of the company, such as a consultant. The task of setting objectives for the meeting is performed by the third party in collaboration with key management figures. General areas for consideration are chosen.
   b. *Collecting Information for the Meeting*—This is accomplished prior to the meeting, using techniques described in the section on Data Feedback.
   c. *The Meeting Itself*—Starting with the agenda, the group has latitude to conduct its meeting in accord with its own set of priorities. The group ultimately produces a list of action items to be implemented and determines who is responsible for each one, then sets a deadline for completion of each.
   d. *Follow-through*—Follow-up sessions are scheduled with the whole group to see that agreed-upon actions are taken and to review problems arising in action implementations.

4. *The Confrontation Meeting*
   The Confrontation Meeting developed by Richard Beckhard[7] is a direct and immediate technique that enables organizations to identify problems, establish priorities, increase total management participation, and gain increased employee input in goal setting. It is designed as an intensive one-day meeting in which all management personnel are called together.
   A number of variations are possible in conducting Confrontation Meetings, but generally an attempt is made to get peer managers together, both interdepartmentally and intradepartmentally, in order to evaluate the existing status of the organization and to recommend planned action changes. Once the problems and recommendations are formulated, the peer managers as a group meet in "confrontation" with the highest-level management personnel in the organization. In this meeting, these high-level managers make commitments openly regarding the recommendations they will or will not accept. When recommendations are not accepted, the reasons for their nonacceptance are discussed. At the end of the confrontation session, follow up plans are made to insure the implementation of the actions, and a follow-up review meeting is scheduled for a later date.
   The specific phases of the Confrontation Meeting are discussed in detail in chapter 11, "Techniques of Group Leadership and Decision Making."

5. *Force Field Analysis*
   Force field analysis is a useful tool
   a. for identifying and analyzing conditions that require change and
   b. for establishing a systematic strategy of change that can be achieved with a minimum of effort and disruption.
   The Force Field model was proposed by Kurt Lewin, who saw behavior in organizations not as static habits or patterns but as a dynamic balance of forces working in opposite directions within the social-psychological space of the organization. The model assumes that any

6. J.K. Fordyce and R. Weil, *Managing with People* (Reading, Mass.: Addison-Wesley, 1971).
7. R. Beckhard, *Harvard Business Review*, 45 (1967).

Figure 13.1

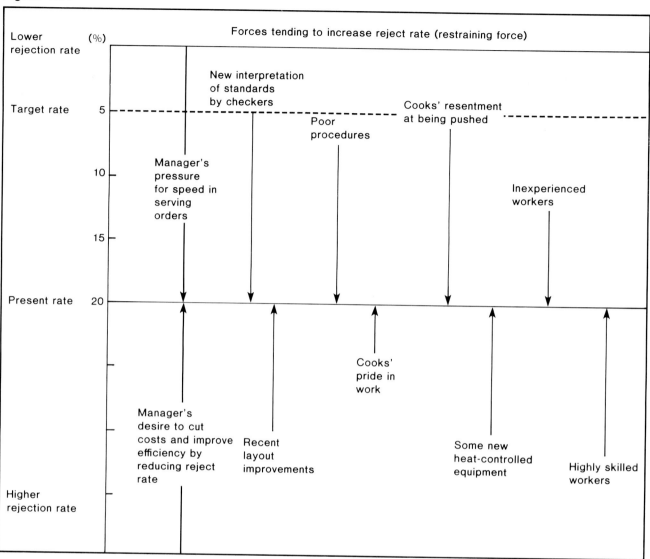

interpersonal situation represents a state of equilibrium at any given moment, balancing counterposed forces acting to change the situation and acting to keep it the same.

The following diagram characterizes the Force Field Model.

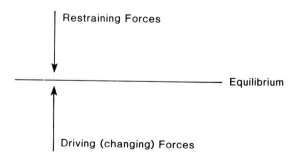

Prior to bringing about a change, the individual or group that feels the change is desirable should identify all of the driving and restraining forces and assign arrows to them.

Example: A group of supervisors are disturbed by the output quality of food preparation coming out of the kitchen. Twenty percent of the items are rejected for not meeting the standards for appearance, warmth, and portion control. They want to establish an MBO goal to reduce the reject level of items not meeting the standards to 5 percent. During a brainstorming session, they identified all pertinent forces and represented them as arrows. The length of the arrows were proportioned to represent the magnitude of the force.

All of this is shown in figure 13.1. When the driving forces that threaten or pressure people are increased, the resistance is also likely to be increased. It is better to increase those driving forces that do not increase resistance, to work on reducing restraining forces, or to consider new driving forces that can be brought into play. By concentrating on forces that are easiest to change, the supervisors are able to maximize the payoff and to alter performance in the least disruptive fashion.

DATA FEEDBACK

One barrier to change within organizations lies in the absence of meaningful objective feedback of events and situations that might be contributing to various outcomes. When scales drop dramatically, the restaurant manager usually makes changes, but unfortunately the changes may be impulsive and reactive rather than planned and systematic. Skillful managers can learn much about an organization's culture and its problems by carefully gathering data by means of interviews, questionnaires, and observations. Regardless of how much data is collected, however, it is not of much value unless put to *use*.

Data Feedback represents an OD technique for bringing about change in which data are fed back to the persons who generated them and then an action plan is developed on the basis of the data feedback. Mann identifies five characteristic conditions for data feedback that enhance its efficiency as a means of changing organizational systems.[8]

1. Employees participate in the *collection, interpretation,* and *analysis* of data, developing a feeling of ownership in the proposed solutions.

2. Employee family groups discuss data that are relevant to their functioning. They do not discuss abstract principles.

3. The process of feedback provides employees with immediate feedback concerning the success or failure of various actions steps, so to give added motivation to their efforts.

4. Group involvement supports individual efforts.

5. By involving management at the top, the process of feedback is accepted throughout the company.

METHODS OF COLLECTING DATA

Data collection has an ominous ring for many managers. It sounds too much like research, which often implies using complex and esoteric methods, bringing in outside consultants, and coming up with long-term projects that cannot help "right now."

This section describes some of the simpler, easier techniques of data collection that can be used in organizational development projects and that can provide groups with immediate feedback, so they can make "right now" decisions.[9] Data collection for organizational development purposes is somewhat different from collecting traditional research data. In traditional research, careful emphasis is placed on the research methodology and on making sure that the data are collected by totally unbiased and objec-

tive methods, inasmuch as the research *concludes* with final results. OD data collection is, by contrast, a *beginning* point, a point from which to provide decision-making groups with a frame of reference for their efforts. OD data collection should avoid bias and unreliable procedures, of course, but the methodology should not impede the process of providing the decision-making groups with feedback data to consider. As long as the groups are aware of the techniques used for accumulating the data, they can decide for themselves how "pure" the data may be.

Questionnaire

The questionnaire is an economical and popular technique for gathering data. A questionnaire can be a formal instrument used to survey general attitudes and behavior (see chapter 11) or it can be constructed for a specific *ad hoc* purpose. One of the desirable features of a questionnaire is the anonymity it assures to a respondent, which in turn often results in strong sentiments being brought out into the open. On the other hand, a questionnaire does not permit "prodding" to find out what feelings and thoughts may lie beyond the taking of a particular position. Questionnaires can be constructed to obtain objective, factual data or subjective data based on the feelings of the respondent. Objective data are much easier to tabulate and provide an easy means for making comparisons between groups. Subjective data, though difficult to quantify, offer potentially rich clues concerning underlying problems and issues. Most questionnaires should be constructed to provide both objective and subjective data.

Some sample questionnaire items are listed below.

Objective items
"On the average, how many customers do you see in a day?"
"How many waitresses report to the dining room supervisor?"
"What would be an ideal number to report to the supervisor?"

Subjective items
"How do you rate morale in the company? Please explain."
"What do you think we could do to increase efficiency?"
"What factors seem to be holding back our company?"

---

8. F.C. Mann, "Studying and Creating Change: A Means to Understanding Social Organization," in *Research in Industrial Human Relations,* ed. C.M. Arensberg et al. (New York: Harper and Brothers, 1957).
9. Adapted from J.K. Fordyce and R. Weil, *Managing with People* (Reading, Mass.: Addison-Wesley, 1971).

Interviewing

Prior to starting an OD exercise, such as a team-building meeting, it is common practice to interview participants. Because of the sensitivity of the data, interviews are usually undertaken by a third party (e.g., a consultant, a member of the personnel department, or someone not involved directly with the situation being explored). The interviewer is concerned with exploring ways for the group to be more effective, such as feelings related to a situation, people interactions, or personal concerns that have never been voiced. The interviewer usually treats the data anonymously, though reporting general findings and interpretations to the group. Interviews can be conducted on an individual or subgroup basis.

The interviewer is interested in learning about feelings and observations of participants, not in leading them to his conclusions. Interview questions should be "open-ended" and directed toward getting substantive information about the organization. Questions can be general, specific about management, concerned with relationships, or even personal. The keys to interviewing lie in the rapport and trust the interviewer establishes and in the assurance of maintaining confidentiality in using the data.

The following are examples of leading questions.

"What changes would you like to see made?"
"What is Ms. X like as a manager?"
"Can you give me some examples of unresolved problems in the organization?"

Its effectiveness notwithstanding, interviewing has limitations. One problem lies in the time required and the massive amount of data that must be organized and presented. In addition, interview data are always subject to an interpretation of the findings by the interviewer. With interviewers lacking rapport or acceptability with the group, the findings can be rejected, particularly if sensitive or controversial data is presented. In such cases, interviewing can lead to adverse rather than positive results and can polarize the group process.

Sensing

Sensing is an OD method by which managers can learn about problems, needs, and ideas of individuals within the organization with whom they would ordinarily have little contact. Sensing involves an unstructured interview held with a group of employees for the sole purpose of educating the manager. Depending on the receptivity of the group, the sessions are often tape recorded to provide an accurate transcript of issues covered.

When properly used, sensing can be a highly effective technique that enables employees to make their feelings known directly to top management. Care must be taken to explain fully to both supervisors and employees that the sessions are not intended for "spying" on the supervisors nor will they be used to reprimand, judge, or "sell" anything to employees. They do not take the place of any regular management-employee meetings nor are they intended to solve a myriad of problems. Mostly, they attempt to explore feelings or ideas connected with one or a few main issues.

Example: The general manager of a multiple-restaurant operation is involved with a group of technical experts in establishing a company-wide pension plan. The experts have demonstrated that a variety of plans are possible with the same basic dollar outlay, depending on the needs and wishes of the company. Each plan has some definite advantages and disadvantages. Before a plan is adopted, the general manager had planned to have it discussed with the employees. Now the thinking of the general manager is that the pulse of the employees needs to be taken even before a plan is drafted, so that the plan will most nearly reflect the wishes of the employees. Several sensing sessions with various employees at the units are planned by the general manager.

Polling

Sometimes groups become stalemated, but the "real" issues are often hidden. Polling offers a way for a group to evaluate "where it is" in order to be able to get on with the tasks at hand. Polling is a quick, interesting, and simple technique. Questions and polling procedures can be devised easily by anyone in the group, but the whole group takes part in the process and feels a commitment to the results.

Example: The unit managers have been meeting regularly to devise planning goals for making improvements in the units. The discussions do not seem to be going anywhere. The discussion leader suggests polling the group to determine their outlook for coming up with desired changes on a "Scale of Optimism," which is quickly devised by the leader. The group agrees to participate, and the leader draws the scale of optimism on the chalkboard.

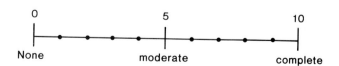

Each unit manager is asked to assign a number to his or her degree of optimism. The responses cluster around 3. The polling procedure triggers a group discussion concerning its pessimism. Various members acknowledge their own inertia and the difficulty in planning for change when they are so busy with day-to-day operations trying to make up for staff shortages. Some hidden resentment surfaces concerning the unreasonableness of the task established by the general manager under present circumstances. A meeting between the general manager and the unit managers is scheduled, and it proves to be quite productive in bringing a number of hidden issues to the surface. The manager, feeling frustrated with some of the unit managers, was using the group project as a way to "motivate" all managers rather than attempting to deal specifically with problem managers. The managers, though recognizing a need to keep change-oriented, felt the change expectations were simply another demand on an already full schedule. Once issues were resolved, the managers were able to incorporate a systematic program of change coordinated within the framework of their existing MBO program.

Another Example: The dining room crew must work together as a close group. They have regular planning meetings, but the meetings are not always productive. One member finally expresses the feelings that the group is not productive because of certain relationships among members, and that the group has been avoiding facing up to real issues.

The third party in the group suggests that each member respond to two questions:

- Which two persons in the group do I *like* working with *most?*
- Which two persons in the group do I *like* working with *least?*

The responses were collected on signed slips of paper. On the basis of the tabulations, figure 13.2 grid was developed. Once the data brought the relationship issues into the open, the group was also able to deal with other issues designed to improve the relationships.

INTERGROUP PROBLEM SOLVING

One of the most prevalent and compelling forces in American society is the high value placed on competition. Healthy competition, obviously, is not only desirable but inevitable. Our free enterprise system is predicated on fundamental beliefs in the positive values of competition. We also recognize that competition can be destructive and that a free enterprise system without controls leads to highly undesirable consequences for individuals and our society as a whole.

Figure 13.2

Chosen \ Choosers	Mary	Marge	Sue	Rita	Tina	June
Mary	▓	X	✓	✓	X	✓
Marge		▓		✓		
Sue	✓		▓	X	✓	X
Rita	✓	✓	✓	▓	✓	✓
Tina	X	✓	X		▓	X
June	X	X	X	X	X	▓

✓ = most   X = least

Because competition is so vital a part of organizational development, a large amount of research has been directed at exploring its effects on industries and businesses. One significant conclusion is uncontested: organizations are so structured that competition between departments and groups is the *rule* rather than the exception. Almost any newcomers to the hotel-restaurant field quickly recognize the antipathy between kitchen and dining room workers, hotel versus restaurant personnel, labor and management, skilled and unskilled workers, staff and line, and other subgroups.

Sherif and Sherif have noted that once initiated, competition between groups tends toward stability and is perpetuated over time. By contrast, collaborative behavior often remains unstable and groups must work constantly to develop collaborative behavior.[10]

When work groups compete, considerable stereotyping of the other group occurs, much like the stereotyping that occurs among competing political or religious groups. Each tends to devalue the contributions of the competing group and to overassess its own flexibility and reasonableness. Competing groups tend to polarize each other to the point of causing many of the major problems in industries to arise due to the inability of management to bring about collaborative working relationships among various factions and subgroups of workers.

A case example: As organizations grow, more and more departments are created. With the creation of new departments, need also arises for systems to be developed to coordinate the flow of work and communications between departments. The possibility also exists for excessive competition between departments.

---

10. M. Sherif and C. Sherif, *Social Psychology* (New York: Harper and Row Publishers, 1969).

A consultant to a restaurant organization was asked by management to assist in trying to resolve a major systems problem within the organization involving movement of food from a commissary to various operating units. A number of departments were involved in the system, including unit managers, general manager, data processing, warehousing, commissary, and accounting.

Recognizing the possibility of intergroup competition as a basis for the problem, the intervention procedure selected was the "Confrontation Meeting" approach, described elsewhere in this chapter and in chapter 11. Representatives of each involved department were assembled in small discussion groups with representatives from other departments. The groups were asked simply to define the problem through their discussions and to come up with recommendations for improving the situation.

Most participants came into the group meetings feeling that other participants were adversaries and competitors. Most felt their departments were working hard to make the system work but felt that one or more of the other departments were not cooperating. After approximately two hours, a dramatic thing happened. As group members explored the systems problem with other departmental representatives, each gradually came to the realization that the reason the system was not working resided in the fact that *there was no system!* Each department was merely doing its part of the system, but basic flaws existed that could only be seen through a collaborative effort. Rather than collaborate, each department was getting more defensive and less cooperative as the problems became more acute. Once the basic flaws were detected, the groups quickly developed a more efficient system and a major company problem that had persisted for over a year was lessened significantly in a matter of hours.

OD techniques, which focus on intergroup problem solving and team building, strive to bring about *intergroup trust* and to get the groups working toward a *superordinate goal,* i.e., a goal that one group alone cannot attain. To bring about intergroup trust, groups must have dialogue. They must be free to discover that the stereotypes they have built in their minds are not necessarily valid and may in fact be erroneous. They must also discover that they *need* the other group; that together the two groups can accomplish what neither can accomplish on its own.

The Confrontation Meeting is an excellent technique for bringing about intergroup collaboration. Most Data Feedback techniques also have direct application to intergroup problem-solving situations. More specifically, the Intergroup Team-Building Meeting is presented below as another example of a procedure that can be used to increase intergroup collaboration.

The Intergroup Team-Building Meeting[11]

The Intergroup Team-Building Meeting is designed specifically to improve working relationships between two groups. Going into the meeting, both groups recognize that the working relationship is not ideal and that positive changes in the relationship are desirable. The following steps are recommended:

Step 1: Objective Setting. A planning committee, consisting of the managers of the respective groups and a third party establish the scope and objectives of the meeting.

Step 2: Data Collection (optional).

Step 3: The Meeting: All participants are informed fully as to why they are meeting, what the meeting hopes to accomplish, and what procedures will be followed.

Each group meets separately to prepare three lists describing positive experiences in working with the other group, negative experiences in working with the other group, and an empathy list predicting what the other group will say about it.

The groups come together and a spokesman for each group presets the lists. The total group prepares a working agenda and sets priorities concerning the most significant items. No attempt is made to resolve issues. Subgroups are formed that consist of representatives of both groups. Each group is given one or more items from the agenda to work through in terms of improving relationships between the groups. The total group reassembles to formulate a list of action items that it commits itself to carry out. The action items are assigned and scheduled.

Step 4: Follow-up. Follow-up activity and meetings are scheduled to see that items have been performed and that the open communications developed at the meeting are continued.

SUMMARY

Organizational Development (OD) is an educational strategy adopted to bring about a planned organizational change. OD takes place within an organization in a real life setting and arises from the exigencies of real problems or crises.

---

11. J.K. Fordyce and R. Weil, *Managing with People* (Reading, Mass.: Addison-Wesley, 1971).

A number of specific techniques for bringing about change can be considered. Techno-Structural Interventions involve changing the organizational structure in the direction of providing greater participation opportunities for employees. Two Techno-Structural possibilities include incentive plans and Job Enrichment practices.

Team Development is concerned with bringing about greater harmony and decision making among overlapping work units. A number of specific techniques apply to developing a team-like approach, including Diagnostic Team Meetings, Family Group Diagnostic Meetings, Family Group Team-Building Meetings, Confrontation Meetings, and Field Force Analyses.

Data Feedback provides an avenue for a group interested in bringing about change to perform research on itself and to use the data to plan effective changes. Methods of collecting data include questionnaires, interviewing, sensing, and polling.

Intergroup problem solving attempts to minimize competition among rival groups and to increase collaboration toward a superordinate goal. The Confrontation Meeting and The Intergroup Team-Building Meeting offer relevant approaches for increasing intergroup collaboration.

14

"If you own a shaggy dog, vacuum him instead of the floors and rugs, clothes and furniture."

The foregoing advice might be changed to read: "If you manage a shaggy hotel or restaurant, analyze the operation to discover better ways of performing the work and developing systems that will make the work easier." In other words, hotel or restaurant management must step back periodically, examine the work being done to see if it can be simplified, tasks combined or eliminated, employees rescheduled, work assembled for minimizing physical and mental effort. Every operation performed can be examined to see if it is economical to substitute equipment for manpower, machines for muscle power, electronic devices for routine mental chores.

Traditionally, hotel or restaurant keeping has been a handicraft business—people working with their hands. Much of it still is hand work—salad making, luggage carrying, waiter service. Personal service has been one of its great offerings to the public. Today the service is still there but much is being mechanized. Conveyor belts running a half block or more, carrying soiled dishware, and moving up and down through several stories, carrying food; cafeteria serving lines on wheels, that can feed up to fifteen people a minute; computers whirring and clicking away doing payrolls for employees hundreds of miles away, keeping food inventories, doing accounts receivable and accounts payable, and keeping guest charges up to the second—all make the hotel and restaurant business a much more efficient business than it was in the past— a business that demands a higher level of education and management sophistication.

EXCESSIVE WAITING AND CLEANING TIME IN HOTELS AND RESTAURANTS

It has been stated that the average kitchen employee performs productive work only 55 percent of the time—that much of that person's time is spent watching food cook,

waiting for something or someone. Careful research is not available to substantiate that statement, but it is apparent from gross observation of the usual kitchen that at a given moment many people cannot perform productive work. Most studies have shown that with certain pieces of equipment as much as 50 percent of an employee's time is spent in sanitation, the term defined broadly. The cycle of business in hotels and restaurants is such that some ingenuity is required to maintain work flow in a variety of jobs: cashiers, front desk clerks, bellpersons, and all waiting personnel. Most check-ins that take place in a hotel or motel occur between the hours of 4 and 8 P.M. What can the bellperson do the rest of the time? Restaurant cashiers are busy during the meal periods. Can other work be assigned to them during the periods of lull? Is it necessary for all the tableware to be washed during the meal periods, or can the work be spread throughout the day or over several days?

Does it pay to purchase convenience foods or even frozen meals? Will the customers accept instant mashed potatoes, dehydrated onions, the use of soup and gravy bases in sauces, and products made from bakery mixes? Some convenience foods definitely have a cost advantage, others do not. One study showed that the cost per portion of fresh potatoes was almost twice as much as for instant potatoes when the expense of labor was included. Dehydrated onions cost 10¼ cents a pound as compared with 18 cents a pound for fresh onions prepared by hand. The dehydrated onions were satisfactory for cooked dishes but could not be used in sandwiches.

The administration of the state mental hospitals of New York State found that it was less expensive to purchase canned, boned chicken than to have chicken purchased, cooked, and deboned within the hospital kitchens.

Why not buy prepared frozen foods and do away with chefs and cooks within the establishment completely? In one of the most successful food operations in the country, Howard Johnson's, most of the food is frozen. No one in the Howard Johnson restaurant could properly be called a cook.

In general, it can be said that food processing can be done more economically using mass production methods in a factory than it can be done within a restaurant or hotel kitchen. Everyone agrees, however, that the very best food available is made from fresh food prepared to order and served to the patron at once. Truite Bleu, made from live swimming trout kept in a tank in the kitchen, has a considerably different taste than frozen trout. Peas prepared from fresh peas shelled by hand generally are more tasty than canned peas. The specialty of the house usually gives the patron something a little bit different than he can get elsewhere and constitutes a part of its appeal, yet the preparation costs must be considered. Labor cost in making a pie is somewhere between fifty cents and one dollar; the cost of preparing boeuf à la mode is high; the time required to prepare stuffed sole Normande is considerable and the skill required does not come cheap, yet they may be "right" for a particular restaurant.

Although utility costs in hospitality operations are quite high (they can be as high as 5–6 percent of the total sales dollar), human labor costs are much higher. Hotels, restaurants, hospitals, and clubs must see to it that personpower is used only when the work requires artistry, personal service, or brain power. Let machines substitute for muscles whenever and wherever possible. Human life is much too valuable even in its lowest cash terms to be used as no more than mindless mechanical power.

It is estimated that in 1850 only 26 percent of the work energy consumed in the United States came from power-driven machines. Today the figure is 94 percent. We employ ten times as much energy per person in the United States as the average for the rest of the world. The larger chain operations in our field are industrializing. The little French restaurant with its four tables and its food prepared by the owner can be a thing of beauty and artistry, but not very profitable.

Wages continue upward over the years. Hours are being reduced to forty a week or less. Maximum productivity from manpower is essential.

Labor costs in hotels, restaurants, hospitals, industrial feeding operations, and clubs are one of the biggest and most difficult to control of all costs. In commercial hotels they are 30 percent or more of the gross revenue. In restaurants, labor costs are 20 to 40 percent of the gross sales. Clubs often run a labor cost of over 40 percent of the gross income. On top of these percentages, the United States Chamber of Commerce states that hotels pay 9.4 percent more in nonwage labor payments (meals, social security, unknown exemptions, and the like). Fringe benefits can go as high as 30 percent of wages, and they are rising. There are few operations in which alert and informed management cannot with system, controls, and good personnel techniques reduce labor costs several percentage points.

According to Harris, Kerr, Forster accountants, 50 percent of hotel jobs should have variable schedules. Only a small percentage actually do have them. The same firm states that only 15 percent of the hotel repairs are emergency repairs and that 85 percent of them can be scheduled, thus reducing maintenance men's many hours of riding up and down on service elevators for emergency repair jobs.

Labor cost is relative and most meaningful in terms of cost per unit of production: cost to wash a window, cost to prepare a guest room, cost per salad, cost per portion of roast beef, and so on. In food operations labor cost and food cost are two sides of the same coin. Skilled, well-paid labor may result in a higher-than-average labor cost but a lower-than-average food cost. Using frozen meals, for example, means an increase in food cost and a decrease in labor cost. Low-paid management may well cost an operation thousands of dollars of unnecessary food costs.

SCHEDULING PERSONNEL TO FIT THE WORK LOAD

Scheduling personnel to fit work load is a major factor in reducing labor costs. Harold Van Ormon, Jr., a well-known hotelman, states that up to one-third of the labor in hotels is wasted through lack of personnel scheduling. Production requirements in hotels and restaurants vary widely throughout the day, the week, and the year. Meals in a restaurant, for example, may range from 500 for a Monday evening to 25 for Sunday breakfast. Within the same day the number of dinners served may be only a fraction of the number of luncheons served. The number of meals vary seasonally as well as follow a weekly pattern.

Sales in restaurants during January, February, March, and April are low compared to sales during the other months of the year. Across the country as a whole July and August bring peak sales, then there is a gradual drop-off until November. December picks up a bit only to have January drop precipitously.

In figure 14.1, we see that Monday through Thursday in a typical successful Downtowner Motor Inn finds the house full. On Fridays the occupancy drops to 45 percent. In many commercial hotels around the country, Saturday and Sunday occupancy falls below 40 percent, and there are wide swings in business volume on a seasonal basis. Generally December is by far the lowest month for the hotel business, and Christmas Day finds many hotels with less than 10 percent occupancy. Some cities have a high spring occupancy; others reach their peak in the summer. Scheduling employees to fit such variations in sales challenges management to the utmost.

Figure 14.1 Average Daily Occupancy-Downtowner Motor Inns

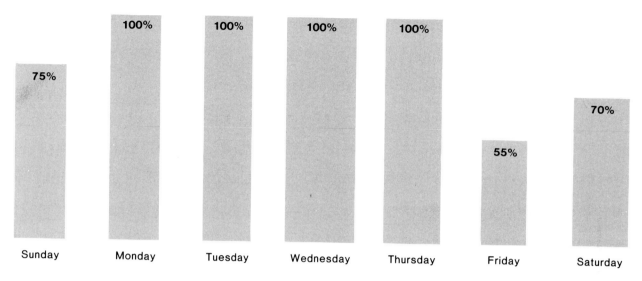

Figure 14.2 Production Curve

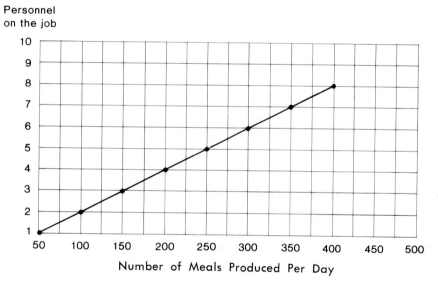

In hundreds of industrial food-service operations the difference between profit and loss comes from the fact that most of the serving personnel are employed for only two hours a day, drawn from employees of the company being served who hold other regular jobs. It has been found in many restaurants that people who ordinarily would not take a full-time job are interested in working up to four hours daily. These people are a boon to the food-service business.

Ideally, the number of personnel scheduled would correspond to the production turned out. Such a production curve would look like figure 14.2.

Conceivably such a curve would be achieved in an industrial feeding operation or cafeteria with a fixed volume. In most hotels it will remain an ideal only. Key personnel must be kept on regardless of the volume. However, here are some scheduling practices that have increased efficiency in food operation:

1. **Schedule personnel on split shifts.**
   Waiters and waitresses can be scheduled for a noon meal, for example, then be off until the dinner meal, or until a night banquet. This is especially feasible in downtown operations where personnel live close to the business and have things to do at home. In other operations, split shifts are not practical.

Table 14.1   Staffing Table for Kitchen

Jobs to be Filled	For 0–49 Patrons	For 50–99 Patrons	For 100–175 Patrons	For 175-plus Patrons
Chef	1	1	1	1
Cook	1	2	3	4
Salads—Pantry	1	2	2	3
Dishwasher	1	2	3	3
Potwasher	1	1	1	1
Cleaner	0	1	1	1
Storeroom Clerk	0	1	1	1
Baker	0	1	1	1

Table 14.2   Staffing Table for Dining Room
(Based on Number of Patrons)

Jobs to be Filled	For 0–37	For 38–58	For 59–75	For 76–95	For 96–112	For 113–129	For 130–145	For 146–166	For 167–Plus
Hostess	1	1	1	1	1	1	1	1	1
Waiter—Waitress	2	3	4	5	6	7	8	9	10
Bus Person	1	2	2	3	3	3	3	4	5
Bar Waitress	1	1½	1½	2	2	2½	2½	2½	2½

2. Where possible, schedule personnel irregularly to fit the pattern of work requirements.

Some personnel may need to be scheduled to start at noon one day, morning another day, and at four o'clock still another day. Be careful in scheduling that no one is overworked or inconvenienced too much.

3. Use part-time personnel.

In many operations part-time employees should be used extensively. In operations where meals and functions are confined mostly to the evenings, only a core of full-time employees is needed. A large staff of full-time personnel in such instances not only creates an excessive labor cost but leads to generally slipshod operation. Keep a file of part-time help on hand. With training they can be an effective part of the work force.

4. Use of staffing table.

Manpower can to a large degree be budgeted just as are materials or equipment. The staffing table is an excellent labor cost control device and can be applied to any operation. As efficiency and equipment are introduced, the staffing table is changed. The tables show that as patrons increase the number of employees increase. Conversely, as patrons decline in number, the number of staff should decrease. Because of differences in layout, services offered, and equipment, each operation must necessarily construct a staffing table to fit its operation.

Tables 14.1 and 14.2 show hypothetical staffing for a restaurant—kitchen and dining room.

Controlling Housekeeping Labor Costs

Cost of preparing a room in a hotel may be as high as $4 or $5 a room, depending upon the number of rooms cleaned, wages paid to the cleaners, and linen costs.

An obvious way to reduce cleaner costs in hotels and motels is to change the work schedules to fit the demand—the rooms to be cleaned. A transient roadside motel may experience 90 percent of its checkouts before 8 A.M., in which case cleaners can be scheduled to begin work at 8 or earlier. If, on the other hand, 50 percent of the guests in a resort property don't get up before 10 A.M., there is no point in scheduling more than half of the maid force until 10 A.M. City hotels often neglect to schedule enough cleaners for afternoon and evening shifts to cover late checkouts.

Figure 14.3 Sales Curve/Work-Schedule Chart

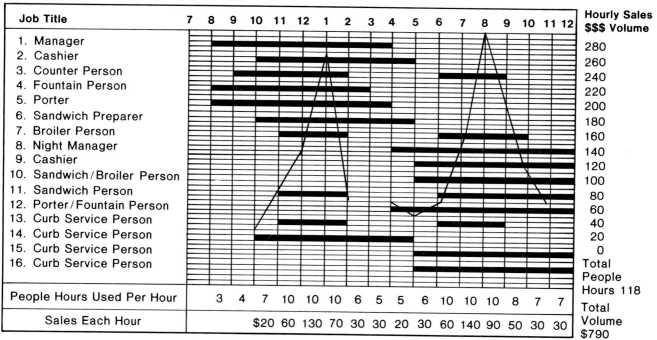

Job Title	7	8	9	10	11	12	1	2	3	4	5	6	7	8	9	10	11	12	Hourly Sales $$$ Volume
1. Manager																			280
2. Cashier																			260
3. Counter Person																			240
4. Fountain Person																			220
5. Porter																			200
6. Sandwich Preparer																			180
7. Broiler Person																			160
8. Night Manager																			140
9. Cashier																			120
10. Sandwich/Broiler Person																			100
11. Sandwich Person																			80
12. Porter/Fountain Person																			60
13. Curb Service Person																			40
14. Curb Service Person																			20
15. Curb Service Person																			0
16. Curb Service Person																			Total People Hours 118
People Hours Used Per Hour		3	4	7	10	10	10	6	5	5	6	10	10	10	8	7	7		
Sales Each Hour			$20	60	130	70	30	30	20	30	60	140	90	50	30	30			Total Volume $790

A Miami Beach hotel experiences a number of early checkouts, several at 6 A.M. It also experiences several late checkouts at 5 P.M. To assure that these rooms are ready at once, a cleaner and houseperson team is scheduled for early morning and another team for beginning in the afternoon.

The Sales-Labor Chart

Most food-service operations can afford the time to make a graph of the relationship between sales per hour and the number of person-hours used each hour. Graphs are a means of breaking down a complicated subject and putting it into a form that enables management to comprehend it and to reschedule employees to fit sales volume. All that is necessary is to keep a record of the sales made each hour and to plot such sales on the curve hour by hour. (In many restaurants, personnel tally sales at the end of each hour.) The sales curve is overlaid on a work-schedule graph. Figure 14.3 is a hypothetical graph.

In the sales-person-hour chart it is seen that the peak sales periods are from 12:00 to 2:00 P.M., and from 6:00 to 9:00 P.M. During these rush periods ten people-hours are being used per hour, which seems appropriate. During the period from 10:00 to 11:00 in the morning only $40 has been taken in in sales, yet seven people-hours were consumed, and after 10:00 in the evening only $60 an hour was taken in while seven people-hours were used per hour. The graph suggests that perhaps the wayside restaurant represented should close at 10:00 P.M. The man-

ager beginning the shift at 4:00 in the afternoon could probably start at 5:00 or 6:00 just as well. Three of the curb service personnel could well be off between the hours of 4:00 and 6:00. As always, there would be other factors to consider in rescheduling, but the chart is a point of departure for analysis.

Once scheduling has been revised, systems are needed to keep it in line with work requirements. The Harris, Kerr, Forster system is an elaborate one suitable for large operations. A restaurant can use a more elementary system effectively. Figure 14.4, the "Sales and Employee Forecast" chart is one that is used in a cafeteria chain. Every day each cafeteria manager predicts what his breakfast, lunch, and dinner sales will be for the following day. The forecast is based on the sales made on a given day of the week the previous year, taking into consideration weather forecasts, unusual situations in the area that increased or decreased business, and the general trend of business—whether it was up or down.

Getting the manager to make the forecast is difficult because of multitudinous other tasks and being so involved with day-to-day operation.

The number of employees who were used for each meal in the kitchen, at the serving table, and in the dining room is recorded. From the statistics it is often evident that on certain days too many employees are on hand—on other days too few. The sales income by employee is computed and a standard of sales per employee per day established.

The chart is simple enough to be understood; the system requires no special person such as a Food and Beverage Controller to operate.

Figure 14.4   Sales and Employee Forecast

Date _____

Weather Today: _____
Conventions in Town:

Party Business: _____

Other Factors Affecting Sales:

Forecasted Sales in Dollars:	Breakfast	Lunch	Dinner
	_____	_____	_____

Adjusted Food Order &
Production:

Number of Employees:	Breakfast	Lunch	Dinner
Kitchen	_____	_____	_____
Counter	_____	_____	_____
Dining Room	_____	_____	_____

Actual Sales:	Breakfast	Lunch	Dinner
	_____	_____	_____

Sales patterns continually shift. Many restaurants are advised to close for the winter. Some should not serve breakfasts. Breakfast charts provide information for such decisions.

The Mechanics of Employee Scheduling

Even in the best run houses, employees come in to work only to find that there has been a mistake in scheduling and that they are not needed. At other times the manager or supervisor is frantically on the phone trying to locate employees with days off who can fill in, again because of mistakes in scheduling. Managers need all the help they can get in routinizing the forecast and the scheduling of employees. In industry various shifts come and go as a group, a situation which is seldom practical in a hotel or restaurant. Restaurants opened for lunch only can more readily schedule employees by block. School lunch programs usually require a group of servers, most of whom come on at a certain hour and then leave together at a certain hour. In some food-service establishments it may be possible to stack schedules as seen below:

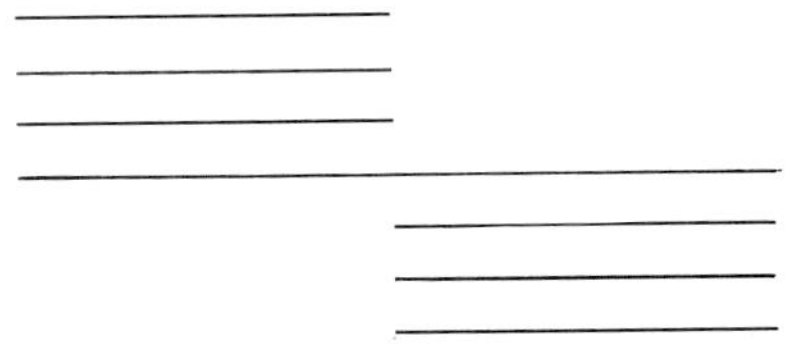

Other food-service operations may have two primary shifts with a small group of employees overlapping the two. One shift might begin at 7 A.M. and go home at 3 P.M. To carry the noon rush a few part-time employees might start at 11 A.M. and work until 1 P.M. The overlap schedule can be depicted as below:

The most efficient scheduling for most food operations turns out to be the staggered schedule, employees scheduled to fit the varying volume of sales. Scheduling to fit the sales picture can be time-consuming and something like putting together a jigsaw puzzle. Part-time employees are scheduled to cover rush periods, part-time hosts or hostesses can be employed to cover the peak meal periods, dishmachine operators may be scheduled on into the night.

Dining room employees are often scheduled on a rotating basis to assure all employees of being on the floor an equal amount of time when tips are greatest. Mimeographed charts expedite the scheduling. A sample is seen on page 268.

Name	Position	Mon.	Tues.	Wed.	Thurs.	Fri.	Sat.	Sun.
	A	X	X					
	B		X	X				
	C			X	X			
	D				X	X		
	E					X	X	
	F						X	X
	G	X						X

The Work Schedule Sheet

The final result of scheduling appears in the form of a work schedule, a sample of which is shown as figure 14.5.

The sample assumes that the employees will work forty-hour weeks. As mentioned, costs can be reduced by scheduling many or most of the employees part-time. If dining room employees do not need maximum income they perform better when scheduled part-time because of the tremendous nervous energy required in a high-volume restaurant. The usual employee is fairly well exhausted after four or five hours of waiting, busing, or cooking, under pressure. From the house viewpoint, it is also better to have fresh employees, part-timers who are not on the floor after running out of energy.

Figure 14.6 is another example of scheduling, this one tied in with the forecasting system. This schedule breaks the kitchen down into sections and records subtotals of the hours worked by each section. It is seen that the sample schedule for an "average motor inn" resulted in a total of 535 hours worked in the kitchen for the week covered. A staffing chart would have been budgeted for that particular kitchen—so many kitchen personnel in each category budgeted for a forecast of so many meals. The manager would then compare the actual hours worked with those budgeted for the period.

It is interesting to see the variable schedule worked by the different personnel. Bill, the morning cook, came in at 6 A.M. on Sunday and worked until 5 P.M. The rest of the week he came in at 6 A.M. and left at 3 P.M.

Frank, the afternoon cook, came in early on Sunday; Bud, the cook's helper, came in two hours late on Friday and worked two hours longer; Dave, a part-time warewasher, worked a highly variable schedule, probably to fill in as needed: all day Sunday, from 3 P.M. in the afternoon to 11 P.M. on Thursday, and from 7 A.M. to 4 P.M. on Saturday.

COMPUTERS AND LABOR SAVING

At one point in computer development it was believed by many that the computer would displace a sizable portion of the work force, a belief that has not yet been substantiated. Computers have been introduced gradually into the hotel and restaurant business, mostly into hotels of 300 rooms or more. At first the programming and then the maintenance problems more than offset any advantages gained from computer use. As early as 1963 the New York Hilton management decided to computerize most of its paperwork, and much publicity was generated about computerized reservations, registration, and accounting. Once installed, the management probably wished they had never heard of computers because of so many breakdowns, lost information, and the resulting confusion. Gradually computers began to be widely used by chains for reservations and for automating payroll computations and check writing. But it was not until the appearance of the minicomputer—a small, less expensive computer—that computers were very widely used in the hotel business other than for mechanizing the reservation system.

Does the computer reduce the payroll? The consensus of opinion seems to be that computer applications in the hotel and restaurant business seldom reduced the total cost but did provide much speedier information and the possibility of rapid analysis of costs and income. Market analysis is also quickly done. For example, each day the computer can print out a list of all guests in the house, grouping them by city of residence, pinpointing those areas most suitable for the concentration of promotion and advertising money.

Computer terminals can be placed wherever needed and information can be fed into the computer in a hotel; or the computer can be placed miles away and reached via telephone lines. The Sheraton-Boston Hotel, for example, has terminals at reservations, at the front desk, at guest registration, with the front office and restaurant

Figure 14.5 Staff Coverage Work Schedule*

WORK SCHEDULE

Unit _____   Period _____

Approved by: _____

Name	Position	Mon.	Tues.	Wed.	Thurs.	Fri.	Sat.	Sun	Total Hours
	A	6:00 / 2:30	6:00 / 2:30	6:00 / 2:30	6:00 / 2:30	6:00 / 2:30	X	X	40
	B	X	X	6:00 / 2:30	6:00 / 2:30	6:00 / 2:30	6:00 / 2:30	6:00 / 2:30	40
	C	7:00 / 3:30	7:00 / 3:30	X	X	7:00 / 3:30	7:00 / 3:30	7:00 / 3:30	40
	D	8:00 / 4:30	8:00 / 4:30	8:00 / 4:30	8:00 / 4:30	X	X	8:00 / 4:30	40
	E	X	8:00 / 4:30	8:00 / 4:30	8:00 / 4:30	8:00 / 4:30	8:00 / 4:30	X	40
	F	8:00 / 4:30	X	X	8:00 / 4:30	8:00 / 4:30	8:00 / 4:30	8:00 / 4:30	40
	G	11:00 / 7:30	11:00 / 7:30	11:00 / 7:30	X	X	11:00 / 7:30	11:00 / 7:30	40
	H	11:00 / 7:30	11:00 / 7:30	11:00 / 7:30	11:00 / 7:30	11:00 / 7:30	X	X	40
	I	X	X	11:00 / 7:30	11:00 / 7:30	11:00 / 7:30	11:00 / 7:30	11:00 / 7:30	40
	J	11:00 / 7:30	11:00 / 7:30	X	X	11:00 / 7:30	11:00 / 7:30	11:00 / 7:30	40
	K	2:30 / 11:00	2:30 / 11:00	2:30 / 11:00	2:30 / 11:00	X	X	2:30 / 11:00	40
	L	X	2:30 / 11:00	2:30 / 11:00	2:30 / 11:00	2:30 / 11:00	2:30 / 11:00	X	40
RELIEF									
	M	B	B	C	X	X	A	A	40
	N	E	X	X	C	D	D	E	40
	O	X	F	F	G	G	H	X	40
	P	I	I	J	J	X	X	H	40
	Q	L	X	X	EXTRA	K	K	L	40
TOTAL HOURS		96	96	96	104	96	96	96	680

*Source: Robert D. Buchanan, "How to Determine Staffing Needs," *Food Service Marketing*, August 1977.

Figure 14.6

Positions	Sunday		Monday		Tuesday		Wednesday		Thursday		Friday		Saturday		Weekly Total
Names of Staff	Schedule	Hrs	Schedule	Hrs	Schedule	Hrs	Schedule	Hrs	Schedule	Hrs	Schedule	Hrs	Schedule	Hrs	Hours
John—Steward	OFF		6A-3P	8	6A-3P	8	6A-3P	8	6A-3P	8	6A-3P	8	7A-4P	8	48
Bill—AM Cook	6A-5P	10	6A-3P	8	6A-3P	8	5A-3P	9	6A-3P	8	6A-3P	8	OFF		51
Frank—PM Cook	1P-11P	10	3P-11P	8	3P-12P	9	3P-11P	8	OFF		3P-11P	8	2P-11P	9	52
Tim—Extra Cook	4P-8P	4											3P-6P	3	7
Sub-Total Hours															158
Bud—Cook's Helper	7A-4P	8	7A-4P	8	OFF		7A-4P	8	7A-4P	8	9A-6P	8	7A-4P	8	48
Ken—Cook's Helper	OFF		3P-11P	8	7A-4P	8	6A-3P	8	3P-11P	8	OFF		OFF		32
Sub-Total Hours															80
Elaine—Pantry	5A-3P	9	6A-3P	8	6A-3P	8	OFF		5A-3P	9	6A-3P	8	6A-3P	8	50
Ruth—Pantry	1P-11P	10	OFF		OFF		3P-11P	8	3P-11P	8	3P-11P	8	2P-11P	9	43
Sub-Total Hours															93
Jess—Warewasher	6A-4P	10	7A-4P	8	7A-4P	8	7A-4P	8	7A-4P	8	7A-4P	8	OFF		50
Bob—Warewasher	2P-11P	9	3P-11P	8	3P-11P	8	3P-11P	8	OFF		3P-11P	8	3P-12P	9	50
Dave—Warewasher	8A-5P	8							3P-11P	8			7A-4P	8	24
Otto—Potwasher	OFF		8A-5P	8	8A-5P	8	10A-7P	8	8A-5P	8	8A-5P	8	OFF		40
Tom—Night Cleaner	11P-8A	8	11P-8A	8	OFF		OFF		11P-8A	8	11P-8A	8	11P-8A	8	40
Sub-Total Hours															204
Weekly Total Hours															535

Source: Thomas W. Lattin, "Systems Approach to Labor Cost Control," *Cooking For Profit.*

cashiers, in housekeeping, in the Accounts Receivable department, and at the telephone switchboard. Printed reports are generated for these departments and also for the hotel sales director, the executive offices, and the food and beverage offices. The accounting office in the Sheraton-Boston prepares guest bills in a matter of minutes. Master billing for a group of 1,000 people can be done in one hour by the Receivable Clerk in Accounting.

Charges made in any of the restaurants with computers can be fed directly into a computer almost instantaneously. For example, a businessperson hurrying to catch a plane can rush into one of the restaurants for a quick breakfast and head from there straight to the front desk to check out. The cashier in the restaurant records every transaction into the computer using the terminal keyboard, and the transaction is automatically fed onto the guest's folio so that it is ready by the time the guest reaches the desk.

Terminals are located adjacent to the telephone operator stations and the computer supplies the room number. If a Mr. Smith is called, the computer prints on a screen the name of every Smith registered at the hotel and the rooms they are occupying.

In Housekeeping a computer publishes a room status report each night that can be used to assign housekeepers for the next day. As rooms are vacated the information is fed from the front desk to the computer and updated when the rooms have been cleaned and are ready for occupancy.

Using a computer, tips indicated on restaurant and bar bills can be charged directly to room numbers or credit cards and stored in the computer. By pushing a button at the end of a day, the payroll department will get an accurate tip total for each waiter and waitress in the house.

The computer can also be used as part of hotel security. When a guest checks in that person tells the clerk what 4-digit number he or she would like to use as a room combination. The clerk sets a number on a console. Throughout the guest's stay that person simply punches the number in the proper sequence to get into his or her room. It is a keyless lock system. Cleaners enter a room using a special housekeeping combination. When the guest checks out the clerk cancels the guest's particular combination. In case of emergency, the front desk can override individual combinations with a key. By appropriate programming the hotel can eliminate the room rack.

The widest application of computers in hotels has been with reservation systems. Two hotels in Hawaii are using a computerized reservation system for booking group sales and have programmed it to take reservations up to the year 2000. The EECO System used is set up so that hotels within a radius of ten miles can all share the same computer. Computers can also be programmed to automatically generate letters requesting advance deposits of guests who hold reservations.

In 1977 most hotel personnel familiar with computers felt that a computer would be useful in hotels of 150 rooms or more if computer costs were reduced. A few felt they could be installed in smaller properties and still pay off. The computer can be used to keep track of guests' demographics, information to be used in planning market strategy. It can be programmed to pinpoint the type of traveler, length of stay, company affiliation, hometown, expenditures while in the hotel, or any other information fed into the system.

The System 7 developed by IBM involves an auto-wake-up system that can provide simultaneous wake-up service for any time specified. The Peach Tree Plaza in Atlanta uses a system that can wake up as many as 900 guests at precisely 7 A.M. The system is interfaced with the national weather reporting service to include the weather report as part of the wake-up call.

Some managers are still skeptical about the reliability of computers and include one or two computers for backup in the event of failure of the main system.

CRT (cathode ray tubes) terminals are used to display any information requested that is part of the computer's programming. The employee talks with the computer and the information requested is displayed in black and white on the cathode ray tube.

Some of the functions performed by computers include the following:

—Printing out lists of next day's arrivals, the type of space required and the length of stay.
—Producing lists of guests checking out and of "no-shows" for the previous day.
—Providing accurate room status.
—Locating available rooms.
—Keeping a running total of rooms available for sale.
—Completing accurate guests' folios with every charge clearly indicated.
—Preparing Accounts Receivable reports, revenue reports, departmental reports.
—Providing each department with daily status reports, including budget performance, if required.
—Printing out reports that give current sales revenue for each department and a total house count.
—Computing automatically the average revenue per room, average number of guests per room.
—Posting tax to the guest's folio and handling all mathematical computations.

Usually a hotel installs a system that can be added to as the staff becomes familiar with the equipment, as the computer proves itself, or as new features can be afforded.

Other computer applications include:

—Providing instant information as to who is in the house, who will stay, how long, who is left, and who will arrive late.
—A daily forecast of rooms.
—An inventory of which rooms are available, those on change, and those that are being rehabilitated.
—Information pertaining to any individual guest can be called up for display on a screen—phone charges, hotel charges, gift shop charges, restaurant charges, and a total for all of them immediately, coincidentally with the guest's checking out.
—The computer can be programmed each day to supply the latest information concerning local events, weather information, in-house menus, entertainment available.
—The computer will produce payroll checks automatically, deducting income tax, workmen's compensation insurance, unemployment taxes, and other deductions.
—The computer can keep track of accounts receivable, accounts payable, and inventories.
—Groups who spend the most money in restaurants and gift shops can readily be identified.
—Lodging quarters cleaners can dial information directly into the computer showing room status.
—Key information is quickly available from the nerve centers in the six vital hotel areas: reservations, registration, cashier, housekeeping, telephones, and back-office accounting.

Eventually as has already been demonstrated, computers will react to verbal commands and questions. Is it too much to expect hotels to someday provide computer-matched dating services for lonely guests?

Computer Bookkeeping and Control

Restaurants not in hotels seldom employ food and beverage checkers, and most hotel kitchens are eliminating that position. The smaller restaurant is likely to employ a part-time person working at home who does the restaurant bookkeeping on a day-to-day basis. An accounting firm is employed to prepare a monthly statement and help with the income taxes. Chain operations ordinarily do most of the bookkeeping and operating analysis at the home office. Record-keeping at the unit level is minimal.

A few chains use the computer extensively. The Jerrico Company, parent company of the Long John Silver chain, centralizes bookkeeping by computer in their Lexington, Kentucky, office. All data from the day's operation in each store is sent over long-distance phone lines to the central computer during the night, when long-distance rates are inexpensive. Their system, "computer talking to computer," is highly sophisticated. The Lexington-based computer in effect calls the computer at the unit level. The computer in the store then feeds the daily data of the store's operation to the central computer, wherein it is analyzed and printed out for operating executives of the company. Top management knows every day what the food costs, labor costs, and other statistics were for the entire chain for the previous day.

Eliminating the Cashier

Magnolia's Peach, a fine restaurant in Upland, California, with sales in excess of 1 million dollars a year, has a novel way of eliminating the cashier function. Each waiter brings his own bank, makes all of his own change, and at the end of his shift pays the house what he owes based on what has been "bought" from the kitchen and bar. He "buys" all of the food and beverages from the kitchen and from the bar. Each bill is fed into a minicomputer, which presents the total owed by the waiter at the end of the shift. It has often been said that being a waiter or waitress is like being in business for oneself. This plan carries the metaphor one step further. The plan, by eliminating the many trips to and from a cashier, eliminates the need for a cashier and speeds turnover of customers.

The On-Premise Controller/Bookkeeper

Few restaurants employ a full-time bookkeeper, especially one that is on the premises. Restaurant Adventures, the small chain of restaurants in California, has a different idea. Each of their restaurants gross more than a million dollars in sales annually, and each has a full-time book-keeper, or auditor, who comes on duty in the afternoon and has all transactions audited by two o'clock in the morning. The day's business is completely recorded and analyzed by later that morning. Labor, food, and other percentage ratios are computed daily. The auditor is usually a more mature person who does not mind the late hours and likes working on one's own. The job pays well.

The Upward Push on Job Classifications

Food-service managers in governmental units such as school lunch programs and food services in colleges, universities, and governmental offices are likely to find that labor costs rise excessively because semiskilled jobs gradually are upgraded by one means or another so that the job classification calls for an inordinately high wage scale. Custodians receive the same income as highly skilled employees, secretaries become office administrators, file clerks move up to the secretary classification. Shrewd employees work at moving the job into a higher job category than is justified. It is virtually impossible to reclassify a job downward. The manager is then locked into an excessive labor cost about which little can be done. Civil service systems are often filled with highly capable people who spend much of their time figuring ways to extract the most from the system. Nor are managers adverse to building empires for the simple reason that their own job classification can be moved upward along with the others; the more employees, the higher the job classification.

As part of work simplification studies, jobs can often be reclassified or taken apart and made into jobs that better reflect their true value to an organization. It is strange how often this happens when a hotel chain is bought the number of corporate positions that disappear without noticeable effect on operations.

Standards Useful as Guides in Work Simplification

While the objective in work simplification is to achieve maximum work production with minimal effort, knowing what is possible to achieve or has been achieved in other establishments gives the analyst goals toward which to shoot. The American Dietetic Association, for example, has published the following chart showing the number of meals produced for one people-hour of effort in various kinds of food-service establishments. It is seen that hotels produce the least number of meals per hour expended while the school lunch, for apparent reasons, can produce as many as fifteen meals per hour of effort.

Meals Produced Per People-Hour of Labor Used	
Type Institution	No. of Meals
Hotels	1.25– 1.50
Restaurants	1.50– 1.87
Cafeterias	3.60– 8.75
School Lunch	5.45–15.00
College Dormitories	3.38– 9.07
Hospitals	4.76

As might be expected, productivity per employee varies tremendously with the volume of sales. In the restaurant, at least, there seems to be no point of diminishing returns

Table 14.3   Breakdown of Payroll by Function—Ratios to Total Payroll, 1975

Functions	California Restaurants			Table-Service Restaurants United States 1975
	Full-Service Dinner Houses	Coffee Shops		
		All	Net Income	
Service	32.1%	37.6%	36.4%	30.6%
Bartenders	11.4	8.6	9.7	8.3
Preparation	25.2	30.9	30.6	25.6
Sanitation	10.0	5.2	5.5	7.6
Administrative and general	19.6	15.8	16.0	23.3
Other	1.7	1.9	1.8	4.6
TOTAL	100.0%	100.0%	100.0%	100.0%

as regards the amount of sales that can be produced per employee. Restaurants that have sales volumes of $100,000 per year have an employee productivity of usually less than $10,000. When the sales volume increases to $500,000 per year the productivity per employee more than doubles and can be as high as $25,000. For those restaurants that do 1 million dollars in sales (there are many around the country) sales volume per employee usually exceeds $25,000. In those restaurants doing over 2 million dollars per year in sales, the average productivity per employee reaches $38,000 and up.

Labor Analysis, a Division of Labor

For many restaurants and cafeterias labor costs can be divided into three parts: one-third direct preparation labor, one-third service, and one-third supervision, sanitation, and cleaning. These ratios vary with the restaurant style of operation (e.g., a coffee shop, dinner house, or fast-food operation) and with the area in which the establishment is located. Table 14.3, taken from a study by Laventhol and Horwath, shows the breakdown of payroll by function for the year 1975.[1]

In this breakdown the service function in restaurants across the country was about 31 percent of the total labor cost. Food preparation took about one-fourth of the total, while sanitation, administrative and general labor costs consumed about 30 percent of the total labor cost. The coffee shop manager, for example, would be interested mainly in how the breakdown of service preparation and administrative labor costs compared with those of other coffee shops in the area. A full-service dinner house man-

ager would see that about 11 percent of the total labor costs went to bartenders, and 10 percent for sanitation (about double that for coffee shops).

WORK SIMPLIFICATION QUESTIONS

Work simplification is a frame of mind and a procedure of analysis. Analysis of a job or group of jobs for the express purpose of increasing efficiency is properly called work simplification. Work simplification asks:

1. **Can it be eliminated?**
   Will the use of a wall-washing machine make it unnecessary to wash walls by hand? Will the use of a rinse injector in the dish machine eliminate time-consuming stain removal from serving trays? Will the use of a wetting agent eliminate toweling of silverware?

2. **Can it be combined?**
   Can the night clerk do food and beverage auditing? Can the clerk act as night engineer also? Can bellpersons do maintenance and repair work? If the partitions are cut out of the front office, can one employee do several jobs during slow periods?

3. **Are there unnecessary delays?**
   Is service delayed by waiters piling up at the service bar? Is there a delay in getting the food from the kitchen to the pantry? Are rooms unavailable because they are not made up by the housekeeping department?

---

1. Laventhol and Horwath, *California Restaurant Operations, 1976,* Los Angeles, 1976.

Figure 14.7   Conventional Shelving Layout
(71+ Sq. Ft. of Storage Capacity)

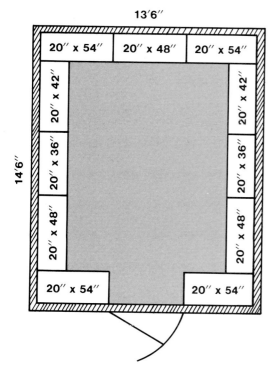

Figure 14.8   New Movable Aisle System
(111+ Sq. Ft. of Storage Capacity)

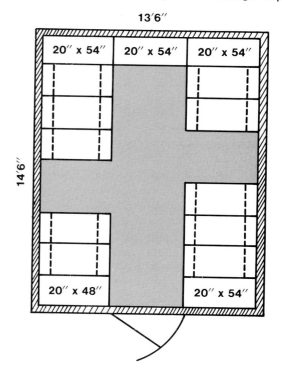

4. Is there misdirected effort?

Can frozen orange juice be profitably used in place of fresh oranges? Can a conveyor belt (instead of muscle power) be profitably used in carrying food and dishes? Can a kitchen be steam-cleaned rather than hand scrubbed?

5. Are skills used properly?

Does the janitor use the proper stroke in mopping? Might the high school graduate working as a dish attendant be more effectively used in a higher-level job? Are you using a highly paid cook to do clean-up work that can be done by a lesser paid employee?

6. Are employees doing too many unrelated tasks?

Are we reducing the effectiveness of the host or hostess by requiring that person to take phone reservations? Are we using the assistant manager as a clerk rather than as an executive? Does our chef have too many personnel duties to perform that could be done by the personnel manager? Are you spending too much time doing club work on company time?

7. Is work spread unevenly?

Are the dishwashers finished and standing idle while the kitchen clean-up person never finishes? Are the housepersons overworked while the cleaners take it easy? Does the service elevator operator get the same rest periods as the desk clerks?

Looking at an Old Problem in a New Way

Experience and tradition often crystallize the way one looks at things. A fresh perspective or view by an outsider can often restructure the way anything is seen. A good example of this is the traditional storeroom layout. Seen below is a conventional shelving layout of a storeroom that has shelving arranged around the perimeter of the room. The conventional layout provides seventy-one square feet of storage capacity as seen in figure 14.7.

The same space can be seen differently (see fig. 14.8). In this instance movable shelving has been substituted for fixed shelving. The result: 111 square feet of storage capacity versus the 71 square feet in the conventional layout.[2]

What Is Efficiency?

An engineering definition of efficiency is simple enough:

$$\text{efficiency} = \frac{\text{output}}{\text{input}}$$

---

2. Adapted from a talk by J. Roger Sanderson, Market Forge Company, *The Consultant* (International Society of Food Service Consultants), April 1977.

In other words, efficiency is the percentage of productivity that results from the amount of effort involved. The formula can be applied to mental effort as well as to physical effort and is useful in speaking about efficiency. In relating it to human effort several qualifications must be made. The human machine must rest, must be inspired, must have goals, must think highly of itself to be creative, must rest periodically, and can be thrown out of alignment easily.

It has been said that the mind is not used to more than 10 percent of efficiency. In physical terms perhaps this is true, and any effort or technique that will increase the efficiency of the mind should probably be considered. Philosophers and religious leaders have struggled with the problem of increasing human mental efficiency over the centuries, and much of what they advise is useful in the business world. The Greek emphasis on a balanced life is sound for most people, although we find people like Elsworth Statler, one of the geniuses in the hotel field, whose interest and energies were focused on the hotel business in a way that would be considered "unbalanced," according to some standards. He was able to get along on three or four hours of sleep a night, which increased his creative hours.

Caesar Ritz was a perfectionist in a field in which perfection is dangerous. In times of stress he would add to his stress by insisting upon perfection and paid the penalty by spending the last years of his life in a state of depression.

Most of us should balance rest with activity, and we should offset the frustrations usually found on the job with "reward" activities outside of business hours. Each person must follow a cycle of activity that is unique to that individual to obtain maximum performance. We need rest pauses and should encourage coffee breaks or their equivalents in establishing work schedules for employees. We need to gain satisfactions off the job such as bridge playing, golf, tennis, and travel in order to reintegrate the ego after the frazzling experiences on most jobs. Whatever is said about human efficiency must be stated in terms of the individual psyche, at least to some extent, but there are wide areas where efficiency can be increased.

Rest Before You Get Tired

Since the hotel and restaurant business can be a stress business, management must be sensitive to those cues indicating that stresses are piling up. The tired person cannot handle new problems or new ideas with equanimity or enthusiasm. Avoid letting situations develop to the point where stress makes rest absolutely necessary. Conferences usually should be scheduled in the morning when people are fresh. Tough problems should be tackled when a person is at peak level. For most people this is in the morning, but some people don't really get wound up until late in the day.

When the individual organism begins to lose its alacrity in response, it is time to rest and replenish. This can be done by a change of work, a change of pace, a change of focus. Do not build up a debt of energy by overworking. Recovery time varies with the individual, goes down with age. The person who works himself to the bone is maltreating not only self but the business as well, for that person's decisions will be less effective and relations with other people, guests, and employees less than optimal. A fifty- or sixty-hour week is fine for someone who has a variety of challenges, is highly motivated, can move in and out of an environment at will. The executive who is conducting business at a cocktail party is not really working in the sense of the paid manager who is on the floor of the restaurant or in the hotel lobby. Many studies show that for most routine jobs forty or forty-two hours a week are about maximal for maintaining efficiency. Hours worked beyond this level mean a fast drop-off in productivity. When exhaustion appears, extreme frustration comes easily and frequently, sometimes leading to panic.

Where possible, establish work schedules that reflect optimal efficiency in management and among employees. Avoid those schedules that make for exhaustion.

TIME MANAGEMENT

A supervisor or manager is more concerned with time management than the hourly worker, presumably having greater discretion as to the use of available time. The first-line supervisor may have considerably more discretion than the president. Generally speaking, as one climbs in the hierarchy more demands are made on getting one's attention, and there is less discretionary time at one's disposal. Paradoxically the higher one is in the hierarchy, the more time one should spend on planning, which requires discretionary time. Consequently, management personnel must place priorities on every effort and ration that time throughout the day, throughout the week, the month, and the year. All chores are shed which can be passed down to someone else, leaving oneself time for the more important things.

Time management is critical. It starts when the executive gets out of bed and only ends when that individual falls asleep at night. Before arriving at the office the executive probably has in mind or on paper a list of the day's hoped-for accomplishments. Each item has an order of priority (low priorities just fade away).

1. Call "Just Wonderful Tours" to set up a luncheon for possible scheduling of the tour into the hotel.
2. Meet with food and beverage department head to discuss why food costs for the month were up two points and to find ways of correcting.
3. Talk with chief engineer about tighter scheduling of the engineering crew.
4. Invite advertising agency head to lunch for discussion of brochure.
5. Dictate replies to correspondence.

The weight placed on various activities, the priorities given, are measures of the executive's judgment. Some people never have time to do the important things because of being bogged down with the unimportant ones. Business can become a millstone around one's neck.

Since time is inexpansible, control of time is perhaps more important than the control of money. If the executive's job entails constant interactions with other people, the length of those interactions must be controlled in some way. Executives have developed a number of techniques for so doing. Here are some recommended techniques:

1. Avoid casual conversation. Don't have conversation pieces around—prints, family photos, trophies, statues, or the like—that invite conversation.
2. Set up a signal system with your secretary so that the secretary calls after so many minutes, insuring that the visitor doesn't overstay the allotted time.
3. When you want the visitor to leave stand up and ease yourself towards the door. The visitor will probably stand and begin walking in the same direction.
4. Scheduling meetings in your office just before lunch or late in the day provides a good reason for breaking them off. People are anxious to get to their meal or to get home and so are less likely to overstay their time.
5. See salespeople on a particular half-day or day only (every Tuesday morning for salespeople).
6. When giving the same instructions to several employees, call them together rather than talking to them individually.
7. Transact as much business as possible over the phone rather than by face-to-face contacts.
8. During conferences defer all calls. Have your secretary get the number and call back after the conference. But do call back.

Peter Drucker, the well-known management consultant, tells his clients to plan their time rather than their work. According to him those executives who really get things done don't start with their work. They start with their time. Doing so requires perseverance and self-discipline.

Maximize Yourself

In the early 1900s, Frank Gilbreth, a former brick mason, began serious analysis of personal efficiency and pointed out that time could be saved in such mundane activities as bathing, dressing, and using the bathroom. He suggested using two bars of soap, one in each hand, to lather one's body in bathing. He also recommended buttoning the vest using two hands, one buttoning from the bottom, the other from the top. He arranged for his children to learn the Morse code while using the toilet. His "motion economy" studies searched out better ways for arranging a desk. He recommended placing items like a pen and other much-used equipment within an easily reachable distance and in a position to be easily grasped. Cabinet makers have long organized their work spaces by placing tools in fixed positions to be easily reached and placed. Why shouldn't an executive give the same attention to one's work area, the desk? Piling papers on top of a desk is not efficient because of the necessity of rifling through the entire pile to find what is needed. Files are much more efficient but take time to organize. "Take time to organize" is a key concept in motion economy and in increasing productivity.

There are dozens of techniques that can be helpful in increasing one's personal efficiency. The notebook in the pocket to keep a record of appointments, things to do, ideas to investigate can keep the mind uncluttered for absorbing new information and attacking new problems.

Bucking things that can be done by other people on down the line frees the manager for considering problems and making decisions that are appropriate for a manager. A good secretary is like a right arm and can often do the routine things better than the manager, and if that individual has talent will welcome being given routine responsibilities beyond typing and filing. Personal efficiency extends to dress, housing, transportation. If efficiency is a primary objective—and it should not always be—managers will live close to their operation, avoiding hours of commuting to and from work. They would probably wear clothes made of synthetics, such as mixtures of nylon and dacron and wool, and would probably drive compact cars. It is quite possible to travel around the world with nothing but a bag for carrying all the clothes that are needed. Some of the most successful executives in the hotel and restaurant business have 10' × 15' offices, do much of their dictating on portable machines, telephone rather than write, and have developed an efficient pattern of life without really planning to do so. As with most things in life, values soon become involved in considerations of efficiency. The manager of a resort catering to the wealthy probably needs to drive an expensive car to maintain status in the eyes of the guests. One resort manager has 150 sport jackets, each costing in excess of $200. For this individual the sport jackets may be necessary.

Over the years students in hotel classes have been asked to come up with suggestions for time management. Here is a selected list of such suggestions, some more humorous than practical.

To increase your personal efficiency:

1. Wash hair while taking a shower, instead of doing it separately and using extra soap, time, and water.

2. Live on the first floor of a residence to avoid the stairs and time in an elevator.

3. Avoid all waiting lines by avoiding rush periods at the dining halls, movies, traffic.

4. Have your papers and groceries delivered to your home.

5. Use review notes instead of reading the textbooks.

6. Eat TV dinners instead of preparing a full meal.

7. Trim your own hair avoiding cost and time at the barber shop.

8. Always make appointments to avoid waiting.

9. Take courses where you get double reward. For example, senior lifesaving badge in the swimming class in Physical Education.

10. Drink powdered milk to save refrigeration and the problem of getting fresh milk.

11. Use pullover shirts or sweaters instead of button shirts.

12. Only purchase gasoline when going by a station; always fill the tank.

13. Place articles where they are going to be used—the TV guide on top of the TV set; the dictionary at your desk.

14. When typing, use correction paper rather than erasing.

15. Cash only one large check a week instead of several; this saves time and money.

16. Get up before the rest of the family and use the bathroom at your leisure.

17. Use teflon-lined pans and pots to avoid scrubbing.

18. Never search for anything physically if it can be done by the phone.

19. Plan your day so that the major problems or hardest studies are done at the time when you are freshest; save the easier reading for a period when you are getting tired.

20. Learn to speed-read.

21. Spray your shoes with silicone spray to avoid having to shine them.

22. Buy food in large quantities and freeze if necessary.

23. Cut off the legs of old pants and make Bermuda shorts. Cut off the sleeves of shirts and make short sleeved shirts.

24. Carry a small note pad and jot down all of the ideas you don't want to forget.

25. Serve food from pans in which they are cooked. Using casserole dishes saves handling and washing.

26. Have a memo pad beside the telephone for ready use.

27. Cook all foods on top of stove instead of oven, saving time and fuel cost.

28. Arrange dresser drawers so that the most used items are in the top drawer.

29. Arrange your clothes in the closet according to those used the most. Clear out closet of clothes that are out of season.

30. Make clear notes the first time for lectures or use portable tape recorder.

31. Get up when the alarm goes off instead of fighting it.

32. Get your auto keys out before arriving at the car or at a door so as not to have to wait.

33. Do assignments after they have been discussed in class. Don't waste time puzzling over a poorly organized textbook.

34. Live as close to the campus as possible.

35. Make a list each morning of things to be done for the day.

In glancing over these guidelines to efficiency it quickly becomes obvious that efficiency can become not only a way of life but can develop into fanaticism. Recommendations such as the above are anathema to one who pictures oneself as the gentleperson searching for the well-rounded life, who may feel that the behavior recommended would mechanize life to the point where the person becomes a machine. People, they say, should take time to smell the flowers. Well and good, but if things can be done efficiently, things that are valued, more discretionary time is left to do as one pleases. Of course, it may be more efficient to live in a monk's cell and wear a burlap bag, but who wants to? It is more efficient to drive a Volkswagen than a Cadillac, also more dangerous in case of an accident. It is more efficient to live on bread, milk, and vitamin pills, but probably not as pleasing to most. It is more efficient to limit all interviews to, say, ten minutes, but perhaps not so enjoyable. Everything said about efficiency must be framed in light of the individual needs and values, not forgetting the reactions of associates and members of the family.

The story is told of the visitor who questioned an Indian sitting by the side of the road day after day:

Visitor: What are you doing sitting by the side of the road all day?
Indian: Why do you work hard all day?
Visitor: So that I can build up security and retire.
Indian: I've already retired.

To win at any game usually requires complete immersion, doing those things that must of necessity be done in order to win. If one wants to become efficient and productive one has to change one's life-style accordingly. Something is given up and something is gained—the old "trade-off" game.

The executive on the job quite naturally wants to make the work accomplished as productive as possible, still leaving room for the amenities of life. As an organized person, the individual organizes a desk in an executive manner, placing materials most frequently used closest at hand. In other words files that will be used most frequently are those closest to the desk and chair. The use of a telephone tickler system saves time, and having a desk facing the door so that visitors can be readily seen makes good sense. It is sometimes useful to have a few chairs around so that small conferences can be called extemporaneously in the office. It also makes good sense to arrange the day's work so that those efforts that require the greatest mental alacrity are done when the person is at peak mental level. Some people are brightest in the morning, others in the evening or at other times.

It makes for greater productivity to go through all the mail at once, think about it, and answer as much as can be done quickly by transcribing it for the secretary to do later. A secretary whose time is less valuable than that of the executive, should open all mail and lay it out on the executive's desk. Let a travel agent make most travel arrangements; it is the job of a specialist, one that costs the traveler nothing. Have tickets for travel mailed rather than having to pick them up at the travel agency. To avoid delays in reaching others by phone try to schedule phone calls for less busy times of the day (other than 10–11:30 A.M.).

Efficiency in the Kitchen

The principle of examining the way things are done to see if the procedures can be improved applies especially to the kitchen, where hand work reigns supreme. The general principle, "put things on wheels," has several applications. A cart can be used to collect soiled pots and pans for delivery to the pot and pan sink. The clean ware can be distributed to the various kitchen stations using the cart. Staples such as flour, rice, and sugar can be placed in bins having attached wheels. Many of the heavy pieces of cooking equipment, such as gas-fired broilers and ranges, can be placed on wheels so they can be moved readily and the spaces behind them cleaned easily.

If there is a continuous flow of anything from one point to another consider the conveyor belt. Such belts are widely used in cafeterias for moving soiled ware from the dining area to the dishwashing room. The conveyor belt is used to transport plated food from kitchen to dining area in some restaurants, two examples being the Brasserie and the Trattoria, in New York. Prepared food, plated and covered, moves on the top part of the belt to the dining area. Soiled ware is returned to the kitchen via the lower part of the continuous belt. An electric eye automatically stops the belt if plated food is not taken off the belt before it reaches the turn-around point.

With imagination standard kitchen equipment can be given multiple use. For example the french fry cutter can be used to cut carrot sticks, celery, and apples. A butter slicer can be used to slice bananas and eggs. The pastry blender will cut and slice hard cooked eggs. The slicer can be used to cut bread if the bread is frozen. A pastry wheel is useful in marking a sheet cake for slicing. A no. 2 can with one end removed can be used as a cutter for stamping out hamburger buns. The same can if squeezed into an oblong shape will stamp out hot dog buns. A pitcher or a bent no. 10 can could be used for pouring batter into muffin tins. Hamburger patties portioned with the use of a scoop can be flattened with the bottom of a can that has been dipped in cold water (two cans make it possible to use both hands at the same time). If ground meat is spread over the entire surface of a shallow pan it can be flattened with a rolling pin and waxed paper then cut into squares for hamburgers. Counter pans can be used both for cooking such items as macaroni and cheese and as a serving utensil.

The pastry bag can be used for stuffing eggs, celery, and other items.

Organize, Organize, Organize

Many kitchen tasks can be done more efficiently if greater thought is given to organization. The breading of fish, scallops, or other items may be done faster if a team of two or three people work together at it. With a team, one member can keep a hand wet and sticky doing the wet part of the job while the others do the tasks that require relatively dry hands. When one individual does the complete task of breading, one hand can be the "wet hand," the other the "dry hand." Salad making can sometimes be done more efficiently by a team, members passing the salad along, each contributing something. Sandwiches can be made eight or twelve at a time by spreading all of the bottom slices at one time. The filler is then added all at one time. Finally the tops are all placed on the bread and the sandwiches are sliced at one time. To speed the operation both hands can be used to add ingredients, such as ham or cheese slices, rather than having one hand hold the ham while the other deals the slices out onto the bread. Sandwiches can be made thirty-six at a time, in rows of four each and piled three deep, each pile sliced together.

Instead of fighting to free gelatin desserts and salads and having to warm the sides by immersing the container in water or by using a knife to slice around between the food and the container, grease the container with cooking oil. Also oil the sides and bottom of pans in which noodles, spaghetti, rice, or apples are cooked. The oil prevents them from boiling over and from sticking to the pan.

Oftentimes a simple little trick will speed a task and make it much easier. For example, when weighing out ingredients for any recipe simply add the ingredients onto the scale, piling one ingredient on top of the next. Add the total weight rather than weighing each item separately and combining later.

Items such as raisins, cranberries, and liver, which are difficult to grind in a meat grinder, can first be frozen. The experienced cook knows that the easiest ways to remove skins from tomatoes is to dip them in boiling water or to apply a little heat to the surface over a gas flame.

Specialization of Function

In heavy industry the attempt has been made to specialize every job so that each employee does only a limited number of tasks and makes few decisions. The employee on the assembly line epitomizes this viewpoint, perhaps putting a few nuts and bolts on a part of a piece of equipment as it passes. Productivity is increased and for some employees such work is probably satisfactory. One of the appeals of the hotel and restaurant business is that there are few such specialized jobs to perform: employees are able to start and complete a task such as greeting a guest and rooming the guest, taking an order and serving a meal and collecting for it. This is one of the several appeals that the hotel and restaurant field has for employees and it should not be aborted. There are many jobs, however, that can be more highly specialized than they are at present. Many jobs, especially those in the kitchen, have too much time wasted in the "make-ready and the put-away" phases of the task, too little time devoted to the production phase. For example, the time needed to make five apple

pies is almost as great as that needed to make twenty-five apple pies because of the make-ready and the put-away aspects of the job. Why not make twenty-five pies or fifty pies, if they can be frozen and used later?

Why should each cook go to the storeroom to get the ingredients for one recipe, return to the kitchen, and make up the recipe? Why not have the storeroom person assemble all ingredients for recipes, assemble the pans to be used for the recipe, and wheel them to the cook? This is done in many establishments and is worth considering even in relatively small operations. The storeroom person who does the receiving, sorting, and issuing can also do the recipe assembling. That person may also be called upon to be a kitchen utility person or even a cook if the operation is small. By using the storeroom assembly method, or "ingredient room" assembly method as it is called in some hospitals, desirable specialization of function is achieved.

Avoiding Bottlenecks in Service

As with any company offering service to the public, a hotel or restaurant will find that bottlenecks can occur, just as they do in the assembly of an automobile or the manufacture of any product. Speed of a cafeteria line, for example, depends upon the speed of the cashier. Other bottlenecks in cafeteria service can be created by improper layout or a pileup due to excessive work being done at one station. Carving or sandwich-making stations are likely to cause delays in the serving line.

The front desk of a hotel is a critical service spot where the tired guest is likely to appreciate the fastest service possible. To expedite the check-in procedure most of the clerical work can be done beforehand by preregistration. The guest folios can be completely filled in so that registration procedure for the guest consists of merely the signing of the person's name. In effect, the hotel has transferred some of the work of registration from the guest to hotel personnel. The registration procedure is cut from several minutes to less than a minute. Preregistration is a much-appreciated guest service. To make the registration procedure even more pleasant for the guest, some hotels have installed stools or chairs for guests use while registering.

"Batching" Work

In doing almost any work, a warm-up period is required of the workers before they hit their stride. A worker is able to maintain that stride for varying lengths of time, then there is a fall-off in quality or quantity. When a worker is required to shift from task to task a natural loss

Figure 14.9   Flow Process Chart (Otis-type)

O—An operation: frying, warming, carving, boning, totaling a check, etc.
T—Transportation: carrying a tray, moving dirty dishes, trucking dirty linen, lifting a pot, etc.
I—Inspection: a food checker inspecting portions, a floor housekeeper checking a room for readiness, a storekeeper weighing in fresh food, etc.
S—Storage: linen in a closet, food in bins, glasses in a rack, meat in a refrigerator, etc.
D—Delay: a bottleneck caused by crowding at the service bar, a waiting period for clean glasses, etc.

Travel in feet	in seconds	Symbol					Description
		O	T	I	S	D	
		O	T	I	S	D	
		O	T	I	S	D	
		O	T	I	S	D	
		O	T	I	S	D	
		O	T	I	S	D	
		O	T	I	S	D	
		O	T	I	S	D	
		O	T	I	S	D	
		O	T	I	S	D	
		O	T	I	S	D	
		O	T	I	S	D	
		O	T	I	S	D	

	Totals

O
T
I
S
D

Summary

of efficiency is experienced. The secretary who is typing a letter and must answer the phone loses typing continuity and rhythm. The manager who is calling a series of purveyors for quotations loses efficiency when interrupted by the appearance of a cook or someone else. Every task can be "batched" to make a unit that can be performed efficiently by a person. What constitutes an optimal size varies with the individual, but there are guidelines. Some jobs need to be divided and made more specialized; others need to be enlarged to hold worker interest, create a sense of responsibility and anticipation, and avoid monotony. What is monotonous to one person is challenging to another.

One employee can prepare all the potatoes and do all of the baking for several operations more efficiently than several employees in different locations can ready the same amount in smaller quantities. "Batching" accounts for the desirability of situating much of the preparation and cooking of food in the central commissary if the operations being served are not too large. Centralized commissary preparation offers no advantage when it serves food-service units that are large enough to be individually efficient. Commissary operation is advantageous when it serves a number of smaller operations, each of a size not efficient in itself. It would make no sense to

prepare food centrally and deliver it to a restaurant that has over 1 million dollars in sales and is large enough to prepare its own food on a production basis.

"Batching" is a practice that can be applied to almost any work to be done; for example, the manager who must plan an employee schedule, order food for the next day, and dictate letters in answer to the current day's mail is usually well advised to schedule available time so that each of these tasks is done as a unit rather than having them interspersed throughout the day. The manager would try to do all dictation in the morning to get the secretary started, might do all of the food purchasing after 6:00 P.M. when the purveyors would be less busy and could take calls personally, and could make up the employee schedule in the afternoon during a break following the noon rush period.

THE FLOW PROCESS CHART

To detect bottlenecks and improve efficiency in work flow, special tools have been devised. One of the best known of these tools is the process chart, a means of identifying each step in a process or activity. Five symbols, standardized by practice, are used as signs for (1) opera-

Figure 14.10   Otis-type Process—From Pantry to Guest

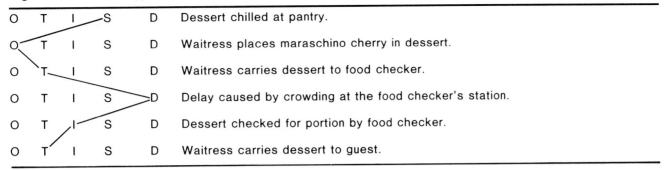

O	T	I	S	D	Dessert chilled at pantry.
O	T	I	S	D	Waitress places maraschino cherry in dessert.
O	T	I	S	D	Waitress carries dessert to food checker.
O	T	I	S	D	Delay caused by crowding at the food checker's station.
O	T	I	S	D	Dessert checked for portion by food checker.
O	T	I	S	D	Waitress carries dessert to guest.

Figure 14.11   Work-Process Chart

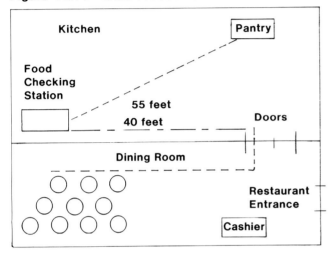

tions, (2) transportation, (3) storage, (4) inspection, and (5) delay. In analyzing the flow of food through a kitchen to the guest or for any other work process, the symbols serve as a simple recording device. The Otis-type flow chart is shown as figure 14.9.

The process of getting a fruited gelatin dessert from a pantry to a guest might proceed as shown in figure 4.10.

The *flowing* of the dessert from the pantry to guest can in this way be followed in a systematic way and a more satisfactory analysis made.

To clarify this problem of the movement of the dessert from the pantry to the guest, a diagram of the process can be made showing the routes followed and the number of steps taken between key points. For example, we might find by plotting the route over which the dessert is taken that our diagram or work-process chart resembles that in figure 14.11.

In this case the diagram suggests that either the food checker be moved or that the doors between the kitchen and dining room be moved.

The recommendation for making such changes, would of course, be dependent on other factors not considered in the diagram. The flow of food from other kitchen stations such as the range and soup station would need to be considered. The heat conditions at the present checking station and the proposed one would also make a difference in our decision. Similarly, costs and the way the personnel involved respond to the change would play important parts in the problems.

TIME AND MOTION STUDY

Time and motion study is an attempt to simplify work and reduce effort. A job or series of tasks is broken down into the elementary motions performed by the worker. By carefully analyzing the motions used and the time spent in making them, it is often possible to eliminate some of the motions, to substitute more economic ones, and to rearrange the sequence of motions so that the work is simplified or made easier to perform.

Some principles on which such study is made include:

1. Both hands should begin motions simultaneously. This increases rhythm and eliminates loss of time due to overlapping motions.

2. Both hands should complete motions simultaneously.

3. Both hands should not be idle at the same instant.

4. Work should be so arranged that the arms will move in opposite and symmetrical directions. This gives the worker balance that is lacking when both arms move in the same direction.

5. The fundamental motions of a task should be limited to as few as possible.

6. The motions made should be within the radius of the worker, thus should not be unduly fatiguing. This precludes reaching in any direction so far as to necessitate bending the trunk.

7. The hands should be relieved of work that can be done by the feet, provided there is other work for the hands to do at the same time.

8. The faster motions should be taught first.

9. Sequences of motions should be arranged so as to build a rhythm and to use curved-line rather than straight-line movements.

10. The uses of the different parts of the body should be restricted to as few as possible.

It is apparent that the principles listed above will apply most readily to jobs that are repetitive and include only a small number of tasks.[3]

Methods study is particularly appropriate to room cleaning. Work flow and individual cleaning tasks can be examined, and almost invariably, improved methods developed. Not unusually, as much as one-third of the cleaning time can be lopped off. Better equipment can be suggested, work-paths rerouted, and dozens of steps saved. The principles of motion economy applied to separate cleaning tasks results in additional labor cost reduction.

The Cleaning Sequence in a Motel Room

The general sequence of work done by the cleaner in a motel room proceeds as follows:

1. Makes bed

2. Cleans up loose trash and empties ash trays into waste basket

3. Cleans bathroom, doing the floor last

4. Cleans Venetian blinds

5. Wet-mops floor

6. Arranges furniture, lays rug, and finishes

This sequence of work has been common in the hotel and motel for a number of years. Methods study engineers have developed refinements in the sequence of work and several improvements in the work methods used. Classic work in methods study applied to room cleaning was done in 1948 at Chicago's Sherman Hotel. Members of the staff of the Motion and Time Study Laboratory of Purdue University, stopwatches in hand, timed every task in the job of preparing a guest room. An ingenious camera that took one picture every second was trained on the cleaner at work. When the cleaner who was performing the work opened the door the camera duly recorded it as taking five seconds. When she walked twenty feet to the bathroom an assistant wrote on his clipboard "20 feet." The cleaner left her equipment, then turned and went into the bedroom where she left the bed linen on a stool at the foot of the bed.

As she continued cleaning, the university observers and the camera noted everything she did to the room: "To window—open window—to bed—strip bed—pick up soiled linen—to bath—open door"—and so on until the room was neat and ready for the next guest.

Later the film was developed and analyzed. Besides describing every component of the job the staff plotted a track of the cleaner's movements around the bed, around the room, and around the bathroom. It was duly noted that it took 302 seconds to make the bed, 234 seconds to sweep and carpetsweep the rug, 248 seconds to dust the furniture, and 171 seconds to hang the shower curtains.

After everything had been reduced to seconds, totals were taken. It took the maid 1,835 seconds to prepare the room. She had walked a total of 439 feet.

The Purdue team then set about to find an improved way of doing the job. They were relatively certain of success, for their guiding philosophy is fixed: "There is always a better way." Although they knew practically nothing about housekeeping as such they did know a great deal about how to ask questions. Their question-asking had helped some of them to find better ways of doing everything from stacking tobacco in the field to typing letters. Also, they could draw on the work of at least three studies that had already been made on bedmaking.[4]

Systematically they examined each task to see if it could be done with less energy, less time. They asked themselves "can it be combined, can it be eliminated?" They were interested in the overall pattern of the work, the sequence in which tasks were done.

To aid in the analysis every step in the room-cleaning process was itemized and listed on a chart. Each part of the process was timed. The times and the distances walked by the cleaner as she went about her work were included in the chart.

Later when improved methods had been introduced, the new room-cleaning method was plotted on another chart. The charts, one for the old method and one for the new method, are shown together as figure 14.12. Both can be profitably studied. An insight into methods study can be gained that cannot otherwise be acquired.

To further aid in the analysis the cleaner was "tracked" as she went about her work. Her path of work was plotted and a drawing made of the bedroom and bathroom. The old and new track of work taken by the cleaner as she cleaned the bathroom is shown in figures 14.13 and 14.14. The old method shows a surprising number of trips around

3. For a comprehensive discussion of work analysis see Edward A. Kazarian, *Work Analysis and Design for Hotels, Restaurants and Institutions* (Westport, Conn.: Avi Publishing Co., 1976).

4. "Easier Homemaking," Station Bulletin 529 (Lafayette, Ind.: Purdue University, 1948).

Figure 14.12 Hotel Sherman Memo-O-Motion Chart

Maid Cleaning Room 1018-3/4/48
Date of Analysis 3/9/48

	Old Method				Proposed Method	
Distance	Time	Explanation		Distance	Time	Explanation
6	5	Open door			5	Open door
20	1	To bath		20	8	To beside bed
8	2	Open door			29	Remove soiled linen
10	2	Leave equipment inside			29	Remove soiled linen
7	4	To foot of bed			7	Place soiled linen in cart
	1	Put linen on stool			7	Lay clean linen on bed
	1	To window—right		10	4	To window—left
	8	Open window		10	6	Open window
	2	To window—left		20	8	To window—right
20	6	Open window			6	Open window
3	3	To bed		5	4	To bath with cart
	29	Remove soiled linen		5	6	Place equipment in bath
80	29	Remove soiled linen			4	Gather soiled towels
	5	Pick up soiled linen			2	To cart
	2	Open door			4	Dispose of soiled towels
80	1	Inside bath			2	To bath
	4	Picked up soiled linen			62	Clean tub and rags
	31	To linen closet			60	Clean walls
6	10	Dispose of and pick up linen			50	Clean sink
	31	To bath			40	Clean toilet
	7	Get equipment			40	Clean floor
	3	To tub		5	2	To cart
	93	Clean tub		5	5	Get shower curtain, towels, and stool
	78	Clean walls			2	To tub
	60	Clean sink			15	Place bath towels
	40	Clean toilet			85	Hang shower curtain
	53	Clean floor				Gather equipment
20	6	To foot of bed		5	5	To cart
	5	Get stool and towels		16	5	Place equipment on cart
20	10	To bath			5	Pick up sweeper and rags
	15	Place bath towels			6	To bed
	171	Hang shower curtains			217	Make beds
	4	Gather equipment		10	4	To window—left
20	8	To foot of bed			57	Clean window and blind
	5	Store equipment		12	5	To window—right
	392	Make beds			47	Clean window and blind
6	3	To equipment		5	2	To equipment
20	8	To foot of bed			200	Dust room
	5	Store equipment			150	Sweep rug
	392	Make beds			5	Pick up equipment
6	3	To equipment		5	2	To cart
	14	Get equipment		15	5	Place equipment on cart
10	4	To window—left			6	Out door
	57	Clean window and blind			3	Close door
12	5	To window—right		**148 feet**	**1218 seconds**	
	47	Clean window and blind				
12	4	To window—left				
	4	Pick drapes off floor				
30	20	To door				
	7	Put out soiled linen				
30	6	To window—left				
	4	Pick up broom				
	234	Sweep and car. sw. rug				
	248	Dust furniture				
	3	Pick up stool in bath				
15	5	To bed				
	10	Dust stool				
18	5	To bath				
	7	Gather equipment				
6	13	To door				
	3	Out door				
439 feet	**1835 seconds**					

Analysis by M. E. Mundel and the staff of the Motion and Time Study Laboratory of Purdue University.

Figure 14.13 Cleaning Bathroom—Old Method

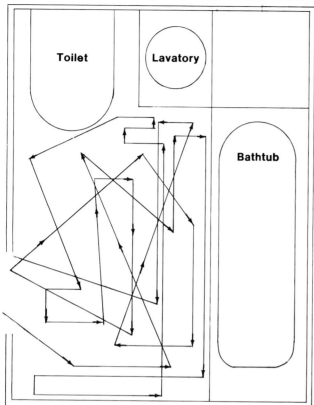

Figure 14.14 Cleaning Bathroom—New Method

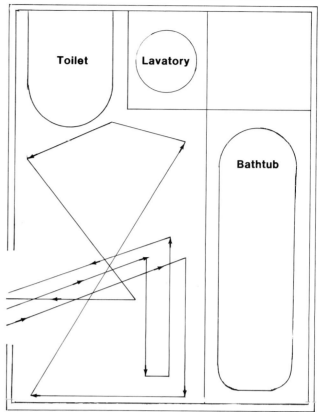

the bathroom. The World War II phrase "Is this trip necessary?" was most appropriately asked by the researchers. The new method of cleaning the bathroom shows that a good many trips around the bathroom were eliminated.

Savings on details add up. Here is an example. The cleaner used a rag to wash the lavatory bowl, tub, and the wainscotted walls of the bathroom. When she was through she washed it out in the lavatory—necessitating an additional bowl-washing. The motion-study staff recommended carrying it dirty to the next room to be cleaned and washing it in the dirty bowl before beginning the cleaning there.

A suggestion for sweeping and dusting the room was to start in the farthest corner, work back, making sure that each stroke barely overlapped with the previous one. Much time is wasted in haphazard sweeping and dusting.

The Purdue study results: A new method that took 1,218 seconds.

With no new equipment the work was simplified so that the time was cut by one-third. The number of feet the maid walked was reduced from 439 to 148.

How to Make a Bed

Most of us make a bed by putting on the first sheet, tucking it in on the sides and mitering it on the corners at the foot of the bed. We repeat this with the second sheet, the blanket and the spread. Each piece of linen requires our running around the bed at least once. The track we make is similar to the one shown as the old method in figure 14.15. Time for this method was six minutes, thirty-two seconds.

The new way of making beds entails but 1.75 trips around the bed. The diagrams (fig. 14.15) show the old and new process. The major difference between the old and new methods is that all of the linen is placed on the bed at once, all adjusted at one time at each of the four corners of the bed. The head is made completely before anything is done to the foot.

A few of the steps in the new method are pictured above. The sequence of steps is as follows:

1. Standing at the left head of the bed the cleaner spreads the bottom sheet and tucks it in for the few feet closest to her. The sheet can be thrown to cover the bed and the cleaner does not leave her position to adjust the sheet at other corners.

Figure 14.15 Bedmaking Methods

Bedmaking—Old Method   Bedmaking—New Method

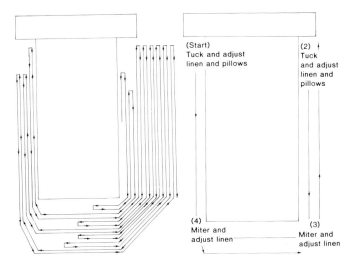

wear unevenly—shoulder, hip, and feet areas get the most wear—it is good practice to change ends frequently. It is estimated that by changing sheets end-for-end, frequently up to six months more usage will be obtained.

Seconds Translate Into Dollars

The few seconds saved on a number of details add up to minutes. Minutes saved on each room total hours by the end of the day. Add these together and in a relatively small operations these hours become hundreds of dollars. In a large operation the figures have three or more digits.

For example, if the Sherman Hotel succeeded in cutting their room cleaning by ten minutes the profit equation became: 1,360 rooms $\times$ 10 minutes saved each room = 13,600 minutes or 226⅔ hours saved each day; 226⅔ hours $\times$ 365 days = 82,733 hours saved per year; and 82,733 hours $\times$ $1.80 (cleaner's wage) = $148,919.40 saved a year.

Division of Room-Cleaning Duties

Applying industrial engineering techniques to the study of room cleaning, Holiday Inns has divided the room-cleaning jobs so that the job is done by two persons, a dispatcher and the cleaner. Dispatchers come to work an hour before the cleaners and strip the used linen from the room and leave the fresh. They also empty the trash. The dispatchers work from a large supply cart.

The cleaner enters the room with a small two-wheel cart, parks it in the room, closing the door after her. She follows a twenty-eight-step cleaning procedure that covers everything from getting the room-cleaning assignment in the morning to restocking supplies at the end of the day. The cleaning within the room starts with the bath and vanity. Then the cleaner moves on to the wardrobe rack, bed, television, nightstand, dresser, air conditioner, lights, table, and chairs. Vacuuming and raking the shag carpet are done just before leaving the room. The new room-cleaning procedure is completed in twenty-three minutes. The procedure increases the number of rooms that can be done in a day from fourteen up to about twenty or twenty-two rooms.

Bringing the cart inside the room, says the analysts, makes the worker more comfortable and saves energy, since the heat or air conditioning does not escape as before when carts were parked outside and had to be returned to frequently for supplies.[5]

2. Remaining in the same spot the top sheet is spread—but not tucked in. Tucking in the top sheet takes time and is unnecessary.

3. The blanket is spread and adjusted.

4. The spread is thrown and adjusted.

5. A pillow is picked up from the opposite side of the bed, encased, folded, and spotted in its correct place.

6. The cleaner then walks around the bed to the other side of the head of the bed and repeats these 5 steps.

7. Next she walks to the foot of the bed nearest her last standing position and miters the sheets and adjusts the blankets and spread.

8. The last step comprises doing step 7 at the other foot of the bed.

In another study the old way took five minutes and thirty-two seconds. The old method was well established in the cleaner's habit-system. The new way, which was done without training and the establishment of habits, took four minutes twenty-nine seconds—or a reduction of sixty-three seconds and at least four trips around the bed.

To speed bedmaking even more, use a contour or fitted sheet for the bottom sheet. Contour sheets being of less weight save on laundry costs when laundry is paid for on the basis of weight.

To save time and sheets have the sheets made with identical small seams. This eliminates the need for locating the top of the sheet each time it is used. More important, it provides for automatic changing of the position of the sheet since by chance one end will be at the head of the bed one time, and at the foot the next. Since sheets

5. "Industrial Engineering Comes to Holiday Inns," *Hotel and Motel Management,* January 1978, pp. 27–29. The introduction of the new method done under Mimi Scott, Innkeeper.

The small two-wheel cart used by the maid in the Holiday Inn system. The cart is wheeled into the guest room and parked. Photo courtesy of Holiday Inns.

Large cart used by "dispatchers" using the Holiday Inn system. The cart remains in the hall or outside each guest room. Photo courtesy of Holiday Inns.

Necessity for Considering Feelings and Individual Differences

Job changes inevitably include changes in human relations. The human relations changes are usually more important than the job changes. The supervisor who gets an idea that will reduce by half the movements for a particular task can, by introducing the change in a wrong way, actually decrease the efficiency of the operation. The feelings of the employee or employees who are involved must be considered as well as the facts of the job change. Employees who are invited to participate in work simplification and are consulted when job changes occur are likely to accept the change and make it work. Job changes thrust on the workers from above arouse anxieties and resentment. Later chapters will discuss more fully the means and implications of gaining employee support for new ideas.

Individual differences must also be considered in a work-simplification program. There is no best way of performing a task. People vary widely in their temperaments

and abilities. One person may enjoy a highly repetitive job and for that individual the job is efficiently set up. Another needs change and challenge. A repetitive job may need to be broken up and the worker given more responsibility. For this person the job is inefficiently set up.

Further Illustrations of Work Simplification

To illustrate the effectiveness of work-simplification studies and to give the reader an idea of the number of jobs to which work simplification can be applied, summaries of fifteen case studies conducted by Sanford E. Maus, of Harris, Kerr, Forster and Company follow.

Case One

Situation: A small dish pantry was staffed for years on the basis of service for three meals a day. Later when the morning meal was eliminated management neglected to change the work schedule.

Time and effort are saved by letting the butter on the bread pick up the sandwich spread material. Otherwise, the chopped egg or other filling must be placed on the sandwich bit by bit.

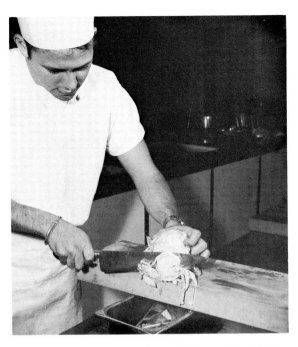

Letting gravity work for the cook. The sliced lettuce falls directly into the pan rather than having to be collected and lifted into it.

Onions cause no tears if scalding water is poured over them. They can be quartered quickly when the top and root are first sliced off.

Why use one French knife to chop onions when two will double the cutting action?

These oranges peel readily and the peels come off in large pieces because the oranges were parboiled enough to loosen the skins, not enough to cook the orange.

Cole slaw is quickly "assembled" when needed if the ingredients are prepared ahead of time. Final assembly must be done just before serving to have a crisp product.

Results of analysis: A bar graph was drawn up that plotted the work schedule and rated the amount of work done by periods throughout the day.

Photographs illustrating work simplification appear on following pages.

Case Two

Situation: A certain hotel served an average of 500 room service breakfasts from about 7 to 11 A.M. However, most of the soiled dishes did not reach the dishwashing station until about 10 A.M. In the dining room the bulk of the service took place from 8:30 to 9:30. The complete dishwashing crew reported for work at 7 A.M.

At night, after the dining room closed, only the dance room remained open. It closed about 2:00 A.M.; a complete dishwashing crew remained until that time.

Results of analysis: Employees were not needed on the morning shift until 9 A.M. On the night shift only one of the two personnel was required between 9 P.M. and 2 A.M. One-third of the employees were not needed.

Case Three

Situation: The accounting procedure of a large hotel required that restaurant checks be totaled twice by the dining room cashier and again by the night revenue controller.

Parsley can be crisped and dried quickly by rolling it in cheesecloth, placing it under running water, then ringing it out while still in the cheesecloth. Excellent for French frying.

Figure 14.16   XYZ Hotel Job Ticket

Name of Employee _____   Date _____

Time No. _____   Location _____

Time Job Commenced _____   Time Job Concluded _____

Describe nature of job briefly _____

Results of analysis: Accounting procedure was changed so that the restaurant cashier totaled checks once except in instances where a page of the restaurant control report failed to balance. The position of night revenue control was eliminated by incorporating it in day revenue control.

Case Four

Situation: A new municipal regulation required that a fire watch be maintained at all public functions in hotels of a particular city. The regulation was sprung on the management of a particular hotel in the midst of a public function. Casting about for someone to fill the watch, the management pressed into service a plumber who had not gone home. The plumber continued the job of fire watch at time-and-a-half wages. No one thought to hire less expensive labor.

Results of analysis: Another employee was hired to do the job, at a savings.

Case Five

Situation: In a particular hotel, outside contractors were previously engaged to paint blocks of rooms. Now painters on the hotel staff were doing the job.

Results of analysis: The hotel's staff required twice as many person-hours to paint a given area as did the crew of the outside contractor. Although the hotel painters received considerably less wages per hour, the total cost of painting was almost as great using hotel painters as it was to engage the outside contractor. Taking into account the fact that the hotel painters took longer and consequently reduced revenue by keeping rooms unrentable, the outside contractor may have been more economical. It was concluded that poor supervision and training accounted for the inefficiency of the hotel painters.

A simple form (see fig. 14.16) was devised that could be used for aiding supervision of all maintenance employees.

The form permits the supervisor to appraise the industriousness of the employee and to spot soldiering on the job. For example, if an employee takes an hour and a half to replace a washer in a faucet, probably one of three things is wrong. The employee is loafing; is incompetent; or the whole faucet needs replacing.

Case Six

Situation: In one hotel each cleaner's daily quota of rooms was sixteen. A check on the cleaner's performance showed an average of about thirteen rooms cleaned per day. Extra payments had to be made for rooms cleaned above thirteen.

Results of analysis: A study showed that 20 percent of the cleaners' working time was spent in getting linen from the linen room. This was caused by a linen shortage that made proper stocking of the floor linen closets virtually impossible. A par system of stocking linen and other supplies was installed for floor closets. The cleaners were then able to report to their floors and to work without interruption. Cleaners were able to do their quota of sixteen rooms and were saved considerable exasperation. Extra rooms payments were eliminated. Guests complaints subsided. Wear and tear on the service elevator was reduced, and the hotel saved 10 percent on the housekeeping payroll.

Case Seven

Situation: It was believed necessary in a certain hotel to employ three bellpersons during the morning watch. One spent 1½ hours of the morning in picking up the mail at the post office and doing duties other than bellhopping.

Results of analysis: It was found that the person who relieved the elevator operator had a lull of almost two hours at approximately mail time. This individual was assigned the job of picking up the mail and doing the other extra tasks done by the third bellperson, who was no longer needed.

Case Eight

Situation: With a problem of morning and evening rush hours, management of a medium-sized hotel considered it necessary to schedule three passenger elevators at practically all times except during the midnight shift.

Results of analysis: By computing the relationship between passenger traffic demands and potential round trips per hour, it was determined that two elevators could handle the passenger traffic. However, it was necessary at times in the evening periods to detain "up" cars two to four seconds at the ground floor to avoid dispatching sparsely filled elevators. This delay was unimportant to passengers already in the elevators, and saved considerable waiting time on the part of guests coming to the lobby.

Case Nine

Situation: Management of a hotel having two entrances stationed a doorman at the main entrance and believed it necessary to station a doorman at the other entrance (an annex entrance) at least part of the time.

Result of analysis: An analysis showed that room guest traffic was negligible at the annex entrance and that the entrance was used mainly by luncheon guests. The part-time service of a doorman at the annex entrance appeared to do more harm than good, since in the guests minds it appeared as inconsistent service.

Case Ten

Situation: The front office of a hotel appeared to be overstaffed, yet it had difficulty in getting the work done.

Results of analysis: Analysis of the jobs of room clerk and cashier showed a large portion of time lost through poor work planning. It was found that too often the room clerk and cashier wished to occupy the same space at the same time. The front office was rearranged and the assistant manager and reservation clerk were moved from a second-floor office to a space in the lobby near the front office. The reservation clerk or the assistant manager was available to cover relief and help in periods of unusual activity. Moreover, the reservation clerk could perform additional duties, such as the typing of front office accounts and the stacking of supplies.

Case Eleven

Situation: In one dining room it was found that the average production per waiter fell three covers below that which could reasonably be expected.

Results of analysis: Each waiter was given an additional day off per week. As a result each waiter could do more covers per day, and come up with average daily earnings. The hotel saved $800 per year. Its service did not suffer, and the waiters earned approximately the same in five days as they formerly did in six.

Case Twelve

Situation: A restaurant maintained a staff of five waiter's assistants. It appeared that only four were needed.

Results of analysis: It was found true that four assistants could handle all busing tasks. When one assistant left the remaining crew readily absorbed all the work.

Case Thirteen

Situation: Management of a certain hotel was very payroll conscious. It kept the hotel staff at a minimum. However, an analysis of the kitchen payroll showed excessive overtime.

Results of analysis: It was found that the present employees could not complete all the work required in normal working hours. Two employees were hired to reduce the tremendous pressure on the minimum staff. This eliminated most of the overtime payments, with a reduction in aggregate salary expense.

EFFICIENCY IN WORK METHODS

Some of the more successful cafeterias seek consistently to develop greater efficiency in labor utilization and operating practices. This section lists some efficient work methods observed in a study conducted in 1969.[6]

Rotary Assembly Table

A labor-saving device makes use of a rotary or lazy-susan table in the salad and bakery departments. The photographs show a salad preparer getting tossed salads ready, and a bakery assistant filling pie shells, both using this type of table.

With a hand movement, the preparer revolves the table, moving the plates directly in front of her, thus reducing the walk and reach requirements of this task. The various ingredients were taken from an adjacent table or cart and assembled into the final product on the rotary table.

A lazy-susan salad table tested in a midwestern cafeteria showed these advantages:

---

6. J. F. Freshwater, J. C. Bouma, and R. M. Lammiman, *Labor Utilization and Operating Practices in Commercial Cafeterias.* U.S. Department of Agriculture, *Agriculture Research Service,* Marketing Report no. 824, 1969.

Salad-making is more efficient when the rotary assembly table is used.

Bakery assistants also benefit from the use of the rotary assembly table.

1. Increased productivity of from 43 to 217 percent, depending on the type and number of salads assembled at one time

2. Fresher salads (because they are made closer to the time of sale)

3. Less operator fatigue

4. Ingredients more easily accessible

The chief disadvantages were that the table:

1. Is specialized equipment

2. Has no storage space for raw ingredients

3. Needs more floor space than conventional table

Soiled Pot and Pan Conveyor

Another labor-saving device is a conveyor that transports soiled pots from the meat and vegetable cooking area to the pot and pan washing area. An inclined skate-wheeled conveyor is connected to the back of the pot and pan sink. The meat and vegetable cook places soiled pots and pans upon the conveyor on which they are rolled to the opposite end where they are washed. The conveyor is illustrated in the photo to the right.

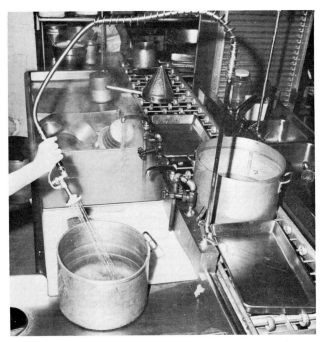

The soiled pot and pan conveyor is another labor-saving device that increases worker productivity in the cafeteria and restaurant setting.

Analyzing and Simplifying Work/291

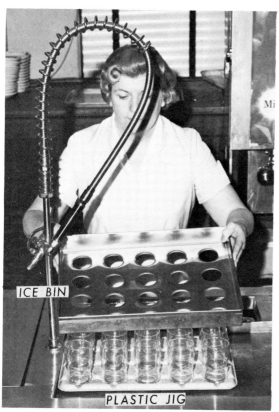

This cafeteria worker is using the plastic jig and ice bin to increase her efficiency while filling water glasses.

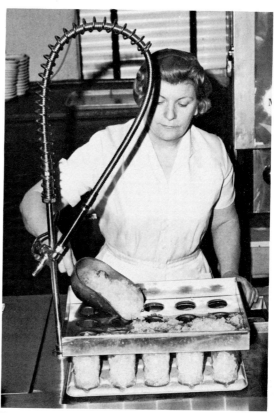

The ice is easily and quickly distributed into the individual water glasses when the ice bin is used.

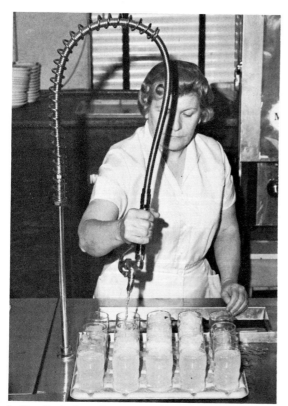

In the final step, the water glasses are filled from a water faucet with a flexible overhead arm.

Mobile Cooler Racks

Some operators have equipped the walk-in coolers and freezers with mobile racks. With mobile racks, employees can conveniently roll food productions directly from the box during the cleaning operation. This type of shelf storage was superior to the stationary type in that each item of food did not need to be handled in order to clean the walk-in box.

Filling Water Glasses

A unique labor-saving feature is used to fill glasses with ice and water. A plastic jig, which fits over the base of the glasses, is positioned over the glasses while they are in the dish machine rack. The rack is then turned over and removed leaving the glasses free-standing, mouth up. A stainless steel bin approximately three inches deep, with twenty circular openings matching the mouths of the glasses is then placed on top of the glasses. Ice is scooped into the bin and distributed into the water glasses. The bin is removed and the twenty glasses are filled by dispensing water from a flexible overhead arm.

Beverage Dispensers

One way to reduce labor costs on the serving line is to design as many self-service features as possible into the line. Two types of self-service milk dispensers were observed. In one cafeteria, milk was sold in cartons. An inclined shelf was mounted over a refrigerator base cabinet. Milk cartons were mechanized on this inclined, gravity-fed shelf. As the customer selected a carton of milk, the carton directly behind slid to the front of the shelf; thus the beverage station person was not required to move the milk cartons forward after each customer selection. In another cafeteria, milk was sold by the glass. The customer obtained a standard eight-ounce glass from a glass-rack and positioned it beneath the pouring spout. The glass was filled by depressing a button that activated an automatic dispenser.

A labor-saving method of dispensing carbonated beverages on the serving line was also observed. A three-head, carbonated beverage dispenser was located on the line. The dispensing heads were adjacent to the rail, making it a self-service unit; thus the beverage person did not have to serve the customer.

Wrapped Silver Storage

One operator reduced the travel or walking requirements of employees handling wrapped silver at the serving line by installing a roller conveyor. An inclined roller conveyor stacked with the standard cafeteria trays of wrapped silver extended from the serving line rail, through the partition behind the line, and into the kitchen. As the silver supply on one tray was exhausted, the tray was removed and placed on a tray stand. This allowed the next tray with wrapped silver to roll down the conveyor for customer use.

Order-call System

Some of the cafeterias studied offered cooked-to-order items, such as grilled steaks. One operator offering grilled steaks increased line speed by installing an order-call system. The various steak cuts were merchandised on ice in a portable food cart. The cart and a telephone of an inter-communication system were located at the entrance of the serving line. The second telephone was located at the grill station behind the hot food section of the serving line. The customer telephones an order into the grill attendant from the entrance of the serving line. The grill attendant in turn supplies the customer with an order number. When the customer arrives at the grill station on the serving line, the steak can be picked up with that order number. If the steak is not cooked upon the patron's arrival at the grill station, the customer picks up the identification number and proceeds through the serving line to a table. The grill cook signals dining room employees for delivery of the steak.

Food Preparation Hints[7]

Meat

Hamburger patties may be made in quantity using one of several methods:

1. Spread ground meat evenly over the entire surface of an 18″ × 26″ baking pan, cover with wax paper, and flatten with a rolling pin. Cut into square hamburger portions before cooking.
2. Portion ground meat with a scoop on an 18″ × 26″ baking pan. Cover with wax paper and place a second 18″ × 26″ baking pan on top. Push gently to flatten meat patties. Your second pan is ready for filling.
3. Patties can also be flattened with the bottom of a can dipped in cold water. Use both hands, a can in each hand.
4. Slice frozen ground beef for hamburger patties to save portioning and shaping. Place frozen beef in the refrigerator the day before it is to be used. It will be thawed enough to slice the next morning.
5. Place meat patties in rows three layers deep in a baking pan, separating layers with strips of aluminum foil just wide enough to cover each individual row of patties.

Cut meat loaf into individual portions before baking. Slices separate easily when cooled.

Place bacon slices on an 18″ × 26″ bun pan and cook in oven. Bacon will brown evenly without turning.

Eggs

For easier peeling, crack hard-cooked eggs when hot, put in cold water to cool, then peel.

Peel hard-cooked eggs by slipping a spoon under the cracked shell at the large end.

When opening eggs, have a pan ready in which to drop the shells. This saves rehandling the shells when you are ready to dispose of them. Break an egg in each hand simultaneously.

Baking

Mix all dry ingredients together and all liquid ingredients together before blending into each other.

When creaming butter and sugar, add some of the liquid called for in the recipe. The contents will cream faster with less sticking to the bowl.

---

7. *Koch Food Service Bulletin* no. 644, prepared by Research and Educational Department of Koch Refrigerators, Inc.

For a real time-saver, roll yeast or quick bread dough to about one-quarter-inch thickness, spread generously with softened butter, and then fold in half and cut out the rolls. When baked, the rolls are already sliced and buttered.

Roll out and bake cobbler crust on a cookie sheet and then cut into squares and place on the warm fruit, which has been cooked, thickened, and portioned into serving dishes.

Vegetables

To remove skins from tomatoes:

1. Dip them into boiling water until the skin will slip. Cool immediately by placing them in cold water. Remove the skins and place the tomatoes in the refrigerator.

2. Rub the back of a knife over the entire surface to loosen the skin.

3. Insert a fork into a firm tomato and hold it over a low flame until the skin wrinkles and splits.

When preparing lettuce for salad cups, don't cut out the core. Grasp the core firmly and twist once and it will come out rather easily. Let water run through the core hole into the lettuce and it will loosen and separate the leaves.

Hold onions under lukewarm water when cleaning and cutting. This will help you avoid discomfort and tears.

Cut unpeeled onions in quarters from top to bottom, then remove skin from quarters by pulling skin out and down.

Cooking potatoes in their jackets saves food value and prevents waste in peeling. Boiled potatoes may be peeled faster by hand than uncooked potatoes.

Gelatin

Plain gelatin does not need to be softened if there is sugar in the recipe. Simply mix the gelatin and sugar together and dissolve in hot liquid.

Gelatin desserts and salads can be removed from containers more easily if the containers have been coated with cooking oil.

Milk and Cream

When heating milk in a steam-jacketed kettle, coat the inside with butter. This will prevent milk deposits and scorching and will make the cleaning operation easier.

When whipping cream, chill bowl, beater, and cream, and the cream will whip in half the time.

Do not reconstitute nonfat dry milk solids or powdered eggs if they are to be used for cooking or baking.

1. Combine these with flour and other dry ingredients.

2. Add the liquid used in reconstituting these products with the other liquid ingredients in the recipe.

Equipment

Save time by using the correct tool.

Weigh all ingredients in a recipe to assure accurate measurements.

Where scales are not available, use only calibrated metal measuring cups and/or spoons for measuring ingredients:

1. When the recipe calls for four cups of an ingredient use the quart measure rather than measuring one cup four times.

2. Measure all dry ingredients first and you then may use the same cup for measuring shortening.

3. If, in addition to shortening, the recipe calls for molasses, syrup, or honey, measure the shortening first, then the liquids will not stick to the cup.

Use scoops for filling muffin tins, measuring sandwich fillings, serving mashed potatoes, rice, etc. To assure standardizing portions, keep records of the sizes of scoops used.

Use aluminum foil to make a tight-fitting lid on pans in which food is being cooked in the oven.

Nonelectrical equipment and parts of equipment that are small enough to fit may be efficiently washed in a dishwasher.

A pair of scissors is a useful item in the kitchen. It will come in handy for cutting such foods as meats and various vegetables for salads, and especially handy for such items as marshmallows. Dip scissors in water and the marshmallows won't stick to the blades.

Use a three-inch pastry brush for greasing pans instead of a small pastry brush.

Grind such foods as onions, meats, cheese for sandwiches, etc. Doing so will save time and give more uniform results.

1. A little butter run through the meat grinder before grinding onions, meats, cheese, nuts, or raisins, makes cleaning easier.

2. After using the electric meat grinder, put several slices of bread through the grinder. This will be an aid in cleaning fat and grease out of the grinder.

Fasten a plastic bag over the mouth of the shredder-slicer hopper to catch food as it is being cut. Fill each bag to your exact portion requirement for use when you need it.

Select the knife specifically designed for the job to be done:

1. Use a French knife and a cutting board when slicing or chopping foods by hand.

2. Use a slicing knife to slice meat.

3. Utility knives may be used for coring vegetables, peeling, etc.

Always use cutting boards for chopping foods. Never cut against your thumb.

If a knife starts to fall, watch your feet and step aside, but let it fall.

Cut through a cluster or bunch of celery stalks, carrots, weiners, pickles, etc., instead of slicing one piece at a time.

When cutting either cake or ice cream, dip the knife in hot water to make a smoother cut.

An egg slicer may be used to cut cooked carrots, potatoes, hard-cooked eggs, bananas, and other soft foods.

Use a wire whip beater to make smooth gravies and sauces.

Work Areas

Arrange the work area so that you can work without undue stretching or reaching:

1. Average reaching height is 72″.
2. Average stooping height is 28″.
3. Average surface reach: (a) close reach is 16″ to 18″, (b) maximum extended reach is 29″.

Correct working height of work tables reduces fatigue and permits an even flow of work.

1. There should be four to six inches between the work surface and the bend of the elbow of the worker.
2. The immediate work area may be adjusted to the proper height by: (a) using a two-inch wooden chop board or, (b) place a two-inch wooden chop board across a 12″ × 20″ pan (the depth of the pan will depend upon the height the work area needs to be raised).

Always work with both hands to:

1. Put lettuce on two salad plates at a time.
2. Place two biscuits on the baking pan.
3. Dish fruit or desserts; one hand positions the dish, the other dips the food.
4. Wash counter tops and dining room tables; one hand washes, the other dries.
5. Make sandwiches; one hand positions bread and moves the filled sandwiches while the other hand spreads the filling.

CONSERVING EMPLOYEE ENERGY BY PICK-UP AND DELIVERY

All of us have a finite amount of energy. If much of it is consumed in getting to and from work, how much is left to do the work? How much of a hassle is it for a particular employee to get to work and to get home again? At some locations, isolated resorts for example, employees may spend one or two hours getting to and from work even though the straight-line distance between home and work is short. Public transportation may be unavailable or the routings circuitous. The employee may be at least partially exhausted before getting to the job and then expend considerable energy in getting home. Disadvantaged employees often live on the edge of town and do not own automobiles. The hours of work may be such that public transport is available only after long intervals of waiting, or unavailable completely. How much better—if at all practicable—to have a station wagon pick up and deliver such employees as is done by numerous hotels and restaurants? Sometimes it is advisable to provide a large automobile for one of the employees who then picks up others and delivers them home as he commutes to work. Most of us have a finite supply of energy. Much of it can be consumed unnecessarily before arriving at work.

SUMMARY

Most restaurants and hotels lack system in utilizing labor and equipment efficiently. One major way to reduce labor cost is through proper scheduling. Experts feel that 50 percent of hotel jobs should be scheduled on a variable basis, but only a small percentage actually do. Scheduling practices to increase efficiency include the following: (a) schedule personnel on split shifts, (b) where possible schedule personnel irregularly to fit one pattern of work requirements, (c) use part-time personnel, and (d) use a staffing table.

Examples are available to demonstrate efficient ways to graph relations between sales per hour and number of people-hours used each hour as a tool to help management in scheduling. On the basis of published reports and surveys, standards have been established that serve as useful guidelines in undertaking work simplification. Work simplification asks: (a) Can it be eliminated? (b) Can it be combined? (c) Are there unnecessary delays? (d) Is there misdirected effort? (e) Are skills used properly? (f) Are employees doing too many unrelated tasks? (g) Is work spread unevenly?

Time management is critical for managers who must constantly place priorities on every effort and ration their time. Those chores others can handle must be passed down. Managers need to plan their time rather than their work. A number of examples are available depicting possibilities for managing one's time more efficiently.

The kitchen is a place in which considerable automation and organization can save time, effort, and money. Managers need to continually be alerted to new ideas. Specialization of function and "batching" of work are useful techniques to consider.

The process flow chart is a well-known tool to help detect discrepancies in logical work flow by identifying and analyzing each step in a process or activity. Time and motion studies can help simplify work and reduce effort by breaking down a job or series of tasks into the elementary motions performed by the worker.

The Harris, Kerr, Forster Payroll
Cost Control System

15

Chapter 1 outlined the functions of management, one of which is to systematize work where possible. Systems, of course, can be overdone. They can also guide an organization along pathways that permit repetition and alleviate confusion. The human animal likes a certain amount of routine and repetition. Systems can organize work and establish habits that carry us through the workday, simplify work, and create efficiency. A system, to be effective, should have a self-correcting device built into it, similar to a thermostat, which keeps the system on track.

The hotel and restaurant business, with its wide variations and sales volume from day-to-day, week-to-week, and throughout the year, can well use a labor cost control system, an attempt to make available the number of personnel hours needed to perform the work at hand. Without such a system either too many or too few employees are likely to be employed for the number of covers to be served or the number of guests accommodated.

A labor or payroll cost control system establishes procedures for forecasting sales so that department heads can adjust their staff schedules to meet the predicted work load. The forecast gives the employees advance notice of changes that will affect their working schedules. The longer the forecast the less accurate it is likely to be, but the more beneficial it will be to department heads and employees in setting up work schedules. The forecast can be made for a year in advance, a month in advance, a week in advance, or updated day by day. A rooms forecast is usually initiated by the reservations manager after consulting the file of reservations and adding anticipated stay-overs for each day of the forecast. The forecast is then adjusted in the light of any additional information, including the number of *no-shows* and *walk-ins* experienced in the past.

The firm of Harris, Kerr, Forster and Company, accounting specialists, has developed a labor cost control system that has proved effective in many hotels, clubs, and other institutions. It is called a *Payroll Pre-control*

System, since emphasis is placed on the forecasting and budgeting of labor requirements. Through the generosity of this firm, their system is presented here in abbreviated form.

The purpose of the system is to achieve maximum utilization of peoplepower through planning, coordination, and control of personnel. The system involves setting work standards, forecasting volume of business, and matching labor requirements with the business volume. It is a *cycle of control* since it begins with planning, then compares forecasted results with actual results, and finally arranges for corrective action. Since at least 50 percent of the jobs in the typical full-service hotel require variable scheduling of personnel, much of the savings that result from precontrol come from scheduling employees to fit the actual work loads. The determination of production standards for each job also accounts for increased personnel efficiency.

ELEMENTS OF THE LABOR PRECONTROL SYSTEM

The precontrol system has six major elements.

1. The determination of work performance standards for each job classification within a particular establishment. These standards are expressed in terms of the *physical* unit rather than *dollar* units. Examples are number of occupied rooms per employee, number of food covers served per restaurant employee, number of laundry pieces processed per laundry employee, number of rooms cleaned per cleaner. The physical unit does not change as does the dollar unit and is more reliable as a unit of measurement and control. Work standards are determined through job analysis, analysis of past performance, and comparison with established standards of employee productivity for various jobs. Any change in the job itself, of course, necessitates a review of the job standard.

The job standards are assembled in table form and show the personnel requirements by job and job group for the various normal volumes of work in a particular department. The tables are called *Range Tables of Staffing Guides at Varying Volume Levels.*

2. The consideration of each job as a unit. Every job is assigned a number that represents it alone, a particular work schedule, and a particular work area or station. Each employee is assigned a job number, and no employee can be placed on the regular payroll unless a management-approved job number is open. All jobs are classified and grouped in each department according to their degree of variability in work volume. Jobs such as cleaners, waiters, waitresses, warewashers, and bellpersons, which experience much variation in work load, are termed *prime variables* and given special attention.

3. A regular system of forecasting work loads by a forecasting committee. Work loads are forecast in three stages:
   a. By months for a year in advance.
   b. Regular weekly forecasts for the coming week.
   c. Regular daily refinements and modifications of the weekly estimates for three days in advance.

4. A formal system of accurate daily reporting of payroll by each department head. The report is a record of the number of full-time employees and hours by job classification. It does not include dollars of payroll since, again, all the standards are expressed in terms of physical units rather than money.

5. A formal system of control for the hiring and use of extra employees and overtime work. Department heads must request all overtime or extra labor before the labor is hired. The requisition itself, once approved by management, serves as authority for the payroll department to make the necessary wage payments.

6. A regular review of the results of the overall system. A daily report is made by each department head of all time worked in terms of equivalent full-time employees and by job classification or group. A summary report is then compiled at the end of each payroll period. This is sent to the general manager and all department heads. It shows the number of employees set for each department and for the hotel as a whole.[1]

The weekly report constitutes an evaluation of the results of the overall system—the number of personnel days over or under the standards set as a result of the forecasts.

The precontrol payroll system sets job standards, forecasts the number of people-days that will be needed, then reviews to see how many people-days were used over or under the forecasted needs.

From the tables and figures in this section we see the system as it operates through its paper forms. Study the forms and the comments on each. If necessary, go back to the six elements of the overall plan.

1. Table 15.1 on page 299 is the weekly report that goes to the general manager and to each department head. It is the summary sheet showing the results of the precontrol plan for each department. For example, it is seen that the front office used exactly the number of people-days as forecasted, while housekeeping used 1.4 people-days more than was budgeted. Based on this report remedial action can be taken to bring the people-days used in line with the forecasted people-days.

2. Table 15.2 (see page 300) is a job number control list. Each job has an assigned number that represents a specific work area or station, and a definite work schedule. All personnel are assigned a job number that represents their station and work schedule. Only jobs that have numbers can be filled.

3. The figure 15.1 on page 301 form is used by department heads for making all job changes. It goes to the payroll department for use in maintaining job number control. Use of the form assures that all job changes are made within the staffing tables as set up in the Job Number Control list.

4. The room occupancy forecast (table 15.3 on page 301) is usually made by the front office manager and presented to the committee that makes the weekly forecast. The form is prepared in duplicate, one copy going to the individual responsible for forecasting the number of covers to be served in the restaurant, the second going to the weekly forecast committee.

   The weekly forecast committee makes the occupancy forecast based on the additional facts they have. The adjusted forecast then goes to the payroll control office to be used in setting up the weekly volume forecast and payroll budget.

5. The daily and weekly food cover forecast (table 15.4 on page 302) is similar to the room occupancy forecast in that it is the first approximation of the business that is expected and is made by the department head, in this case usually the food controller.

---

1. Used with the permission of the Harris, Kerr, Forster Company.

The food cover forecast then goes to the weekly forecast committee and is adjusted by them. The adjusted forecast is sent to the payroll controller and posted to the volume forecast (table 15.5 on page 303) and payroll budget. Delivery of the daily forecast is made by the superintendent of service to all department heads by a specified time each day.

As with the room occupancy forecast, the forecasted volume of business is used as a basis for determining the number of employees needed.

6. The volume forecast is the summary of the room forecast and all of the food forecasts. It is made up from the room and food cover forecasts by the payroll control office. The beverage revenue forecast is made as a percentage of the food cover forecast. The percentage used is based on past experience.

This summary sheet goes to all operating department heads to help them determine their personnel requirements.

The superintendent of service sees to it that the volume forecasts are distributed to the department heads.

7. Figure 15.6 on page 304 is range tables that give estimates of the number of personnel who will be needed at varying volumes of work. The tables are used as guides in budgeting the number of personnel needed and also to evaluate performance results.

Since every hotel has a different layout and type of service, the range table must be made for the individual hotel. Work standards are developed from an analysis of past performance and reference to an established standard of employee productivity. Each department has its own range table.

8. Table 15.7 on page 304 is used by department heads in planning for their day-to-day requirements of personnel and also by the payroll controller in measuring and evaluating daily production.

These tables are developed from the range tables to show daily averages and, of course, must be prepared for the various individual departments.

9. The volume forecast and payroll budget form (table 15.8 on page 305) is a further step in payroll planning for the coming week. It is made by the payroll control office for the department heads and shows the number of covers anticipated for each day of the week and the number of personnel required to service the particular volume of business. It too is made up for the various individual departments.

10. The daily room occupancy forecast (table 15.9) is used by the department heads in planning for the day-to-day personnel needs. It is an adjusted forecast made every day for three days in advance. It is delivered to the department heads by a specified time daily.

11. A daily personnel report (table 15.10 on page 307) is a record of all time worked in terms of people-days. It is filled out by the individual department head and sent to the payroll control office. The department head posts the actual time worked in all job categories for each day. Notice that time worked is expressed in terms of people-days broken down into regular, overtime, and extra employment.

12. The extra personnel requisition form (fig. 15.2 on page 308) serves as a control on extra labor requirements and encourages planning for such labor. Before any extra employees can be hired, this form must go to the manager for approval. The approved form is returned to the department head and is that individual's authority for hiring the extra labor.

13. The requisition for overtime authorization (fig. 15.3 on page 308) is similar in purpose to the extra personnel requisition. It encourages planning and is a control in that the manager must approve overtime work in advance.

14. Figure 15.4, a summary form, is a compilation of the actual volume worked the preceding day. (See page 309.) It is made by the auditor's office. It is a breakdown by job classification or group showing the number of employees for each grouping and also the number of guests, food covers, beverage revenue, and total revenue for the hotel. It is used by the payroll control office as an overall picture of the labor results as compared with the production standards for a particular day.

15. The production analysis form (table 15.11 on page 309) is a daily record of units of output by job classification or group that shows the number of employees who were used to perform a particular volume of work. The number of employees is divided into the total volume of work for each classification and the result is the output per employee, an excellent guide for measuring performance by departments.

The operation of the Precost Control System can be traced through the use of the forms enumerated above.

It is seen that the system utilizes three agencies: the department heads who make the first forecast; the forecasting committee that adjusts and refines the forecast; and the payroll controller who coordinates the system and prepares the operating results for analysis and remedial action by general management and the department heads. The system is precontrolled in that the number of personnel who will be needed is predicted ahead of actual utilization.

The prediction proceeds by four steps:

1. A business forecast for the ensuing week is made by the department head.

Table 15.1 Summary of Departmental Payroll Comparison Reports for Week Ended June 14

Hotel

Department		Average Number of Employees on Duty		Difference Under-[Over]		Equivalent Payroll Cost
		Actual	Standard	Employees	% of Standard	
Front Office		5.5	5.5	—		
Housekeeping		22.1	20.7	[1.4]		
Food Service		14.6	15.1	.5		
Food Preparation		27.0	25.5	[1.5]		
Steward		25.0	26	1.		
Food Storeroom		2.5	2.5	—		
Food Service	Dining Room	10.2	10.2	—		
	Room Service	5.5	5.5	—		
	Coffee Shop	12.9	12.4	[.5]		
	Banquets	20.2	18.7	[1.5]		
Total Food Service		48.8	46.8	[2.]		
Beverage Preparation		7.2	7.2	—		
Lounge Service		7.6	7.2	[.4]		
Telephone		4.7	4.7	—		
All Others		47.5	47.5	—		
Totals		212.5	208.7	[3.8]		

Volume Statistics

Total Sales	$50,400.00
Occupied Rooms	2,632
Food Covers Served	10,210
Beverage Sales	$ 6,600.00

2. This forecast is adjusted by the forecasting committee.

3. Based on the business forecast and using productivity standards for the various jobs, the number of personnel needed is predicted.

4. After the forecasted period is over, the actual number of personnel used is compared with the amount that was budgeted.

Control of extra labor or overtime labor is achieved by requiring that prior approval be received from management for their employment. The total process is a continuous one, review and adjustment being built into the system. Work standards change as new methods, equipment, and layout are introduced. Labor usage is tied directly to work volume. All in all the system represents a marked advance in management in the hospitality field. While the system would not be used in its entirety in a small operation, the principles are applicable to any hospitality or institutional operation, be it a private club of 100 members, a 50-bed hospital, or a 1,000-room hotel.

A restaurant can make use of a modified form of the forecast and control system illustrated here. Each restaurant encounters factors that influence the number of patrons coming at any given time—weather, sporting events, day of the week, season, etc. The forecast precedes as in the Harris, Kerr, Forster System.

1. Last year's sales on a particular day.

2. Add to or subtract from last year's sales to account for special factors such as weather conditions, convention in town, etc.

3. Add or subtract a percentage to account for the trend of business. If sales are up, one would generally add on 10 percent to the forecast. If sales are down, the reverse would be true.

4. Schedule the number of employees needed according to the forecast.

Table 15.2	Job Number Control List

Steward

Hotel _____

Job or Clock Card Number	Job Classification	Work Area or Station	Work Schedule
220	Warewasher	Coffee Shop	7:00 A.M.– 4:00 P.M.
221	Warewasher	Coffee Shop	11:00 A.M.– 8:00 P.M.
222	Warewasher	Coffee Shop	4:30 P.M.– 1:30 A.M.
223	Warewasher, Relief	Coffee Shop	Variable
224	Open		
225	Open		
226	Warewasher	Main Kitchen	9:00 A.M.– 6:00 P.M.
227 thru 229	Warewashers	Main Kitchen	11:00 A.M.– 8:00 P.M.
230 thru 232	Warewashers	Main Kitchen	12:00 noon– 9:00 P.M.
233 thru 236	Warewashers	Main Kitchen	1:00 P.M.–10:00 P.M.
237 thru 242	Warewashers	Main Kitchen	3:00 P.M.–12:00 Mid.
243 thru 250	Warewashers	Main Kitchen	6:00 P.M.– 3:00 A.M.
251 and 252	Warewashers, Relief	Main Kitchen	Variable
253 and 254	Open		
255 and 256	Kitchen Cleaners		5:00 P.M.– 2:00 A.M.
257	Kitchen Cleaner		12:00 Mid.– 9:00 A.M.
258	Kitchen Cleaner, Relief		Variable
259	Open		
260	Potwasher	Main Kitchen	7:00 A.M.– 4:00 P.M.
261	Potwasher	Main Kitchen	1:00 P.M.–10:00 P.M.
262	Potwasher	Pastry Shop	12:00 Noon– 9:00 P.M.
263	Potwasher, Relief		Variable
264	Food Runner	Coffee Shop	6:00 A.M.– 3:00 P.M.
265	Food Runner	Coffee Shop	2:30 P.M.–11:00 P.M.
266	Runner	Main Kitchen	6:00 A.M.– 3:00 P.M.
267	Open		
268	Open		
269	Open		
270	Open		
271	Yardworker		6:00 A.M.– 3:00 P.M.
272	Yardworker		3:00 P.M.–12:00 Mid.
273	Open		
274	Silver Burnisher		7:00 A.M.– 4:00 P.M.
275	Open		
276	Kitchen Steward		6:00 A.M.– 3:00 P.M.
277	Kitchen Steward		3:00 P.M.–12:00 Mid.
278	Kitchen Steward, Banquets and Relief		Variable
279	Open		

Figure 15.1 Wage and/or Position Change

Hotel _____

Employee's Name _____ Effective Date of Change _____

The records of the foregoing named employee should be changed as follows:

	From	To	Remarks
Position	Warewasher	Kitchen Steward	
Work Area	Main Kitchen	Banquets and Relief	
Work Schedule	9:00 A.M.–6:00 P.M.	3:00 P.M.–12:00 Mid.	
Department	Steward	Same	
Job Number	226	278	
Rate	$24.80	$33.50	
Meals	2	2	

Changed:

Clock Card _____ **Earnings Record** _____ **Contract Card** _____ **ID Card** _____

Approved by:

Department Head _____ **Auditor** _____ **Manager** _____

Table 15.3 Weekly Room Occupancy Forecast for Period Ending June 14

Hotel

		Sun.	Mon.	Tues.	Wed.	Thurs.	Fri.	Sat.	Total
Permanent		108	108	108	108	108	108	108	756
Conventions	A	85	142	142	142	12	—	—	523
	B				60	60	60	60	240
	C					36	36		72
Total Conventions		85	142	142	202	108	96	60	835
Transients with Reservations		33	85	108	110	122	81	21	560
Transients w/o Reservations		18	30	45	9	40	56	50	248
Other (employees, etc.)		8	8	8	11	11	11	8	65
Total Estimated Occupancy		252	373	411	440	389	352	247	2,464
Rooms Out of Order		5	5	5	—	—	—	3	18
Rooms Vacant		183	65	24		51	88	190	598
Total Rooms Available		440	440	440	440	440	440	440	3,080
Occupancy Percentage		57.2%	84.7%	93.4%	100.0%	88.5%	80.0%	56.1%	80.0%

Table 15.4   Daily and Weekly Food Cover Forecast for Period Ending June 14

Hotel _____

	Date 8	9	10	11	12	13	14	
	Day Sun.	Mon.	Tues.	Wed.	Thurs.	Fri.	Sat.	Total for Week
Dining Room Luncheon		180	200	225	190	175	110	1,080
Dinner	400	120	150	175	160	135	290	1,430
Total	400	300	350	400	350	310	400	2,510
Room Service Breakfast	60	35	50	50	65	40	20	320
Luncheon	5	10	10	20	15	10	25	95
Dinner	20	35	45	40	50	35	45	270
Total	85	80	105	110	130	85	90	685
Banquets Breakfast	—	—	—	30	—	—	—	30
Luncheon	—	50	85	210	80	25	115	565
Dinner	—	250	120	60	170	40	630	1,270
Total	—	300	205	300	250	65	745	1,865
Coffee Shop								
Breakfast	140	220	275	290	290	250	200	1,665
Luncheon	—	290	300	300	285	260	290	1,725
Dinner	270	110	175	190	165	150	120	1,180
Total	410	620	750	780	740	660	610	4,570
Total Food Covers	895	1,300	1,410	1,590	1,470	1,120	1,845	9,630

Table 15.5   Volume Forecast for Period from June 8 **thru** June 14

Hotel _____

	Date	8	9	10	11	12	13	14	Total for Week
	Day	Sun.	Mon.	Tues.	Wed.	Thurs.	Fri.	Sat.	
Rooms Forecast Occupied Rooms		252	373	411	440	389	352	247	2,464
Occupancy Percentage		57.2%	84.7%	93.4%	100.0%	88.5%	80.0%	56.1%	80.0%
Guest Count		300	450	500	525	470	425	300	2,970
Arrivals (Rooms)		136	121	70	64	90	20	35	536
Departures (Rooms)		53	—	32	35	141	57	140	458
Food Cover Forecast Dining Room									
Luncheon		—	180	200	225	190	175	150	1,080
Dinner		400	120	150	175	160	135	290	1,430
Total		400	300	350	400	350	310	400	2,510
Room Service Breakfast		60	35	50	50	65	40	20	320
Luncheon		5	10	10	20	15	10	25	95
Dinner		20	35	45	40	50	35	45	270
Total		85	80	105	110	130	85	90	685
Banquets Breakfast		—	—	—	30	—	—	—	30
Luncheon		—	50	85	210	80	25	115	565
Dinner		—	250	120	60	170	40	630	1,270
Total		—	300	205	300	250	65	745	1,865
Coffee Shop Breakfast		140	220	275	290	290	250	200	1,665
Luncheon		—	290	300	300	285	260	290	1,725
Dinner		270	110	175	190	165	150	120	1,180
Total		410	620	750	780	740	660	610	4,570
Total Food Covers		895	1,300	1,410	1,590	1,470	1,120	1,845	9,630
Beverage Revenue Forecast Bar A		$ —	$325	$ 460	$475	$400	$400	$ 720	$2,780
Bar B		220	430	550	500	425	530	1,065	$3,720
Total Beverage Forecast		$220	$755	$1,010	$975	$825	$930	$1,785	$6,500

Table 15.6   Tentative Range Tables of Staffing Guides at Varying Volume Levels
Steward

Hotel _____

| | | | Normal Volume Range of Total Weekly Food Covers | | | | | | |
| | | | 10,000 Employees | | 9,600 Employees | | 9,200 Employees | | |
Job Classification or Group	Hours in Work Week	Upper Limit	On Staff	On Duty	On Staff	On Duty	On Staff	On Duty	Lower Limit
Warewashers	40		21.2	15.1	20.2	14.5	19.2	13.7	
All Others									
Kitchen Cleaners	40		2.0	1.4	2.0	1.4	2.0	1.4	
Potwashers	40		3.0	2.1	3.0	2.1	3.0	2.1	
Food Runners	40		1.7	1.2	1.5	1.0	1.5	1.0	
Silver Burnisher	40		1.0	.7	1.0	.7	1.0	.7	
Kitchen Stewards	40		3.0	2.1	3.0	2.1	3.0	2.1	
Total All Others			14.6	10.6	14.4	10.4	14.4	10.4	
Total Stewards			35.8	25.7	34.6	24.9	33.6	24.1	

Table 15.7   Schedule of Staffing Guides and Daily Output Standards
Steward

Hotel _____

| Normal Volume Range of Total Food Covers | | Warewashers | | All Others | | Total | |
Weekly	Daily Average	Employees on Duty	Output	Employees on Duty	Output	Employees on Duty	Output
9,600 ↑	1,371	14.5	94.5	10.4	131.8	24.9	55.0
10,000 ↓	1,430	15.1	94.7	10.6	134.9	25.7	55.6

Table 15.8   Volume Forecast and Payroll Budget for Week of June 8

Steward

Hotel _____

Food Cover Forecast for Week

	Sun.	Mon.	Tues.	Wed.	Thurs.	Fri.	Sat.	Total for Week
Main Kitchen								
Regular Covers	485	380	455	510	480	395	490	3,195
Banquet Covers	—	300	205	300	250	65	745	1,865
Total Main Kitchen	485	680	660	810	730	460	1,235	5,060
Coffee Shop Covers	410	620	750	780	740	660	610	4,570
Total Food Covers	895	1,300	1,410	1,590	1,470	1,120	1,845	9,630
Warewashers on Duty	9.5	13.8	14.9	16.8	15.6	11.9	19.5	14.6

Payroll Budget for Week

Job Classification	Planned Staff
Warewashers	14.6
All Others	110.7
Total Staff	25.3

Table 15.9	Daily Room Occupancy Forecast				
Hotel					
	Date	**June 9**	**June 10**	**June 11**	**June 12**
	Day	**Today**	**Tuesday**	**Wednesday**	**Thursday**
Previous Night's Count		263	393	435	440
Reservations		155	49	66	82
Arrivals without Reservations		38	15	—	18
Employees and Others		—	—	3	—
Estimated Departures		63	22	64	140
Total Estimated Occupancy		393	435	440	400
Occupancy Percentage		89.3%	98.8%	100.0%	90.9%
Guest Count		484	525	525	480
Comments					

Table 15.10   Daily Personnel Report

Hotel

Steward _____

Day Monday   **Date** June 9   **Signed** A. Steward
                                                                    _____
                                                                    Department Head

Job Classification or Group	Equivalent Full-time Employees (compute to nearest ⅛)				Absent with	Temporary Assignment	
	Regular	Overtime	Extra	Total	Pay	Time	Job
Warewashers							
Coffee Shop	3			3			
Main Kitchen	7	⅝	2	9 – ⅝		1	Kitchen Cleaner
Total Warewashers	10	⅝	2	12 – ⅝			
All Other							
Kitchen Cleaners	2			2	1		Vacation
Potwashers	2			2			
Food Runners	1			1			
Icemen	1	⅜		1 – ⅜			
Yardmen	2			2			
Silver Burnisher	1			1			
Kitchen Stewards	2			2			
Total All Other	11	⅜		11 – ⅜			
Total Staff on Duty	21	1	2	24			
Total Employees Off Duty	9						
Total Staff	30						

Figure 15.2   Extra Personnel Requisition

Hotel _____

Department _____

Date Extra Labor Required ___June 9___

Signed _____
      Department Head

Extra Labor Requested		Number of Employees		
Job Classification	Function or Room Assignment	Requested	Approved	Remarks
Warewashers	F.N.O.W.—Blue Room	3	2	
	(250 expected)			

Date Approved ___June 9___

Signed ____A. Manager____
      Manager of Representative

Figure 15.3   Requisition for Overtime Authorization

Hotel _____

Department ___Steward___

Time Card Number ___268___

Name of Employee ___John___

Job Title ___Potwasher___

Date Overtime Worked ___6/6/52___

State Reason in Detail for Overtime Unanticipated late business.

No. of Overtime Hours Required ___1–½___

Signed ___A. Steward___

Approved ___A. Representative___
      Manager or Representative

Began Overtime Work at ___3:00 P.M.___

Finished Overtime Work at ___6:00 P.M.___

Total Overtime Hours Worked ___3___

Overtime Hourly Wage Rate ___$3.25___

Total Overtime Wages ___$9.75___

Signed ___A. Steward___
      Department Head

Figure 15.4 Auditor's Daily Volume Statistics Report

Day _____ Date _____   Hotel _____

Occupied Rooms	
Permanent	108
Transient	268
Employees	8
Total Occupied Rooms	384
Guest Count	492
Food Covers	
Dining Room	295
Room Service	76
Banquets	332
Coffee Shop	657
Total Food Covers	1,360
Beverage Revenue	
Lounge Bar	$ 340.00
All Other	419.00
Total Beverage Revenue	$ 759.00
Total Hotel Revenue	$5,125.00

Please deliver to Payroll Controller by 12:00 noon

Table 15.11 Production Analysis for the Week Ended June 14

Hotel

Classification	Sunday			Monday			Tuesday			etc.
	Empl.	Vol.	Output	Empl.	Vol.	Output	Empl.	Vol.	Output	
Food Preparation Chefs and Cooks	10.7	880	82.2	12.2	1,360	111.4	12.5	1,465	117.2	
Pantry	6.0	880	146.6	7.1	1,360	191.5	7.3	1,465	200.6	
All Others	5.2	880	169.2	6.5	1,360	209.2	6.5	1,465	225.3	
Total	21.9	880	40.1	25.8	1,360	52.7	26.3	1,465	55.7	
Steward Warewashers	10.5	880	83.8	11.6	1,360	117.2	13.4	1,465	109.3	
All Others	8.3	880	106.0	11.4	1,360	119.2	12.0	1,465	122.0	
Total	18.8	880	46.8	23.0	1,360	59.1	25.4	1,465	57.6	

Wage and Salary Administration

16

The hotel and restaurant business, as with most service industries, experiences a constant press for higher wages and shorter hours; wages are increasing both in amount and as a percentage of the gross income of the business. In full-service hotels, labor cost constitutes about 35 percent of the gross income; in motels, labor costs are considerably less, ranging from about 12 percent in the smaller operations where part of the work is done by the owner-operator to around 30 percent in the larger motels that have food services and bars. The larger motor hotels are in effect hotels offering most hotel services.

In commercial restaurants labor cost varies widely, depending upon the menu offered, the efficiency, and amount of sales. In a restaurant serving mostly steaks, the labor costs may run as low as 20 percent of the gross income, while in a luxury restaurant with all of its service, labor cost may go as high as 40 percent of the gross income. There is a wide range of productivity per employee and consequently of labor costs within the restaurant business. In table-service restaurants, for example, productivity dropped 15 percent from 1973 to 1978. Labor costs vary from 15 percent of gross sales to over 45 percent. The most common labor cost found varied from between 25 and 29 percent of sales. Labor costs for the restaurant industry averaged about 31 percent in 1977 (payroll plus employee benefits). All service industries have high labor costs as a percentage of income.

WAGES IN THE INDUSTRY*

Generally speaking, wages of hotel and restaurant employees were found by the U.S. Bureau of Business to be near the bottom of the wage scale. Around the country there are marked differences in wages paid. In the South, outside of the cities, wages in restaurants are low.

The fairness of the wage or salary and the response of the person receiving it is a judgment made by the indi-

vidual based on that person's attitudes, beliefs, level of aspiration, and the comparative wage or salary being received by co-workers in the hotel or restaurant, or on a level commensurate with the person in the industry. Of two people with similar abilities, skills, and experience, one may consider three dollars an hour a munificent wage, the others view it as contemptible. The individual's expectations, level of ambition, financial obligations, and social background are reflected in personal attitudes towards the wage or salary. Such attitudes can change rapidly.

About the only constant in the reaction to a particular wage or salary is the emphasis placed by most people on what is being received by others considered to be on the same level. A cook in one restaurant may receive $200 a week and consider himself or herself as well paid, being the highest paid individual in the kitchen. Across the street another cook may be receiving $400 a week and be dissatisfied because the person considered to be an equal or less is receiving a higher wage.

A manager of a hotel or restaurant may be quite happy as far as present salary is concerned until attending a convention and learning that a former classmate who is doing about the same work is receiving more. Many persons are quite content with a modest salary if they are given stock options or included under a plan by which they will share in the profits or growth in equity of the hotel or restaurant. Usually the more ambitious, energetic, freewheeling type of individual is more eager for a compensation plan under which, though receiving a relatively small salary, this person can share in the prosperity of the enterprise if it goes well.

The value system of society partly determines how rewards of the society are ladled out. In the United States, white-collar jobs traditionally have been more highly rewarded than blue-collar ones. Some of the most miserable jobs have been the least rewarded—ditch diggers,

*The American Hotel and Motel Association, 88 7th Ave., N.Y., N.Y., 10019 makes periodic wage and salary surveys of the hotel and motel industry.

coal miners, pot and pan washers. Some of the most desirable and glamorous jobs have received the highest rewards—airline pilots, senators, college professors. In Russia the coal miner is paid in terms of the unpleasantness of the job and the danger that must be undergone. Consequently, that job is one of the highest paid in the society. Union pressures in special situations also influence rewards. Merchant Marine officers, tugboat captains, political patronage jobs are comparatively highly overrewarded. Since so many of the jobs in the hotel, restaurant, and club business are entry positions and can be filled by most able-bodied people, pressure for higher rewards has been minimal. Disadvantaged groups such as newly arrived immigrants and minority groups have traditionally been pleased to fill the entry positions. This situation is changing. Hundreds of jobs such as lodging quarters cleaner, porter, and dishwasher are open in the cities on any given day despite the fact that the nation is experiencing a high unemployment rate. Inevitably wage rates will be increased and the cost will be passed on to the consumer.

Tips and Other Factors

Ironically the persons who are the most skilled or who do the least desirable work often get less pay than the tipped employees. It is not unusual in a restaurant to find waiters making $300 a week as compared with the chef's salary of $250. Waiter's assistants may make as much as thirty or forty dollars a day while the pot and pan washer, performing the most disagreeable and one of the hardest of jobs, receives the minimum wage. As previously noted, extraneous factors often influence wages in food-service establishments. Where food service is operated by a school, college, or industrial plant the food-service employees are likely to be covered under a civil service contract and receive double the wages of a similar employee in a commercial establishment. In 1978, for example, in many industrial, college and university, and school food services the minimum starting wage ran about $4.10 an hour. Some dishwashers received as much as $12,000 a year—especially for in-flight food-service operations (to which they would indeed be entitled if paid on the basis of disagreeableness of the job). One of the reasons why contract food-service operators have grown rapidly is a desire on the part of industrial and college management to extricate themselves from the higher wage agreements.

Federal Minimum Wage Rates

In 1977 the U.S. Congress passed a new wage rate for restaurants that set the minimum wage at $2.30 an hour and moved the rate by stages to $3.35 an hour as of January 1, 1981. Employers had previously been allowed to reduce the minimum wage up to 50 percent to allow a deduction for tips. By 1980 this credit will be reduced to 40 percent.

Restaurants doing less than $275,000 as of July 1, 1978 were not covered by the national minimum wage. The dollar-volume-of-coverage test is to be moved to $362,500 by December 31, 1981. State laws supercede the Federal law if the minimum wage is set at a higher rate, as it is, for example, in California and Alaska.

The absence of minimum wage regulations would inevitably mean low wages for hotel and restaurant employees in large sections of the country. The buying public would get a little lower food check, a hotel room for a little less money in these areas. Low wages usually mean less sharp management, less intelligent planning, the use of obsolescent equipment, less system, and, in the last analysis, less attractive service for the public. With low wages there is not the push to replace people with equipment to increase efficiency, to get the maximum productivity per employee.

With minimum wages and union negotiation forcing increased wages, the extra cost is passed on to the customer.

Why should the hospitality business subsidize the public any more than any other industry? The automobile industry, the coal industry, the shoe industry long ago gave up this notion.

When a minimum wage is introduced into an area all operators are forced to increase their wages together and, consequently, the prices they charge their customers. There is an adjustment in what can be given to a customer and a larger share of the income goes to the employee. In an industry where many of the employees are less advantaged, it would seem well to welcome minimum wage legislation. As a result the entire industry will gain status, because its employees can live in a decent American style.

It is true that a minimum wage forces an increase in the wages of the other employees, since a differential between wages is usually maintained. Wages tend to move up together, with differentials remaining about the same. Of course, if wages are forced up too high, the public will change to other forms of entertainment and service, at least to some extent.

Productivity Does Not Keep Pace with Industry in General

While wages and salaries in the United States rise nearly every year, so too does productivity (most of the time). As long as the rise in productivity keeps pace with the rise in wages and salaries there is no problem.[1] Prices to the consumer remain about the same. In the hotel and restaurant business, however, relying as it does almost exclusively on people-effort rather than the work of machines, productivity has not risen much over the years.

A 1976 Survey of Table Service Restaurant Operations conducted by the NRA showed the total sales per full-time equivalent employee ranging from $15,545 in the lower quartile of those surveyed to a high of $25,869 in the upper quartile. Payroll per full-time equivalent employee ranged from $4,057 to $6,614, a labor cost of close to 25 percent of sales.

Sales per employee, a simple measure of productivity in restaurants, varies widely, usually increasing as volume of sales increases. A few restaurants experience as much as $50,000 sales per employee.

THE FAIR LABOR STANDARDS ACT

The Fair Labor Standards Act (FLSA) contains provisions and standards concerning minimum wages, equal pay, maximum hours, overtime pay, recordkeeping, and child labor.* Included under FLSA are hotels, restaurants, and clubs. The FLSA was enacted in 1938, but through the years a number of amendments and new interpretations have arisen. This is not the complete picture, however, inasmuch as most states have wage laws of their own.

Food-service work cannot easily be programmed, regulated, or scheduled. Split shifts are not uncommon. Definite lulls occur between peak periods. An employee may come to the end of a shift but prefer to wait for a customer to complete the meal in anticipation of a tip. The employer could afford to pay for overtime at the regular rate but would not want to pay a premium wage for the convenience of the employee. In 1979, the overtime rate for covered employees was at least one and one-half times the regular rate for hours worked in excess of forty per week. Closing hours are highly variable in the hospitality industry. It is the nature of the industry to gear itself to the whims of its customers.

It is true that bigger dish machines may call for fewer dishwashers per hundred covers washed, or that self-bussing eliminates bussing personnel, or that computers can replace bookkeepers. It does not seem possible to increase the amount of service dispensed by the individual employee to any large extent. Therefore the cost of increased wages must be passed on to the consumer—the guest in the hotel and the patron in the restaurant. This is being done.

Equal Pay Provisions

The employer may not discriminate on the basis of sex or age.

Minimum Age Requirements

The basic minimum age in hotels and motels is sixteen, though some minors aged fourteen and fifteen may be employed in specific occupations for a limited number of hours. Such occupations include office and clerical work, waiter's assistants, kitchen helpers (except cooking), waiters and waitresses, cleaners, bellpersons, and attendants at soda fountains and cafeteria counters. Minors under eighteen may *not* be employed in hazardous occupations.

Employers can protect themselves from unintentional violation of the child labor provisions by obtaining and keeping on file an employment or age certificate for each young person employed to show that the individual is at least the minimum age for the job. Heavy fines are assessed for violations.

Records

Employers are required to keep records, though no particular form of recordkeeping is required. Some of the specific recordkeeping items required are the following:

1. Full name of employee
2. Home address, including zip code
3. Date of birth, if under nineteen
4. Sex and occupation
5. Time of day and day of week on which the employee's workweek begins
6. Regular hourly rate of pay in any workweek in which overtime premium is due; basis of wage payment (such as $3/hr., $21/day, $100/wk. plus 5 percent commission).
7. Daily and weekly hours of work
8. Total daily or weekly straight time earnings

---

1. Over the period 1952 to 1972 output per people-hour in the United States gained an average of 3 percent a year as shown by a survey based on government statistics. From 1973 to 1978, productivity gains have been lower.
*See "Restaurants Under the Fair Labor Standards Act," U.S. Department of Labor, Employment Standards Administration, Wage and Hour Division, revised October, 1978.

9. Total overtime excess compensation for the workweek where applicable

10. Total additions to or deductions from wages paid each pay period

11. Total wages paid each pay period

12. Date of payment and the pay period covered by the payment

Wage Garnishments

Effective July 1, 1970 federal law limited the amount of an employee's disposable earnings subject to garnishment (collected by a creditor from an employee through the employer). The maximum part of the total disposable earnings of an individual that is subject to garnishment in any workweek may not exceed the *lesser* of (*a*) 24 percent of the disposable earnings for that week; or (*b*) the amount by which the individual's disposable earnings for that week exceeds thirty times the federal minimum hourly wage.

Various states have also added restrictions regarding wage and salary garnishment. Laws, regulations concerning employment and their interpretation, continually change and without continuous information about the changes the hospitality operator can face legal problems. Ready access to such information is usually available through state restaurant and hotel associations and from the National Restaurant Association, headquartered in Washington, D.C., and from the American Hotel and Motel Association, with principal Offices in New York City.

PROFIT SHARING PLANS

A number of profit sharing plans have been established by hotels and restaurants. Such plans have decided tax advantages, both for the employer and the employee. They can also build morale by creating in the employee a sense of ownership in the company. As a part-owner, the employee quite naturally takes a more personal interest in efficiency and cost saving.

In some cases a primary motive for instituting a profit sharing plan has been to exclude the union. A well-known hotel that instituted a profit sharing plan in 1946 has seen the plan eroded by the inclusion of the majority of employees in union programs. At its inception, it included close to 1,000 employees; as of 1974 it applied to 100, all of whom were in the white-collar category.

For a period of years in the late 1960s, hotel and restaurant stocks soared, with stocks selling as high as fifty or sixty times what was being earned per share each year. Since then some of the stock sold in the market place for only three or four times earnings. Several of the profit sharing plans had invested all of the contributions made by the company and by the employee in their own company's stock. When the stock plummeted, the visions of sugar plums dancing in the heads of employees, visions of million dollar estates being built up through the profit sharing plan, vanished.

Probably the most pronounced value of a profit sharing plan from the point of view of the employer is that such plans tend to encourage employee stability. The employee who has a stake in a profit sharing plan, and who may lose it by leaving, is more likely to think twice before taking a job elsewhere. Some plans enable the employee to build up remarkably large estates even though the employee may hold a low-paying job. The two largest employers in the hotel and restaurant field, Holiday Inns and Marriott, instituted plans that are worth study.

The Marriott Corporation Profit Sharing Savings and Retirement Plan

The Marriott plan, as explained in its employee booklet, has produced astoundingly large estates for the employees who were eligible for taking part in the plan and who remained with the company at least twenty years.[2] An employee who made $2 an hour would have accumulated a retirement account of $10,900 at the end of ten years of employment, $68,300 at the end of twenty years, and $385,000 at the end of thirty years of employment. The person who had a weekly rate of pay of $200 conceivably could end up with an estate of close to a million dollars. Total contribution to the plan by the employee would be only $34,500; the rest would have been contributed by the company and by earnings made from the money invested in the profit sharing trust.

The key to understanding how such large estates could be accumulated is the fact that while the Marriott Corporation contributed 8 percent of its consolidated profits before income taxes and before bonus payments were made, only those employees who had a total of three years service with the company were eligible to participate. Also important is the fact that if an employee who is partici-

---

2. "Profit Sharing, Savings and Retirement Plan," Marriott Corporation, 1970.

pating left the company, that person's share of the money contributed by the company was reapportioned to the remaining participants.

An assumption is made that the money in this profit sharing trust would continue to appreciate as it had in the past. The plan from 1961 at its inception to 1969 had a remarkable appreciation record. Total contributions by employees (who were allowed to contribute between 5 and 10 percent of their gross wages) was $5,692,615. The company contribution plus earnings of the profit sharing trust was $13,589,164. In other words, for every dollar contributed by the employee, well over two dollars came from the company contribution and investment income.

The Marriott Corporation employees profit-sharing, savings, and retirement plan and Trust was revised in 1976. The optimistic picture of what the profit sharing plan would produce for the individual employee was drastically changed in 1970, 1973, 1974, and 1975. The company contribution accounts showed heavy losses because of a sharp decline in the investments owned by the profit sharing fund. These investments included stocks and bonds in the Marriott Corporation stock.

Even so, the company contributed over 24 million dollars of profits to the profit sharing plan from fiscal year 1961 through fiscal year 1976, or $1.19 for each dollar that the employee contributed.

Under the new plan, the company contribution to the employee account is based on the employees' contribution, 5 percent of wage or salary. An employee, can, however, contribute up to 10 percent of wage or salary, which is tax free until the time the employee begins drawing upon it, usually after retirement when the person is in a lower tax bracket. The portion of the money contributed by the employee is 100 percent guaranteed by the company, and draws interest.[3]

The Holiday Inns Profit Sharing Plan

Holiday Inns, the largest accommodation company the world has ever known, has a profit sharing plan similar in structure to that of Marriott's. Like Marriott's plan, for a time it generated large sums of money for the employees who participated in it for any length of time.

In 1976 the profit sharing plan was changed to permit the employee to participate without a contribution or with a contribution at the employee's choice. The company sets aside 5 percent of its profits each year for profit sharing, half of which is distributed to all employees regardless of their contribution. That distribution varies according to the employee's earnings and years of service. The other 50 percent of the sum set aside for profit sharing is distributed to those who make contributions during the year.

Employees may contribute between 2 and 6 percent of their wages or salary. The company contributes an amount equal to these contributions—or $1,000—whichever is less.

All contributions are deposited in a Plans Trust Fund administered by Trustees. The money is invested and may increase or decrease in value, depending upon the value of the investments.[4]

Holiday Inns Company also provides a retirement plan to which employees do not contribute. It is tied in with social security, the goal being to provide individual employees who retire at age sixty-five with an annual income of about half of what they received each year from the company during their last few employment years.

Tax Savings for Owners through Profit Sharing

The federal government will allow the establishment of a profit sharing plan in any business provided the plan meets certain Internal Revenue Service specifications. In effect the government encourages profit sharing plans by allowing a certain percentage of profits to go untaxed if the money is placed into a profit sharing plan to be shared in by all employees. Such plans must be approved by the Internal Revenue Service before initiation. Under these plans a restaurant operator, for example, may be able to reduce personal taxes by allocating a certain percentage of pretaxed profits to an employee profit sharing plan. The employer shares in the profit sharing plan. Income from the plan is deferred until a time when the operator's income may place him or her in a lower bracket with a lower tax rate, usually on retirement. Employees similarly benefit by having an estate built up for them that is paid back at retirement when their taxable income is reduced. They are still eligible to participate in federal social security plan and upon retirement can draw social security payments while also receiving the benefits of the profit sharing plan.

RETIREMENT PLANS

At the turn of the century there were very few pension systems—American Express, Railroad Retirement—and those in effect were designed to afford a measure of protection for widows and orphans. Since the life span then was about forty years, few workers lived long enough to

---

3. Employees' Profit Sharing, Savings and Retirement Plan and Trust, Marriott Corporation, July 31, 1976.
4. "Your Profitsharing Plan Benefits," Corporate Employee Benefits Office, Holiday Inns, Inc., Memphis.

qualify for superannuation benefits. The life span has increased dramatically. A man retiring in 1977 had an additional thirteen years to live, while a woman retiring in the same year had seventeen years.

Independent hotels and restaurants change hands frequently and their owners have given little thought to retirement plans for employees. A few of the larger chains have established profit sharing plans that supplement federal social security retirement benefits.

EMPLOYEE STOCK OWNERSHIP PLANS

Since the late 1960s and the early 1970s the federal government has encouraged the distribution of company stock to employees by giving tax advantages for doing so. For closely held companies, especially those owned by the operating officers, the Employee Stock Ownership Plan (ESOP) has advantages. The owners of a hotel or restaurant corporation can use profits ordinarily paid in federal taxes to buy stock from themselves and distribute the stock to the corporation employees. The owners still retain control of the company but also are able to withdraw part of their equity.

Under the Pension Reform Act of 1974 (ERISA) a company can contribute its own stock to a trust and makes a tax deduction for the fair market value of the stock subject to the same deduction limitations as a profit sharing plan. In effect the company buys the stock from the owners and contributes it to a trust. An ESOP trust accumulates its funds tax free—it pays no tax on contributions it receives over the years and pays no tax dividends, interest, or other income received as a result of its holding and investing the contributed funds. When a retired employee sells the stock the previously untaxed, unrealized appreciation is taxable—but as long-term capital gain.

It is true that the owners are diluting their ownership, but they are also beneficiaries of the stock and are able in effect to sell their stock to their own employees without the employees paying for it. The original controlling owners of the stock can retain stock voting rights even though the employees are the beneficial owners. An ESOP does not have to include union employees if such employees are covered by a collective bargaining agreement and there is evidence that the retirement benefits presently available were the subject of good-faith bargaining. Another advantage of an ESOP to the present owners and to long-time employees is that those employees who terminate with less than ten years service usually forfeit part of their interest in the trust; those with less than four years' service forfeit all of their interest.[5] Their shares are then added to those owned by the remaining employees.

The International Restaurant Supply Company of Los Angeles, introduced an ESOP in 1973, and has found it very effective in stimulating efficiency, cost control, and pride in the company. Profits that ordinarily would have been paid to the federal government in the form of corporation taxes have been used to purchase company stock. Ownership that had been closely held is now shared with employees according to each employee's wage or salary and length of service with the company. The original stockholders expect to pass control of the company to the employees, but since the old owners are also active in management, they too receive shares of the stock and have seen the value of their stock increase.

Each year the company contributes to a trust, which continues to buy the company stock at a price determined by outside experts or by the stock market. The maximum that a company can contribute each year is 15 percent of the compensation of the participants in the plan. That amount is treated as a tax deduction for the company. Since the corporation normally pays 50 or more percent of its profits in corporation taxes, the company in effect contributes nothing.

EMPLOYEE BENEFITS

What an employee receives in wages is one thing, what the individual gets in total goods, services, and other benefits is something else. Kitchen and dining room employees have customarily received meals while on the job. Some establishments have eliminated this practice, since such a benefit is often taken for granted. The employee does not consider it in computing wages and benefits. Resort employees are usually provided lodging as well as meals at a reduced cost. Other fringe benefits for the usual hotel and restaurant employee includes uniforms while on the job. Many hotels supply special suits or jackets for front office employees. Nearly every hotel supplies bellpersons' uniforms and cleaners' uniforms. Waiters and waitresses in some establishments are asked to provide their own uniforms; the cost of doing this cannot be shifted to the employee if it results in reducing the hourly rate below the minimum wage; in others, uniforms are provided and so too is laundering. Health and medical insurance may be provided. In some cases dental care is a fringe benefit. The number of fringe benefits tends to increase with time. The hotel, restaurant, and club business necessarily reflects society as a whole: as three-week vacations become more common in industry as a whole, hotel and restaurant employees expect the same treatment.

---

5. *Levanthal and Howath Perspective*, Spring/Summer 1976, Chicago.

FRINGE BENEFITS, PERQUISITES, STOCK OPTIONS

Fringe benefits can almost be said to be limited only by the imagination. A fringe benefit is whatever the person receiving it feels has value. For example, titles are often offered as benefits. Companies may have several vice-chairpeople, several executive vice-presidents. The executive washroom is stepped up to become a private washroom with a private bath. How many executives can usher visitors into their own private restroom?

Then there is a chauffeured limousine to pick up the executive at home—to take the executive to and from airport—and on and on. Hotel chains usually offer free rooms to employees on vacation and VIP's in the company get all expenses paid plus babysitting costs.

In the one-upmanship benefits game there is the original art tactic. How many executives have a (company-owned) Picasso or a Monet in their office? And how about a company yacht to be used for the entertainment of customers, for conferences, and now and then for a company meeting?

When the really top executive travels, a secretary goes along to carry the briefcase and the money. The executive carries a Hewlett-Packard calculator and a Gucci briefcase (again, both are company-owned). For the busy executive who cannot commute home, there is the company apartment, complete with decor by a famous decorator.

If the company is closely held, there is auto insurance for the family. For the harried executive, there is the annual retreat to the Greenbrier, or a similar spa, for a medical check-up and recuperation at company expense. There may even be a group legal plan, which is ready for the employee who encounters legal problems.

Perquisites for managerial employees in the hotel restaurant and club business are extensive. Managers and their spouses may attend hotel conventions or shows, all expenses paid by the company. Hotel managers often have entertainment accounts, some permitting the manager to spend several hundred dollars a month in entertainment. Management personnel typically eat and drink in the first-class dining room at no expense to themselves. A manager who lives in may receive complete household maintenance. Membership in the country club and at least one civic club may be provided at company expense.

Fringe benefits are usually better than wages or salary in that the goods or services are received without the need for state or federal tax payments. If a person is in a 40 percent income bracket, a dollar received in the form of a perquisite is really worth close to $1.65. Here are some tax-free fringe benefits accorded to many hotel, restaurant, and club executives:

1. All car expenses
2. Paid-up life insurance at company cost
3. Vacation travel that can be combined with business to be tax deductible
4. Medical expenses reimbursed, including drugs
5. Loans at no interest charge

This last item can be a sizeable fringe benefit. Suppose an executive takes a $60,000 mortgage on a house at 9 percent interest. Over twenty-five years more than $90,000 in interest would be paid on that mortgage. An interest-free loan from the company would have the effect of the executive's being given an extra $90,000.

Stock options—key executives are often given the right to purchase company stock at a fixed price. As an example an executive could be given the right to buy 1,000 shares of company stock at $10 a share. Suppose ten years later the stock is selling for $30 a share. (Ordinarily there is a three-year waiting period before the stock can be purchased.) If the executive had exercised the option to purchase the thousand shares at $10 a share that individual would in effect have made $20,000. This is better than $20,000 in salary because the maximum tax is about 25 percent of the appreciation. If the stock is held for a year and then sold, the executive would get this beneficial tax treatment. In the form of salary the executive would have had to pay in accordance with the tax bracket in which he/she falls, which would ordinarily be more than 25 percent.

The owner of a hotel or restaurant can incorporate the business and receive all of the above fringe benefits. By choosing to take profits in the form of benefits rather than in dollars, the individual's tax obligation is considerably reduced.

SUMMARY

Hotel and restaurants are labor-intensive, therefore a large percentage (20–40) of sales are paid out in wages and salaries. Salaries in the business can be compared, in general, to those of other management jobs bearing similar responsibilities in other business areas.

By virtue of its emphasis on service, the hotel and restaurant industry does not generally show increased productivity to offset rises in wages and salaries. The cost of increased wages must be passed on to the consumer, but the fear always exists that in doing so, the consumer will change to other forms of entertainment and services.

The most important legislation bearing on wages and salaries involves the Fair Labor Standards Act of 1938 and its amendments. While less than 5 percent of the eating places in America are covered under FLSA, most are covered under state fair labor acts. The future will undoubtedly see more enterprises covered under FLSA and greater uniformity among state legislation.

Federal and state legislation controls the minimum wage that can be paid. FLSA also establishes guidelines relative to nondiscrimination, minimum ages of workers, wage garnishments, and records required by employees. Since employment regulations are constantly changing, the employer is advised to join the state or national hospitality trade associations in order to keep alert to changing regulations.

Some of the larger hotels and restaurants have utilized profit sharing plans to an advantage.

Union Relations

17

Management and union relations in the hotel business date back well over 100 years, to a time when craft-oriented groups of waiters and bartenders banded together for mutual protection and fraternal association. The Hotel and Restaurant Employees Union and Bartenders Union (AFL-CIO), headquartered in Cincinnati, and numbering over 430,000 members in 1977, evolved from these early efforts. The Union's annual income is close to $18 million. Since more than 4 million persons are employed in the hotel and restaurant business, the number unionized represent less than 15 percent of the total.

The reasons are several: high turnover, especially among restaurant employees; thousands of small hotels and restaurants that make union organizing effort costly and difficult; lack of strong union leadership; fighting within the union itself; and an unfavorable union reputation in several cities, especially Chicago and New York. Semiskilled and unskilled jobs in the hotel and restaurant business partly account for the unusually large turnover experienced in the field and provide a major reason why the Union is not stronger. Something like 30 percent of the employees in the food-service industry are teenagers; about 70 percent are women. A majority of them can be easily replaced.

UNION STRENGTH IN CITIES

Unionization in the hotel business is strongest in the North and in major cities, particularly in the Northeast and on the West Coast. The larger hotel chains are likely to be organized.

In 1975, H. & R. E. Union membership was concentrated in the larger cities as follows:

New York City	51,370
Los Angeles	22,028
Las Vegas	21,369
San Francisco	19,878
Detroit	15,010
Minneapolis/St. Paul	10,219
Miami/Ft. Lauderdale	10,068
Chicago	8,332[1]

The union is weakest in the South. Only the Miami Beach hotel group is well organized where some fifty hotels are unionized. Eleven of the nation's twenty right-to-work states are in the South. These laws forbid employer-union contracts that require all workers to join a union.

Hotels in some cities such as San Francisco, Honolulu, and New York have had the Hotel and Restaurant Employees' Union representing their employees for many years, and management bargains as a group with the various other unions involved.

BRIEF HISTORY OF HOTEL AND RESTAURANT UNIONIZATION

In the period 1860–70, societies of cooks and waiters were organized in several of the major cities of the United States. They included English- , German- , French- , and Spanish-speaking culinary workers. In 1887 a number of locals representing various hotel and restaurant employees were affiliated with the American Federation of Labor. Among those represented were the trades of waiters, cooks, bartenders, and bakers. In 1891 the unions were amalgamated to form the "Waiters and Bartenders' National Union," which held its first national convention in 1892 and changed its name to "Hotel and Restaurant Employees' National Alliance."

Almost from the inception of the newly organized union there was open antagonism between it and the hotel operators. At the second convention, held in 1893, the

---

1. Source—Hotel and Restaurant Employees' and Bartenders' International Union.

318

union condemned the United States Hotel Association and Saloon Keepers. The employers were criticized for denouncing agitators in the labor movement, for blacklisting (excluding from employment) employees who belonged to the unions, and for operating employment bureaus. The charges were just for saloon keepers and head waiters, who often worked together to demand a percentage of the employee's pay, either in the form of cash or in drinks. The waiters labeled this the "vampire system."

Another common form of malpractice among employers was that of permitting the head waiter to extract a "kick in" from the waiters under his supervision. Under this practice, each Saturday night the waiter was expected to "kick in" a portion of his tips to the head waiter as a price for keeping his job. Under the guise of claiming payment for "breakage," some employers were guilty of similar practices.

It was not until the Franklin Roosevelt administration in 1932 that unions gained strength in numbers. In that year the Norris-LaGuardia Act drastically reduced the freedom of courts to grant injunctions against strikes (injunctions had been widely used by employers). The Wagner Act of 1935 publicly encouraged and facilitated collective bargaining through unions and prohibited certain actions on the part of the employer that were defined as "Unfair Labor Practices." As part of the act, the National Labor Relations Board was created; it determined appropriate bargaining units, certified unions as bargaining agents, and acted to prevent unfair labor practices.

In 1937, a major hotel strike was called in San Francisco by a confederation of separate unions acting through a local joint board. At the end of a few days almost 10,000 workers were out on strike, but the unions carefully avoided calling out the employees in the smaller hotels. The strike ended after eighty-nine days and set the stage for San Francisco's becoming one of the most strongly unionized of cities. Similar strikes were called in Seattle and Los Angeles. In Detroit, the Statler and Book-Cadillac Hotels experienced "sit-ins," a new weapon that had been used by employees in automobile factories. The employees simply refused to leave the hotel.

The 1930s, depression years, were favorable for unions in that the National Industrial Recovery Act (NIRA), which was passed in 1933, encouraged union growth. Protection for the individual worker was needed, as seen in the union contract signed in 1939 between the Association and Council in New York City which provided, among other things, for a forty-eight-hour, six-day workweek for most workers, fifty-four hours for waiters and busboys. Maids received $14.50 a week; waiters $9.00 a week; and bellmen $4.00 a week.[2]

During World War II, the War Labor Board was established to mediate wage disputes for the duration of the war. Following the war in 1946, a number of strikes occurred.

Strikes cost both the union and the employer. The Miami Beach strike, which lasted from April 13, 1955, until January 5, 1957, cost the union in excess of $1.5 million for legal fees and other costs. The hotel owners worked together to stave off closing down their properties. To keep the hotel operating while recruiting efforts were speeded up to replace the strikers, flying squads of department heads and key employees were rushed to each hotel as it was picketed.

The strength of the union is augmented in those locations where the Teamsters' Union is strong. Often that union will refuse to make deliveries of supplies to hotels and restaurants that are being picketed.

Prior to 1959, the hotel industry operated under the various state laws regarding union relations, a condition favored by the union until about 1955. After a series of petitions by the union to the National Labor Relations Board, requesting that jurisdiction be taken over by that Board, the case was finally taken to the U.S. Supreme Court. On November 24, 1958, the Supreme Court's ruling was such that the NLRB assumed jurisdiction over most of the hotel industry.

The NLRB bases much of its conduct and decisions on the Taft-Hartley Act going back to 1935. Section 7 of the act specifies the rights of employees to join employee organizations and to bargain collectively through representatives of their own choosing. Section 8 of the act defines what will be considered unfair labor practices. Paraphrasing these sections:[3]

—The employer may not interfere with, restrain, or coerce employees regarding their right of self-organization and collective bargaining.
—The employer cannot dominate or interfere with the formation of a labor organization nor contribute financially to its support.
—The employer may not discriminate in hiring or retaining an employee as a matter of encouraging or discouraging membership in a labor organization.
—The employer may not discharge or otherwise discriminate against an employee who has filed charges against the employer or given testimony under the Taft-Hartley Act.

---

2. Quoted in "Resolution of Grievances in Service Industries: The New York City Contract Model," *Cornell H & R Quarterly*, May 1977, p. 35.
3. Those interested should read the law itself, which is legally phrased and more detailed.

The union is enjoined from doing certain things that are declared unfair labor practices:

—The union may not restrain or coerce employees in their collective bargaining rights, nor may the union restrain or coerce an employer in the selection of representatives for the purposes of collective bargaining or for the adjustment of grievances.
—The union may not refuse to bargain collectively with an employer if the union represents the employees.
—The union may not influence employees to strike or otherwise try to force an employee or self-employed person to join a particular labor union or employee organization.
—The union may not force or require an employer to recognize or bargain with a particular union if another union is already certified to represent those employees.

Union Groups Bargain With Employer Groups

In the larger cities, where several unions may be involved with the hotel and restaurant business, unions may act together under a single umbrella to bargain with employers who also form a group for bargaining purposes. The idea apparently originated in New York City where in the 1930s a "Trades Council" was formed to bargain for all employees in the hotel industry in New York City. On the other side of the bargaining table was the New York City Hotel Association. This arrangement exists today in such cities as Chicago, San Francisco, Washington, D.C., Boston, and Los Angeles.

MANAGEMENT AND LABOR VIEWPOINTS

Theoretically, labor and management favor the health and prosperity of all concerned. There are differences in opinion, however, as to how such goals are to be achieved. Labor generally presses for greater security, more wages, and improved benefits. Labor believes that higher wages and other benefits will be passed on to the consumer. Management, on the other hand, contends that raising rates and prices reduces the market. Taking the broad view, it can be said the nontip, semiskilled employees in the hotel and restaurant business have been at the bottom of the economic heap. Low wages and long hours have benefited the public as seen in prices.

Comparing many job requirements in the hotel and restaurant business with similar ones in other semiskilled

fields, a strong case can be made for higher hotel and restaurant wages. Civil servants, meat cutters, newspaper assembly workers, and supermarket employees in certain locations receive double the wages for job skills and working conditions not much different than those found in hotels and restaurants. Indeed, the added labor costs in these businesses have been passed on to the public.

Confusing the picture is the fact that tip employees in food service usually do well financially, especially in bars, dinner houses, and in many hotel restaurants; while cleaners and maintenance personnel have almost invariably received the minimum wage allowed by law.

In hotels, service personnel and cleaners comprise by far the largest numbers of employees, one reason why they are among the first to be approached by union organizers. In much of the United States cleaners and maintenance personnel are likely to be members of minority groups, blacks in the South and in cities, Mexican-Americans and Mexicans in the Southwest. Unionization can provide greater security and independence for them.

In a highly competitive society it can hardly be expected that people in power, managers and owners, will willingly cede some of their power and control to others. Similarly, it is understandable that employees would like the support of fellow employees and talented, aggressive people from the outside in negotiating wages and benefits. It is also quite understandable that people who are not assured of a job and who lack highly salable skills would like assurances in writing that their job is at least somewhat secure.

A union, if sincerely interested in its membership, can provide checks and balances to management and ownership, exert pressure to push up wage rates, and exact better working conditions. In doing so, costs of goods and services are almost always increased and those increases are usually passed along to the consumer.

Management's Position Vis-à-vis Unionization

Generally speaking, if given a choice, management prefers not dealing with a union for the simple reason that unions are in business to get more wages, benefits, and rights for employees, especially higher wages. Some managements forestall union efforts in every legal way possible. They see unionization as an attempt to usurp management rights or, at the very least, restrict them. Some owners devote considerable time and effort to keeping out the union. The Marriott Corporation, one of the largest in the hospitality field, is such a company and for many years had no union representation until the Essex Hotel in New York City was purchased (where the hotel was already unionized). Other companies, such as the Sheraton Corporation, have assigned a senior vice-president to deal with unions and unionization.

The "Hard-Line" Management View

The hard-line management position has been that free enterprise and rugged individualism are rewarded by success. If workers do not like the work, they may go elsewhere. No one is forced to continue working for a harsh employer. By self-sacrifice and personal risk taking, the owners and operators of hotels and restaurants made themselves successful. Since it is their business and they take the risks, they can hire whoever they like and run their business as they please. The owners are not going to let anyone tell them what they can or cannot do. They are especially opposed to having "their" workers form groups and then try to tell them, the owners, who worked hard for what they have, and have taken risks with their capital, how the hotel or restaurant will operate.

Over the years successful hotel management tended to be paternalistic. The owner or manager saw himself as "Big Daddy" with "his" employees as members of an extended family to be treated somewhat as relatives or children, to be rewarded and punished as family members. As a father the owner/manager made pay advances, often took care of hospital bills, stood bail for employees, got them out of jail, and provided pensions for old and loyal workers. There were no contracts between employer and employees, and sometimes none were needed to assure the employee of fair treatment. (This approach was not appreciated in large cities, where turnover was high and where ownership was corporate with frequent manager turnover.)

The management position against unionization includes the following points:

—The union will force higher labor costs, not only in wages, but costs in lost working time, strikes, time consumed in grievance settlements, and union activity.
—Since the union's major appeal is increased wages, union officers must pressure management for higher wages in order to keep their own jobs.
—Union contracts often interfere with efficiency by forcing the employee to do only the work called for in the job classification. A pastry cook, for example, may not do the work of a sous chef; and the dishwasher may not do the work of a glass washer. Some contracts call for the entire banquet crew to be called in even though only a few employees are needed.
—A union contract forces divided loyalty between the union and the company.

—Unionization encourages antagonisms toward management and encourages people with hostilities to express them toward management and to stir up trouble generally.
—Much time is taken by management in justifying personnel actions, such as layoffs, promotions, terminations.
—Under a union contract, the individual employees are not free to negotiate for their own wage or salary, a factor that reduces the incentive to produce.
—Union officials are in business to serve themselves, not the union membership. The union is corrupt—it has been Mafia-dominated in some places, and it resorts to violence to gain its ends. Union leadership is not elected democratically and does not reflect the wishes and desires of the membership.

Factors Favoring Unionization

Management in a number of instances, however, say they welcome a union contract. The contract establishes guidelines: management has certain rights and responsibilities; employees have theirs; wages and hours are clearly specified; benefits are spelled out; grievances are defined and procedures for resolving them detailed.

The union may be a good source of employees. A large hotel, for example, may need one hundred banquet waiters for a Thursday night. The union sends them over.

The union claims that in some places the retirement, medical, and dental plans under union contract can be had at less cost than could be provided by the employer.

Employee relations are spelled out. Benefits are detailed, grievances defined, and the procedures for resolving them are made a part of the contract. In many locations a union may be a good source of employees. A large hotel, for example, may be able to get a hundred or more banquet waiters for a particular night through the union on short notice.

Another factor: union business may be important to the convention property. Union representatives will not patronize a nonunion hotel.

Employee Viewpoint

In the past, the employee had no real assurance of not being fired capriciously or dealt with unjustly in case of ownership or management change. Usually the employee had few alternatives. High employee turnover, apathy, and management resistance to organization made it difficult or impossible to gain union recognition. In some cities, especially New York and Chicago, mobster control and strong-arm tactics in the past gave the union an unsavory reputation. Questionable loans made by the union added to the reputation.[4] Moreover, the principal union, Hotel and Restaurant Employees Union, has not been known for consistently strong leadership or ability. Even so, a contract usually brings a more structured relationship between employer and employee and safeguards for the employee.

The unionized employee bargains not as an individual but as a member of the entire group of employees; and the individual may also be covered by relatively inexpensive retirement, medical, and dental plans. Ideally, the union is there to protect the individual employee against arbitrary, selfish, or capricious actions on the part of management.

The union's biggest appeal to the employee, of course, is to the pocketbook. Strongly unionized communities and businesses usually have higher wage rates than those that are nonunion. According to Jerry M. Eisen, vice president of Ramada Inns, employees within a given area receive about the same rates of pay, union or not. Nonunion and partially unionized companies are likely to keep wages close to those of unionized companies. But, says Eisen, unionization adds 25 percent to the cost of labor in terms of benefits and other elements, such as inefficiency and ineffectiveness brought on by unneeded employees, narrowly defined jobs, restrictive production, strikes, and shutdowns.

If the local union leadership is fair and aggressive, the employee probably has greater job security, more wages, and more benefits than would be the case if the union were not present. It is well known that semiskilled employees in the hotel and restaurant business, especially cleaners, utility personnel, and waiting personnel, have received the lowest allowable minimum wage, and in the past, have been asked to work split shifts and longer-than-usual hours. On the other hand, tip employees in food service usually do well financially, especially in dinner houses and in many hotel restaurants. They often favor the union because of its position that all tips are the property of the server and cannot arbitrarily be divided among other employees or supervisors as is sometimes done in nonunion houses even in the face of wage and hour laws. ("Service charges" can legally be kept by the operator.)

Fringe benefits for unionized employees can be substantial. The Los Angeles Labor Agreement for 1974, for example, added forty-six cents an hour to all wages to cover costs of medical and dental insurance plans for employees and their families.

Among the reasons why employees join unions are the following:

Obviously, and primarily, to improve wages and working conditions and to benefit from better working hours. Fringe benefits, such as medical and dental insurance, are a part of the union package.

The union employee has greater job security and more stable employment, since the employer must justify personnel actions, such as terminations and promotions.

Major reasons, according to union officials, have to do with bad management, unfair labor practices, tactlessness, and capricious treatment of the employee. The employee comes to feel that without union protection there is little likelihood of getting equitable treatment.

Union relations experts maintain that a company getting a union deserves what it gets because management has neglected to do a number of things:

—Failed to eliminate sources of complaints that unions can exploit, such as confusing pay practices or inconsistent disciplinary procedures.
—Failed to erect roadblocks to union organizing drives, such as, for example, to discourage workers from signing union recognition cards.
—Failed to publicize union problems—to describe union scandals and internal friction, for example.
—Failed to pay as well as or better than the prevailing wages in the community.
—Failed to provide adequate employee benefits or to adequately administer benefit plans.
—Failed to provide an open-door policy for hearing employee complaints.
—Failed to point out the cost of union dues.

A catalog of grievances that favor the joining of a union includes such factors as:

• Management favoritism
• Overtime problems
• Nepotism (employment of relatives of management or owners)
• Unfair tip distribution
• Poor employee scheduling and overwork
• Poor equipment
• Lack of training
• Timecard errors
• Criticism of employees in front of others
• Management indifference and ineptitude
• Poor employee meals and unpleasant employee dining room
• Undignified treatment of employees by management

---

4. See *Institutions/Volume Feeding,* October 1975.

KEEPING THE UNION OUT

For those companies and individuals determined to keep the union out, a number of strategies and tactics are used. The best one of all, of course, is to provide topflight management and offer better than prevailing wages, benefits, and working conditions.

Companies like Ramada Inns and Marriott Corporation work at remaining nonunion. Information is constantly being fed to management and supervisors from corporated offices about how to remain nonunion and to do so within guidelines established by the National Labor Relations Act. What is legal and what is illegal activity on the part of management is emphasized.

Aside from doing everything that is recommended for good employer/employee relations, some employee-relations experts feel that the best way to keep out unions is to weed out those potential malcontents long before the union calls. Employees who are lazy or inadequate, or who complain excessively, or shirk their duties should be eliminated, say some experts. Overqualified employees are also potential sources of trouble. Often respected by other employees, their interest in the union could be contagious.

Countering Union Tactics

Quite naturally the union has a number of tactics designed to gain recognition in the quickest possible way. One such tactic is to call or write a letter demanding union recognition because "a majority of your employees have signed up with the union." One should be careful in the way one reacts to such a demand; or you risk finding yourself in the position of jeopardizing relations with the National Labor Relations Board by being forced to recognize a union even without a secret ballot. The American Hotel and Motel Association recommends that certain things not be done:[5]

1. Do not agree to look at any proof of majority support, such as union cards, membership applications, a petition.
2. Do not ask to be shown any proof of majority support.
3. Do not enter into any unnecessary discussion with the union representative.
4. Do not agree to a "card check" or any form of device for proof of majority status that might be suggested.
5. Do not agree to have a "neutral" party, such as a priest, minister, or rabbi "check" for majority status.
6. Do not poll your employees to see if they really did "sign up."

7. Do not ask for an election and then proceed to commit unfair labor practices in an effort to destroy the union's alleged majority.
8. Do not decline recognition and then try to dissipate the union's alleged majority by unfair labor practices.

According to Siegel, the author of the A.H.&M.A. guide, when confronted by such a tactic, the employer should reply "We must decline to extend recognition to your labor organization unless and until it is certified by the National Labor Relations Board and a unit appropriate for collective bargaining."

The employer who examines the union's proof of majority may forfeit the right to insist upon an NLRB election.

In trying to keep the union out, the company is free to communicate with its employees individually or in groups, even though a number of employees have signed union cards. They are still free to vote and work against the union. The vote conducted by the NLRB is absolutely secret.

The company can remind its employees what it has done for them in the past, including fringe benefits offered, health insurance, paid holidays, paid sick leave, vacations, and free uniforms.

The company can point out the cost of being a union member, including the cost of dues and special assessments, and the cost of a strike if one should be called. "Why should you join a union when you have better working conditions, wages, and benefits than places that are organized? And you don't have to pay union dues."

The employer can point out the misdeeds of the union if it has had a bad record, such as connections with criminals, bombings that have taken place in such cities as Chicago, and the like.

Union representatives may be prohibited from soliciting interest in the union during working times and in working areas. It cannot be restricted from soliciting during lunch hours or coffee breaks, or before work begins and after it ends, even though it be within the hotel or restaurant. But the employer can ban solicitation in the customer or sales area of the restaurant, even though the employees are on the coffee or lunch break, because doing so may disturb guests and patrons. Neither may the union distribute literature in customer areas.

The no-solicitation rule must, however, be applied to everyone equally, including charitable organizations who may wish to solicit on the premises.

---

5. Allen G. Siegel, *When the Union Knocks, A Guide for Non-Union and Union Employees in the Hotel and Motel Industry* (New York: A.H.&M.A., 1976).

The company is perfectly free to discuss union activities with employees individually or in groups, as long as the conversation is "noncoercive." The employer or the employer's representative may not visit the home of an employee to discuss the union, and it is not a good policy to discuss the union in a supervisor's office, an area that could be construed as having a "coercive" atmosphere.

Do's and Don'ts in Labor Disputes

The period prior to a union election takes on the character of a political campaign. Speeches and promises are made; the other side is denounced; the rhetoric may get hot and heavy. As with political campaigns, the promises made do not legally have to be kept, nor does what the union representatives say necessarily have to be true. Neither do union predictions about the company laying off employees, reducing wages, or benefits, etc., necessarily have to take place. The National Labor Relations Board feels that such statements are similar to those made in a political campaign—made for effect, sometimes being unadulterated rhetoric.

In the emotional atmosphere of an election the sides necessarily develop thick skins. Ridicule and insults may be tossed back and forth with impunity.

In the fight to keep a union out, it is believed by some experts, almost any ploy should be used if it will be successful and not expressly illegal. Management may do a number of things quite legally:

—It has the right to state its reasons for opposing a
   union.
—It can send "truth sheets" to employees presenting
   the facts in a positive manner.
—Messages can be stuffed into pay envelopes to
   show the amount of dues that will be deducted if
   employees vote for unionization. The cost of a
   strike can be dramatized with charts and graphs.
—Meetings can be held on company time presenting
   the company viewpoint. (These presentations
   should be taped.) A series of meetings is deemed
   most effective, the last one being held just prior to
   the election.
—Since people tend to remember what has been
   done for them recently and forget benefits awarded
   sometime in the past, management should do
   something tangibly beneficial prior to the election.
   Besides publicizing what has been done for
   employees, the company could sponsor a dance or
   picnic. It might even add a special holiday, with
   double pay for those who work.

One thing management may not do: threaten in any way what management may do in case the union wins.

At this time, management should be careful to reflect confidence and calm. Supervisors and department heads are part of management. Both the National Labor Relations Board and various courts have held that in the sensitive area of labor relations all supervisors are, in fact, management, and that the company is legally responsible for their actions.

Every member of the management team, particularly department heads and first-line supervisors, should know what they may and may not do, what may and may not be said, and how the supervisors' attitudes, opinions, and actions may be construed under the law.

When an Election Takes Place

A point that is likely to be overlooked in an election is that a union needs only 51 percent of the vote to legally represent the employees. This means that if an establishment has 100 employees and only 11 of them vote, but of those 11 voters 6 of them vote for the union, the union is the representative for all the employees, even though almost 90 percent of them did not vote at all! It would therefore behoove the management team opposed to union representation to inform all employees about the issues involved and to "get out the vote."

Herbert K. Witzky in his book, *The Labor-Management Relations Handbook for Hotels, Motels, Restaurants and Institutions*, lists ten instances in which hotel managements made mistakes, some of them quite innocently, in labor relations. In each case the National Labor Relations Board ruled against management.[6]

—A hotel manager employed a spy to attend
   employee meetings called by the union. The spy
   reported the names of employees who signed union
   cards and union strategy and plans. The employees
   who signed were fired. The union filed a complaint
   with the NLRB. Obviously, this was a case of
   dirty pool on the part of management.
Result: The hotel was made to rehire the employees
   and pay them in full for all lost wages. A notice
   had to be inserted in each pay envelope advising
   employees they were free to join the union of their
   choice.

6. Herbert K. Witzky, *The Labor-Management Relations Handbook* (Boston: Cahners Books, 1975).

—A hotel manager fired thirteen employees who signed union cards and stated that they had been fired because business was slow. Business was not slow. Again, a blatant case disregarding the intent of the National Labor Relations Act.

Result: The manager was forced to rehire them.

—Another hotel owner had a different ploy, arranging for the preparation of false reports of guest complaints against two employees suspected of unionism.

—A New Jersey hotel operator hired only people who had been cleared by the union. The NLRB interpreted this action as coercing applicants into joining the union and as discriminating against nonunion persons.

Result: The hotel had to back pay all employees' initiation fees, union dues, and other collected monies from the time the contract had gone into effect. In this instance the employer could well have believed he was "cooperating" and trying to make the contract with the union work. It could have been an instance where goodwill backfired because of lack of knowledge.

—In negotiating with a union, hotel management insisted on a no-strike clause with full union liability for any injury or damage caused by any violation. It also insisted that the liability be extended to the full resources of the International Union.

Result: The NLRB ruled that the hotel company could not insist on an "or else" tag when negotiating, which in their view was a refuse-to-bargain condition.

—An employee who asked to pass out union cards to fellow employees at a hotel was fired. Management claimed it had a strict rule forbidding all solicitation at the hotel.

Result: It was found that such a no-solicitation rule was not in effect at the hotel. The individual was ordered rehired with return of all back wages.

—In private sessions with employees, a hotel manager promised a raise if the employees would not vote to join the union.

Result: The NLRB ruled that the hotel was interfering with the rights of employees to organize.

—A California motel owner fired an employee for passing out the union cards of a local hotel and restaurant union. The owner invited an organizer from a different union to speak to the employees, who was able to convince them to join that union.

Result: The NLRB ordered withdrawal of recognition of the union and forced the owner to reimburse all employees for the dues they had paid into it.

The owner could have formed the second union, feeling that it would be more fair and would better represent the hotel employees. The owner may also have had an understanding with the second union leadership that a "sweetheart contract" would be forthcoming, one that would be more favorable to management.

—A hotel owner arranged to have employees who were thinking about joining a union called in by the personnel manager and told that if they joined the union they would have to pay their own insurance, that bonuses would be cut off, that some would be laid off, and that the workload would be increased for the remaining personnel.

Result: The NLRB ruled that this was an unfair labor practice.

—The management of a 200-room hotel in the Northeast helped create an Employee Relations Committee, and for seven years covered the expenses of operating it.

Result: The NLRB interpreted the Employee Relations Committee as being in effect a labor union. Management was told to stop dealing with the committee in any way unless an NLRB election was held, proving that a majority of employees wanted the committee to represent them.

In this instance the hotel management may have been sincerely interested in developing employee representation. Or the motivation could have been a desire to keep other and stronger unions from coming in.

LABOR NEGOTIATIONS

Once a union gains recognition, the firm must then sit down with union representatives and negotiate a labor agreement, which is then subject to negotiation if either party desires every year or so.

Labor negotiations is a specialty in itself. Few hotel or restaurant operators are well enough informed or experienced to get involved in labor relations without expert help. Government regulations concerning labor relations change. So too do legal interpretations of regulations. It might be expected that the larger hotel or restaurant chains would maintain fairly large labor or industrial labor relations departments. Such is not the case. In one large hotel chain one vice-president conducts nearly all of the labor negotiations throughout this country for the company. This individual, highly skilled at this specialty and well-read on changes in laws and what is happening around the country in labor negotiations, is usually confronted across the bargaining table by equally experienced representatives from the international union. The individual operator would be at a serious disadvantage in such a bargaining situation.

Those hotel and restaurant operators whose employees are represented by the union meet periodically with union representatives to agree upon wages, hours, conditions of work, and related subjects. The agreement may take a few minutes; sometimes it requires days or weeks, depending upon the attitudes of the representatives present.

To many, the bargaining process is a game of psychology, the object being to get the opposing members into a frame of mind that will cause them to agree to demands. There are many widely used techniques for this purpose. One of the most common is to make blue-sky demands—demands that are ridiculously extravagant. A common technique is to ask for twice as much as you expect to get. Some negotiators attempt to beat their opponents down by force of logic. Others attempt to secure agreements that are in the face of the law, or that can be sidestepped in practice.

Undoubtedly some persons are better traders than others, and they use that ability to their advantage at the bargaining table. If the trading can be done so that all parties are satisfied, well and good. If, however, one wins one's demands at the expense of the enmity of the other party, the victory is a hollow one.

Many persons skilled in industrial relations believe it unwise to have negotiators who are of a legalistic trend of mind. Such negotiators, it is believed, are too concerned with technicalities and with winning the case. The negotiator should know the law, but should not try to profit at the expense of the other negotiators. The contract should be shown to a lawyer for consideration of legal aspects after the negotiations.

The individual restaurant operator can call upon the state restaurant association or the National Restaurant Association for help if the restaurant is a member of either. The individual hotel operator likewise can call upon the American Hotel and Motel Association through the state hotel association for collective bargaining advice. Undoubtedly strong-arm tactics have been employed by local unions and often the individual operator is comparatively helpless. The individual operator may be called upon to put money under the table to avoid a strike. Picket lines can be placed around the establishment, damage may be done to food and beverage deliveries, and "accidents" may happen within the establishment. If the property is picketed the Teamsters Union will usually refuse to cross the picket line to deliver supplies.

Pointers for Negotiating Contracts

According to a guide for dealing with the union, a number of tactics can be employed during negotiations with the union that will work to the employer's advantage.[7]

- —The company should come into the negotiations with its own proposals and avoid being placed completely on the defensive by listening to only those proposals made by the union.
- —Before yielding to a union demand, insist upon a corresponding concession.
- —In responding to a wage proposal an employer can make a counterproposal so low as to have ample room to negotiate.
- —The general posture during negotiations should be one of flexibility and resourcefulness.
- —Be patient.
- —Never lose your cool.
- —Keep your word, especially about "off the record" discussions.
- —During negotiations, be wary of showmanship on the part of the union, showmanship that may be in the form of dramatics, table pounding, screaming, or intimidation. Other union negotiators may use the "honey" approach.
- —If the union presents exorbitant wage demands, do not make a counterproposal until the demands are reduced to reasonable proportions.
- —The employer may use certain ploys, such as creating "straw men"—proposing certain items which, while desirable, are not essential—demands that can be withdrawn in exchange for concessions.
- —It is best to have negotiations on "company ground," either in a company conference room, in the company lawyer's office, or in other space rented by the company.
- —Keep complete notes of the proceedings: the National Labor Relations Board tends to believe the side that keeps the best notes.

When Demands Are Unreasonable

Bearing in mind that in negotiations both sides often overstate their demands and expect to back off as a form of tactics, some overstatement can be expected at the outset of a bargaining session. When a side seems to hold to a position that appears ridiculous or unreasonable, certain tactics are in order:

1. Say that the position is ridiculous.
2. Ask that the question be referred to a third party.

---

7. Siegel, *When the Union Knocks.*

3. Ask that the position be made public.

4. Refer to industry norms for such things as wages, hours, and benefits, bearing in mind that these vary widely from city to city and from region to region.

Beware of Contract Clauses that Restrict Productivity

Union clauses in some cities forbid a lodging quarters cleaner from handling food service in any way, which results in a distasteful display of leftover food and glasses full of cigarette butts sitting in hallways of hotels, waiting for someone in the food-service department to collect them.

Another union rule requires that if the kitchen is open at all, every station must be manned, obviously very costly when serving early breakfasts or late snacks. The cost is, of course, passed on to the consumer and can drive many of the hotel's guests outside the hotel to less expensive restaurants.

Another idiotic rule requires waiters to operate only in their own station, never to as much as fill a water glass or provide additional rolls or butter for a guest at another station.[8]

The Right Number to Negotiate

It is sometimes felt that there is strength in numbers, each side of the bargaining table bringing in a large group to represent it. This tactic probably has some psychological advantage, but it has been pointed out that if good faith bargaining is to take place, only one or two spokesmen for each side should be named. Otherwise the meeting can get bogged down. Like "too many cooks spoil the soup," too many negotiators spoil the bargaining session.

Look for the Points of Agreement

In any disagreement it is a good policy to concentrate on those points which the parties agree on. Stress agreement rather than disagreement, and narrow down the areas of disagreement. Spell out differences definitely so that everyone knows about what is being argued. Too often disagreements turn out to be minor when the verbiage is cleared away.

If No Agreement Is Possible

When disagreement is pointed and has reached the stage of impasse, the points of disagreement may be referred to a third party. Or they can be tabled for a later date or indefinitely. Federal and many state laws require notification of state and federal mediation services. These services can be made available only with the consent of both parties.

THE CONTRACT OR LABOR AGREEMENT

As a result of collective bargaining, labor agreements are drawn up in written form, usually published in a handbook, and made available to all who participated and to the employees covered by the contract. As a matter of custom and practice, agreements tend to follow a pattern covering such matters as the following:

1. A statement recognizing the union as a bargaining agent for the employees covered in the contract, and the period of time covered by the contract. For example the Uniform Contract between Restaurant-Hotel Employer's Council of Southern California, Inc., and the Los Angeles Joint Executive Board of the Hotel and Restaurant Employees' and Bartenders' Union AFL-CIO, agreed upon a contract to be effective between 1975 and 1980.

2. A section covers the arrangements by which new employees must become union members.

3. A contract may stipulate that the employer must call the union first when new employees are needed.

4. A check-off clause, which means that the employer agrees to deduct union dues from an employee's wages and salaries and remit them to the union.

5. A section covering health, welfare, and retirement funds; the employer agrees to make specified remittances to such funds. (Some are pleased to comply since they feel it reduces the amount of time spent by union representatives on the property.)

6. A guarantee that authorized union representatives be permitted to come on the employer's premises to investigate conditions and interview employees at times other than during rush hours.

7. A clause that states that employees may wear union buttons and may not be discharged for any proper union activity.

8. A section that spells out the way in which grievances are to be handled. The Los Angeles contract reads in part:

"All questions, grievances or controversies pertaining to the application or interpretation of this AGREEMENT shall be handled in the following manner:

A. The EMPLOYER and the UNION shall attempt to settle the matter within seven (7) days. Claims of alleged violation of the terms and provision of this AGREEMENT should not be considered unless one of the parties hereto notifies the other of such violation within sixty (60) days after the occurrence thereof; and in any event

---

8. William B. Tabler, "Hotels in Today's Difficult Times," Statler Lectures-1974, University of Massachusetts.

no retroactive adjustment if required shall exceed sixty (60) days from the day the grievance is first submitted to EMPLOYER, or his designated representatives, by the EMPLOYEE or by the UNION."

The Los Angeles agreement goes on to say that if a settlement is not reached within a week the grievance must be submitted in writing within another week to the other party. If it still is not disposed of within two weeks, the grievance may be passed on to an impartial arbitrator, elected jointly by the union and the employer. In the Los Angeles contract the arbitrator is picked from a list of five qualified arbitrators. The arbitrator's expenses are shared jointly.

9. Vacations that must be granted employees are listed. Under the Los Angeles contract, employees receive one week of vacation after one year, and varying additional amounts of time up to four weeks after twenty years of employment.

10. Holidays for which special pay must be awarded are listed. The Los Angeles contract calls for double pay if the employee works on a designated holiday and two and one-half times the employee's regular rates of pay if required to work on a holiday that is also the sixth or seventh day of that employee's regular workweek.

11. Split Shift Limitations: In the past employers often took advantage of employees to require that they work split shifts, which meant that even though a worker might be on the job only eight hours, that individual was tied up for a much longer time. Union contracts spell out the workday and how the workday may be split. For example: In the Los Angeles contract: "Dining Room employees shall not work more than eight (8) hours in eleven (11) hours. There shall not be more than one split in a shift. There shall be no split between the hours of 6:00 P.M. and 4:00 A.M. Split and short shifts shall be permitted only in the dining room."

12. Other conditions of employment are carefully described—the number of consecutive days that may be required of an employee to work, extra pay for night work, and the like.

13. Meals on the job: Culinary workers generally are entitled to meals while on the job and time off to eat them.

14. Uniforms, linens and their cleaning: Who pays for uniforms, linens and for cleaning them is usually covered by the contract.

Uniforms can be a touchy subject; who pays for them, who launders them? Some hotels supply front desk clerks with special clothing, jackets, and ties. In concept restaurants waiter/waitress uniforms can be unique and expensive. After Caesar Ritz put his waiters in formal dress in the 1890s, the first-class waiter had quite a wardrobe. Writing in *The American Waiter* in the early part of the century, an author listed clothing that the first-class waiter should own:

One black serge jacket
One black low-cut vest
Two white jackets
One full-dress coat and vest
One tuxedo coat
One low-cut white vest
Two pairs white gloves
Two black bow ties
Two or three pairs doe or cheviot black pants
Two white ties
One pair of good shoes with rubber heels
Six white shirts, with cuffs and collars

Mr. Goins, the author, pointed out that shirts should be changed as often as twice a week. In winter, he said, underwear should be changed twice a week and in summer daily.[9]

Federal law states that "Expenses associated with the purchase and maintenance of employer-required uniforms cannot be shifted to the employee if it results in reducing hourly earnings below the required minimum."[10] Many states have a more stringent law. For example, in Colorado, the employer either provides and maintains the uniform, or the employee receives an extra 5 cents an hour to do so himself. (Ordinary white uniforms are excepted.)

15. A prohibition against strikes, picketing, and boycotts.

16. Many contracts state that a union employee may not be required to cross a picket line.

17. A statement of management prerogatives.

18. A statement describing what is bargainable.

19. A statement of how gratuities are to be distributed. In the past management often collected tips and distributed them as they saw fit, sometimes keeping part for themselves.

20. The section of most interest to employees is that dealing with wage scales.

21. As an illustration of the variety and kinds of jobs found in the classification of cooks, the relevant section in the Los Angeles contract is seen in table 17.1.

9. *Cornell H & R Quarterly,* May 1977, p. 35.
10. NRA, Washington Report, Sept. 18, 1978.

Table 17.1   Schedule "A"*

Hotels, Motels, Restaurants,
Clubs and Night Clubs

Cooks	Effective 3/16/75 Per Day	Effective 9/16/76 Per Day	Effective 4/1/78 Per Day
Chef . . . Open . . . Minimum 10% per day above highest classification rate of pay			
Sous Chef Open . . . Minimum 10% per day above highest classification rate of pay			
Second Cook Saucier	34.35	36.75	39.32
Night Chef	34.35	36.75	39.32
Pastry Chef	34.35	36.75	39.32
Second Pastry Chef	30.37	32.50	34.77
Pastry Cook	28.42	30.41	32.54
Head Baker	34.35	36.75	39.32
Second Baker	30.37	32.50	34.77
Baker	28.42	30.41	32.54
Roast Cook	33.18	35.50	37.98
**Carver	33.18	35.50	37.98
Broiler Cook	33.18	35.50	37.98
Head Fry Cook	33.18	35.50	37.98
Fry Cook	30.37	32.50	34.77
Dish-Up Man	28.42	30.41	32.54
Head Garde Manager	34.35	36.75	39.32
Second Garde Manager	30.37	32.50	34.77
Other Garde Manager	28.42	30.41	32.54
Head Delicatessen Manager	38.26	40.94	43.81
Delicatessen Man	34.75	37.18	39.78
Delicatessen Carver	34.75	37.18	39.78
Combination Delicatessen Man-Frycook (less than 4 hours per day as Delicatessen Man)	32.43	34.70	37.13
Head Butcher	34.35	36.75	39.32
Butcher	30.37	32.50	34.77
Poultry and Fish Butcher	28.42	30.41	32.54
Head Pantryman	30.37	32.50	34.77
Pantryman	28.42	30.41	32.54
All Assistants & Helpers	32.66	25.32	27.08
Vegetable Cook	28.42	30.41	32.54
First Relief Cook	34.35	36.75	39.32
Second Relief Cook	30.37	32.50	34.77
Extra Cook, 8 hours or less	34.35	36.75	39.32

The Employer may have the option of either furnishing Cooks' uniforms or paying 50 cents per day in lieu thereof; but such linens shall be laundered by the Employer.

Extra Cooks shall be a separate classification with a flat rate of pay for eight hours or less.

Relief Cooks shall be a separate classification with a flat rate of pay for eight hours or less.

Chef and Sous Chef classifications, which are now open, shall be paid a minimum of 10% per day above the highest classification rate of pay.

New Years' Eve Extra Work	39.70	42.48	45.45

*Taken from: Uniform Contract Between Restaurant-Hotel Employer's Council of Southern California, Inc. and Los Angeles Joint Executive Board of Hotel and Restaurant Employees and Bartenders Unions, AFL-CIO, March 16, 1975 through March 15, 1980.

**Exhibition carving from carving from carts for a majority of the shift.

Job Definitions

What constitutes a job is sometimes specified in the contract. Employers naturally want freedom to ask employees to do a variety of tasks; labor contracts usually restrict the kind of work that can be done by a person holding a particular job. For example, mechanics and maintenance employees "shall not perform the work involving major structure alterations. Any dispute as to whether the work constitutes mechanical maintenance work or major structural alterations shall be determined by arbitration as any other dispute arising under this agreement." Collective bargaining agreements can include definitions that restrict work performance unnecessarily. For example, contracts have stated that glasswashers may not wash dishes, which may mean that when no soiled glasses are available for washing the "glasswasher" stands idly by while dishwashers may be overworked.

The disadvantages of setting up rigid job classifications has been around for centuries. Despite the fact that Louis XV had nearly 3,000 persons in his employment, and his queen had 2,000, the queen's bed still did not get dusted. The Duc de Luynes reports that one day in 1747 the queen noticed that the woodwork at the end of her bed was covered with dust. Her lady-in-waiting sent for the *valet de chambre-tapissier,* who declined to touch it, maintaining that he and his aides were responsible for making the queen's bed but not for polishing the furniture, or even for dusting it. That was the work of another body of servants known as the *Garde-Meuble.*[11] In another anecdote the Duchess de Rohan is said to have come back hungry from a ride and ordered a lackey to bring her something to eat. He refused point-blank, and as the maitre d'hotel could not be found, the Duchess went hungry.

Union Hiring Office

The union may insist on operating an employment office and that new employees should be employed through that office. The New York agreement specifies that a joint Union-Hotel Association employment office be opened for hiring all employees except banquet waiters, waitresses, and captains. If the employer does not find an applicant who has been referred by the office to be satisfactory, the employer is free to hire someone else. (As of 1979 the normal practice in New York City was to recruit through the State Employment Service.)

Management Rights

It may seem strange that a labor contract should include management rights but management should and does insist that it has certain rights that are distinctively man-

agement, "inalienable" if management is to manage. The New York contract reads: "The employer shall have the right to direct and control its employees. The employer shall have the right to lay off, promote, or transfer any employee. Promotion shall not be subject to contest or review. The union shall, by representative designated by it, have the right to confer with the employer in behalf of any laid off or transferred employee. If the union claims that a layoff or transfer results in any abuse of the rights of employees the grievance shall be subject to the Grievance in Arbitration provisions . . . The employer shall have the right to discharge any employee. The union may question whether an employee's discharge was for just cause."

Work Schedules

While it was once possible to require hotel and restaurant employees to come in or check out at management's desire, some union contracts now stipulate that work schedules must be posted in advance. For example, the contract between the Hotel Restaurant Employees and Bartenders Union Local 5 in Honolulu with some of the larger Hawaiian hotels reads:

> Work schedules must be posted no later than Saturday afternoon, Friday noon for maintenance. Kitchen schedules are subject to change on forty-eight-hour posted notice. In case of emergencies schedules may be adjusted without penalty provided the employees are given reasonable notice and the union is promptly notified of the reasons. In making changes, the employer must give consideration to any prior arrangements the employee has made; for example, babysitters. The union tells its members that if you fail to notify your supervisor at least twenty-four hours before the schedule is posted that you will be unable to work a shift, the supervisor will substitute a junior employee for that shift.[12]

GRIEVANCE AND ARBITRATION PROCEDURES

While it is nice to think that labor and management have the same or common goals, such is not the case. Management is usually concerned with maximizing profits, labor with maximizing wages and other benefits. Differences are certain to arise. To resolve such disagreements, ground rules for discussion are necessary. Disagreement can be broadly divided into those that arise in the contention which takes place when contracts are hammered out or reopened—"contract negotiation disputes"—and

11. James Laver, *The Age of Illusion* (New York: David Mackay Company, 1972).
12. Summary of Hilton Hawaiian Village, Kahala Hilton Hotel, Kelly Hotels, Sheraton Hawaii Corporation, and Waikiki Biltmore Hotel agreements, 1970.

those that come about as a matter of interpretation of agreements already reached. These latter are usually called *grievances,* although the term is somewhat misleading. The vast majority of disputes arise over grievances.

No matter how amiable and amicable the relationship between employers and employees, some grievances are to be expected. A low grievance rate according to the experts is defined as one grievance per year for every 100 employees.[13] The number and nature of grievances reflect management policies, union political considerations, the size the establishment, and the personality of key union and company representatives.

Discussion and compromise usually resolve grievances and other differences, but if they cannot be resolved, both parties may agree to turn the dispute over to a third party—a mediator or an arbitrator. In labor negotiations, a mediator often provided by the National Labor Relations Board acts as a disinterested party, talks with both sides, and tries to produce a solution agreeable to both sides. An arbitrator does the same thing but presents a solution that is binding on both parties despite the fact one or both may disagree. The expenses of the arbitrator are shared. Arbitration can be handled by one person or a board. The board may be a three-person panel—an arbitrator from management, one from the union, and one neutral. The arbitration decision is presented in written form along with a summary of the problems presented and the reasons why a particular decision or solution was reached.

The New York agreement calls for an impartial chairman as the permanent umpire, whose compensation and whose office expenses are shared by the Association and the Union. The decisions of the impartial chairman has "the effect of a judgment entered upon an award made, as provided by the Arbitration Laws of the State of New York, entitling the entry of a judgment in a court of competent jurisdiction against the defaulting party who fails to carry out or abide by such decision."

Ordinarily, grievances move through formal stages with discussion and settlement possible at any stage. The stages of a grievance are:

Step 1: Employee grievance discussed with the supervisor.

Step 2: Union representative and employee discuss grievance with the department head.

Step 3: The business agent joins in the discussion.

Step 4: Arbitration.

Whether or not a grievance has any basis in objective conditions, it is always real to the person having it. Often the stated cause of a grievance may not have any logical connection to the complaint. An employee may complain of not being able to stand the work in a kitchen because of a draft caused by an open window. To satisfy the employee the window is closed and now the grievance changes to "it is too hot in this kitchen." An interview with the employee may disclose the real cause of the individual's complaint to be a feeling against a certain loudmouthed cook who the employee works alongside. Since the stated cause of the grievance does not correlate with the facts, should management disregard such complaints? Obviously not. The fancied grievance about the draft is just as real to the employee as though it were fact. Management, as management, attempts to make all conditions correct for optimal efficiency. If the grievances were disregarded, management would be falling down on its job. Stated grievances give management opportunity to change conditions that impair morale and production. The mere expression of a grievance to a sympathetic listener may settle it. The real causes of many grievances are injured feelings, a lack of friendship, a need to confide in someone. Supervisors who understand such feelings can, by attentive listening and a genuine expression of interest in the employee's stated problem, often solve the unstated problem. Where real deficiencies exist in the work situation, pay rates, or personal relationships, the grievance procedure is a valuable means of calling attention to them so that they can be corrected.

Of course, if employees do not know and understand the grievance procedure, it is of no value. Real or imagined injustices are permitted to simmer and finally erupt. The employee feels subject to the whims of the supervisor, without a means for appeal. Thus the employee's feeling of security, which is necessary for job satisfaction and best job performance, is seriously impaired.

A policy that permits any employee to appeal to top management for a review of his or her case in the event the employee's supervisor or department head places the person's job in jeopardy is one calculated to increase employee security and the all-important feeling of belonging. Some chain operations provide a system of appeals by which an employee in a branch house may appeal to the home office for a review of a grievance. This would appear to be an excellent policy as long as it is handled so as not to undermine the supervisor's or branch manager's leadership.

Other Clauses

The union demands that no employee be discharged or laid off because of union activities. (Certain protections are legally provided by provisions of the NLRB.)

---

13. *Cornell H & R Quarterly,* May 1977, p. 37.

Interestingly, in New York City the Association and the union have agreed to establish a joint program for training employees for promotion and advancement. Employers contribute a dollar to the program each month for each employee.

Contracts spell out vacations and holidays. The New York contract says there would be one week vacation after one year of work, two weeks after two years, twelve days after five years, and three weeks after ten years of employment. Employees who are asked to work on legal holidays as defined by the contract receive double pay.

The New York City contract also specifies that uniforms be supplied by the employer when required for work.

Any number of other special clauses can be introduced into an agreement. For example, in the agreement between Local 5 Hawaii and certain Hawaiian hotels the employer makes up the difference between what the employee could receive on the job and what that employee is paid for jury duty in the event of being called for that duty. Funeral leave is included as a right. "In case of the death of a parent, spouse, child, brother or sister, the employee is entitled to two days paid leave and up to five more calendar days of unpaid leave." Some contracts and state regulations call for premium pay when an employee works a split shift or a short shift.

A University Food-Service Contract

A number of food services in universities have been unionized. A university contract, for example, may stipulate:

—All regularly scheduled employees must become members within thirty days of being hired.
—Once an employee signs an authorization card, the university payroll department must deduct dues and initiation fees, which sum is turned over to the union.
—Employees work a forty-hour week, five consecutive days, with time-and-a-half for regular overtime on the sixth day, double time on the seventh day, and double-time-and-a-half for holidays.
—There are twelve paid holidays.
—Regular employees who work twenty or more hours a week receive $3,000 in free life insurance.
—A hospitalization, medical, and major medical plan includes family coverage.
—A pension plan is in effect: 1 percent of yearly earnings based on the highest income year in the last five years prior to retirement, multiplied by total years of service; the plan is completely employer funded.

—Funeral leave: three paid days.
—Sick leave: twelve days per year after six months of service; cumulative up to 200 days.
—The university supplies and launders uniforms for employees.
—Vacations: two weeks after one to four years; three weeks after five to nine years; four weeks after ten to nineteen years; five weeks after twenty or more years.
—Records must be kept whenever an employee is tardy, and a formalized warning must be issued to the employee.
—At Harvard University, fringe benefits, in a large part brought about by union pressure, amount to forty-two cents for every payroll dollar.

Shop Stewards and Business Agents

Once an establishment has been unionized, the union appoints shop stewards in each department to represent the employees or the steward is elected by the employees in the department. The shop steward is not paid by the union, but it is important to note that most frequently the person is appointed, not elected by the employees of the department. When grievances arise they are taken to the shop steward, who in turn takes them up with the supervisor or, if necessary, the business agent. In a large city like Los Angeles, the union has a dozen or more business agents, each one concerned with a geographical area and a particular group of employees. Most grievances are handled on the first or second level, but if they cannot be resolved they move on to a higher level and eventually, if not settled, to arbitration. The union is just as eager as management to avoid going to arbitration because the cost can run up into several hundred or even thousands of dollars per arbitration case.

Care in Discharging Employees

There is no question but that union activity and labor contracts have forced management in many parts of the country to be more careful and to have second thoughts about discharging employees. Indiscriminate firing will, of course, be resisted by the union. It will irritate not only the person discharged but will create anxiety among remaining employees. To show good faith, a manager in a hotel or restaurant may give an employee who is not performing well (for whatever reason) a series of written warnings. By discussing the problem employee with the shop steward, the business agent, or the union official in charge, a minimal amount of ill feeling is created. But it is important to talk to the employee first and then to send a memo or letter summarizing the conversation to that individual, pointing out areas of dissatisfaction—tardiness, discourtesy, high breakage, appearance, disinterest, slow performance, and so on.

If performance continues on a low standard, have a second discussion and send a second memo. If this fails, the third discussion and memo should be sufficient to justify any discharge and usually will if the union representative and the employees have not been unnecessarily antagonized previously and been kept aware of the concern over performance.

Some operators favor giving the unproductive or disruptive employee a day off—with pay—to decide if the job is what the employee can and/or will perform. Such action causes the employee to take a serious look at the job and whatever is affecting performance.

Take a Union Official to Lunch

What better place to discuss mutual personnel problems than over lunch with the relevant union official? Some restaurant and hotel managers make a point of having lunch at least once a month with the union official, just to avoid misunderstandings. If indeed the luncheon is used to reach a more amicable relationship, it is an excellent investment in time and food.

SUMMARY

We have seen that unionization is strong in larger hotels, particularly in the cities (exception—the South). Unionization has advantages and disadvantages, at least theoretically. It is likely to provide checks and balances on management. Overall it exerts upward pressure on wages and provides some protection for the individual employee. Unionization requires additional time and effort on the part of management and supervisors and often reduces efficiency in operations by restricting productivity.

In many locations unionization is a fact of life, and management must learn to work within the parameters established by the union contract and the federal and state laws covering labor/management relations. In others, management is strongly adverse to unionization and can do a number of things to avoid having employees vote for collective bargaining. A number of legal practices as well as those regarded as "unfair labor practices" are discussed. The best shields against unionization are good management-employee relations and wages, salaries, and working conditions as good as or better than those prevailing in the area.

Fire and Safety Programs

18

Fire protection and safety programs have one thing in common: both require the active interest of top management to be effective. Fire and accident prevention are functions of management, reflecting management alertness and its relation to employees. Both involve human life, misery, and high costs if neglected. Hundreds of lives and millions of dollars have been lost in hotel/motel and restaurant fires. Accidents can cause lifetime impairment. Contrary to what might be expected, hotels, motels, and restaurants are relatively hazardous places insofar as accidents and fires are concerned.

Accidents are costly. Premiums for workman's compensation insurance were over three times as costly in 1978 than those of 1952. Weekly compensation paid to out-of-work employees (those who've been injured, laid off, etc.) have been increased regularly. Medical and hospital costs continue to climb sharply. And courts of law continue to award generous sums to individuals in settlement of their civil suits brought against an employer.

THE OCCUPATIONAL SAFETY AND HEALTH ACT OF 1970

The Occupational Safety and Health Act of 1970 (OSHA) is one of the most far reaching labor statutes ever enacted by Congress. No longer can increased safety be considered merely a desirable goal for American industry. Safety is demanded by law.

Every employer in the food service industry is covered. As of this writing, there is an effort in Congress to lessen substantially OSHA's regulatory powers over small operations. To assure compliance, the act provides for penalties of sizeable fines.

Government agencies are stepping in to insist that safety training programs be instituted. In California, for example, every employer is mandated to inaugurate and maintain an accident prevention program that includes the following:

A training program designed to instruct employees in general safety work practices and specific instructions with respect to hazards unique to the employee's job assignment.

Scheduled periodic inspections are conducted to identify and correct unsafe conditions and work practices that may be found.

The state supplies consultants from the Division of Industrial Safety who assist in the development of training programs for employers and employees on such subjects as safety and health and advise on safety standards and their application to specific situations.

Health and Safety Standards

Minimum safety standards have been published by state and federal agencies relating to such things as safe walking and working areas; adequate sanitation; elimination of fire and accident hazards; supplying safety equipment, including medical and first aid where it is obviously needed; maintaining permissible noise and pollution levels; providing required guards for machinery (high speed slicers and grinders); adopting necessary safety factors for ovens, furnaces, industrial gas piping equipment, oil burning equipment, boilers, pressure cookers, and elevators; installing required coverings for fuel systems; and proper groundings for electrical outlets.[1]

The Occupational Safety and Health Act of 1970 established the National Institute for Occupational Safety and Health (NIOSH) under the Department of Health, Education and Welfare and the Occupational Safety and Health Administration (OSHA) under the Department of Labor. In some states the federal government has del-

---

1. "Interim Occupational and Health Standards," *Federal Register,* part 2, May 29, 1971. On April 28, 1973, permanent Occupational and Health Safety Standards were issued. These serve as the final authority spelling out all aspects of the law.

334

egated enforcement authority for occupational safety and health to state governments. Although state standards sometimes differ, they must be at least as effective as the federal standards. NIOSH (the technical arm of OSHA) has published the "Health and Safety Guide for Hotels and Motels."[2] This guide describes safe practices and includes requirements under federal regulations, and suggests a number of accepted good safety practices.

Much of the maintenance of occupational health and of environmental control is based on common sense—common sense that many of us fail to exercise from time to time. An employee should not be placed in a noisy environment, but what is a noisy environment? The NIOSH regulations say that no one should be exposed to ninety decibels for more than eight hours, and even this level of noise may result in hearing damage to some individuals. At ninety decibels a person must shout at a distance of two feet to be heard. Some dishrooms could reach this level, and a high-speed ventilating fan might give off this amount of noise.

Most of us recognize that we should not stand on the top rung of a ladder for the simple reason that there is no support for balance at this level and very little at the next rung down. Metal ladders, good conductors of electricity, can be dangerous when used in electrical work.

It makes good sense to put nonskid material on quarry tile, because quarry tile becomes very slick when damp or wet.

Most of us know that oily rags are capable of spontaneous combustion, yet it may seem like too much trouble to put them in a metal receptacle or to dispose of them daily.

It is perfectly obvious that a first-aid kit should be available in every establishment and that someone should be around who is trained in first aid. But how often is this commonsense practice overlooked?

Meat slicers are a major hazard in a kitchen because they are purposefully kept razor sharp. Even disassembling them for cleaning can be highly dangerous. Are personnel who are working these slicers properly warned and trained? A number of shortened fingers will attest to the sad fact that something was omitted.

The booklet "Health and Safety Guide for Hotels and Motels" contains some eighty pages of regulations and recommendations to maintain health and safety. Most of us won't read it so it would be helpful to invite a representative of the company accident insurance carrier to look over the establishment and make recommendations.

Offhand it would be expected that a hotel or restaurant is a very safe place in which to work. No so. The guest may be a considerable factor in the safety, or lack of it, in a hotel. Up in the guest rooms, a guest may be smoking in bed and may drop off to sleep with a lighted cigarette in hand—a major fire hazard.

Down in the kitchen, employees are scurrying about on damp, quarry tile floors, which are setups for falls and serious injuries. The exhaust ducts over the cooking equipment are probably laden with grease and ready to ignite the second something on the stove catches on fire and the flames reach the hood. Chefs are cutting away with knives and meat slicers, often cutting themselves.

In dining rooms around the country, guests are drinking, talking, often failing to cut their meat into bite-sized pieces. All too frequently the large chunks of meat lodge in a guest's throat and the person chokes to death. Hotels and restaurants can be hazardous places in which to work and to frequent as guests.

The Bureau of Labor Statistics collects data on work-related injuries and illnesses in a number of industries. In 1974 eating and drinking places experienced 170,300 occupational injuries and illnesses. About 52,000 of these caused lost workdays, the average number of workdays being lost was 11.[3]

Record Keeping

The OSHA law requires every employer to make and preserve records of occupational injuries and illnesses so as to develop information that will aid in preventing industrial accidents and illnesses. Specifically, three types of records must be maintained: (1) a log of all reportable occupational injuries and illnesses, (2) an annual summary of the total number of reportable occupational injuries and illnesses including deaths, and (3) an annual general report required by the Secretary of Labor. Details can be obtained from the state hotel and restaurant association.

Recognizing that small business may endure unusual hardships in maintaining records, provisions are made by which a company can petition the Labor Department to permit alternate methods of record keeping. In order to meet the provisions of the act, small businesses may also be eligible for loans from the Small Business Administration to upgrade facilities to meet new health and safety standards.

2. "Health and Safety Guide for Hotels and Motels," U.S. Department of Health, Education and Welfare, Division of Technical Services, Cincinnati, Ohio, 1975. Obtainable from the U.S. Government Printing Office, Washington, D.C.
3. "Health and Safety Guide for Hotels and Motels," U.S. Department of Health, Education and Welfare. Cincinnati, Ohio, 1975.

FIRE PREVENTION AND THE GUEST

Cigarette smoking, particularly smoking in bed, is the number one cause of hotel and motel fires. In Texas, for example, the Board of Insurance Commissioners reported that 74 percent of the hotel fires in that city were caused by careless disposal of cigarettes and matches. The cigarette falls on the carpet or bedding and a fire starts. How to prevent such habits? The answer is not in posting "No Smoking!" signs, for one cannot change habits fixed over a period of years by the use of signs.

Fireproofing as much of the room furnishings as possible helps. The placing of ash trays in swivels that permit the trays to swing close to the prone smoker helps. One motel with two parallel lines of sleeping units introduced swiveled ash trays in one line of units and left the other line as before. During the succeeding year several fires occurred in the units without the swiveled ash trays, none in the other units.

Another preventive method is to make the guest pay. The city of Houston has an ordinance that makes it a misdemeanor for guests to cause a hotel fire through carelessness. Guilty guests pay not only the fire damage to the hotel but also a fine to the city. Detroit has a similar ordinance.

Notifying Guests of Fire

State laws require that the innkeeper exercise "reasonable and ordinary care in the safety of guests." The hotel is responsible for notifying guests immediately of any danger. A fire in a Texas hotel started at 4:20 A.M. and by 4:30 it was beyond control. Employees tried to extinguish the blaze but failed to notify the guests by telephone or otherwise. Several people died, and the hotel was held liable because of the ten-minute delay in warning guests.

A guest of a western hotel charged that he detected smoke and told the desk clerk. Nothing was done and about two hours later the guest awoke in a smoke-filled room. Getting no response on the telephone, he tried to take the elevator but it was not running. Escaping by means of a rope fire escape, the rope parted. The hotel proprietor was held liable for failing to notify all guests and do everything to save them from danger.

All employees should be trained to notify the telephone operator at the first indication of fire. Seconds count. The telephone operator then calls the closest fire fighting organization and sets off the system for fighting fires within the hotel. Some hotels have made the mistake of requiring notification of the general manager before notifying outside firefighting organizations. Too often the general manager cannot be found immediately. In the small hotel or motel, notification of the owner, who is probably on the premises, might be a desirable first course of action.

The American Hotel and Motel Association (AH&MA) issued this fire prevention bulletin for summer resort hotels. The first five items need daily check. The others should be examined once or twice during the season.

1. Make sure that *No Smoking* regulations are enforced. Modern practice is to confine smoking to a special *safe smoking area* supplied with plenty of ash trays or sandpails for the disposal of smoking materials. State and municipal laws must, of course, be considered here.

2. Store painters' supplies in an outlying building or other safe storage space. Keep everything including drop cloths in this area, except for immediate requirements. Make sure that rags and oily waste are put in tight, metal containers and removed at the end of each day.

3. Do not leave unattended salamanders (portable stoves or incinerators) in a building at any time.

4. Provide fire extinguishers and a fire watch for operations involving cutting or welding equipment. (See the following section on cutting and welding.)

5. Maintain good housekeeping conditions. Do not allow combustible trash to accumulate; rather, remove it daily and burn it in a safe location.

6. Clear excessive underbrush around principal buildings and make sure that grass and weeds are close cut. A well-groomed space of 100 to 300 feet is advisable depending on the amount of combustible undergrowth and dry grass beyond the clearing space.

7. Make certain that your employees know how to turn in an alarm to your local fire department and understand the need for immediate action in the event of fire.

8. Check to see that water has been turned on in hose standpipes or other fire protective equipment and that extinguishers have been recharged.

9. Arrange storage outdoors or in a small outlying building for any larger quantities of furnishings, plumbing, fixtures, etc., that are delivered in combustible wrappings or light crating.

10. Provide watch guards at night and at other times when the premises are unattended.

11. Notify your insurance carrier of any structural alterations made or being made.

12. To ensure the safest means of heating your buildings, use your own heating plant or portable Underwriters' Laboratories listed oil-heat units. If salamanders must be used, place them on a solid, noncombustible footing away from woodwork or tarpaulins. Coke or coal are the safest fuels for salamanders.

13. Use only flameproof tarpaulins.

14. Check electrical circuits to make sure they are properly fused, and that frayed lamp and appliance cords have been replaced.

15. Make certain that light arrester and lightning rod wire grounds are in good condition.

Cutting and Welding

Since cutting and welding are important methods for severing or joining piping and structural steel, they are frequently used in hotel maintenance. Both present hazards, although oxyacetylene equipment is more dangerous in welding than either gas or electrical equipment.

Here are the precautions that should be taken before and during such operations:

1. Sweep clean and wet down the surrounding floor.

2. Relocate combustible storage thirty to forty feet away and use asbestos or flameproof tarpaulins to protect any storage that cannot be moved.

3. Provide extinguishing equipment such as hose lines, extinguishers, or water pails at the scene of operations.

4. Keep the area under watch for at least a half hour after the work is completed. It is necessary to extend this care to any location on floors above or below where metal globules may go. (When a piece of pipe or a steel building member is cut, small globules of molten metal are thrown out in a heavy shower resembling rain. The globules may bounce and roll for as far as thirty to forty feet from the actual cutting operations; sometimes they get through pipe holes or cracks to the floor below. They can easily start smoldering fires that burst into flame when no one is present.)

5. Appoint someone from your own staff to designate areas where cutting or welding can be done. It is unwise to give outside workers unlimited choice in this matter.

6. Make sure that at least one helper is available to use extinguishing equipment if necessary. A small fire may not be visible to the cutting equipment operator while wearing dark glasses.

Avoiding Spontaneous Ignition

Spontaneous ignition can be easily avoided if you observe these simple safety rules:

1. Use cans with tight, self-closing covers for the storage of materials that may heat spontaneously. (Garbage cans with tight lids may also be used for this purpose.)

2. Empty the cans at the end of the day.

3. Make sure that all waste and sweepings are burned in a well-arranged incinerator, trucked away, or otherwise safely removed.

Materials in common use that heat spontaneously include: (a) vegetable oils such as linseed, cottonseed, coconut, palm, olive, peanut, and soybean; (b) animal oils including lard and tallow; (c) certain solids including soft coal. All forms of fermenting or decaying organic matter (hay or silage) produce some heat, although temperatures seldom become high enough for ignition.

Properly stored, these materials are harmless. Take linseed oil, for example. It will not heat spontaneously in a bottle because of the small surface exposed. If thinly spread fiber-waste is soaked with linseed oil, the exposed surface area is greatly increased and oxidation takes place. However, the thinly spread waste affords no insulation and the heat is dissipated rapidly enough so that ignition is unlikely. Now take the same oil-soaked waste and wad it up in a ball. Oxidation proceeds at the same rate, but the outer layers of the ball provide insulation so that heat is not so readily lost from the center. The heat at the center of the wad rises. The chances that it will rise high enough to ignite the wadding are increased. If the whole package is placed in a warm place, look out!

Foam Rubber Products

In recent years foam rubber has been used more and more as filling for upholstered chairs, sofas, pillows, mattresses, and seating equipment. It may vary considerably in its composition, but foam rubber is about as easy to ignite as feathers, cotton stuffing, or hair. When it is covered with a combustible textile as it usually is in mattresses, pillows, and chairs, the ignition hazard becomes that of textile covering; rapid surface burning of the foam rubber will then result. When foam rubber materials are taken from a laundry drying tumbler and placed in a hamper where they are effectively insulated by other materials, spontaneous heating can result in ignition. Once ignited, foam rubber or foam latex burns rapidly under most conditions.

Foam rubber releases almost as much heat when it is burned as gasoline. It not only burns rapidly, but gives off dense clouds of heavy smoke. Thus the storage of large piles of foam rubber pillows or mattresses presents a serious fire hazard. The danger is not so much from spontaneous ignition under normal storage conditions, but in

Figure 18.1

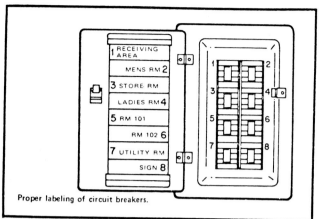

Proper labeling of circuit breakers.

the intense burning rate and rapid flame spread once the material has been ignited from any source. Storage of large quantity of foam rubber requires automatic protection engineered to meet these conditions.

Circuit Breakers and Fuses

Circuit breakers and fuses are the safety valves of electrical circuits. Their purpose, of course, is to shut an electrical circuit when it becomes overloaded. Heat in or around a fuse box indicates that circuits are overloaded and fuses with too high a rating are being used. If the circuits are seriously overloaded, the fuse box itself may be warm to the touch. If the wiring is overloaded, the temperature of the wire rises and this can be detected at the fuse box.

If a fuse blows out, for example, it does not solve the problem to replace it with a fuse rated too high or by placing a coin behind a plug fuse. That only increases the chances that the safety equipment will be unable to function properly. Fuses with a *time-lag* have been available in recent years. These fuses permit the overload to continue for an interval. With the starting of a motor the time-lag fuse permits a momentary overload; but the fuse will blow if the overload persists. Call your electrician for advice if fuses of the proper rating cannot be used without continued interruptions of service. These interruptions serve as warnings of overloaded circuits that may cause fires.

The *Health and Safety Guide for Hotels and Motels* states that "more fires are caused by electrical malfunction than any other cause." Ironically, the guide also states that standards pertaining to electrical equipment and their use have been cited as violations more frequently than any others. How many times have you seen a circuit-breaker box without labels? An obvious violation and one easily corrected (see fig. 18.1):

How often have you seen frayed and deteriorating flexible cords running to vacuum cleaners? A shocking situation, perhaps the cause of the next hotel fire.

PREVENTION OF ELECTRICAL FIRES

Analysis of a study of 122 hotel fires showed that 21 percent were attributed to electrical deficiencies—defective wiring, motors, and appliances. In a similar study of 75 motel fires, 16 percent were classified as "electrical."

Used periodically, the following checklist will help to prevent most types of electrical fires.

1. Replace temporary or makeshift wiring promptly with a permanent safe installation.
2. Use explosion-proof equipment where needed, as in rooms where paints are stored or mixed.
3. Replace damaged cords, switches, or plugs immediately.
4. Avoid overcrowding outlets, as this causes deterioration of wiring.
5. Never allow unprotected light bulbs to be used.
6. Clean all motors periodically to prevent buildup of grease and dirt.
7. Prohibit use of wiring run under carpets for additional lamps, etc. This unsafe practice permits the wires to be stepped on and the insulation to be worn off, thus causing the heated wires to come in contact with the rug.
8. Check to see that electric cords are not strung over metal piping or nails where deterioration or breakage can occur.
9. Never allow use of "octopus" multisocket connections.
10. Limit extension cords to fifteen feet in length and do not use multiple interconnected extension cords.
11. Make sure that fuses or circuit breakers are of correct capacity.
12. Inspect and maintain all motors according to a planned schedule.
13. Insist that cooling coils on refrigeration equipment be clean and well ventilated.
14. Keep light bulbs and other "hot" appliances clear of combustible material.
15. Buy and use only those appliances and accessories approved by an underwriters laboratory.[4]

---

4. "Fire and Accident Prevention," *Operations Bulletin* (New York: American Hotel & Motel Association, November, 1968).

A FIRE PROTECTION PROGRAM

A complete fire protection program is more than fire prevention in the usual sense of the word. It is more than a set of rules of what not to do, of where to store inflammables, and the upkeep of fire extinguishers. The best fire prevention program sometimes fails. It is at such a time that the need for a more complete program is glaringly evident.

Training in ways of combating fires is a necessity. The training should not be perfunctory or sporadic. It must be continuous, instilled by regular drills. Every key person in the organization must know their particular duty assignment. The training must be such that in case of fire, a trained fire brigade is already on the scene.

Who Should Be Responsible for Fire Training?

Since every hotel and nearly every large restaurant is a fairly well-contained unit, usually within a single building with its own power, light, and heat supply, the logical person to head the fire protection program is the manager of the business. Just as aboard a ship all responsibilities center under the office of one individual, the captain of the ship, so it is in a hotel or restaurant. If a fire occurs, the manager or a representative of the manager is responsible. As aboard a ship, however, no one individual can perform all the duties for which the captain is responsible. The manager who attempts directly to control the training, hiring, firing, and other jobs rightly performed by the personnel manager or an assistant is a jack-of-all-trades, master of none. In the large manufacturing establishment the responsibility for fire prevention is usually delegated to a safety department. The hotel and restaurant do not have such a specialized department. In large hotels the chief engineer is often assigned the fire fighting and training responsibility. In some hotels the security chief is in charge.

Training for Fire Fighting

During the period preceding World War II, the United States Navy believed its fire fighting program to be adequate. The war soon dispelled such notions. More ships were lost as a result of fires than from any other reason. Drastic steps were taken. Almost every man in the seagoing Navy was required to spend an intensive period of training during which he was literally sent into the flames to extinguish roaring oil and gasoline fires. Aboard ship continuous drills made his knowledge of fire fighting equipment a workable, active knowledge. In the case of

actual fire his reactions could be predicted. He acted automatically. He knew his fire station, he knew his piece of equipment and, more importantly, he had been so conditioned that he would not panic. Ship losses due to fires were greatly reduced. The Navy training program followed well-known principles, namely learning by doing, and learning by repetition. Fire drills were repeated until the individual acted automatically. He had learned the manner in which to act so thoroughly that thought was unnecessary.

Some factories dealing with dangerous inflammables have several fires every day. No one gets particularly excited, and no one becomes frightened. The fires are quickly extinguished by highly trained fire teams. The hotels and restaurants can so train their personnel that, given proper equipment, fires will offer no danger during working hours. (Nighttime fires are something else.)

Training Fire Brigades

Several hotels have introduced a plan of fire protection patterned after the Navy plan. In the plan all key personnel are assigned fire stations. All stations and the names of personnel assigned to the stations are posted. Monthly fire drills are held.

Keeping the fire bill (roster of personnel and their duties in case of fire) effectively current at all times is a continuous job on the part of the director of the fire program. Employee turnover and changes in shifts necessitate rearrangement in the fire organization. Often the fire organization is least effective at night, when serious danger is most likely to develop.

Working closely with the director of the fire protection program is the chief engineer. The engineer's responsibility is to see that the fire fighting equipment is in working order. Too often fires have become uncontrollable because of faulty equipment or lack of an adequate water supply.

Telephone operators are also key personnel in any fire protection program. Because telephone operators are in control of communication, it is recommended by the National Safety Council that they set up these procedural instructions:

1. Notification of municipal fire department.
2. House officers to be notified, and in what order.
3. Procedure for warning guests.
4. Wires to be kept open for emergency use only.

Of course, periodic drill is essential if the personnel are to learn their duties. Instruction in the use of the fire fighting equipment is also necessary. The nearest fire station personnel are usually available for teaching. Instruction can be reinforced by periodic demonstration lectures. Every possible emergency should be investigated and the steps to be taken gone over in drill. Leaving matters to a general understanding is not enough. When the emergency arises, general understanding becomes general confusion.

Every employee should be so trained that in case of fire his or her first act will be to do one of two things. If the fire is small, the person will fight it alone. If it is of any size, the employee will immediately notify the hotel switchboard operator, who notifies the municipal fire department. Immediate and swift action is imperative. The first few moments of a fire determine whether it can be extinguished without damage or whether loss of property and perhaps loss of life will result.

Fighting some fires, even small ones, can be highly dangerous. A cleaner's cart with cleaning chemicals, for example, can give off poisonous fumes if the cart catches fire.

Employees will respond enthusiastically to fire brigade training if it is properly presented. When employees understand the importance of fire prevention and gain an ego reward from participation in prevention programs, the program is likely to be a success.

The patrons of the hotel and restaurant are probably more of a hazard in case of fire than are flames, smoke, and other attendant dangers. Television news scenes of panic-stricken guests leaping to their deaths and killing one another only serve to emphasize the need for careful planning. Key personnel must be trained to direct the flow of patrons to the proper exits. Security personnel, engineering, and front desk people are often trained. Such personnel must be schooled in the proper course of action for any of the possible emergencies that may arise. Should the front exits be blocked, they must know of other routes. Guests should never ride the elevators, those could stall, leaving them helpless between floors where the fire is most dangerous. Elevator cabs may be death traps.

Bell Code System for Locating Fire

Coded alarm systems for dispatching employees to the scene of the fire immediately are used. Bells and alarms have been installed at strategic points throughout the hotel: manager's office, assistant manager's desk, apartment, linen room, engineer's office, halls, and public areas. Fires are reported to the telephone operator who, by referring to a chart, rings the bells identifying the fire's location.

The code is set up so that the fire location is quickly identified. For example, three short bells followed by four long bells means that a blaze has started in section three of the fourth floor.

KITCHEN FIRES

Fires in Unprotected Areas

A fire attributed to the explosion of a liquid gas cylinder burned down a modern hotel in Seoul, Korea, taking many lives. Care must be taken to guard against range fires in kitchens, flue fires, and dining room fires in which sparks from such things as a flambé cart may prove disastrous.

As might be expected, the kitchen with its open flames, flammable oils, and personnel pressures is the origin of many fires in hotels and restaurants. It only takes a few moments for the oil in a deep fat fryer or for the fat in some meats to burst into flames if left unattended while cooking. Until 1946 most deep frying was done without thermostatic control and on top of a stove. The oil could quickly reach above 600°F, the flash point. Today most deep frying is done in deep-fry kettles with thermostatic controls, but the controls can fail. When this happens, flames shoot to the ceiling and up into the exhaust ducts. Exhaust ducts that have not been given a recent cleaning have a fat buildup along the insides of the ducts. These ducts often extend all the way to the top of a multi-storied building. A roaring fire inside an exhaust duct can act as a match to ignite the rest of the building. Throwing water on an oil fire only spreads the fire. The water droplets form steam, explode, and splatter little fire bombs of oil in all directions. If they hit people, they cause instant and deep burns because of the intense heat.

A study by the National Fire Protection Association found that 18½ percent of restaurant fires originated in grease hoods and ducts, or spread into hoods and ducts from cooking equipment under the hoods. To fight grease fires smother them with baking soda, cover them with a pan so that the oxygen is eliminated, or use a fire extinguisher.

GOOD HOUSEKEEPING

Good housekeeping prevents fires. In modern fire-resistant structures there is still the danger of fires from accumulated inflammable materials in non-fire-resistant storage places or other rooms. Adequate storage of inflammables, precautions in the use of the incinerator, and rapid disposal of refuse are a part of good housekeeping. In guest rooms where a primary cause of fires is carelessness in smoking, a good supply of ash trays handy to the guest is good housekeeping. One way of insuring good housekeeping is by means of the Periodic Inspection Checklist. The department head, manager, or the personnel director should make biweekly or monthly inspections. Each inspection is recorded on a special form; defects are noted. Part of the checklist supplied by the National Safety Council appears as figure 18.2.

Figure 18.2

( ) Indicates satisfactory		(x) Indicates unsatisfactory	
Kitchens		**Stewards**	
Floors and stairs	( )	Floors	( )
Power-driven equip.	( )	Hand trucks	( )
Ranges	( )	Hand tools	( )
Utensils	( )	Storage of materials	( )
Dishes	( )	Others	( )
Glassware	( )		
Knives, cleaver, etc.	( )		
Light	( )		
Doors	( )	**Service Dept.**	
Steam tables	( )		
Housekeeping	( )	Floors	( )
Others	( )	Elevators	( )

Of course, perfunctory inspection is not sufficient. Follow-up of all defects is usually delegated to specific persons. In addition to reducing fire hazards, a periodic inspection program improves working conditions and raises morale.

ACCIDENT PREVENTION

Employers are constantly seeking to gain further information concerning the causes and prevention of accidents. In the larger cities employers form associations for the purpose of developing and disseminating safety information. In New York, the Greater New York Safety Council is a clearinghouse for such information, and it actively sponsors safety training conferences. A national organization, the National Safety Council is the best known and perhaps the most active of all safety organizations. Founded in 1913 as a nonprofit coordinating institution, it collects and publishes accident statistics of all types. It also provides films and posters and works with the American Hotel and Motel Association. It furnishes lecturers for the various topics concerning safety.

The National Safety Council offers a complete accident and fire prevention service to hotels. According to the Council, its members have 30 to 40 percent fewer accidents than nonmembers. Among its services:

1. Industrial hygiene and technical materials including Hotel Accident Prevention Manual, Bibliography of Safety and Health, data sheets, safe practices manual, *Industrial Supervisor* magazine, and technical releases;

2. Education and training materials including posters, safety instruction cards, safe worker magazine, *Broken Glass*, waiter's assistant cards, and a quantity of the *Safety Register*, a twenty-page employee booklet in fundamentals of safety;

3. Accident analysis and records, including the accident analysis chart and the Periodic Inspection Checklist;

4. An opportunity for consultation services, participation in the largest lending library on safety in the world, and participation in nationwide safety contests; and

5. Safety calendars, posters, and hotel room and guest literature to promote public relations by assuring the guest of an active safety and fire prevention program.

COMPARATIVE ACCIDENT RATES

Is the hotel or restaurant a safe place to work?

Figure 18.3 shows occupational injury and illness incident rates of several industries for comparative purposes. In 1975 some 158,000 work-related injuries and illnesses took place in eating and drinking places, somewhat below the average of most of the industries reported on, but more than those experienced in drug stores, furniture stores, and apparel and accessory stores.

The injury and illness rate for hotels and motels (not included in chart) was slightly above that for eating and drinking places.[5]

Danger lurks everywhere. Averting danger depends upon the care with which people work and live. People fall on perfectly flat surfaces. They cut their fingers wrapping packages. Bruises are incurred by walking into walls in broad daylight. Danger is very much a function of people.

---

5. Economic Report, *NRA,* October 3, 1977.

Figure 18.3   Occupational Injury and Illness Incidence Rates, 1974–75
(Incidence rates per 100 full-time workers)

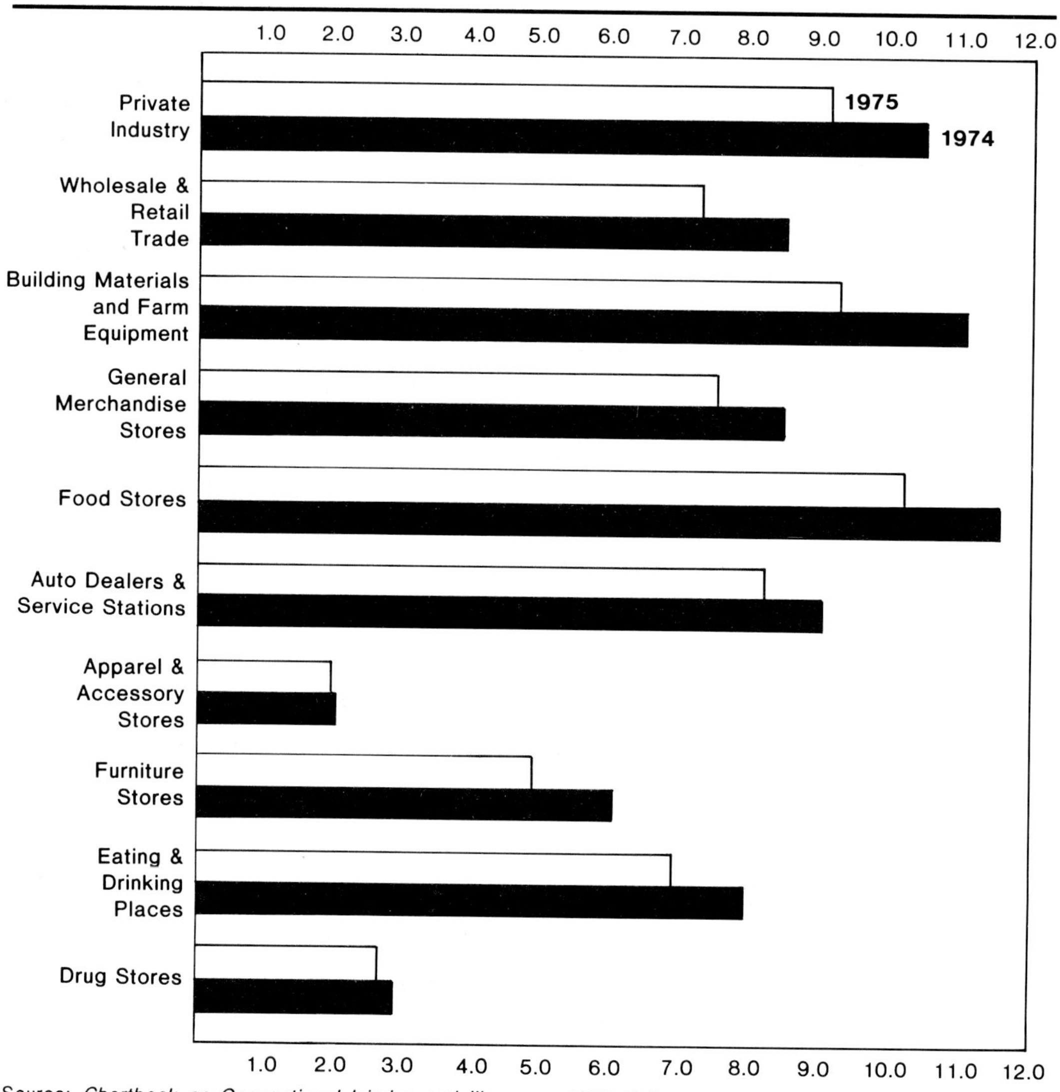

Bar chart categories (1975 = white bars, 1974 = black bars):

- Private Industry: 1975 ≈ 9.3, 1974 ≈ 10.4
- Wholesale & Retail Trade: 1975 ≈ 7.3, 1974 ≈ 8.6
- Building Materials and Farm Equipment: 1975 ≈ 9.3, 1974 ≈ 11.1
- General Merchandise Stores: 1975 ≈ 7.6, 1974 ≈ 8.6
- Food Stores: 1975 ≈ 10.2, 1974 ≈ 11.6
- Auto Dealers & Service Stations: 1975 ≈ 8.2, 1974 ≈ 9.1
- Apparel & Accessory Stores: 1975 ≈ 1.9, 1974 ≈ 2.1
- Furniture Stores: 1975 ≈ 5.0, 1974 ≈ 6.1
- Eating & Drinking Places: 1975 ≈ 6.9, 1974 ≈ 8.0
- Drug Stores: 1975 ≈ 2.7, 1974 ≈ 3.0

Source: *Chartbook on Occupational Injuries and Illnesses, 1975, BLS.*

Types of Accidents in Hotels/Motels

Heading the list in number and cost of all accidents in hotels/motels, as represented in the state of Florida, are strains due to lifting or handling materials. The Florida Department of Industrial Safety tabulated 410 such accidents occurring in Florida hotels and motels in one year.

Typical of these accidents were the following cases:

1. A housekeeper was lifting wet linen from a washing machine when her foot slipped on a wet floor.

2. A maintenance man was lifting a cement flower pot when he felt a severe pain in his back. He had ruptured an intervertebral disk, which necessitated an operation.

3. A PBX operator received a lumbar strain from doing nothing more than lifting a guest card file case.

Hernias and back strains are commonplace in any work that involves lifting. Many times there exists a history of strains, and the current accident has only precipitated what has gone before. Where medical examinations are not given during the employment procedure, employees can come on the job with already existing hernias and back ailments, and later claim that an accident on the job was the cause. No one can disprove their claims. When lifting, it is important to keep the back as straight as possible and make use of the leg muscles.

The next largest cause of hotel and motel accidents, as found by the Florida Department of Industrial Safety, was slipping on a level area. Illustrative of such cases are the following:

Table 18.1   Injury and Illness Record of Hotel Chain

Type of Injury	Percent of Total Injuries	Average Cost
Falls on level surfaces	16	$ 750
Cuts on sharp objects (knives, broken glass, etc.)	11	100
Lifting	11	600
Struck by doors, carts, etc.	10	600
Pushing objects (carts, beds, furniture, etc.)	7	1,350
Caught in-under-between	6	200
Struck against	6	150
Foreign particles in eyes (soaps, cleaners, dust, etc.)	5	300
Hand tools	5	90
Burns (hot objects spilled hot water, coffee, etc.)	5	400
Falls from elevated surfaces (ladders, etc.)	4	600
Dermatitis (from soaps, cleaners, etc.)	3	140
Machine in operation	2	1,000
Inhalation, ingestion, skin absorption of toxic chemicals	2	800
Bending, stooping	2	1,250
Miscellaneous	6	—
Average cost per injury or illness was $650.		

*Source: *Health and Safety Guide for Hotels and Motels* U.S. Dept. Health, Education and Welfare, 1975.

1. An office clerk tripped over her own feet, fell, struck an object, and broke her arm.

2. A dining room captain slipped while walking into the kitchen and struck the back of his head, causing a cerebral concussion.

3. A cleaner slipped on a waxed floor, fell, and broke her wrist.

4. A waitress received a permanent partial disability by falling while carrying a glass pitcher. Her left hand was severely lacerated.

5. A cleaner broke her toe when she stepped on a dog's foot. The dog jerked suddenly, and she struck her toe against the bed.

To avoid such accidents, see to it that rugs or mats that are wrinkled, have upturned edges, or that have been rolled up are not left lying so as to present a tripping hazard. Keep all floors dry, and if you have large waxed areas, use a nonskid wax.

Falls from one level to another were third among the most frequently occurring kinds of accident in Florida in one year. Falls from stairs or steps occurred 130 times. Here are two examples:

1. A repairman was working above the ceiling of a room when he fell through the ceiling joists and landed on a concrete floor, fracturing his ankle.

2. A houseman was painting while standing on an eight-foot scaffold. The telephone rang, he lost his balance, fell, and broke his wrist.

Use safety ladders and prevent people who become dizzy while working on ladders from doing that kind of work. Spend time in getting ready to work. Never use boxes, chairs, and other makeshifts in place of ladders.

Many accidents fall into strange categories. For example, there was the case of the dignified assistant manager whose sense of propriety and chivalry was offended when the muscular swimming instructor passed a few remarks to a waitress. The assistant manager fought with the swimming instructor. Result, a possible concussion for the assistant manager.

Accidents strike in many forms. A can of trash that contained mango peels and seeds caused a mango rash on the face, neck, and arms of the cleaner who was carrying it.

The housekeeper did nothing more than open a door when a heavy gale was blowing outside. She was jerked off her feet and thrown to the ground.

Fire and Safety Programs/343

An accident that could happen to anyone using a power mower occurred to a man who tried to clear the choked reel while the motor was still running. His hand and fingers were severely lacerated.

Kitchen Hazards

Ellsworth Statler, perhaps the most innovative of all hotelmen, died because of burns received from a coffee maker that exploded. The accident, which happened around the turn of the twentieth century, was not the immediate cause of his death; but his body was so scarred that later in 1928, when he contracted pneumonia, the normal breathing mechanism of the skin could not be fully used to help combat the disease.

Any closed vessel that contains a liquid and is heated constitutes a potential bomb. As pressure increases the steam, a jacketed kettle or other utensil holding the liquid could explode.

The kitchen contains several of the elements of accidents: high temperatures, liquids under pressure, highly flammable material such as oil and cooking gas. Gas, when it does not burn in an oven, for example, fills the oven and when finally ignited, explodes. Gas that escapes into the kitchen is poisonous to people and causes unconsciousness and death. Lack of oxygen in a kitchen caused by the consumption of oxygen by combustible gas can deplete the oxygen level to the point where it is dangerous to the people working there. Electricity too has its hazards: exposed wiring and heating elements on top of a stove can explode when overheated.

Wet floors are a big cause of accidents in a kitchen. Slipping and falling on a damp floor can cause all sorts of damage to the individual, including broken bones, possible concussions, and disfigurement. Kitchen floors are usually made of quarry tile because it is easier to clean and provides maximum durability. A few kitchens are now being carpeted, thus reducing slips and falls.

According to a report by the New York State Department of Labor, the two greatest accident sources in a restaurant kitchen are broken glass and burns. Wait personnel are frequently cautioned against putting broken drinking glasses and crockery among soiled dishes. Dishwashers must often work so rapidly that they cannot examine each piece carefully before handling. Kitchen personnel must be particularly careful to guard against burns.

In California the largest cause of disabling injuries were cuts and bruises, followed by slips or falls. Burns came next, then strains and sprains.

Cuts and bruises	31 percent
Slips or falls	26 percent
Burns	14 percent
Strains and sprains	13 percent
Caught in or between	10 percent
Miscellaneous	6 percent

To help prevent accidents in restaurants the Southern California Restaurant Association compiled the following "Safe Work Habits":

SAFE WORK HABITS

A. *Fall Prevention Practices*
   Many injurious and disabling accidents in the food-service industry involve falls. All accidents are unfortunate, but the most unfortunate thing is the fact that almost every fall could have been prevented by proper safety precautions. Here are some simple reminders to help avoid many falls:
   1. If you spill it, wipe it up.
   2. If you drop it, pick it up.
   3. Keep floors clean and dry.
   4. Mop and "dry mop" small areas at a time.
   5. Watch your step on tile floors.
   6. Walk; do not run.
   7. Remove or report all aisle obstructions.
   8. Report leaks or dripping equipment immediately.

B. *Safe Use of Knives*
   1. When using a knife, focus on the job at hand.
   2. Cut away from your body.
   3. Keep knife edge away from you.
   4. Always use a cutting board.
   5. Keep knives properly stored; do not leave them in the sink.
   6. Keep knife edges keen.
   7. Use proper knife for the job, such as boning, carving, paring, etc.
   8. Use knives as cutters, not openers or hammers.

C. *Use of Kitchen Machinery*
   1. Know the hazards of the machine before using it.
   2. Always switch off or pull the plug before cleaning or adjusting a machine.
   3. Machines should always be switched off before being plugged in.
   4. Do not start mixing machines until bowl is properly placed and beater is fastened securely.
   5. Always use hopper and wooden tampers when grinding meat.
   6. Never reach into a vegetable chopper, meat grinder, patty machine, or ice grinder when these machines are switched on.

D. *China and Glassware*
1. Handle with care.

2. Discard chipped or broken ware immediately, depositing in special container provided.

3. Do not mix with metal pots and pans.

4. Do not store pins or tacks in china or glassware.

5. If you know or suspect the presence of broken glass in soapy water, drain water first, then remove broken pieces.

6. Use pan and brush or broom to sweep up broken glass.

7. Use damp paper towel to pick up glass slivers.

8. Do not deposit discards in wastebaskets, garbage bins, or refuse cans.

E. *Heat, Electricity, and Gas*
1. Never shut off or handle any electric switch with wet hands or wet towels.

2. Do not stand on a wet floor when turning on electricity.

3. Always report frayed electrical cords and ungrounded electrical plugs.

4. Never turn on a gas burner without lighting it.

5. Always note whether the pilot light is burning before turning on any gas burner.

6. When handling the dishwashing machine, learn to distinguish between the hot water, steam, and waste valves.

7. When lifting the cover from a stock pot or any cover from boiling food, pull the cover forward and tilt the back up.

8. Do not pour water into the coffee urn or transfer pot so rapidly that it splashes over.

9. Avoid holding arm over open part of coffee urn when removing lid. Slide the lid to one side instead of lifting straight up.

10. Use dry potholders when handling hot utensils.

11. Keep stove top and hood grease-free.

12. Always ventilate oven and stand to one side before lighting burner.

F. *Food Preparation*
1. Do not attempt to retrieve a spoon or any other article that may drop into the bowl of the mixer while it is in motion.

2. When using the french fryer, it should never be filled more than half full of oil, and only dry food should be put into it.

3. Use a minimum amount of water when boiling.

4. Do not place cooking utensils with handles jutting out over the edge of stove.

5. Always keep cooking utensils off the floor.

6. Use long-handled tongs to keep clear of spattering fat while frying or browning.

G. *Serving and Clearing*
1. Avoid overloading trays.

2. Remove defective glass or china.

3. Avoid overfilling liquid containers.

4. Report broken duckboards and damaged or curled floor mats.

5. Stop and wipe up spills or food particles immediately.

6. Wear sensible work shoes.

7. Keep uniform clear of pins or jewelry.

8. Stack dishes in such a manner that they will not topple.

9. Give proper warning when passing anyone carrying hot food or dishes.

10. Keep to the right when rounding corners.

H. *Receiving and Storage*
1. Always remove staples and nails from cartons and crates; do not bend them down.

2. Store heavy material on lower shelves and lighter material above, in orderly fashion.

3. Keep food containers covered.

4. Keep a clean and orderly work area.

5. Keep stored material at least 18 inches away from light bulbs and sprinkler heads.

6. Use safe ladders for obtaining material from storage, and avoid overreaching. Do not use chairs and boxes as platforms.

I. *For a Safe Lift, Always*
1. Get help with extra-heavy loads.

2. Keep the load close to your body.

3. Bend your knees and keep your back straight, raise body and load together by straightening your legs.

Other common accident hazards in restaurants lie in improper lifting, resulting in hernias and strained backs, collisions in cramped quarters, and finger pinching.

In a study of 1,561 accidents to hotel employees conducted by the Liberty Mutual Insurance Company, percentages of accident by cause were listed for the various departments in a hotel.

Since accidents to guests and to the public are also a reflection of personnel training and alertness, it might be well to examine a chart that lists the cause of accidents to the guests and the public. It was drawn up by the Liberty Mutual Insurance Company from data on 393 guest and public accidents in eighteen major hotels over a fifteen-month period. It will be noted that slips and falls and defective equipment account for about 60 percent of all the accidents.

Figure 18.4

UNIVERSAL CHOKING SIGN

FIRST AID FOR
CHOKING

If victim can cough, speak, breathe ➡ *Do not interfere*

If victim cannot
COUGH
SPEAK
BREATHE
IS BLUISH

HAVE SOMEONE CALL FOR HELP

PHONE: _____

Figure 18.5

TAKE ACTION: FOR CONSCIOUS VICTIM•SITTING OR STANDING

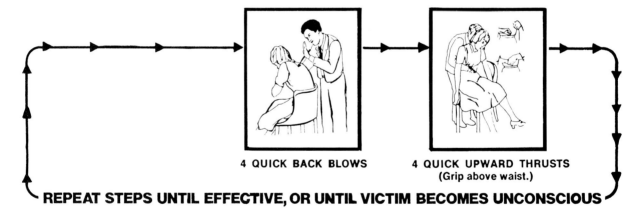

4 QUICK BACK BLOWS   4 QUICK UPWARD THRUSTS
(Grip above waist.)

REPEAT STEPS UNTIL EFFECTIVE, OR UNTIL VICTIM BECOMES UNCONSCIOUS

FIRST AID FOR CHOKING VICTIMS

A number of people have died in restaurants from having food lodged in their windpipe, food that shuts off the possibility of breathing. Many restaurants have taken up the challenge of preparing at least some of their people in how to dislodge the food and, if necessary, how to give mouth-to-mouth and cardiopulmonary resuscitation. Local Red Cross chapters stand ready to instruct interested persons in these resuscitation methods. Legislative proposals have been made to require restaurant personnel to act in case of someone choking on the premises, but the liability features of such requirements have prevented the proposals from becoming law.

The universal choking sign is seen as part of figure 18.4, a poster provided by the National Restaurant Association. If the victim can cough, speak, or breathe, do not interfere. If the victim cannot cough, speak, or breathe, and is turning bluish, have someone call for help and take the action as soon as possible, as shown in figure 18.5 diagrams. The Heimlich Maneuver, shown in figure 18.5, is easily learned. Untrained persons should probably not try the resuscitation methods, but it would be helpful if everyone could know how to perform them if for no other reason than that there exists the possibility that someone close to them may die for lack of resuscitation.

Restaurant diners in particular seem susceptible to the choking problem. Animated by food, drink, and the excitement of conversation with friends, it is easy for one to forget about cutting one's meat into small pieces or to bother to chew it well before swallowing. In most of the choking incidents in restaurants, pieces of meat three or four inches long are found to be causing the blockage. In one coffee shop chain in one year some seventeen choking victims were aided by restaurant personnel, who probably saved their lives.

If, after the food has been dislodged, and the victim is still not breathing, mouth-to-mouth resuscitation by a trained person is highly recommended. All the more reason why one or several people in a restaurant should take the Red Cross training in mouth-to-mouth resuscitation and cardiopulmonary resuscitation. Hundreds of people have been saved from death caused by heart attacks, drowning, and other catastrophes when someone in the family or some other person is available immediately to administer mouth-to-mouth resuscitation. The life you save could be that of a close relative.

If the choking victim cannot speak or breathe, aid can be given by either hitting the victim on the back or by grasping the person from behind and administering quick upward thrusts as seen in the diagram in figure 18.5.

Recognizing that the possibility of a law suit with resultant damages will often discourage even qualified persons from rendering emergency medical assistance, many states have passed "Good Samaritan Laws," which insulate from legal liability certain classes of persons who do render such assistance. All states have enacted Good Samaritan Laws in one form or another. Giving the wrong assistance or even the wrong advice can make the hotel or restaurant liable. A case in point occurred in a Hilton Hotel in 1973:

A customer slipped and fell backwards, banging his head on a wall. The fall resulted in a large bump, considerable pain, and subsequent vomiting. A request was made for assistance and a woman, claiming to be a licensed, practical nurse, came forward. Her diagnosis was one of nonserious injury. When the customer later obtained the services of a qualified doctor, even major surgery could not prevent brain damage. Suit was brought against the hotel and the court acknowledged that even though the hotel was under no obligation to obtain or provide medical assistance or aid, once undertaken, it was under a duty to supply competent assistance. The court then assessed damages in the amount of $210,000.00.[6]

Little wonder that people are reluctant to step forward and help an injured person—fearful that they may do something wrong or be said to be at fault. Complicating the matter is the possibility that a state legislature will require that aid be given in cases of choking or the like, further complicating the legal status of the individual who leaps forward to help the victim. The operator may be placed in the position of "damned if one does, damned if one doesn't."

FIRST AID AND IMMEDIATE MEDICAL AID

The availability of immediate first aid and knowing what to do to reach medical services can save life and limb of guests and employees. Merely having a first aid kit at hand has made it possible to save partially severed fingers, stop excessive blood loss, and save lives. The following questions focus attention on the kind of planning needed to provide for quick first aid and medical services:

—Are medical personnel readily available for advice and consultation regarding injury or illness on the job?
—Is someone on premise adequately trained in first aid?
—Are first aid materials handy and in sanitary and usable condition?
—Are frequent inspections of first aid materials made, and is a good supply maintained?
—Are facilities for quick drenching or flushing of the eyes and body available when someone has been exposed to corrosive substances?
—If ambulance service is unavailable within thirty minutes, are stretchers, blankets, or other warm coverings available?
—Can an injured person be transported to medical help from isolated locations in the building?

When accidents happen to employees or guests, very often none of the people at the scene have a clear idea of what to do. Frequently some bold person steps forward and does the wrong thing. A person who has fallen and is unable to move or who has some broken bones should not be moved because of the possibility of tearing skin or muscles, or in some way exacerbating the condition. Someone who knows a little bit about first aid is likely to rush in with a tourniquet to stop bleeding, a procedure that should not be used if a dressing with a gauze pad will stop the bleeding.

---

6. NRA Washington Report, November 1, 1976.

Here, then, are some general first aid instructions intended for use in emergencies involving accidents or illness. These procedures are not to be used as a substitute for medical attention, but only as emergency measures until a physician can get to the scene.

- Keep seriously injured persons lying down.
- Never try to give liquids to an unconscious person.
- Control bleeding by pressing on the wound with a gauze pad.
- Restart breathing with mouth-to-mouth artificial respiration.
- Keep broken bones from moving or being moved.
- Cover burns with thick layers of cloth.
- Keep heart attack cases quiet.
- Fainting cases: Place head lower than heart.
- Cover eye injuries with gauze pad.
- ALWAYS CALL A DOCTOR

The National Restaurant Association has developed, in poster form, instructions for the emergency treatment of burns and of wounds. The posters condense a great deal of first aid information, parts of which are seen in figures 18.6 and 18.7. It is worth pointing out that the best treatment for first-degree burns (minor burns where the skin is reddened) and for second-degree burns (where blisters form) is to immerse the affected area in cold water or, if that is not possible, to apply clean cloths that have been soaked in ice water. For third-degree burns (severe) a patient should be treated for shock, and the burn area should be covered with clean, dry cloth. The objective in the latter cases is to get the victim to the hospital or doctor immediately.

There are many misconceptions about the proper treatment for burns. Contrary to what many have believed for a long time, burns should not be treated with butter, lard, or fat. The salt content in these "treatments" is high; consequently, the skin is robbed of vital moisture necessary to heal burns.

Another first aid procedure about which there is considerable confusion deals with the treatment of a bruise. Cold compresses are the answer, inasmuch as they restrict the flow of blood to the area—blood that otherwise collects and can cause further tissue damage.

In treating a person for shock, keep the individual in a prone position with feet elevated (unless other injuries prevent or contraindicate this) and make sure the person is warm. Heavy blankets, table linen, or coats can be used. Avoid giving the shock victim any liquids, especially alcoholic beverages, or drugs. Any of these "treatments" may further aggravate the shock condition.

From the foregoing discussion and presentation of accident figures it is apparent that the hotel and restaurant industry is nonhazardous by reputation only. That the restaurant industry can be a hazardous field is borne out in the accident figures of the state of Pennsylvania. In one year that state had a total of 3,000 time-loss injuries and 14 fatalities in its eating and drinking places. These figures are about two and a half times that of the frequency in industry in general and more than four times those in the steel industry.

ACCIDENT PREVENTION IN A CAFETERIA CHAIN

Illustrative of what can be done to reduce accidents is the experience of Morrison Cafeterias, a large company with headquarters in Mobile, Alabama.

- As part of the continued training process, all management and supervisory personnel are brought to the home office in groups for three days of instruction and workshop. The basic first aid course is incorporated into this program period.
- An established safety team conducts routine inspections of each operation, and the reports are analyzed and reviewed by the division and district management along with the company safety officers. The results of the findings are then discussed with the operation's manager for any necessary action.
- Prior to the opening of a new cafeteria, a three-hour safety orientation class is conducted by the safety department for all new employees. As part of the program, two company-developed safety films are presented; the films are followed by a question and answer period. These films stay at the cafeteria for the manager's use in the continuing safety-education program.
- Morrison officials routinely instruct builders to incorporate built-in safety features to their operations as they are constructed or remodeled. The base areas under a dish machine are depressed, for example, so that water will not seep out onto the working area. Areas in front of ice machines are recessed and nonslip grids are installed, so that employees will not slip while removing ice from the machine. The free-swinging doors leading from the serving lines into the kitchen have been reduced in width and a two-inch soft rubber sweep has been installed to eliminate jammed fingers.

The emphasis on accident prevention and the fact that Morrison Cafeterias owns its own insurance company have reduced their workers compensation insurance costs substantially.

Figure 18.6

EMERGENCY TREATMENT OF BURNS

1ST DEGREE BURNS

MINOR BURNS

Skin is reddened

TREATMENT

Apply cold water applications to the affected area or submerge the burn area in cold water. (A dry dressing may be applied.)

DO NOT APPLY BUTTER, LARD OR FAT

2ND DEGREE BURNS

BLISTERS FORMED

Shock likely with extensive 2nd degree burns.

TREATMENT

1. Immerse burned area in cold water bath — or under cold running water — or apply ice water soaked **clean** cloths until pain subsides.
2. Blot dry and apply **clean dry** cloth or dressing and send to doctor.

DO NOT OPEN THE BLISTERS

DO NOT APPLY BUTTER, LARD, FAT OR BURN OINTMENT

3RD DEGREE BURNS

SEVERE BURNS

Involve entire skin layers. Burns are deep, charring the skin. (Includes electrical burns because these are deeper than they appear.)

TREATMENT

1. Protect burned area by covering with **clean dry** cloth
2. Treat for shock
3. Get patient to hospital or doctor IMMEDIATELY!

DO NOT APPLY BUTTER, LARD, FAT OR BURN OINTMENT

DO NOT REMOVE ADHERED PARTICLES OF CLOTHING

EXTENSIVE BURNS

If over 15% of body is burned, WASTE NO TIME Give appropriate first aid and get patient to hospital immediately!

BURNS INVOLVING EYES

Needs IMMEDIATE First Aid Attention and Medical Assistance

IF SPLASHED BY HOT OIL OR GREASE —

Flush with a slow stream of cool water for at least 15 minutes

IF BURNED BY FLAME OR EXPLOSION —

Apply cold, wet towel or other cold pack

DO NOT APPLY OIL OR OINTMENT

1. Place sterile dressing over eyes to immobilize the lids
2. Take patient to doctor or hospital

CHEMICAL BURNS

- Immediately wash away chemical with large quantities of running water for at least five minutes.
- Remove victim's clothing from areas involved.
- Then treat as for any similar heat burn.

Figure 18.7

EMERGENCY TREATMENT OF WOUNDS

CUTS, WOUNDS AND ABRASIONS

Immediately cleanse wound and surrounding skin with soap and warm water, wiping away from wound.

Hold a sterile pad or clean cloth over the wound until the bleeding stops.

Replace sterile pad or clean cloth and bandage lightly.

If hand injury, raise hand above the level of the heart.

DO NOT put mouth over a wound

DO NOT breathe on wound

DO NOT allow fingers, used hankerchief or other soiled material to touch the wound

DO NOT use an antiseptic on the wound

WHEN TO SEEK MEDICAL ATTENTION

1. If there is spurting bleeding (this is an emergency).
2. If slow bleeding continues beyond 4 to 10 minutes.
3. If there is foreign material in the wound that does not wash out easily.
4. If the wound is a deep puncture.
5. If the wound is long or wide and may require stitches.
6. If a nerve or tendon may be cut (particularly in hand wounds).
7. If the wound is on the face or wherever a noticeable scar would be undesirable.
8. If the wound is of a type that cannot be completely cleansed.
9. If the wound has been in contact with unclean material.
10. At the first signs of infection (pain, reddened area around wound, swelling).

SHOCK

Shock will be present with many injuries.

A person in shock will be cold, pale, perspiring and may pass out.

TREATMENT

1. Telephone for emergency ambulance or doctor.
2. Treat for shock by:

    Placing patient in prone position with feet elevated unless contraindicated.

    Covering only enough to prevent loss cf body heat.

    Do not give any fluids.

    Do not administer any drugs.

    Do not give alcoholic beverages.

OTHER INJURIES

BRUISES

Apply ice bag or cold compress for 25 minutes. If skin is broken, further treatment is the same as for a cut.

BLISTERS

Keep clean with mild soap and water and protect from further irritation. If blister has broken, treat it as an open wound. If infected, seek medical assistance.

FOREIGN BODY IN EYE

If particle is located—do not rub eye. Gently touch with point of clean moist cloth and flush eye with water. If unsuccessful or if pain persists, refer to physician.

Do not attempt to remove foreign object by inserting a match, toothpick or any other instrument. Do not use dry cotton around the eye.

GAS HEATER SAFETY IN MOTOR HOTELS

Gas-fueled space heaters used in sleeping rooms are safe only under specific conditions. If for some reason the burning gas is extinguished, the gas may continue to flow, soon poisoning the occupants of the room. To guard against this, all gas heaters must have 100 percent automatic safety cutoffs. When the flame is extinguished, these cutoffs automatically turn off the supply of gas.

Most gas-operated heating equipment requires about fifty-four cubic feet of air to burn; they exhaust one cubic foot of low-pressure gas fuel. All sleeping rooms using gas heaters, therefore, must have a constant intake of fresh air. Two manufacturers of gas heaters make equipment that draws an air supply directly from outside the building and exhausts it directly outside. With this equipment no air is taken from the room and no exhausted air from the heater reenters the room. These are the only kind that the authors can recommend for motel use.

With equipment that does not draw fresh air from the outside, permanent and unclosable openings for fresh air must be made in the room. The Florida Hotel and Restaurant Commission requires all Florida motels to meet a code stating that the opening be not less than ten square inches and that a minimum of one square inch of opening be made for each one thousand BTU (British Thermal Units) output by the heaters.

Opening a window by nailing it open or putting permanent supports under it is not satisfactory. Guests feeling a draft may unwittingly block the opening and endanger themselves.

Heaters not designed to exhaust the burned gases directly to the outside must be properly vented to discharge the exhaust fumes.

Although the sealed-in type of intake and exhaust heater initially costs more than the old type, the cost of venting the old type makes it almost as expensive as the sealed-in type.

Do not tamper with the lives of guests by using equipment that is anything less than entirely safe!

THE SUPERVISOR: KEY TO SAFETY SUCCESS

Safety is largely a matter of training; the supervisor, usually the trainer, is also largely responsible for identifying and correcting safety hazards. Unless the kitchen manager sets up and follows through with a regular schedule of cleaning the grease filters in the hood over the ranges, the filters are not likely to be cleaned, and fires may result. Unless the dish pantry supervisor is insistent that the floors in the pantry are kept dry, they will remain wet and someone may fall and be injured.

The supervisor's interest, attitude, and enthusiasm for safety can be transmitted to the employees. A disinterested attitude will be quickly reflected in employees' attitudes. The supervisor must recognize that safety is an integral part of supervision. Faulty performance that leads to accidents is on a par with faulty performance that leads to other wastes and to general inefficiency.

Safety Committees

A number of hotels and restaurants have organized safety committees. This is one area wherein labor-management committees can attract little criticism. Management has everything to gain and little to lose by arranging for the function of committees representing the various departments in which hazards are greatest. Rotating the membership serves to stimulate the feeling among employees that they are a real part of the organization. It also serves to introduce new ideas and maintain enthusiasm for the safety program. The safety committee may also include fire protection in its program. One large hotel has a safety supervisor who investigates all accidents, keeps accident records, and makes recommendations.

A prominent New York restaurant has a program in which two safety inspections are made weekly by members of the restaurant staff. The inspection committee sees to it that all belts, pulleys, and other moving machinery parts are covered or sheathed. In addition to the staff biweekly inspections, a store mechanic checks freight elevators daily to make certain they are in proper working order. Kitchen and pantry floors are kept free from litter to minimize the danger of falls.

A thorough safety program that functions through a safety committee pays dividends in lower compensation insurance costs and accident figures.

ARE ACCIDENTS ACCIDENTAL?

In raising the question as to whether accidents are accidental, we consider the psychology of the accident as well as the physical situation in which an accident may occur. We are immediately faced with a paradox in two apparently contradictory statements often expressed by the same person. The firm conviction that "accidents will happen" is often countered by the equally strong belief that "it can't happen to me." There is also the imputation that it is sportsmanlike to take risks and that somehow it reflects on the person's sportsmanship to introduce safety measures and devices. The problem of accidents is complex and tied up with many facets of the personality.

Most of us are likely to have an accident sometime in our lives. Such accidents may be entirely unavoidable.

Figure 18.8

ACCIDENTS

TO EMPLOYEES

% BREAKDOWN BY DEPARTMENTS

	% OF ALL REPORTS	HOUSEKEEPING	ENGINEERING	FOOD	SERVICE	ALL-OTHERS
MISC. BUMPS & CUTS — Striking Objects, Nails & Splinters, Dropping Objects, Pinched Between Objects, Falling Material, Door Pinches & Bumps	28.0	35.6	13.8	33.0	12.4	5.2
SLIPS & FALLS	15.6	32.4	10.7	42.6	9.8	4.5
HANDLING MATERIAL STRAINS	12.9	28.4	16.4	40.2	11.0	4.0
BURNS FROM HOT SUBSTANCES	7.4	20.0	27.0	51.3	1.7	
FLYING OBJECTS IN EYES	7.1	23.4	27.0	27.0	18.0	4.6
GLASS & CHINA	7.0	25.5	4.5	68.2		1.8
HAND IMPLEMENTS	4.7	9.6	12.3	75.5	1.3	1.3
OPERATION OF ELEVATOR	3.8	3.4	6.8	6.8	83.0	
RAZOR BLADES	1.7	96.3			3.7	
MACHINERY	1.5	46.1	7.8	46.1		
ALL OTHERS	10.3	27.9	11.2	35.4	8.1	17.4
TOTAL ACCIDENTS REPORTED BY DEPT'S.		454	227	616	186	78
% OF TOTAL ACCIDENTS REPORTED		29.1%	14.5%	39.5%	11.9%	5%

Figure 18.9

ACCIDENTS

TO GUESTS AND THE PUBLIC

CAUSE		%
SLIPS & FALLS		47.4
DEFECTIVE EQUIPMENT	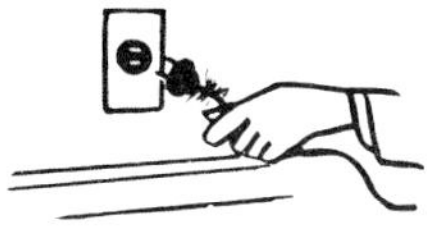	13.2
FOOD Foreign Substances Illness Spilled		10.4 2.0 1.8
STRUCK By DOORS		4.1
STRIKING STATIONARY OBJECTS		3.8
ELEVATOR DOORS & GATES		3.5
FALLING OBJECTS		2.6
MISCELLANEOUS		11.2

SLIPS & FALLS AGENCIES		
PUBLIC ROOM FLOORS		29.6
STAIRS & STEPS		25.3
SIDEWALK ENTRANCES		10.7
ROOMS		8.6
DOORS— ENTRANCE	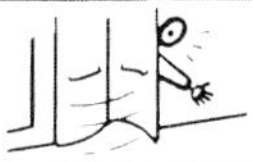	4.8
ELEVATORS		3.2
ALL OTHER		17.8
AGENCIES OF DEFECTIVE EQUIPMENT		%
GLASS & CHINA		34.6
FURNITURE		21.2
BURNS FROM ELECTRICAL APPLIANCES		15.4
PLUMBING FIXTURES		9.6
ALL OTHER		19.2

Studies of taxicab drivers and other industrial employees seem to show, however, that many accidents are not accidental. In some studies of industrial concerns it has been found that 20 percent of the personnel consistently have a higher total of accidents that the other 80 percent. Such individuals are called *accidentprone*. By use of certain tests, many of these individuals can be identified and placed in jobs in which hazards are at a minimum. Often the accidentprone person has a physical disability.

One of the largest causes of accidents is defective vision. Measured by the standard eye charts, such as the Snellen or The American Medical Association Chart, many employees test 20–20 vision. However, when tested by more adequate instruments, an individual's vision may be found to be insufficient for certain jobs. Some clerical work calls for good vision at close distances and other visual requirements not measured by the standard eye charts. By research, the visual requirements of every job in the house can be established. It can be predicted within a certain range of error whether or not one will have an accident on a particular job if one's total vision is known. Often employees who appear to have excellent vision may be subject to severe headaches and other strains because of poor vision.

Several jobs in the hotel and restaurant are susceptible to accidents. Kitchens with temperatures exceeding 110°—common occurrence during the summers—exhaust the employee and make accidents more likely. Summer resort employees who work long schedules (six- and seven-day weeks have been common) are also likely candidates for accidents. As the summer season advances, accidents increase in the resort hotel kitchen. One drops a can on one's toes; cuts oneself with a knife; receives a burn from a hot pan. Quite naturally as fatigue sets in, sensory reaction time diminishes. It is a sad note that kitchen employees in resorts are so often scheduled for continuously long hours, hours that are certain to induce fatigue, reduce resistance to frustration, and increase accidents.

Heat or excitement induces epileptic seizure among epileptoids (people who have a tendency toward such seizures). An epileptic seizure in a kitchen is a frightening experience. The subject, having lost conscious control of all motor activity, may thrash about, throw himself on a hot stove, bite his tongue off and even swallow it. The only treatment for the moment is to get the person out of the danger area into a cool, quiet place, held so that there is no possibility for self-inflicted injury. Persons with a history of epilepsy should never be assigned to pressure jobs or jobs with undue heat or noise.

Another predisposing condition for accidents is alcohol in the kitchen. It has been the custom in hotels and restaurants that follow the European tradition to provide beer and other alcohol in the kitchens, especially when the pressure builds. Alcohol is, of course, a depressant to the senses, which is exactly the opposite of what is needed. Alcohol does deaden the feelings of muscular fatigue, but causes excessive sweating and a loss of discriminatory reactions needed in handling knives, slicers, meat saws, and hot pots and pans.

Coffee is a temporary stimulant but acts to create an energy debt that must be paid in full. As one physician put it "the coffee drinker is the most tired of persons." Stimulants and depressants, especially in the kitchen, are hazardous.

Other physical disabilities predispose the employee to an undue number of accidents. Partial paralysis, arthritis, defects of the equilibrium sense, or poor muscle coordination may set the stage for accidents. Such disabilities do not disqualify the individual from employment per se, but should be considered in placing the person. Many jobs in the hotel and restaurant are relatively nonhazardous and may be filled by accidentprone employees.

The hotel and restaurant, in addition to having accident problems unique to their industry, have many of the problems of the typical industrial plant. Engineering department personnel are exposed to boiler accidents, repair shop personnel to the hazards of various types of power driven tools. With the refrigerating system there is the possibility of escape of the refrigerant. Electrical, upholstery, and carpentry shops present fire hazards and the possibility of muscular strains, cuts, and bruises. The laundry department and its machinery, the engineering department, the service department, the steward's department, housekeeping, and the other departments all present special problems.

Elevator Accidents

A relatively common occurrence in hotels is the stalling of elevators between floors. If this should occur, call the elevator maintenance company. Unless specifically trained, the hotel engineering personnel should not attempt to handle such incidents.

Management's role in such incidents is to prevent further problems by reassuring the occupants of the stalled elevator and insisting that the elevator company's personnel can and will handle the situation. Management should reassure the trapped occupants by voice or by phone. Some people become hysterical and need all the reassurance they can get. Astute managers have been known to send (and with good results) a bottle of champagne to those trapped.

SAFETY TIPS

Following are thirty safety tips that are reminders of value to any hotel or restaurant employee. Use them as points of discussion in safety meetings.

1. When lifting, keep the back straight and lift with the legs.
2. Don't try to carry too many bags at one time.
3. When carrying any heavy load, call for help.
4. Don't stand on the edge of a tub when putting up shower curtains. It's too easy to slip and fall.
5. Never pick up razor blades with your hands. Use a dustpan or a piece of cardboard and wipe the blade onto the container with a dust cloth or rag.
6. Don't pick up broken glass with your hands; use a damp cloth.
7. Never reach into a wastebasket with your hands to empty it. Pick up the basket and pour the trash into the receptacle.
8. When washing glasses, inspect them for nicks so that you do not cut your hands. Nicked glasses are harboring spots for bacteria.
9. When turning a mattress, lift it by the side straps, set it on its side, then lower into place.
10. Keep loose articles off the floors to avoid tripping accidents.
11. Place electrical cords behind furniture and away from traffic to avoid tripping accidents.
12. When opening doors, use the doorknobs; grasping the door itself can mean bruised fingers.
13. Don't pull knives toward the body. When not in use store them in racks where they cannot hurt you.
14. If a glass is broken while it is being washed, drain the sink and pick up the pieces with a dishcloth or rag.
15. Don't dry the inside of a glass by forcing a towel inside. The glass may break in your hands.
16. Don't use a glass as an ice scoop. Use a metal scoop that cannot break in your hands.
17. In using stepladders, check them for any defective parts. Don't overreach while on a ladder. Taking a little time may save a lot of time.
18. Note all defects in guest rooms and correct them at once.
19. Before lighting a gas oven, check for evidence of leaking gas.
20. Stand to one side when lighting a gas oven and use a taper rather than a match.
21. Use pads for handling hot pots, pans, and other utensils.
22. Wear protective gloves when using steel wool or strong cleaning compounds.
23. Use knee pads for scrubbing bathroom floors or similar areas.
24. Do not crowd elevators above their rated capacities.
25. Permit only authorized personnel to operate elevators.
26. Close service and/or freight elevators at each landing.
27. Do not overload bus trays.
28. Use glass racks for transporting or storing glassware.
29. Place warning tags on all machinery undergoing repairs.
30. Never work on moving machinery.

Whenever you get any kind of cut, apply first aid immediately. Avoid infection. Safety is largely a matter of attitude. Think; be careful; be safe.

RESEARCH IN ACCIDENT PREVENTION

As with many other personnel functions, for best results it is necessary to bolster our reasoning with facts and figures. Keeping adequate records of accidents can help in accident control. So that they can be compared, accident rates usually are kept according to a formula. Two rates, the frequency rate and the severity rate, are commonly recorded. The frequency rate equals the number of accidents that result in lost working time per million person-hours worked. The severity rate is defined as the number of days lost per thousand person-hours.

$$FR = \frac{\text{Lost-time accidents}}{\text{person-hours} \div 1,000,000}$$

$$SR = \frac{\text{Days lost}}{\text{person-hours} \div 1,000}$$

Studying the cause of the accident may suggest ways of eliminating further mishaps. A standard record of an accident might include the items shown in figure 18.10.

The National Safety Council publishes an *Accident Analysis Chart* that can be obtained at nominal cost. Figure 18.11 is a portion of that chart.

Since every hotel and restaurant has a more or less unique set of conditions regarding fire protection and accident prevention, the programs developed will vary from one house to another. Obviously, plans and programs must be instituted and changed to meet changing conditions. However, aids developed by such organizations as the National Safety Council are very worthwhile and will fit any fire and accident prevention program.

Figure 18.10   Hotel Hamilton Accident Report Form

Name of injured person _____

Social Security number _____

Any witnesses? _____ If so, list names and addresses _____

_____

_____

Describe nature and severity of accident _____

_____

_____

What type of work was the employee performing at the time of the accident? _____

_____

Was there some observable physical or mechanical cause? _____

_____

If so, name such cause _____

Statement by the injured _____

_____

_____

Statement from the supervisor or department head _____

_____

_____

Was something done to prevent a recurrence of the accident? _____

If so, what? _____ Reported by _____

Figure 18.11   Accident Analysis Chart

					Injury				

Tabulation

Period   to

1. Temporary total
2. Permanent partial
3. Deaths and permanent total
4. Total (1, 2, & 3)

5. Man hours worked
6. Frequency rate
   (line 4 × 1,000,000
   Line 5)
7. First aid treatments

Accident No.	Date of Accident	Name of Injured	Occ. or Dept.	Injury			Desc. of Accident (Give exact details)	Corrective Action Taken
				Nature & Location	Class (1, 2, 3, 7)	Days Lost		

SUMMARY

The Occupational Safety and Health Act of 1970 demands safety by law. Every employer in the hotel and restaurant industry is covered. Penalties of fines of more than $20,000 and imprisonment of up to one year can be levied on those employers who fail to comply. The government has published interim and permanent standards. An important part of OSHA requires every employer to make and preserve records of occupational injuries and illnesses so as to develop information that will aid in preventing industrial accidents and illnesses. Small businesses may be eligible for SBA loans to upgrade facilities and to meet new health and safety standards.

Fire and accident prevention requires concerted effort of all employees through careful application of standards, inspections, and training. The kitchen is particularly vulnerable to accidents. The National Safety Council offers a complete accident and fire prevention service to hotels, claiming that it reduces accidents 30 to 40 percent.

Appendix: Statistical Tools Useful
in Personnel Management

As indicated throughout this book, research is a prime responsibility of the personnel administrator. Statistics provide a simple language for the development of research. Through statistics it is possible to (a) summarize and interpret vital personnel information conveniently; (b) make possible comparisons from one company or area to others on such important variables as labor turnover, absenteeism, productivity, and morale; (c) promote the continued evaluation practices; and (d) enhance the general understanding of management functions.

The appendix provides a review of the important statistical concepts with which personnel administrators need to become familiarized.

PERSONNEL STATISTICS

It is not intended in this section to provide information concerning the formulae or computation of statistics. These can be found with "cookbook" application in any basic text on statistics. Rather, the intent is to provide some understanding of the basic concepts of statistics used in personnel management functions, in order to guide the personnel worker to the most appropriate use of specific statistical techniques.

GRAPHIC PRESENTATION

A valuable statistical tool is the representation of data through graphs and charts. A fundamental principle to remember is that "a picture may be worth ten thousand words" if it is done properly. Personnel analysts constantly are called on to "sell" ideas and facts to management, but ideas and facts that are not understood are of little value, regardless of their potential importance.

A wide assortment of graphic possibilities are available to the person interested in utilizing them. Examples can be found daily in popular newspapers and magazines of such techniques as bar graphs, pie graphs, line graphs, belt graphs, pictographs, map graphs, histograms, and frequency polygons. Figure A.1 shows just one example

of how very complex, technical data can be depicted with clarity by means of a simple graphic presentation.

AVERAGES

The Mean

The mean (M) is the most widely used average because it lends itself easily to statistical formulation. It is computed easily by adding the variable such as ages, test scores, or hours worked by individuals and dividing the sum by the total number of cases. A disadvantage occurs when using the mean with a small number of cases, because a few extreme scores may create a serious distortion.

The Median

The median (Md) is the middle person or score in a distribution of persons or scores. In a group of five waitresses standing in the order of their height, the third waitress from either end represents the median of the group. Medians are used as a means of obtaining a quick estimate or when a few extremes might distort the mean.

The Mode

The mode (Mo) represents the value that appears most frequently in an array of figures. For example, 100 waiters may vary in height from five feet five inches to five feet eleven inches, but the most common height, or mode, might be five feet nine inches.

Index Numbers

Much of the information used in business—for example, cost of living, wage rates, production totals—is expressed in terms of base indexes. The base is selected to express

Of Each 10 Applicants Whose Restaurant Test Battery Total Score Is in the	Will Not Be Accepted By Restaurant	Will Be Accepted and Will Be Rated by His Supervisors after Three Months as			
		A Failure	Just Acceptable	Satisfactory	Outstanding
Highest Quarter ○ ○ ○ ○ ○ ○ ○ ○ ○ ○		◖	○ ◖	○ ○ ○ ○ ○ ◖	○ ○ ○ ◖
Second Quarter ○ ○ ○ ○ ○ ○ ○ ○ ○ ○	○ ◖	◖	○ ◖	○ ○ ○ ○ ○ ◖	◖
Third Quarter ○ ○ ○ ○ ○ ○ ○ ○ ○ ○	○ ○ ◖	○ ◖	○ ○ ◖	○ ○ ○	
Lowest Quarter ○ ○ ○ ○ ○ ○ ○ ○ ○ ○	○ ○ ○ ○ ○ ○ ◖	○ ◖	○ ◖	◖	

what a representative, or normal, rate may be and then all further figures are expressed in terms of that base. Research, for example, may establish a base rate for the daily hourly working average of waitresses at seven hours per day during a one-month period. If a waitress averaged eight hours per day during the next month, her relative index of work would be 114.7 or 8/7; if she averaged only six hours per day, her relative index would be 85.9 or 6/7.

MEASURES OF VARIABILITY

It is possible for two groups of workers to have similar (even identical) average values and yet to be quite different. The individual values of one group may be spread much more widely than the values in another group, but there is no way to explain this variability without the proper statistics to tell us how scattered, or spread, values may be. The following measures are used in personnel to show variability within a group of persons or scores.

Range

The range simply represents the difference between the highest and lowest value in a group. If age were the variable, the range would show the oldest and the youngest person.

Centile (or Percentile)

This is the value on a scale below which are given any percentage of the cases in a group. For example, the seventy-fifth percentile is the point below which are seventy-five percent of the cases and the nineteenth percentile is the point below which are nineteen percent of the cases.

The Standard Deviation

The standard deviation is a widely used statistic that is used to describe the variability of groups for which the means have been determined. Arithmetically, it is equal to the square root of the mean of the squared deviations from the group mean.

One vital function of the standard deviation is in making interpretations from the normal curve. In a normally distributed group, 34.13 percent of the area lies between the mean and a point that is one standard deviation away from it. One standard deviation above the mean combined with one standard deviation below the mean accounts for about two-thirds of the area, or 68.26 percent. Thus when we know that the hours Mary worked last month were more than one standard deviation above the mean number of hours worked by all of the other women, we see that Mary worked longer hours than did two-thirds of the other women. (Actually, the comparison can be ascertained even more precisely, as is described in the section following, which deals with the normal curve.)

The symbol for standard deviation is σ, sigma.

Correlation

The most important statistic available to the personnel analyst is the correlation coefficient. There are several types of correlation coefficients and there are special conditions that justify the use of one instead of another. Bas-

Figure A.2   The Normal Probability Curve

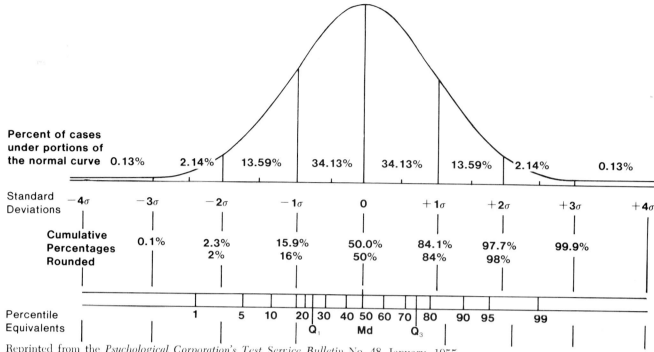

Percent of cases under portions of the normal curve 0.13%   2.14%   13.59%   34.13%   34.13%   13.59%   2.14%   0.13%

Standard Deviations -4σ -3σ -2σ -1σ 0 $+1\sigma$ $+2\sigma$ $+3\sigma$ $+4\sigma$

Cumulative Percentages Rounded   0.1%   2.3%   15.9%   50.0%   84.1%   97.7%   99.9%
2%   16%   50%   84%   98%

Percentile Equivalents   1   5   10   20 30 40 50 60 70   80   90   95   99
Q_1 Md Q_3

Reprinted from the *Psychological Corporation's Test Service Bulletin* No. 48, January, 1955.

ically, the correlation simply shows us the degree of relationship between two variables or measures. Thus, if we can ascertain a relationship between education, age, school grades, or a placement test on the one hand with some measure of a person's work performance on the other hand, we may have some information that is vital to us in our future selection.

Another use of the correlation coefficient is as a basis for prediction. For example, we may find that a correlation exists between job success as a cook and scores made in a training course. We then can predict one's chances for success on the job by virtue of that individual's score in the training course.

The most frequent use of a correlation coefficient is to determine statistically whether a relationship or an observation that we discover is a genuinely significant relationship or is due merely to chance. The significance of the correlation coefficient in this latter sense is related to the theoretical normal curve and the laws of probability.

The normal curve is a theoretical distribution that follows the laws of chance and represents the approximate range and difference of human variability. Personnel analysts find it useful in three main ways:

1. If it is discovered that large numbers of personnel data approximate a normal distribution, it can be assumed that the personnel data was representative;

2. The curve—as a distribution of probability—is used to determine the reliability and significance of many measures of personnel performance. It is thus possible to determine if such measures are the result of certain consistent factors or if they were due merely to chance factors; and

3. By following standard laws, the curve is used in a scaling sense in order to compare different units in terms of a standard scale.

DETERMINING THE EFFECTIVENESS OF TESTS[1]

Personnel workers in business and industry have considerable opportunity for evaluating tests used in their own employee selection and placement programs. Even rather small samples can be useful in bettering our understanding of tests, especially if the group is well-defined. In this section we want to suggest several ways in which validation studies may be carried out by test users.

Basic to all validation studies is the notion that we are interested in *predicting* one variable (the criterion) from

1. Reprinted in part from the *Psychological Corporation's Test Service Bulletin* no. 37 "How Effective Are Your Tests?"

another variable (the test score). The *criterion* is always some measure or index of the employee's success or proficiency on the job. Included among the many types of criteria that we find in industrial and business situations are supervisors' ratings, rate of production, proportion of spoilage in pieces produced, number of sales, commissions earned, and the like. A test is *valid* if it predicts, with dependable accuracy, what the applicant's or employee's criterion score or rating *will* be at some time subsequent to the testing.

The problem of securing a satisfactory measure of the criterion—one that is a reliable and correct description of the standard of workmanship attained—is a tough nut to crack. It is in this respect that personnel research and practice are most often deficient today. However, we shall assume that the personnel worker does have a satisfaction criterion measure on the jobs for which validation of the test is desired.

The validation process then becomes one of determining the *relationship* between the two variables—the test and the criterion. The extent of this relationship—the correlation between the two variables—may be expressed in a number of different ways, some very simple and others very complex. Usually the nature of our criterion data determines the way in which we can best express the relationship between the test and the criterion. This is due to the great variety of ways in which criterion measures may be secured and expressed. Test results generally, but not always, are expressed as a continuous series of scores and are adaptable to almost any type of statistical analysis.

The many ways of expressing the relationships between tests and criteria may be classified in two major groups. There are the methods (*a*) that apply statistics to the data so that a single number is secured that expresses the extent of relationship between the two variables and those (*b*) that give a summarized picture of relationship without an over-all summarizing numerical value. Both types of methods are useful for expressing the correlation between two variables. Selection of one or another depends, of course, on the situation. For purposes of convenience, we shall call the first group of methods "correlational techniques" and the second group "summarizing techniques." Let us now consider the various methods and some instances where each of them would be applicable.

Correlation Techniques

Product-Moment Correlation Coefficient

The oldest and still the most widely used method for expressing the degree of relationship between test scores and proficiency measures is the product-moment coeffi-

cient of correlation, the Pearson *r*. The product-moment coefficient is usually computed from a scatter diagram or correlation chart in which the scores on each variable have been grouped into classes. An example of test validation by the technique of product-moment correlation is shown in figure A.3. The test scores, in this instance, are taken from an experimental edition of the *Store Personnel Test, Form FS,* given to 155 trainees for jobs in a large retail grocery organization. These scores are based on the price computation and verbal reasoning items that are in Part II of this test. The criterion consists of ratings, carefully made by the training staff, on learning ability, working speed, and overall qualifications for grocery work. For each individual the ratings on these three aspects of job fitness were summed to give a combined rating that could range from a low score of zero to a high of twelve. From the scatter diagram in figure A.3 it is a relatively simple matter to compute the product-moment correlation coefficient. (The computational method is given in practically all textbooks on statistics, and commercially available correlation charts facilitate the actual work.) In this sample, $r = 0.46$ which is gratifyingly high for a validity coefficient.

When a product-moment coefficient is to be calculated, the number of groups in which each variable is divided (class intervals) should be at least nine or ten. If the number of class intervals is less than nine, the "coarseness" of grouping may result in distortion of the coefficient. Very often, however, criterion data do not permit of more than four or five classes. For such instances alternative correlation methods are available. Notable among these alternatives are the biserial coefficient and the tetrachoric coefficient.

Biserial Correlation Coefficient

The biserial coefficient, r_{bis}, may be computed when one of the variables is expressed as a "dichotomy," that is, as either one or the other of just two alternative categories. (An underlying assumption, which is generally not violated by criterion data, is that a normal distribution is possible on the dichotomized variable if more refined measurement were practicable.) One example would be an industrial training situation where the ratings of employees can be most properly given as "pass" or "fail." The relationship of test scores to such a criterion may be evaluated by use of a biserial coefficient.

Another situation frequently encountered is one where criterion ratings fall into four possible classes. In table A.1 are shown the test scores of fifty-two employed stenographers on the *Seashore-Bennett Stenographic Proficiency Test* and the ratings of these people by their supervisors on the criterion of stenographic ability. The criterion ratings fall into four classes: Below Average,

Error Scores on Store Personnel Test, Form FS

Trainer Ratings (Sum of learning ability, working speed, and over-all-fitness)	56–54	53–51	50–48	47–45	44–42	41–39	38–36	35–33	32–30	29–27	26–24	23–21	20–18	17–15	14–12	11–9	8–6	5–3	2–0
12											2	2	1		1	1			
11										1	2		3	3	1	5	1		
10											3	1	3	1	1	2	2		
9									1		5	4	3	6	4	3	1		
8										1	4	4	2	2	2	2	1		
7										3	4	3	1	2	2	4			
6							2			2	6	2	1		2	1			
5								1	1	4	3		1	2	1	1			
4						1	1	3		1	1	1							
3		1				1	1	1			3			1	3				
2							1	1	1		1					1			
1														1					

Table A.1   Ratings on Stenographic Ability

Test Scores	Below Average	Average	Above Average	Excellent
19		1	3	2
18		3	3	5
17		1	2	2
16		1	—	2
15		8	5	
14		2	—	
13		3	—	
12		1	1	
11		—	—	
10	2	2	1	
9	—	—		
8	1	1	—	
Subtotals	3	23	15	11
Totals		26		26
		(Group 1)		(Group 2)

Average, Above Average, and Excellent. Since four classes are too few for proper use of the product-moment method, one may put Below Average and Average into one group, and Above Average and Excellent into a second group, so that a biserial r may be computed. In Table I, $r_{bis} = 0.60$. The actual computation is not shown, but it is an easily mastered process that consumes relatively little time.

The biserial coefficient may be interpreted in the same way as the product-moment r; it is a method developed specifically for estimating the extent of correlation when one variable is in the form of a dichotomy. Usually it is the criterion variable that is expressed in two broad categories, but it is possible to have the reverse situation. Consider the situation in which a test classifies workers as either "20/20 vision or better" or "needing visual correction" and the criterion can be expressed in number of units of work turned out. In this case, the test is the dichotomized variable and the criterion may have a wide range. The biserial coefficient is equally applicable to this situation.

We have discussed only two of the better-known correlational techniques. There are a number of others such as the coefficient of contingency, Phi-coefficient, point-biserial *r,* and correlation ratio that are useful in special instances. In almost all cases, the data and the purpose will determine which is the most appropriate method. The general plan of plotting numbers of cases in squares or cells is fundamental to all correlation methods. Personnel workers may use fine or coarse groupings. As the number of groups or classes becomes large and if the data are continuous, the Pearson *r* may be used to advantage. But there are numerous situations where rather coarse groupings may be investigated effectively by available techniques.

Summarizing Techniques

We have used the words "summarizing techniques" merely for convenience in referring to several methods of expressing the relationship between predictors and criteria that depend only on common sense and simple arithmetic. We shall illustrate only two methods although the reader can doubtlessly think of many more. The principal advantages of these methods are that they take very little time and are relatively easy to interpret. The methods described do not have well-established names, and the names we give them here are simply handy ones.

Differences in Average Scores in Criterion Subgroups

Let us suppose we have classified our workers into five grades on the basis of rated or measured proficiency and that we also have test scores for these workers. We can easily compute the average score on the test for each of the five categories of workers. If the average scores decrease as the ratings become poorer and if the differences are considerable, we can conclude, without the necessity for elaborate statistical computations, that the test is working quite well.

Sometimes the criterion for a test is not a job rating but something else, such as occupational level or level of earnings. An intelligence test, for example, might reasonably be expected to distinguish between groups of different earning capacity. Presumably, the brighter people are capable of greater earnings, and this state of affairs should be reflected in the average scores of the various groups. An illustration of this type of analysis is given in table A.2, which presents the average scores of different occupational groups on the *Wesman Personnel Classification Test* (a test of verbal reasoning and numerical ability).

Table A.2   Average Score

Group	N	Verbal	Numerical	Total
Executive Trainee Candidates	584	30.3	15.7	46.0
Life Insurance Salespeople	414	23.9	11.7	35.6
Nursing School Applicants	123	19.9	10.6	30.5
Mechanical Apprentice Applicants	194	14.1	7.0	21.1
Chain Store Clerks	174	11.7	6.2	17.9

The order of the groups on the test corresponds almost exactly to their order according to level of earnings (or potential earnings in the case of the executive trainee candidates). The average scores on the parts and total of the *Wesman PCT* show a definite upward trend as the level of earnings increases. This, of course, is not conclusive nor is it a thorough analysis, but it gives easily grasped evidence of the validity of the test.

Occasionally this sort of "inspectional" analysis may be misleading—i.e., it may be hard to decide whether an observed difference between the average scores of two groups is really dependable or merely due to chance. It is possible, however, to evaluate the significance of the difference between two averages by means of a standard statistical test and to estimate the likelihood that the difference found is due to chance.

Percentage of Success in Each Category of Test Rating; Expectancy Tables

At the time of testing, the personnel worker can classify the sample of persons into several categories, say five, based on their test scores. Theoretically, if the test is perfectly valid for predicting a given type of performance, *at some later date* all of the top-ranking group on the test should be successful on their jobs and all of the bottom group should have failed on the job or be the least competent persons. In between there would be gradations in the percentage of successful persons.

Figure A.4, taken from a study made by the Industrial Division of The Psychological Corporation, shows how practical such a method of analyzing the correlation between test predictors and performance criteria can be. At the time of employment, the personnel experts rated

Figure A.4

	Satisfactory Production	Unsatisfactory Production	Error Scores on Test	Low (1–3)	Below Average (4–6)	Above Average (7–9)	High (10–12)	Totals
Excellent	94%	6%	0- 8	-	-	2 (33%)	4 (67%)	6
Very Good	62%	38%	9-17	4 (8%)	7 (13%)	27 (51%)	15 (28%)	53
Average	46%	54%	18-26	6 (9%)	15 (22%)	30 (45%)	16 (24%)	67
Below Average	25%	75%	27-35	4 (17%)	13 (57%)	5 (22%)	1 (4%)	23
Poor	17%	83%	36-44	2 (40%)	3 (60%)	-	-	5
			45-53	1 (100%)	-	-	-	1

all workers on the basis of test scores and interview procedures, although due to the scarcity of labor at the time, all who applied had to be hired. The ratings were ignored in employing people and were not made known to the supervisors. Later the relative success of the employees on a piece-work criterion was reported, with the results shown in the figure. It is apparent that the combination of tests and judgments of interviewers is potentially effective, and that if a standard is set to cut off, say, all applicants in the bottom 40 percent on test and interviewer rating, considerable improvement in the output of the work force would be achieved.

In figure A.4 we have rearranged the data in the previous figure so as to illustrate an "expectancy table." This table says that 67 percent of those with zero to eight errors on the test were rated High, 33 percent Above Average, and none Below Average or Low. It says, at the other extreme, that all (six cases) of those with thirty-six or more errors on the test rated Below Average or Low. If a number of new applicants are now tested by this company, the employment manager can use the expectancy table to estimate how many of those scoring in each category may be counted on to develop into satisfactory workers. This method of studying the validity of a test is an important one and will probably be used more and more. Observe that we can draw lines across this table and quickly secure the four figures needed for computing r_{tet}.

			Rank Correlation Method—Test A			
Person Number	1 Test Score	2 Perf. Rating	3 Test Score Ranked	4 Perf. Rat. Ranked	5 Absolute Difference	6 Difference Squared
A1	8	5	4.5	7.5	3.0	9.00
A2	9	7	2.5	3.0	0.5	0.25
A3	7	8	6.0	2.0	4.0	16.00
A4	6	5	7.5	7.5	0.0	0.00
A5	8	6	4.5	5.0	0.5	0.25
B1	5	4	9.0	9.5	0.5	0.25
B2	9	6	2.5	5.0	2.5	6.25
B3	6	6	7.5	5.0	2.5	6.25
B4	11	10	1.0	1.0	0.0	0.00
B5	4	4	10.0	9.5	0.5	0.25
					ΣD^2 =	38.50

1. Rank from highest to lowest (1 to 10) the scores and ratings in columns 1 and 2, recording ranks in columns 3 and 4.

2. Calculate absolute difference between values in columns 3 and 4, recording differences in column 5.

3. Square each difference in column 5, recording squares in column 6.

4. Sum (Σ) column 6.

5. Multiply 6 times ΣD^2, obtaining 231.00

6. Multiply N (the number of sets of data) by N^2-1, obtaining 990.00.

7. Divide value obtained in step 5 by value obtained in step 6, obtaining 0.23.

8. Subtract result of step 7 from 1.00, obtaining 0.77, the rank correlation.

Note: The formula for and solution of the rank correlation is:

$$\rho = 1 - \frac{6\Sigma D^2}{N(N^2-1)} = 1 - \frac{6(38.50)}{10(100-1)} =$$

$$1 - \frac{231}{10(99)} = 1 - \frac{231}{990} = 1 - 0.23 = 0.77$$

1. Square individual test scores and ratings in columns 1 and 2, recording products in columns 3 and 4.

2. Multiply individual test scores in Column 1 by individual ratings in column 2, recording products in column 5.

3. Sum (Σ) all 5 columns.

4. Multiply N (number of sets of data) by ΣXY, subtracting ΣX times ΣY from it, obtaining 277.

5. Multiply N by ΣX^2, subtracting the product of ΣX times itself from it, obtaining 401.

6. Take square root of value found in step 5, obtaining 20.02.

7. Repeat steps 5 and 6 for corresponding Y values (ΣY^2 and ΣY), obtaining 17.57.

8. Divide value found in step 4 by the product of the values found in steps 6 and 7, obtaining 0.79, the linear correlation.

Note: The formula for and solution of the linear correlation is:

$$r = \frac{N\Sigma XY - \Sigma X \Sigma Y}{\sqrt{N\Sigma X^2 - (\Sigma X)^2} \ \sqrt{N\Sigma Y^2 - (\Sigma Y)^2}} =$$

$$\frac{4730 - 4453}{\sqrt{5730 - 5329} \ \sqrt{4030 - 3721}} =$$

$$\frac{277}{\sqrt{401} \ \sqrt{309}} = \frac{277}{20.02 \times 17.57} = \frac{277}{351.75} = 0.79$$

Linear Correlation Method—Test A				
1 Test A X	2 Perf. Rat. Y	3 Test A X^2	4 Perf. Rat. Y^2	5 Cross Product XY
8	5	64	25	40
9	7	81	49	63
7	8	49	64	56
6	5	36	25	30
8	6	64	36	48
5	4	25	16	20
9	6	81	36	54
6	6	36	36	36
11	10	121	100	110
4	4	16	16	16
$\Sigma X = 73$	$\Sigma Y = 61$	$\Sigma X^2 = 573$	$\Sigma Y^2 = 403$	$\Sigma XY = 473$

Index